Across Cultures

A Reader for Writers

Across Cultures

A Reader for Writers

SIXTH EDITION

Sheena Gillespie
Robert Becker

Queensborough Community College
City University of New York

PEARSON
Longman

New York • San Francisco • Boston
London • Toronto • Sydney • Tokyo • Singapore • Madrid
Mexico City • Munich • Paris • Cape Town • Hong Kong • Montreal

Senior Vice President/Publisher: Joseph Opiela

Executive Marketing Manager: Ann Stypuloski

Production Manager: Ellen MacElree

Project Coordination, Text Design, Electronic Page Makeup:
    Stratford Publishing Services

Cover Designer/Manager: Wendy Ann Fredericks

Cover Illustration: Copyright © Jose Ortega/Stock Illustration Source, Inc.

Manufacturing Buyer: Lucy Hebard

Printer and Binder: R. R. Donnelley and Sons Company

Cover Printer: Phoenix Color Corps.

Library of Congress Cataloging-in-Publication Data

Across cultures : a reader for writers / Sheena Gillespie, Robert Becker.—6th ed.
        p.   cm.
    Rev. ed. of: Across cultures / Sheena Gillespie, Robert Singleton.
    5th ed. 2001
    ISBN 0-321-21318-1
    1. College readers.   2. English language—Rhetoric—Problems, exercises,
etc.   3. Multiculturalism—Problems, exercises, etc.   4. Report writing—
Problems, exercises, etc.   5. Culture—Problems, exercises, etc.   6. Readers—
Multiculturalism.   7. Readers—Culture.   I. Gillespie, Sheena.   II. Becker,
Robert (Robert J.)
    PE1417.A27   2004
    808'.0427—dc22   2004011365

Please visit our website at http://www.ablongman.com

ISBN 0-321-21318-1

    5 6 7 8 9 10—DOH—07 06

*To Gabe, Amanda, and in memory
of Callum (1992–2003).*

*To S.G., for your encouragement,
support, and friendship.*

Contents

Asterisks after titles identify student writings.

Literacy Narratives   **390**

The Knowing Eye   **400**

Rhetorical Contents

DESCRIPTION

PERSUASION

Preface for the Teacher

There is no such thing as a neutral educational process. Education either functions as an instrument which is used to facilitate the integration of the younger generation into the logic of the present system and bring conformity to it, or becomes "the practice of freedom," the means by which men and women deal critically and creatively with reality and discover how to participate in the transformation of their world.

—Richard Shaull

ACROSS CULTURES: A READER FOR WRITERS is a reader that invites students to look beyond their own society and culture. The title embodies our guiding image of a reaching out—moving beyond the immediate and the parochial to an acknowledgment and acceptance of pluralism and diversity within and among cultures. In our usage, such reaching out does not mean blending or blurring or assimilating (or hybridizing, in the biological sense). The outreach we mean may be found, first, in the selection of readings by authors from and about many countries: by North Americans writing about other cultures and about United States culture and subcultures; by members of ethnic subcultures in the United States, such as immigrants or their children, African-Americans, or Native Americans, writing about the United States; and by persons from other cultures writing about those cultures. Second, this reaching out is encouraged by the text's apparatus, in aids to the student. Perspectives (quotations); chapter introductions; text selection headnotes; the end-of-lesson trio Interpretations, Correspondences, Applications; and Additional Writing Topics are found in every chapter.

We began the first edition of *Across Cultures* in 1989, and since then, the number of students coming from homes that are bilingual and bicultural has almost doubled in campuses across the country. In a recent essay in the *Chronicle of Higher Education*, Isabelle de Courtivron, professor of foreign languages and literature at Massachusetts Institute of Technology, notes that although we hear daily about the many facets of globalization, little "has been written about the impact of this cross-cultural movement on the lives of our students and the texture of education." She exhorts educators to "build on the strengths that our students increasingly display, and to begin a conversation about the new linguistic realities" by developing curricula not only on college campuses but in elementary schools. We agree with her assessment and have endeavored to include in the sixth edition texts and apparatus that address the "new linguistic realities" of our students, a topic much debated currently by educators and politicians. Consequently, we hope to learn more about the ramifications of "tapping into" the rich cultures, languages, experiences, and values of our students.

The sixth edition of *Across Cultures* reflects other extensive revisions. We have added at the request of many reviewers a new first chapter on "Writing, the 'Writing Process,' and You," in which we ask students to think of themselves as writers joining a community of writers who will assist one another as they engage in the various stages of writing texts.

We have expanded the literacy narratives beyond the linguistic to better reflect the other kinds of literacies that students are engaged in, including the visual arts, performing arts, and technology.

Our decision to increase the number of images in most chapters is to encourage more complex and varied writing topics. The new prompts invite students to sharpen their observational skills, play with different voices, and make connections between the images and the chapter's texts.

In the apparatus, we have added more questions on rhetorical strategies in the Interpretations and Correspondences sections. We have also made more extensive use of group work and/or writing assignments in the Applications sections by adding an additional topic for each text. Last, in response to the influence on pedagogy of theories of multiple intelligences and literacies, we have developed Applications questions and exercises that tap into these additional ways of knowing.

The outreach implied by the title *Across Cultures* is an outgrowth of our understanding of the term *culture*. To define culture is a task not to be limited to a mere dictionary definition. Distinguished anthropologists A. L. Kroeber and Clyde Kluckhohn have devoted a sizable volume, *Culture: A Critical Review of Concepts and Definitions*, to this topic. Their effort continues whenever anthropologists communicate. In assembling this textbook, we have found Bronislaw Malinowski's essay on culture in the *Encyclopedia of the Social Sciences* (vol. IV), and Kluckhohn's 1962 essay, "The Concept of Culture," particularly useful. In those works the following definitions appear: Culture is the "artificial, secondary environment" that human beings superimpose on the natural, and (from Kluckhohn),

> Culture, then, is . . . that part [of human life] which is learned by people as the result of belonging to some particular group, and is that part of learned behavior which is shared with others. It is our social legacy, as contrasted with our organic heredity. It is the main factor which permits us to live together

in a society, giving us ready-made solutions to our problems, helping us to predict the behavior of others, and permitting others to know what to expect of us.

From these definitions, then, these characteristics of culture follow: culture is social, it is a human achievement, and human achievements are designed to serve an end or good; that is, the good of human beings. The world of culture is a world of values. Although the good may be immaterial—truth, beauty, honor, glory—cultural good must be realized in temporal and material form. Culture consists as much in conserving values as in realizing them. And finally, culture is pluralistic. It is society's attempt to realize a large number of values, some of them highly complex.

The selections we offer in *Across Cultures* cover a much greater variety of cultural trends than the table of contents indicates. For example, work, the subject of Chapter 5, leads to such related subjects as affirmative action, immigration, cultural displacement, family narratives, and definitions of success. Traditions, the subject of Chapter 6, leads to questions of family life, the roles of men and women, class differences, and rituals and ceremonies of all kinds.

The chapters are also interconnected in ways that the table of contents cannot indicate. For example, *work* exists within a matrix of traditions, relationships, education, and choices. Hence our inclusion of Correspondences throughout the book. These questions ask students to make connections and draw comparisons between the Perspectives (brief quotations at the beginning of each chapter) and the texts in that chapter, between the selections within the chapter, and between the texts in different chapters.

Each chapter begins, as we have said, with Perspectives, brief provocative quotations that stimulate thought and discussion on the chapter topic. Next come the texts—myths, folktales, essays, and short stories. Whereas many of the essays and stories reflect the seemingly endless—often tumultuous—changes in current events, our rationale for including myths and folktales is to show culture in its conserving role. Although *Across Cultures* probably pays more attention to shifts in population and to political and economic changes around the world, these changes occur against backgrounds of centuries of history and tradition, of treasured stories of origins and beginnings that give direction to the current shifting allegiances. Such stories may actually revive and sustain some cultures.

The opening texts of each chapter are myths and folktales that remind us of how culture sustains us. These stories are regarded as holy, as scripture, as culturally indispensable; they link time and the timeless. As N. Scott Momaday says of the storyteller in Native American tradition: "[He] creates himself and his listeners through the power of his perception, his imagination, his expression, his devotion to important details. He is a holy man; his function is sacred."

Cultural commentary in our text is direct and explicit. Each chapter includes one section on general American culture by an American writer, two or three texts by writers from diverse ethnic groups within the United States writing either on the experience of those groups or on individuals within them, and several texts by writers from cultures elsewhere in the world. A Geographical Index at the back of the book indicates the worldwide scope of these texts, the better to place American culture and its own diversity in a world context for comparison.

Each text is proceded by a biographical/cultural headnote and is followed by questions—Interpretations—that provoke thinking and discussion, probe comprehension, call attention to important rhetorical features, and help the reader relate the text to the chapter topic. Comparison or cross-examination is the purpose of the questions called Correspondences, which also follow each text. The Applications section provides writing and discussion topics and follows each group of Perspectives and each text. These activities call on the student to analyze cross-cultural similarities and differences and sometimes to place themselves at crossroads.

We are grateful to the following reviewers for their excellent critiques and suggestions for the sixth edition of the text: Jennifer Whetham, Shelly L. Brulotte, Lori Ann Stephens, Lorraine S. Lipoma, Carla Witt, Tammy Frankland, Shari Horner, and Robert Roth.

Special thanks too to Emma Wunsch for revising the biographical headnotes and to Ann Agranoff, Theo Callendar, Cynthia Chase, and Jean Darcy for submitting student essays.

We acknowledge our gratitude to Gladys DeBuccio, Patricia Gorton, and Kathy Howard for their generous assistance in the preparation of the manuscript, to Eden Kram of Longman for her prompt and expert processing of permission requests, and to Isabel Pipolo for her meticulous preparation of the instructors' manual.

Preface for the Student

We are in the middle of an extraordinary social experiment: the attempt to provide education for all members of a vast pluralistic democracy.

—Mike Rose

Narrative is radical, creating us at the very moment it is being created.

—Toni Morrison

AS TEACHERS, WE SHARE MIKE ROSE'S EXCITEMENT at being part of a unique intellectual and social experiment that seeks to provide education for a culturally diverse student population. In *Across Cultures*, we invite you to celebrate this historically unprecedented multicultural experiment by reading the narratives of writers of other cultures, both within the United States and abroad. Toni Morrison, a Nobel Prize–winning author, believes in the power of narrative to help us understand ourselves and others. As an African-American, Morrison is particularly concerned that the writer's words and stories be the windows through which both writer and reader gain knowledge not only of the self but also of the self in relation to people of other cultures.

This book points toward possibilities hardly imagined in the world of your parents. Through business travel, tourism, governmental foreign aid, immigration, and an explosion in all kinds of communication, cultural interactions are occurring at a greater rate than ever before.

Old cultures, and even some not so old, such as that of the United States, like to think, "We are the world." But once cultures cross—whether such meetings add to or subtract from the sum of their parts—they are never again the same: they can never again claim absoluteness, exclusivity, or monopoly. To promote such meetings, or crossings, is the purpose of *Across Cultures: A Reader for Writers*.

Cultural meetings can occur in many ways. By *culture* we mean that "artificial, secondary environment" (Malinowski) that human beings superimpose on the natural environment. Wherever people make their mark on nature, they are creating a culture; a great deal of effort goes into a "creative conversation" about the value of these marks. A society expends a great deal of effort in attempting to conserve what it deems to be most valuable. Chapter 6, Traditions, deals with such efforts. The other eight chapters suggest some of the many ways in which cultural meetings can occur: in the family, community, gender relationships, in education, in work, encounters, choices, and through popular culture.

At the center of each chapter are readings on a common subject or meeting ground, but you are introduced to the chapter through a group of brief quotations (Perspectives) to stimulate personal responses in journal entries and collaborative explorations in group projects. Each text is introduced with a biographical headnote that places the author in a particular historical-geographical context. After most texts are three sets of questions: Interpretations, to provoke thinking and discussion and to call attention to specific rhetorical features; Correspondences, to encourage comparisons of cultures; and Applications, exercises to develop critical thinking and writing skills. Accordingly, you will often be asked to compare texts within, between, and among chapters.

In each chapter there is also a paired reading. Correspondences and Applications follow the second reading.

The first one or two texts in each chapter are myths or folktales. These stories show culture in its conserving role. The stories purport to explain a people's origin or trace their values to earliest times. Each chapter also has texts by authors from and about a variety of countries: by North Americans writing on other cultures or about United States culture and subcultures; by members of ethnic subcultures within the United States, writing about themselves (often as outsiders); and by foreigners writing about their native cultures.

Several features of the book will assist you in applying the readings to your study of writing. We have also added to this edition a new first chapter on "Writing, the 'Writing Process,' and You" in which we ask you to think of yourselves as writers joining a community of writers who will help one another as you engage in the various stages of writing texts. The Perspective section can be used to stimulate journal writing. Applications questions provide specific opportunities for you to convey what you think on a particular issue to a wider audience than just your peers through more structured writing and discussion activities. The Additional Writing Topics at the end of each chapter require you to conduct interviews, engage in debate, take positions, or reach conclusions. We have also expanded the range of writing topics to include creative writing, topics that draw upon different kinds of intelligences, as well as topics that ask/assist/require you to use the Web.

Since you are also a visual generation, we are adding images in each chapter to encourage more complex and varied writing topics. The new prompts invite you to sharpen your observational skills, play with different voices, and make connections between the images and the chapter's texts.

When you look around your classes and your campus, you probably see a student body diverse in its many countries, ethnicities, and age. We hope that *Across Cultures* will encourage you to "tap into" the rich cultures, languages, experiences, and values of your fellow students.

Across Cultures

A Reader for Writers

1

Writing, the "Writing Process," and You

Who are you? What is your name? How old are you? Where are you from? Who is in your family? What are you interested in? Why are you here? Where do you want to be in five years? Your answers to these questions will help you to define yourself, to place you in a context, to help you to realize your self-identity. You are a man or a woman. Maybe you are eighteen years old, or twenty-five, or forty, or seventy, or any number between or beyond. You're from the city, the suburbs, the country. You want to be an accountant, a physician, a musician, a teacher, a professional athlete, a movie star.

Whatever your thoughts and responses are to the above questions, one thing is for certain—you are a writer. While you may not have included this answer among those offered to the questions above, as a member of the class you are enrolled in you are a writer. Sure, in the outside world you are a son or daughter, a mother or sister, a brother or uncle. You are an artist, a someday All-Star, entrepreneur of the year, or attorney of the month. You want to become a fashion designer, a Grammy winner, a Nobel Prize winner, the President.

However, when you walk through the door into your English class, you are a writer participating in a community of writers. Here your thoughts and ideas will be committed to the written page, and the identity you establish for yourself as a writer will prove to be as important as any you might have invented prior to this time. The sooner you commit to this perception of yourself, the sooner you will trust yourself to get your words down on paper, and the easier the process of writing will become.

Yet this transformation into and acceptance of being a writer is not undemanding.

First of all, writing is not the same as speaking. Writing utilizes different physical actions as well as unique cognitive processes. Rather than merely translating speech into a written form, writing allows one to select more consciously the language that will be used to communicate. When you speak, you probably don't spend much time considering each word that you will use—words usually just seem to flow. Sometimes they seem to flow much too easily and quickly! Did you ever experience having words come out of your mouth and as you were saying them you thought to yourself, "Whoops! I probably shouldn't have said that!" Too late! Sometimes it seems as if words bypass our brains and emerge into the ears of our listeners all by themselves!

Writing, on the other hand, is a more deliberate and physical act. The words we want to use are still there, but now we can take our time and luxuriate in our choice of them as we put them down on the page. In fact, we can often change a word before it is committed to paper, and even when it's down we can still modify it to suit our needs. It is our ability to control more carefully the presentation of language that makes writing a unique verbal act; however, this uniqueness is—as you will see—a double-edged sword.

In this day of email and instant messaging, we are closer than ever to emulating speech in our writing. It is quite possible to have the same "Whoops" response after replying to an IM all too quickly! The incorporation of technology into writing is a revelation that has sprouted a revolution.

Despite the changes that technology (specifically computer-based word processing programs, email, and instant messaging) has brought to writing, there is still one fundamental truth concerning writers and writing—as a writer, you are unique. Although many writers may share similarities, it is most unlikely that two writers will do *exactly* the same thing. In fact, it is not unusual for any single writer to alter how she or he approaches writing depending upon the task at hand. This approach to writing—the *writing process*—is unique to each writer, and, it may be argued, unique to each project undertaken. Yet there are important lessons to be learned from an examination of the choices that all writers make when encountering a writing task.

The first choice a writer makes is how to begin. How do you actually start a writing project? Some people like to sit quietly before they write, giving themselves a chance to gather their thoughts before committing them to paper. Other people like to engage in some physical activity— taking a walk or shooting some baskets—to help them clear their minds before starting. Others like to jump in, get that first sentence down and keep on going from there. While one of these actions might describe the way that you get started, there are other techniques that writers use to get them past that blank piece of paper staring them in the face. Three of these are freewriting, brainstorming, and journal–writing. Since you are a unique person and a unique writer, not all of these techniques will work for you. However, by giving each a serious try (indeed, the old "college try"), you might discover a tool that will help make you a more comfortable and effective writer. When this occurs, take this technique with you and incorporate it into your own writing process.

For many writers getting started is the hardest part. A bare sheet of paper can be intimidating, and the sooner that you can put words on it, the better. *Freewriting* is a technique where you write down whatever comes into your mind without consideration of language, grammar, or content. But all you'll get is garbage, you say? The idea is not to evaluate your thoughts but merely to generate them. You will have much time to consider and reconsider the words and ideas that will become your final text, but the real trick for a writer is just to get going! Sit down in a quiet place. Set a timer for five minutes and begin to write. Don't let yourself be interrupted. Don't stop for anything. If you have an itch, don't scratch it—write about scratching it. If you are feeling hungry, don't stop to grab for that cookie—write about the intensity of your hunger pains. If you get stuck and have nothing to write about, write down the colors of the rainbow, the days of the week, or the months of the year until your mind picks up a thread and starts going along it. One thing about your mind: it moves pretty quickly, and keeping up with it might prove a challenge. Do the best you can to follow it. If it stops in mid-thought and moves to another, stay with it! When freewriting, try to train yourself to stop in mid-sentence to follow your brain as it moves through the back alleys of your consciousness.

At the end of five minutes, or whenever you have set your timer to go off, go back and read what you have written. (Note how your handwriting may have deteriorated as you have gone forward!) What is the most interesting (or important) idea that you have written? What topic seems to crop up more than any other? What intriguing idea would you like to pursue? The best piece of writing that you can create is the one about something that you are interested in. Practice freewriting regularly and use it to help you find those topics that are meaningful to you.

Another technique to help you to get started is *brainstorming*. Brainstorming is similar to freewriting in that you may use it to generate ideas, but it is different in that you simply create a list of those points you think you want to make about a topic. Often, brainstorming is done as a group activity. When used in this way, group members call out responses to a recorder who sets down on paper or a chalkboard the ideas that are generated. As with freewriting, the idea is not to make judgments about the contributions that are being brainstormed. That will come later, in preparation for creating a first draft of a writing task. Rather, the object of brainstorming is to get those juices flowing and place ideas out there!

Yet another means of generating ideas is *journal-writing.* Setting your ideas to paper three or more times a week is a way to create a record of your thoughts and feelings. Note, however, that keeping a journal is not like writing in a diary. Whereas a diary is primarily a posting of daily events, journals may be quite varied and contain many kinds of entries. Sure, you might write about what happened to you during the day, but you should also be experimenting with new forms and diverse topics. Write a letter to a friend or a famous person, create lyrics to a song or a poem, sketch a landscape or a portrait, cut out and paste in a quotation, picture, or recipe that you find interesting. Of course, as you include material in your journal, be sure to comment on it. What is it about those lyrics that you find most interesting? How do they apply to your life? That picture you cut out of the magazine— what do you find intriguing about it? Why would you want to visit that place? What do you think you would find there? And that recipe you included in your journal so as not to forget it—what was the response to it when you served it to your family and/or friends? What was the verdict? Was it worth making or did you have to order in a couple of pizzas as an emergency measure?

Whatever you decide to do with your journal, remember that it should be a representation of who you are and what you think. If you choose to write only daily diary-like entries, don't be surprised if the sameness of that form causes you to lose interest in the enterprise. By giving a journal a fair try—by making it as unique as *you* are—you will not only see more clearly who you are, but you will also discover many topics to write about, some of which you might never have thought about before.

Freewriting, brainstorming, and *journal-writing* are techniques that will help you to generate ideas and get your writing started. Now that you no longer have a blank page or screen in front of you, what will you do with all that stuff?

Once you have some raw material for an essay, there are certain questions that you—and all writers—need to answer to create an effective piece. Primarily, you must consider *what* you want to say, to *whom* you want to say it, and *why* you want to convey the information.

The first decision you have to make concerns the "what"—what is it that you want to communicate? Generating ideas about your topic might have opened up several aspects of your topic to you; now you need to think about what the main point is that you want to express. This main idea about your general topic, when stated as a clear and direct sentence, is your *thesis*. There's nothing fancy about a thesis statement. It's simply a one-sentence expression of the main idea that you want to convey to your readers.

Another matter that you need to address concerns the person or people who will read your writing. This readership is called an audience and you need to take them into account when you create your work. Who will your readers be? How old are they? How much formal education do they have? What are their interests? Why are they reading your work? Your answers to these questions will help you to target your audience. Depending upon your topic and whom you are writing for, you may need to adjust your vocabulary, treatment of ideas, the complexity of language, and even the form that your writing takes.

Yet another concern that writers take into account when considering audience is *tone*—how one presents himself or herself to an audience. How do you want yourself and your topic to appear to your readers? Do you want to take a forceful stance with them, letting them know who's boss and in control of the information being presented? Do you want to win their sympathies and come over to your way of seeing things? Do you want to appear impartial and sway your audience with a logical presentation of information? The relationship you form with your readers—the tone that you supply to your writing—will be created by your choice of language, how you appeal to their hearts and minds, and your approach to your topic.

One final consideration you need to address is *why* you are writing your piece. Yes, you are in a writing class and you want to get a good grade. However, this answer to the question addresses your *motives* for writing rather than your *purpose*. Basically, if you are seeking some kind of tangible, material compensation—primarily either grades or money—then you are talking about motives. Your purpose for writing concerns non-material objectives: you may want to entertain your readers, inform them, vent your emotions to them, or even provide a memory for them to preserve in their own minds. Chances are, you won't be able to settle on a single purpose for writing; indeed, it seems the more complex the work, the more purposes a writer has in mind for writing it. However, by assessing your purpose, audience, and meaning before creating your first draft, you will be able to more closely approach what it is that you want to convey to your readers and how you want to say it.

So now we get to putting all of this preparatory work into action, into that work of writing that we have called a first draft. Just its name implies that there will be (at least!) one more, so what's unique about a first, as opposed to a second, third, or fourth, draft?

First drafts are where you get to work out on paper the real answers to those questions asked earlier. While you have generated ideas and thought about your meaning, purpose, and audience, a first draft is the place where you get to try out your ideas and intentions.

When you create this draft, try to stick to your main idea (thesis), and organize information in a way that best addresses your view of audience and that achieves your purpose for writing. However, don't be surprised if when you complete this draft and read it over, you have found a new main point or discovered additional answers to some of the questions you asked yourself earlier. Quite often a first draft is where a writer truly discovers what he or she has to say. It is not unusual for a writer to declare after completing a first draft, "*Now* I have found what I really want to talk about!" There's a simple truth to this statement. How do we know what we want to say until we have said it?

Going back to the earlier discussion of speech and writing, sometimes when we speak we discover the truth of a statement only when it is too late. However, making such a discovery when creating a first draft is like finding gold! Now that you have found what you want to say, you may create a second draft that capitalizes on this knowledge. Now an opportunity presents itself for you to refine and sharpen your topic in view of your discovery. You might also re-evaluate your assessment of your audience and how you might best approach your readers. In essence, a first draft is a critical step in creating an interesting and effective final essay.

But wait! With your first draft in hand, how will you go about transforming it into a completed essay? Most students try to touch up a first draft by making surface changes to it. They may alter the structure of a sentence or two, and are likely to change a few words and fix spelling errors and minor grammatical slips. While these changes will help to increase the clarity of the essay, they will not capitalize on the hard work you have already done creating the first draft and then reassessing your meaning, purpose, and audience. To improve a first draft significantly most often calls for a writer to revise it thoroughly. Those changes mentioned above really concern *editing* and will be discussed later. What experienced writers do to a first draft almost always involves the use of *revising strategies*. These strategies are available to all writers and are the only techniques available to transform a promising first draft into a truly effective piece of writing. Here are the revising techniques available to you:

Addition: Use this technique to offer additional information to your reader. You might add only a phrase to clarify an idea, but sometimes you might need to add a sentence or even a whole paragraph to make your point strongly and clearly.

Deletion: The exact opposite of addition, deletion is used when you have too much information in your essay. Perhaps you repeat yourself or stray from your thesis. In these instances, remove that information to create a tighter, more effective, essay.

Substitution: A combination of addition and deletion, substitution requires you to replace ineffective text with phrases, sentences, or paragraphs that convey your ideas more exactly and clearly.

Rearrangement: Whereas the previous techniques have to do with the amount and effectiveness of the information you provide, rearrangement concerns the *organization* of the information in your essay. There are three techniques involved in rearranging an essay:

Moving: Use this technique to take information from one place in the essay and position it elsewhere. Sometimes a sentence or group of sentences really belongs somewhere else—move them to where they will function more effectively.

Combining: On occasion you will notice that sentences referring to the same idea appear in varied places in your essay. If you determine that these ideas ought to be placed together, you would use combining to bring them to a new location, perhaps creating a new paragraph to accommodate them.

Redistributing: The opposite of *combining,* this technique would be used to de-emphasize information by taking ideas from one location and placing them in several related areas. Sometimes a body paragraph that supports your thesis tangentially can be broken up and the relevant sentences placed in other paragraphs. This will eliminate the digression you have made and strengthen the body paragraphs that are already in place.

These techniques—*adding, deleting, substituting, rearranging*—will help you to change the substance of your essay. By doing so, they will enable you to change your meaning and better adapt it to your purpose and audience. These revision strategies will encourage you to do much more than alter a word or punctuation mark, and they will help you make the kinds of changes that first drafts require to bring them to completion.

Let the power of your computer's word-processing program help you use these revising strategies. Your text is flexible and not set in stone. Highlight and cut and paste those sentences that are giving you a problem. How do they look in their new location? Not too good you say? Hit the undo icon and your text is as it was. To be doubly sure that no harm will come to your original, save the first draft (as Draft1), open the file, and immediately save the working copy as Draft2. Now if something goes terribly wrong and you can no longer undo the changes you have made, you can always revert back to your original document, Draft1. Play with your text—add, delete, substitute, and rearrange—but be sure to save your work often! Becoming familiar with the power of revision is a prerequisite to becoming a more effective writer.

By now your revised essay is pretty much where you want it. You have said what you had intended to say and have achieved your purpose in view of your intended audience. Before handing your work to your instructor or submitting it for publication, you need to take the final two steps to maximize its effectiveness—*editing* and *proofreading*.

Both of these stages have been discussed briefly earlier. *Editing* occurs when you read over your draft and examine and modify each sentence for clarity and effectiveness. Sharpen your choice of language to make certain that every word is accurate, that every word says what you want it to say. You might add, delete, or substitute a word or phrase here and there to increase the effectiveness of your text.

Proofreading is when you go over your piece for the last time, paying attention to the accuracy of every word and punctuation mark. Check the spelling of each and every word sentence by sentence—don't trust a spellchecker to find and correct errors since it will not recognize wrong word choices (*form* instead of *from*, for example). Check grammar and punctuation to make sure that minor slips are corrected.

One problem with proofreading is that you are probably the worst person to check your work at this time! Since you have read your essay so many times, your mind often will tell your eye what to see and slight errors will go unnoticed. It's helpful to exchange papers with a classmate and to alert each other to those minor errors that fall into the proofreading category. Should you be unable to share your work, you might read your essay backwards, beginning with the last sentence and ending with the first. Doing this will decontextualize your essay so that your mind does not know what to expect and your eyes will be put to work! After completing this final stage of the "writing process," your essay should be one that you are proud of and that represents your best efforts. Indeed, you have done the work that all writers need to do to write effectively.

Even so, this process of writing and revising might not be completed. Perhaps, after reading your essay, your peer group or instructor may suggest additional revisions or things to think about. In that case, assess the comments that were made and use your writing process to accommodate a new set of changes. This exchange of ideas and perceptions between a writer and his or her audience is invaluable. Learning how readers view your work and respond to your words is an important experience and an essential part of any writer's writing process. Indeed, it is by exposing yourself to these writing situations that you earn the title and identity of "writer."

What has been summarized above are those techniques that make up the writing process. Remember, however, that every writer formulates his or her own plan to successfully complete a writing task. *Your* writing process is the sequence of steps that you find to be most helpful in creating an essay. You do not need to apply each of these steps, and frequently, steps are not followed in order. It is the nature of writing that makes these processes recursive; that is, a writer usually goes back and forth among them as the written work is produced. Oftentimes, writers revise works in process—even in the most preliminary stages. Conversely, it is plausible to generate ideas even when a piece is nearing completion.

Most important, experiment with your writing process to find the most effective way to write for *you*! Make those techniques and strategies that work best part of your personal armory of writing techniques. For example, some writers, when composing an essay, begin with the essay's body and leave the introduction for last. Their rationale is that they need to know what they have written before creating the paragraph that introduces the work. Whatever your personal preferences, keep your mind open to new techniques. Allow yourself to enjoy the freedom and potential for self-discovery that every writer may experience when setting ideas to paper.

Literacy Narratives

In *Across Cultures*, the essays by Sherman Alexie (p. 74), Susan G. Madera (p. 79), Paule Marshall (p. 210), Vincent Cremona (p. 219), Gloria Naylor (p. 390), and Kenneth Woo (p. 394) are "literacy narratives." A *narrative* may be defined as a story that makes a point. What, however is *literacy*? According to *The American Heritage Dictionary of the English Language, Fourth Edition,* one definition of literacy is "The condition or quality of being literate, especially the ability to read and write." Certainly, the authors named above are concerned with reading and writing; this kind of literacy—linguistic literacy—is central to their personal stories. Yet, perhaps other kinds of literacy are also being addressed in these stories.

A second definition presented in *The American Heritage Dictionary* is of literacy as "the condition or quality of being knowledgeable in a particular subject or field." In this case, our representation of literacy must expand to encompass what we know and how we know it. In these instances, who we are as individuals and as individuals within society will help to form our knowledge of ourselves and our world. The things we do and the people we do them with will help to shape our definitions.

- What kind of literacy is required when hiking a trail or negotiating a subway system?

- What does one have to know to work in an office or a factory?

- How does one begin to master the technological literacy required by today's world?

- What kinds of literacy are required to play a song or create a painting?

- If you attend a house of worship, what kinds of literacy are invoked? What would someone who practices another religion need to know in order to become literate in your faith?

- How does one know how to dance, ice skate, or perform gymnastics?

- What kind of literacy is required to participate in a team sport, to be involved in a relationship, to be a member of a family?

- What does "literacy" mean to you? What kinds of literacy have you mastered? Which are you currently in the midst of learning?

Sometime this semester, your instructor might ask you to write your own literacy narrative. Perhaps, if you are asked to share your story with a classmate, a group of your peers, or with your whole class, you might observe types of literacy that you had not thought about. As your classmates share their stories, what do you notice about their literacy narratives? How is the general idea of literacy being described? What kinds of literacy are being addressed? How do these narratives compare with those published in this book?

And, as you read the literary narratives in *Across Cultures*, think about what common themes or kinds of literacy the authors are writing about. Consider how their stories resemble yours, how their depictions of literacy relate to your story and the stories of your classmates.

Composing Your Own Literacy Narratives

If you have been asked to write a literacy narrative, there are several approaches to the assignment that you may take. Below is a method to help you formulate your ideas about your involvement with language. By following the sequence of assignments from beginning to end, you will create the kind of essay that is represented by the authors who have published their literacy narratives in the chapters of this book.

PROMPTS

- Remember back to your first writing memory, either at home or at school.

- When was the first time you realized that a piece of your writing had an effect on someone?

- When have you seen or felt language doing "harm" or causing "hurt"?

- Describe the physical location where you do your writing in as much detail as you can.

- Characterize your writing process using the metaphor of a meal. For example: What kinds of food? Home cooked? Fast food? A holiday celebration? How many courses and of what kind? Who is present when you eat? What does the table look like where you eat? Silverware? Napkins? Drinks? Rests between parts of the meal? While watching TV? Is there dessert?

- What is your favorite book? When did you read it? Why is it your favorite?

- Describe a person who has been an influence on your writing/reading/language use.

- When did you first become aware of your private voice in a public context?

- What kind of stories did you enjoy hearing as a child? Can you remember creating a story of your own?

JOURNAL WRITING

Select one of the prompts above and, without stopping, write for five minutes on anything that comes to mind related to the prompt. When the five minutes are up, select another prompt and write again for five minutes. Repeat the process again so that you have three freewritten chunks of text. Now go back and look for connections across the three chunks and rewrite them so that they form one comprehensive journal entry.

CONNECTIONS

Based upon what you have written, look through the texts in the chapter and find at least one that you can link to. Are there issues in the text that help you make sense of your journal entry? How can you use these to expand on your literacy narrative? Remember that points of conflict may be as helpful as those in common, as you think about them in relation to your own writing.

REFLECTIONS

Read over the new material you have added to your narrative. How did the process of reading literacy narratives, reseeing other texts as literacy narratives, and writing your own narrative help you to think of these issues in different contexts? What insights did you gain about yourself coming into language? Do you better understand the differences between your public and private voices? How might you develop them? As you negotiate among your various roles and cultures, how will you use language to create understanding? In what contexts might you engage in the discourse of persuasion? Write a journal entry on any of these issues that seem pertinent to your literacy narrative.

CHAPTER

2

Family and Community

A REVIEW OF THE PERSPECTIVES on family, friends, and community in this chapter reflect incredible variations in cross-cultural views of social relationships, but one theme remains constant: we are social beings. The variations that exist in family, friendship, and community have been built on the changeless desire and need to reach out to one another.

The thousand-year-old parable of the Good Samaritan establishes a clear definition of *neighbor,* a definition that transcends tribal and even family differences and calls on us to value service to others over our own comfort. Even those who accept this definition as an ideal, however, admit that it is very difficult to practice.

The American poet Walt Whitman described the self as a "miracle of miracles, beyond statement, most spiritual and vaguest of earth's dreams, yet hardest basic fact, and only entrance to all facts." The self, as Whitman indicates, is indeed paradoxical, and if it is to remain dynamic, it must constantly evolve. To ensure self-growth, we must evaluate all that happens to us, however seemingly insignificant.

What you will encounter as you read the texts on these issues is that regardless of their ethnic and cultural backgrounds, the writers have a common interest in knowing and understanding themselves and others. You will meet people like yourself with complex personalities composed of conflicting desires, attitudes, and expressions. Like them, you play many roles—parent, child, sibling, friend, lover, employee, student. Although each of us is unique, we are also influenced by those who share our daily and communal lives. When our own personality, individualism, and sense of identity become all-important, who helps us reconcile self and society, independence and interdependence? The cross-cultural examples in this chapter may suggest some answers.

Family members and the places we grew up are often important catalysts for reconstructing and understanding ourselves. Dana Wehle and Mahwash Shoaib, for example, invite us to their family homes in New York and Pakistan respectively, to present their responses to the deaths of a parent and grandparent.

Emma Wunsch focuses on family relationships in the nineties in the United States; Lewis (Johnson) Sawaquat reveals his aspirations for his daughter, while Tom Montgomery-Fate uses the analogy of a balancing act to describe the complexities of parenthood.

Immigrant family relationships add different voices to this conversation. Immigration can put a heavy strain on family solidarity. The immigration of Maxine Hong Kingston's family from China to California makes her an angry feminist. Cultural differences in the way female children are treated are great between China and America, and Kingston must leave her family to find herself. The parent-child relationship is badly strained. The struggle turns Kingston into a "woman warrior." In "Two Lives," Malayasian immigrant Shirley Geok-Lin Lim reflects on her lack of identity as a "resident alien." "Without family, house or society, she views herself through the eyes of citizens: guest, stranger, outsider, misfit, beggar."

The basic importance and influence of family members, even those about whom we are ambivalent, are apparent in this cross-cultural survey of relationships. All of the texts reinforce how much of our personal and cultural identities are rooted in our need for community.

Perspectives

Civilization progresses at the expense of individual happiness.

—*Sigmund Freud*

No people are ever as divided as those of the same blood.

—*Mavis Gallant*

All parents realize, or should realize, that children are not possessions, but are only lent to us, angel boarders, as it were.

—*John Gregory Dunne*

"Family" is not just a buzz word for reactionaries; for women, as for men, it is the symbol of the last area where one has any hope of control over one's destiny, of meeting one's most basic human needs, of nourishing that core of personhood, threatened now by vast impersonal institutions and uncontrollable corporate and government bureaucracies.

—*Betty Friedan*

Relationships and communion are the most significant clues surrounding the mystery of our human nature. They tell us the most about who we are.

—*Susan Cahill*

Friendship is by its very nature freer of deceit than any other relationship we can know because it is the bond least affected by striving for power, physical pleasure, or material profit, most liberated from any oath of duty or constancy.

—*Francine du Plessix Gray*

Some people are your relatives but others are your ancestors, and you choose the ones you want to have as ancestors. You create yourself out of those.

—*Ralph Ellison*

Talents are best nurtured in solitude; character is best formed in the stormy billows of the world.

—*Johann Wolfgang von Goethe*

Friendship marks a life even more deeply than love.

—*Elie Wiesel*

Your children need your presence more than your presents.

—Jesse Jackson

The price of hating other human beings is loving oneself less.

—Eldridge Cleaver

In search of my mother's garden I found my own.

—Alice Walker

Every man's neighbor is his looking glass.

—English Proverb

Fate makes relatives, but choice makes friends.

—DeLile

I have three chairs in my house; one for solitude, two for friendship, three for society.

—Henry David Thoreau

Each friend represents a world in us, a world possibly not born until they arrive, and it is only by this meeting that a new world is born.

—Anaïs Nin

The family, not the individual, is the real molecule of society, the key link in the social chain of being.

—Robert Nisbet

Home is the place, when you have to go there, they have to take you in.

—Robert Frost

The moment we cease to hold each other, the minute we break faith with one another, the sea engulfs us and the light goes out.

—James Baldwin

We are people in search of a national community.

—Toni Morrison

Children have more need of models than of critics.

—Joseph Joubert

The family is the basic cell of government: it is where we are trained to believe that we are human beings or that we are chattel, it is where we are trained to see the sex and race divisions and become callous to injustice even if it is done to ourselves, to accept as biological a full system of authoritarian government.

—Gloria Steinem

All happy families resemble each other; each unhappy family is unhappy in its own way.

—Leo Tolstoy

Not people die but worlds die in them.

—Yevgeny Yevtushenko

APPLICATIONS

1. Review the perspectives on family and discuss them with your group. With whose views of family are you in agreement? With whom do you disagree? Write a journal entry explaining your responses.

2. Brainstorm on your associations with home. How do they differ from Frost's definition? Write your definition of home and share it with your group. Summarize what you learned about different concepts of home.

3. Discuss Morrison's perspective with your group. What is your interpretation of a "national community"? To what extent are Americans searching for it? Is it a dream of yours? Is it attainable? Write a specific summary of the highlights of your discussion.

The Good Samaritan

LUKE 10:29–37

The parable of the Good Samaritan is one of a number of stories told by Jesus to his followers. The original city of Samaria was the center of a sect whose worship at a separate temple (on Mt. Gerizim) and whose recognition of the authority of only the Pentateuch (the first five books of the Bible) led to continual tension with the Jews of Jerusalem and elsewhere. As you read the parable, brainstorm on your associations with the word "neighbor."

THEN ONE OF THE EXPERTS IN THE LAW stood up to test him and said,
"Master, what must I do to be sure of eternal life?"

"What does the Law say and what has your reading taught you?" said Jesus.

"The Law says, 'Thou shalt love the Lord thy God with all thy heart and with all thy soul and with all thy strength and with all thy mind—and thy neighbor as thyself,'" he replied.

"Quite right," said Jesus. "Do that and you will live."

But the man, wanting to justify himself, continued, "But who is my 'neighbor'?"

And Jesus gave him the following reply:

"A man was once on his way down from Jerusalem to Jericho. He fell into the hands of bandits who stripped off his clothes, beat him up, and left him half dead. It so happened that a priest was going down that road, and when he saw him he passed by on the other side. A Levite also came on the scene, and when he saw him he too passed by on the other side. But then a Samaritan traveler came along to the place where the man was lying, and at the sight of him he was touched with pity. He went across to him and bandaged his wounds, pouring on oil and wine. Then he put him on his own mule, brought him to an inn and did what he could for him. Next day he took out two silver coins and gave them to the innkeeper with the words: 'Look after him, will you? I will pay you back whatever more you spend, when I come through here on my return.' Which of these three seems to you to have been a neighbor to the bandits' victim?"

"The man who gave him practical sympathy," he replied.

"Then you go and give the same," returned Jesus.

INTERPRETATIONS

1. The lawyer wants to "test" Jesus and, after hearing Jesus' first answer, to "justify himself." How do you think he feels after hearing the parable and correctly answering Jesus' question? How do you explain the change?

2. Jesus connects salvation (inheriting "eternal life") with kind service to needy people. How important do *you* consider service to needy people? What's the best way to be of service? Can one do wrong in doing right? Do good works also require sensitivity and intelligence? Health and wealth? Why or why not?

3. "Love thy neighbor" turns out to be, in this parable, something quite practical. What is *your* idea of love?

4. Jesus answers the lawyer's second question—"And who is my neighbor?"—with a story instead of a definition. What definition does the story imply? Do you agree with the definition? Why or why not? How does Jesus tailor his story to his audience? Why does he choose a Samaritan as the hero of his story?

CORRESPONDENCES

1. "Every man's neighbor is his looking glass." What point is this English proverb making about behavior? How might that point apply to the parable of the Good Samaritan?

2. Review Goethe's perspective (page 17) and discuss its application to "The Good Samaritan."

APPLICATIONS

1. Discuss with your group the concept of community, a central theme in "The Good Samaritan." What emotional, sensory, and visual associations does the word evoke for you? When did you most feel part of a community? Is it possible to have a sense of community living in a city as opposed to a small town? What images do you associate with community? Can people from different cultures share a sense of community? Write a summary of your group's discussion citing specifics.

2. Write a journal entry describing your concept of an ideal community and the roles you can imagine yourself fulfilling in such a place.

3. Brainstorm on your associations with the word "neighbor." What images does it evoke? How has the concept of neighbor changed with time? What factors have contributed? How well do you know your next-door neighbor? Write a concise summary of the points discussed in your group.

In Search of Balance

TOM MONTGOMERY-FATE

Tom Montgomery-Fate (b. 1960) grew up in a small town in Iowa. Currently a professor of English at College of DuPage in Glen Ellyn, Illinois, he is the author of Beyond the White Noise *(1997), a collection of personal essays about teaching in the Philippines. His work has appeared in* The Boston Globe, The Chicago Tribune, Manoa, Puerto Del Sol, *and has aired on National Public Radio. This essay originally appeared in* Mothering *magazine, and is included in his forthcoming book,* Steady and Trembling. *Montgomery-Fate is searching for "balance" as a parent. What connotations does "balance" hold for you?*

EACH SPRING a trail that parallels the railroad tracks near our home converts itself from a frozen dirt path through a silhouette of trees and dried brambles into a leafy green tunnel. Stinkweed, nettles, and wild rhubarb spring from the warming earth. Sumac, bittersweet, and scrub hardwoods fill in the middle tier. Overhead, new leaves define a growing network of maple, oak, and cottonwood branches, which soon block much of the light. By summer the wooden frame homes and apartments that line the path disappear behind the swaying walls of green. You can no longer see around the trail's frequent bends and turns. It is a comforting blindness, one I look forward to. When I coast along the bumpy path on my old Raleigh 3-speed through the heart of suburbia with my two young daughters riding ahead of me, there is nothing I want to know less than exactly where we are or where we're going.

We never go very far. But for the girls, the simple path along the tracks may as well be a national forest. Tessa is 7 and likes to race ahead of us and double-back while I roll slowly along with Abby, who is 4, and learning to ride Tessa's old bike. Still in love with her red trike, Abby is skeptical. She is both excited and afraid of the hand-me-down two-wheeler. It is a little too big for her, the seat a little too high, even in its lowest position. The gritty bearings make pedaling difficult and the training wheels are rust-locked a bit out of position. When I first lifted her onto the seat and she tried to pedal, she became worried. It felt too tippy. Determined, she got back on and practiced. As she slowly cranked the wheels forward and rattled down the path, she began to lean her torso and shift her shoulders when the bike began to tip. Soon she found her balance.

That night at supper Tessa recalled her own fear when she first rode a two-wheeler. Like Abby, she didn't trust that the training wheels would "catch her." But what I most remember is when we took the training wheels off. Over and over I sprinted behind Tessa down the path with my hand on the small of her back as she pedaled and coasted and wobbled and dipped. It was awkward because I was both slightly pushing her forward and trying to hold her up—wanting to both keep her going and keep her from falling. As I panted along behind I encouraged her and reiterated two instructions: "keep the handlebars straight," and "don't shift your butt in the seat." Her face was screwed so tightly in concentration that I don't know if she heard. She was listening more to her body—to what it knew about balance—to what it feels like to roll upright into the wind on two thin rubber tires in spite of gravity. Seeing her confusion, I stopped talking, other than an occasional "You're doing great!" She didn't say a word the first few attempts. Though when she finally fell in the dirt she looked up at me like I had let her down. I consoled her, inspected her scrapes, and then said what my Dad had said: "Get right back on. You can do it!" After a half dozen more attempts she could nearly balance herself. Then she began to say it. The same thing I said to my Dad: "Let go!" "Let go!"

I finally did. She abruptly veered off the path onto a connected sidewalk, careened off someone's picket fence, bumped through their front yard, dodged a tangled garden hose, slowed her bike, and gently fell into a forsythia bush. I walked over to find her laughing.

When I tell this story to my friend Jim, a psychologist, he explains how balance works: Neurons in Tessa's inner ear are constantly firing to monitor her body's position and movement in space. "We learn it only by doing," Jim says. "The hands teach the brain. That's why once you learn how you never forget." It's called kinesthesis—a primitive, survival behavior—something we share with monkeys and dogs. Psychological balance, however, is a uniquely human concept.

I wish parenting was like riding a bike, or taping drywall, or playing a C scale on the piano—something you could master and remember. But once you learn how you always forget, because the how keeps changing. Coasting is rare. Pedaling up hill into the wind isn't: Fatigue grows into a roaring tantrum. Scissors are the only solution to a grape bubble-gum hairball. It's five minutes too late to replace the permanent set of markers with the washable ones. Barbie's head gets "accidentally" flushed down the toilet and is jammed somewhere inside.

My friend Dan used to take his daughters for rides on his tandem bike around their farm in Michigan. When they were small, Dan rode in front so he could steer. But as the girls got older they grew tired of their father's wide back and large head blocking their view of the vineyards and wildflowers. They wanted to control the bike themselves, to take their father for a ride rather than vice versa. So Dan moved to the rear. As his girls guided him along the bumpy gravel lanes he noticed that they pedaled slower than him and were less concerned about their destination. Still tall enough to see where they were going, he learned to enjoy riding in back. And the bike was more stable with his greater bulk in the rear position.

Bonnie, one of my former teachers, remembers when her son, Chris, first learned to ride a bike. After several practice sessions, he still couldn't quite balance himself. Then early one morning, while dressing, Bonnie and her husband looked out their bedroom window to see Chris riding all alone on the front sidewalk. As he triumphantly wobbled by he turned to look up at them. "I don't need you anymore," he yelled in a moment of joy.

Some nights I lie awake in bed next to my wife Carol long after she is asleep and the house has grown dark and I wonder how our children can both devastate and sustain me. I listen to the elm branches scratching in the wind at our wooden siding, to the wind-up alarm clock quietly ticking on my cluttered nightstand, and I start to remember things.

Does it matter that I can't tell whether these memories are from my childhood or theirs, that what separates my life as a son and as a father feels more like a membrane than a hard line?

Some nights this blurring of our lives is all I have to right myself: We swashed brilliant grass-green paint across the bottom of white paper, swiped raw blue strokes of sky across the top, and floated a yellow sun ball in between. We concocted silly songs and knock-knock jokes while locked in a traffic jam. We hid in the forts we built from wet snow or dead limbs or blankets and chairs, delighting in the dark refuge. We buried hamsters and gerbils and turtles and goldfish and had funeral services for each one. We played house and dress-up and pranced in the sprinkler and tried to count the stars. We flicked our wrists and watched a knot of worm fly out over the river, trailed by a red and white bobber and a double kerplunk. We learned to wait, to dream of the world beneath the moving water, to believe in the unseen.

Things didn't change as much as I thought they would during that long, bumpy ride from son to father. I am still my parents' child. I *still* struggle to fit in, and to stand out, and to feel at home somewhere. I still wonder if I am good enough, and fear I am missing something. I still teeter on the wheels of instinct and reason, never quite in balance.

My own father is nearly 80 now. About forty years ago he taught me how to ride a bike. I don't recall exactly how old I was or how many days it took me to learn. But I remember the bike: a little blue stingray with a sparkly, vinyl banana seat. I remember the desperate struggle to stay upright, the falling, the startling joy of not falling. I remember a fantasy I shared with a friend: with enough raw down-hill speed and the help of our unzipped coats snapping in the wind behind us, we could lift off the ground like the Wright brothers and pedal into the sky. I remember I trusted my father. "You can do it," he said. More a promise than an expectation, these words were sometimes unspoken—a kind of faith, which I suppose told him when to let go of his four sons. I still hear those words now, as I run behind my daughters, gently pushing, trying to hold them up—along with myself. "You can do it," I say, listening to my father, and preparing to fall.

INTERPRETATIONS

1. To what extent has the author seemed to have found a sense of balance? Cite examples to support your point of view.

2. The author suggests that the vulnerability a parent feels is not necessarily a sign of weakness or flaw, but evidence of the humanity he or she shares with his or her child. Do you agree? Why or why not?

3. Montgomery-Fate contrasts psychological and physical balance. How would you describe the importance of balance in a family or in an individual? How would you recognize it? Do you consider your family "balanced"? Cite evidence.

4. The essay focuses on the writer's children, on himself, and on his father. How does this continuity of family affect him?

5. This essay was published in *Mothering*, a magazine that rarely includes male writers. Why do you think it was selected? How does mothering or fathering differ from parenting?

6. How do you interpret the "comforting blindness" the author refers to in the introduction? How does this apply to what he says about parenting?

CORRESPONDENCES

1. Compare and contrast Montgomery-Fate's concept of fathering with that of Sawaquat.

2. Review Dunne's perspective on the parent–child relationship and discuss its relevance to Montgomery-Fate's text.

APPLICATIONS

1. Discuss with your group your views about parenting. Do you think that parenting and/or growing up has become easier, harder, or about the same? How important is it to preserve a sense of balance in family relationships? Summarize your conclusions.

2. Using this essay as a model, experiment with writing an extended essay on a different topic, perhaps on some other issue relating to family life.

3. Is there a family member who, in the present or in the past, caused you to see yourself in new ways? How was your self-concept changed by this relationship? To what extent was this person aware of the changes to which he or she contributed? Explain.

We Kissed the Tomato
and Then the Sky

DANA WEHLE

Dana Wehle (b. 1954), born in Queens, New York, now lives in Brooklyn. She is a classically trained painter with a Masters of Fine Arts. The daughter of two Holocaust survivors, her work has been recognized for its effectiveness in communicating the impact of the Holocaust on the second generation. She has a Master's degree in Social Work and is a certified psychoanalyst with a private psychotherapy practice in New York. As you read Wehle's essay, list in your journal her conflicting emotions about her mother. To what extent does she resolve them?

MY PARENTS' BIG BED was not the kind to take refuge in when I was little. The two twin beds, connected by an elegant walnut headboard, were each clearly assigned. One was his, one was hers. After my father died, my mother made the monumental decision to make his side hers after forty-three years of it being the other way. She defensively explained that her motive was not to help resolve her loss, but simply to be closer to the door. In fact, the increasing number of times she got up during the night became a matter of concern to us all.

When I visited her once she was alone, I knew she would have preferred my sleeping next to her but, always needing my space, I awkwardly told her I preferred to sleep upstairs in my old room. Our love was deep and passionate, but our differences were equally as strong. For years, I had perched on a ledge waiting patiently, and sometimes not so patiently, for an opening for her to let me love her and for her to return that love for an extended period of time without tense interruption. It might have happened that the clock ran out before that opening presented itself. But, like a seagull watching for signs of food, I didn't miss my chance.

Just a year and a half after my father died, as cancer slowed her down and her need to lead was increasingly balanced by her willingness to be led, I cherished sleeping next to her. Two grown women, mother and daughter in corny, flowery nightgowns, filled this once forbidding bed in precious unity. Night after night, our arms stretched across the crack between the beds as our hands warmly joined. With just one reading light easing the darkness, I now viewed the room from her vantage point. In this space that enveloped us both, my mother would share her disbelief at her illness, her increasing symptoms and pains and even her unanswerable questions. I would say, "Pfeh!"; and she would say, "That's right. Pfeh!" Each lying on our own side, we were fully on the same side in sharing the sadness and the anger. We talked about Karl, her first husband, and my father and how blessed she felt for having loved two such loving men. She asked me if I was happy with my husband, and I said "very." We bonded as two women who shared the thankfulness of knowing this type of love.

Once, I crawled on her side and kissed her soft cheek. She gave me her special "Safta"* kiss. I kissed her hand and retreated to my side of the enormous bed. In the middle of the night, I was awakened by her moans of pain, which she did not recall in the morning. Keeping to her routine, I made the bed in just the right way: the bedspread did not touch the floor, the quilts were not bumpy, and the throw pillows were not carelessly placed. In spite of this, she became cold when the temperature was warm; full when she ate only a spoonful; and tired when her day had barely begun.

The big bed, now perfectly made in its flowery pastel-colored spread with matching pillows, holds all these memories plus the last— her lying there no longer able to warmly hold my hand.

• • •

Who would have believed that in my lifetime I would have gotten to share meditation space with my mother? But in her last weeks, when the pain of cancer slowed her down, this fast-moving, always self-sufficient woman was too tired to run. She did not stop running all at once, however. It was gradual, more like the increasing presence of the left hand in a piano composition, where the effect of the grave bass notes emerges in time.

For my mother, shopping was once the beginning of a long day that included swimming forty laps, cooking up a storm, writing letters, doing "administrative work," and trying to sit down to write the last essay in a series on her Holocaust experiences. At this time, shopping alone wore her out. As she would say, "she couldn't anymore." How trapped she must have felt. Her survivor instincts told her she had to find new doors. Though she could no longer will her body to do more, she still had command over her mind and soul. At seventy-nine, this

---

*"Safta" means grandmother in Hebrew. This kiss had no name when my siblings and I were young but my mother called it "the safta kiss" with the grandchildren. It can't be described, it has to be experienced.

Czech Jewish woman who was set in her ways opened herself up to a "New Age" experience.

We meditated in two green-and-white lawn chairs, inhaling and exhaling as we felt the earth's energy travel through our bodies. We visualized ourselves as eagles flying above Floral Park and landing at Jones Beach. We watched the ocean come forward and recede as we observed our breathing doing the same. We felt the rhythm of nature and the universe and experienced ourselves being part of the whole. Guided by ancient wisdom, we tried to find balance within the extremes and centeredness in the moment. After we embraced memories of the past at Jones Beach and absorbed the ocean's lessons, we slowly traveled back to Queens. We landed and gently opened our eyes. My mother and I were sitting in the driveway in the sun, hearing the birds sing, the neighbors rattle their garbage cans, and the dogs bark as we listened to the silence.

One week later, two weeks before her death, we sat in a sculpture park with two dear friends. My mother enthusiastically suggested that she lead us through a meditation. I got to share this sacred space with her; this space she could create only because even at this desperate time, she was open to expansion. I still hear her saying "I feel the wind caressing my face."

• • •

She sat there with a weak smile on her face as her fading eyes suddenly filled with the recognition of a world once known. Around the large dining room table, my mother, my sisters, and I were assembled. My brother went between this room and another, changing CDs as we all tried to decide which music to play at her funeral. The surrealism of the moment was not lost.

I sat directly across from her and caught the flash of light in her sunken eyes as the Beethoven piece we played at my father's funeral filled the air. I think the others missed this flash as they continued to discuss the options. I requested that we be silent and share the experience.

If music can be worn out, this Beethoven concerto would have been destroyed by how often my mother listened to it after my father's death. After a year or so, however, this same CD became lethal for her as she could no longer bear the pain that it evoked. On this day before her own death and one and a half years after my father's, with fresh ears, she received this music as an offering from heaven.

My mother described our relationship as love/hate. But at that time, when only I seemed to know what filled her heart, I knew what she meant by her last direct words to me: "It always amazed me how you would sometimes know what I was feeling without my saying the words."

Dear Ma, I had a dream a few days after you died and all I remember is you sitting at the end of the table smiling at me as you knew I knew the profound joy you were feeling at the moment Daddy's music filled your soul.

• • •

Oddly, my mother's death has given me a sense of completion in a way similar to my finishing a painting. Drawn studies, painted studies, notes, and art materials fill my studio as the residue of final works. Audio tapes and journals crammed with ponderings about my parents' future deaths fill my drawers, which, with my memories, are the stuff of my latest final work. I prepared for the day when I could no longer hear their voices by taping their sweetest answering machine messages. One year after my father's death Ma left these:

Are you home? Daninko? OK. I just came from the city. I wanted to report to you, OK? Thank you, Bye-bye. (October 1996)

Hi Dana. Are you there? Are you home? Oh. What a pity. Channel 13. Danny Kaye. So, I thought you would laugh. Anyhow, Bye-bye. (December 1996)

My mother's urgency defined her life-affirming existence, yet it was also a constant reminder to me of her emotional scars. She beat death so many times, from the gas chambers to critical illnesses. She was just beginning to beat her paralyzing grief after my father's death. Now, her obsessive race, which she so ably finessed over her lifetime, was over.

This seventy-nine-year-old woman was a juggler extraordinaire, but a juggler's art is both exhilarating and unsettling to watch. Warding off the sound of shattering plates, my mother looked straight ahead till the very end. One quiet night, however, she did confess that she was not sure whether she or the cancer was in control. When the terror of death found its way through her thick defenses, my mother found solace in knowing she would be with my father when she died.

The last of her messages was left thirty-four days before her end, and it went like this:

Hi Dana. I am just reporting. I am chewing my breakfast very slowly. I came from swimming . . . and I will rest . . . and then I will go to get the drug. And I had a very good, peaceful night.

And also Dr. Li called me, how I am feeling after that tea. So, that was very nice. I hope you are fine. I am just reporting. Bye-bye. (May 1997)

I suppose it's because she had no regrets, and because I now have many answers to questions that occupied me since I was young, that I feel some sense of completion. Both finishing a painting and saying goodbye to someone you love require time to reflect upon moments that are just right as well as unanswered questions.

Hello? Dani? Are you home? That's Ma. Are you there? Dana? OK, so I just wanted to know what is going on. I didn't hear from you, so I wanted to make sure that you are OK. So call me if you feel up to it. OK? Bye-bye. (March 1997)

Ma. I'm here. Where are you?

• • •

The house is still intact; the pillows on the couch are still scrunched from someone's weight; the flowers in the vases are still more alive than dead; the mail is still coming to a woman who was alive less than a month ago and to a man long gone. My home. My house where I grew up. My parents' house. My mother's house.

Soon my mother's beloved tomato plants, still green, will bear the red harvest that she knew she would not live to see. The piano, which once eloquently spoke for my father through his strong fingers and passionate heart, will be among the things removed. The smell of cardboard boxes mingling with the sight of frenzied dust particles will signal that the pain of saying goodbye is near.

I comfort myself by knowing that my mother's refined artistic sensibility will filter into my home when some of her artwork and belongings will become my own. I look forward to honoring my promise to my father to organize "the stuff downstairs" into an archive. This stuff (rare, browning photographs and documents from before the war; my parents' published writings as witnesses to the Holocaust; materials from my father's years as administrative head of the Jewish Community in Prague, hospital administrator, and Czech Jewish historian; as well as newer family memorabilia) has always been, and will always be, a defiant symbol of their survival. I feel calmed by the honor of this task.

Though the breakdown has not yet started, I have already felt compelled to rescue a remnant of my mother's favorite shirt from being used simply as a rag. The familiar battle between a need to hold on and a voice that says let go has begun. I guess that saying goodbye to her, to him again, and to the house will mean separating from the rags. I guess that the struggle itself will bestow honor upon them and the home they created.

• • •

Today is September 4, 1997, and always counting the time since my father died, I just realized that today is exactly one year and ten months since his death. Ma died on June 11 and I now count both their days, though hers is still counted only in months. The house has been totally dismantled, and its stark emptiness is especially pronounced when strangers come to check out whether they want to make it their home. Like the sound of a wailing Greek chorus, the lamenting of old neighbors, family, and dear friends counters the silent indifference of those who pass through with no feeling. A sweet, subtle reminder of the way Ma sounded when she answered the phone by one of those who loved her the most brings it all back.

Last week, my husband and I picked a juicy red tomato off the stem. Holding each other tightly, we kissed this symbol of life, each other, and then the sky. Our hands could not part. This was our goodbye. Later on, my sister and I held each other. We cried. We prayed. We laughed in our childhood bedroom, as we got one last touch of the textured linoleum tiles that used to bruise our hands while we endlessly practiced to be in the "Jacks Olympics." Filled with the joy of sharing, we said our goodbye.

• • •

Today is September 4, 2000 and I still have not stopped saying goodbye. Tonight, about five years since my father died and about three years since my mother died, the beautiful bright moon suddenly appeared outside my window. Memories of my parents, like the moon, often emerge unexpectedly as sources of light surrounded by darkness. Some nights, when sleep is alluding me, I am struck by the power of memory. Once, while thinking about someone's wedding plans, my eyes got overwhelmed with tears because all I could think about was how gleaming my father's eyes were when he shared in the joy of my wedding just two weeks before he died. Another time, while watching a poignant late night "Roseanne" rerun, I suddenly cried reckless tears because all I could think about was how loving my mother was when she brought me homemade soup while I was recovering from surgery one year before she died.

Each time my tears of loss turn into tears of gratitude, I say good-bye again. Each time my tears of loss turn into tears of gratitude, I feel the wind caressing my face.

INTERPRETATIONS

1. The author refers several times to her mother's urgency. Does this word also describe the author? What examples can you cite? What is the underlying reason for her urgency?

2. Time is an important theme in this essay. What direct and indirect techniques does the author use to suggest the passing of time?

3. Characterize the author's relationship with her mother. What different aspects of this relationship does she portray in the essay?

4. Analyze her father's role in the essay. What symbols does the author associate with him? How do these add unity to the memoir?

CORRESPONDENCES

1. Walker's perspective reflects upon the links between her mother and herself. To what extent is this also true of Wehle's text?

2. Cahill's perspective addresses relationships and communion. Find examples of each in Wehle's text and analyze their effect.

APPLICATIONS

1. Wehle uses many literary techniques to enhance theme. With your group members, cite examples of foreshadowing, similies, and metaphors. To what senses do they appeal? Are there examples that indicate Wehle's interest in the visual arts? Why does she end her essay with a line that occurs earlier? How has its meaning changed?

2. Wehle discusses part of her mother's history and the values she communicated. Write an essay analyzing the impact that your family's history and values has had on you. Be specific.

3. Review the answering machine tapes in Wehle's essay. What do they reveal about her mother? What do they add to knowledge of the author? Is this an effective method for writing memoirs? Why or why not?

Focusing on Friends

STEVE TESICH

Steve Tesich (1943–1996) was born in Yugoslavia and immigrated to the United States when he was fourteen. He is best known for the original screenplay Breaking Away *(1979), for which he won an Academy Award. He also wrote the screenplays* Eyewitness *(1981) and* Four Friends *(1981); many plays for the theater, including* Passing Game *(1977),* The Road *(1978), and* Division Street *(1980); and a novel,* Summer Crossing *(1982). A recurring theme in Tesich's work is the plight of the outsider. Before reading Tesich's essay, brainstorm on the word "friend."*

WHEN I THINK OF PEOPLE who were my good friends, I see them all, as I do everything else from my life, in cinematic terms. The camera work is entirely different for men and women.

I remember all the women in almost extreme close-ups. The settings are different—apartments, restaurants—but they're all interiors, as if I had never spent a single minute with a single woman outside. They're looking right at me, these women in these extreme close-ups; the lighting is exquisite, worthy of a Fellini or Fosse film, and their lips are moving. They're telling me something important or reacting to something even more important that I've told them. It's the kind of movie where you tell people to keep quiet when they chew their popcorn too loudly.

The boys and men who were my friends are in an entirely different movie. No close-ups here. No exquisite lighting. The camera work is rather shaky but the background is moving. We're going somewhere, on foot, on bicycles, in cars. The ritual of motion, of action, makes up for the inconsequential nature of the dialogue. It's a much sloppier film, this film that is not really a film but a memory of real friends: Slobo, Louie, Sam. Male friends. I've loved all three of them. I assumed they knew this, but I never told them.

Quite the contrary is true in my female films. In close-up after close-up, I am telling every woman who I ever loved that I love her, and then lingering on yet another close-up of her face for a reaction. There is a perfectly appropriate musical score playing while I wait. And if I wait long enough, I get an answer. I am loved. I am not loved. Language clears up the suspense. The emotion is nailed down.

Therein lies the difference, I think, between my friendships with men and with women. I can tell women I love them. Not only can I tell them, I am compulsive about it. I can hardly wait to tell them. But I can't tell the men. I just can't. And they can't tell me. Emotions are never nailed down. They run wild, and I and my male friends chase after them, on foot, on bicycles, in cars, keeping the quarry in sight but never catching up.

My first friend was Slobo. I was still living in Yugoslavia at the time, and not far from my house there was an old German truck left abandoned after the war. It had no wheels. No windshield. No doors. But the steering wheel was intact. Slobo and I flew to America in that truck. It was our airplane. Even now, I remember the background moving as we took off down the street, across Europe, across the Atlantic. We were inseparable. The best of friends. Naturally, not one word concerning the nature of our feelings for one another was ever exchanged. It was all done in actions.

The inevitable would happen at least once a day. As we were flying over the Atlantic, there came, out of nowhere, that wonderful moment: engine failure! "We'll have to bail out," I shouted. "A-a-a-a-a!" Slobo made the sound of the failing engine. Then he would turn and look me in the eye: "I can't swim," he'd say. "Fear not." I put my hand on his shoulder. "I'll drag you to shore." And, with that, both of us would tumble out of the truck onto the dusty street. I swam through the dust. Slobo drowned in the dust, coughing, gagging. "Sharks!" he cried. But I always saved him. The next day the ritual would be repeated, only then it would be my turn to say "I can't swim," and Slobo would save me. We saved each other from certain death over a hundred times, until finally a day came when I really left for America with my mother and sister. Slobo and I stood at the train station. We were there to say goodbye, but, since we weren't that good at saying things and since he couldn't save me, he just cried until the train started to move.

The best friend I had in high school was Louie. It now seems to me that I was totally monogamous when it came to male friends. I would have several girl friends but only one real male friend. Louie was it at that time. We were both athletes, and one day we decided to "run till we drop." We just wanted to know what it was like. Skinny Louie set the pace as we ran around our high-school track. Lap after lap. Four laps to a mile. Mile after mile we ran. I had the reputation as being a big-time jock. Louie didn't. But this was Louie's day. There was a bounce in his step and, when he turned back to look at me, his eyes were gleaming with the thrill of it all. I finally dropped. Louie still looked fresh; he seemed capable, on that day, of running forever. But we were the best of friends, and so he stopped. "That's it," he lied, "I couldn't go another step farther." It was an act of love. Naturally, I said nothing.

Louie got killed in Vietnam. Several weeks after his funeral, I went to his mother's house, and, because she was a woman, I tried to tell her how much I had loved her son. It was not a good scene. Although I was telling the truth, my words sounded like lies. It was all very painful and embarrassing. I kept thinking how sorry I was that I had never told Louie himself.

Sam is my best friend now, and has been for many years. A few years ago, we were swimming at a beach in East Hampton. The Atlantic! The very Atlantic I had flown over in my German truck with Slobo. We had swum out pretty far from the shore when both of us simultaneously thought we spotted a shark. Water is not only a good conductor of electricity but of panic as well. We began splashing like madmen toward shore. Suddenly, at the height of my panic, I realized how much I loved my friend, what an irreplaceable friend he was, and, although I was the faster swimmer, I fell back to protect him. Naturally, the shark in the end proved to be imaginary. But not my feelings for my friend. For several days after that I wanted to share my discovery with him, to tell him how much I love him. Fortunately, I didn't.

I say fortunately because on reflection, there seems to be sufficient evidence to indicate that, if anybody was cheated and shortchanged by me, it was the women, the girls, the very recipients of my uncensored emotions. Yes, I could hardly wait to tell them I loved them. I did love them. But once I told them, something stopped. The emotion was nailed down, but, with it, the enthusiasm and the energy to prove it was nailed down, too. I can remember my voice saying to almost all of them, at one time or another: "I told you I love you. What else do you want?" I can now recoil at the impatient hostility of that voice but I can't deny it was mine.

The tyranny of self-censorship forced me, in my relations with male friends, to seek alternatives to language. And just because I could never be sure they understood exactly how I felt about them, I was forced to look for ways to prove it. That is, I now think how it should be. It is time to make adjustments. It is time to pull back the camera, free the women I know, and myself, from those merciless close-ups and have the background move.

INTERPRETATIONS

1. Contrast Tesich's treatment of male and female friends in his cinematic imagination and in his real life.

2. To what extent do you agree with Tesich that telling a person you love him or her "nails down" the emotion?

3. By moving from the general to the specific, Tesich is able to present Slobo, Louie, and Sam in some detail. How do his portrayals of them clarify his purpose? How do they affect you as his audience?

CORRESPONDENCES

1. Review the Nin perspective on friendship (page 18). How does it apply to Tesich's relationships with his male friends?

2. Apply the du Plessix Gray perspective on friendship (page 17) to Tesich's portrayal of his friendships with women. To what extent do you treat male and female friends differently?

APPLICATIONS

1. In addition to contrasting friendships between men and women and women and men, Tesich also defines friendship in general. Discuss his ideas about friendship with your group. To what extent do you agree with his gender distinctions? Do your friendships fit into the categories he discusses? Write a summary of your conclusions.

2. From the title to the last sentence, much of the language is from the world of filmmaking. How does this language help Tesich clarify his meaning and purpose? Support your point of view with specific examples.

3. How do you differentiate between an acquaintance and a friend? Do you consider someone you "hang out" with frequently your friend? Write a journal entry on these questions.

from White Tigers

MAXINE HONG KINGSTON

Maxine Hong Kingston (b. 1940) was born to Chinese immigrant parents in Stockton, California and did not speak English until she started school. Kingston went on to excel academically and graduated from the University of California, Berkeley. In 1976, while teaching in Hawaii, she published her most successful and critically acclaimed autobiographical novel The Woman Warrior: Memoirs of a Girlhood Among Ghosts. *Kingston's other books include:* China Men *(1980),* Hawaii One Summer *(1987),* Tripmaster Monkey: His Fake Book *(1989),* The Literature of California: Native American Beginnings to 1945, Volume 1 *(2000) [Editor], and* To Be The Poet *(2002). Kingston's most recent novel,* The Fifth Book of Peace, *was published in 2003. Record in your journal, several responses to Kingston's opening sentence.*

MY AMERICAN LIFE has been such a disappointment.

"I got straight A's, Mama."

"Let me tell you a true story about a girl who saved her village."

I could not figure out what was my village. And it was important that I do something big and fine, or else my parents would sell me when we made our way back to China. In China there were solutions for what to do with little girls who ate up food and threw tantrums. You can't eat straight A's.

When one of my parents or the emigrant villagers said, "Feeding girls is feeding cowbirds," I would thrash on the floor and scream so hard I couldn't talk. I couldn't stop.

"What's the matter with her?"

"I don't know. Bad, I guess. You know how girls are. 'There's no profit in raising girls. Better to raise geese than girls.'"

"I would hit her if she were mine. But then there's no use wasting all that discipline on a girl. 'When you raise girls, you're raising children for strangers.'"

"Stop that crying!" my mother would yell. "I'm going to hit you if you don't stop. Bad girl! Stop!" I'm going to remember never to hit or to scold my children for crying, I thought, because then they will only cry more.

"I'm not a bad girl," I would scream. "I'm not a bad girl. I'm not a bad girl." I might as well have said, "I'm not a girl."

"When you were little, all you had to say was 'I'm not a bad girl,' and you could make yourself cry," my mother says, talking-story about my childhood.

I minded that the emigrant villagers shook their heads at my sister and me. "One girl—and another girl," they said, and made our parents ashamed to take us out together. The good part about my brothers being born was that people stopped saying, "All girls," but I learned new grievances. "Did you roll an egg on *my* face like that when *I* was born?" "Did you have a full-month party for *me*?" "Did you turn on all the lights?" "Did you send *my* picture to Grandmother?" "Why not? Because I'm a girl? Is that why not?" "Why didn't you teach me English?" "You like having me beaten up at school, don't you?"

"She is very mean, isn't she?" the emigrant villagers would say.

"Come, children. Hurry. Hurry. Who wants to go out with Great-Uncle?" On Saturday mornings, my great-uncle, the ex-river pirate, did the shopping. "Get your coats, whoever's coming."

"I'm coming. I'm coming. Wait for me."

When he heard girls' voices, he turned on us and roared, "No girls!" and left my sisters and me hanging our coats back up, not looking at one another. The boys came back with candy and new toys. When they walked through Chinatown, the people must have said, "A boy—and another boy—and another boy!" At my great-uncle's funeral I secretly tested out feeling glad that he was dead—the six-foot bearish masculinity of him.

I went away to college—Berkeley in the sixties—and I studied, and I marched to change the world, but I did not turn into a boy. I would have liked to bring myself back as a boy for my parents to welcome with chickens and pigs. That was for my brother, who returned alive from Vietnam.

If I went to Vietnam, I would not come back; females desert families. It was said, "There is an outward tendency in females," which meant that I was getting straight A's for the good of my future husband's family, not my own. I did not plan ever to have a husband. I would show my mother and father and the nosy emigrant villagers that girls have no outward tendency. I stopped getting straight A's.

And all the time I was having to turn myself American-feminine, or no dates.

There is a Chinese word for the female I—which is "slave." Break the women with their own tongues!

I refused to cook. When I had to wash dishes, I would crack one or two. "Bad girl," my mother yelled, and sometimes that made me gloat rather than cry. Isn't a bad girl almost a boy?

"What do you want to be when you grow up, little girl?"

"A lumberjack in Oregon."

Even now, unless I'm happy, I burn the food when I cook. I do not feed people. I let the dirty dishes rot. I eat at other people's tables but won't invite them to mine, where the dishes are rotting.

If I could not eat, perhaps I could make myself a warrior like the swordswoman who drives me. I will—I must—rise and plow the fields as soon as the baby comes out.

Once I get outside the house, what bird might call me; on what horse could I ride away? Marriage and childbirth strengthen the swordswoman, who is not a maid like Joan of Arc. Do the women's work; then do more work, which will become ours too. No husband of mine will say, "I could have been a drummer, but I had to think about the wife and kids. You know how it is." Nobody supports me at the expense of his own adventure. Then I get bitter: no one supports me; I am not loved enough to be supported. That I am not a burden has to compensate for the sad envy when I look at women loved enough to be supported. Even now China wraps double binds around my feet.

When urban renewal tore down my parents' laundry and paved over our slum for a parking lot, I only made up gun and knife fantasies and did nothing useful.

From the fairy tales, I've learned exactly who the enemy are. I easily recognize them—business-suited in their modern American executive guise, each boss two feet taller than I am and impossible to meet eye to eye.

I once worked at an art supply house that sold paints to artists. "Order more of that nigger yellow, willya?" the boss told me. "Bright, isn't it? Nigger yellow."

"I don't like that word," I had to say in my bad, small-person's voice that makes no impact. The boss never deigned to answer.

I also worked at a land developer's association. The building industry was planning a banquet for contractors, real estate dealers, and real estate editors. "Did you know the restaurant you chose for the banquet is being picketed by CORE and the NAACP?" I squeaked.

"Of course I know." The boss laughed. "That's why I chose it."

"I refuse to type these invitations," I whispered, voice unreliable.

He leaned back in his leather chair, his bossy stomach opulent. He picked up his calendar and slowly circled a date. "You will be paid up to here," he said. "We'll mail you the check."

If I took the sword, which my hate must surely have forged out of the air, and gutted him, I would put color and wrinkles into his shirt.

It's not just the stupid racists that I have to do something about, but the tyrants who for whatever reason can deny my family food and work. My job is my own only land.

To avenge my family, I'd have to storm across China to take back our farm from the Communists; I'd have to rage across the United States to take back the laundry in New York and the one in California. Nobody in history has conquered and united both North America and Asia. A descendant of eighty pole fighters, I ought to be able to set out confidently, march straight down our street, get going right now. There's work to do, ground to cover. Surely, the eighty pole fighters, though unseen, would follow me and lead me and protect me, as is the wont of ancestors.

Or it may well be that they're resting happily in China, their spirits dispersed among the real Chinese, and not nudging me at all with their poles. I mustn't feel bad that I haven't done as well as the swordswoman did; after all, no bird called me, no wise old people tutored me. I have no magic beads, or water gourd sight, no rabbit that will jump in the fire when I'm hungry. I dislike armies.

I've looked for the bird. I've seen clouds make pointed angel wings that stream past the sunset, but they shred into clouds. Once at a beach after a long hike I saw a seagull, tiny as an insect. But when I jumped up to tell what miracle I saw, before I could get the words out I understood that the bird was insect-size because it was far away. My brain had momentarily lost its depth perception. I was that eager to find an unusual bird.

The news from China has been confusing. It also had something to do with birds. I was nine years old when the letters made my parents, who are rocks, cry. My father screamed in his sleep. My mother wept and crumpled up the letters. She set fire to them page by page in the ashtray, but new letters came almost every day. The only letters they opened without fear were the ones with red borders, the holiday letters that mustn't carry bad news. The other letters said that my uncles were made to kneel on broken glass during their trials and had confessed to being landowners. They were all executed, and the aunt whose thumbs were twisted off drowned herself. Other aunts, mothers-in-law, and cousins disappeared; some suddenly began writing to us again from communes or from Hong Kong. They kept asking for money. The ones in communes got four ounces of fat and one cup of oil a week, they said, and had to work from 4 A.M. to 9 P.M. They had to learn to do dances waving red kerchiefs; they had to sing nonsense syllables. The Communists gave axes to the old ladies and said, "Go and kill yourself. You're useless." If we overseas Chinese would just send money to the Communist bank, our relatives said, they might get a percentage of it for themselves. The aunts in Hong Kong said to send money quickly; their children were begging on the sidewalks and mean people put dirt in their bowls.

When I dream that I am wire without flesh, there is a letter on blue airmail paper that floats above the night ocean between here and China. It must arrive safely or else my grandmother and I will lose each other.

My parents felt bad whether or not they sent money. Sometimes they got angry at their brothers and sisters for asking. And they would not simply ask but have to talk-story too. The revolutionaries had taken Fourth Aunt and Uncle's store, house, and lands. They attacked the house and killed the grandfather and oldest daughter. The grandmother escaped with the loose cash and did not return to help. Fourth Aunt picked up her sons, one under each arm, and hid in the pig house, where they slept that night in cotton clothes. The next day she found her husband, who had also miraculously escaped. The two of them collected twigs and yams to sell while their children begged. Each morning they tied the faggots on each other's back. Nobody bought from them. They ate the yams and some of the children's rice. Finally Fourth Aunt saw what was wrong. "We have to shout 'Fuel for sale' and 'Yams for sale,'" she said. "We can't just walk unobtrusively up and down the street." "You're right," said my uncle, but he was shy and walked in back of her. "Shout," my aunt ordered, but he could not. "They think we're carrying these sticks home for our own fire," she said. "Shout." They walked about miserably, silently, until sundown, neither of them able to advertise themselves. Fourth Aunt, an orphan since the age of ten, mean as my mother, threw her bundle down at his feet and scolded Fourth Uncle, "Starving to death, his wife and children starving to death, and he's too damned shy to raise his voice." She left him standing by himself and afraid to return empty-handed to her. He sat under a tree to think, when he spotted a pair of nesting doves. Dumping his bag of yams, he climbed up and caught the birds. That was when the Communists trapped him, in the tree. They criticized him for selfishly taking food for his own family and killed him, leaving his body in the tree as an example. They took the birds to a commune kitchen to be shared.

It is confusing that my family was not the poor to be championed. They were executed like the barons in the stories, when they were not barons. It is confusing that birds tricked us.

What fighting and killing I have seen have not been glorious but slum grubby. I fought the most during junior high school and always cried. Fights are confusing as to who has won. The corpses I've seen had been rolled and dumped, sad little dirty bodies covered with a police khaki blanket. My mother locked her children in the house so we couldn't look at dead slum people. But at news of a body, I would find a way to get out; I had to learn about dying if I wanted to become a swordswoman. Once there was an Asian man stabbed next door, words on cloth pinned to his corpse. When the police came around asking questions, my father said, "No read Japanese. Japanese words. Me Chinese."

I've also looked for old people who could be my gurus. A medium with red hair told me that a girl who died in a far country follows me wherever I go. This spirit can help me if I acknowledge her, she said. Between the head line and heart line in my right palm, she said, I have the mystic cross. I could become a medium myself. I don't want to be a medium. I don't want to be a crank taking "offerings" in a wicker plate from the frightened audience, who, one after another asked the spirits how to raise rent money, how to cure their coughs and skin diseases, how to find a job. And martial arts are for unsure little boys kicking away under fluorescent lights.

I live now where there are Chinese and Japanese, but no emigrants from my own village looking at me as if I had failed them. Living among one's own emigrant villagers can give a good Chinese far from China glory and a place. "That old busboy is really a swordsman," we whisper when he goes by, "He's a swordsman who's killed fifty. He has a tong ax in his closet." But I am useless, one more girl who couldn't be sold. When I visit the family now, I wrap my American successes around me like a private shawl; I *am* worthy of eating the food. From afar I can believe my family loves me fundamentally. They only say, "When fishing for treasures in the flood, be careful not to pull in girls," because that is what one says about daughters. But I watched such words come out of my own mother's and father's mouths; I looked at their ink drawing of poor people snagging their neighbor's flotage with long flood hooks and pushing the girl babies on down the river. And I had to get out of hating range. I read in an anthropology book that Chinese say, "Girls are necessary too"; I have never heard the Chinese I know make this concession. Perhaps it was a saying in another village. I refuse to shy my way anymore through our Chinatown, which tasks me with the old sayings and the stories.

The swordswoman and I are not so dissimilar. May my people understand the resemblance soon so that I can return to them. What we have in common are the words at our backs. The ideographs for *revenge* are "report a crime" and "report to five families." The reporting is the vengeance—not the beheading, not the gutting, but the words. And I have so many words—"chink" words and "gook" words too—that they do not fit on my skin.

INTERPRETATIONS

1. Much of the "disappointment" Kingston has experienced is the result of an ingrained favoritism of sons over daughters. How much of this attitude in these particular parents is traditional and

how much is heartfelt? Cite details. Do you believe tradition is powerful enough to make parents truly hate a daughter?

2. How does Kingston react to her parents' treatment of her?

3. What obstacles lie in the way of Kingston making herself a "warrior" or "swordswoman"? What is her attitude toward these obstacles—self-pity, humor, philosophical acceptance? How can you tell?

4. Check the Glossary for definitions of *tone*. What is the tone of the sentence, "Nobody in history has conquered and united both North America and Asia"? Where do you find other sentences in this same tone?

5. Speaking of marriage, the author says, "Even now China wraps double binds around my feet." What does she mean?

6. "From the fairy tales, I've learned exactly who the enemy are." What fairy-tale elements does the author weave into her narrative? What do these elements contribute to the narrative?

Mother Tongue

AMY TAN

Amy Tan (b. 1952) had a wide variety of jobs, including bartending and car-
ing for developmentally disabled children, before writing The Joy Luck Club
(1989) for which she won the LA Book Award and The National Book Award.
Tan's other books include The Kitchen God's Wife *(1991),* The Moon
Lady *(1992),* The Hundred Secret Senses *(1995), and* The Bonesetter's
Daughter *(2000).* The Opposite of Fate, *a work of non-fiction was pub-*
lished in 2003. In addition to writing, Tan is a member of The Rock Bottom
Remainders, a rock band that includes Stephen King, Dave Barry, Ridley
Pearson, Scott Turow, and Matt Groening. To what extent do you, like Tan,
use "different Englishes"?

I AM NOT A SCHOLAR OF ENGLISH or literature. I cannot give you much more than personal opinions on the English language and its variations in this country or others.

I am a writer. And by that definition, I am someone who has always loved language. I am fascinated by language in daily life. I spend a great deal of my time thinking about the power of language—the way it can evoke an emotion, a visual image, a complex idea, or a simple truth. Language is the tool of my trade. And I use them all—all the Englishes I grew up with.

Recently, I was made keenly aware of the different Englishes I do use. I was giving a talk to a large group of people, the same talk I had already given to half a dozen other groups. The nature of the talk was about my writing, my life, and my book, *The Joy Luck Club*. The talk was going along well enough, until I remembered one major difference that made the whole talk sound wrong. My mother was in the room. And it was perhaps the first time she had heard me give a lengthy speech, using the kind of English I have never used with her. I was saying things like, "The intersection of memory upon imagination" and "There is an aspect of my fiction that relates to thus-and-thus"—a speech filled with carefully wrought grammatical phrases, burdened, it suddenly seemed to me, with nominalized forms, past perfect tenses, conditional phrases, all the forms of standard English that I had learned in school and through books, the forms of English I did not use at home with my mother.

Just last week, I was walking down the street with my mother, and I again found myself conscious of the English I was using, the English I do use with her. We were talking about the price of new and used furniture and I heard myself saying this: "Not waste money that way." My husband was with us as well, and he didn't notice any switch in my English. And then I realized why. It's because over the twenty years we've been together I've often used that same kind of English with him, and sometimes he even uses it with me. It has become our language of intimacy, a different sort of English that relates to family talk, the language I grew up with.

So you'll have some idea of what this family talk I heard sounds like, I'll quote what my mother said during a recent conversation which I videotaped and then transcribed. During this conversation, my mother was talking about a political gangster in Shanghai who had the same last name as her family's, Du, and how the gangster in his early years wanted to be adopted by her family, which was rich by comparison. Later, the gangster became more powerful, far richer than my mother's family, and one day showed up at my mother's wedding to pay his respects. Here's what she said in part:

"Du Yusong having business like fruit stand. Like off the street kind. He is Du like Du Zong—but not Tsung-ming Island people. The local people call putong, the river east side, he belong to that side local people. That man want to ask Du Zong father take him in like become own family. Du Zong father wasn't look down on him, but didn't take seriously, until that man big like become a mafia. Now important person, very hard to inviting him. Chinese way, came only to show respect, don't stay for dinner. Respect for making big celebration, he shows up. Mean gives lots of respect. Chinese custom. Chinese social life that way. If too important won't have to stay too long. He come to my wedding. I didn't see, I heard it. I gone to boy's side, they have YMCA dinner. Chinese age I was nineteen."

You should know that my mother's expressive command of English belies how much she actually understands. She reads the *Forbes* report, listens to *Wall Street Week,* converses daily with her stockbroker, reads all of Shirley MacLaine's books with ease—all kinds of things I can't begin to understand. Yet some of my friends tell me they understand 50 percent of what my mother says. Some say they understand 80 to 90 percent. Some say they understand none of it, as if she were speaking pure Chinese. But to me, my mother's English is perfectly clear, perfectly natural. It's my mother tongue. Her language, as I hear it, is vivid, direct, full of observation and imagery. That was the language that helped shape the way I saw things, expressed things, made sense of the world.

Lately, I've been giving more thought to the kind of English my mother speaks. Like others, I have described it to people as "broken" or "fractured" English. But I wince when I say that. It has always bothered me that I can think of no way to describe it other than "broken," as if it were damaged and needed to be fixed, as if it lacked a certain wholeness and soundness. I've heard other terms used, "limited English," for example. But they seem just as bad, as if everything is limited, including people's perceptions of the limited English speaker.

I know this for a fact, because when I was growing up, my mother's "limited" English limited *my* perception of her. I was ashamed of her English. I believed that her English reflected the quality of what she had to say. That is, because she expressed them imperfectly her thoughts were imperfect. And I had plenty of empirical evidence to support me: the fact that people in department stores, at banks, and at restaurants did not take her seriously, did not give her good service, pretended not to understand her, or even acted as if they did not hear her.

My mother has long realized the limitations of her English as well. When I was fifteen, she used to have me call people on the phone to pretend I was she. In this guise, I was forced to ask for information or even to complain and yell at people who had been rude to her. One time it was a call to her stockbroker in New York. She had cashed out her small portfolio and it just so happened we were going to go to New York the next week, our very first trip outside California. I had to get on the phone and say in an adolescent voice that was not very convincing, "This is Mrs. Tan."

And my mother was standing in the back whispering loudly, "Why he don't send me check, already two weeks late. So mad he lie to me, losing me money."

And then I said in perfect English, "Yes, I'm getting rather concerned. You had agreed to send the check two weeks ago, but it hasn't arrived."

Then she began to talk more loudly. "What he want, I come to New York tell him front of his boss, you cheating me?" And I was trying to calm her down, make her be quiet, while telling the stockbroker, "I can't tolerate any more excuses. If I don't receive the check immediately, I am going to have to speak to your manager when I'm in New York next week." And sure enough, the following week there we were in front of this astonished stockbroker, and I was sitting there red-faced and quiet, and my mother, the real Mrs. Tan, was shouting at his boss in her impeccable broken English.

We used a similar routine just five days ago, for a situation that was far less humorous. My mother had gone to the hospital for an appointment, to find out about a benign brain tumor a CAT scan had revealed a month ago. She said she had spoken very good English, her best English, no mistakes. Still, she said, the hospital did not apologize when they said they had lost the CAT scan and she had come for nothing. She said they did not seem to have any sympathy when she told them she was anxious to know the exact diagnosis, since her husband and son had both died of brain tumors. She said they would not give her any more information until the next time and she would have to make another appointment for that. So she said she would not leave until the doctor called her daughter. She wouldn't budge. And when the doctor finally called her daughter, me, who spoke in perfect English—lo and behold—we had assurances the CAT scan would be found, promises that a conference call on Monday would be held, and apologies for any suffering my mother had gone through for a most regrettable mistake.

I think my mother's English almost had an effect on limiting my possibilities in life as well. Sociologists and linguists probably will tell you that a person's developing language skills are more influenced by peers. But I do think that the language spoken in the family, especially in immigrant families which are more insular, plays a large role in shaping the language of the child. And I believe that it affected my results on achievement tests, IQ tests, and the SAT. While my English skills were never judged as poor, compared to math, English could not be considered my strong suit. In grade school I did moderately well, getting perhaps B's, sometimes B-pluses, in English and scoring perhaps in the sixtieth or seventieth percentile on achievement tests. But those scores were not good enough to override the opinion that my true abilities lay in math and science, because in those areas I achieved A's and scored in the ninetieth percentile or higher.

This was understandable. Math is precise; there is only one correct answer. Whereas, for me at least, the answers on English tests were always a judgment call, a matter of opinion and personal experience. Those tests were constructed around items like fill-in-the-blank sentence completion, such as, "Even though Tom was _____, Mary thought he was _____." And the correct answer always seemed to be the most bland combinations of thoughts, for example, "Even though Tom was shy, Mary thought he was charming," with the grammatical structure "even though" limiting the correct answer to some sort of semantic opposites, so you wouldn't get answers like, "Even though Tom was foolish, Mary thought he was ridiculous." Well, according to my mother, there were very few limitations as to what Tom could have been and what Mary might have thought of him. So I never did well on tests like that.

The same was true with word analogies, pairs of words in which you were supposed to find some sort of logical, semantic relationship— for example, "*Sunset* is to *nightfall* as _____ is to _____." And here you would be presented with a list of four possible pairs, one of which showed the same kind of relationship: *red* is to *stoplight, bus* is to *arrival, chills* is to *fever, yawn* is to *boring*. Well, I could never think that way. I knew what the tests were asking, but I could not block out of my mind the images already created by the first pair, *"sunset* is to *nightfall"*—and I would see a burst of color against a darkening sky, the moon rising, the lowering of a curtain of stars. And all the other pairs of words—red, bus, stoplight, boring—just threw up a mass of confusing images, making it impossible for me to sort out something as logical as saying: "A sunset precedes nightfall" is the same as "a chill precedes a fever." The only way I would have gotten that answer right would have been to imagine an associative situation, for example, by being disobedient and staying out past sunset, catching a chill at night which turns into feverish pneumonia as punishment, which indeed did happen to me.

I have been thinking about all this lately, about my mother's English, about achievement tests. Because lately I've been asked, as a writer, why there are not more Asian Americans represented in American literature. Why are there few Asian Americans enrolled in creative writing programs? Why do so many Chinese students go into engineering? Well, these are broad sociological questions I can't begin to answer. But I have noticed in surveys—in fact, just last week—that Asian students, as a whole, always do significantly better on math achievement tests than in English. And this makes me think that there are other Asian-American students whose English spoken in the home might also be described as "broken" or "limited." And perhaps they also have teachers who are steering them away from writing and into math and science, which is what happened to me.

Fortunately, I happen to be rebellious in nature and enjoy the challenge of disproving assumptions made about me. I became an English major my first year in college, after being enrolled as pre-med. I started writing nonfiction as a freelancer the week after I was told by my former boss that writing was my worst skill and I should hone my talents toward account management.

But it wasn't until 1985 that I finally began to write fiction. And at first I wrote using what I thought to be wittily crafted sentences, sentences that would finally prove I had mastery over the English language. Here's an example from the first draft of a story that later made its way into *The Joy Luck Club,* but without this line: "That was my mental quandary in its nascent state." A terrible line, which I can hardly pronounce.

Fortunately, for reasons I won't get into today, I later decided I should envision a reader for the stories I would write. And the reader I decided upon was my mother, because these were stories about mothers. So with this reader in mind—and in fact she did read my early drafts—I began to write stories using all the Englishes I grew up with: the English I spoke to my mother, which for lack of a better term might be described as "simple"; the English she used with me, which for lack of a better term might be described as "broken"; my translation of her Chinese, which could certainly be described as "watered down"; and what I imagine to be her translation of her Chinese if she could speak in perfect English, her internal language, and for that I sought to preserve the essence, but neither an English nor a Chinese structure. I wanted to capture what language ability tests can never reveal: her intent, her passion, her imagery, the rhythms of her speech and the nature of her thoughts.

Apart from what any critic had to say about my writing, I knew I had succeeded where it counted when my mother finished reading my book and gave me her verdict: "So easy to read."

INTERPRETATIONS

1. Tan's mother reads all kinds of books with ease. Why is it so much easier to "receive than to send"—to understand a new language than to speak it?

2. What several "Englishes" do you speak and why? What examples can you offer?

3. Good writing, according to Tan, is easy reading. How good according to this criterion is this essay? What do you think contributes most to easy reading?

4. How can being bilingual make a writer better in both languages?

CORRESPONDENCES

1. Kingston and Tan, Asian-American writers, describe their families' interactions with language. What role does English play in each selection? How do language barriers affect relationships among various family members?

2. Review Gallant's perspective on families. To what extent do you agree or disagree? How does it apply to Kingston's and/or Tan's essay?

APPLICATIONS

1. Point of view concerns the narrator of a written work and answers the question "Who is telling the story?" Read over the excerpt

from *White Tigers* by Maxine Hong Kingston. What would happen if the story were told from *another* character's perspective? Select one character (e.g., the mother, a villager, the boss at the art supply store, a relative) and rewrite a section of the story from that character's perspective. Pay close attention to what that character is thinking, feeling, and experiencing. Also, be sure to include specific details that capitalize on the character's knowledge of the event that you are writing about.

2. Although your lifestyle may differ greatly from that of your parents and/or grandparents, are there issues pertaining to family on which you agree? Discuss this subject with your group including in your considerations the role of the family in communicating and preserving human values.

3. Prepare a presentation for a Parent Teacher Association meeting on the following topic: "Parental expectations of children often produce negative effects." What *tone* should you adopt to best reach your audience?

4. Write a journal entry on the significance of Tan's title "Mother Tongue."

Treasures

MAHWASH SHOAIB

Mahwash Shoaib (b. 1973), a native of Pakistan, is a graduate of the University of Punjab and currently a graduate student at the Graduate School and University Center of CUNY in New York City. She is a poet, a writer, and a translator of poetry from her native Urdu language into English. Keenly interested in philosophy as a way of life, she devotes her time between the study of language and literature, writing, and bibliophilia. Her aim is to realize her creative potential in both fiction and poetry. Before reading Shoaib's essay, freewrite on one of your "treasures."

> *Pakistan, formerly a part of India, became a dominion in 1947. In 1956, an Islamic Republic was proclaimed. For the next thirty-five years, government consisted of a series of elected prime ministers alternating with military coup d'etats. In 1988, Benazir Bhutto became the first female leader of a Muslim nation when she was elected prime minister. In the nine years that followed, three governments were successively dissolved on the allegation of corruption and mismanagement. Although Nawaz Sharif was appointed the prime minister in 1996 through a landslide vote, the country itself faces an uncertain future on the fiftieth anniversary of its conception.*

THEY ARE ALL WAITING FOR ME. I slowly lift the dress out of the wrappings of tissue. It is indeed beautiful. The velvet is a majestic russet color; the embroidery is of real silver thread and fills the neck of the kameez[1] *in the shape of a bow. The slightly dull sequins still blink on the velvet. There are solid creases where the cloth was folded; here the velvet shines with a fiercer intensity than below the folds which reveal lighter mysteries. When I pass my hand over it, the velvet smooths down. As I wear the dress for the first time, I am amazed at how snugly it fits me, as if it were made just for me. The dress is not mine; it was a part of my grandmother's trousseau. In fact, this is what my grandfather brought for her to wear on their* nikkah.[2] *She wore it only once and then put it away; then my youngest* khala,[3] *her last daughter to be married, wore it; and now, the dress is being worn for the third time by me. I feel it on my body and try to imagine how my grandmother must have felt on the nuptial day, adorned*

---

[1] A long shirt worn with pants called shalwar.
[2] Traditional Muslim marriage ceremony.
[3] Aunt, mother's sister.

in this dress. My young cousins ask me impatiently from outside the door if I need any help. I open the door and come out feeling a little shy. Everyone stops talking and tells me how nice I look in her dress, the women admiring how immaculately preserved it is and how much it would cost today to have something like that made.

Everyone, young and old, his children and grandchildren, called him Abbaji, with love. Last year, January 1 was a very joyous occasion for us because we celebrated Abbaji's ninety-fifth birthday. Eleven of his fifteen children managed to gather in the same house that day. I promised him that five years from now we would celebrate his century-marking birthday and everyone would be there.

Today there is an unusual number of people in my grandfather's house because it is Eid, *the day at the end of* Ramazan, *when we celebrate the end of fasting and offer prayers of gratitude to Allah. Not only are two of my* khalas *here with their families, but just a few moments ago my grandmother's brother, my mother's* mamoon,[4] *came in with his wife and daughters. Their bright, jocund voices shimmering through the walls, now everyone is sitting together in the living room talking and drinking tea while the children are playing all over the house. Spicy aromas emanating from the family kitchen are mingling with delicate perfumes on crisply-ironed clothes to form one warm embrace.*

Although every time the phone rang at night we would be filled with dread, no one was prepared for the news. This year on the midnight of January 1, we were awakened by a phone call telling us that Abbaji had died. Later on I found out that Abbaji had died calling out for every one of his children, few of whom were with him at that time. That is why I cannot reconcile the fact that I wasn't there at the time when he wanted to gather all his seeds. The distance does nothing to dissipate the agony and anger; only it makes the grief more unbearable. How can you triumph distance and time to tell someone that you love him, something you thought you would always have time for?

After a few minutes I excuse myself and go to my grandfather's room to show him the dress. My eldest mamoon *is sitting beside my grandfather and when he sees me entering with my cousins behind me, he leaves the room grumbling that these children do not leave any corner of the house in peace. The girls, somewhat bored now, run off to play. As I sit down on his bed, my* khala *also comes in the room after having served the latest guests. Abbaji is*

[4]Uncle, mother's brother.

lying in his bed, supported by pillows, and smiles at me kindly. Through the open door I see the tree casting a long shadow in the coral evening.

My earliest memories are associated with Abbaji because I spent my early childhood under the eyes of my grandparents in their *haveli*, the huge fort-like house that Abbaji had before he moved to the smaller house, after my grandmother's death. His voracious appetite for reading instilled in me a respect for books. Once when I was ten or eleven years old, we went to spend our winter vacations with him. I brought along my arsenal of books to while away time and one of the books was Robert Louis Stevenson's *Treasure Island*. One afternoon when I was tired of playing with my cousins, I went to look for the novel. After a long search I came out on the veranda and found Abbaji basking in the hazy sunlight and reading the book. I remember feeling a concoction of mild surprise and delectation even then that my own grandfather was reading and enjoying the same book that had made me so happy. Then at times he would tell me a tale within a tale. One evening very long ago when he was young, Abbaji was sitting on a rock by a frothy river reading a book. In the book an incident was described in great detail in which a snake slithers off a rock and falls into the river; at that very moment, a snake, out of nowhere, sprang on the rock right in front of him and landed into the gushing waters. At the end of the tale, Abbaji would chuckle with merry perplexity; I would try to picture a young boy with a book in his hands at the edge of a river, his shadow extending before him, frightened by the sudden appearance of a lithe snake, and my blood would race with adventure. This is what a child's trove of bright and diffused memories is made up of—shared words and shared silences.

I ask him, Abbaji, how does the dress look? He puts on his glasses and looks at me from head to toe, tells me that it is very beautiful and asks when did I have it made. I do not realize but my khala *guesses immediately and laughingly asks him if he does not recognize it. My grandfather, with a short embarrassed laugh, says no. I then tell him that it is the dress that my grandmother wore for her wedding. He asks incredulously if it is true, and we talk about how many people came to visit us today and how much I'll miss this day when I go back. After some time I come out of his room a little hurt and disappointed.*

When I look at the pictures I took of Abbaji last year, I still wonder at the kind smile touching the tired liquid eyes of a man who had seen life and still found it amusing. His presence was a spiritual focus to which his scattered progeny drifted back time and again. Family legend has it that when he was sixteen or seventeen, Abbaji ran away from his home in Afghanistan because of an escalating bloody dispute about his father's estate, to which he was the sole heir. And I ask myself, what do I truly know of my grandfather? I do remember so many times when he came to visit us at our house in Lahore, the weddings, births and birthdays we celebrated. But I also remember the times when he used to pick up the loosened skin from his hands remorsefully. So, in sad nostalgia, what matters most . . . the freedom from pain of a loved one or the lost inert moments of happiness induced by him?

There are still a lot of guests in the living room and I mingle with them. One of my cousins and I pose for a special picture of me in the dress. Just when the camera flashes, I remember that I forgot to take off the thick woolen socks peeking from under it.

I have lost my bearings. It seems that right when I was beginning to convince myself that the tunnel was not so dimly lit, life slapped me full in the face of my meager certitude. A catharsis is unwelcome and the fear for the mortality of my loved ones is fresh. I have found that treasures that bind you by the spirit are hard to keep. The dress, the pictures are still tangible; the person whose presence was hope is no more. I keep returning to times and events and places and images in a tiding circuit until I am unsure of where I started from. Suddenly I am frightened of the new year.

INTERPRETATIONS

1. Why do you think Shoaib begins her essay with a detailed description of her grandmother's wedding dress?
2. Shoaib's memoir juxtaposes past and present in alternating paragraphs. Analyze the effects of this technique on her purpose and meaning. How does she use this technique to reflect on her relationship with Abbaji?
3. Characterize Abbaji. Which of his traits have most influenced the author? How would you describe their relationship? Do you have a similar relationship with any member of your family?

CORRESPONDENCES

1. In their essays, Kingston and Shoaib each focus on their extended family and their family traditions. Contrast their attitudes toward both. What factors might account for any differences in the two authors' points of view?

2. Shoaib and Wehle write about the death of a close family member. Compare and contrast their responses to loss.

APPLICATIONS

1. Shoaib's essay focuses on her portrayal of her grandfather, but in the italicized passages she also reveals herself. Write a portrait of the author using these paragraphs.

2. Freewrite about an older family member who intrigues you and about whom you would like to know more. Interview family members or friends for information about him or her, and write a description based on your interviews.

3. Shoaib and Wehle recall an experience that represents a turning point in their lives. If you have had such an experience (it need not be about death), write an essay comparing its effects when it first occurred and now as you view it in retrospect.

4. Note how Shoaib uses visual cues in the text to signal different voices and tones. If you examine the italicized and the non-italicized sections of the essay, what kinds of music are evoked by each of these font types? How would you describe these kinds of music to a reader?

5. It is possible to look at Shoaib's first paragraph as a journal entry. Try to write a journal entry about something that is happening in this essay from the perspective of one of the other participants.

Two Lives

SHIRLEY GEOK-LIN LIM

Shirley Geok-Lin Lim (b. 1944) was born in Malacca, Malaysia, a small town on the coast of the Malay Peninsula. Lim received her Ph.D. in English and American Literature from Brandeis University in 1973. Her first book of poems, Crossing The Peninsula *(1980), won the Commonwealth Poetry Prize. Lin has published four additional books of poetry and three collections of short stories. Her memoir,* Among The White Moon Faces: An Asian-American Memoir of Homelands *(1997) received the American Book Award. Lim's first novel* Joss and Gold *was published in 2001. Lim is currently the Chair Professor of English and head of the English Department at the University of Hong Kong, as well as Professor of English and Women's Studies at the University of California, Santa Barbara. What associations, if any, do you have with the phrase "resident aliens?"*

No ONE WHO HAS NOT LEFT EVERYTHING behind her—every acquaintance, tree, corner lamp post, brother, lover—understands the peculiar remorse of the resident alien. Unlike the happy immigrant who sees the United States as a vast real-estate advertisement selling a neighborly future, the person who enters the country as a resident alien is neither here nor there. Without family, house, or society, she views herself through the eyes of citizens: guest, stranger, outsider, misfit, beggar. Transient like the drunks asleep by the steps down to the subway, her bodily presence is a wraith, less than smoke among the 250 million in the nation. Were she to fall in front of the screeching wheels of the Number Four Lexington line, her death would be noted by no one, mourned by none, except if the news should arrive weeks later, twelve thousand miles away.

A resident alien has walked out of a community's living memory, out of social structures in which her identity is folded, like a bud in a tree, to take on the raw stinks of public bathrooms and the shapes of shadows in parks. She holds her breath as she walks through the American city counting the afternoon hours. Memory for her is a great mourning, a death of the living. The alien resident mourns even as she chooses to abandon. Her memory, like her guilt and early love, is involuntary but her choice of the United States is willful.

For what? She asks the question over and over again. At first, she asks it every day. Then as she begins to feel comfortable in the body of a stranger, she asks it occasionally, when the weekend stretches over the Sunday papers and the television news does not seem enough, or when the racks of dresses in the department stores fail to amuse. Finally, she forgets what it feels like not to be a stranger. She has found work that keeps her busy, or better still, tired. She has found a lover, a child, a telephone friend, the American equivalents for the opacity of her childhood. The dense solidity of Asian society becomes a thin story. At some point, she no longer considers exchanging the remote relationships that pass as American social life for those crowded rooms in Asia, the unhappy family circles. And were those rooms really that crowded, the family so intensely unhappy? . . .

It was the waste of time I minded most, a sludgy feeling that took over October and November. In September, almost a year after my arrival at Brandeis, Father had written to say he had been diagnosed with throat cancer. He was seeking medical care in Malacca. "Don't come home," his letter ended, "I don't want you to interrupt your studies."

I told no one. Food stuck in my throat whenever I thought of Father. The thought was like a fishbone, sharp and nagging. I couldn't speak of him.

Another short letter arrived from China without a return address. I read it over and over in the safety of my room. "I am doing well," it said. "My white blood cells have gone up, and I am feeling stronger." The small black-and-white photograph that fell out of the envelope showed that he was lying. The shirt draped over his body like a sheet over a child, although his face was old and sad.

For a few months, the letters came from China without a forwarding address: he was staying near the clinic in Canton, noted for its cancer cures. He wrote irregularly. Like a careful student, perhaps because he was lonely, he sent the laboratory reports on his white blood count. His letters were optimistic to begin with. The white blood-cell numbers had improved; he was enjoying this Chinese city he had never seen before, visiting parks, zoos, and museums, with a new friend also undergoing treatment at the clinic. Then a letter arrived complaining of homesickness. He wanted to be home with the family; he missed Malaysian food.

When Thanksgiving came, the Castle emptied out. Julie and Carol returned to Brooklyn and Missouri. On Friday I picked up a letter from my mailbox. The rice-paper-fine aerogramme rustled as I spread it out to read the ball-point print that smeared across the crumpled blue surface. It was a letter from Second Brother, and I was immediately afraid, for Second Brother had never written to me before. "We buried Father two weeks ago," he wrote.

I stared at the words and calculated the time. Two weeks ago, and a week for the aerogramme to cross the world to reach me in

Massachusetts. It was unimaginable that Father, the source of whatever drove me, that total enveloping wretchedness of involuntary love, my eternal bond, my body's and heart's DNA, had been dead for almost a month. The world had a hole in it, it was rent, and I would never heal.

Maggie came knocking at my door just as I finished reading Second Brother's letter. An orphan left with a trust fund, she was slowly completing her graduate studies, while spending most of her time volunteering to help with the animals in the zoo. She wanted to know if I had had any pumpkin pie yet for Thanksgiving. Would I go with her to the cafeteria for a piece of pie? I was still holding Second Brother's blue aerogramme in my hand.

"My father's dead," I said to her. Why was I telling her this? Would I have said the same thing if the janitor had knocked on the door to fix the radiator? "He died three weeks ago."

"Oh," she said. "I'm sorry." I could see that she was. Tall and big-boned, Maggie was deep water, quiet-spoken, all reserve.

I paid for my pie and coffee at the cafeteria and watched her eat. She left the crust and scraped the brown gooey filling carefully with her fork till it was all gone. My throat hurt. Then I returned alone to my room. I knew Maggie would never visit me again. I had been too painful for her.

At first I didn't cry. It wasn't Father's death that drove hardest at me, it was that he had been dead for more than two weeks already, and I hadn't known all that time that he had gone. "We didn't think you should come home," Second Brother wrote. The grief and the guilt lay beyond tears. Months later, in Brooklyn where I was sharing a studio apartment with Charles, the Brandeis graduate student whom I would later marry, I woke up in the middle of the night my face drenched with tears. I had wept in my sleep for Father.

A month after the news of Father's death, Second Brother sent me a package of papers from Father's belongings. Father had kept all my old school record books, annual school certificates of achievement, examination diplomas, yellowed letters of recommendation from high school teachers, and Malaysian citizenship documents. On an unmailed aerogramme sheet, Father had scrawled in a shaky hand, "I want you to come home now."

My brother also sent me a diary Father had kept in the last weeks of his life. Only a few pages were filled, and all the entries were addressed to me. In the early entries, he wrote he was hopeful he would recover, and he did not want me to return home because it was so important for me to continue my studies. In the second to last entry, he asked that I hurry home; he didn't believe he had much time left and he wanted to see me. In the very last entry, addressing me as his dear daughter, he wrote that although he knew I would do so, still he asked that I promise to take care of my brothers and sister, Peng's children. The entry was very short and the handwriting erratic. My father had willed his children to me.

The day I received the package, I emptied my bank account and sent the few hundred dollars in it to Peng. With it, my letter promised that I would send her as much as I could each month. For a long time, every U.S. dollar rang as precious Malaysian currency for me to remit. A ten-dollar shirt? I paid for it and guiltily counted the groceries the money could have bought for Father's family. I disapproved of my growing consumerism. The pastries that gleamed, sugar-encrusted, at Dunkin' Donuts, which I eyed longingly, would buy copy books for my half-brothers. For the next few years, I carried my father's ghostly presence through department stores and restaurants. His sad smile was a mirage of poverty. I saw my half-siblings ragged and hungry whenever I glanced at a sales tag, and every month, I made out a bank draft to Peng and mailed it out as an exorcism.

An exorcism I could not explain to Charles, my American husband. How could one eat well if one's family was starving? For Chinese, eating is both material and cultural. We feed our hungry ghosts before we may feed ourselves. Ancestors are ravenous, and can die of neglect. Our fathers' children are also ourselves. The self is paltry, phantasmagoric; it leaks and slips away. It is the family, parents, siblings, cousins, that signify the meaning of the self, and beyond the family, the extended community.

In writing the bank drafts I remained my father's daughter, returning to Father the bargain we had made. This is the meaning of blood— to give, because you cannot eat unless the family is also eating. For years, I woke up nights, heart beating wildly. Oh Asia, that nets its children in ties of blood so binding that they cut the spirit.

INTERPRETATIONS

1. How does Lim characterize the "resident alien" in paragraphs one and two? What is the connection between the "resident alien" and the "alien resident"?

2. What is the effect of Lim's recording the process of her father's illness and death?

3. Why does she include the entries from her father's diaries? How would you describe the relationship she and her father shared?

4. How do you interpret the last line of her essay? What examples of her spirit's being "cut" can you cite?

CORRESPONDENCES

1. Dana Wehle and Lim record their responses to the death of a parent. Compare and contrast their reactions to that experience.

2. How do Shoaib and Lim use mood and tone to enhance theme?

APPLICATIONS

1. Write a journal entry on the title of Lim's essay.

2. Lim writes that she disapproves of her "growing consumerism." What examples does she cite? Do you and your group members think of yourselves as consumers? Is it easy to resist being a consumer in today's society? Summarize your group's discussion.

3. Lim writes about her sorrow and guilt as she distances herself from her native culture. If you have had a similar experience, write a short essay describing how you resolved the paradox of being a "resident alien" and "an alien resident."

4. Who is Lim describing in paragraphs one and two of this essay? What do you imagine this person to look like? Draw a sketch of this individual. Then, using your sketch to guide you, write a detailed description of this person.

For My Indian Daughter

LEWIS (JOHNSON) SAWAQUAT

Lewis (Johnson) Sawaquat (b. 1935) was raised in Harbor Springs, Michigan, where his great-grandfather was the last official chief of the Potawatomi Ottawas. A retired surveyor, Sawaquat is currently the cultural adviser of The Grand Travers Band of Ottawa and Chippewa Indians. In "For My Indian Daughter," the author portrays his personal odyssey toward greater ethnic pride and cultural awareness. He adopted his Indian name after this essay was published.

According to tradition, the Ottawas, the Ojibway, and the Potawatomi were originally one tribe living north of the Great Lakes. After the Ottawas separated, they were active in the Indian Wars as allies of the French. After joining the Huron at Mackinaw in Michigan (adjacent to the area of Johnson's home town of Harbor Springs and nearby Burt Lake), the Ottawa dispersed over a wide area. When first encountered by whites (in the seventeenth century), the Potawatomi lived mainly near the mouth of the Green Bay in Wisconsin. By the end of the century, they had settled along both sides of the southern end of Lake Michigan. The majority of the tribe still lives in Michigan.

MY LITTLE GIRL IS SINGING HERSELF to sleep upstairs, her voice mingling with the sounds of the birds outside in the old maple trees. She is two and I am nearly 50, and I am very taken with her. She came along late in my life, unexpected and unbidden, a startling gift.

Today at the beach my chubby-legged, brown-skinned daughter ran laughing into the water as fast as she could. My wife and I laughed watching her, until we heard behind us a low guttural curse and then an unpleasant voice raised in an imitation war whoop.

I turned to see a fat man in a bathing suit, white and soft as a grub, as he covered his mouth and prepared to make the Indian war cry again. He was middle-aged, younger than I, and had three little children lined up next to him, grinning foolishly. My wife suggested we leave the beach, and I agreed.

I knew the man was not unusual in his feelings against Indians. His beach behavior might have been socially unacceptable to more civilized whites, but his basic view of Indians is expressed daily in our small town, frequently on the editorial pages of the county newspaper, as white people speak out against Indian fishing rights and land rights, saying in essence, "Those Indians are taking our fish, our land." It doesn't matter to them that we were here first, that the U.S. Supreme Court has ruled in our favor. It matters to them that we have something they want, and they hate us for it. Backlash is the common explanation of the attacks on Indians, the bumper stickers that say, "Spear an Indian, Save a Fish," but I know better. The hatred of Indians goes back to the beginning when white people came to this country. For me it goes back to my childhood in Harbor Springs, Michigan.

Harbor Springs is now a summer resort for the very affluent, but a hundred years ago it was the Indian village of my Ottawa ancestors. My grandmother, Anna Showanessy, and other Indians like her, had their land there taken by treaty, by fraud, by violence, by theft. They remembered how whites had burned down the village at Burt Lake in 1900 and pushed the Indians out. These were the stories in my family.

When I was a boy my mother told me to walk down the alleys in Harbor Springs and not to wear my orange football sweater out of the house. This way I would not stand out, not be noticed, and not be a target.

I wore my orange sweater anyway and deliberately avoided the alleys. I was the biggest person I knew and wasn't really afraid. But I met my comeuppance when I enlisted in the U.S. Army. One night all the men in my barracks gathered together and, gang-fashion, pulled me into the shower and scrubbed me down with rough brushes used for floors, saying, "We won't have any dirty Indians in our outfit." It is a point of irony that I was cleaner than any of them. Later in Korea I learned how to kill, how to bully, how to hate Koreans. I came out of the war tougher than ever and, strangely, white.

I went to college, got married, lived in La Porte, Indiana, worked as a surveyor and raised three boys. I headed Boy Scout groups, never thinking it odd when the Scouts did imitation Indian dances, imitation Indian lore.

One day when I was 35 or thereabouts I heard about an Indian powwow. My father used to attend them and so with great curiosity and a strange joy at discovering a part of my heritage, I decided the thing to do to get ready for this big event was to have my friend make me a spear in his forge. The steel was fine and blue and iridescent. The feathers on the shaft were bright and proud.

In a dusty state fairground in southern Indiana, I found white people dressed as Indians. I learned they were "hobbyists," that is, it was their hobby and leisure pastime to masquerade as Indians on weekends. I felt ridiculous with my spear, and I left.

It was years before I could tell anyone of the embarrassment of this weekend and see any humor in it. But in a way it was that weekend, for all its silliness, that was my awakening. I realized I didn't know who I was. I didn't have an Indian name. I didn't speak the Indian language. I didn't know the Indian customs. Dimly I remembered the Ottawa word for dog, but it was a baby word, *kahgee*, not the full word, *muhkahgee*, which I was later to learn. Even more hazily I remembered a naming ceremony (my own). I remembered legs dancing around me, dust. Where had that been? Who had I been? "Suwaukquat," my mother told me when I asked, "where the tree begins to grow."

That was 1968, and I was not the only Indian in the country who was feeling the need to remember who he or she was. There were others. They had powwows, real ones, and eventually I found them. Together we researched our past, a search that for me culminated in the Longest Walk, a march on Washington in 1978. Maybe because I now know what it means to be Indian, it surprises me that others don't. Of course there aren't very many of us left. The chances of an average person knowing an average Indian in an average lifetime are pretty slim.

Still, I was amused one day when my small, four-year-old neighbor looked at me as I was hoeing in my garden and said, "You aren't a real Indian, are you?" Scotty is little, talkative, likable. Finally I said, "I'm a real Indian." He looked at me for a moment and then said, squinting into the sun, "Then where's your horse and feathers?" The child was simply a smaller, whiter version of my own ignorant self years before. We'd both seen too much TV, that's all. He was not to be blamed. And so, in a way, the moronic man on the beach today is blameless. We come full circle to realize other people are like ourselves, as discomfiting as that may be sometimes.

As I sit in my old chair on my porch, in a light that is fading so the leaves are barely distinguishable against the sky, I can picture my girl asleep upstairs. I would like to prepare her for what's to come, take her each step of the way saying, there's a place to avoid, here's what I know about this, but much of what's before her she must go through alone. She must pass through pain and joy and solitude and community to discover her own inner self that is unlike any other and come through that passage to the place where she sees all people are one, and in so seeing may live her life in a brighter future.

INTERPRETATIONS

1. What audience besides his daughter is Sawaquat writing for? Cite evidence. Why do you suppose he waited until he was nearly fifty and had a daughter—he has three other children, boys—to express these thoughts?

2. "I didn't know who I was." What do we have to know about our-
    selves before we know who we are? How important is ancestry to
    a sense of identity? What should be our attitude toward our ances-
    try—or ancestries?

3. Until he asked his mother, Sawaquat did not know his Indian
    name. Why do you suppose she withheld it? How do you think
    you would feel to discover that you had another name? Why?

4. What was involved in Sawaquat "finding himself"? Why must
    such a search be conducted with others? How did white society
    delay the search and make it difficult?

CORRESPONDENCES

1. Feelings of alienation and displacement are expressed by both Lim
    and Sawaquat. Explain their causes and effects. How are they rec-
    onciled in each text?

2. Review Morrison's perspective and discuss its relevance to
    Sawaquat's essay. Does pursuing ethnic identity preclude search-
    ing for a national community? Explain.

APPLICATIONS

1. "We come full circle to realize other people are like ourselves, as dis-
    comfiting as that may be sometimes." To what extent do you agree
    with Sawaquat? Write a summary of your group's discussions.

2. Write an essay on a part of your cultural heritage you might some-
    day want to share with your children.

3. In paragraph 14 Sawaquat says of his daughter: "She must pass
    through pain and joy and solitude and community to discover her
    own inner self that is unlike any other . . ." To what extent do you
    agree? Write a journal entry of an experience that corresponds to
    Sawaquat's comment.

4. In this essay Lewis Sawaquat writes: "The chances of an average
    person knowing an average Indian in an average lifetime are
    pretty slim." Hopefully, the following Web sites will help a reader
    begin to bridge this knowledge gap.

    http://www.indiancountry.com/

    http://www.turtletrack.org/

    http://www.navajohopiobserver.com

Noah

DANIT WEHLE

Danit Wehle (b. 1973) was born in Israel and raised in Teaneck, New Jersey. During her sophomore year of high school, her mother gave birth to her third child, Noah. Danit's essay "Noah" depicts how the relationship with her new brother developed and how it continued to grow while she was attending the University of Massachusetts at Amherst.

I ALWAYS HAD A VERY NORMAL HOME LIFE. You know, the typical two parents, two kids. My mother and father used to take my brother and me on a family outing every weekend and occasionally during the school week. I remember it was always so exciting when my father would come home from work early because that meant we could all hang out together and play cards or Monopoly. It was always the four of us. I mean as I got older I did go out with my friends but when I came home my parents were always there and even though I didn't spend as much time with them as I had, when I did it was still the four of us and still just as much fun.

My life changed drastically when I was fifteen years old. My mother announced to my brother and me that she was going to have a baby. My first instinct was to cry and scream at her. How could she forget about us? We were her kids. Didn't she love us? Weren't we what she wanted? Was she getting sick of us? But then I thought about it some more and it sounded great. How exciting! I loved babies and now I'd have my own little brother or sister. I became very involved with her pregnancy. I read up on all her books and kept track of the developing stages of the baby. I remember the whole nine months all we talked about was the baby's name. We each had our list and agreed that we didn't all have to love the name, but we all had to at least be able to tolerate it. (My parents wanted us to be involved so we wouldn't feel like they were leaving us and now moving on to a new generation of kids.) It was good to be involved because it brought us all together again.

The last month I rarely left the house and if I did, I called about every five minutes to see if my mother was in labor. I drove her crazy but finally it happened. The day my mother had the baby, I was at my piano lesson. My teacher told me my mother was at the hospital and he would drive me home. I don't remember exactly what I felt that day. I mean I know it was intense excitement but I remember thinking then that when I look back at this day in a few years, I'll forget how happy I was. So I don't remember how it felt but I do know that I've never been so happy as the day when my little brother Noah was born.

The minute I saw him in the hospital, I fell in love with him. He was so tiny and soft. He came home the next day and I carried him into the house. From that day on, I was his little mother. I dressed him, fed him, bathed him, watched him grow and watched him develop. I was so proud.

It sounds like I adjusted perfectly but actually I didn't. Every once in a while I would blow up at my parents for ignoring me or for piling too much responsibility on me. Many times I wished that Noah was never born and our life was back to normal: how it used to be. It wasn't the four of us anymore. Our rhyming names didn't even work any-more. It was always Danit, Amit, Ronit, and John and now it was Danit, Amit, Ronit and John . . . and Noah. This all bothered me on and off for a while but really every time I saw Noah I forgot about my anger and just remembered how much I loved him.

Well, months went by and I spent a great deal of time with Noah. I watched him sit, crawl, stand, eat by himself, walk, talk. I was so proud of him. I was like a typical mother; carrying pictures of him in my wallet. He was my baby.

Noah and I were very close. He really had fun with me. I taught him cute little sayings like, "Homey don't play dat" or "K-Mart sucks." I spoke to him as if he were my age so he began to talk like a little man. I couldn't get enough of him. He was a little man in an adorable body. I loved him.

A few days before college I took Noah to his first movie: *101 Dalma-tians*. It was our special day. I bought him popcorn, M&M's, and a lemonade. I'll never forget his face. He was sitting on the big theater seat holding a little bag of popcorn and a huge cup of lemonade, staring at the big, big TV screen in awe.

It was the hardest to say goodbye to Noah. I knew that my parents and I would be able to keep in touch over the phone or in letters. My brother the same thing. But Noah needed to see me, play with me. I remember I took him to the backyard and I told him that I'd be back in a little while, that he could send me pictures, talk to me on the phone, visit me. I told him never to forget that I love him and that he'll always be my little guy. Just as I was pulling out of the driveway, Noah shouted after me, "Danit, I love you!"

INTERPRETATIONS

1. Compare Wehle's relationship with Noah and her relationship with the rest of her family. To what extent did the interfamily relationship before Noah's birth prepare Wehle for a new sibling?

2. Wehle says she was like a fifteen-year-old mother. How was her situation like that of a real mother? How was it different?

3. Wehle changed from initial resentment to eager acceptance of her mother's pregnancy. How adequate is Wehle's treatment of this change? How would the essay be affected if Wehle included her *brother's* reaction to the birth and growing up of Noah?

CORRESPONDENCES

1. Review Friedan's perspective on family (page 17) and discuss its relevance to Wehle's essay.

2. "For My Indian Daughter" is told from the point of view of a parent, while "Noah" is narrated from the perspective of a sibling. Analyze the differences in your responses to both selections. How does point of view affect purpose and meaning as well as audience response?

APPLICATIONS

1. How might the age at which a woman becomes a mother affect the way she feels and acts toward her child? Discuss the advantages and disadvantages of young parenthood.

2. Sometimes we can best illustrate the importance of a relationship by focusing on a particular event. Choose an event, action, or conversation to best explain a relationship that is important to you. Before writing, review Wehle's account of taking Noah to his first movie.

3. To what extent does family life foster independence or dependence; freedom or control? Write an essay citing three reasons why, in your opinion, the effects of family life contribute to individual freedom or group conformity.

Learning to Fly

EMMA WUNSCH

Emma Wunsch (b. 1975) holds a B.A. from Binghamton University and expects to receive an M.F.A. from Brooklyn College in 2004. Wunsch has published in the Aura Arts Literary Review, PoetryMemoirStory, New England Writers Network, *and* Hanging Loose. *Her short story "Sugar Cereal" was published in 2003 in the* Vermont Literary Review. *Before reading Wunsch's essay, define your concept of "a family room family."*

I'M SITTING AT MY KITCHEN TABLE, doing physics homework. "An airplane whose air speed is 200 km/hr is supposed to fly in a straight path 25 degrees North of East. But a steady 50km/hr wind is blowing from the north. In what direction should the plane fly to reach its destination?" I can't do this problem. It never works out. I can't do a lot of physics problems. So many, that I think physics is becoming a problem.

In the living room, my mother is making my ten-year-old brother practice piano. She wants so badly for him to be talented. To be good. Over and over again he plays his scales: C, A minor, G, E-flat minor. He plays the scales so well that it is almost mechanical. He never makes a mistake. He used to; he used to hit wrong notes. That was before he went to Mrs. Paulie for lessons. My mother thinks Mrs. Paulie is amazing because after only two lessons my brother's scales were flawless. My father doesn't think Mrs. Paulie is worth sixty-five dollars an hour, but since my mother seems to like her so much, he doesn't push it. My father doesn't push a lot of things. That's why I told him about the physics test I got back, instead of my mother. My mother would have been hysterical . . . calling tutors, my teacher, and helping me make flash cards. She's very big on flash cards. My father said he wanted me to do better, signed the test, and dropped it.

I asked my brother how he learned to play his scales . . . what was so magical about Mrs. Paulie?

"She made me practice over and over," he said.

Deep. But I'm hoping that this advice will work for physics. Maybe if I keep doing the problems over and over, it will sink in.

• • •

My mother comes into the kitchen. I hope she's going to start dinner, but instead she starts opening and closing drawers. I ignore her and read over my plane problem.

"Have you seen the nail clipper? Sammy's fingernails are too long and they click on the keys."

I have not seen the nail clipper. Why would it be in the kitchen anyway? My mother looks annoyed with me, as if I'm purposefully withholding the nail clipper, so she'll go crazy listening to Sammy's nails click.

She calls my father up from refinishing the basement. She wants us to call it the "family room." Sammy and I will not. We're not a "family room" family. My father has not seen the nail clipper. He asks if my mother is going to make dinner. She does not answer. The scales stop. We remain still; my mother calls for Sammy to continue. There is another moment of silence before the reassuring notes are heard again. My mother is deep in thought. She reaches for the phone and makes a call. My father gets a beer out of the fridge and looks at me. We wonder what my mother is up to. She hangs up the phone.

"I want you to go out to the pharmacy and pick up a pair of nail clippers. You can get a pizza for dinner, too."

My father looks at her. It is January and 13 degrees outside. The pharmacy is twenty minutes away. I hold my breath.

In the end, the nail clippers win. My father and I climb in his '77 Chevy which takes awhile to start. We drive in silence. It is too cold to speak, even with the heat on. There is nobody else in the pharmacy. My father spends ten minutes picking out the best nail clipper. Which one is the cheapest? Which one is made in America? In the end he buys two. And a pack of Lifesavers for me.

In the car, I turn on the radio. Bob Dylan is singing "Positively 4th Street." Bob Dylan is my father's generation.

"Why do you kids keep listening to this old music? What's wrong with your generation?"

Sometimes I think my father can read my mind.

"Nothing's wrong with my generation, I just like this music better," I say.

"Something's wrong with every generation."

He gets deep and cynical when he's hungry. I offer him a Lifesaver.

"I like Dylan. I think he's cool. Didn't you ever listen to him when you were growing up?"

We've had this conversation before.

"No. I was at college."

"That's no excuse, Dad. At college. Does that mean you couldn't be cool?"

"I had a lot of work to do. I studied hard."

"You didn't study ALL day. What did you do in your free time?"

I know the answer before he even says it.

"I read."

My father always reads. He's an editor for a small publishing company. Even when he doesn't like what he's editing, he's always, in some way, excited by it. I like to read, too. But I do other things. I explain this to my father; he smiles at me. We stop at a red light.

"Why couldn't you have been into your generation? I don't understand. The one thing we could really have in common is the Sixties and you read through the decade. Didn't you even go to one hootenanny or Be-in, just to see what all the excitement was about?"

"No. I didn't care about tie-dye or pot or peace. I was happy just sitting in my dorm, listening to Mozart, thinking."

"You're such a nerd, Dad." We turn into the driveway.

"Groovy," he replies.

• • •

We forgot the pizza. For dinner we have tuna fish on rye bread with mayonnaise. For dessert we have raisins. I'm depressed. Dinner was gross, and I still haven't done my physics. My mother is depressed. Mrs. Paulie telephoned to say she is retiring; she's moving to Florida for her arthritis. Now what is Sammy going to do? Without Mrs. Paulie, my brother will be lost. Forever. Sammy is depressed. He doesn't seem to care about Mrs. Paulie, but he wasn't invited to Adam Green's birthday party. He doesn't know why. My father is not depressed. He is happy to go into his study and edit.

After dinner my mother makes several phone calls about finding a new piano teacher. I'm still figuring out exactly where I have to fly. My mother tells the woman on the phone that Sammy is gifted. Gifted. What an odd word. I'm not gifted. Especially not in physics. Sammy is a gifted pianist, but he's not as talented as my mother hopes and thinks he is. My father is a talented editor and nerd. My mother is a talented mother, enthusiast, nag. I'm not particularly good at anything. I don't even listen to music from my generation.

Yet, I am only sixteen. Sammy is young, too. He will probably not be a musician. He will never figure out why Adam did not invite him. He will probably learn to hate the piano . . . my mother will make that happen. That will be too bad. I'll miss his songs. My father is not young, but he is happy. My mother is not young either, but she will continue to pride herself on being a concerned mother. So concerned that she will continue to buy index cards by the gross so her children will not go without flash cards; so concerned that she insists her husband build her children a "family room."

I can't do physics. I stuff my notebook in my bag, grab an apple, and head up to my room. I want to finish a novel I'm reading. I want to write a novel. Maybe I'll listen to Sammy play. Maybe I'll listen to Dylan; maybe I'll listen to music from my generation. I'm no longer depressed about my physics. I realize that it's not so much where the wind takes me, but that one day, I'll fly.

INTERPRETATIONS

1. Characterize the parents in "Learning to Fly."

2. Do you agree with Sammy and the narrator that theirs is "not a 'family room' family"? How would you define each type of family?

3. What portrait of the narrator emerges from the story? Describe her role in the family. How is it similar to or different from Sammy's?

CORRESPONDENCES

1. Contrast the tone of "Learning to Fly" with that of "Noah." How do differences in tone affect purpose, meaning, and audience response?

2. Both Wunsch and Danit Wehle focus on family life in the nineties. What does each author imply about the importance of family?

APPLICATIONS

1. Write an essay analyzing the implications of the title of Wunsch's short story. How does she use the title as a framing device for her text?

2. Write an essay about a family member you once considered rather ordinary but now appreciate and value highly. Focus on one event or experience that was most significant in transforming your view of this person.

3. Assume the persona of a parent and write an essay explaining why you would prefer your child to take risks despite the fact that doing so may make life more difficult for him or her.

The Joy of Reading and Writing: Superman and Me

SHERMAN ALEXIE

Sherman Alexie (b. 1966) grew up on the Spokane Indian Reservation in Wellpinit, Washington. Shortly after graduating from Washington State University, he received the Washington State Arts Commission Poetry Fellowship. In 1991 Alexie published his first poetry collection, The Business of Fancydancing. *Alexie received the National Endowment for the Arts Poetry Fellowship in 1992, and* The Lone Ranger and Tonto Fistfight in Heaven, *a collection of short stories, was published in 1993.* Reservation Blues, *Alexie's first novel, was published in 1995. His second novel,* Indian Killer *(1996), was a* New York Times *Notable Book. The basis for the screenplay was "This is What it Means to Say Phoenix, Arizona." A short story was released as the film* Smoke Signals *in 1998. To date, Alexie has published 14 books, including his most recent collection of short stories.* Ten Little Indians *(2003). Record in your journal your responses to Alexie's title.*

Approximately 1,100 Spokane Tribal members live on the reservation where Alexie grew up. Alexie's father is a Coeur d'Alene Indian, and his mother is a Spokane Indian. The Spokane Indians are of the Interior Salish group, which has inhabited northeastern Washington, northern Idaho, and western Montana for centuries. "Spokane" is generally accepted as meaning "Sun People" or "Children of the Sun." The living cycle of the Spokane was integral to their economic and social life. In the spring, the winter camps dispersed to gather food, hunt, and fish. By early summer, salmon fishing, hunting, and root digging were the main activities. Summer was the time of year when inter-tribal activities were at the highest, since neighboring tribes joined the Spokanes for root and berry gathering. This tradition of socializing is carried on today with the Indian "Pow Wows," which begin in June and end in September. Visiting, games, and ceremonial dancing are an important part in the social life of today's Indians.

I LEARNED TO READ WITH A *SUPERMAN* COMIC BOOK. Simple enough, I suppose. I cannot recall which particular Superman comic book I read, nor can I remember which villain he fought in that issue. I cannot remember the plot, nor the means by which I obtained the comic book. What I can remember is this: I was three years old, a Spokane Indian boy living with his family on the Spokane Indian Reservation in eastern Washington state. We were poor by most standards, but one of my parents usually managed to find some minimum-wage job or another, which made us middle-class by reservation standards. I had a brother and three sisters. We lived on a combination of irregular paychecks, hope, fear, and government surplus food.

My father, who is one of the few Indians who went to Catholic school on purpose, was an avid reader of westerns, spy thrillers, murder mysteries, gangster epics, basketball player biographies, and anything else he could find. He bought his books by the pound at Dutch's Pawn Shop, Goodwill, Salvation Army, and Value Village. When he had extra money, he bought new novels at supermarkets, convenience stores and hospital gift shops. Our house was filled with books. They were stacked in crazy piles in the bathroom, bedrooms, and living room. In a fit of unemployment-inspired creative energy, my father built a set of bookshelves and soon filled them with a random assortment of books about the Kennedy assassination, Watergate, the Vietnam War, and the entire twenty-three book series of the Apache westerns. My father loved books, and since I loved my father with an aching devotion, I decided to love books as well.

I can remember picking up my father's books before I could read. The words themselves were mostly foreign, but I still remember the exact moment when I first understood, with a sudden clarity, the purpose of a paragraph. I didn't have the vocabulary to say "paragraph," but I realized that a paragraph was a fence that held words. The words inside a paragraph worked together for a common purpose. They had some specific reason for being inside the same fence. This knowledge delighted me. I began to think of everything in terms of paragraphs. Our reservation was a small paragraph within the United States. My family's house was a paragraph, distinct from the other paragraphs of the LeBrets to the north, the Fords to our south, and the Tribal School to the west. Inside our house, each family member existed as a separate paragraph but still had genetics and common experiences to link us. Now, using this logic, I can see my changed family as an essay of seven paragraphs: mother, father, older brother, the deceased sister, my younger twin sisters, and our adopted little brother.

At the same time I was seeing the world in paragraphs, I also picked up the *Superman* comic book. Each panel, complete with picture, dialogue, and narrative, was a three-dimensional paragraph. In one panel, Superman breaks through a door. His suit is red, blue, and yellow. The brown door shatters into many pieces. I look at the narrative above the picture. I cannot read the words, but I assume it tells me that "Superman is breaking down the door." Aloud, I pretend to read the words and say, "Superman is breaking down the door." Words, dialogue, also float out of Superman's mouth. Because he is breaking down the door, I assume he says, "I am breaking down the door." Once again, I pretend to read the words and say aloud, "I am breaking down the door." In this way, I learned to read.

This might be an interesting story all by itself. A little Indian boy teaches himself to read at an early age and advances quickly. He reads *Grapes of Wrath* in kindergarten when other children are struggling through Dick and Jane. If he'd been anything but an Indian boy living on the reservation, he might have been called a prodigy. But he is an Indian boy living on the reservation and is simply an oddity. He grows into a man who often speaks of his childhood in the third-person, as if it will somehow dull the pain and make him sound more modest about his talents.

A smart Indian is a dangerous person, widely feared and ridiculed by Indians and non-Indians alike. I fought with my classmates on a daily basis. They wanted me to stay quiet when the non-Indian teacher asked for answers, for volunteers, for help. We were Indian children who were expected to be stupid. Most lived up to those expectations inside the classroom but subverted them on the outside. They struggled with basic reading in school but could remember how to sing a few dozen powwow songs. They were monosyllabic in front of their non-Indian teachers but could tell complicated stories and jokes at the dinner table. They submissively ducked their heads when confronted by a non-Indian adult but would slug it out with the Indian bully who was ten years older. As Indian children, we were expected to fail in the non-Indian world. Those who failed were ceremonially accepted by other Indians and appropriately pitied by non-Indians.

I refused to fail. I was smart. I was arrogant. I was lucky. I read books late into the night, until I could barely keep my eyes open. I read books at recess, then during lunch, and in the few minutes left after I had finished my classroom assignments. I read books in the car when my family traveled to powwows or basketball games. In shopping malls, I ran to the bookstores and read bits and pieces of as many books as I could. I read the books my father brought home from the pawnshops and secondhand. I read the books I borrowed from the library. I read the backs of cereal boxes. I read the newspaper. I read the bulletins posted on the walls of the school, the clinic, the tribal offices, the post office. I read junk mail. I read auto-repair manuals. I read magazines. I read anything that had words and paragraphs. I read with equal parts joy and desperation. I loved those books, but I also knew that love had only one purpose. I was trying to save my life.

Despite all the books I read, I am still surprised I became a writer. I was going to be a pediatrician. These days, I write novels, short stories, and poems. I visit schools and teach creative writing to Indian kids. In all my years in the reservation school system, I was never taught how to write poetry, short stories, or novels. I was certainly never taught that Indians wrote poetry, short stories, and novels. Writing was something beyond Indians. I cannot recall a single time that a guest teacher visited the reservation. There must have been visiting teachers. Who were they? Where are they now? Do they exist? I visit the schools as often as possible. The Indian kids crowd the classroom. Many are writing their own poems, short stories, and novels. They have read my books. They have read many other books. They look at me with bright eyes and arrogant wonder. They are trying to save their lives. Then there are the sullen and already defeated Indian kids who sit in the back rows and ignore me with theatrical precision. The pages of their notebooks are empty. They carry neither pencil nor pen. They stare out the window. They refuse and resist. "Books," I say to them. "Books," I say. I throw my weight against their locked doors. The door holds. I am smart. I am arrogant. I am lucky. I am trying to save our lives.

INTERPRETATIONS

1. The purpose of an introduction is to engage the reader. How well does Alexie's first paragraph accomplish this? Cite effective examples.

2. What role does his father play in his literacy acquisition? Is there someone who played a similar role in your learning to read?

3. How effectively does Alexie use the metaphor of a fence as a framing device for his essay? Trace its development in each paragraph.

4. In paragraph 4, Alexie returns to the theme of literacy as empowerment. Why does he reintroduce Superman? To what effect?

5. Alexie devotes subsequent paragraphs to personal history and cultural stereotypes. Explain the effects of the latter with respect to teachers, non-Indian, and Indian students.

6. Review Alexie's conclusion. Why does he devote so much time to visiting Indian schools? What is the effect of his ending his essay with the symbol of the door?

APPLICATIONS

1.   "I read anything that had words and paragraphs. I read with equal parts of joy and desperation. I loved those books, but I also knew that love had only one purpose. I was trying to save my life." Write a journal response to each of Alexie's statements. What is the effect of juxtaposing joy and desperation? How do you react to his linking reading with saving his life?

2.   Alexie writes ". . . I realized that a paragraph was a fence that held words." To what extent is this metaphor dependent upon an understanding of another kind of literacy? What literacy is being invoked?

3.   In his second paragraph, Alexie writes: "My father, who is one of the few Indians who went to Catholic school on purpose . . ." What do the last two words of this quoted phrase tell you about the literacies present on the reservation?

One Voice

SUSAN G. MADERA

Susan G. Madera was born and raised in Little Italy, in Manhattan. She lives with her husband and two children in Queens, New York. She received her Associate in Arts degree from Queensborough Community College in 2003. She currently attends Queens College where she majors in English and minors in Secondary Education. Record in your journal your responses to Madera's first paragraph.

GROWING UP, I KNEW TWO LANGUAGES: English, and neighborhood. The former was taught at school, and the latter was learned at home, from family and friends. I could read and write in English, but I spoke neighborhood. "What is neighborhood?" you may ask. That is the language spoken in the neighborhood of my youth, Little Italy. It is a language full of slang words, and colloquialisms. Where I grew up, almost everyone spoke neighborhood.

As a child, I attended Transfiguration, a small Catholic grammar school in Chinatown. This school was several blocks away from our cramped, fifth floor apartment in a walk-up building on Broome Street. It was a financial hardship for all five children in our family to attend this school. My father worked two strenuous jobs so that we could enjoy the benefits of a good education. I wore my plaid jumper, crisp white blouse, and red uniform tie with pride each day. I was getting the best education that money could buy. My father said that if I studied hard, I was going to be "someone" when I grew up.

In grammar school, the most difficult subject I studied was English. There were so many complicated rules to memorize! To me, it was a foreign language—mysterious, and intriguing, but not a language that I spoke fluently. I was not alone in my feelings of dismay. Many of the students in my class were having difficulty learning this new language.

I remember Dominick Mazzocchi asking, "How can you say *ain't* ain't a word?"

The teacher responded, "Not only is it not a word, but that was a double negative!"

Dominick responded, "Double what? I wish you would talk English! None of us is understanding you."

"You mean, none of us *are* understanding you," remarked the teacher.

Dominick screamed, "We don't talk like you do!" He was sent to the principal's office.

The truth is, we did not speak alike. Although we were getting a great education in school, it was the language we learned outside of school that determined our speech. Amy Tan writes that the way your friends speak to you, while you are growing up, will have a great impact on you (page 48). The effect on my language skills was a tremendous one, albeit negative. I could not speak English properly.

Once outside the neighborhood, this language hindered me. I was not always understood clearly, or was mocked. "What do you mean, you want to 'take' a haircut?," asked the hairdresser. "Where do you want to take it?" He began to laugh at me. I was so embarrassed. How could he not understand me? The language I picked up on the streets was a part of me, but as I grew up I wanted to get as far away from it as possible. It embarrassed me. In this case, being bilingual was not a blessing, it was a curse.

In high school, I began to use the rules taught to me in my English classes in grammar school. More than anything, I wanted to speak like everyone else. I tried my best, but was unsuccessful. The only way I could stop speaking neighborhood was to take a knife and cut the tongue from my mouth! In my junior year, I was approached by my English teacher who asked if I would like to write for the school paper. "I can't do that!," I exclaimed, "I don't talk right!" She then told me that although I did not speak correctly, I wrote correctly. My written work showed no trace of my flawed speech. She had so much confidence in me that she wanted me to edit the paper as well. I was flabbergasted, and quickly accepted the position. When my first story was published, I was amazed at the response I received from my peers. No one believed that I had written it! I could, indeed, write in proper English. This gave me hope. Perhaps, one day, I might also be able to speak correctly. I felt very much like M. Bella Mirabella, who described how she felt when she accomplished her goals. She wrote, "I was no longer the proverbial small child looking in the shop window."[1] I too was no longer on the outside looking in.

Success at last!

After high school, I attended Brooklyn College. Walking on campus for the first time was like browsing through a travel brochure. I was transformed into a tourist. There were trees everywhere. Although I was

[1]M. Bella Mirabella. "The Education of an Italian-American Girl Child." *Liberating Memory*. Ed. Janet Zandy. (Rutgers University Press, 1995), pp. 162–172.

only in Brooklyn, I felt far from the city streets of Manhattan. I was in a different world. This was not like the small Catholic schools I had attended. I was alone, and afraid, but determined.

On the first day of classes, I was overwhelmed with feelings of anxiety. I was so excited, I could hardly breathe. That feeling of excitement was soon transformed into a feeling of terror. One of my professors had decided to make my life miserable. He taught Speech 101. On the first day of class, he had each student read aloud from our text book to determine the quality of their speech. He then proceeded to demean me, my heritage and my education. That day was only the first of many. He proceeded to make a fool of me each and every day our class met. That first, and last, semester at Brooklyn College was a dream that turned into a nightmare. José Torres (page 178) writes that you should not let someone else's opinion of you affect your self worth. Unfortunately, this professor's opinion of me was so low, and his personal attacks were so painful, that I had lost all confidence in myself. It took years for me to gain that confidence back. I decided that college was not for me, and I went into the working world.

I was lucky enough to get a position as a typist in a very prestigious company, Morgan Guaranty. I began my career in the typing pool, typing on an IBM typewriter. Within a year, word processors came into the office, and I was thrilled to be picked as one of the people trained to use one. During this time, I met a wonderful man who would change my life forever—Michael. We dated for two years, and were married at Most Precious Blood Church, in Little Italy.

My personal life was wonderful, so too was my professional life. Over the next few years, I got small promotions within my department. Each promotion brought much more responsibility, with a little more money. One day, at review time, I was called into a meeting. When I walked into the dimly lit conference room, I was surprised to see several assistant vice presidents and a vice president with my supervisor. I immediately broke into a cold sweat. What had I done wrong? My years of "dedication, hard work, and knowledge of the English language" had brought me to their attention. Knowledge of the English language! They were joking, they had to be. They proceeded to make me an offer I could not refuse—my own department. I was dumbfounded when offered this position, but accepted quickly, before they changed their minds. I headed a department of word processors in the investment research department. This success was much larger than the one achieved in high school. I was now being accepted in the business world.

I eventually left Morgan on maternity leave with my first child. Upon my return, I was to be trained on the new IBM computers, and become supervisor of an even larger group of people. Once our son was born and I looked into his sparkling eyes, I knew I could not leave him to the care of a baby-sitter. When I returned three months later, it was to resign my position.

I am still a supervisor, but of our home. Michael is now twelve years old, and Matthew is six. Unfortunately, our children have a bit of neighborhood in them. I take the blame for this. As Dr. Benjamin Spock says about childhood development, "Between 3 and 5 years they were, generally, cozy, affectionate family children who proudly patterned their activities, table manners, and speech after their parents."[2] Our children's speech patterns were picked up from the main caregiver in our home, me. When I hear one of our boys say something incorrectly, I explain why it is wrong, and tell him the correct way to say it. My husband often tells me that I should be an English teacher because I am always correcting their grammar. I want our children to have the benefit of a strong background in English. I know the downfalls of not speaking properly, and I do not want them to experience them, as I have.

To say that I have conquered all my fears of the English language would be untrue. Twenty-one years after walking away from Brooklyn College, I am back in school at Queensborough Community College. What was the first class I decided to take? Why English, of course. I am as determined as ever to speak English as well as possible. I am doing well in my class, and I am proud of myself. I am also quite glad that QCC has decided to give me the three credits I earned in Speech at Brooklyn College, although I barely passed, with a grade of D. I could not have taken that class again.

Over the years, I have gained confidence in myself as a writer. The way I speak does not exemplify who I am; however, my writing is a true expression of the person I am inside. When I write, words come from deep inside of me, and spill out onto the page. I never stop to correct myself, as I would if I were speaking. I may speak two languages, but I write with one voice.

INTERPRETATIONS

1. What distinctions does Madera make between the language of school and the language of the neighborhood?

2. Why does she regard being bilingual as a "curse" rather than a "blessing"?

[2]Dr. Benjamin Spock, and Michael B. Rothenberg, M.D., *Dr. Spock's Baby and Child Care* (New York: Pocket Books, 1985).

3. What roles do her teachers play in her acquisition of written language?
4. What point does she make about her "two languages" in her conclusion?

APPLICATIONS

1. Do you like Madera have a "writing self" and a "speaking self"? How do they differ? What does each express about your identity?
2. The opening sentence to Susan G. Madera's essay is: "Growing up, I knew two languages: English, and neighborhood." What literacies are implied in this statement? What is involved in the literacy of "neighborhood"? What knowledge do you bring to your understanding of your neighborhood?
3. What literacy is presented in Madera's anecdote about Dominick Mazzocchi? What assumptions about literacy are made?
4. How does Madera ultimately resolve the conflict between the literacies of English and neighborhood? To what extent have you negotiated these same literacies and the demands they make upon you?

The Knowing Eye

Venus and Serena Williams. *New York Times*, August 31, 2000

READING IMAGES

1. Which of these photographs depict "family"? Which show "community"? Explain your answers.
2. Crucial to many definitions of family or community is the idea of sharing or giving. As you examine these photographs, what do you think is being shared or given?

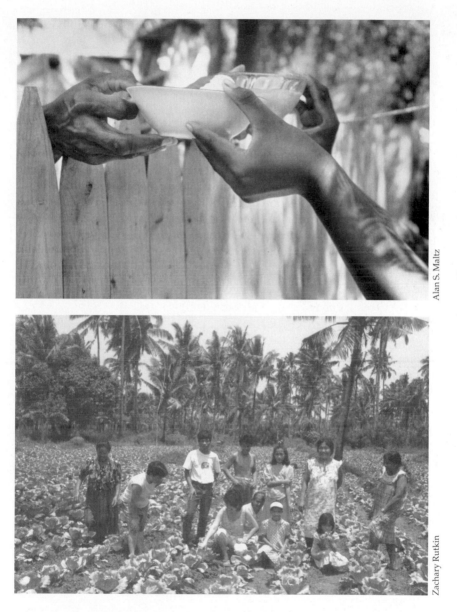

Alan S. Maltz

Zachary Rutkin

MAKING CONNECTIONS

1. Which essay (or essays) in this chapter seem(s) to match these photographs? What similarities do you notice?

2. Select one "Perspective" (see pages 17–19) to summarize each photograph. After making your choices, are the quotations and

photographs interchangeable? What have you learned about the interplay of words and images?

WORDS AND IMAGES

1. Which image do you like more? Why? Present your findings in an argumentation and persuasion essay.

2. As you examine the photograph of the tennis players, what do you think they might be saying to each other? First, write a dialogue of ten lines that illustrates the conversation they might be having *as sisters*. Now, write another dialogue of ten lines with the assumption that the women are *not related*. What do you observe about the dialogues you have created? How does the presence or absence of family relations influence the dialogues you have written?

Additional Writing Topics

1. Motherhood is an important theme in the texts by Dana Wehle, Amy Tan, and Maxine Hong Kingston. Analyze their respective viewpoints in an essay on motherhood that also includes your evaluation of the topic.

2. Several writers in this unit focus on the complex roles that memory plays in constructing the self. Write an essay in which you recount at least two memories and explain their significance in shaping your identity.

3. Several selections focus on family members and their influence. Why are families so important? Write an essay answering this question. Use examples from this chapter and your own experience.

4. Does the observance of customs, rituals, or traditions promote unity and continuity within the family? What rituals have your family shared over the years? How have these contributed to family relationships? Write an essay explaining how the observance of rituals helps preserve the family.

5. Review Nin's perspective on friendship (page 18). What does it suggest about possibilities in relationships? Are old friends necessarily one's best friends? Write an essay comparing two friendships of varying durations. How has each contributed to your knowledge of yourself? How do the relationships differ?

6. You have been introduced to several families in this chapter. Imagine being invited to spend a weekend with one of them. Which family would you choose and why? What would you expect from such a visit? Cite evidence from the text to support your expectations.

7. Several writers in this chapter discuss the transition from family to community. Write an essay focusing on a particular experience that enabled you to have such a transition. To what extent were you able to make a connection between your private and public worlds?

8. Interview three members of your group or three friends about their family structure and parental roles. Focus on at least three specific areas that might include information regarding economic issues, discipline, decisions, and other factors you consider relevant. Write an essay analyzing your findings.

9. According to the contemporary writer and critic Susan Sontag, "a family's photograph album is generally about the extended family—and, often, is all that remains of it." What role do photographs play in your immediate and extended family? Write an essay describing selected family photographs that support Sontag's thesis.

CHAPTER

3

Gender Issues

Few aspects of contemporary life in North America and other parts of the world have changed more radically in the last two decades than those focusing on women in the workplace, gender roles in marriage, women's sexuality, divorce, communication between men and women, child custody, and sexual preference.

The texts on gender issues present a number of points of view on the relationship between men and women and their perceptions of each other. The writers explore, among other things, why various cultures have constructed different images of men and women at different points in their history.

They invite you to examine these changing cross-cultural concepts of masculinity and femininity and to evaluate the degree to which they have affected both men and women in their individual quests for identity, as well as the radical changes in the structure of the family. Some of the writers ask you to decide whether gender conflicts should be confronted or avoided, while others pose possibilities for freeing both sexes from the confines of traditional roles.

The most recurrent and controversial aspects of gender relations found in these texts is the debate between patriarchs and feminists. In some, the traditional idea of male supremacy has left its mark, and in others it is vigorously rejected, shattering intrapersonal and intracultural harmony.

Sexual orientation and sexual preference are current controversies particularly in the realm of "Queer Theory" in which scholars propose that human sexuality is a social construct based on culture rather than nature. They argue that in many cultures outside of the United States bisexuality and homosexuality are accepted, releasing both males and females from the confines of traditional sexual roles. Obviously, such reconsiderations are complex, involving not only individual and social values but moral and religious beliefs.

The ramifications, personal, familial, and cultural, of women's return to the workplace are the focus of the texts by Barbara Dafoe Whitehead and Dorsett Bennett. Both writers analyze the impact of rising divorce rates, single motherhood, changing roles of fathers, and child custody laws. Jason Barone and Leslie Norris write about an experience many children share: realizing that parents are fallible and cannot protect them. Paul Theroux critiques traditional concepts of masculinity in the United States, while Rose Del Castillo Guilbault contrasts definitions of macho in Hispanic culture with those of mainstream America. Jerry Rockwood presents the complexities of preparing a sensitive son to function in a culture in which masculinity and aggressiveness are considered synonymous. The controversial topic of sexual preferences is the focus of the texts by Dennis Altman and Anna Quindlen.

As you join the debate concerning feminists, patriarchs, homosexuals, and lesbians in these texts from various cultures and traditions, you are invited to speculate on questions such as the following: Are men rightly in charge of the family and tribe? Should women be accorded the same personal, political, and economic rights as men? Can the family survive the challenge to traditionalism created by changing personal and economic gender roles? Are women who return to the workplace surrendering their matriarchal role of nurturing the family and tribe? How have cultural attitudes toward homosexuals and lesbians resulted in political and sexual exclusion? What new definitions are needed for the concept of love?

Perspectives

Masculinity and Femininity may stand on either side of a mile-high wall, yet women and men share beds and homes, histories and children. So while racial and ethnographic stereotypes are fueled by segregation and prohibit familiarity . . . sexual stereotypes are formed in intimacy. This is what makes them unique, and uniquely troubling.

—Judith Levine

Marriage is a lottery in which men stake their liberty and women their happiness.

—Virginia des Rieux

We need to draw on images of collaborative caring by both men and women as a model of responsibility.

—Mary Catherine Bateson

Marriage must be a relation either of sympathy or of conquest.

—George Eliot

In sum, "homophobia" is a form of acute conventionality. We should do our best to help humankind over this illness, since heterosexuals who are free of it tend to have much better lives than heterosexuals who are not.

—George Weinberg

Indeed, it is my experience that both men and women are fundamentally human, and that there is very little mystery about either sex, except for the exasperating mysteriousness of human beings in general.

—Dorothy Sayers

Marriage comes with more myths attached to it than a six-volume set of ancient Greek history.

—Steven Tesich

A good marriage is that in which each appoints the other the guardian of his solitude.

—Rainer Maria Rilke

Love will redeem a man and change his entire character and existence; lack of love will literally drive a woman crazy.

—Jean Anouilh

A child becomes an adult when he realizes that he has a right not only to be right but also to be wrong.

—*Thomas Szasz*

The word love has by no means the same sense for both sexes, and this is one of the serious misunderstandings that divide them.

—*Simone de Beauvoir*

Growing up homosexual was to grow up normally but displaced; to experience romantic love, but with the wrong person; to entertain grand ambitions, but of the unacceptable sort; to seek a gradual self-awakening, but in secret, not in public.

—*Andrew Sullivan*

Women have served all these centuries as looking-glasses possessing the magic and delicious power of reflecting the figure of man at twice its natural size.

—*Virginia Woolf*

The legal subordination of one sex to another is wrong in itself and now one of the chief hindrances to human improvement.

—*John Stuart Mill*

Males become so accustomed to masking their true emotions that it seems like second nature.

—*Mark Zmarzly*

APPLICATIONS

1. Review the various perspectives on marriage. What do they suggest about this intimate relationship? Select the one with which you are most in agreement and compare your choice with those of your group. What consensus, if any, did you reach?

2. Working with members of your group, devise a questionnaire that asks respondents about positive traits associated with masculinity and femininity. Distribute the questionnaire to ten or twelve classmates or co-workers. Write an analysis of their responses.

3. Discuss Zmarzly's perspective with your group. To what extent do you agree with him? What cultural and social factors account for males suppressing their emotions? What solutions are there?

Women

CHINESE FOLKTALE

Milton Rugoff in his A Harvest of World Folk Tales *introduced this old Chinese story this way:*

> *Popular conceptions of China's isolation notwithstanding, Chinese folktales have been no more free of international influence than those of Europe or America. Coming mostly from India through the medium of Buddhism, but also from the Near East, many familiar themes, including those of "Cinderella," the Master Thief, and the trapping of a jinni (genie) in a bottle, appear in Chinese folklore. But the national temperament asserts itself in many ways. Ripened by centuries of a religious philosophy that makes for serenity, the Chinese have lent their stories many distinctive qualities: a gentle whimsicality, fantasy, pathos, the uncanny, a quiet resignation to fate.*

AFTER HE WAS MARRIED, Chang the Third no longer wanted to go to work. He sat at home the whole day and played with his wife. He gazed endlessly at her beautiful face, and the longer he looked the less he wanted to go out. Finally, he gave up his job and remained night and day with his wife. He went on in this way for six months, and then for a year; but even the largest fortune is soon exhausted if one does nothing, and Chang had merely lived on his earnings. In two years, all his wife's jewels, the chairs, the tables, the linen, the clothes, in fact everything they had, was pawned or sold, and they were left without a penny.

His wife was really unusually beautiful, but she thought to herself, "Since his marriage, my husband has never left the house. Day and night he sits around doing nothing but eat. In a short while we shall no longer have the wherewithal to live." So she upbraided him, saying, "You really can't stay at home all day. All men must go to work." But Chang saw her beauty and he thought anxiously, "If I went out another man could come and make love to her." And instead of listening to her words, he remained at home, preferring to eat the most miserable food.

But eventually their poverty became unbearable. They could no longer live if he did not work. Finally, one morning, he said good-by to his wife and decided to go to a village. On his way he met a fine-looking man of about fifty years, who said to him, "Which is the way to such and such a village?" Chang answered, "I am going there myself, so we can go together." During their walk Chang told the stranger his story. "I am so unhappy at leaving my wife," he said. "But I must look for work to enable us to live."

The stranger replied, "The simplest thing is to bottle up your wife. I will give you the bottle, and every day, when you leave, you will only need to look at your wife and blow into the bottle, and she will vanish inside at once. As you can always take it with you, you will never lose your wife. I must now take another road, so farewell." Then he handed Chang a large three-inch bottle from his bag and disappeared. Chang dropped the bottle into his bag, noting what the man had said, and set off gaily for the village. The next day he tried the gift. As his wife was combing her hair before the mirror, he secretly blew into the bottle. The woman saw in the mirror the reflection of her husband blowing into a bottle, but then she lost consciousness and woke up to find herself inside the bottle. Chang put the bottle in his pocket and went off to his work in the village. He was quite contented, for now no other man could flirt with his wife. In the evening he tipped the bottle, and his beautiful wife stood before him as before.

One day, however, he was forced to leave his wife at home to do the washing. He begged her not to leave the house when the washing was finished, and then set off to the village, forgetting to take the bottle with him.

After her husband's departure, the wife went down to the river to wash the clothes. While she was rinsing a shirt she suddenly felt a long, hard thing between her fingers. She took it out and looked at it carefully. "It's a bottle," she said to herself. "Every morning my husband blows into it and I vanish inside. Why has he forgotten it today?" While she was pondering over the matter, a handsome young man passed by on the other bank. She looked up at him, and without thinking what she was doing blew into the bottle, whereupon the young man disappeared. When she had finished the washing, she replaced the bottle in her husband's clothes.

When the man arrived home, he immediately asked for the bottle he had left behind, and his wife handed it to him without a word. The next day when he went out he blew into the bottle as usual, and his wife disappeared, and again he flattered himself that she was safe from the caresses of other men.

That evening on his return he tipped the bottle, but this time two people appeared, his wife and a handsome young man. He was very much surprised and said to himself, "How strange! I thought my wife was quite safe shut up in the bottle, but now she has got a man with her! How odd it is! And how impossible it is to keep a beautiful wife to oneself."

INTERPRETATIONS

1. Describe the relationship between Chang and his wife. How does it change in the course of the story?

2. What type of marriage does the bottle symbolize? What does the mirror symbolize?

3. What seems to be the point (moral) of this tale?

4. Do you think the title works? Why or why not? Would an equally good title be "Men"?

Apollo and Daphne

GREEK LEGEND

Greece reached the height of its achievements and power in the fifth century B.C. Its accomplishments in art, architecture, science, mathematics, philosophy, drama, literature, and democracy became legacies for future generations in countries all over the world. In later centuries, Greece fell under the rule of Rome, Turkey, and other nations. In 1829, it won independence from Turkey and became a kingdom. A republic was formed in 1924. During World War II, occupation by Germans, Italians, and Bulgarians was met by guerrilla warfare against the occupying armies. Subsequent struggles led to the reestablishment of the monarchy, juntas, and finally socialist government.

DAPHNE [GREEK FOR "LAUREL"] was a wood nymph, the daughter of the river god Peneus. She was one of those free-spirited women in mythology who was more interested in hunting and fishing than in men. Her father despaired that she would ever marry; he was more interested in grandchildren than in having still more game to eat.

The god Apollo saw Daphne one day and fell instantly in love with her. He was unable to think of anything but her and he pursued her to no avail. Daphne was absolutely indifferent to his attentions; it mattered not whether he was god or mortal. She also knew that relationships with gods were often complicated and even dangerous. She was, after all, half divine, yet mortal. Finally Apollo chased her through the forests until she was stricken with fear. There was no way that she could outrun him, so she cried for her father to save her with a miracle.

Suddenly, she felt her feet become rooted in the earth. She could not move. Leaves began to sprout from her arms—she had become a living laurel tree. The gods have a way of sorting things out of the most desperate situations, so they made the laurel tree the sacred tree of Apollo.

To this day, whether at poetry contests or athletic events, both within the purview of Apollo, the winner is crowned with laurels.

INTERPRETATIONS

1. Do you think of yourself as a "free spirit"? Explain.
2. To what extent are Daphne's father's expectations typical? Do you empathize with her? Why or why not?
3. Consult a source on laurel trees and explain their significance with respect to Daphne.
4. Is there a victor in this myth? Explain.

CORRESPONDENCES

1. Review the Rilke perspective (page 91). To what extent do you agree with his point about solitude in relationships? What might Chang the Third (of "Women") have learned from Rilke?
2. To what extent are Apollo and Chang the Third responsible for their fates?

APPLICATIONS

1. Personal space and its effect on gender relationships differs among cultures. Using "Women" as a point of departure, compare your ideas on personal space and romance with group members from other cultures.
2. Discuss with your group the degree to which Daphne's being a free spirit conflicts with parental expectations. To what extent is this still the case? Write a summary of your group's conclusion.
3. Discuss the issue of possessiveness in intimate relationships. Focus on dating perspectives from male and female members of your group and discuss the degree to which they affect attitudes toward freedom in close gender relationships.

The Male Myth

PAUL THEROUX

Paul Theroux (b. 1941), who is adept at writing fiction and nonfiction, was born in Medford, Massachusetts, and educated at the University of Maine, the University of Massachusetts, and Syracuse University. As a Peace Corps volunteer in the Congo, he became too friendly with local politicians who were not in good standing with the country's dictator. His association with these leaders led to his deportation. However, he returned to Africa and eventually travelled in Asia, Europe, and Central America, teaching and writing. The Mosquito Coast *(1982),* My Secret History *(1989),* Milroy the Magician *(1994), and* Kowloon Tong *(1997) are just a few of his numerous novels.*

Theroux's travel books include: The Great Railway Bazaar *(1975),* Riding the Iron Rooster *(1988),* To The Ends of the Earth *(1990),* Fresh Air Fiend *(2000), and* Dark Star Safari *(2002). Theroux currently divides his time between Cape Cod and Hawaii, where he is a professional beekeeper. Theroux makes many provocative statements to engage his readers. Which do you find most effective?*

THERE IS A PATHETIC SENTENCE in the chapter "Fetishism" in Dr. Norman Cameron's book *Personality Development and Psychopathology*. It goes: "Fetishists are nearly always men; and their commonest fetish is a woman's shoe." I cannot read that sentence without thinking that it is just one more awful thing about being a man—and perhaps it is the most important thing to know about us.

I have always disliked being a man. The whole idea of manhood in America is pitiful, a little like having to wear an ill-fitting coat for one's entire life. (By contrast, I imagine femininity to be an oppressive sense of nakedness.) Even the expression "Be a man!" strikes me as insulting and abusive. It means: Be stupid, be unfeeling, obedient and soldierly, and stop thinking. Man means "manly"—how can one think "about men" without considering the terrible ambition of manliness? And yet it is part of every man's life. It is a hideous and crippling lie; it not only insists on difference and connives at superiority, it is also by its very nature destructive—emotionally damaging and socially harmful.

The youth who is subverted, as most are, into believing in the masculine ideal is effectively separated from women—it is the most savage tribal logic—and he spends the rest of his life finding women a riddle and a nuisance. Of course, there is a female version of this male afflic-tion. It begins with mothers encouraging little girls to say (to other adults), "Do you like my new dress?" In a sense, girls are traditionally urged to please adults with a kind of coquettishness, while boys are enjoined to behave like monkeys toward each other. The nine-year-old coquette proceeds to become womanish in a subtle power game in which she learns to be sexually indispensable, socially decorative and always alert to a man's sense of inadequacy.

Femininity—being ladylike—implies needing a man as witness and seducer; but masculinity celebrates the exclusive company of men. That is why it is so grotesque; and that is also why there is no manliness without inadequacy—because it denies men the natural friendship of women.

It is very hard to imagine any concept of manliness that does not belittle women, and it begins very early. At an age when I wanted to meet girls—let's say the treacherous years of thirteen to sixteen—I was told to take up a sport, get more fresh air, join the Boy Scouts, and I was urged not to read so much. It was the 1950s and, if you asked too many questions about sex, you were sent to camp—boys' camp, of course; the nightmare. Nothing is more unnatural or prisonlike than a boys' camp, but if it were not for them, we would have no Elks' Lodges, no pool-rooms, no boxing matches, no marines.

And perhaps no sports as we know them. Everyone is aware of how few in number are the athletes who behave like gentlemen. Just as high-school basketball teaches you how to be a poor loser, the manly attitude toward sports seems to be little more than a recipe for creating bad marriages, social misfits, moral degenerates, sadists, latent rapists and just plain louts. I regard high-school sports as a drug far worse than marijuana, and it is the reason that the average tennis champion, say, is a pathetic oaf.

Any objective study would find the quest for manliness essentially right wing, puritanical, cowardly, neurotic and fueled largely by a fear of women. It is also certainly philistine. There is no book hater like a Little League coach. But, indeed, all the creative arts are obnoxious to the manly ideal, because at their best the arts are pursued by uncompet-itive and essentially solitary people. It makes it very hard for a creative youngster, for any boy who expresses the desire to be alone seems to be saying that there is something wrong with him.

It ought to be clear by now that I have an objection to the way we turn boys into men. It does not surprise me that when the President of the United States has his customary weekend off, he dresses like a cow-boy—it is both a measure of his insecurity and his willingness to please. In many ways, American culture does little more for a man than prepare him for modeling clothes in the L. L. Bean catalogue. I take this as a personal insult because for many years I found it impossible to admit to myself that I wanted to be a writer. It was my guilty secret, because being a writer was incompatible with being a man.

There are people who might deny this, but that is because the American writer, typically, has been so at pains to prove his manliness. But first there was a fear that writing was not a manly profession—indeed, not a profession at all. (The paradox in American letters is that it has always been easier for a woman to write and for a man to be published.) Growing up, I had thought of sports as wasteful and humiliating, and the idea of manliness as a bore. My wanting to become a writer was not a flight from that oppressive role playing, but I quickly saw that it was at odds with it. Everything in stereotyped manliness goes against the life of the mind. The Hemingway personality is too tedious to go into here, but certainly it was not until this aberrant behavior was examined by feminists in the 1960's that any male writer dared question the pugnacity in Hemingway's fiction. All that bullfighting and arm-wrestling and elephant shooting diminished Hemingway as a writer: One cannot be a male writer without first proving that one is a man.

It is normal in America for a man to be dismissive or even somewhat apologetic about being a writer. Various factors make it easier. There is a heartiness about journalism that makes it acceptable—journalism is the manliest form of American writing and, therefore, the profession the most independent-minded women seek (yes, it is an illusion, but that is my point). Fiction writing is equated with a kind of dispirited failure and is only manly when it produces wealth. Money is masculinity. So is drinking. Being a drunkard is another assertion, if misplaced, of manliness. The American male writer is traditionally proud of his heavy drinking. But we are also very literal-minded people. A man proves his manhood in America in old-fashioned ways. He kills lions, like Hemingway; or he hunts ducks, like Nathanael West; or he makes pronouncements, like "A man should carry enough knife to defend himself with," as James Jones is said to have once told an interviewer. And we are familiar with the lengths to which Norman Mailer is prepared, in his endearing way, to prove that he is just as much a monster as the next man.

When the novelist John Irving was revealed as a wrestler, people took him to be a very serious writer. But what interests me is that it is inconceivable that any woman writer would be shown in such a posture. How surprised we would be if Joyce Carol Oates were revealed as a sumo wrestler or Joan Didion enjoyed pumping iron. "Lives in New York City with her three children" is the typical woman-writer's biographical note, for just as the male writer must prove he has achieved a sort of muscular manhood, the woman writer—or rather her publicists—must prove her motherhood.

There would be no point in saying any of this if it were not generally accepted that to be a man is somehow—even now in feminist-influenced America—a privilege. It is on the contrary an unmerciful and punishing burden. Being a man is bad enough; being manly is appalling. It is the sinister silliness of men's fashions that inspires the so-called dress code of the Ritz-Carlton Hotel in Boston. It is the institutionalized cheating in college sports. It is a pathetic and primitive insecurity.

And this is also why men often object to feminism, but are afraid to explain why: Of course women have a justified grievance, but most men believe—and with reason—that their lives are much worse.

INTERPRETATIONS

1. What is Theroux's definition of *manly*? To what extent do you agree with it?

2. How does Theroux define *femininity*? What observations does he make about society's attempts to stereotype women?

3. Theroux makes several comments about "the sinister silliness of men's fashions." What is the context for his analysis? To what extent do you agree with him?

Americanization Is Tough on "Macho"

ROSE DEL CASTILLO GUILBAULT

Rose Del Castillo Guilbault (b. 1952) is a columnist on Hispanic issues, an associate editor at Pacific News Service, and director of editorials and public affairs at a San Francisco television station. She examines the differing meanings of macho in mainstream America and in her ethnic culture.

WHAT IS MACHO? That depends which side of the border you come from.

Although it's not unusual for words and expressions to lose their subtlety in translation, the negative connotations of *macho* in this country are troublesome to Hispanics.

Take the newspaper descriptions of alleged mass murderer Ramon Salcido. That an insensitive, insanely jealous, hard-drinking, violent Latin male is referred to as *macho* makes Hispanics cringe.

"Es muy macho," the women in my family nod approvingly, describing a man they respect. But in the United States, when women say, "He's so macho," it's with disdain.

The Hispanic *macho* is manly, responsible, hardworking, a man in charge, a patriarch. A man who expresses strength through silence. What the Yiddish language would call a *mensch*.

The American *macho* is a chauvinist, a brute, uncouth, selfish, loud, abrasive, capable of inflicting pain, and sexually promiscuous.

Quintessential *macho* models in this country are Sylvester Stallone, Arnold Schwarzenegger, and Charles Bronson. In their movies, they exude toughness, independence, masculinity. But a closer look reveals their machismo is really violence masquerading as courage, sullenness disguised as silence and irresponsibility camouflaged as independence.

If the Hispanic ideal of *macho* were translated to American screen roles, they might be Jimmy Stewart, Sean Connery, and Laurence Olivier.

In Spanish, *macho* ennobles Latin males. In English it devalues them. This pattern seems consistent with the conflicts ethnic minority males experience in this country. Typically the cultural traits other societies value don't translate as desirable characteristics in America.

I watched my own father struggle with these cultural ambiguities. He worked on a farm for twenty years. He laid down miles of irrigation pipe, carefully plowed long, neat rows in fields, hacked away at recalcitrant weeds and drove tractors through whirlpools of dust. He stoically worked twenty-hour days during harvest season, accepting the long hours as part of agricultural work. When the boss complained or upbraided him for minor mistakes, he kept quiet, even when it was obvious the boss had erred.

He handled the most menial tasks with pride. At home he was a good provider, helped out my mother's family in Mexico without complaint, and was indulgent with me. Arguments between my mother and him generally had to do with money, or with his stubborn reluctance to share his troubles. He tried to work them out in his own silence. He didn't want to trouble my mother—a course that backfired, because the imagined is always worse than the reality.

Americans regarded my father as decidedly un-*macho*. His character was interpreted as non-assertive, his loyalty non-ambition, and his quietness, ignorance. I once overheard the boss's son blame him for plowing crooked rows in a field. My father merely smiled at the lie, knowing the boy had done it, but didn't refute it, confident his good work was well known. But the boss instead ridiculed him for being "stupid" and letting a kid get away with a lie. Seeing my embarrassment, my father dismissed the incident, saying "They're the dumb ones. Imagine, me fighting with a kid."

I tried not to look at him with American eyes because sometimes the reflection hurt.

Listening to my aunts' clucks of approval, my vision focused on the qualities America overlooked. "He's such a hard worker. So serious, so responsible," my aunts would secretly compliment my mother. The unspoken comparison was that he was not like some of their husbands, who drank and womanized. My uncles represented the darker side of *macho*.

In a patriarchal society, few challenge their roles. If men drink, it's because it's the manly thing to do. If they gamble, it's because it's how men relax. And if they fool around, well, it's because a man simply can't hold back so much man! My aunts didn't exactly meekly sit back, but they put up with these transgressions because Mexican society dictated this was their lot in life.

In the United States, I believe it was the feminist movement of the early '70s that changed *macho*'s meaning. Perhaps my generation of Latin women was in part responsible. I recall Chicanas complaining about the chauvinistic nature of Latin men and the notion they wanted their women barefoot, pregnant, and in the kitchen. The generalization that Latin men embodied chauvinistic traits led to this interesting twist of semantics. Suddenly a word that represented something positive in one culture became a negative prototype in another.

The problem with the use of *macho* today is that it's become an accepted stereotype of the Latin male. And like all stereotypes, it distorts truth.

The impact of language in our society is undeniable. And the misuse of *macho* hints at a deeper cultural misunderstanding that extends beyond mere word definitions.

INTERPRETATIONS

1. In paragraphs 5 and 6, Del Castillo Guilbault defines Hispanic and American concepts of *macho*. How are they different? What would you add to her definitions?

2. What portrait of the author's father emerges from her essay? How does his inclusion either strengthen or detract from her argument?

3. How, according to the author, did the feminist movement of the seventies change the meaning of *macho*? What other factors might also be taken into account?

CORRESPONDENCES

1. Compare and contrast Theroux's definition of *manly* with Guilbault's definition of *macho*. You might consider her comments on patriarchy as well as his comments in his concluding paragraph.

2. Characterize the tones of each author. As their purpose was to persuade, whose tone did you find most convincing? Did your group reach a consensus? Why or why not?

APPLICATIONS

1. "I have always disliked being a man." With this sentence, Paul Theroux begins the second paragraph of his essay "The Male Myth." As you read through the essay, extract sentences that support this viewpoint. Now, imagine how someone who disagrees with Theroux would respond to these statements. (Perhaps, select someone famous who typifies the kind of "manliness" that Theroux seems to be questioning.) Try to create a conversation (dialogue) between these two individuals.

2. Guilbault depicts two kinds of "macho" in her essay: American macho and the Hispanic ideal. What do you imagine these two types to *look* like? Draw a portrait that represents the American type of macho and one that represents the Hispanic type. What characteristics are discernible in your drawings that define these types? How did the author's text help you to create these images?

3. Discuss with your group the degree to which society and culture influence our concepts of masculinity and femininity. To what extent is it possible or desirable to go beyond stereotypical definitions?

4. Review Sayers's perspective (page 91) and write an essay defending or rewriting her point of view. Consider, for example, the degree to which your own sense of "mystery" has been shaped by your gender.

5. Bring to class four advertisements from current magazines featuring dress styles for men and women. Analyze with your group the images they intend to communicate. To what extent are they based on gender stereotypes? What do they "promise" the consumer?

Life Intrudes

JERRY ROCKWOOD

Jerry Rockwood (b. 1927) is an actor, director, and author who has taught at the Stella Adler Studio and the American Academy of Dramatic Art. Rockwood is the author of The Craftsmen of Dionysus: An Approach to Acting, *which was published in 1966. "Life Intrudes" was originally published in 1988 in* The New York Times Magazine *as part of the "About Men" series. To what extent do you empathize with Rockford's first paragraph?*

I NEVER SPOKE BACK. I was quiet and obedient. And so I grew up without aggression, at least the kind of aggression that can be seen on the surface.

It has cost me dearly. I think one reason I became an actor was to be able to vent my squelched aggression and hostility through the characters I played on the stage. But one needs loads of personal aggression to make it in the theater, and, as a result, I never had the success I wanted. Eventually, I turned to teaching acting in college.

Now I have been watching my son, Matthew, a year out of college, display a similar lack of aggression. He reminds me of myself—the way I used to find myself shrinking back or turning away from unpleasantness. Matthew uses "I choose not to" as an excuse for avoiding things he ought to face. It troubles me. It makes me wonder about the values we impose in raising our children.

Education, to a Cherokee father, meant teaching his son to hunt with a bow and arrow, to tread noiselessly through the woods. To an Eskimo father, it meant showing his boy how to tap ice for strength and thickness, how to gauge the depth of the water. Education for these boys meant learning to deal with the environment.

Was it so with Matthew when he was a boy? I think not. His was a good school. Private. Expensive. With all the right and beautiful philosophies intended to help kids grow up to be interested and sincere and sensitive and cooperative and creative and aware—to shun violence and war and vice and double-dealings. Disputes in Matthew's school were mediated by sympathetic and understanding teachers. Feelings were aired, points of view pointed out, alternatives proposed. The right stuff.

But I cannot forget an episode that occurred when Matthew was nine years old. A boy named Kevin, the leader of a small gang of bullies, had it in for him. I remember saying something like, "Look, Math, if Kevin calls you filthy names and teases you, then he's not a very nice kid, and the best thing to do is to ignore him. Laugh it off and walk away."

"But he follows me. And then he starts shoving me. And today he knocked over a bike on me. I don't know what to do!"

Well, what do you do? Tell me, educators and psychologists, what should I have told my son to do? He had discovered that the world inside his fabulously equipped, psychologist-staffed and superior-teacher-laden school was not like the real world outside.

What I did do is this: when I learned that Matthew was determined to fight with Kevin, I first tried to talk him out of it. I asked him if he could beat Kevin. He said yes. I saw that he was determined, and so I agreed and even accompanied him. "My father is coming," Matthew had explained to the other boys, "just to make sure that two of you guys don't jump me at once."

We all walked along the beach looking for a secluded place. "Whatever happens, Dad," Matthew said on the way, "don't break it up." I said I wouldn't break it up.

I stood against a telephone pole, gripping with one hand the lowest of the metal spikes used for climbing it. A dozen or more kids stood nearby. Matthew was sturdier than the wiry Kevin: they were the same height. Each waited for the other to move first. Kevin sprang and, in an instant, had Matthew down and in a headlock. His fist smashed again and again into Matthew's face. There was no contest. Kevin was an accomplished street fighter; Matthew simply didn't know how to fight. At last, "Do you give up?" "Yes."

Matthew rose to his feet, his nose bleeding, his lips bloody and swollen. He tried to hold back the tears, but the anger and humiliation were too much. He made a lunge, and Kevin reached all the way back with his right fist and threw all his weight into a solid punch in the neck. There was an audible intake of breath from the spectators at the sound of the punch. Matthew was stunned and gave a strangulated cry. "Do you give up?" A nod of the head. I put my arm around my son's shoulder and took him home to bathe his wounds.

Later, I tucked him in bed and kissed him goodnight. I knew that his bruises would heal, but I wasn't sure about the humiliation. Even now, all I'm sure of is that Matthew remembers the incident as vividly as I.

I am puzzled. I reluctantly allowed my son to have his confrontation, and he did not shrink from it. But was that enough? Should I have taught Matthew to be a street fighter, as well? Should he have been trained to co-exist in this other world? The idea is monstrous to me. But so is the idea of his being beaten up by any punk who comes along. Are we wrong in presenting only half the picture? Do you train a sailor by showing him the ropes and neglect to tell him about wind direction and tides?

"Life intrudes," was one of the pet expressions of Stella Adler, a wonderful acting teacher with whom I worked for years. Life intrudes. No matter how solidly we build our dream cabin, we can't ever completely seal up all the cracks. Life will sneak in, force itself upon us. It is there no matter how often we mutter our yeses and noes and ifs and buts and maybes. It is there, and it may be unwise to pretend it is not.

I don't have an answer, just the uncertainty of how to wish the best for Matthew and all of us. If we can't train the street fighters to be gentlemen, must we train the gentlemen to be street fighters? Should we all be Boy Scouts? Be Prepared? Or is that akin to the craziness of putting a hair trigger on the gun?

INTERPRETATIONS

1. What evidence does Rockwood present to support his point that being unaggressive has cost him? How has his lack of aggression affected his son?

2. What does the incident with the bully reveal about Matthew? About his father? To what extent do you agree that Matthew probably "remembers the incident" as vividly as does his father?

3. Review paragraphs 14–16. What is Rockwood puzzled about? Should he have taught Matthew to be a street fighter? Has he failed as a father? Why or why not?

CORRESPONDENCES

1. What conversation can you imagine taking place between Bennett and Rockwood on the subject of fatherhood? What issues would you add to their discussion?

2. To what extent have rigid gender roles imposed emotional limitations on men? Compare Theroux and Rockwood's points of view on this issue.

APPLICATIONS

1. Review paragraph 15 and discuss with your group the thematic significance of Rockwood's title. Can parents protect their children from "dangers"? How do fathers help their sons (and daughters) to deal with violence and aggression? Summarize your discussion.

2. Write a journal entry on your first encounter with a bully. When and where did it occur? What emotions do you associate with the experience? Were the effects long-lasting? Did it involve your parents?

3. Assume Matthew's persona and write a portrait of his father referring to specific incidents and/or statements in Rockwood's essay.

4. Rockwood writes about his perception of his son's fight with Kevin and its repercussions. What do you think Matthew would say about this incident? Create a detailed journal entry that Matthew might write the day after the event.

The Unromantic Generation

BRUCE WEBER

Bruce Weber (b. 1953) is the drama critic for The New York Times. *His short story collection* Look Who's Talking: An Anthology of American Short Stories *was published in 1986. "The Unromantic Generation," was published in the April 5, 1987 issue of The New York Times Magazine. To what extent would you term your generation romantic or unromantic?*

HERE IS A CONTEMPORARY LOVE STORY.

Twenty-four-year-old Clark Wolfsberger, a native of St. Louis, and Kim Wright, twenty-five, who is from Chicago, live in Dallas. They've been going together since they met as students at Southern Methodist University three years ago. They are an attractive pair, trim and athletic, she dark and lissome, he broad-shouldered and square-jawed. They have jobs they took immediately after graduating—Clark works at Talent Sports International, a sports marketing and management company; Kim is an assistant account executive at Tracy-Locke, a large advertising agency—and they are in love.

"We're very compatible," she says.

"We don't need much time together to confirm our relationship," he says.

When they speak about the future, they hit the two-career family notes that are conventional now in the generations ahead of them. "At thirty, I'll probably be married and planning a family," says Kim. "I'll stay in advertising. I'll be a late parent."

"By thirty, I'll definitely be married; either that or water-skiing naked in Monaco," Clark says, and laughs. "No. I'll be married. Well established in my line of work. Have the home, have the dog. Maybe not a kid yet, but eventually. I'm definitely in favor of kids."

In the month I spent last winter visiting several cities around the country, interviewing recent college graduates about marriage, relationships, modern romance, I heard a lot of this, life equations already written, doubt banished. I undertook the trip because of the impression so many of us have; that in one wavelike rush to business school and Wall Street, young Americans have succumbed to a culture of immediate gratification and gone deep-down elitist on us. I set out to test the image with an informal survey meant to take the emotional temperature of a generation, not far behind my own, that *seems* so cynical, so full of such "material" girls and boys.

The sixty or so people I interviewed, between the ages of twenty-two and twenty-six, were a diverse group. They spoke in distinct voices, testifying to a range of political and social views. Graduate students, lawyers, teachers, entertainers, business people, they are pursuing a variety of interests. What they have in common is that they graduated from college, are living in or around an urban center, and are heterosexual, mirrors of myself when I graduated from college in 1975. And yet as I moved from place to place, beginning with acquaintances of my friends and then randomly pursuing an expanding network of names and phone numbers, another quality emerged to the degree that I'd call it characteristic: they are planners. It was the one thing that surprised me, this looking ahead with certainty. They have priorities. I'd ask about love; they'd give me a graph.

This isn't how I remember it. Twelve years ago, who knew? I was three years away from my first full-time paycheck, six from anything resembling the job I have now. It was all sort of desultory and hopeful, a time of dabbling and waiting around for some event that would sprout a future. Frankly, I had it in mind that meeting a woman would do it.

My cultural prototype was Benjamin Braddock, the character played by Dustin Hoffman in Mike Nichols's 1967 film *The Graduate*, who, returning home after his college triumphs, finds the prospect of life after campus daunting in the extreme, and so plunges into inertia. His refrain "I'm just a little worried about my future," served me nicely as a sort of wryly understated mantra.

What hauls Benjamin from his torpor is love. Wisely or not, he responds to a force beyond logic and turns the world upside down for Elaine Robinson. And though in the end their future together is undetermined, the message of the movie is that love is meant to triumph, that its passion and promise, however naïve, are its strength, and that if we are lucky it will seize us and transform our lives.

Today I'm still single and, chastened by that, I suppose, a little more rational about what to expect from love. Setting out on my trip, I felt as if I'd be plumbing a little of my past. But the people I spoke with reminded me more of the way I am now than the way I was then. I returned thinking that young people are older than they used to be, *The Graduate* is out of date, and for young people just out of college today, the belief that love is all you need no longer obtains.

"Kim's a great girl; I love her," Clark Wolfsberger says. "But she's very career-oriented. I am, too, and with our schedules the way they are, we haven't put any restrictions on each other. I think that's healthy."

"He might want to go back to St. Louis," Kim Wright says. "I want to go back to Chicago. If it works out, great. If not, that's fine, too. I can handle it either way."

They are not heartless, soulless, cold, or unimaginative. They *are* self-preoccupied, but that's a quality, it seems to me, for which youthful generations have always been known. What distinguishes this generation from mine, I think, is that they're aware of it. News-conscious, media-smart, they are sophisticated in a way I was not.

They have come of age, of course, at a time when American social traditions barely survive. Since 1975, there have been more than a million divorces annually, and it is well publicized that nearly half of all marriages now end in divorce. Yet the era of condoned casual promiscuity and sexual experimentation—itself once an undermining of the nation's social fabric—now seems to be drawing to a close with the ever-spreading plague of sexually transmitted disease.

The achievements of feminist activism—particularly the infusion of women into the work force—have altered the expectations that the sexes have for each other and themselves.

And finally, the new college graduates have been weaned on scarifying forecasts of economic gloom. They feel housing problems already; according to *American Demographics* magazine, the proportion of young people living at home with their parents was higher in 1985 than in the last three censuses. They're aware, too, of predictions that however affluent they are themselves, they're probably better off than their children will be.

With all this in mind, today's graduates seem keenly aware that the future is bereft of conventional expectations, that what's ahead is more chaotic than mysterious. I've come to think it ironic that in a youth-minded culture such as ours, one that ostensibly grants greater freedom of choice to young people than it ever has before, those I spoke with seem largely restrained. Concerned with, if not consumed by, narrowing the options down, getting on track, they are aiming already at a distant comfort and security. I spoke, on my travels, with several college counselors and administrators, and they concur that the immediate concerns of today's graduates are more practical than those of their predecessors. "I talk to them about sex," says Gail Short Hanson, dean of students at George Washington University, in Washington. "I talk about careers. And marriage, with women, because of the balancing act they have to perform these days. But love? I can't remember the last conversation I had about love."

Career-minded, fiercely self-reliant, they responded to me, a single man with a good job, with an odd combination of comradeliness and respect. When the interviews were over, I fielded a lot of questions about what it's like to work at *The New York Times*. How did I get my job? Occasionally, someone would ask about my love life. Considering the subject of our discussions, I was surprised it happened so rarely. When it did, I told them I'd come reasonably close to marriage once, but it didn't work out. Nobody asked me why. Nobody asked if I was lonely.

Micah Materre, twenty-five, recently completed an internship at CBS News in Chicago and is looking for a job in broadcast journalism. Like many of the young people I talked to, she is farsighted in her romantic outlook: "I went out with a guy last fall. He had a good job as a stockbroker. He was nice to me. But then he started telling me about his family. And there were problems. And I thought, 'What happens if I fall in love and we get married? What then?'"

It may be a memory lapse, but I don't recall thinking about marriage much at all until I fell in love. I was twenty-nine; late, that's agreed. But the point is that for me (and for my generation as a whole, I believe, though you hate to make a statement like that), marriage loomed only as an outgrowth of happenstance; you met a person. Today's graduates, however, seem uneasy with that kind of serendipity. All of the married couples I spoke with are delighted to be married, but they do say their friends questioned their judgment. "I heard a lot of reasons why I shouldn't do it," one recent bride told me. "Finally, I just said to myself, 'I feel happier than I've ever felt. Why should I give this up just because I'm young?'"

Most of them too young to remember the assassination of *either* Kennedy, they are old enough to have romantic pasts, to have experienced the trauma of failure in love. What surprised me was how easily so many of them accepted it; it seems a little early to be resigned to the idea that things fall apart. In each interview, I asked about past involvements. Were you ever serious about anyone? Any marital close calls? And virtually everyone had a story. But I heard very little about heartbreak or lingering grief. Instead, with an almost uniform equanimity, they spoke of maturity gained, lessons learned. It isn't disillusionment exactly, and they *are* too young to be weary; rather, it sounds like determination.

Twenty-five-year-old Peter Mundy of San Francisco, for example, says that until six months ago he'd had a series of steady girlfriends. "I'm down on romance," he says. "There's too much pain, too much pressure. There are so many variables, and you can't tell until you're in the middle of it whether it'll be positive. It's only in retrospect that you can see how things went wrong. In the meantime, you end up neglecting other things."

The prevalent notion is that chemistry is untrustworthy; partners need to be up to snuff according to pretty rigorous standards. Ellen Lubin, twenty-six, of Los Angeles, for example, has just gotten engaged to the man she's been living with for two years. When she met him, she says: "I wasn't that attracted to him right away. But there were things about him that made me say, 'This is what I want in a man.' He's bright. He's a go-getter. He was making tons of money at the age of twenty-five. He's well-connected. He was like my mentor in coming to deal with life in the city."

At the end of *The Graduate*, Benjamin Braddock kidnaps his lady love at the altar, an instant after she has sealed her vows to someone else, and they manage to make their escape because Benjamin bolts the church door from the outside with a cross. That was the 1960s, vehement times. When I graduated, we were less obstreperous. Sacraments we could take or leave. And marriage wasn't much of an issue. If we put it off, it wasn't for the sake of symbolism so much as that it didn't seem necessary. In the last few years, I've been to a number of weddings among my contemporaries, people in their thirties, and that impression of us is still with me. What we did was drift toward marriage, arriving at it eventually, and with some surprise. Some of us are still drifting.

Today's graduates have forged a new attitude entirely. In spite of the high divorce rate, many of those I spoke with have marriage in mind. Overwhelmingly, they see it as not only desirable, but inevitable. Because of the odds, they approach it with wariness and pragmatism. More cautious than their parents (for American men in 1985, the median age at the time of their first marriage was 25.5, the highest since the turn of the century; it was 23.3 for women, a record), they are methodical in comparison with me.

Perhaps that explains why I find the way they speak about marriage so unromantic. Men and women tend to couch their views in different terms, but they seem to share the perception that marriage is necessarily restricting. Nonetheless they trust in its rewards, whatever they are. Overall, it doesn't represent the kind of commitment that seems viable without adequate preparation.

"I've been dating someone for a year and a half," says Tom Grossman, a twenty-four-year-old graduate of the University of Texas. "We don't talk about marriage, and frankly I don't think it'll occur." Currently area sales manager in San Antonio for the John H. Harland Company, a check-printing concern, Grossman says he has professional success in mind first. "I want to be really well off financially, and I don't want that struggle to interfere with the marriage. There are too many other stress factors involved. I want to be able to enjoy myself right away. And I never want to look back and think that if I hadn't gotten married, I could have accomplished more."

Many young women say they responded with some alarm to last year's [1986] *Newsweek* report on the controversial demographic study conducted at Harvard, which concluded that once past thirty, a woman faces rapidly dwindling chances of marrying. At a time when women graduates often feel it incumbent on them to pursue careers, they worry that the possibility of "having it all" is, in fact, remote.

Janie Russell, twenty-five, graduated from the University of North Carolina in 1983, left a serious boyfriend behind, and moved to Los Angeles to pursue a career in the film industry. Working now as a director of production services at New Visions Inc., like many other young women she believes the independence fostered by a career is necessary, not only for her own self-esteem but as a foundation for a future partnership. "I look forward to marriage," she says. "But this is a very selfish time for me. I have to have my career. I have to say to myself, 'I did this on my own.' It makes me feel more interesting than I would otherwise. Of course, what may happen is that I'll look up one day and say, 'O.K., husband, where are you?' And he won't be there."

About halfway through my trip I stopped interviewing married couples because they tended to say similar things. They consider themselves the lucky ones. As twenty-four-year-old Adam Cooper put it, at dinner with his wife, Melanee, also twenty-four, in their Chicago apartment: "The grass is not greener on the other side."

I came away thinking it is as true as ever: all happy families are the same. But the couples I spoke with seemed to me part of a generation other than their own, older even than mine. Calling the Coopers to arrange an interview, I was invited for "a good, home-cooked meal."

The next day, I met Micah Materre, who expressed the prevailing contemporary stance as well as anyone. Outgoing and self-possessed, she gave me a long list of qualities she's looking for in a man: good looks, sense of humor, old-fashioned values, but also professional success, financial promise, and a solid family background. "Why not?" she said. "I deserve the best." But as I was folding up my notebook, she added a plaintive note: "I'll get married, won't I? It's the American way, right?"

Very early on in my sexual experience I was flattered by a woman who told me she ordinarily wouldn't go to bed with men who were under twenty-six. "Until then," she said, "all they're doing when they're with you is congratulating themselves." For whatever reason, she never returned my calls after that night. Not an untypical encounter, all in all. Congratulations to both of us.

We were a lusty, if callow, bunch, not least because we thought we could afford to be. Encouraged by the expansive social mores spawned by the sexual revolution, fortified by the advent of a widespread availability of birth control, and fundamentally unaware of germs, we interpreted sex, for our convenience, as pure pleasure shared by "consenting parties." If it feels good, do it. Remember that?

It is an attitude that the current generation inherited and put into practice at an early age. Asked about her circle of friends in Los Angeles, Lesley Bracker, twenty-three, puts it nonchalantly: "Oh, yeah, we were all sexually active as teenagers. When we were younger, it was considered O.K. to sleep around."

Now, however, they are reconsidering. In general, on this topic, I found them shy. They hesitate to speak openly about their sex lives, are prone to euphemism ("I'm not exactly out there, you know, mingling"), and say they worry about promiscuity only because they have friends who still practice it. According to Laura Kavesh and Cheryl Lavin, who write a column about single life, "Tales from the Front," for the *Chicago Tribune* that is syndicated in some sixty other papers around the country, a letter from a reader about the virtues of virginity generated more supportive mail than anything that has appeared in the column in its two years of existence. I'm not about to say there's a new celibacy among the young, but my impression is that even if they're having twice as much sex as they say they're having, it's not as much as you would think.

The AIDS scare, of course, is of primary relevance. "I talk about AIDS on first dates," says Jill Rotenberg, twenty-five, publishing manager of a rare-book company in San Francisco. "I talk about it all the time. I've spoken with the guy I'm dating about taking an AIDS test. Neither one of us is thrilled about condoms. But we use them. The first time we had sex, I was the one who had one in my wallet."

Not everyone is so vehement. But seriously or jokingly, in earnest tête-à-tête or idly at dinner parties, they all talk about it. To some, the new concern is merely a source of disappointment. Several of the young people I spoke with express the sense of having been robbed. It's tough to find sex when you want it, tougher than it used to be, is the lament of many, mostly men. As it was put to me at one point, "I wish I'd been born ten years earlier."

Jill Rotenberg says she feels betrayed: "I've had one long relationship in my life. He was my first lover, and for a long time my only one. So I feel I've had an untainted past. Now I feel I'm being punished anyway, even though I've been a good girl."

"I feel like I'm over the hurdle," says Douglas Ertman, twenty-two, of San Francisco, who got engaged last summer. "I'm really lucky to know that I'll have one sexual partner forever."

Most agree that the solution is monogamy, at least on a temporary basis. "It's a coupled-up society," says Alan Forman, twenty-six, a law student of George Washington University who, for the last several months, has been in a monogamous relationship. "Now more than ever. A lot of people I know are feeling the pressure to get hooked up with somebody."

I ask Forman and his girlfriend, twenty-four-year-old Debra Golden, about their future together. They say they don't know ("I'm too insecure to make a decision like that," she says), and I get the sense they never talk about it. Then she turns to him, genuinely curious. "Say you break up with me and go to New York next year," she says.

"I don't know," he says. "If I meet someone and I like her, what do I have to do, ask her to take a blood test?"

A decade ago, one of the privileges that my contemporaries and I inferred from our sexual freedom was more or less to deny that there might be, in the sexual act, an innately implied emotional exchange. It's no longer feasible, however, to explain away sex as frivolity, inconsequential gratification. And that has complicated things for all of us, of course, whatever age, single or not.

But for young people, it's an issue, like marriage, that has been raised early: what does sex mean, if it doesn't mean nothing?

It's clearly a struggle for them. In one of my first interviews, twenty-five-year-old Karl Wright of Chicago told me: "Maybe there's a silver lining in all this. Maybe AIDS will bring back romance." The more I think about that, the more chilling it gets.

Beverly Caro, a twenty-five-year-old associate in the Dallas law firm of Gardere & Wynne, graduated from Drake University, in Des Moines, in 1983, and attended law school there as well. Her office high above the street looks out on the city's jungle of futuristic skyscrapers. She had offers from firms in Denver and her hometown of Kansas City, Missouri, she says, but chose to come to Dallas because "I see upward mobility here; that's what I was looking for."

Ms. Caro has an attractive, thoughtful manner and a soft voice, but like many of her contemporaries, given the chance to discuss her personal goals, she speaks with a certitude that borders on defiance. Currently, she sees two men "somewhat regularly," she says. "I'd like to have a companion. A friend, I guess. But finding a man is not a top priority. I want to travel. I want to establish myself in the community. I don't see any drastic changes in my life by the time I turn thirty. Except that I'll be a property owner."

During my interviews, the theme of getting on track and staying there surfaced again and again. I came to think of it as the currency of self-definition. As a generation, they are not a particularly well-polled group, but certain figures bear out my impression.

According to annual surveys of 300,000 college freshmen conducted by the Higher Education Research Institute at the Graduate School of Education of the University of California at Los Angeles, young people today, by the time they *enter* college, are more inclined to express concrete life objectives than they've been for many years. Of those surveyed last fall, 73.2 percent cited being "very well off financially" as an essential or very important objective. That's up from 63.3 percent in 1980, 49.5 percent in 1975. Other objectives that the survey shows have risen in importance include "obtain recognition from colleagues for contributions to my special field"; "have administrative responsibility for the work of others"; "be successful in my own business"; and "raise a family." At the same time, the percentage of freshmen who consider it important to "develop a meaningful philosophy of life" has declined from 64.2 percent in 1975 to 40.6 percent last year.

Many of the people I spoke to feel the pressure of peer scrutiny. A status thing has evolved, to which many seem to have regretfully succumbed. Several expressed a weariness with meeting someone new and having to present themselves by their credentials. Yet, overwhelmingly, asked what they're looking for in a romantic partner, they responded first with phrases such as "an educated professional" and "someone with direction." They've conceded, more or less consciously, that unenlightened and exclusionary as it is, it's very uncool not to know what you want and not to be already chasing it.

"Seems like everyone in our generation has to be out there achieving," says Scott Birnbaum, twenty-five, who is the chief accountant for TIC United Corp., a holding company in Dallas.

Birnbaum graduated from the University of Texas in 1984, where, he says, "For me, the whole career-oriented thing kicked in." A native Texan with a broad drawl, he lives in the Greenville section of the city, an area populated largely by young singles. His apartment is comfortably roomy, not terribly well appointed. He shakes his head amiably as he points to the television set propped on a beer cooler. "What do I need furniture for?" he says. "Most of my time is taken up going to work."

Confident in himself professionally, Birnbaum was one of very few interviewees who spoke frankly about the personal cost of career success. Many speculated that they'll be worried if, in their thirties, they haven't begun to settle their love lives; this was more true of women than men. But Birnbaum confesses a desire to marry now. "It's kind of lonely being single," he says. "I'd hate to find myself successful at thirty without a family. Maybe once I'm married and have children, that might make being successful careerwise less important."

The problem, he goes on, is the collective outlook he's part and parcel of. "Here's how we think," he says. "Get to this point, move on. Get to that point, move on. Acquire, acquire. Career, career. We're all afraid to slow down for fear of missing out on something. That extends to your social life as well. You go out on a date and you're thinking, 'Hell, is there someone better for me?' I know how terrible that sounds but it seems to be my problem. Most of my peers are in the same position. Men and women. I tell you, it's tough out there right now."

When I returned to New York, I called Alex de Gramont, whom I'd been saving to interview last. I've known Alex for a long time, since he was a gawky and curious high school student and I was his teacher. Handsome now, gentle-looking, he's a literary sort, prone to attractive gloom and a certain lack of perspective. He once told me that his paradigm of a romantic, his role model, was Heathcliff, the mad, doomed passion-monger from Emily Brontë's *Wuthering Heights*.

A year out of Wesleyan University in Middletown, Conn., Alex has reasons to be hopeful. His book-length senior thesis about Albert Camus has been accepted for publication, and on the strength of it, he has applied to four graduate programs in comparative literature. But he's unenthusiastic, and he has applied to law schools, too. In the meantime, he is living with his parents in New Jersey.

He tells me that last summer he went to West Germany in pursuit of a woman he'd met when he was in college. He expected to live there with her, but he was back in this country in a couple of weeks. "Camus has a line," Alex says, "'Love can burn or love can last. It can't do both.'" Like Benjamin Braddock, Alex is a little worried about his future.

Dustin Hoffman is forty-nine. I'm thirty-three. Both of us are doing pretty well. Alex, at twenty-three, confesses to considerable unease. "Every minute I'm not accomplishing something, I feel is wasted," he says, sort of miserably. "I feel a lot of pressure to decide what to do with my life. I'm a romantic, but these are very unromantic times."

INTERPRETATIONS

1. The message of *The Graduate* is that love "is all you need." Weber believed that message when he was in college, and now he finds that his interviewees do not. Do you? Why or why not?

2. Can you formulate a definition of love as Weber and his interviewees are using it? Is it the same as sex? Can you define *romantic* as Weber uses it in his title and throughout the essay? Is *romantic* the opposite of *realistic*? Is it possible that there is an intellectual,

nonromantic type of love that is not reducible to feelings? If so, frame your definition of love accordingly.

3. "Today's graduates ... seem uneasy with ... serendipity." How have divorce statistics, feminism, and "forecasts of economic gloom" converged to make today's graduates careful "planners"? Do you think being a planner and being open to pleasant surprises (serendipity) are mutually exclusive? Why or why not?

4. What is the main point of Weber's interview with Alex de Gramont? Why do you think he wanted to save that interview for last and to report on it last?

5. Is Weber's main purpose to inform or to persuade? Cite evidence to support your opinion.

CORRESPONDENCES

1. Anouilh's perspective on human relationships (page 91) states that love is a powerful emotion. How is his concept similar to (or different from) those expressed by Weber's interviewees? To what extent are their points of view attributable to what Weber terms "self-preoccupation"?

2. Review Bateson's perspective on relationships (page 91) and write a journal entry regarding your imagined responses of two of Weber's interviewees.

APPLICATIONS

1. Most recent graduates, says Weber, accept marriage as "inevitable." What effect might this attitude have on their marriages? Will other factors offset this fatalism? What effect might the AIDS scare have? Will AIDS "bring back romance"? How? Do you consider such a return a desirable development?

2. Most of the young people Weber interviewed felt a great pressure to accomplish much in a short time. To what extent does your generation share their ambition and sense of urgency? How do these factors affect your personal relationships? For example, do you spend time with people who may not further your career?

3. Weber's essay was published in 1987. How have attitudes and expectations about gender relationships changed since then? Are dating practices different? Does "unromantic" apply to your

generation? Consider these issues with your group and write a concise summary of your discussion.

4. In the first page of his essay, Weber uses the term "life equation." What is your "life equation" for happiness? Try to compute a mathematical formula such as $a + b + c + \ldots = x$, where a, b, and c stand for life's variables (e.g., *spouse, career, home . . .*) and x equals "*happiness*." Review Weber's essay for additional variables that might factor into your "life equation."

Women and the Future
of Fatherhood

BARBARA DAFOE WHITEHEAD

Barbara Dafoe Whitehead, received a B.A. at the University of Wisconsin and an M.A. and Ph.D. in American social history at the University of Chicago. Dafoe Whitehead writes on issues of marriage, family, and child well-being. She is the author of The Divorce Culture *(1999) and* Why There Are No Good Men Left *(2003). Dafoe Whitehead is also the author of the widely acclaimed 1993* Atlantic Monthly *article "Dan Quayle Was Right," which was nominated for the National Magazine Award and won an Exceptional Merit in Media award. Other publications Dafoe Whitehead has written for include:* American Enterprise, Commonweal, Woodrow Wilson Quarterly, Times Literary Supplement, Washington Post, Atlanta Journal-Constitution, The Los Angeles Times, *and* The Boston Globe. *Brainstorm on your associations with "women."*

MUCH OF OUR CONTEMPORARY DEBATE over fatherhood is governed by the assumption that men can solve the fatherhood problem on their own. The organizers of last year's [1995] Million Man March asked women to stay home, and the leaders of Promise Keepers and other grass-roots fatherhood movements whose members gather with considerably less fanfare simply do not admit women.

There is a cultural rationale for the exclusion of women. The fatherhood movement sees the task of reinstating responsible fatherhood as an effort to alter today's norms of masculinity and correctly believes that such an effort cannot succeed unless it is voluntarily undertaken and supported by men. There is also a political rationale in defining fatherlessness as a men's issue. In the debate about marriage and parenthood, which women have dominated for at least thirty years, the fatherhood movement gives men a powerful collective voice and presence.

Yet however effective the grass-roots movement is at stirring men's consciences and raising their consciousness, the fatherhood problem will not be solved by men alone. To be sure, by signaling their commitment to accepting responsibility for the rearing of their children, men have taken the essential first step. But what has not yet been acknowledged is that the success of any effort to renew fatherhood as a social fact and a cultural norm also hinges on the attitudes and behavior of women. Men can't be fathers unless the mothers of their children allow it.

Merely to say this is to point to how thoroughly marital disruption has weakened the bond between fathers and children. More than half of all American children are likely to spend at least part of their lives in one-parent homes. Since the vast majority of children in disrupted families live with their mothers, fathers do not share a home or a daily life with their children. It is much more difficult for men to make the kinds of small, routine, instrumental investments in their children that help forge a good relationship. It is hard to fix a flat bike tire or run a bath when you live in another neighborhood or another town. Many a father's instrumental contribution is reduced to the postal or electronic transmission of money, or, all too commonly, to nothing at all. Without regular contact with their children, men often make reduced emotional contributions as well. Fathers must struggle to sustain close emotional ties across time and space, to "be there" emotionally without being there physically. Some may pick up the phone, send a birthday card, or buy a present, but for many fathers, physical absence also becomes emotional absence.

Without marriage, men also lose access to the social and emotional intelligence of women in building relationships. Wives teach men how to care for young children, and they also encourage children to love their fathers. Mothers who do not live with the father of their children are not as likely as married mothers to represent him in positive ways to the children; nor are the relatives who are most likely to have greatest contact with the children—the mother's parents, brothers, and sisters—likely to have a high opinion of the children's father. Many men are able to overcome such obstacles, but only with difficulty. In general, men need marriage in order to be good fathers.

If the future of fatherhood depends on marriage, however, its future is uncertain. Marriage depends on women as well as men, and women are less committed to marriage than ever before in the nation's history. In the past, women were economically dependent on marriage and assumed a disproportionately heavy responsibility for maintaining the bond, even if the underlying relationship was seriously or irretrievably damaged. In the last third of the twentieth century, however, as women have gained more opportunities for paid work and the availability of child care has increased, they have become less dependent on marriage as an economic arrangement. Though it is not easy, it is possible for women to raise children on their own. This has made divorce far more attractive as a remedy for an unsatisfying marriage, and a growing number of women have availed themselves of the option.

Today, marriage and motherhood are coming apart. Remarriage and marriage rates are declining even as the rates of divorce remain stuck at historic highs and childbearing outside marriage becomes more common. Many women see single motherhood as a choice and a right to be exercised if a suitable husband does not come along in time.

The vision of the "first stage" feminism of the 1960s and '70s, which held out the model of the career woman unfettered by husband or children, has been accepted by women only in part. Women want to be fettered by children, even to the point of going through grueling infertility treatments or artificial insemination to achieve motherhood. But they are increasingly ambivalent about the ties that bind them to a husband and about the necessity of marriage as a condition of parenthood. In 1994, a National Opinion Research survey asked a group of Americans, "Do you agree or disagree: One parent can bring up a child as well as two parents together." Women split 50/50 on the question; men disagreed by more than two to one.

And indeed, women enjoy certain advantages over men in a society marked by high and sustained levels of family breakup. Women do not need marriage to maintain a close bond to their children, and thus to experience the larger sense of social and moral purpose that comes with raising children. As the bearers and nurturers of children and (increasingly) as the sole breadwinners for families, women continue to be engaged in personally rewarding and socially valuable pursuits. They are able to demonstrate their feminine virtues outside marriage.

Men, by contrast, have no positive identity as fathers outside marriage. Indeed, the emblematic absent father today is the infamous "dead-beat dad." In part, this is the result of efforts to stigmatize irresponsible fathers who fail to pay alimony and child support. But this image also reflects the fact that men are heavily dependent on the marriage partnership to fulfill their role as fathers. Even those who keep up their child support payments are deprived of the social importance and sense of larger purpose that comes from providing for children and raising a family. And it is the rare father who can develop the qualities needed to meet the new cultural ideal of the involved and "nurturing" father without the help of a spouse.

These differences are reflected in a growing virtue gap. American popular culture today routinely recognizes and praises the achievements of single motherhood, while the widespread failure of men as fathers has resulted in a growing sense of cynicism and despair about men's capacity for virtuous conduct in family life. The enormously popular movie *Waiting to Exhale* captures the essence of this virtue gap with its portrait of steadfast mothers and deadbeat fathers, morally sleazy men and morally unassailable women. And women feel free to vent their anger and frustration with men in ways that would seem outrageous to women if the shoe were on the other foot. In *Operating Instructions* (1993), her memoir of single motherhood, Ann LaMott mordantly observes, "On bad days, I think straight white men are so poorly wired, so emotionally unenlightened and unconscious that you must approach each one as if he were some weird cross between a white supremacist and an incredibly depressing T. S. Eliot poem."

Women's weakening attachment to marriage should not be taken as a lack of interest in marriage or in a husband-wife partnership in child rearing. Rather, it is a sign of women's more exacting emotional standards for husbands and their growing insistence that men play a bigger part in caring for children and the household. Given their double responsibilities as breadwinners and mothers, many working wives find men's need for ego reinforcement and other forms of emotional and physical upkeep irksome and their failure to share housework and child care absolutely infuriating. (Surveys show that husbands perform only one-third of all household tasks even if their wives are working full-time.) Why should men be treated like babies? women complain. If men fail to meet their standards, many women are willing to do without them. Poet and polemicist Katha Pollitt captures the prevailing sentiment: "If single women can have sex, their own homes, the respect of friends, and interesting work, they don't need to tell themselves that any marriage is better than none. Why not have a child on one's own? Children are a joy. Many men are not."

For all these reasons, it is important to see the fatherhood problem as part of the larger cultural problem of the decline of marriage as a lasting relationship between men and women. The traditional bargain between men and women has broken down, and a new bargain has not yet been struck. It is impossible to predict what that bargain will look like or whether there will even be one. However, it is possible to speculate about the talking points that might bring women to the bargaining table. First, a crucial proviso: There must be recognition of the changed social and economic status of women. Rightly or wrongly, many women fear that the fatherhood movement represents an effort to reinstate the status quo ante, to repeal the gains and achievements women have made over the past thirty years and return to the "separate spheres" domestic ideology that put men in the workplace and women in the home. Any effort to rethink marriage must accept the fact that women will continue to work outside the home.

Therefore, a new bargain must be struck over the division of paid work and family work. This does not necessarily mean a 50/50 split in the work load every single day, but it does mean that men must make a more determined and conscientious effort to do more than one-third of the household chores. How each couple arrives at a sense of what is fair will vary, of course, but the goal is to establish some mutual understanding and commitment to an equitable division of tasks.

Another talking point may focus on the differences in the expectations men and women have for marriage and intimacy. Americans have a "best friends" ideal for marriage that includes some desires that might in fact be more easily met by a best friend—someone who doesn't come with all the complicated entanglements of sharing a bed, a bank account, and a bathroom. Nonetheless, high expectations for emotional intimacy in marriage often are confounded by the very different understandings men and women have of intimacy. Much more than men, women seek intimacy and affection through talking and emotional disclosure. Men often prefer sex to talking, and physical disrobing to emotional disclosing. They tend to be less than fully committed to (their own) sexual fidelity, while women view fidelity as a crucial sign of commitment. These are differences that the sexes need to engage with mutual recognition and tolerance.

In renegotiating the marital bargain, it may also be useful to acknowledge the biosocial differences between mothers and fathers rather than to assume an androgynous model for the parental partnership. There can be a high degree of flexibility in parental roles, but men and women are not interchangeable "parental units," particularly in their children's early years. Rather than struggle to establish identical tracks in career and family lives, it may be more realistic to consider how children's needs and well-being might require patterns of paid work and child rearing that are different for mothers and fathers but are nevertheless equitable over the course of a lifetime.

Finally, it may be important to think and talk about marriage in another kind of language than the one that suffuses our current discourse on relationships. The secular language of "intimate relationships" is the language of politics and psychotherapy, and it focuses on individual rights and individual needs. It can be heard most clearly in the personal-ad columns, a kind of masked ball where optimists go in search of partners who respect their rights and meet their emotional needs. These are not unimportant in the achievement of the contemporary ideal of marriage, which emphasizes egalitarianism and emotional fulfillment. But this notion of marriage as a union of two sovereign selves may be inadequate to define a relationship that carries with it the obligations, duties, and sacrifices of parenthood. There has always been tension between marriage as an intimate relationship between a man and a woman and marriage as an institutional arrangement for raising children, and though the language of individual rights plays a part in defining the former, it cannot fully describe the latter. The parental partnership requires some language that acknowledges differences, mutuality, complementarity, and, more than anything else, altruism.

There is a potentially powerful incentive for women to respond to an effort to renegotiate the marriage bargain, and that has to do with their children. Women can be good mothers without being married. But especially with weakened communities that provide little support, children need levels of parental investment that cannot be supplied solely by a good mother, even if she has the best resources at her disposal. These needs are more likely to be met if the child has a father as well as a mother under the same roof. Simply put, even the best mothers cannot be good fathers.

INTERPRETATIONS

1. To what extent do you agree or disagree with Whitehead that women should *not* be excluded from the contemporary fatherhood movement?

2. Why, according to the author, have women become less committed to marriage today than they were in the past?

3. "Men, by contrast, have no positive identity as fathers outside marriage." What evidence does Whitehead offer to support her thesis? Do you agree with her point of view? Why or why not?

4. In the last paragraph of her essay, Whitehead focuses on the needs of children. What points does she make? Are children being affected by parental pursuit of individual identity? How?

CORRESPONDENCES

1. Review Bateson's perspective on gender roles (page 91) and discuss its relevance to Whitehead's essay.

2. Whitehead and Bennett focus on responsibilities of raising children. Should these tasks be shared equally in your opinion? What gender differences are pertinent in your view in raising male children?

APPLICATIONS

1. Discuss with your group the causes and effects of generational changes in the roles of fathers in raising children.

2. How has your mother or father served as a role model for you? Focus on a particular event or experience and describe it in specific detail.

3. According to Whitehead, "women see single motherhood as a choice and a right to be exercised if a suitable husband does not come along in time." Discuss this issue and its possible effects on raising children, should single motherhood become more prevalent.

I, Too, Am a Good Parent

DORSETT BENNETT

*Dorsett Bennett is an attorney in Roswell, New Mexico. His essay was origi-
nally published in the "My Turn" section of* Newsweek *on July 4, 1994.
What is your definition of a good parent?*

DIVORCE IS A FACT OF MODERN LIFE. A great number of people simply
decide that they do not wish to stay married to their spouse. A divorce
is not a tremendously difficult situation unless there are minor children
born to the couple. If there are no minor children, you simply divide the
assets and debts. But you cannot divide a child. The child needs to be
placed with the appropriate parent.

In my own case, my former wife chose not to remain married to me.
That is her right and I do not fault her decision. My problem is that I do
not believe it is her right to deny me the privilege of raising our children. Some fathers want to go to the parent/teacher conferences, school
plays, carnivals and to help their kids with homework. I have always
looked forward to participating on a daily basis in my children's lives.
I can no longer enjoy that privilege—the children live with their
mother, who has moved to a northern Midwest state.

I tried so hard to gain custody of my children. I believe the evidence
is uncontradicted as to what an excellent father (and more important,
parent) I am. My ex-wife is a fairly good mother, but unbiased opinions
unanimously agreed I was the better parent. Testimonials were videotaped from witnesses who could not attend the out-of-state custody
hearing. I choose to be a father. When I was three years old, my own
father left my family. While I've loved my father for many years, I did
and still do reject his parental pattern.

A couple of centuries ago, a father and mother might have shared
equally in the care and raising of children above the age of infancy. But
with the coming of the Industrial Revolution the father went to work
during the day, leaving the full-time care of the young to the mother, who
stayed at home. It was easier to decide who should get child custody
under those circumstances. That would be true today even if the mother
were put into the position of working outside the home after the divorce.

Now, a majority of married mothers are in the workplace—often
because the family needs the second income to survive. With the

advent of the working mother, we have also seen a change in child care. Not only have we seen an increase in third-party caregivers; there is a decided difference in how fathers interact with their children. Fathers are even starting to help raise their children. I admit that in a great many families there is an uneven distribution of child-care responsibilities. But there are fathers who do as much to raise the children as the mother, and there are many examples where men are full-time parents.

But, because we have this past history of the mother being the principal child caregiver, the mother has almost always been favored in any contested child-custody case. The law of every state is replete with decisions showing that the mother is the favored custodial parent. The changes in our lifestyles are now being reflected in our laws. In most, if not all, states, the legislature has recognized the change in child-care responsibilities and enacted legislation that is gender blind. The statutes that deal with child custody now say that the children should be placed with the parent whose care and control of the child will be in the child's best interest.

This legislation is enlightened and correct. Society has changed. We no longer bring up our children as we did years ago. But it is still necessary to have someone make the choice in the child's best interest if the parents are divorcing and cannot agree on who takes care of the kids. So we have judges to make that enormous decision.

The state legislature can pass laws that say neither parent is favored because of their gender. But it is judges who make the ultimate choice. And those judges are usually *older males* who practiced law during the time when mothers were the favored guardians under the law. These same judges mostly come from a background where mothers stayed home and were the primary caregivers. By training and by personal experience they have a strong natural bias in favor of the mother in a child-custody case. That belief is regressive and fails to acknowledge the changed realities of our present way of life. Someone must be appointed to render a decision when parents cannot agree. I would ask that those judges who make these critical decisions re-examine their attitudes and prejudices against placing children with fathers.

After the videotaped testimony was completed, one of my lawyers said he had "never seen a father put together a better custody case." "But," he asked me, "can you prove she is unfit?" A father should not be placed in the position of having to prove the mother is unfit in order to gain custody. He should not have to prove that she has two heads, participates in child sacrifice or eats live snakes. The father should only have to prove that he is the more suitable parent.

Fathers should not be discriminated against as I was. It took me three years to get a trial on the merits in the Minnesota court. And

Minnesota has a law directing its courts to give a high priority to child-custody cases. What was even worse was that the judge seemed to ignore the overwhelming weight of the evidence and granted custody to my ex-wife. At the trial, her argument was, "I am their mother." Other than that statement she hardly put on a case. Being the mother of the children was apparently deemed enough to outweigh evidence that all the witnesses who knew us both felt I was the better parent; that those witnesses who knew only me said what an excellent parent I was; that our children's behavior always improved dramatically after spending time with me; that my daughter wished to live with me, and that I had a better child-custody evaluation than my wife.

So I say to the trial judges who decide these cases: "Become part of the solution to this dilemma of child custody. Don't remain part of the problem." It is too late for me. If this backward way of thinking is changed, then perhaps it won't be too late for other fathers who should have custody of their children.

INTERPRETATIONS

1. Characterize Bennett. Why does he want custody of his children? Are his reasons valid in your opinion? Why or why not?

2. According to Bennett, many states have enacted legislation in child custody cases that is "gender blind." What factors account for this new legislation?

3. To what extent do you agree with Bennett's advice for trial judges?

CORRESPONDENCES

1. "But there are fathers who do as much to raise the children as the mother, and there are many examples where men are full-time parents." What conversations on this subject can you imagine taking place between Bennett and Whitehead?

2. What is Bennett's purpose in writing about parental custody? How would you describe his style? Is it accessible to a general audience? How does it differ from Whitehead's?

APPLICATIONS

1. Brainstorm with your group on your concepts of fatherhood. What images and emotions does the word evoke? What responsibilities are fathers expected to assume in the family? How has the role of father changed in the last decade?

2. Write a journal entry on the kind of parent you would like to be using examples from your childhood, if appropriate. What personal qualities would you most like to communicate to your children?

3. Should the responsibilities of raising children be shared equally by both parents or should one be the primary caregiver? What gender characteristics, if any, do you think are pertinent to the task of raising children?

4. Bennett's argument hinges on changing the way American legislative and judicial systems view the relationship between gender roles and custody laws. Do you think that his entreaty to judges to "Become part of the solution to this dilemma of child custody" has been heard? Check the following Web sites and come to a conclusion. Remember to consider the reliability of your sources.

    http://www2.state.ga.us/Courts/Supreme/cecustdy.htm

    http://www.glennsacks.com/fathers_bear_the.htm

    http://www.menweb.org/throop/custodydivorce/joint/henry.10-442.html

Why Are Gay Men So Feared?

DENNIS ALTMAN

*Born in 1943 in Sydney, Australia, Dennis Altman is a Reader in Politics at
La Trobe University in Melbourne, Australia. Among his works are* AIDS in
The Mind *(1986) and* Paper Ambassadors *(1991). The excerpt from the
article below appeared in the* New Internationalist *in November 1989.*

GAY MEN ARE THE VICTIMS of insults, prejudice, abuse, violence, sometimes murder. Why are gay men hated by so many other men? Some
maintain that homosexuality is unnatural or a threat to the family.
But celibacy is also unnatural, yet nuns and priests are not regularly
attacked. And there is also a good case to be made that homosexuality
actually *strengthens* the family by liberating some adults from childbearing duties and so increasing the pool of adults available to look
after children.

But the real objection to homosexuality (and lesbianism) is
undoubtedly more deep-seated: It is threatening because it seems to
challenge the conventional roles governing a person's sex, and the
female and male roles in society. The assertion of homosexual identity
clearly challenges the apparent naturalness of gender roles.

Men are particularly prone to use anger and violence against those
they think are undermining their masculinity. And it is here that we can
find at least some of the roots of homophobia and gay-bashing.

As Freud understood, most societies are built upon a set of relationships between men: Most powerful institutions like parliaments and
business corporations are male-dominated. And this "male bonding"
demands a certain degree of sexual sublimation.

In many societies, the links between men are much stronger than
the relations that link them to women. But these bonds are social rather
than individual, and for this reason need to be strictly governed.
Armies, for example, depend upon a very strong sense of male solidarity, though this does not allow for too close an emotional tie between
any *specific* pair of men.

Thus the most extreme homophobia is often found among tightly
knit groups of men, who need to deny any sexual component to their
bonding as well as boost their group solidarity by turning violently
on "fags" or "queers," who are defined as completely alien. This is a

phenomenon found among teenage gangs, policemen, and soldiers. A particularly prominent example of this was Germany's Nazi Party, which shortly after coming to power purged those of its members who were tempted to turn the hypermasculinity of Nazism into an excuse for overt homosexual behavior.

Many observers of sexual violence have argued that the most virulent queer-basher is attacking the homosexual potential in himself—a potential that he has learned to suppress. Because homosexuality is "un-masculine," those who struggle with feelings of homosexuality (often unacknowledged) will be particularly tempted to resolve them through "masculine" expressions of violence. In court cases involving violence against gay men, the idea of preserving one's male honor is often pleaded as a defense.

Homophobia has effects that go far beyond those individuals against whom it is directed. Like racism and sexism, it is an expression of hatred that harms the perpetrator as well as the victim; the insecurities, fears, and sexual hang-ups that lead young men to go out looking for "fags" to beat up are dangerous to the entire society.

Those societies that are best able to accept homosexuals are also societies that are able to accept assertive women and gentle men, and they tend to be less prone to the violence produced by hypermasculinity.

INTERPRETATIONS

1. To what extent do you agree with Altman that homosexuality and lesbianism are feared because they challenge "the apparent naturalness of gender roles"?

2. What, according to Altman, is the connection between homosexuality and violence?

CORRESPONDENCES

1. Review Sullivan's perspective (page 92) and discuss its application to Altman's essay.

2. Review Weinberg's perspective on homophobia (page 91) and discuss its application to Altman's essay. How does it support or contradict Altman's point of view?

APPLICATIONS

1. Discuss with your group the question posed in Altman's title. To what extent do you agree that both homosexuals and lesbians are feared?

2. Review paragraph 8 of Altman's essay and write a persuasive essay agreeing or disagreeing with his point of view. You may include your emotional as well as your intellectual responses to his thesis.

3. Theroux and Rockwood share the difficulties of growing up male in a culture in which stereotypes of masculinity are pervasive. What conversation can you imagine them having with Altman? What would you add to the discussion?

Gay

ANNA QUINDLEN

Anna Quindlen (b. 1953) joined The New York Times *in 1977 and became deputy metropolitan editor in 1983. In 1990 she became the third woman in the paper's history to write a regular column for its Op-Ed page. Shortly after winning a Pulitzer Prize for Commentary in 1992, Quindlen left journalism to write fiction.* Blessings, *her most recent novel, was published in 2002. Her other novels include:* Object Lessons *(1991),* One True Thing *(1994), and* Black and Blue *(1998). Quindlen is also the author of the nonfiction books,* Living Out Loud *(1988),* How Reading Changed My Life *(1998), and* A Short Guide to A Happy Life *(2000). Quindlen returned to journalism when she took over the "Last Word" on the back page of* Newsweek *in 1999. Before reading Quindlen's essay, brainstorm on your associations with her title.*

WHEN HE WENT HOME LAST YEAR, he realized for the first time that he would be buried there, in the small, gritty industrial town he had loathed for as long as he could remember. He looked out the window of his bedroom and saw the siding on the house next door and knew that he was trapped, as surely as if he had never left for the city. Late one night, before he was to go back to his own apartment, his father tried to have a conversation with him, halting and slow, about drug use and the damage it could do to your body. At that moment he understood that it would be more soothing to his parents to think that he was a heroin addict than that he was a homosexual.

This is part of the story of a friend of a friend of mine. She went to his funeral not too long ago. The funeral home forced the family to pay extra to embalm him. Luckily, the local paper did not need to print the cause of death. His parents' friends did not ask what killed him, and his parents didn't talk about it. He had AIDS. His parents had figured out at the same time that he was dying and that he slept with men. He tried to talk to them about his illness; he didn't want to discuss his homosexuality. That would have been too hard for them all.

Never have the lines between sex and death been so close, the chasm between parent and child so wide. His parents hoped almost until the end that some nice girl would "cure" him. They even hinted broadly that my friend might be that nice girl. After the funeral, as she helped with the dishes in their small kitchen with the window onto the backyard, she lost her temper at the subterfuge and said to his mother: "He was gay. Why is that more terrible than that he is dead?" The mother did not speak, but raised her hands from the soapy water and held them up as though to ward off the words.

I suppose this is true of many parents. For some it is simply that they think homosexuality is against God, against nature, condemns their sons to hell. For others it is something else, more difficult to put into words. It makes their children too different from them. We do not want our children to be too different—so different that they face social disapprobation and ostracism, so different that they die before we do. His parents did not know any homosexuals, or at least they did not believe they did. His parents did not know what homosexuals were like.

They are like us. They are us. Isn't that true? And yet, there is a difference. Perhaps mothers sometimes have an easier time accepting this. After all, they must accept early on that there are profound sexual differences between them and their sons. Fathers think their boys will be basically like them. Sometimes they are. And sometimes, in a way that comes to mean so much, they are not.

I have thought of this a fair amount because I am the mother of sons. I have managed to convince myself that I love my children so much that nothing they could do would turn me against them, or away from them, that nothing would make me take their pictures off the bureau and hide them in a drawer. A friend says I am fooling myself, that I would at least be disappointed and perhaps distressed if, like his, my sons' sexual orientation was not hetero. Maybe he's right. There are some obvious reasons to feel that way. If the incidence of AIDS remains higher among homosexuals than among heterosexuals, it would be one less thing they could die of. If societal prejudices remain constant, it would be one less thing they could be ostracized for.

But this I think I know: I think I could live with having a son who was homosexual. But it would break my heart if he was homosexual and felt that he could not tell me so, felt that I was not the kind of mother who could hear that particular truth. That is a kind of death, too, and it kills both your life with your child and all you have left after the funeral: the relationship that can live on inside you, if you have nurtured it.

In the days following his death, the mother of my friend's friend mourned the fact that she had known little of his life, had not wanted to know. "I spent too much time worrying about what he was," she said. Not who. What. And it turned out that there was not enough time, not with almost daily obituaries of people barely three decades old, dead of a disease she had never heard of when she first wondered about the kind of friends her boy had and why he didn't date more.

It reminded me that often we take our sweet time dealing with the things that we do not like about our children: the marriage we could not accept, the profession we disapproved of, the sexual orientation we may hate and fear. Sometimes we vow that we will never, never accept those things. The stories my friend told me about the illness, the death, the funeral and, especially, about the parents reminded me that sometimes we do not have all the time we think to make our peace with who our children are. It reminded me that "never" can last a long, long time, perhaps much longer than we intended, deep in our hearts, when we first invoked its terrible endless power.

INTERPRETATIONS

1. Why do you think the gay man's parents would prefer "to think that he was a heroin addict rather than that he was a homosexual"?

2. To what extent do you agree with Quindlen that parents are reluctant to accept children who are too different from them?

3. What is Quindlen's supposition about being the mother of a homosexual? Do you agree with her? Why or why not?

CORRESPONDENCES

1. Compare and contrast societal attitudes toward sexual preference in the texts by Quindlen and Altman.

2. Is Quindlen seeking only to inform her audience or does she wish also to persuade? Compare her purpose and tone with that of Altman.

APPLICATIONS

1. Imagine yourself as the young gay man and write a letter to your parents explaining your sexual preference.

2. Discuss with your group the implications of AIDS for your generation and its effects on gender relationships and on individual and family lives.

3. The film *Lifetime Companion* portrays the responses of a group of friends confronting the reality of AIDS. Rent the videotape and write a review of the film including the characters' reactions to their situation.

4. If the young man discussed in Quindlen's essay had written a poem to his mother entitled "Dear Mom," what would he have said in it? Create this poem. If you would like, set it to music. What kind of melody would you choose to accompany your lyric? What is the relationship between your words and your music?

The Gravity of Mark Beuhrle

JASON BARONE

Jason Barone (b. 1982) was born in Queens, New York and at age four moved to Canada. He lived in Oakville for fifteen years before returning to New York. He is currently pursuing his B.A. in Media Studies at Hunter College and hopes to become a sports writer for a major publication or for the Anaheim Angels. As you read about Barone's expectations of his father, compare them with your idea about what a father should be.

I LIVE IN PARADISE as well as Pandemonium. I grew up in a beautiful town of Oakville, which lies only a 30-minute car ride west of Toronto. During my elementary years my life was a much younger version of *Everybody Loves Raymond.* In fact, when you look closely, you will find a great deal of similarities between the fictional Barone's on that show and the real life Barone's in my family. During high school I attended Appleby College, which was a private high school that backs onto Lake Ontario. The old red brick school buildings that spread throughout the campus and our quaint little chapel complete with stain glass windows could make you believe that life just could not get any better. My house was part of a collection of houses in the "Fairway Hills" community that slowly crept onto the Glen Abby golf course. For those of you who watch the PGA, you have probably seen my house in the background when the Canadian Open is played.

Over the years my friends have more or less have stayed the same. The only real change with them has been the setting for where we hung out: from the portable steps to the dining hall and now at the downtown pub, The King's Arm's. It would all sound like paradise if not for the fact that five years ago my parents got divorced.

This heart crushing news was delivered to family and friends in January 1998. I found out in December 1997, just as Christmas Eve passed into Christmas. To no surprise, Christmas has turned from an exciting time into nothing. I overcompensate for this by always wanting to have the tree, the lights, and our *Alvin and the Chipmunks Christmas* CD all roaring at full force a few weeks before Christmas. My guess is that I do this so that my mother, younger brother, and sister are too distracted to see how empty my eyes are.

We had come down from Canada to visit my Mom's side of the family and were staying with an Uncle in New Jersey. It was on the ride back to Jersey when my brother, sister, and I had all fallen asleep in the back of my Dad's Jeep. I had awakened, but my eyes for some reason had not opened; it had never happened before, and it's never happened since. To be truthful, I don't know how long I was up, I just remember the fighting. Everything was "discussed." Have you ever cried while frantically trying to keep motionless and expressionless? It's like a shiver that doesn't end. My parents still think I was asleep the whole time.

After that, I found myself praying every day, sometimes even multiple times. A sense of doom had overcome me and I was reaching out to the one person who might be able to help save my family. This went on for about a month until one Saturday afternoon while I was talking on the phone with my friend Patrick. I've heard how when bad news is delivered, the recipient seems to know what is going to be said before a word is spoken. Personally, I never bought into that. However, when my mother—in a calm and monotonous tone—said "Tell your friend you'll call him back, I need to tell you something," I immediately knew.

I have never received the Eucharist since.

• • •

"Did you talk to your mother?"
"Yes."
"OK, well."
"Did you cheat on her?"
"Yes."

I still wish that I had slammed the phone down at that moment; something to put him in his place. After my mom had told me, we sat there in silence for what felt like ten minutes (in truth it was closer to ten seconds). It was during that time that I was screaming at myself to keep composed, for Mommy. Eventually, I broke down. I had not even been on the job for two minutes and already I broke down; how was I going to do this for years after?

After a divorce most children and their fathers are not able to maintain a close relationship as the years pass. By the time most of these children are young adults, they often have little or no emotional intimacy left with their father. When they do talk, write, or get together—which is not often—too many of these fathers and their young adult children feel uncomfortable and emotionally distant. Their relationship has often dwindled into a fairly superficial one—more like a distant uncle who knows as little about the children's present lives as they know about his. Usually there is not animosity or resentment as much as indifference, awkwardness, and an underlying anxiety about what to say or do around each other. But for other young adults and their fathers, the lingering animosity and pain related to the parents' divorce continues to drive a wedge between them (Nielsen).

It was then that I decided I needed a new role model because I could no longer look at my dad in awe. I now shake my head while I let out a big sigh. Before the divorce, my dad and I used to really have something special. He came to all my baseball games and the majority of my practices. He himself had been all state in baseball and he was able to teach me things about the game that many kids didn't know. When we went to Blue Jays games, he always pointed out things like positioning, stance, and vision. Whenever I had a question about anything, he always had the answer. Now to most this may seem boring, but I couldn't get enough of it. I gorged myself on baseball, and he was my chef. In the years since, it became a big deal if we had a conversation that was longer than a few syllables. Some days I could go through a whole conversation with little more than a few low hums of acknowledgment to whatever he said. It became apparent that unless we were talking about sports, we would end up fighting. Yet whenever he called, there was a private joy inside of me. Knives were flying at my mother's back from all directions.

My father has since moved to Cleveland, and while we are now able to get along it's more of a friendly relationship than that of a father and son. His words no longer carry any weight.

There are times when I miss my dad. I remember once I was at my best friend's house, and he, his dad, and I were standing around the kitchen talking and joking around. My friend told his dad "You're not so tough now that I'm as tall as you." So as one could imagine, this had to be proved, and a friendly wrestling match ensued. As I watched my friend embarrass himself, I found myself envious because it was things like this that I realized I was unable to experience. Every once in a while, one of my friends would tell a funny story that they remember about my dad. I would nod and give a half-hearted smile, but it didn't matter any more. It had all been tarnished.

Last summer I visited him in Cleveland, and we had decided to take a little road trip to Detroit to see the Tigers play the White Sox. In the bottom of the first, we saw the White Sox pitcher take the mound. A few of his season's statistics flashed on the scoreboard under his name, Mark Buehrle. "Is he any good?." The question took me by surprise, more so when I looked over to see my dad looking up at me the way I used to do to him when I was younger. I rattled out an answer, but I could not get over the question. Wasn't *I* supposed to be asking *him* that? For five years before that, we rarely spoke. Silence had reversed our roles.

• • •

WORKS CITED:

Nielsen, Linda. "College Aged Students With Divorced Parents: Facts And Fiction." *College Student Journal* 33.4 (1999): 543–73.

INTERPRETATIONS

1. What associations do you have with the words "paradise" and "pandemonium"? What effect does Barone achieve by juxtaposing them in the first sentence?

2. Why does Barone focus on his responses to at least six Christmases after the divorce of his parents?

3. Throughout the essay Barone inserts short, objective, declarative statements such as "I have never received the eucharist since" to reflect his subjective states. Find at least two others and discuss what they reveal about his emotional responses to the divorce.

4. What is the effect of including Nielsen's citation in his essay? Which of the possible responses that Nielsen cites best parallels Barones's?

5. Characterize Barone's relationship with his father before the divorce. How does it change? Does he judge his father too harshly? Why or why not?

CORRESPONDENCES

1. According to Yevtushenko's perspective, "not people die but worlds die in them." Discuss its relevance to the texts by Barone and Norris. In what sense did their "worlds die"? Explain.

2. Barone and Norris portray the emotional impact of disruptions in gender relations through the point of view of a child. How do you respond emotionally to the conclusion of each text? What insights did you gain?

APPLICATIONS

1. Analyze with your group the thematic and symbolic significance of the title of each text.

2. Assume the role of Barone's father and write an essay imagining how he would explain his unfaithfulness, his emotional reactions to the changes in their relationship and the reversal of roles that occurs.

Blackberries

LESLIE NORRIS

Leslie Norris (b. 1921), a poet, novelist, and critic, was brought up in Merthyr Tydfil, Wales. Educated at Coventry College and the University of Southampton, Norris is currently a Humanities Professor of Creative Writing at Brigham Young University in Utah and a Fellow of the Royal Society of Literature and Fellow of the Welsh Academy. He has published twelve collections of poetry, two collections of short fiction, critical biography, and literary criticism. His books include The Loud Winter *(1967),* Ransoms *(1970),* Finding Gold *(1976),* Sliding *(1974), and* The Girl from Cardigan *(1988). Most recently Norris published* Kershisnik: Painting from Life *(2002) and the children's book* Albert and the Angels *(2000). Record your first memory of feeling alone despite being surrounded by family members.*

Merthyr Tydfil, located in the north side of the Taff Valley in Wales, often served as the subject of Norris's poetry. These poems often depict a town of boxing, whippet racing, pigeon breeding, rugby, and comic gossip carried by inhabitants of the Valleys. The early eighteenth century saw the establishment of iron-works complexes, which made Merthyr the Iron Capital of the World. In the past twenty years, there has been a remarkable transformation in both the working practices and topography of the area, with considerable land reclamation work creating environmental improvements.

MR. FRENSHAM OPENED HIS SHOP at eight-thirty, but it was past nine when the woman and the child went in. The shop was empty and there were no footmarks on the fresh sawdust shaken onto the floor. The child listened to the melancholy sound of the bell as the door closed behind him and he scuffed his feet in the yellow sawdust. Underneath, the boards were brown and worn, and dark knots stood up in them. He had never been in this shop before. He was going to have his hair cut for the first time in his life, except for the times when his mother had trimmed it gently behind his neck.

Mr. Frensham was sitting in a large chair, reading a newspaper. He could make the chair turn around, and he spun twice about in it before he put down his paper, smiled, and said, "Good morning."

He was an old man, thin, with flat white hair. He wore a white coat.

"One gentleman," he said, "to have his locks shorn."

He put a board across the two arms of his chair, lifted the child, and sat him on it.

"How are you, my dear? And your father, is he well?" he said to the child's mother.

He took a sheet from a cupboard on the wall and wrapped it about the child's neck, tucking it into his collar. The sheet covered the child completely and hung almost to the floor. Cautiously the boy moved his hidden feet. He could see the bumps they made in the cloth. He moved his finger against the inner surface of the sheet and made a six with it, and then an eight. He liked those shapes.

"Snip, snip," said Mr. Frensham, "and how much does the gentleman want off? All of it? All his lovely curls? I think not."

"Just an ordinary cut, please, Mr. Frensham," said the child's mother, "not too much off. I, my husband and I, we thought it was time for him to look like a little boy. His hair grows so quickly."

Mr. Frensham's hands were very cold. His hard fingers turned the boy's head first to one side and then to the other and the boy could hear the long scissors snapping away behind him, and above his ears. He was quite frightened, but he liked watching the small tufts of his hair drop lightly on the sheet which covered him, and then roll an inch or two before they stopped. Some of the hair fell to the floor and by moving his hand surreptitiously he could make nearly all of it fall down. The hair fell without a sound. Tilting his head slightly, he could see the little bunches on the floor, not belonging to him any more.

"Easy to see who this boy is," Mr. Frensham said to the child's mother. "I won't get redder hair in the shop today. Your father had hair like this when he was young, very much this color. I've cut your father's hair for fifty years. He's keeping well, you say? There, I think that's enough. We don't want him to dislike coming to see me."

He took the sheet off the child and flourished it hard before folding it and putting it on a shelf. He swept the back of the child's neck with a small brush. Nodding his own old head in admiration, he looked at the child's hair for flaws in the cutting.

"Very handsome," he said.

The child saw his face in a mirror. It looked pale and large, but also much the same as always. When he felt the back of his neck, the new short hairs stood up sharp against his hand.

"We're off to do some shopping," his mother said to Mr. Frensham as she handed him the money.

They were going to buy the boy a cap, a round cap with a little button on top and a peak over his eyes, like his cousin Harry's cap. The boy wanted the cap very much. He walked seriously beside his mother and he was not impatient even when she met Mrs. Lewis and talked to her, and then took a long time at the fruiterer's buying apples and potatoes.

"This is the smallest size we have," the man in the clothes shop said. "It may be too large for him."

"He's just had his hair cut," said his mother. "That should make a difference."

The man put the cap on the boy's head and stood back to look. It was a beautiful cap. The badge in front was shaped like a shield and it was red and blue. It was not too big, although the man could put two fingers under it, at the side of the boy's head.

"On the other hand, we don't want it too tight," the man said. "We want something he can grow into, something that will last him a long time."

"Oh, I hope so," his mother said. "It's expensive enough."

The boy carried the cap himself, in a brown paper bag that had "Price, Clothiers, High Street" on it. He could read it all except "Clothiers" and his mother told him that. They put his cap, still in its bag, in a drawer when they got home.

His father came home late in the afternoon. The boy heard the firm clap of the closing door and his father's long step down the hall. He leaned against his father's knee while the man ate his dinner. The meal had been keeping warm in the oven and the plate was very hot. A small steam was rising from the potatoes, and the gravy had dried to a thin crust where it was shallow at the side of the plate. The man lifted the dry gravy with his knife and fed it to his son, very carefully lifting it into the boy's mouth, as if he were feeding a small bird. The boy loved this. He loved the hot savor of his father's dinner, the way his father cut away small delicacies for him and fed them to him slowly. He leaned drowsily against his father's leg.

Afterwards he put on his cap and stood before his father, certain of the man's approval. The man put his hand on the boy's head and looked at him without smiling.

"On Sunday," he said, "we'll go for a walk. Just you and I. We'll be men together."

Although it was late in September, the sun was warm and the paths dry. The man and his boy walked beside the disused canal and powdery white dust covered their shoes. The boy thought of the days before he had been born, when the canal had been busy. He thought of the long boats pulled by solid horses, gliding through the water. In his head he listened to the hushed, wet noises they would have made, the soft waves slapping the banks, and green tench looking up as the barges moved above them, their water suddenly darkened. His grandfather had told him about that. But now the channel was filled with mud and tall reeds. Bullrush and watergrass grew in the damp passages. He borrowed his father's walking stick and knocked the heads off a company of seeding dandelions, watching the tiny parachutes carry away their minute dark burdens.

"There they go," he said to himself. "There they go, sailing away to China."

"Come on," said his father, "or we'll never reach Fletcher's Woods."

The boy hurried after his father. He had never been to Fletcher's Woods. Once his father had heard a nightingale there. It had been in the summer, long ago, and his father had gone with his friends, to hear the singing bird. They had stood under a tree and listened. Then the moon went down and his father, stumbling home, had fallen into a blackberry bush.

"Will there be blackberries?" he asked.

"There should be," his father said. "I'll pick some for you."

In Fletcher's Woods there was shade beneath the trees, and sunlight, thrown in yellow patches on to the grass, seemed to grow out of the ground rather than come from the sky. The boy stepped from sunlight to sunlight, in and out of shadow. His father showed him a tangle of bramble, hard with thorns, its leaves just beginning to color into autumn, its long runners dry and brittle on the grass. Clusters of purple fruit hung in the branches. His father reached up and chose a blackberry for him. Its skin was plump and shining, each of its purple globes held a point of reflected light.

"You can eat it," his father said.

The boy put the blackberry in his mouth. He rolled it with his tongue, feeling its irregularity, and crushed it against the roof of his mouth. Released juice, sweet and warm as summer, ran down his throat, hard seeds cracked between his teeth. When he laughed his father saw that his mouth was deeply stained. Together they picked and ate the dark berries, until their lips were purple and their hands marked and scratched.

"We should take some for your mother," the man said.

He reached with his stick and pulled down high canes where the choicest berries grew, picking them to take home. They had nothing to carry them in, so the boy put his new cap on the grass and they filled its hollow with berries. He held the cap by its edges and they went home.

"It was a stupid thing to do," his mother said, "utterly stupid. What were you thinking of?"

The young man did not answer.

"If we had the money, it would be different," his mother said, "Where do you think the money comes from?"

"I know where the money comes from," his father said. "I work hard enough for it."

"His new cap," his mother said. "How am I to get him another?"

The cap lay on the table and by standing on tiptoe the boy could see it. Inside it was wet with the sticky juice of blackberries. Small pieces of blackberry skins were stuck to it. The stains were dark and irregular.

"It will probably dry out all right," his father said.

His mother's face was red and distorted, her voice shrill.

"If you had anything like a job," she shouted, "and could buy caps by the dozen, then—"

She stopped and shook her head. His father turned away, his mouth hard.

"I do what I can," he said.

"That's not much!" his mother said. She was tight with scorn. "You don't do much!"

Appalled, the child watched the quarrel mount and spread. He began to cry quietly, to himself, knowing that it was a different weeping to any he had experienced before, that he was crying for a different pain. And the child began to understand that they were different people; his father, his mother, himself, and that he must learn sometimes to be alone.

INTERPRETATIONS

1. What is meant by the final paragraph of the story? To what extent has Norris led up to these ideas? What examples in the text can you locate to support your answers?

2. What gender issues are presented by Norris? What specific examples can you provide to illustrate these issues?

3. Mr. Frensham is the first character presented in the story. What is his relation to the other major characters?

4. Where does this story take place? To what extent does this setting influence the tensions presented? What tensions do you find to exist in this story?

5. On page 147, the boy's father says: "On Sunday . . . we'll go for a walk. Just you and I. We'll be men together." How accurately does this statement summarize the gender issues of this story? Explain your answer fully.

CORRESPONDENCES

1. What is your perception of the father in "Blackberries"? To what extent does he represent the type of man Theroux describes in "The Male Myth"?

2. Analyze with your group the thematic and symbolic significance of the title of Barone's and Norris's texts.

APPLICATIONS

1. Of the characters in this story, which of them have names? Which do not? Why would Norris choose to make this decision? Write a description of an object without actually naming the object. If you were to read this description to your classmates, would they be able to guess the object? What writing techniques must you use to create an accurate description without naming the object or giving away its identity too easily?

2. Notice the details that Norris uses to depict the events occurring in the story from the perspective of the child. Which specific details stand out in your mind that best capture the boy's perspective? Write a story that depicts an event from a child's viewpoint. What must you do with your choice of words, sentence structures, and selection of details to present this perspective effectively?

3. Assume the role of Barone's father and write an essay imagining how he would explain his unfaithfulness, his emotional reactions to the changes in their relationship, and the reversal of roles that occurs at the end of the essay.

4. If you *really* wanted to get to know someone, what questions would you ask of that person to learn about him or her?

    Think carefully about questions that would provide little information and those that would yield essential facts and insights. Now, make up a list of the five questions you think are most important to ask. Next, pair up with a classmate who you do not know very well and ask that person your five questions. Be sure to take notes as your questions are answered! After you have asked your questions, reverse the process.

    After all five questions have been asked and answered by both you and your classmate, separate from each other and use your notes to create a "character sketch." (Perhaps the first thing you might do is change the name of the person you interviewed to preserve his or her privacy!) When creating your sketch, what information will you include and what will you leave out? What information might you manipulate to make your "character" more interesting? While working on this sketch, reflect on the characters that Norris has invented and presented in "Blackberries." How has Norris helped you to get to know his characters? What techniques has he used that you might use in creating your character?

The Knowing Eye

Michelle V. Agins/*The New York Times*

READING IMAGES

1. How does each photograph address "gender issues"? What message about gender and identity is being given by each photographer?

2. One theory about art is that at its center is ambiguity. What does the word ambiguous mean? How does each photograph embrace ambiguity? How are these treatments of ambiguity similar or different?

MAKING CONNECTIONS

1. How does the photograph of the women boxers relate to the essays by Theroux, Del Castillo Guilbault, and Rockwood?

2. What is the tone or mood presented in the photograph of the faces? Which essays do you think best correspond to this feeling?

Emma Wunsch

WORDS AND IMAGES

1. What would the people from the first and second photographs say to each other? Create a dialogue that captures this conversation.

2. The photograph of the women boxers directly confronts the issue of gender roles. Are there certain jobs that you think are gender specific? If so, what are they? Why do you think they should be available only to men or to women? After thinking and writing about these questions, compare your responses with those from the members of your peer group. How are your ideas similar to and different from those of your classmates? What consensus opinion has been formed?

Additional Writing Topics

1. To what extent have your concepts of gender roles and gender relationships changed during the last five years? Write an essay that analyzes the factors that contributed to your modifying your point of view on these issues.

2. Write an essay discussing whether it is realistic to expect marriage to last a lifetime today. What expectations do most people have about marriage? What expectations should they have?

3. Parental roles is a controversial issue in the essays by Bennett and Whitehead. Evaluate their views. To what extent do you find consensus? What might you add to the debate?

4. Whitehead and Bennett raise the issue of power within the family. How does this use of power affect other family members? Using your own experience as well as these essays as sources, write an essay analyzing an aspect of power within the family.

5. Are gender roles more rigidly assigned in the United States than in other countries? In some cultures, for example, it is not unusual for men to express affection for one another or even to cry in public. Discuss how cultural expectations affect gender stereotypes.

6. Societal and familial attitudes toward homosexuality are explored by Altman and Quindlen. Write an essay analyzing your emotional associations with this topic.

7. Societal and cultural attitudes toward masculinity are the focus of the essays by Theroux, Rockwood, and Del Castillo Guilbault. How does your attitude toward this emotionally charged subject compare to theirs? Write an essay defining your concept of masculinity and analyzing your emotional reactions to it.

8. Many young women in the United States today are balancing a career and family. Explore the issue of working mothers by consulting articles that have appeared in magazines and newspapers over the past decade. Look specifically for pieces that enumerate the problems faced by these women when it comes to running the home, caring for the children, and advancing on the job. Using this material as your evidence, write a paper analyzing the various problems faced by working mothers.

CHAPTER
4

Education

H UMAN BEINGS SHOW a wonderful capacity to learn and unlearn—if it were not so you would not see such diversity in this and all the other chapters of this book. "The greatest happiness of man as a thinking being," said Goethe, "is to know what is knowable and quietly to revere what is unknowable." Several cross-cultural texts in this chapter clearly support Goethe's notion of the joy of learning, including "Poets in the Kitchen," "The Rain Makes the Roof Sing," and "The Mistress of Make Believe."

Education is also an important issue to politicians, educators, and parents, and the pendulum swings back and forth constantly as to what aspects of the educational system should be reevaluated. Currently, the national spotlight is on assessment and measuring students' performance through a series of standardized tests beginning in third grade and continuing through college.

Another "hot" issue is bilingual education, a matter of controversy in several states despite the large numbers of students in public schools for whom English is not a first language. Critics of bilingual education claim that this approach delays the acquisition of English and a student's ability to achieve proficiency in the language of public discourse. The more extreme groups view bilingualism as a threat to national unity, and that has prompted the formation of English-only movements.

Defenders of bilingualism argue that forcing students to abandon their private language is pedagogically unsound, and often psychologically debilitating. For example, Eva Hoffman, forced to leave her native Poland in 1959 at age thirteen, describes in her memoir *Lost in Translation*, the trauma of linguistic dispossession as she struggled to learn English in school in Vancouver, Canada. "Blind rage, helpless rage is rage that has no words—rage that overwhelms one with darkness."

Several texts in this chapter focus also on the crucial and controversial implications of the connections between language and culture. Is it desirable and possible for public schools to perform this mission without robbing students of their natal language and culture? Is it possible to achieve biculturalism, as well as bilingualism? Is it possible to tolerate, even respect, other religions, systems of law, forms of art, and languages without losing respect for one's own? Is our idea of culture clear and distinct enough to speak of absolute boundaries between cultures? If we accept the concept of cultural differences, even cultural boundaries, is cultural exclusiveness the goal we want to pursue?

Several texts in this chapter focus also on the controversial connections between language and culture and between language and gender. Deborah Tannen, for example, shares how her research on the effects of gender on conversational styles caused her to radically change her teaching strategies. James Baldwin argues that Black English was developed to enhance communications among African-Americans, enabling them to acquire a deeper "communal identity," while José Torres emphasizes the importance of education and the link between language and power, and Chang-Rae Lee recalls his mother's powerlessness expressed by her silence as a Korean immigrant in a suburb in the United States.

Education also involves learning about ramifications of social inequities, the focal point of the texts by Isabel Pipolo, and Toni Cade Bambara.

Is a person educated who knows only his or her own culture as it is at that moment? Anyone who knows the history of his or her own culture expects change. But at what price? By what vehicle? Preparation for the global village of the twenty-first century surely requires your generation to formulate new definitions of an educated person.

Perspectives

Only the curious have, if they live, a tale worth telling at all.

—Alastair Reid

Not to transmit an experience is to betray it.

—Elie Wiesel

I hear and I forget. I see and I remember. I do and I understand.

—Chinese Proverb

Education is what survives when what has been learnt has been forgotten.

—B. F. Skinner

Sexist language, racist language, theistic language—all are typical of the policing languages of mastery, and cannot, do not, permit new knowledge or encourage the mutual exchange of ideas.

—Toni Morrison

Learning to read books—or pictures, or films—is not just a matter of acquiring information from texts, it is a matter of learning to read and write the texts of our lives.

—Robert Scholes

What I wish for all students is some release from the clammy grip of the future. I wish them a chance to savor each segment of their education as an experience in itself and not as a grim preparation for the next step. I wish them the right to experiment, to trip and fall, to learn that defeat is as instructive as victory and is not the end of the world.

—William Zinsser

Education is not a product: mark, diploma, job, money—in that order: it is a process, a never-ending one.

—Bel Kaufman

Education is hanging around until you've caught on.

—Robert Frost

Put yourself in a different room, that's what the mind is for.

—Margaret Atwood

Shall I teach you what knowledge is? When you know a thing, to recognize that you know it, and when you do not know a thing, to recognize that you do not know it. That is knowledge.

—*Confucius*

Education! Which of the various me's do you propose to educate, and which do you propose to suppress?

—*D. H. Lawrence*

By doubting we are led to enquire: By enquiry we perceive the truth.

—*Abelard*

The greatest difficulty in education is to get experience from ideas.

—*George Santayana*

It is above all by the imagination that we achieve perception, and compassion, and hope.

—*Ursula K. Le Guin*

I have always come to life after coming to books.

—*Jorge Luis Borges*

Power is the ability to take one's place in whatever discourse is essential to action and the right to have one's part matter.

—*Carolyn Heilbrun*

. . . That is what learning is. You suddenly understand something you've understood all your life, but in a new way.

—*Doris Lessing*

Knowledge is power.

—*Francis Bacon*

The mind is an enchanting thing.

—*Marianne Moore*

But it is not hard work which is dreary; it is superficial work. That is always boring in the long run, and it has always seemed strange to me that in our endless discussions about education so little stress is ever laid on the pleasure of becoming an educated person, the enormous interest it adds to life. To be able to be caught up into the world of thought—that is to be educated.

—*Edith Hamilton*

APPLICATIONS

1. Discuss Hamilton's description of an educated person. To what extent has your education been pleasurable? How has it made your life more interesting? What does it mean to you "to be caught up in the world of thought"?

2. Abelard and Reid focus on the importance of curiosity in acquiring knowledge and becoming an interesting person. Have you been encouraged by your teachers to ask questions? Do you consider yourself curious? Has curiosity played a positive role in your education? Cite one or two examples.

3. Discuss Zinsser's perspective on education. To what extent do you agree that it is important "to trip and fall" and that defeat or failure may be used constructively? How can these views be reconciled with the pressures facing today's college students? Write a summary of your group's discussion.

The Creation of the Crow World

CROW LEGEND

The Crow, who were one of the most powerful tribes in Montana, are members of the second largest Indian language group north of Mexico (the Siouan; the largest is the Algonquian). They lived along the Yellowstone River and its tributaries and hunted across the plains and into the Rocky Mountains. Their reservation is in Montana near Billings. The name "Crow" is thought to be a mistranslation of their name for themselves, Apsaruke.

From the several versions of the Crow creation myth that have been recorded, this one has been selected because it is the most revealing of the material culture of the tribe and because it has less similarity with creation myths of other tribes.

LONG BEFORE THERE WAS ANY LAND and before there was any living thing except four little ducks, the Creator, whom we call Old Man, came and said to the ducks, "Which one of you is brave?"

"I am the bravest," replied one duck.

"Dive into the water," Old Man said to the duck, "and get some dirt from the bottom. I will see what I can do with it."

The brave duck went down and was gone a long time. It came up again carrying on its beak some dirt that it gave to Old Man. He held it in his hand until it became dry. Then he blew the dirt in all directions and thus made the land and the mountains and the rivers.

Old Man, who was all-powerful, was asked by the ducks to make other living things. So he took more dirt in his hand and, after it had dried, he blew it off. And there stood a man and a woman, the first Crow Indians. Old Man explained to them how to increase their number. At first they were blind; when their eyes were opened and they saw their nakedness, they asked for something with which to clothe themselves.

So that they might have food and clothing, Old Man took the rest of the dirt brought up by Duck and made animals and plants. Then he killed one of the buffalo he had made, broke a rock, and with one of the pieces cut up the animal. Then he explained its parts and told the man and woman how to use them.

"To carry water," he said, "take the pouch from the inside of the buffalo and make a bucket. Make drinking cups from its horns and also from the horns of the mountain sheep. Use the best pieces of buffalo for food. When you have had enough to eat, make a robe from the hide."

Then he showed the woman how to dress the skin. He showed the man how to make arrowheads, axes, knives, and cooking vessels from hard stone. "To make a fire," said Old Man, "take two sticks and place a little sand on one of them and also some of the driest buffalo chips. Then take the other stick and roll it between your hands until fire comes."

Old Man told them to take a large stone and fasten to it a handle made from hide. "With it you can break animal bones to get the marrow for making soup," he said to the woman. He also showed her how to scrape skins with a bone from the foreleg of an animal, to remove the hair.

At first, Old Man gave the man and woman no horses; they had only dogs for carrying their things. Later he told them how to get horses. "When you go over that hill there, do not look back, no matter what you hear." For three days they walked without looking back, but on the third day they heard animals coming behind them. They turned around and saw horses, but the horses vanished.

Old Man told them how to build a sweat lodge and also explained its purpose. And he told the man how to get dreams and visions. "Go up in the mountains," he said, "cut a piece of flesh from yourself, and give it to me. Do not eat while you are there. Then you will have visions that will tell you what to do."

"This land is the best of the lands I have made," Old Man said to them. "Upon it you will find everything you need—pure water, vegetation, timber, game animals. I have put you in the center of it, and I have put people around you as your enemies. If I had made you in large numbers, you would be too powerful and would kill the other people I have created. You are few in number, but you are brave."

INTERPRETATIONS

1. How important is Old Man's role as a teacher?

2. How apt are the Crows as students? What is the point of Old Man's lesson on how to get horses?

3. Old Man's last lesson is about the Crows' relations with other peoples—foreign affairs. How do you interpret this lesson? What does this lesson indicate about Old Man's nature, character, or qualities?

CORRESPONDENCES

1. Compare "The Creation of the Crow World" with the creation stories in Chapter 6 and discuss the significance of differences in their emphases.

2. Review the Abelard perspective on education (page 158). What role does enquiry play in "The Creation of the Crow World"? In your educational experiences?

APPLICATIONS

1. "The Creation of the Crow World" is part of the oral tradition of the Crow Indians. What cultural and educational functions does the oral tradition perform? Write a journal entry on what the Crow legend communicates about teaching and learning.

2. Review the Chinese proverb and discuss its application to "The Creation of the Crow World." Do you agree that we learn by seeing and doing rather than by listening? Cite supporting examples.

3. "The Creation of the Crow World" links disobedience with punishment. Have you ever learned something valuable by breaking the rules? If so, write a journal entry on the experience.

Gender in the Classroom

DEBORAH TANNEN

Deborah Tannen (b. 1951) holds an M.A. and Ph. D. in Linguistics from the University of California, Berkeley. Currently Tannen is a University Professor at Georgetown University where she teaches linguistics. To date Tannen has published 19 books, including You Just Don't Understand, That's Not What I Meant!, *which was on* The New York Times *Best Seller list for nearly four years. Tannen's latest book,* I Only Say This Because I Love You: Talking to Your Parents, Partner, Sibs, and Kids When You're All Adults *(2001) was awarded the 2001 Books for a Better Life Award in the Relationships category. Tannen has been featured in and has written for most major newspapers and magazines including* The New York Times, Newsweek, Time, USA Today, People, The Washington Post, *and* The Harvard Business Review. *In addition to her linguistic research and writing. Tannen has published poetry, short stories, and personal essays. Her play,* "An Act of Devotion," *is included in* The Best American Short Plays: 1993–1994. *According to Tannen, gender roles often affect class participation. To what extent do you agree or disagree with her point of view?*

WHEN I RESEARCHED AND WROTE my latest book, *You Just Don't Understand Women and Men in Conversation*, the furthest thing from my mind was reevaluating my teaching strategies. But that has been one of the direct benefits of having written the book.

The primary focus of my linguistic research always has been the language of everyday conversation. One facet of this is conversational style: how different regional, ethnic, and class backgrounds, as well as age and gender, result in different ways of using language to communicate. *You Just Don't Understand* is about the conversational styles of women and men. As I gained more insight into typically male and female ways of using language, I began to suspect some of the causes of the troubling facts that women who go to single-sex schools do better in later life, and that when young women sit next to young men in classrooms, the males talk more. This is not to say that all men talk in class, nor that no women do. It is simply that a greater percentage of discussion time is taken by men's voices.

The research of sociologists and anthropologists such as Janet Lever, Marjorie Harness Goodwin, and Donna Eder has shown that girls and boys learn to use language differently in their sex-separate peer groups. Typically, a girl has a best friend with whom she sits and talks, frequently telling secrets. It's the telling of secrets, the fact and the way that they talk to each other, that makes them best friends. For boys, activities are central: Their best friends are the ones they do things with. Boys also tend to play in larger groups that are hierarchical. High-status boys give orders and push low-status boys around. So boys are expected to use language to seize center stage: by exhibiting their skill, displaying their knowledge, and challenging and resisting challenges.

These patterns have stunning implications for classroom interaction. Most faculty members assume that participating in class discussion is a necessary part of successful performance. Yet speaking in a classroom is more congenial to boys' language experience than to girls', since it entails putting oneself forward in front of a large group of people, many of whom are strangers and at least one of whom is sure to judge speakers' knowledge and intelligence by their verbal display.

Another aspect of many classrooms that makes them more hospitable to most men than to most women is the use of debate-like formats as a learning tool. Our educational system, as Walter Ong argues persuasively in his book *Fighting for Life* (Cornell University Press, 1981), is fundamentally male in that the pursuit of knowledge is believed to be achieved by ritual opposition: public display followed by argument and challenge. Father Ong demonstrates that ritual opposition—what he calls "adversativeness" or "agonism"—is fundamental to the way most males approach almost any activity. (Consider, for example, the little boy who shows he likes a little girl by pulling her braids and shoving her.) But ritual opposition is antithetical to the way most females learn and like to interact. It is not that females don't fight, but that they don't fight for fun. They don't *ritualize* opposition.

Anthropologists working in widely disparate parts of the world have found contrasting verbal rituals for women and men. Women in completely unrelated cultures (for example, Greece and Bali) engage in ritual laments: spontaneously produced rhyming couplets that express their pain, for example, over the loss of loved ones. Men do not take part in laments. They have their own, very different verbal ritual: a contest, a war of words in which they vie with each other to devise clever insults.

When discussing these phenomena with a colleague, I commented that I see these two styles in American conversation: Many women bond by talking about troubles, and many men bond by exchanging playful insults and put-downs, and other sorts of verbal sparring. He exclaimed: "I never thought of this, but that's the way I teach: I have students read an article, and then I invite them to tear it apart. After we've torn it to shreds, we talk about how to build a better model."

This contrasts sharply with the way I teach: I open the discussion of readings by asking, "What did you find useful in this? What can we use in our own theory building and our own methods?" I note what I see as weaknesses in the author's approach, but I also point out that the writer's discipline and purposes might be different from ours. Finally, I offer personal anecdotes illustrating the phenomena under discussion and praise students' anecdotes as well as their critical acumen.

These different teaching styles must make our classrooms wildly different places and hospitable to different students. Male students are more likely to be comfortable attacking the readings and might find the inclusion of personal anecdotes irrelevant and "soft." Women are more likely to resist discussion they perceive as hostile, and, indeed, it is women in my classes who are most likely to offer personal anecdotes.

A colleague who read my book commented that he had always taken for granted that the best way to deal with students' comments is to challenge them: this, he felt it was self-evident, sharpens their minds and helps them develop debating skills. But he had noticed that women were relatively silent in his classes, so he decided to try beginning discussion with relatively open-ended questions and letting comments go unchallenged. He found, to his amazement and satisfaction, that more women began to speak up.

Though some of the women in his class clearly liked this better, perhaps some of the men liked it less. One young man in my class wrote in a questionnaire about a history professor who gave students questions to think about and called on people to answer them: "He would then play devil's advocate . . . i.e., he debated us. . . . That class *really* sharpened me intellectually. . . . We as students do need to know how to defend ourselves." This young man valued the experience of being attacked and challenged publicly. Many, if not most, women would shrink from such a "challenge," experiencing it as a public humiliation.

A professor at Hamilton College told me of a young man who was upset because he felt his class presentation had been a failure. The professor was puzzled because he had observed that class members had listened attentively and agreed with the student's observations. It turned out that it was this very agreement that the student interpreted as failure: Since no one had engaged his ideas by arguing with him, he felt they had found them unworthy of attention.

So one reason men speak in class more than women is that many of them find the "public" classroom setting more conducive to speaking, whereas most women are more comfortable speaking in private to a small group of people they know well. A second reason is that men are more likely to be comfortable with the debate-like form that discussion may take. Yet another reason is the different attitudes toward speaking in class that typify women and men.

Students who speak frequently in class, many of whom are men, assume that it is their job to think of contributions and try to get the floor to express them. But many women monitor their participation not only to get the floor but to avoid getting it. Women students in my class tell me that if they have spoken up once or twice, they hold back for the rest of the class because they don't want to dominate. If they have spoken a lot one week, they will remain silent the next. These different ethics of participation are, of course, unstated, so those who speak freely assume that those who remain silent have nothing to say, and those who are reining themselves in assume that the big talkers are selfish and hoggish.

When I looked around my classes, I could see these differing ethics and habits at work. For example, my graduate class in analyzing conversation had twenty students, eleven women and nine men. Of the men, four were foreign students: two Japanese, one Chinese, and one Syrian. With the exception of the three Asian men, all the men spoke in class at least occasionally. The biggest talker in the class was a woman, but there were also five women who never spoke at all, only one of whom was Japanese. I decided to try something different.

I broke the class into small groups to discuss the issues raised in the readings and to analyze their own conversational transcripts. I devised three ways of dividing the students into groups: one by the degree program they were in, one by gender, and one by conversational style, as closely as I could guess it. This meant that when the class was grouped according to conversational style, I put Asian students together, fast talkers together, and quiet students together. The class split into groups six times during the semester, so they met in each grouping twice. I told students to regard the groups as examples of interactional data and to note the different ways in which they participated in the different groups. Toward the end of the term, I gave them a questionnaire asking about their class and group participation.

I could see plainly from my observation of the groups at work that women who never opened their mouths in class were talking away in the small groups. In fact, the Japanese woman commented that she found it particularly hard to contribute to the all-woman group she was in because "I was overwhelmed by how talkative the female students were in the female-only group." This is particularly revealing because it highlights that the same person who can be "oppressed" into silence in one context can become the talkative "oppressor" in another. No one's conversational style is absolute; everyone's style changes in response to the context and others' styles.

Some of the students (seven) said they preferred the same-gender groups, others preferred the same-style groups. In answer to the question "Would you have liked to speak in class more than you did?" six of the seven who said yes were women; the one man was Japanese. Most startlingly, this response did not come only from quiet women; it came from women who had indicated they had spoken in class never, rarely, sometimes and often. Of the eleven students who said the amount they had spoken was fine, seven were men. Of the four women who checked, "fine," two added qualifications indicating it wasn't completely fine: One wrote in "maybe more," and one wrote, "I have an urge to participate often but feel I should have something more interesting/relevant/wonderful/intelligent to say!"

I counted my experiment a success. Everyone in the class found the small groups interesting, and no one indicated he or she would have preferred that the class not break into groups. Perhaps most instructive, however, was the fact that the experience of breaking into groups, and of talking about participation in class, raised everyone's awareness about classroom participation. After we had talked about it, some of the quietest women in the class made a few voluntary contributions, though sometimes I had to insure their participation by interrupting the students who were exuberantly speaking out.

Americans are often proud that they discount the significance of cultural differences: "We're all individuals," many people boast. Ignoring such issues as gender and ethnicity becomes a source of pride: "I treat everyone the same." But treating people the same is not equal treatment if they are not the same.

The classroom is a different environment for those who feel comfortable putting themselves forward in a group than it is for those who find the prospect of doing so chastening, or even terrifying. When a professor asks, "Are there any questions?," students who can formulate statements the fastest have the greatest opportunity to respond. Those who need significant time to do so have not really been given a chance at all, since by the time they are ready to speak, someone else has taken the floor.

In a class where some students speak out without raising hands, those who feel they must raise their hands and wait to be recognized do not have equal opportunity to speak. Telling them to feel free to jump in will not make them feel free; one's sense of timing, of one's rights and obligations in a classroom, are automatic, learned over years of interaction. They may be changed over time, with motivation and effort, but they cannot be changed on the spot. And everyone assumes his or her own way is best. When I asked my students how the class could be changed to make it easier for them to speak more, the most talkative woman said she would prefer it if no one had to raise hands, and a foreign student said he wished people would raise their hands and wait to be recognized.

My experience in this class has convinced me that small-group interaction should be part of any class that is not a small seminar. I also am convinced that having the students become observers of their own interaction is a crucial part of their education. Talking about ways of talking in class makes students aware that their ways of talking affect other students, that the motivations they impute to others may not truly reflect others' motives, and that the behaviors they assume to be self-evidently right are not universal norms.

The goal of complete equal opportunity in class may not be attainable, but realizing that one monolithic classroom-participation structure is not equal opportunity is itself a powerful motivation to find more diverse methods to serve diverse students—and every classroom is diverse.

INTERPRETATIONS

1. To what extent do you agree with Tannen that males find class participation more "congenial" than do females? What evidence does she offer?

2. According to Tannen, men "ritualize opposition"; women don't. How do the anthropologists she cites explain this difference?

3. Tannen contrasts the "ethics of participation" of male and female students. What differences does she discover? How do they affect female participation?

4. Tannen modified her teaching strategies considerably on the basis of her research. Cite some of the changes she made and your responses to them.

CORRESPONDENCES

1. Review Heilbrun's perspective on power and discuss its implications for Tannen's essay.

2. Compare and contrast the tone of Tannen's and Lee's essays. How is tone related to purpose?

APPLICATIONS

1. In paragraph 3, Tannen focuses on the different ways that boys and girls use language to make friends. Review this paragraph and write an essay on how your own experience of making friends validates or refutes Tannen's observations.

2. Debate with your group Tannen's thesis in paragraph 17 that "no one's conversational style is absolute; everyone's style changes in response to the context and others' styles." What consensus did you reach?

3. Test the validity of Tannen's observations on gender in the classroom with your group. To what extent did your conversational styles mirror Tannen's theories? Summarize your findings.

If Black English Isn't a Language, Then Tell Me, What Is?

JAMES BALDWIN

James Baldwin (1924–1987) was born in New York City's Harlem. Much of his writing, including his first novel, Go Tell It on the Mountain *(1953), and his many collections of essays from* Notes of a Native Son *(1955) to the more recent* No Name in the Street, *is autobiographical and concerned with the complexity of the black man and woman's search for identity. In his essay on black English published originally in* The New York Times *in 1979, Baldwin explains the intricate relationship between language and selfhood.*

ST. PAUL DE VENCE, FRANCE—The argument concerning the use, or the status, or the reality, of black English is rooted in American history and has absolutely nothing to do with the question the argument supposes itself to be posing. The argument has nothing to do with language itself but with the *role* of language. Language, incontestably, reveals the speaker. Language, also, far more dubiously, is meant to define the other—and, in this case, the other is refusing to be defined by a language that has never been able to recognize him.

People evolve a language in order to describe and thus control their circumstances, or in order not to be submerged by a reality that they cannot articulate. (And, if they cannot articulate it, they *are* submerged.) A Frenchman living in Paris speaks a subtly and crucially different language from that of the man living in Marseilles; neither sounds very much like a man living in Quebec; and they would all have great difficulty in apprehending what the man from Guadeloupe, or Martinique, is saying, to say nothing of the man from Senegal—although the "common" language of all these areas is French. But each has paid, and is paying, a different price for this "common" language, in which, as it turns out, they are not saying, and cannot be saying, the same things: They each have very different realities to articulate, or control.

What joins all languages, and all men, is the necessity to confront life, in order, not inconceivably, to outwit death: The price for this is the acceptance, and achievement, of one's temporal identity. So that, for example, though it is not taught in the schools (and this has the potential of becoming a political issue) the south of France still clings to its ancient and musical Provençal, which resists being described as a "dialect." And much of the tension in the Basque countries, and in Wales, is due to the Basque and Welsh determination not to allow their languages to be destroyed. This determination also feeds the flames in Ireland for among the many indignities the Irish have been forced to undergo at English hands is the English contempt for their language.

It goes without saying, then, that language is also a political instrument, means, and proof of power. It is the most vivid and crucial key to identity: It reveals the private identity, and connects one with, or divorces one from, the larger, public, or communal identity. There have been, and are, times, and places, when to speak a certain language could be dangerous, even fatal. Or, one may speak the same language, but in such a way that one's antecedents are revealed, or (one hopes) hidden. This is true in France, and is absolutely true in England: The range (and reign) of accents on that damp little island make England coherent for the English and totally incomprehensible for everyone else. To open your mouth in England is (if I may use black English) to "put your business in the street": You have confessed your parents, your youth, your school, your salary, your self-esteem, and, alas, your future.

Now, I do not know what white Americans would sound like if there had never been any black people in the United States, but they would not sound the way they sound. *Jazz*, for example, is a very specific sexual term, as in *jazz me, baby*, but white people purified it into the Jazz Age. *Sock it to me*, which means, roughly, the same thing, has been adopted by Nathaniel Hawthorne's descendants with no qualms or hesitations at all, along with *let it all hang out* and *right on! Beat to his socks*, which was once the black's most total and despairing image of poverty, was transformed into a thing called the Beat Generation, which phenomenon was, largely, composed of *uptight*, middle-class white people, imitating poverty, trying to *get down*, to get *with it*, doing their *thing*, doing their despairing best to be *funky*, which we, the blacks, never dreamed of doing—we *were* funky, baby, like *funk* was going out of style.

Now, no one can eat his cake, and have it, too, and it is late in the day to attempt to penalize black people for having created a language that permits the nation its only glimpse of reality, a language without which the nation would be even more *whipped* than it is.

I say that this present skirmish is rooted in American history, and it is. Black English is the creation of the black diaspora. Blacks came to the United States chained to each other, but from different tribes: Neither could speak the other's language. If two black people, at that bitter hour of the world's history, had been able to speak to each other, the institution of chattel slavery could never have lasted as long as it did.

Subsequently, the slave was given, under the eye, and the gun, of his master, Congo Square, and the Bible—or, in other words, and under these conditions, the slave began the formation of the black church, and it is within this unprecedented tabernacle that black English began to be formed. This was not, merely, as in the European example, the adoption of a foreign tongue, but an alchemy that transformed ancient elements into a new language: *A language comes into existence by means of brutal necessity, and the rules of the language are dictated by what the language must convey.*

There was a moment, in time, and in this place, when my brother, or my mother, or my father, or my sister, had to convey to me, for example, the danger in which I was standing from the white man standing just behind me, and to convey this with a speed, and in a language, that the white man could not possibly understand, and that, indeed, he cannot understand, until today. He cannot afford to understand it. This understanding would reveal to him too much about himself, and smash that mirror before which he has been frozen for so long.

Now, if this passion, this skill, this (to quote Toni Morrison) "sheer intelligence," this incredible music, the mighty achievement of having brought a people utterly unknown to, or despised by "history"—to have brought this people to their present, troubled, troubling, and unassailable and unanswerable place—if this absolutely unprecedented journey does not indicate that black English is a language, I am curious to know what definition of language is to be trusted.

A people at the center of the Western world, and in the midst of so hostile a population, has not endured and transcended by means of what is patronizingly called a "dialect." We, the blacks, are in trouble, certainly, but we are not doomed, and we are not inarticulate because we are not compelled to defend a morality that we know to be a lie.

The brutal truth is that the bulk of the white people in America never had any interest in educating black people, except as this could serve white purposes. It is not the black child's language that is in question, it is not his language that is despised: It is his experience. A child cannot be taught by anyone who despises him, and a child cannot afford to be fooled. A child cannot be taught by anyone whose demand, essentially, is that the child repudiate his experience, and all that gives him sustenance, and enter a limbo in which he will no longer be black, and in which he knows that he can never become white. Black people have lost too many black children that way.

And, after all, finally, in a country with standards so untrustworthy, a country that makes heroes of so many criminal mediocrities, a country unable to face why so many of the non-white are in prison, or on the needle, or standing, futureless, in the streets—it may very well be that both the child, and his elder, have concluded that they have nothing whatever to learn from the people of a country that has managed to learn so little.

INTERPRETATIONS

1. Baldwin distinguishes between the characteristics of a language and the characteristics of a dialect. According to Baldwin, what are these characteristics and how do they differ?

2. In Baldwin's view, what is the relationship between language and reality?

3. Characterize your response to Baldwin's comment in paragraph 4 that "language is also a political instrument, means, and proof of power." To what extent has this been true in your own experience?

4. What is the effect of the italicized words used in the essay? How would their exclusion affect the impact of the essay? Explain your answer.

Mute in an English-Only World

CHANG-RAE LEE

Chang-Rae Lee teaches at Hunter College in New York where he is a member of the Hunter Creative Writing Community (www.thirdrail.hunter creative writing). He is the author of the novels Native Speaker *(1994);* A Gesture Life *(1999), a study of Japanese-Americans from 1939–1945; and* City Pages: Home & Far Away *(1999). This Op-Ed essay was originally published in* The New York Times *in April 1996.*

WHEN I READ OF THE TROUBLES in Palisades Park, New Jersey, over the proliferation of Korean language signs along its main commercial strip, I unexpectedly sympathized with the frustrations, resentments and fears of the longtime residents. They clearly felt alienated and even unwelcome in a vital part of their community. The town, like seven others in New Jersey, has passed laws requiring that half of any commercial sign in a foreign language be in English.

Now I certainly would never tolerate any exclusionary ideas about who could rightfully settle and belong in the town. But having been raised in a Korean immigrant family, I saw every day the exacting price and power of language, especially with my mother, who was an outsider in an English-only world.

In the first years we lived in America, my mother could speak only the most basic English, and she often encountered great difficulty whenever she went out.

We lived in New Rochelle, New York in the early 70s, and most of the local businesses were run by the descendants of immigrants who, generations ago, had come to the suburbs from New York City. Proudly dotting Main Street and North Avenue were Italian pastry and cheese shops, Jewish tailors and cleaners and Polish and German butchers and bakers. If my mother's marketing couldn't wait until the weekend, when my father had free time, she would often hold off until I came home from school to buy the groceries.

Though I was only six or seven years old, she insisted that I go out shopping with her and my younger sister. I mostly loathed the task, partly because it meant I couldn't spend the afternoon playing catch with my friends but also because I knew our errands would inevitably lead to an awkward scene, and that I would have to speak up to help my mother.

I was just learning the language myself, but I was a quick study, as children are with new tongues. I had spent kindergarten in almost complete silence, hearing only the high nasality of my teacher and comprehending little but the cranky wails and cries of my classmates. But soon, seemingly mere months later, I had already become a terrible ham and mimic, and I would crack up my father with impressions of teachers, his friends and even himself. My mother scolded me for aping his speech, and the one time I attempted to make light of hers I rated a roundhouse smack on my bottom.

For her, the English language was not very funny. It usually meant trouble and a good dose of shame, and sometimes real hurt. Although she had a good reading knowledge of the language from university classes in South Korea, she had never practiced actual conversation. So in America, she used English flashcards and phrase books and watched television with us kids. And she faithfully carried a pocket workbook illustrated with stick-figure people and compound sentences to be filled in.

But none of it seemed to do her much good. Staying mostly at home to care for us, she didn't have many chances to try out sundry words and phrases. When she did, say, at the window of the post office, her readied speech would stall, freeze, sometimes altogether collapse.

One day was unusually harrowing. We ventured downtown in the new Ford Country Squire my father had bought her, an enormous station wagon that seemed as long—and deft—as an ocean liner. We were shopping for a special meal for guests visiting that weekend, and my mother had heard that a particular butcher carried fresh oxtails, which she needed for a traditional soup.

We'd never been inside the shop, but my mother would pause before its window, which was always lined with whole hams, crown roasts and ropes of plump handmade sausages. She greatly esteemed the bounty with her eyes, and my sister and I did also, but despite our desirous cries she'd turn us away and instead buy the packaged links at the Finast supermarket, where she felt comfortable looking them over and could easily spot the price. And, of course, not have to talk.

But that day she was resolved. The butcher store was crowded, and as we stepped inside the door jingled a welcome. No one seemed to notice. We waited for some time, and people who entered after us were now being served. Finally, an old woman nudged my mother and waved a little ticket, which we hadn't taken. We patiently waited again, until one of the beefy men behind the glass display hollered our number.

My mother pulled us forward and began searching the cases, but the oxtails were nowhere to be found. The man, his big arms crossed, sharply said, "Come on, lady, whaddya want?" This unnerved her, and she somehow blurted the Korean word for oxtail, soggori.

The butcher looked as if my mother had put something sour in his mouth, and he glanced back at the lighted board and called the next number.

Before I knew it, she had rushed us outside and back in the wagon, which she had double-parked because of the crowd. She was furious, almost vibrating with fear and grief, and I could see she was about to cry.

She wanted to go back inside, but now the driver of the car we were blocking wanted to pull out. She was shooing us away. My mother, who had just earned her driver's license, started furiously working the pedals. But in her haste she must have flooded the engine, for it wouldn't turn over. The driver started honking and then another car began honking as well, and soon the entire street was shrieking at us.

In the following years, my mother grew steadily more comfortable with English. In Korean, she could be fiery, stern, deeply funny and ironic; in English, just slightly less so. If she was never quite fluent, she gained enough confidence to make herself clearly known to anyone, and particularly to me.

Five years ago, she died of cancer, and some months after we buried her I found myself in the driveway of my father's house, washing her sedan. I liked taking care of her things; it made me feel close to her. While I was cleaning out the glove compartment, I found her pocket English workbook, the one with the silly illustrations. I hadn't seen it in nearly twenty years. The yellowed pages were brittle and dog-eared. She had fashioned a plain-paper wrapping for it, and I wondered whether she meant to protect the book or hide it.

I don't doubt that she would have appreciated doing the family shopping on the new Broad Avenue of Palisades Park. But I like to think, too, that she would have understood those who now complain about the Korean-only signs.

I wonder what these same people would have done if they had seen my mother studying her English workbook—or lost in a store. Would they have nodded gently at her? Would they have lent a kind word?

INTERPRETATIONS

1.   What issues does Lee raise in the first paragraph?

2.   What is his purpose in this essay? Is he seeking to inform or persuade his readers on the English-only debate? Cite evidence for your point of view.

3.   How effectively does Lee's mother's workbook function literally and symbolically in the text?

CORRESPONDENCES

1. Baldwin and Lee discuss the relationship between language and power. Which examples do you find most convincing? Explain.

2. Compare and contrast the tone of Baldwin's and Lee's texts. How is purpose related to tone?

APPLICATIONS

1. Baldwin makes a case for the recognition of Black English. For additional information about this issue, explore the following Web sites:

   http://www.jaedworks.com/shoebox/oakland-ebonics.html

   http://www.linguistlist.org/topics/ebonics/lsa-ebonics.html

   http://www.stanford.edu/~rickford/ebonics/SJMN-OpEd.html

   http://www.cal.org/ebonics/

2. Discuss with your group Baldwin's thesis that language "reveals the private identity, and connects one with, or divorces one from the larger, public or communal identity." What experiences can you share that support or refute his thesis? Write a summary of your discussion.

3. Write a journal entry responding to Lee's title. Can you imagine being mute in a culture whose native language is not English? How might you respond in a situation similar to that in the butcher's shop?

4. Which of the following issues regarding language does Lee's essay address: rage, powerlessness, identity, silence, perception? Write a journal entry on the linkage you most related to.

5. Listen to the sounds of a language that you do not understand. Listen for rhythms and melodies. How would you describe this language as a *song*?

A Letter to a Child Like Me

JOSÉ TORRES

José Torres (b. 1936) was raised in poverty in Puerto Rico. After winning a silver medal in the 1956 Olympic Games, he became a professional boxer and had a successful career that culminated in his winning the light-heavywieght boxing championship in 1965. In 1969 he retired, and now frequently writes about boxing and his life experiences. He is the author of In this Corner, Fire and Fear: The Inside Story of Mike Tyson *(1989). In the following essay he offers advice to young people of his ethnic background.*

DEAR PEDRITO:

You're thirteen now, and you must certainly be aware that there are some people in this country who refer to you as "Hispanic." That is, you're a member of a minority group. You read newspapers and magazines, you watch television, so you know that the world is moving into the twenty-first century faced with big problems, enormous possibilities, huge mysteries. I worry that you might not be fully prepared for the journey.

The statistics are scary. They show us Hispanics facing a sea of trouble. The United States has 250 million people, a little more than 20 million of whom are of Hispanic descent. That's only 8 percent of this nation's total population. We're also the youngest ethnic group in the nation. We earn the lowest salaries, and, in cities where we have a large concentration of Hispanics, we have the highest school dropout rate. In New York City, for example, we comprise 25.7 percent of the high school dropouts, 42.7 percent of pregnant teenagers and 8.9 percent of the unemployed.

It should not be too hard for you to understand, my friend, that these statistics hurt us a lot. That means that many of our young people end up badly, as both victims and perpetrators. Some blame us for these conditions, despite our minuscule stock in this country and the fact the overwhelming majority of us are hardworking, decent, law-abiding citizens.

Still, you should realize that the world is not made up of statistics but of individuals. By the year 2030, you'll be my age, and what you do now is going to determine what you'll be doing then.

I've had my defeats; I've made my share of mistakes. But I've also learned something along the way. Let me tell you about a few of them. You didn't ask for this advice, but I'm going to give it to you anyway.

Let's start with a fundamental human problem, and I don't mean race or religion or origin. I mean fear. Fright, my young friend, may be the first serious enemy you have to face in our society. It's the most destructive emotional bogeyman there is. Cold feet, panic, depression, and violence are all symptoms of fear—when it's out of control. But this feeling, ironically, can also trigger courage, alertness, objectivity. You must learn not to try to rid yourself of this basic human emotion but to manipulate it for your own advantage. You cannot surrender to fear, but you *can* use it as a kind of fuel. Once you learn to control fear—to make it work for you—it will become one of your best friends.

I learned this the hard way. I was a boxer. I became a world champion, but on my way up the ladder I found Frankie Kid Anslem, a tough young Philadelphian made of steel. The match proceeded, to my increasing dismay, with me hitting and Anslem smiling. At one point, I remember, I let go a particularly left hook-right cross combination. The punches landed flush on his jaw, but he simply riposted with a smile—and some hard leather of his own.

Suddenly, I found myself struggling for my life. I was afraid. For two rounds—the eighth and ninth—Anslem and I seemed contestants in an evil struggle. My punches seemed to give him energy and pleasure! Unexpectedly, my chest began to burn, my legs weakened, my lungs gasped for air. I felt exhausted. I was dying! Thoughts of defeat and humiliation assailed me. I was grappling with these facts when I saw Anslem's jaw exposed and, reaching from somewhere beyond my terror, I threw a straight right with all my might. And Anslem lost his smile and dropped like an old shoe.

My fatigue disappeared. I felt good, happy, invigorated. Fear had overtaken me, been recognized, then resolved and manipulated for a positive result.

I was obliged to learn about handling fear through the brutal trade of boxing. I didn't have the option now open to you, my young friend. I was one of seven poor kids who lived under many layers of an underdeveloped subculture. I chose a tough profession because two black boxers—a heavyweight champion named Joe Louis, and a middleweight marvel called Sugar Ray Robinson—showed me the way. They lived far away from my hometown in Puerto Rico. But I knew them. I wanted to be like them.

Looking back, I wonder what my choice would have been if real alternatives had been available when I was your age. Don't get me wrong. I'm very proud of my first profession. To be recognized as the best in the world at what you do, even if only for a moment, is a wonderful experience. Still, I was very much aware that boxing was a temporary activity intended only for the young. And so I had a pretty good idea of what your choice should not be if you're given a chance to become an artist, a corporate executive, a doctor, a lawyer, an engineer, a writer, or a prizefighter—though it should be *my* choice.

Whatever your ambition, you must educate yourself. School is a great gift our society offers you. It provides the key for your future. You must accept this gift, not disdain it. School is where you'll learn about your country and your world and your life in both. You also discover the conflicts and contradictions of history. You'll unlock the treasure chest of the world's literature and begin to sense the beauty of music and art. You'll acquire the tools of abstract thinking, of science and mathematics—and the computer, perhaps the primary instrument of the world you'll inherit.

At home, you should learn about compassion and dignity and care. You should realize that the workings of an individual's heart and soul can be as important as the histories of the great battles, military generals, dictators and kings. Most of all, you should learn that it's *you* who are responsible for your future.

There is a basic principle you should never forget: Don't be ruled by other people's low expectation of you! It almost happened to me. I grew up in Playa de Ponce, a small *barrio* in the southern part of Puerto Rico, an island 100 miles long and 35 miles wide, with a dense population today of more than 3.3 million—1,000 human beings per square mile. I was only five when I first noticed the American military men—many of them tall, blond, and blue-eyed—wearing a variety of uniforms, roaming the streets of my neighborhood and picking up the prettiest girls. They seemed to own Playa de Ponce. Their attitude in the streets and their country's constant military victories, which we witnessed at the movie houses, became symbols of these young men's "obvious superiority." By comparison, we Puerto Ricans felt limited, inadequate.

To catch up, I volunteered to serve in the U.S. Army as soon as I became of age. And, for some mysterious reason, I joined its boxing team. My first four opponents were two compatriots and two black men from the Virgin Islands, all of whom I had no trouble disposing of. But just before my fifth fight—against one of those tall, blond, blue-eyed "superior" American soldiers, doubt started to creep into my mind. Yet, despite my worries, after three rounds of tough boxing, I overcame. I won! I had discovered the equality of the human race.

Your best defense against the ignorance of bigots and haters is pride in your own heritage. That's why you must learn your own history. Do it now. Don't wait until you are in college. You don't need teachers. Go to the library. Ask your parents and relatives and friends.

Be proud of your ethnicity and language. Don't be afraid to use it. Don't give up to the stupidity of those know-nothings who insist one language is better than two or three. You should know, and be proud, that in the Western Hemisphere more people speak Spanish than English; that Español was the language of the Hemisphere's first university—the Santo Tomás de Aquino University in the Dominican Republic, founded in 1538—and of the books in its first library. When you discover the long and honorable tradition to which you belong, your pride will soar.

So do not lose the language of your parents, which is also yours. Instead, refine your skill in it. If you're having trouble with grammar or writing, take courses in Spanish. Go to the library and read Cervantes' *Don Quixote*, the first full-fledged novel, or the works of the hundreds of great modern Hispanic authors, such as Gabriel García Márquez, Lola Rodriguez de Tió, Carlos Fuentes, Mario Vargas Llosa, Octavio Paz, Jorge Luis Borges, and Oscar Hijuelos, the 1990 Pulitzer Prize winner in fiction (who writes in English). Read them in both languages; know the strength of both. This is the treasure that no one can ever beat.

Puerto Rico is a nearly imperceptible dot on the map, my friend. Still, this small island recently had five boxing champions at the same time. And consider this: Baseball star Reggie Jackson; the great entertainer Sammy Davis, Jr.; Dr. Joaquín Balaguer, poet, writer and six-time president of the Dominican Republic; the renowned cellist Pablo Casals all had one thing in common—one of their parents was Puerto Rican. The film and stage star Rita Moreno, a Puerto Rican, is one of the few performers ever to win an Oscar, a Tony, a Grammy, and an Emmy award. José Ferrer, a proud Puerto Rican, was once selected as the American citizen with the finest English diction in the United States. Ferrer also won an Oscar for his brilliant performance in the classic film *Cyrano de Bergerac*. Dr. Raul García Rinaidi, a physician of world prominence and a native Puerto Rican, helped invent six instruments now used in cardiovascular surgery. Arturo Alfonso Schomburg, a native Puerto Rican, made extensive investigation into Black history. In his honor, the New York Public Library system erected the Schomburg Center for Research in Black Culture.

The contribution of Hispanics to the development of the United States of America has been vast and unquestionable. But much more remains to be done, my friend. Every member of society must work together in order to survive together.

We live in a country where more than 27 million people can't read or write well enough to take a driving test, and many can't recognize "danger," or "poison." Every eight seconds of the school day a student drops out; every sixty seconds a teenager has a baby; every six minutes a child is arrested for drugs; every year, the schools graduate 700,000 who cannot read their diplomas.

Most of them are *not* Hispanics. Yet, many of these victims are the same people who, day after day, throw themselves in front of a TV set and become passive, docile ghosts, allowing their lives to be easily controlled by others. Television, with its emphasis on package images and quick bites, discourages thought and imagination. Studies indicate that chronic televiewers develop problems with their thinking processes and articulation. Excessive viewing dulls the most indispensable muscle—the brain.

Instead of watching TV, read and write. Words are the symbols of reality, and a well-read person, skilled at decoding those symbols, is better able to comprehend and think about the real world.

Many years ago, the great Japanese artist, Katsushika Hokusai lay on his deathbed at age 89. Experts say no one could paint better than Hokusai during his prime, and many are convinced that his work is as good as—or better than—today's top artists. But Hokusai was never satisfied with his triumphs and successes. "If I could live one more year," he said, "I could learn how to draw."

You, my young friend, would do well to become like Hokusai—a person who can lead a humble but useful and productive life, free of harm and, most important, free of the influences that generate hate, murder, suicide, and death. If you choose to spend your time not reading, thinking, and creating, but watching TV and learning how to deceive, cheat, and lie, then you become another person out there perpetuating the cycle of ignorance that leads to poverty, suffering, and despair. But if you commit yourself to a lifetime of honest work—if you assure yourself that a day in which you are unable to produce anything positive is a tragically misspent day—then, my friend, the twenty-first century is yours.

Go and get it!

INTERPRETATIONS

1. Why does Torres begin his letter by citing mainly negative statistics about Hispanics and then go on to say "that the world is not made up of statistics but of individuals"?

2. Torres tells his young friend that fear may be his greatest enemy. How did Torres overcome his own fear? To what extent do you agree or disagree about the negative power of fear?

3. "School is a great gift our society offers you." What evidence does he cite to support his thesis? How do your experiences with school correspond to Torres's expectation?

4. "Be proud of your ethnicity and language." What evidence did you find most convincing regarding this advice?

5. Respond to Torres's views on watching television, particularly to his comment about television's dulling the brain.

CORRESPONDENCES

1. Baldwin and Torres focus on the connection between language and ethnic pride. How would you differentiate between their methods of presentation? Which did you find more effective? Explain your answer.

2. What conversation can you imagine Torres and Baldwin sharing on the issue of biculturalism? What would you add to the debate?

APPLICATIONS

1. Imagine yourself in Torres's situation. What advice would you offer to a thirteen-year-old preparing for the future?

2. According to Torres, "television, with its emphasis on packaged images and quick bites, discourages thought and imagination." Debate this issue with your group citing examples from your own experience that support or refute Torres. What consensus did you reach?

3. Torres believes in the importance of role models. To what extent do you agree or disagree? How would you define a role model? Is there someone in your past or present who fits your definition? Write a short essay explaining how this person influenced you.

4. Create a concept map of the types of learning or education that Torres presents in his essay "A Letter to a Child Like Me." To learn more about concept mapping, check the following Web sites.

http://www.cotf.edu/ete/pbl2.html

http://users.edte.utwente.nl/lanzing/cm_home.htm

Thinking

ROLANDO JORIF

Rolando Jorif was born in Panama, and was raised in Queens, New York. After attending Catholic parochial school in the 1950s, he graduated from the Bronx High School of Science and continued on to Lehman College–City University of New York (CUNY). A true sixties' drop-out, Jorif left college to become a dancer. Eight years ago, he returned to Hunter College (CUNY) and graduated with a B.S. degree in French and English. He is currently in the doctoral program in American Literature at CUNY Graduate Center and teaches at Queensborough Community College (CUNY). Before reading Jorif's essay, record in your journal your definition of "thinking."

Panama is a Republic on the Isthmus of Panama that connects Central and South America. The capital is Panama City. Christopher Columbus landed in Panama in 1502. In 1510, Vasco Nunez de Balboa was the first European to cross Panama and see the Pacific Ocean. The indigenous population was soon wiped out and Spain established control. In 1821, Panama became a province of Colombia. After a revolt in 1903, Panama declared independence from Colombia. In 1904, the United States began construction of the Panama Canal and established the Panama Canal Zone. Since it was opened in 1914, the status of the Canal has been a feature of Panamanian politics. United States forces intervened in 1908, 1912, and 1918 to protect U.S. interests. Panama has been politically unstable throughout the twentieth century, with a series of dictatorial regimes and military coups. Civil strife during the 1950s and 1960s led to negotiations with the United States for the transfer of the Canal Zone. In 1977, a treaty confirmed Panama's sovereignty over the canal, while providing for U.S. bases in the Canal Zone. The United States agreed to hand over control of the Canal on December 31, 1999. In 1983, General Noriega took control of the National Guard and ruled Panama through a succession of puppet governments. In 1987, the U.S. withdrew its support for Noriega after he was accused of murder, electoral fraud, and aiding drug smuggling. In December 1989, he made himself president and declared war on the U.S. On December 20, 1989, 25,000 U.S. troops invaded Panama. Noriega was captured in January 1990 and taken to the United States for trial. Pere Balladares was elected president in 1994.

Thinking is a very nice exercise when you are young. I used to think a great deal about freedom when I was a child. My ideas developed slowly. No matter what I thought, though, I would try my ideas out to see what would happen. I didn't do this deliberately. It's just how things worked out. I can easily recall three experiences.

My first or second winter in school, I reached over and took a handful of snow off the windowsill and ate it—cold, delicious snow. I was newly-arrived in this country and snow was still a marvel. I should tell you that I had waited until the nun had left the room and that she had chosen my greatest enemy to be the monitor. I'm not making excuses, I'm only setting the scene. If the fool hadn't been left in charge, someone else who took his work seriously would have been left to watch us. Someone else, though, might have understood why I did what I did and might have left me alone. In any case, I was reported for my "bad behavior." I was sent down to the principal's office where that formidable woman told me that eating snow off windowsills would not do; my attempt at an explanation only made more trouble for me.

I learnt my first lesson about freedom that day: you had better be discreet in your expression of it.

My second lesson happened because I had lost a button from my school shirt. We wore uniforms, and the dress code included the proper maintenance of our clothes. I spent my childhood in terror of not being properly dressed in school, or any place else, for that matter. In any case, I had lost a button from my shirt and it needed to be replaced. I approached my very tired mother (she worked to support us) for help. The good woman got up, left the room and returned with needle and thread. She taught me to sew.

My second lesson about freedom was that you had better be able to take care of your own needs.

My third lesson was a bit more painful to learn.

I was an immigrant and I had entered the school system a cultural virgin. Very quickly, I learned about prejudice and "truth, justice, and the American way." Despite what my parents did to encourage me by telling me that we had not come to America to be anyone's friend, or that I was as good as anyone (I did not tell them very much of what really happened to me), I felt that things were hopeless. One day we were told to read the Declaration of Independence. I was thunderstruck; these people knew all the stuff about freedom that I had learned. I memorized the first paragraph and repeated it to myself every chance I had. One day, we were asked to recite it; I was the only one who knew it. Not only that, but when I recited it, the audience of blank faces meant that I was the only one who understood it. Freedom, I learned, was a secret and it meant being all alone in the crowd.

Thinking is a very nice exercise when you are young. What I had thought was freedom was something else, and I had to examine myself and the world around me to correct my error. It spared me a great deal of trouble, even if it gave me some anxious moments. I don't get very much time to think, now that I am older. I also don't get spared much trouble.

INTERPRETATIONS

1. Jorif recalls three experiences from elementary school which taught him about freedom. What did he learn not only about freedom but about himself?

2. Characterize the tone of his essay. Is it humorous, angry, ironic, or sarcastic? Cite evidence for your point of view.

3. How does Jorif use his introduction and conclusion to unify his essay? Why does he think less as an adult?

CORRESPONDENCES

1. Review Frost's perspective on education and discuss its relevance to Jorif's essay. To what did Jorif "catch on"?

2. According to Bacon's perspective, "knowledge is power." Did Jorif's experiences in school make him feel powerful? Explain.

APPLICATIONS

1. Jorif, an immigrant student from Panama, had to grapple with prejudice in a parochial school in New York City. If you have felt alienated for a similar reason, write a journal entry focusing on your reactions to the experience.

2. Imagine inviting Jorif to join your group discussion on thinking and freedom. What points would you raise with him? What questions would you ask?

3. Jorif's experiences in elementary school took place in the 1950s. To what extent would a Panamanian student today encounter a more friendly environment? What factors would you cite to support your point of view?

The Rain Makes the Roof Sing

TOM MONTGOMERY-FATE

Tom Montgomery-Fate (b. 1960) grew up in a small town in Iowa, and later completed the M.A. in Writing program at the University of Iowa. His thesis for that program, Nicaragua: Rice and Beans and Hope *(published in 1988), was the product of his research in war-torn Nicaragua. He currently teaches writing and literature at College of DuPage in Glen Ellyn, Illinois. This essay, which stems from his recent teaching experience in the Philippines, is taken from his book,* Beyond the White Noise *(1997). What does the author learn about himself from his Nicaraguan students?*

The Malay peoples of the Philippine Islands, whose ancestors probably migrated from Southeast Asia, were mostly hunters, fishermen, and farmers. The archipelago was visited by Magellan in 1521. The Spanish founded Manila in 1571. The Islands, named for King Philip II of Spain, were ceded by Spain to the United States for $20 million in 1898 following the Spanish-American War.

Japan attacked the Philippines on December 8, 1941, and occupied the Islands during World War II. On July 4, 1946, independence was proclaimed in accordance with an act of Congress and a republic was established. In 1972, President Ferdinand Marcos declared martial law. He then instituted a new constitution. In 1983, after bitter elections and demonstrations, Marcos and his wife fled the country. Corazon Aquino, widow of an opponent of the Marcos', was elected president. Her government was plagued by economic problems and widespread poverty, Communist and Muslim insurgents, and ineffective military support. An attempted coup in 1989 was thwarted, and in 1992 Fidel Ramos was elected president. The United States vacated the Subic Bay Naval Station in 1992, ending its long military presence in the Philippines. An autonomous Muslim region was established in 1996, formally ending a rebellion that had lasted for 25 years and cost 120,000 lives.

TYPHOON KADIANG HAS ARRIVED, taking down tree limbs and power lines, blowing rain through the screens, cooling the house. When the electricity goes, I light a small candle and anchor it on a metal lid with a few drops of hot wax. I sit at my desk in the teetering light and try to read the responses of my English composition students to their first in-class writing assignment. I asked them to write a one-paragraph response to the question *What is love?* Not wanting to waste paper, each group of four students shared one 8½-by-11-inch sheet, carefully tearing it into quarters. Most wrote only a sentence or two on their pieces.

Due to the wind, I can't keep all of the wrinkled scraps of love weighted down, the candle lit, or the rain out, so I move to another room, choosing windless and hot over inconvenient but cool. But without the breeze to distract me, the incessant pounding of rain on metal is barely tolerable. I can't hear myself think. I can't hear anything. I am consumed by the barrage of sound that refuses to diminish, and then, after nearly an hour, amazingly, gets louder.

None of the students who live with us seems to notice the torrent of rain, or at least to mind. Mhae, though she surely can't hear herself, is playing her guitar and singing with Lita. I watch them for a moment, but can't tell what song they are mouthing. Narissa is studying intensely a trio of thick candles set up around her. She has positioned them so the flames dance wildly in the wind, but somehow are never extinguished. The shifting light and sinister shadows don't seem to affect her concentration. Eden is outside on the porch talking to her boyfriend under the overhang. Carol, my wife, is reading Jane Smiley's *A Thousand Acres* with a dim flashlight. I dream of Iowa, the place I will always come from. My corn and cows and October frosts have been replaced by rice and water buffalo and typhoons. I feel like one of Smiley's characters. I too am going nuts.

> *Love is like the mango—ripe, sweet, everywhere. Everyone eat the mango. Everyone love.*
> *Love is patient and gentle—like slow bubbling rice.*
> *Love is feeling I have with family that we both know.*
> *I love Yang, our carabao. We depend for each other.*
> *My mother nursing her bebe—up all night. Love is what that is.*

The students' responses pull me out of my frustration. I'm intrigued by the variety. When I give the same assignment at home in the United States, American students, who are more adept at English, write less concrete responses. Most are similar to this: "Love is a strong emotional feeling or bond which a person has for another person or thing." The whole aim of this introductory exercise is to learn to distinguish between writing that tells or explains, and writing that shows or reveals, to move from vague, abstract concepts to concrete imagery. It's interesting how the Filipino students seem to give examples more readily, to try to show what love is rather than attempt to explain it. I wonder if there are any cultural implications.

Caring is love. How do we care. When they dynamite fish in my place they are not caring about the coral. Now there are no fish. No coral or shell. Now there is no love.

My brothers and I work together. We love to work together. We love each other. We trust each other.

Love is not always so easy. Sometime I am hard up for love. Two boys courting me. They play the guitar for me; but I don't think it is love.

Love is banal.

Love is "banal"? This response, one of the shortest and least concrete, confuses me—in part because I haven't heard the word since we arrived in the Philippines. Love is dull, common, ordinary, and mundane? I wonder if I'm missing something. Could she mean that love doesn't need to be extravagant or overly complicated, that it's necessary or routine? I don't think so, at least from the little I know about love in the Filipino culture. "Banal" would seem to describe what love is not.

I ask Lita for help.

"*Banal* means 'sacred' or 'holy,'" she explains.

"It does? I've never heard that definition."

"That's because you don't speak Filipino," she smiles.

I tell her that there is also a word in English spelled b-a-n-a-l. She has never heard of it.

Just then Lita hurries off toward the door. "You're not going out, are you?" I ask. "No, no, someone is tapping at the gate." How in the heck did she hear that? How did she distinguish that faint metallic tapping from the roar of the storm?

It's a neighbor. I've forgotten her name again. She wants to borrow a candle. Lita has some extras and goes to get them. The woman, who is sopping wet despite her best efforts with her umbrella, sits down near me in the flickering light and smiles. "*Adu!*" (A lot!), she says, referring to the rain, trying to be cordial. "*Demasiado*" (Too much), I reply. She laughs. It doesn't seem to bother her that we are yelling. "No, no," she says, then shouts, "*Mayat!*" (It's good!). "What?" I ask, reverting to English. She looks confused. "What? What is good?" I ask again, "The rain, The rain is good," she says, now in English. She points to the metal roof. "Listen," she says. The rain is actually beginning to let up—a machine gun now instead of a jackhammer. "The roof sings," she says, smiling again. "Huh? It what?" I ask. "Listen," she says. "The rain makes the roof sing." She looks at me like we share a secret. I desperately wish we did. I understand what the sentence means, but not her deep, knowing gaze. I wonder if she knows that my affirmative nod is in ignorance.

Lita returns with the candles. The woman says *"Agiamanak"* (Thanks), and heads back out into the downpour.

I keep listening. I wait for the watery rhythms and melodies to reveal themselves. But nothing comes. That's all I need. I had found a specific inanimate target for my general frustration: the rain on the roof. But now the neighbor lady comes along and exonerates it. She claims the rain makes the roof sing! I wonder why she is so happy. I wonder what kind of song or voice she hears. I wonder why I can't hear it. I wonder if I will ever hear the intricacy of Filipino culture above the constant hum of my own.

The next afternoon, the rain almost stops, dwindles to a soft drum. But two days of downpour have deadened my hearing. The depth of the quiet is overwhelming. I find myself yelling, still competing with the sound of rain on metal. When I speak too loudly, Narissa laughs, joking about my needing a hearing aid.

I pull out another folder of student writing. Just to vary things, I asked this class (more than half were religion majors) to respond to the question *What is God?*

> God is not here, I not believe now because of suffering much.
> God is hope.
> God walks in muddy fields. He plants seedlings—new life.
> God is what always there is.
> God is rice. God is rain.

God is rain? Is somebody trying to tell me something? That night after supper, the rain completely stops. It's replaced by the frogs in the flooded banana grove near our house. They are not as loud as the rain, but close. I lie awake sweating and listening to the great burping swamp of noise, the slippery-green, cold-blooded chorus, swelling and then waning, swelling and then waning, seemingly without reason.

I pay closer attention. After an hour of listening, I begin to notice that this is not one huge croaking wave of sound, but a sea of specific croaks, with different rhythms, tones, tunes perpetually interrupting each other. Yet despite the seeming chaos, it is clear they are all singing one song. There is a kind of unity in the cacophony—an odd, unexpected harmonic, a collection of sounds at once chaotic and healing. Harmony: sounds that sound good together precisely because they're different. That night, something changes. I am beginning to hear things.

The next morning, the typhoon is still going strong. Classes are canceled. I slide the capiz-shell windows closed and pull out more student writing.

God is always, but not one thing.
God the source of all things is. God the creator and redeemer.
God? Seuguro adda. Diak ammo. But I think yes.
God is espiritu—everywhere. I never wonder no God is here.

The last two responses confuse me. In Ilocano, *adda* means "is pres-ent" and *diak ammo* means "I don't know." Since there are many Span-ish words in Ilocano, I assume that *seguro* means the same thing in this language as it does in Spanish: "certain." Then I remember that the spelling of some Spanish words integrated into Ilocano stayed the same but their meanings changed while the islands were being colonized. *Seguro* in Ilocano means "maybe," not "certain," as it does in Spanish. I wonder about the historical implications of that.

Did the early Filipinos respond with *seguro* (certainly)—the unquestioning affirmative—to their Spanish masters, but actually mean or think "maybe" in their unwillingness to yield or acquiesce, in their longing for other options? Now the phrase made sense: "Maybe God is here. I don't know, but I think yes."

There is more multilingual confusion in the last response: "I never wonder no God is here." I marvel at how my students balance the regional language (Ilocano), the national language (Filipino), the lan-guage of instruction (English), and, often, a tribal language or two. With my limited Ilocano and non-existent Filipino, I am often confused by the language-hopping in their writing. Here, one word caused the problem: *no. No* means "if" in Ilocano. Again I wonder about the colo-nization process, about Spanish or American conquistadors saying "no" and Ilocanos hearing an "if," hearing possibility in denial or con-demnation, seeing a crack of light seeping beneath a locked door. "I never wonder if God is here." I find myself longing for this student's certainty. But I am thinking more about belief in myself than in God. I want to believe that I can fit into an isolated rice-farming community in the Philippines. And I want to believe that I should be teaching English—"the language of the colonizers" or "the language of money," as one of my students once characterized it while explaining why English should be considered a foreign language.

I put the papers down and listen to the rain, wanting to hear an "if" beyond all of the "no's" I have accumulated in five months of trying to live in a radically different culture, of awkward groping toward inte-gration and acceptance. I start thinking about the English and Filipino definitions of *banal*. Somehow the irony seems related to the "if" I was looking for. How does one learn to see and hear the *banal* (Filipino) in the *banal* (English)? How does one learn to find meaning and value in what at first appears to be meaningless? These questions hang in my head like laundry in the rainy season: forever dripping, perpetually damp, unfinished.

My students and friends were trying to help me understand. In their immense patience, they were trying to teach me to live in the present tense, to pay compassionate attention to the world, to listen and see carefully enough to discern the possibility of the extraordinary in the seemingly ordinary, to hear the sacred music in the off-centered wooden rumble of two wagon wheels and a slow, cloppity ox pulling a rice farmer and his son back to their land, back to that raw green rectangle of life. They were teaching me that "love is like a mango," that "God is rain," that frogs can croak in harmony, that a "maybe" can be better than a "yes," and that an "if" is not always so far from a "no." They were teaching me about the writing process, but also about the difficult process of crossing cultures.

A few hours later, the typhoon finally wanes. The torrents of wind fade, and the driving sheets of rain ease to a steady downpour. People take the opportunity to get out of their homes. They emerge from behind bamboo gates to see how the typhoon has left their world. Around their wooden houses, dozens of mangoes, still too green to bruise, have prematurely blown with soft thuds to the leafy soil. Children collect them in plastic buckets. Then they begin to pick up the wet green tangle of bougainvillaea vines and broken acacia limbs. Finally, they sweep up the tattered banana leaves with short stiff brooms made from the ribs of a palm frond. The dustpan is a large cracker tin cut away on one end and wired to a pole.

A vendor walks by with a long pole balanced on the back of his neck and shoulders; at each end of the pole is a silver pail. "Mami . . . mami," he calls, peddling noodles. As the streets begin to drain, horse-drawn carriages gradually reappear, taxying people to the market or on some other errand long delayed. A neighbor rolls up her pantlegs and stretches an empty rice sack over her head for protection as she wades across the still-flooded banana grove. Three green coconuts, a hubcap, and a freshly drowned rat float by her along the way. She steps over the open sewer and up onto the street on her way to the corner Sari Sari store for some eggs.

I keep listening. The rain becomes light and easy. It softly taps gentle corrugated rhythms. The tapping evolves into a pinging, and I begin to detect tinny, dented melodies. They unroll themselves like banana leaves in the sun, their immense hidden beauty revealing itself without warning or effort. A little later, my wife finishes her book and asks me if I want to go to the market with her to get some milkfish for supper. I tell her I need to finish my papers. But instead I keep listening to the roof, searching for the quiet, miraculous voice of the rain.

INTERPRETATIONS

1. Does the author seem to have "acculturated" in his new home? How do you know?

2. What is the significance of the fact that both languages have a word that is spelled the same but has different meanings?

3. What do the two meanings of "banal" suggest about culture crossing, or about how to listen to a new culture?

4. Are there similarities between how to write and learning how to listen to a new culture? Explain.

CORRESPONDENCES

1. Review the Kaufman perspective on education and discuss its relevance to "The Rain Makes the Roof Sing." In what process is the teacher engaged? What does he learn from his students?

2. Montgomery-Fate and Torres address the relation between language and culture. On which issues do they agree and disagree? With whose point of view do you concur?

APPLICATIONS

1. Describe the teacher/student relationship in Montgomery-Fate's essay. To what extent is it important for students to identify with their teachers and to share common interests?

2. Discuss the Kaufman perspective with your group. Does the notion that education is a lifelong process appeal to you? Are any of the adults you know interested in learning new things? What value does this have for them? For you? Are you likely to pursue further education after graduation? Why or why not?

3. Did you grow up believing in the importance or value of education? Were there family members, teachers, or other adults who influenced your thinking? How has your education contributed to who you are and what you think you can accomplish?

4. Montgomery-Fate finds extended meaning in the sound of the rain on his roof. What natural phenomenon have you experienced that has extended your perception and created meaning? Write about this experience while paying careful attention to your senses.

The Lesson

TONI CADE BAMBARA

Toni Cade Bambara (1939–1995) grew up in New York City, deeply conscious of the inequities of race and class. She graduated from Queens College in 1959 and received her M.A. from City College of New York. Her publications include Gorilla, My Love *(1972),* The Sea Birds Are Still Alive *(1977), and* The Salt Eaters *(1980). This is how she perceived her role as a writer:*

> *Stories are important. They keep us alive. In the ships, in the camps, in the quarters, fields, prisons, on the road, on the run, underground, under siege, in the throes, on the verge—the storyteller snatches us back from the edge to hear the next chapter in which we are the subjects. We, the hero of the tales. Our lives preserved. How it was, how it be. Passing it along in the relay. That is what I work to do, to produce stories that save our lives.*

As you read "The Lesson," set in New York City, pay particular attention to Bambara's use of dialogue.

BACK IN THE DAYS when everyone was old and stupid or young and foolish and me and Sugar were the only ones just right, this lady moved on our block with nappy hair and proper speech and no makeup. And quite naturally we laughed at her, laughed the way we did at the junk man who went about his business like he was some big-time president and his sorry-ass horse his secretary. And we kinda hated her too, hated the way we did the winos who cluttered up our parks and pissed on our handball walls and stank up our hallways and stairs so you couldn't halfway play hide-and-seek without a goddamn gas mask. Miss Moore was her name. The only woman on the block with no first name. And she was black as hell, cept for her feet, which were fish-white and spooky. And she was always planning these boring-ass things for us to do, us being my cousin, mostly, who lived on the block cause we all moved North the same time and to the same apartment then spread out gradual to breathe. And our parents would yank our heads into some kinda shape and crisp up our clothes so we'd be presentable for travel with Miss Moore, who always looked like she was going to church, though she never did. Which is just one of things the

194

grownups talked about when they talked behind her back like a dog. But when she came calling with some sachet she'd sewed up or some gingerbread she'd made or some book, why then they'd all be too embarrassed to turn her down and we'd get handed over all spruced up. She'd been to college and said it was only right that she should take responsibility for the young ones' education, and she not even related by marriage or blood. So they'd go for it. Specially Aunt Gretchen. She was the main gofer in the family. You got some old dumb shit foolishness you want somebody to go for, you send for Aunt Gretchen. She been screwed into the go-along for so long, it's a blood-deep natural thing with her. Which is how she got saddled with me and Sugar and Junior in the first place while our mothers were in a la-de-da apartment up the block having a good ole time.

So this one day Miss Moore rounds us all up at the mailbox and it's puredee hot and she's knockin herself out about arithmetic. And school suppose to let up in the summer I heard, but she don't never let up. And the starch in my pinafore scratching the shit outta me and I'm really hating this nappy-head bitch and her goddamn college degree. I'd much rather go to the pool or to the show where it's cool. So me and Sugar leaning on the mailbox being surly, which is a Miss Moore word. And Flyboy checking out what everybody brought for lunch. And Fat Butt already wasting his peanut-butter-and-jelly sandwich like the pig he is. And Junebug punchin on Q. T.'s arm for potato chips. And Rosie Giraffe shifting from one hip to the other waiting for somebody to step on her foot or ask if she from Georgia so she can kick ass, preferably Mercedes'. And Miss Moore asking us do we know what money is, like we a bunch of retards. I mean real money, she say, like it's only poker chips or monopoly papers we lay on the grocer. So right away I'm tired of this and say so. And would much rather snatch Sugar and go to the Sunset and terrorize the West Indian kids and take their hair ribbons and their money too. And Miss Moore files that remark away for next week's lesson on brotherhood, I can tell. And finally I say we oughta get to the subway cause it's cooler and besides we might meet some cute boys. Sugar done swiped her mama's lipstick, so we ready.

So we heading down the street and she's boring us silly about what things cost and what our parents make and how much goes for rent and how money ain't divided up right in this country. And then she get to the part about we all poor and live in the slums, which I don't feature. And I'm ready to speak on that, but she steps out in the street and hails two cabs just like that. Then she hustles half the crew in with her and hands me a five-dollar bill and tells me to calculate 10 percent tip for the driver. And we're off. Me and Sugar and Junebug and Flyboy hanging out the window and hollering to everybody, putting lipstick on each other cause Flyboy a faggot anyway, and making farts with our sweaty armpits. But I'm mostly trying to figure how to spend this money. But they all fascinated with the meter ticking and Junebug starts laying bets as to how much it'll read when Flyboy can't hold his breath no more. Then Sugar lay bets as to how much it'll be when we get there. So I'm stuck. Don't nobody want to go for my plan, which is to jump out at the next light and run off to the first bar-b-que we can find. Then the driver tells us to get the hell out cause we there already. And the meter reads eight-five cents. And I'm stalling to figure out the tip and Sugar say give him a dime. And I decided he don't need it bad as I do, so later for him. But then he tries to take off with Junebug foot still in the door so we talk about his mama something ferocious. Then we check out that we on Fifth Avenue and everybody dressed up in stockings. One lady in a fur coat, hot as it is. White folks crazy.

"This is the place," Miss Moore say, presenting it to us in the voice she uses at the museum. "Let's look in the windows before we go in."

"Can we steal?" Sugar asks very serious like she's getting the ground rules squared away before she plays. "I beg your pardon," say Miss Moore, and we fall out. So she leads us around the windows of the toy store and me and Sugar screamin, "This is mine, that's mine, I gotta have that, that was made for me, I was born for that," till Big Butt drowns us out.

"Hey, I'm goin to buy that there."

"That there? You don't even know what it is, stupid."

"I do so," he say punchin on Rosie Giraffe. "It's a microscope."

"Whatcha gonna do with a microscope, fool?"

"Look at things."

"Like what, Ronald?" ask Miss Moore. And Big Butt ain't got the first notion. So here go Miss Moore gabbing about the thousands of bacteria in a drop of water and the somethinorother in a speck of blood and the million and one living things in the air around us is invisible to the naked eye. And what she say that for? Junebug go to town on that "naked" and we rolling. Then Miss Moore ask what it cost. So we all jam into the window smudgin it up and the price tag say $300. So then she ask how long'd take for Big Butt and Junebug to save up their allowances. "Too long," I say. "Yeh," adds Sugar, "outgrown it by that time." And Miss Moore say no, you never outgrow learning instruments. "Why, even medical students and interns and," blah, blah, blah. And we ready to choke Big Butt for bringing it up in the first damn place.

"This here costs four hundred eighty dollars," say Rosie Giraffe. So we pile up all over her to see what she pointin out. My eyes tell me it's a chunk of glass cracked with something heavy, and different-color inks dripped into the splits, then the whole thing put into a oven or something. But for $480 it don't make sense.

"That's a paperweight made of semi-precious stones fused together under tremendous pressure," she explains slowly, with her hands doing the mining and all the factory work.

"So what's a paperweight?" asks Rosie Giraffe.

"To weigh paper with, dumbbell," say Flyboy, the wise man from the East.

"Not exactly," say Miss Moore, which is what she say when you warm or way off too. "It's to weigh paper down so it won't scatter and make your desk untidy." So right away me and Sugar curtsy to each other and then to Mercedes who is more the tidy type.

"We don't keep paper on top of the desk in my class," say Junebug, figuring Miss Moore crazy or lyin one.

"At home, then," she say. "Don't you have a calendar and a pencil case and a blotter and a letter-opener on your desk at home where you do your homework?" And she know damn well what our homes look like cause she nosys around in them every chance she gets.

"I don't even have a desk," say Junebug. "Do we?"

"No. And I don't get no homework neither," says Big Butt.

"And I don't even have a home," say Flyboy like he do at school to keep the white folks off his back and sorry for him. Send this poor kid to camp posters, is his specialty.

"I do," says Mercedes. "I have a box of stationery on my desk and a picture of my cat. My godmother bought the stationery and the desk. There's a big rose on each sheet and the envelopes smell like roses."

"Who wants to know about your smelly-ass stationery," say Rosie Giraffe fore I can get my two cents in.

"It's important to have a work area all your own so that . . ."

"Will you look at this sailboat, please," say Flyboy, cuttin her off and pointin to the thing like it was his. So once again we tumble all over each other to gaze at this magnificent thing in the toy store which is just big enough to maybe sail two kittens across the pond if you strap them to the posts tight. We all start reciting the price tag like we in assembly. "Handcrafted sailboat of fiberglass at one thousand one hundred ninety-five dollars."

"Unbelievable," I hear myself say and am really stunned. I read it again for myself just in case the group recitation put me in a trance. Same thing. For some reason this pisses me off. We look at Miss Moore and she lookin at us, waiting for I dunno what.

"Who'd pay all that when you can buy a sailboat set for a quarter at Pop's, a tube of glue for a dime, and a ball of string for eight cents?

It must have a motor and a whole lot else besides," I say. "My sailboat cost me about fifty cents."

"But will it take water?" say Mercedes with her smart ass.

"Took mine to Alley Pond Park once," say Flyboy. "String broke. Lost it. Pity."

"Sailed mine in Central Park and it keeled over and sank. Had to ask my father for another dollar."

"And you got the strap," laugh Big Butt. "The jerk didn't even have a string on it. My old man wailed on his behind."

Little Q. T. was staring hard at the sailboat and you could see he wanted it bad. But he too little and somebody'd just take it from him. So what the hell. "This boat for kids, Miss Moore?"

"Parents silly to buy something like that just to get all broke up," say Rosie Giraffe.

"That much money it should last forever," I figure.

"My father'd buy it for me if I wanted it."

"Your father, my ass," say Rosie Giraffe getting a chance to finally push Mercedes.

"Must be rich people shop here," say Q. T.

"You are a very bright boy," say Flyboy. "What was your first clue?" And he rap him on the head with the back of his knuckles, since Q. T. the only one he could get away with. Though Q. T. liable to come up behind you years later and get his licks in when you half expect it.

"What I want to know is," I says to Miss Moore though I never talk to her, I wouldn't give the bitch that satisfaction, "is how much a real boat costs? I figure a thousand'd get you a yacht any day?"

"Why don't you check that out," she says, "and report back to the group?" Which really pains my ass. If you gonna mess up a perfectly good swim day least you could do is have some answers. "Let's go in," she say like she got something up her sleeve. Only she don't lead the way. So me and Sugar turn the corner to where the entrance is, but when we get there I kinda hang back. Not that I'm scared, what's there to be afraid of, just a toy store. But I feel funny, shame. But what I got to be shamed about? Got as much right to go in as anybody. But somehow I can't seem to get hold of the door, so I step away for Sugar to lead. But she hangs back too. And I look at her and she looks at me and this is ridiculous. I mean, damn, I have never ever been shy about doing nothing or going nowhere. But then Mercedes steps up and then Rosie Giraffe and Big Butt crowd in behind and shove, and next thing we all stuffed into the doorway with only Mercedes squeezing past us, smoothing out her jumper and walking right down the aisle. Then the rest of us tumble in like a glued-together jigsaw done all wrong. And people lookin at us. And it's like the time me and Sugar crashed into the

Catholic church on a dare. But once we got in there and everything so hushed and holy and the candles and the bowin and the handkerchiefs on all the drooping heads, I just couldn't go through with the plan. Which was for me to run up to the altar and do a tap dance while Sugar played the nose flute and messed around in the holy waters. And Sugar kept givin me the elbow. Then later teased me so bad I tied her up in the shower and turned it on and locked her in. And she'd be there till this day if Aunt Gretchen hadn't finally figured I was lyin about the boarder takin a shower.

Same thing in the store. We all walkin on tiptoe and hardly touchin the games and puzzles and things. And I watched Miss Moore who is steady watchin us like she waiting for a sign. Like Mama Drewery watches the sky and sniffs the air and takes note of just how much slant is in the bird formation. Then me and Sugar bump smack into each other, so busy gazing at the toys, 'specially the sailboat. But we don't laugh and go into our fat-lady bump-stomach routine. We just stare at that price tag. Then Sugar run a finger over the whole boat. And I'm jealous and want to hit her. Maybe not her, but I sure want to punch somebody in the mouth.

"Watcha bring us here for, Miss Moore?"

"You sound angry, Sylvia. Are you mad about something?" Givin me one of them grins like she tellin a grown-up joke that never turns out to be funny. And she's lookin very closely at me like maybe she plannin to do my portrait from memory. I'm mad, but I won't give her that satisfaction. So I slouch around the store bein very bored and say, "Let's go."

Me and Sugar at the back of the train watchin the tracks whizzin by large then small then gettin gobbled up in the dark. I'm thinkin about this tricky toy I saw in the store. A clown that somersaults on a bar then does chin-ups just cause you yank lightly at his leg. Cost $35. I could see me askin my mother for a $35 birthday clown. "You wanna who that costs what?" she'd say, cocking her head to the side to get a better view of the hole in my head. Thirty-five dollars and the whole household could go visit Grandaddy Nelson in the country. Thirty-five dollars would pay for the rent and the piano bill too. Who are these people that spend that much for performing clowns and $1000 for toy sailboats? What kinda work they do and how they live and how come we ain't in on it? Where we are is who we are, Miss Moore always pointin out. But it don't necessarily have to be that way, she always adds then waits for somebody to say that poor people have to wake up and demand their share of the pie and don't none of us know what kind of pie she talkin about in the first damn place. But she ain't so smart cause I still got her four dollars from the taxi and she sure ain't gettin it.

Messin up my day with this shit. Sugar nudges me in my pocket and winks.

Miss Moore lines us up in front of the mailbox where we started from, seem like years ago, and I got a headache for thinkin so hard. And we lean all over each other so we can hold up under the draggy-ass lecture she always finishes us off with at the end before we thank her for borin us to tears. But she just looks at us like she readin tea leaves. Finally she say, "Well, what did you think of F. A. O. Schwartz?"

Rosie Giraffe mumbles, "White folks crazy."

"I'd like to go there again when I get my birthday money," says Mercedes, and we shove her out the pack so she has to lean on the mailbox by herself.

"I'd like a shower. Tiring day," say Flyboy.

Then Sugar surprises me by saying, "You know, Miss Moore, I don't think all of us here put together eat in a year what that sailboat costs." And Miss Moore lights up like somebody goosed her. "And?" she say, urging Sugar on. Only I'm standin on her foot so she don't continue.

"Imagine for a minute what kind of society it is in which some people can spend on a toy what it would cost to feed a family of six or seven. What do you think?"

"I think," say Sugar pushing me off her feet like she never done before, cause I whip her ass in a minute, "that this is not much of a democracy if you ask me. Equal chance to pursue happiness means an equal crack at the dough, don't it?" Miss Moore is besides herself and I am disgusted with Sugar's treachery. So I stand on her foot one more time to see if she'll shove me. She shuts up, and Miss Moore looks at me, sorrowfully I'm thinkin. And somethin weird is goin on. I can feel it in my chest.

"Anybody else learn anything today?" lookin dead at me. I walk away and Sugar has to run to catch up and don't even seem to notice when I shrug her arm off my shoulder.

"Well, we got four dollars anyway," she says.

"Uh hunh."

"We could go to Hascombs and get half a chocolate layer and then to the Sunset and still have plenty of money for potato chips and ice cream sodas."

"Uh hunh."

"Race you to Hascombs," she say.

We start down the block and she gets ahead which is O.K. by me cause I'm goin to the West End and then over the Drive to think this day through. She can run if she want to and even run faster. But ain't nobody gonna beat me at nuthin.

INTERPRETATIONS

1. What does Miss Moore hope to accomplish during the class outing? What lesson does she want to teach? Do you agree that the lesson needs teaching? Why? Has Miss Moore chosen an effective method of teaching?

2. What evidence is there that this outing is only the latest in a series of attempts to teach a lesson and that the children already know what they are expected to "learn"? How does that repetition affect your reaction to Sylvia's irritation at Sugar's "treachery" in saying what Sugar believes to be the lesson: "Equal chance to pursue happiness means an equal crack at the dough, don't it?" Has Sylvia failed to understand the lesson or is she irritated at the repetition?

3. Although Sylvia says "I'm mad," she will not admit her anger to Miss Moore. Why not? Does Sylvia know what has made her angry? Do we know?

4. Why do you think Miss Moore never demands change due her from the narrator?

5. What do you consider the more important element of this story, the lesson itself or the personalities and/or attitudes of the three or four main characters? Why?

CORRESPONDENCES

1. Review the Frost perspective on education (page 157) and discuss its relevance to "The Lesson."

2. "White folks crazy" appears twice in "The Lesson." What situations give rise to this conclusion? What emotions are the children expressing through these words? What is the significance of Sylvia's resolve that "ain't nobody gonna beat me at nothin"? How is Sylvia's attitude toward white people similar to or different from that of Baldwin?

APPLICATIONS

1. Write an essay about an adult who has had a positive or negative influence on your education. Include in your portrayal an experience that clearly illustrates that influence.

2. According to fiction writer Grace Paley, "If you say what's on your mind in the language that comes to you from your parents and

your street and friends you'll probably say something beautiful."
Write an essay showing the extent to which "The Lesson" supports Paley's point of view.

3.   According to Miss Moore, "where we are is who we are." To what
extent do you agree? Do you consider yourself the product of your
social class? What other factors have contributed to who you are?

4.   When you are with your friends, listen carefully to their conversation. Pay attention to the words they use and the rhythms of their
sentences. What kind of vocabulary is used? How does the conversation flow? Does one person always wait for another to cease
speaking? Do your friends stick to one topic? If possible, take notes
of what is being said and how it is being said. Next, take your notes
and memories and use them to create a dialogue between two characters that you have invented. How does the conversation that you
have created compare with the dialogue presented in Bambara's
story?

The Mistress of Make Believe

DORIS VILORIA

Doris Viloria (b. 1972) was brought up and educated in Queens, New York, and is a graduate of Queens College–City University of New York (CUNY). As you read Viloria's essay, find evidence to support her introductory paragraph.

SHE WAS HUGE, but in a majestic awe-inspiring way like a mountain that only added to her enigma. The word fat never came to mind.

"Good morning class," she'd briskly salute each day, as she marched in on stiletto heels. Her hair would be piled high on her head, in a fountain of honey blond and gray tendrils that was most undoubtedly dyed. The heady scent of lilacs drenched the room as she entered; a tornado of fragrances, heavy make-up, and shopping bags, her gaudy jewelry sending out smart metallic clinks. She always squeezed herself into tight "form fitting" cashmere turtlenecks, which emphasized her rather copious stomach and voluptuous bosom and created the illusion of a kind of fanciful, woman-caterpillar hybrid. Then shifting her bulk considerably, she would sit atop her tall, rickety wooden swivel chair, crossing her legs jauntily, and bringing one polished long red fingernail to her lips. As her meaty arms settled on her lectern, one perfectly tweezed eyebrow languidly drifted up like a cobra, contemplating the class.

"Aaah," she'd purr in her thick coppery, baritone New England accent, as she towered over us, her mouth curling up in a sly grin. "How many of you are ready to let your imagination take you off to distant mystical lands?"

Together we explored the unbridled savagery of William Golding's *The Lord of the Flies*, the silent yearnings and personal betrayals of John Knowles' *A Separate Peace*, and the coming of age in the heart of injustice of a young girl in Harper Lee's *To Kill a Mockingbird*. Golding's desolate, desperate island sprang to life as she needled us with questions.

"Is man simply a beast temporarily tamed by years of affecting proper etiquette, whose mask might drop if taken out of his 'civilized' environment?" she'd fire at us. "How would any of you react if placed in a jungle where your actions were accountable to no one? Would you aspire to rule as a belligerent dictator, or would you struggle to maintain your moralistic humanity and preserve democracy?"

Having thus spat out these challenges she would take a long draught of steaming black coffee from her styrofoam cup, leaving a sharp stain of fuschia lipstick on the rim. Then in a smokey, hypnotic tone she would read a passage from the book. The mood became trancelike as we followed her into the story. Afterwards, those characters would linger about the room like inspirational phantoms as I slaved over my writing assignment.

Creating solely on pure instinct and guided by the illuminations of those benevolent daimons, I wrote a short story based on a gripping terrifying nightmare I'd had. It was as though I had exorcised all the horrors of my dream from myself, and they had metamorphosized into a story that had a life of its own. With a feeling of deep-seated pride and accomplishment, I turned it in.

Walking out of class one day, I heard that unmistakable voice ask for a moment of my time. I was brimming with curiosity as I approached her desk. Those penetrating blue eyes gazed at me with a mixture of respect and mischief. Tapping my story gently on her desk, she inclined that lion's mane of a head to the side and whispered in a close and confidential way, "Where did it come from?"

My eyes darted about the room as I searched for some response. Finally, I turned to her levelly and said honestly, "It just sort of wove itself."

Nodding her head in understanding after what seemed like an hour, she handed me the paper. "It really is very special," she said with a sigh. "You have a way with words that is a talent, a gift. I expect you to be a woman of great individual distinction."

Those words have bolstered me like iron saviors through countless fits of self-doubt and introspection over the past few years. I walked out of the room that day with charmed visions of exquisitely soaring dragonflies before me. The spell has never waned.

INTERPRETATIONS

1. What scene and what group of people do you assume the author to be describing? How effective is that description? What purpose does the description seem intended to serve?

2. How do you interpret the question "Where did it [the story] come from?" How important to the meaning of the essay is this question?

3. How would this essay be affected if the story itself were included or appended here?

4. The last paragraph is perhaps the most important in terms of the meaning of the essay. Comment on the effectiveness of saving this information until the end.

CORRESPONDENCES

1. Review Moore's perspective (page 158). How does it apply to Viloria's educational experience? How many "enchanting" minds are there in her essay?

2. Review Borges's perspective on books (page 158). To what extent does it apply to Viloria's essay? To your own experiences with reading?

APPLICATIONS

1. Viloria is excited by using language effectively. You may be creative in another medium, such as photography, music, art, or dance. Write an essay describing your creative process and the emotions it evokes.

2. Write a journal entry describing the teacher from whom you learned most. Recreate the classroom environment. How was it conducive to learning? Describe a learning activity that excited you.

3. Write a journal entry comparing and contrasting an experience with reading or writing that took place outside of the classroom. How was it different from reading or writing in school?

4. Notice Viloria's use of details in this essay. From her description, create a drawing of "The Mistress of Make Believe." Which details in the text have you focused upon in your artwork?

Learning To Teach

ISABEL L. PIPOLO

Since writing this essay in 1991, Isabel Pipolo graduated from Cornell Univer-
sity with a B.A. in English. She continues to do volunteer work with two non-
profit organizations in New York City, and she plans to get a masters degree in
social work. Pipolo also does freelance computer graphics and web design.

STUYVESANT HIGH SCHOOL IS RENOWNED as being a math and science high
school, but after practically living there for four years, I can honestly
say that I received the most well-rounded liberal arts education one
could ever hope for. This wasn't only because of the kinds of courses
available, but also because of the opportunity to connect one's learning
to the life of the city around us.

In my junior year, for instance, I worked in a psychology internship
program teaching poor grammar-school children from the neighborhood to read and write. In this program, a group of Stuyvesant students
would go to a nearby grammar school and sit with individual children,
helping them with reading and math for two hours each day. At the
start of the program I was ecstatic. It seemed like a wonderful opportunity not only to learn more about children and teaching, but also to
really make a difference in someone's life. These adorable eight-year-
olds seemed to cry out for our attention. They needed us; they wanted
role models and we wanted to fulfill their ideals.

My child's name was Tamika. She was an affectionate black girl
who lived with her grandmother and younger sister in one of the worst
inner city neighborhoods in New York. Tamika and her sister (who was
six) walked to and from school through a neighborhood that I would
refuse to walk through alone at three o'clock in the afternoon.

From the little I could gather about Tamika's home life, her mother
had disappeared suddenly when she was very young; she never even
mentioned a father. I never met her grandmother, but sometimes I sus-
pected that Tamika was mistreated at home because she occasionally
came to school with bruises on her face and arms, which she refused to
discuss. One day her sister was absent and when I asked her teacher
about it, she became flustered and told me not to ask. Tamika told me
that she wasn't allowed to tell me the reason. Since it really upset her,

I didn't pursue the topic, but the incident only increased my suspicion that Tamika's grandmother was not the ideal parent.

I wanted to make an impact on this girl's life—to be her foster mother, to love her and take care of her. I wanted to open her eyes to the world of education and learning and make a lasting impression on her mind. I wanted to be able to change the course of her life just by caring for her for a few months.

Of course, these wishes were unrealistic. One person could not possibly make that much of a change in a mere fifteen weeks. Tamika was friendly and loving and seemed to enjoy being with me. She wrote little notes and drew pictures for me and always seemed happy to see me. Nevertheless, she continued to be the same hyperactive, restless girl that she was at the beginning. She was easily distracted and often if I insisted that we do her schoolwork, she would burst into tears or run screaming from the room. She had no interest in reading or math or in anything having to do with school. Eight years of bad habits could not be corrected in a few weeks, especially not by someone with minimal training in child psychology.

I soon realized that I really could not single-handedly make a big difference in Tamika's life simply by being a big sister for four and a half months, and that any such hopes that such an internship program could work that quickly were idealistic. Simply because a group of super-smart, well-intentioned Stuyvesant students set their minds to the task, there was no guarantee that it could happen.

Tamika came to symbolize something in the society that I had trouble dealing with. Her problem, multiplied by the hundreds of thousands of students in the public school system, became overwhelming. These feelings were so strong that sometimes when in her neighborhood, I found myself wishing to be back in my safe, suburban, middle-class American home, where life was simple and easy. I was frustrated and confused, but also disappointed and bitter because if we—i.e., Stuyvesant students—were supposedly the "cream of the crop," as our principal so loved to call us, and we couldn't make a difference, then who could?

My experience with Tamika helped me to realize that changing the world would take a lot more than I had bargained for. For a program of this kind to succeed, more people need to devote more time and energy to it. Trying to correct eight years of ineffective education and inadequate parenting requires a commitment by society in general, not just a few enthusiastic teenagers enrolled in a psychology elective in a local high school. Reading and math are certainly important to every child's education, but it is difficult, if not impossible, to teach these when the child does not have a basic sense of security and self-confidence. It is even more important, therefore, to teach children to care about themselves, for it is this that will give them the confidence they need to learn other skills, to succeed, and to have a happy life.

INTERPRETATIONS

1. Pipolo comes to feel that the problem "requires a commitment by society in general." Does that mean that there is nothing individuals can do, acting alone, to help people like Tamika?

2. What portrait of Tamika emerges in the essay? Why might it be difficult for her to concentrate in school?

3. What does Pipolo learn from her experience? Does she inspire you to become a mentor? Why or why not?

CORRESPONDENCES

1. How does point of view affect the meaning and tone in the essays of Viloria and Pipolo?

2. What conversation on mentoring can you imagine Pipolo and Torres having? What advice might he offer regarding Tamika's situation?

APPLICATIONS

1. Do the children of poor, uneducated parents have a right to a good education? If so, whose responsibility is it to provide that education? Did your group reach a consensus? Write an analysis of your discussion.

2. "Reading and math are certainly important to every child's education, but it is difficult, if not impossible, to teach these when the child does not have a basic sense of security and self-confidence." What role can you imagine playing in creating a situation in which Tamika would gain "a sense of security and self-confidence"?

3. Discuss with your group an educational experience that occurred outside of school. What did you learn from it? From the experience of group members?

Literacy Narratives

The literacy narratives of Paule Marshall and Vincent Cremona involve metaphor—a figure of speech that makes an implicit comparison between two dissimilar things. Metaphor is complex, inventive, subtle, and powerful. It can transform people, places, objects, and ideas into whatever the writer imagines them to be. Successful metaphors make it possible for us as readers to "see" things in new ways. What is your response, for example, to the metaphor that "the heart is a lonely hunter"? In Paule Marshall's narrative, her poets inform us that "the sea ain' got no back door," while Vincent Cremona transforms a familiar metaphor from the workplace into one that describes his writing style. As you read their narratives, think of a metaphor that you might use to describe your writing.

from Poets in the Kitchen

PAULE MARSHALL

Paule Marshall (b. 1929) was born into a close-knit West Indian community in Brooklyn, New York. She graduated from Brooklyn College in 1953, and was a librarian before working for Our World, *a popular 1950s African-American magazine. In 1959, Marshall's first novel* Brown Girl, Brownstones *was published; in 1960 she received a Guggenheim Fellowship. Marshall's other novels include* Soul Clap Hands and Sing *(1961),* The Chosen Place, The Timeless People *(1969),* Praisesong for the Widow *(1983), and* Daughters *(1991). Her most recent novel,* The Fisher King, *was published in 2001.*

The history of Barbados, the most easterly of the West Indies, begins with the arrival of an English ship in 1605 and with British settlers at the uninhabited island in 1627. Slavery was abolished in 1834. The island, eighty percent of whose population of 256,000 is of African descent, declared its independence from Britain in 1966 but remains within the Commonwealth.

SOME YEARS AGO, when I was teaching a graduate seminar in fiction at Columbia University, a well-known male novelist visited my class to speak on his development as a writer. In discussing his formative years, he didn't realize it but he seriously endangered his life by remarking that women writers are luckier than those of his sex because they usually spend so much time as children around their mothers and their mothers' friends in the kitchen.

What did he say that for? The women students immediately forgot about being in awe of him and began readying their attack for the question and answer period later on. Even I bristled. There again was that awful image of women locked away from the world in the kitchen with only each other to talk to, and their daughters locked in with them.

But my guest wasn't really being sexist or trying to be provocative or even spoiling for a fight. What he meant—when he got around to examining himself more fully—was that, given the way children are (or were) raised in our society, with little girls kept closer to home and their mothers, the women writer stands a better chance of being exposed, while growing up, to the kind of talk that goes on among women, more often than not in the kitchen; and that this experience gives her an edge over her male counterpart by instilling in her an appreciation for ordinary speech.

It was clear that my guest lecturer attached great importance to this, which is understandable. Common speech and the plain, workaday words that make it up are, after all, the stock in trade of some of the best fiction writers. They are the principal means by which a character in a novel or story reveals himself and gives voice sometimes to profound feelings and complex ideas about himself and the world. Perhaps the proper measure of a writer's talent is his skill in rendering everyday speech—when it is appropriate to his story—as well as his ability to tap, to exploit, the beauty, poetry and wisdom it often contains.

"If you say what's on your mind in the language that comes to you from your parents and your street and friends you'll probably say something beautiful." Grace Paley[1] tells this, she says, to her students at the beginning of every writing course.

It's all a matter of exposure and a training of the ear for the would-be writer in those early years of his or her apprenticeship. And, according to my guest lecturer, this training, the best of it, often takes place in as unglamorous a setting as the kitchen.

He didn't know it, but he was essentially describing my experience as a little girl. I grew up among poets. Now they didn't look like poets—whatever that breed is supposed to look like. Nothing about them suggested that poetry was their calling. They were just a group of ordinary housewives and mothers, my mother included, who dressed in a way (shapeless housedresses, dowdy felt hats and long, dark, solemn coats) that made it impossible for me to imagine they had ever been young.

Nor did they do what poets were supposed to do—spend their days in an attic room writing verses. They never put pen to paper except to write occasionally to their relatives in Barbados. "I take my pen in hand hoping these few lines will find you in health as they leave me fair for the time being," was the way their letters invariably began. Rather, their day was spent "scrubbing floor," as they described the work they did.

Several mornings a week these unknown bards would put an apron and a pair of old house shoes in a shopping bag and take the train or streetcar from our section of Brooklyn out to Flatbush. There, those who didn't have steady jobs would wait on certain designated corners for the white housewives in the neighborhood to come along and bargain with them over pay for a day's work cleaning their houses. This was the ritual even in the winter.

Later, armed with the few dollars they had earned, which in their vocabulary became "a few raw-mouth pennies," they made their way

---

[1] Contemporary American fiction writer.

back to our neighborhood, where they would sometimes stop off to have a cup of tea or cocoa together before going home to cook dinner for their husbands and children.

The basement kitchen of the brownstone house where my family lived was the usual gathering place. Once inside the warm safety of its walls the women threw off the drab coats and hats, seated themselves at the large center table, drank their cups of tea or cocoa, and talked. While my sister and I sat at a smaller table over in a corner doing our homework, they talked—endlessly, passionately, poetically, and with impressive range. No subject was beyond them. True, they would indulge in the usual gossip: whose husband was running with whom, whose daughter looked slightly "in the way" (pregnant) under her bridal gown as she walked down the aisle. That sort of thing. But they also tackled the great issues of the time. They were always, for example, discussing the state of the economy. It was the mid and late 30s then, and the aftershock of the Depression, with its soup lines and suicides on Wall Street, was still being felt.

Some people, they declared, didn't know how to deal with adversity. They didn't know that you had to "tie up your belly" (hold in the pain, that is) when things got rough and go on with life. They took their image from the bellyband that is tied around the stomach of a newborn baby to keep the navel pressed in.

They talked politics. Roosevelt was their hero. He had come along and rescued the country with relief and jobs, and in gratitude they christened their sons Franklin and Delano and hoped they would live up to the names.

If F. D. R. was their hero, Marcus Garvey was their God. The name of the fiery, Jamaican-born black nationalist of the '20s was constantly invoked around the table. For he had been their leader when they first came to the United States from the West Indies shortly after World War I. They had contributed to his organization, the United Negro Improvement Association (UNIA), out of their meager salaries, bought shares in his ill-fated Black Star Shipping Line, and at the height of the movement they had marched as members of his "nurses' brigade" in their white uniforms on Seventh Avenue in Harlem during the great Garvey Day parades. Garvey: He lived on through the power of their memories.

And their talk was of war and rumors of wars. They raged against World War II when it broke out in Europe, blaming it on the politicians. "It's these politicians. They're the ones always starting up all this lot of war. But what they care? It's the poor people got to suffer and mothers with their sons." If it was *their* sons, they swore they would keep them out of the Army by giving them soap to eat each day to make their hearts sound defective. Hitler? He was for them "the devil incarnate."

Then there was home. They reminisced often and at length about home. The old country, Barbados—or Bimshire, as they affectionately called it. The little Caribbean island in the sun they loved but had to leave. "Poor—poor but sweet" was the way they remembered it.

And naturally they discussed their adopted home. America came in for both good and bad marks. They lashed out at it for the racism they encountered. They took to task some of the people they worked for, especially those who gave them only a hard-boiled egg and a few spoonfuls of cottage cheese for lunch. "As if anybody can scrub floor on an egg and some cheese that don't have no taste to it!"

Yet although they caught H in "this man country," as they called America, it was nonetheless a place where "you could at least see your way to make a dollar." That much they acknowledged. They might even one day accumulate enough dollars, with both them and their husbands working, to buy the brownstone houses which, like my family, they were only leasing at that period. This was their consuming ambition: to "buy house" and to see the children through.

There was no way for me to understand it at the time, but the talk that filled the kitchen those afternoons was highly functional. It served as therapy, the cheapest kind available to my mother and her friends. Not only did it help them recover from the long wait on the corner that morning and the bargaining over their labor, it restored them to a sense of themselves and reaffirmed their self-worth. Through language they were able to overcome the humiliations of the work-day.

But more than therapy, that freewheeling, wide-ranging, exuberant talk functioned as an outlet for the tremendous creative energy they possessed. They were women in whom the need for self-expression was strong, and since language was the only vehicle readily available to them they made of it an art form that—in keeping with the African tradition in which art and life are one—was an integral part of their lives.

And their talk was a refuge. They never really ceased being baffled and overwhelmed by America—its vastness, complexity and power. Its strange customs and laws. At a level beyond words they remained fearful and in awe. Their uneasiness and fear were even reflected in their attitude toward the children they had given birth to in this country. They referred to those like myself, the little Brooklyn-born Bajans (Barbadians), as "these New York children" and complained that they couldn't discipline us properly because of the laws here. "You can't beat these children as you would like, you know, because the authorities in this place will dash you in jail for them. After all, these is New York children." Not only were we different, American, we had, as they saw it, escaped their ultimate authority.

Confronted therefore by a world they could not encompass, which even limited their rights as parents, and at the same time finding themselves permanently separated from the world they had known, they took refuge in language. "Language is the only homeland," Czeslaw Milosz, the emigré Polish writer and Nobel Laureate, has said. This is what it became for the women at the kitchen table.

It served another purpose also, I suspect. My mother and her friends were after all the female counterpart of Ralph Ellison's invisible man.[2] Indeed, you might say they suffered a triple invisibility, being black, female and foreigners. They really didn't count in American society except as a source of cheap labor. But given the kind of women they were, they couldn't tolerate the fact of their invisibility, their powerlessness. And they fought back, using the only weapon at their command: the spoken word.

Those late afternoon conversations on a wide range of topics were a way for them to feel they exercised some measure of control over their lives and the events that shaped them. "Soully-gal, talk yuh talk!" they were always exhorting each other. "In this man world you got to take yuh mouth and make a gun!" They were in control, if only verbally and if only for the two hours or so that they remained in our house.

For me, sitting over in the corner, being seen but not heard, which was the rule for children in those days, it wasn't only what the women talked about—the content—but the way they put things—their style. The insight, irony, wit, and humor they brought to their stories and discussions and their poet's inventiveness and daring with language— which of course I could only sense but not define back then.

They had taken the standard English taught them in the primary schools of Barbados and transformed it into an idiom, an instrument that more adequately described them—changing around the syntax and imposing their own rhythm and accent so that the sentences were more pleasing to their ears. They added the few African sounds and words that had survived, such as the derisive suck-teeth sound and the word "yam," meaning to eat. And to make it more vivid, more in keeping with their expressive quality, they brought to bear a raft of metaphors, parables, Biblical quotations, sayings and the like:

"The sea ain' got no back door," they would say, meaning that it wasn't like a house where if there was a fire you could run out the back. Meaning that it was not to be trifled with. And meaning perhaps in a larger sense that man should treat all of nature with caution and respect.

---

[2]Title of novel published in 1947 that has become the seminal metaphor for African-Americans.

"I has read hell by heart and called every generation blessed!" They sometimes went in for hyperbole.

A woman expecting a baby was never said to be pregnant. They never used that word. Rather, she was "in the way" or, better yet, "tumbling big." "Guess who I butt up on in the market the other day tumbling big again!"

And a woman with a reputation of being too free with her sexual favors was known in their book as a "thoroughfare"—the sense of men like a steady stream of cars moving up and down the road of her life. Or she might be dubbed "a free-bee," which was my favorite of the two. I liked the image it conjured up of a woman scandalous perhaps but independent, who flitted from one flower to another in a garden of male beauties, sampling their nectar, taking her pleasure at will, the roles reversed.

And nothing, no matter how beautiful, was ever described as simply beautiful. It was always "beautiful-ugly": the beautiful-ugly dress, the beautiful-ugly house, the beautiful-ugly car. Why the word "ugly," I used to wonder, when the thing they were referring to was beautiful, and they knew it. Why the antonym, the contradiction, the linking of opposites? It used to puzzle me greatly as a child.

There is the theory in linguistics which states that the idiom of a people, the way they use language, reflects not only the most fundamental views they hold of themselves and the world but their very conception of reality. Perhaps in using the term "beautiful-ugly" to describe nearly everything, my mother and her friends were expressing what they believed to be a fundamental dualism in life: the idea that a thing is at the same time its opposite, and that these opposites, these contradictions make up the whole. But theirs was not a Manichaean brand of dualism[3] that sees matter, flesh, the body, as inherently evil, because they constantly addressed each other as "soully-gal"—soul: spirit; gal: the body, flesh, the visible self. And it was clear from their tone that they gave one as much weight and importance as the other. They had never heard of the mind/body split.

As for God, they summed up His essential attitude in a phrase, "God," they would say, "don' love ugly and He ain' stuck on pretty."

Using everyday speech, the simple commonplace words—but always with imagination and skill—they gave voice to the most complex ideas. Flannery O'Connor[4] would have approved of how they made

---

[3]Religious sect founded in 276 A.D. in Persia, which teaches the release of the spirit from matter through asceticism.
[4]American writer (1925–1964).

ordinary language work, as she put it, "double-time," stretching, shading, deepening its meaning. Like Joseph Conrad[5] they were always trying to infuse new life in the "old old words worn thin . . . by . . . careless usage." And the goals of their oral art were the same as his: "to make you hear, to make you feel . . . to make you *see*." This was their guiding esthetic.

By the time I was eight or nine, I graduated from the corner of the kitchen to the neighborhood library, and thus from the spoken to the written word. The Macon Street Branch of the Brooklyn Public Library was an imposing half block long edifice of heavy gray masonry, with glass-paneled doors at the front and two tall metal torches symbolizing the light that comes of learning flanking the wide steps outside.

The inside was just as impressive. More steps—of pale marble with gleaming brass railings at the center and sides—led up to the circulation desk, and a great pendulum clock gazed down from the balcony stacks that faced the entrance. Usually stationed at the top of the steps like the guards outside Buckingham Palace was the custodian, a stern-faced West Indian type who for years, until I was old enough to obtain an adult card, would immediately shoo me with one hand into the Children's Room and with the other threaten me into silence, a finger to his lips. You would have thought he was the chief librarian and not just someone whose job it was to keep the brass polished and the clock wound. I put him in a story called "Barbados" years later and had terrible things happen to him at the end.

I was sheltered from the storm of adolescence in the Macon Street library, reading voraciously, indiscriminately, everything from Jane Austen to Zane Grey, but with a special passion for the long, full-blown, richly detailed eighteenth- and nineteenth-century picaresque tales: *Tom Jones, Great Expectations, Vanity Fair*.

But although I loved nearly everything I read and would enter fully into the lives of the characters—indeed, would cease being myself and become them—I sensed a lack after a time. Something I couldn't quite define was missing. And then one day, browsing in the poetry section, I came across a book by someone called Paul Laurence Dunbar, and opening it I found the photograph of a wistful, sad-eyed poet who to my surprise was black. I turned to a poem at random. "Little brown-baby wif spa'klin'/eyes/Come to yo' pappy an' set on his knee." Although I had a little difficulty at first with the words in dialect, the poem spoke to me as nothing I had read before of the closeness, the special relationship I had had with my father, who by then had become an ardent believer in Father Divine and gone to live in Father's "kingdom" in Harlem. Reading it

---

[5]British fiction writer (1857–1924).

helped to ease somewhat the tight knot of sorrow and longing I carried around in my chest that refused to go away. I read another poem, "Lias! Lias! Bless de Lawd!/Don' you know de day's/erbroad?/Ef you don' get up, you scamp/Dey'll be trouble in dis camp." I laughed. It reminded me of the way my mother sometimes yelled at my sister and me to get out of bed in the mornings.

And another: "Seen my lady home las' night/Jump back, honey, jump back./Hel'/huh han'/an'/sque'z it tight . . ." About love between a black man and a black woman. I had never seen that written about before and it roused in me all kinds of delicious feelings and hopes.

And I began to search then for books and stories and poems about "The Race" (as it was put back then), about my people. While not abandoning Thackeray, Fielding, Dickens and the others, I started asking the reference librarian, who was white, for books by Negro writers, although I must admit I did so at first with a feeling of shame—the shame I and many others used to experience in those days whenever the word "Negro" or "colored" came up.

No grade school literature teacher of mine had ever mentioned Dunbar or James Weldon Johnson or Langston Hughes.[6] I didn't know that Zora Neale Hurston[7] existed and was busy writing and being published during those years. Nor was I made aware of people like Frederick Douglass and Harriet Tubman[8]—their spirit and example—or the great 19th-century abolitionist and feminist Sojourner Truth. There wasn't even Negro History Week when I attended P.S. 35 on Decatur Street!

What I needed, what all the kids—West Indian and native black American alike—with whom I grew up needed, was an equivalent of the Jewish shul, someplace where we could go after school—the schools that were shortchanging us—and read works by those like ourselves and learn about our history.

It was around that time also that I began harboring the dangerous thought of someday trying to write myself. Perhaps a poem about an apple tree, although I had never seen one. Or the story of a girl who could magically transplant herself to wherever she wanted to be in the world—such as Father Divine's kingdom in Harlem. Dunbar—his dark, eloquent face, his large volume of poems—permitted me to dream that I might someday write, and with something of the power with words my mother and her friends possessed.

---

[6]Paul Laurence Dunbar (1870–1906), James Weldon Johnson (1871–1938), Langston Hughes (1902–1967)—African-American poets of the Harlem Renaissance.
[7]African-American novelist (1901–1961).
[8]Frederick Douglass (1817–1895), Harriet Tubman (1820–1913)—African-American abolitionists.

When people at readings and writers' conferences ask me who my major influences were, they are sometimes a little disappointed when I don't immediately name the usual literary giants. True, I am indebted to those writers, white and black, whom I read during my formative years and still read for instruction and pleasure. But they were preceded in my life by another set of giants whom I always acknowledge before all others: the group of women around the table long ago. They taught me my first lesson in the narrative art. They trained my ear. They set a standard of excellence. This is why the best of my work must be attributed to them; it stands as testimony to the rich legacy of language and culture they so freely passed on to me in the wordshop of the kitchen.

INTERPRETATIONS

1. Were the "poets in the kitchen" as interesting on paper as in their conversations? What does Marshall think their orality revealed about them? Cite two or three examples.

2. Marshall's "unknown bards" use language to combat their powerlessness in a culture in which they experienced the "triple invisibility of being black, female and foreigners." Which expressions best reflect this?

APPLICATIONS

1. In what contexts do Marshall's poets view language as a refuge? How do you respond to this concept?

2. What kind of literacy is Marshall writing about when she speaks of her early upbringing? What must a participant in kitchen conversation be aware of? What other kinds of literacy might be invoked by "these unknown bards"?

3. Later on in her life, Marshall comes to understand and value another kind of literacy that she has discovered in the "Macon Street Branch of the Brooklyn Public Library." What kind of literacy is this? How is it related to the kinds of literacies that she has described earlier?

4. "It was around that time also that I began harboring the dangerous thought of someday trying to write myself." Why does Marshall use the word "dangerous"? How does her consideration of becoming a writer affect her perceptions of literacy? What happens to your sense of literacy when you engage upon a writing task?

My Pen Writes in Blue and White

VINCENT CREMONA

Vincent Cremona grew up in a middle-class neighborhood on Long Island, New York. He is currently working full-time while pursuing his education in the evening at Queensborough Community College, CUNY.

SOME PEOPLE SAY THAT THEY SEE THINGS in black and white. I tend to view things a little bit differently. I like to say that I see things in blue and white. Certain things that I will see, or hear, or read, and I will say, "This is blue." Other times I will come to the conclusion, "That is white." Sometimes I can even view things as blue and white at the same time. I have been taught, though unintentionally, to view things in this manner since I first learned to read and write.

The manner in which I now write, and communicate for that matter, has been directly affected by the two major influences in my life, my parents. Even though my parents communicate in two completely different ways, I have borrowed from both of them. I am reminded of the words of Richard Rodriguez when he lamented, "I now speak in the chromium accents of my grammar school classmates . . ." I, myself, have taken the plain, frank, honest words of my father and joined them with the proper and formal words of my mother to form the dialect that I now speak. This combination has given me the ability to communicate in many different ways.

When I say that I see things as blue, I mean that I view them as basic, bold, and workman-like. I see things from a blue-collar point of view. I have learned to view things in this manner from my father. A truck driver by trade, my father was a card-carrying member of the International Brotherhood of Teamsters, Local 851. My father was cut in the Jimmy Hoffa mold, in that Jimmy Hoffa believed that most Americans are basically hard working individuals, who have respect for one another, as they face the trials and tribulations of providing a good home life for their families. As a union man, there is a lot of pride and patriotism in his words. He would say things like, "A day's work for a day's pay." It was said by Barbara Brandt that, "For many Americans today, paid work is not just a way to make money but is a crucial source of their self-worth." These words could easily be used to describe my father's attitude towards work. Work was a way of life for my father.

The most interesting thing to me was not his work, but rather my father's relationship with his co-workers. I would go to union meetings with my father and listen to the men talk about politics, finances, and all aspects of life. I was amazed that at such a young age, I could understand everything that they were saying. They spoke in a plain, although loud and brash, English. When I read their union-oriented propaganda, I noticed that it too was easy to understand. These were not complicated men. No one was out to impress or upstage anyone else. These men were union brothers, unmistakably blue-collared, and proud of it.

While I was listening to my father with one ear, my other was always pointed towards my mother. Although my mother also spoke English, like my father, they hardly sounded similar. My mother speaks what I like to call white-collar English. My mother is an office manager at a law firm. She goes to work all cleaned and pressed, briefcase in hand. When I listen to her talk about work, all I would hear was legalese. My mother uses words with many syllables and plenty of letters. She speaks in a very proper and clear voice. When she writes, she does so in a manner that makes the most ordinary things seem complicated. I remember she once wrote me a note for school that read, "Vincent will be unable to attend the upcoming academic function due to a prior commitment." I think she was trying to tell my teacher that I couldn't go on a class trip because we were going on vacation, but I am not really sure.

My mother aligned herself more with Emily Post because she believed the manner in which you talk, or write, or act in a certain situation would determine whether you have acted with class and dignity. My mother is all about being proper, no matter what the situation. Her I's are always dotted and her T's are always crossed. In my mother's white-collared world, the manner in which you conduct yourself has a direct influence on your career.

Learning to see things from these two different points of view has had a dramatic effect on the way I communicate. It is also very evident in my writing. I recently had to write a letter to an airline that had canceled my flight home from vacation, causing me to miss work on Monday. Needless to say, this cancellation was a tremendous inconvenience to me. I conveyed those feelings to the airline, in the bold, brash words of my father, in the beginning of the letter. Then, I used the poignant and legal sounding terms of my mother to convince them that they had better make restitution to me. I received a check from the airline only a few weeks later.

Since most of my writing is now done at work, I can see examples of my dual dialects all over my desk. I am a foreman at a construction company. The people who work directly under me are union construction workers. When I write their work orders, I do it in plain, ordinary, laymen's terms. I do this not because I think they will not understand, but because I know this is the way they choose to communicate.

When I write the same work orders for my supervisors, I write them completely differently. My supervisors are made up of accountants, architects, and other assorted managers and executives. When I communicate with them, whether it is via email, fax, memo, or report, I do it in a very professional manner. The terms I use are very technical and official sounding. I know this is the way it has to be in the corporate world.

Even the writings that I do for school have the traces of these two viewpoints. When I am asked to do a serious business paper, for instance, I tend to write very professionally. I use the long-winded terms used by my professors and textbooks. On the other hand, when I am asked to write about more common ideas, like my experiences, or about myself, I write differently. I prefer to write in a more basic, everyday English. I like to write to the point and from the heart. When it is appropriate, I can even write from both perspectives at the same time. Some people may have to work at this, but to me it comes naturally.

All of my writing, now, I can see as either blue, or white, or some shade thereof. I used to think this made me write like two different people, with different personalities. Now I feel that I have the voice of one author, with a broadened horizon.

INTERPRETATIONS

1. How effective is Cremona's metaphor for describing his writing process? Try to create one to describe yours.

2. How do his parents' prose styles differ? Which do you prefer? How has he used both to his advantage?

APPLICATIONS

1. Review Cremona's last paragraph. What point does he make about language and identity?

2. What view of literacy does each of Cremona's parents represent? What evidence do you find to support your analysis?

3. In the fourth paragraph of the essay, Cremona recounts going to his father's union meetings. What kind of literacy did he observe at those times?

4. Who is Emily Post (mentioned in paragraph 6)? What kind of literacy does she represent? Who is an "Emily Post" in your life?

5. How does Cremona ultimately integrate the literacies that he presents in the essay? How well do you relate to what the author has written about? In what situations do you find yourself navigating among seemingly conflicting definitions of literacy?

The Knowing Eye

U.S. Fish and Wildlife Service/John and Karen Hollingsworth

READING IMAGES

1. When you hear the word "education," what *image* comes to mind? How do these photographs illustrate your visual definition of the word?

2. Which part of each photograph captures your attention? Why do you think the photographer has chosen to make this person/object the focus of the image?

Arnold Asrelsky

MAKING CONNECTIONS

1. There are many ways to learn, and people generally favor a few
    methods. How do these photographs and the kinds of learning
    they convey relate to the essays you have read in this chapter?
    Which essays seem to address the kind of learning implied by the
    first photograph? Which essays imply the methods presented by
    the second image?

2. Which photograph do you think best illustrates a reading from
    this chapter? Which reading does it recall? What connections do
    you make between the written text and the visual one?

WORDS AND IMAGES

1. These photographs depict different ways that people learn. Which photograph is closer to depicting the way that *you* learn? If you have not already written a "Literacy Narrative" (see pages 10–13), write an essay that describes how you learn things best.

2. Examine the photograph of the museum goers. What does the body posture of the people in the photograph tell you about the physical aspects of learning in this environment? Now, visit an art museum or gallery and concentrate on one work of your choice. Look at this work from one position for a few minutes. Then, take five steps back and reexamine the work. Repeat this procedure from another physical location. Write an essay about what you have learned about viewing art (and about learning in general) from this experience.

Additional Writing Topics

1. Write an essay discussing Baldwin's concept that language is the most vivid and crucial key to identity. Include in your essay specific examples from your own experience.

2. "Words themselves are innocuous; it is the consensus that gives them true power." Using a word that has powerful emotional connotations for you, write an essay defining that word as common usage has defined it and analyzing your emotional reactions to it.

3. Review the Kaufman perspective (page 157). What are the ramifications of viewing education as a process rather than a product? To what extent do the selections in this chapter support or refute Kaufman? Write an essay responding to these questions, concluding with your views on this issue.

4. Select a video or a film that presents issues related to education such as *Stanley and Iris, Hoop Dreams, Stand and Deliver*, or *Mr. Holland's Opus*. After viewing the film, write a brief review for your student newspaper explaining the film's point of view on contemporary education.

5. Should a teacher serve as a role model for students? How important is it that he or she be a member of the students' ethnic group? Do teachers have too much or too little influence on their students? Write an essay that answers these questions.

6. Review Reid's perspective on curiosity (page 157) and write an essay on the role of curiosity in the learning process described by Viloria and Torres. Is it possible to learn without being curious? Why or why not?

7. Review the introduction to Bambara's story. Why does she think stories are important? How have stories that you were told and that you have read contributed to your knowledge of your cultural heritage and to your education? Write a speech for your local school board in which you argue for the inclusion of a storytelling component in each of the elementary grades.

8. Some educational theorists argue that because students have grown up with television they prefer the visual to the linear—the image to the word. For such learners, "a picture is worth a thousand words." To what extent do you agree? How has the visual affected information processing? Should more visual techniques of communication be incorporated into the classroom? Write an essay responding to these questions.

CHAPTER

5

Work

A TTITUDES TOWARD WORK and the workplace are constantly changing. Traditionally, work was viewed as something to endure to support one's family, an effort rewarded by a pension and social security. Younger people have different expectations. Some desire economic success and job satisfaction; others prefer to shun the pressures of the corporate world and work for themselves.

We spend a great deal of our lives choosing, preparing for, and doing our work. "What do you do?" is perhaps the first question we want to ask of a new acquaintance. "Talking shop" is supposed to be taboo everywhere except at the office, factory, or construction site, yet no taboo is more frequently, and more gladly broken. For many people, the workplace is life. Talk about it ranges from the personal to the particular to the abstract, whatever one's culture.

The workplace is also changing rapidly. Technological expertise is in demand and will be rewarded by economic gains for those with innovative ideas and appropriate education. The increasing presence of women poses a challenge to traditional career choices and criteria for promotion, and attitudes toward work itself vary widely. For some, the workplace is a vital community, while others regard it as a location in which to perform a service. The notion of staying with one company for a lifetime or even making only one career choice is alien to many, and the concept of loyalty between employer and employee and vice versa is no longer assumed.

As you will discover, attitudes toward work and its value differ among cultures and exist in a matrix of customs, traditions, education, and class. In the Genesis account, work is viewed as a punishment for human disobedience, while in the Nez Percé selection, work is portrayed as interfering with dreams.

The most negative treatment of work in the United States is Gary Soto's "Black Hair"—a grueling account of a summer job that made him keenly aware of the destructive emotional costs of poverty. Ellen Ullman explains and explodes the stereotypical behavior associated with computer programmers by demonstrating from personal experience how their complex relationship to computers is determined by the nature of programming. In "Warning: This is a Rights-Free Workplace," Barbara Ehrenreich cites many examples of the decline of autonomy and dignity in workplaces throughout the country, while fiction writer R. K. Narayan examines the personal and professional commitment expected by employers in his native India.

The issue of affirmative action in the workplace is discussed from a multicultural perspective in the story by Lalita Gandbhir, while Michael Gnolfo presents his reasons for opposing affirmative action programs in the United States.

As you explore the complexities, even controversies, and changes in the workplace and in attitudes toward work, you may decide that now is a good time to join the conversation on these issues.

Perspectives

Work spares us from three great evils: boredom, vice and need.

—Voltaire

How will you know when you have found work you love? One symptom is that you will lose track of time. You'll look at your watch and wonder where the hours have gone, at your calendar and wonder what happened to the week. And that loss of time sense is a symbol as well as a symptom. We are time-bound creatures, but meaningful work can make us forget our moral limitation—because it helps us transcend it.

—Lynne V. Cheney

If people are highly successful in their professions they lose their senses. Sound goes. They have no time to listen to music. Speech goes. They have no time for conversation. They lose their sense of proportion—the relations between one thing and another. Humanity goes.

—Virginia Woolf

Work is a necessity for man. Man invented the alarm clock.

—Pablo Picasso

Life is a continual distraction which does not allow us to reflect on that from which we are distracted.

—Franz Kafka

Each of you has a call, a vocation, which beckons you from the deepest places of your soul.

—David Hilfiker

He that maketh haste to be rich shall not be innocent.

—Proverbs 28:20

A job as a human right is a principle that applies to men as well as women. But women have more cause to fight for it.

—Gloria Steinem

The workplace performs the function of community.

—Robert Schrank

This book, being about work, is, by its very nature, about violence—to the spirit as well as the body.

—Studs Terkel

In fact, there is perhaps only one human being in a thousand who is passionately interested in his job for the job's sake.

—Dorothy Sayers

More and more, we take for granted that work must be destitute of pleasure. More and more, we assume that if we want to be pleased we must wait until evening, or the weekend, or vacation, or retirement. More and more, our farms and forests resemble our factories and offices, which in turn more and more resemble prisons—why else should we be so eager to escape them? We recognize defeated landscapes by the absence of pleasure from them. We are defeated at work because our work gives us no pleasure.

—Wendell Berry

Increased means and increased leisure are the two civilizers of man.

—Benjamin Disraeli

We are not far from the time when a man after a hard weekend of leisure will thankfully go back to work.

—Russell Baker

APPLICATIONS

1. According to Schrank, "the workplace performs the function of community." To what extent do you agree or disagree? Is it possible to establish community in competitive environments? What factors contribute to your feeling at home in the workplace?

2. Discuss Picasso's perspective with your group. Do you think there is a connection between work and time? What is your attitude toward time? Are you punctual for school, work, and leisure activities? Does lateness in others bother you? Summarize your discussion.

3. According to Berry, "we are defeated at work because work gives us no pleasure." To what kind of work is Berry referring? What factors account for boredom in the workplace? What is the difference between a job and a vocation? How would you diminish drudgery in the workplace?

The Fall

GENESIS 3:1–9

The Genesis account of the Fall explains, among other things, the origin of work, painful childbirth, and death. This seminal story following immediately after the Genesis account of Creation continues to exert an influence on Western culture out of proportion to its modest length.

THE SERPENT WAS MORE CRAFTY than any wild creature that the Lord God had made. He said to the woman, "Is it true that God has forbidden you to eat from any tree in the garden?" The woman answered the serpent, "We may eat the fruit of any tree in the garden, except for the tree in the middle of the garden; God has forbidden us either to eat or to touch the fruit of that; if we do, we shall die." The serpent said, "Of course you will not die. God knows that as soon as you eat it, your eyes will be opened and you will be like gods knowing both good and evil." When the woman saw that the fruit of the tree was good to eat, and that it was pleasing to the eye and tempting to contemplate, she took some and ate it. She also gave her husband some and he ate it. Then the eyes of both of them were opened and they discovered that they were naked; so they stitched fig-leaves together and made themselves loincloths.

The man and his wife heard the sound of the Lord God walking in the garden at the time of the evening breeze and hid from the Lord God among the trees of the garden. But the Lord God called to the man and said to him, "Where are you?" He replied, "I heard the sound as you were walking in the garden, and I was afraid because I was naked, and I hid myself." God answered, "Who told you that you were naked? Have you eaten from the tree which I forbade you?" The man said, "The woman you gave me for a companion, she gave me fruit from the tree and I ate it." Then the Lord God said to the woman, "What is this that you have done?" The woman said, "The serpent tricked me, and I ate." Then the Lord God said to the serpent:

> Because you have done this you are accursed
> more than all cattle and all wild creatures.
> On your belly you shall crawl, and dust you shall eat
> all the days of your life.
> I will put enmity between you and the woman,

between your brood and hers.
They shall strike at your head,
and you shall strike at their heel.

To the woman he said:

I will increase your labour and your groaning,
and in labour you shall bear children.
You shall be eager for your husband,
and he shall be your master.

And to the man he said:

Because you have listened to your wife
and have eaten from the tree which I forbade you,
accursed shall be the ground on your account.
With labour you shall win your food from it
all the days of your life.
It will grow thorns and thistles for you,
none but wild plants for you to eat.
You shall gain your bread by the sweat of your brow
until you return to the ground;
for from it you were taken.
Dust you are, to dust you shall return.

INTERPRETATIONS

1. What attitude toward work does the passage reveal?

2. What attitude toward woman does the story reveal? Does the story explain why the serpent chose to speak to the woman, not the man? Of what significance is this choice?

3. What attributes of God does this story reveal? Does God's ban on the knowledge of good and evil (morality?) play into the serpent's evil designs, making the man and woman unnecessarily vulnerable? Is obedience God's main objective, and is this simply a test case to see whether the new man and woman can obey orders, no matter what the orders?

My Young Men Shall Never Work

CHIEF SMOHALLA
AS TOLD BY HERBERT J. SPINDEN

The Nez Percé are a tribe of American Indians formerly occupying much of the Pacific Northwest whose reservation is in Idaho.

Because Native Americans resisted giving up their homes and nomadic way of life to become farmers, white people have often called them lazy, stubborn, and impractical. But to Indians, whose homes, land, and hunting were sacred, anything that threatened any one of these threatened their whole system of beliefs and values, in short, their very lives.

MY YOUNG MEN SHALL NEVER WORK. Men who work cannot dream and wisdom comes in dreams.

You ask me to plow the ground. Shall I take a knife and tear my mother's breast? Then when I die she will not take me to her bosom to rest.

You ask me to dig for stone. Shall I dig under her skin for bones? Then when I die I cannot enter her body to be born again.

You ask me to cut grass and make hay and sell it and be rich like white men. But how dare I cut off my mother's hair?

It is a bad law and my people cannot obey it. I want my people to stay with me here. All the dead men will come to life again. We must wait here in the house of our fathers and be ready to meet them in the body of our mother.

INTERPRETATIONS

1. Are the Nez Percé objecting to all work? Would you define work to include hunting?

2. What is the Nez Percé's reason for rejecting what they call "work"? What do they value more than work? How common is it for a culture to place the highest value on something other than work? Is work the highest value of American culture? What's the evidence?

3. To what extent is the misunderstanding between the Nez Percé and the whites a matter of language (definition)? Of tradition?

What is the Nez Percé attitude toward the earth? What metaphor extends through and is elaborated within the whole passage?

CORRESPONDENCES

1. Review the Voltaire perspective (page 229). How does it apply to the Genesis account of the origins of work? Which attitude toward work best reflects your own?

2. Review the Kafka perspective (page 229). What does it mean? To what extent does it reflect the sentiments about work expressed by Smohalla of the Nez Percé?

APPLICATIONS

1. "The Fall" portrays work as punishment for disobedience. Can work also be rewarding? Can you imagine living a fulfilled life without work? Write a journal entry on these questions.

2. "Men who work cannot dream and wisdom comes in dreams." Write a journal entry responding to Chief Smohalla. To what extent does involvement in work affect time for dreams?

3. Many college students work at least 20 hours per week. If this is true of you, write a short essay on how you juggle your schedule to meet these responsibilities.

from Living Up the Street
Black Hair

GARY SOTO

Gary Soto (b. 1952) was raised in Fresno, California and is the author of ten poetry collections. New and Selected Poems *(1995) was a finalist for the Los Angeles Book Award and the National Book Award.* Living Up The Street, *Soto's memoir, received a Before Columbus Foundation American Book Award in 1985. In addition to writing, Soto has produced a film and wrote a libretto for the Los Angeles Opera. Soto also serves as Young People's Ambassador for the California Rural Legal Assistance and the United Farm Workers of America. Before reading Soto's essay, write a journal entry on the summer job you most hated. What did you learn from the experience?*

THERE ARE TWO KINDS OF WORK: One uses the mind and the other uses muscle. As a kid I found out about the latter. I'm thinking of the summer of 1969 when I was a seventeen-year-old runaway who ended up in Glendale, California, to work for Valley Tire Factory. To answer an ad in the newspaper I walked miles in the afternoon sun, my stomach slowly knotting on a doughnut that was breakfast, my teeth like bright candles gone yellow.

I walked in the door sweating and feeling ugly because my hair was still stiff from a swim at the Santa Monica beach the day before. Jules, the accountant and part owner, looked droopily through his bifocals at my application and then at me. He tipped his cigar in the ashtray, asked my age as if he didn't believe I was seventeen, but finally after a moment of silence, said, "Come back tomorrow. Eight-thirty."

I thanked him, left the office, and went around to the chain link fence to watch the workers heave tires into a bin; others carted uneven stacks of tires on hand trucks. Their faces were black from tire dust and when they talked—or cussed—their mouths showed a bright pink.

From there I walked up a commercial street, past a cleaners, a motorcycle shop, and a gas station where I washed my face and hands; before leaving I took a bottle that hung on the side of the Coke machine, filled it with water, and stopped it with a scrap of paper and a rubber band.

The next morning I arrived early at work. The assistant foreman, a potbellied Hungarian, showed me a timecard and how to punch in. He showed me the Coke machine, the locker room with its slimy shower, and also pointed out the places where I shouldn't go: The ovens where the tires were recapped and the customer service area, which had a slashed couch, a coffee table with greasy magazines, and an ashtray. He introduced me to Tully, a fat man with one ear, who worked the buffers that resurfaced the white walls. I was handed an apron and a face mask and shown how to use the buffer: Lift the tire and center, inflate it with a footpedal, press the buffer against the white band until cleaned, and then deflate and blow off the tire with an air hose.

With a paint brush he stirred a can of industrial preserver. "Then slap this blue stuff on." While he was talking a co-worker came up quietly from behind him and goosed him with the air hose. Tully jumped as if he had been struck by a bullet and then turned around cussing and cupping his genitals in his hands as the other worker walked away calling out foul names. When Tully turned to me smiling his gray teeth, I lifted my mouth into a smile because I wanted to get along. He has to be on my side, I thought. He's the one who'll tell the foreman how I'm doing.

I worked carefully that day, setting the tires on the machine as if they were babies, since it was easy to catch a finger in the rim that expanded to inflate the tire. At the day's end we swept up the tire dust and emptied the trash into bins.

At five the workers scattered for their cars and motorcycles while I crossed the street to wash at a burger stand. My hair was stiff with dust and my mouth showed pink against the backdrop of my dirty face. I then ordered a hotdog and walked slowly in the direction of the abandoned house where I had stayed the night before. I lay under the trees and within minutes was asleep. When I woke my shoulders were sore and my eyes burned when I squeezed the lids together.

From the backyard I walked dully through a residential street, and as evening came on, the TV glare in the living rooms and the headlights of passing cars showed against the blue drift of dusk. I saw two children coming up the street with snow cones, their tongues darting at the packed ice. I saw a boy with a peach and wanted to stop him, but felt embarrassed by my hunger. I walked for an hour only to return and discover the house lit brightly. Behind the fence I heard voices and saw a flashlight poking at the garage door. A man on the back steps mumbled something about the refrigerator to the one with the flashlight.

I waited for them to leave, but had the feeling they wouldn't because there was the commotion of furniture being moved. Tired, even more desperate, I started walking again with a great urge to kick things and tear the day from my life. I felt weak and my mind kept drifting because of hunger. I crossed the street to a gas station where I sipped at the water fountain and searched the Coke machine for change. I started walking again, first up a commercial street, then into a residential area where I lay down on someone's lawn and replayed a scene at home—my Mother crying at the kitchen table, my stepfather yelling with food in his mouth. They're cruel, I thought, and warned myself that I should never forgive them. How could they do this to me.

When I got up from the lawn it was late. I searched out a place to sleep and found an unlocked car that seemed safe. In the back seat, with my shoes off, I fell asleep but woke up startled about four in the morning when the owner, a nurse on her way to work, opened the door. She got in and was about to start the engine when I raised my head up from the backseat to explain my presence. She screamed so loudly when I said "I'm sorry" that I sprinted from the car with my shoes in hand. Her screams faded, then stopped altogether, as I ran down the block where I hid behind a trash bin and waited for a police siren to sound. Nothing. I crossed the street to a church where I slept stiffly on cardboard in the balcony.

I woke up feeling tired and greasy. It was early and a few street lights were still lit, the east growing pink with dawn. I washed myself from a garden hose and returned to the church to break into what looked like a kitchen. Paper cups, plastic spoons, a coffee pot littered on a table. I found a box of Nabisco crackers which I ate until I was full.

At work I spent the morning at the buffer, but was then told to help Iggy, an old Mexican, who was responsible for choosing tires that could be recapped without the risk of exploding at high speeds. Every morning a truck would deliver used tires, and after I unloaded them Iggy would step among the tires to inspect them for punctures and rips on the sidewalls.

With a yellow chalk he marked circles and Xs to indicate damage and called out "junk." For those tires that could be recapped, he said "goody" and I placed them on my hand truck.

When I had a stack of eight I kicked the truck at an angle and balanced them to another work area where Iggy again inspected the tires, scratching Xs and calling out "junk."

Iggy worked only until three in the afternoon, at which time he went to the locker room to wash and shave and to dress in a two-piece suit. When he came out he glowed with a bracelet, watch, rings, and a shiny fountain pen in his breast pocket. His shoes sounded against the asphalt. He was the image of a banker stepping into sunlight with millions on his mind. He said a few low words to workers with whom he was friendly and none to people like me.

I was seventeen, stupid because I couldn't figure out the difference between an F 78 14 and 750 14 at sight. Iggy shook his head when

I brought him the wrong tires, especially since I had expressed interest in being his understudy. "Mexican, how can you be so stupid?" he would yell at me, slapping a tire from my hands. But within weeks I learned a lot about tires, from sizes and makes to how they are molded in iron forms to how Valley stole from other companies. Now and then we received a truckload of tires, most of them new or nearly new, and they were taken to our warehouse in the back where the serial numbers were ground off with a sander. On those days the foreman handed out Cokes and joked with us as we worked to get the numbers off.

Most of the workers were Mexican or black, though a few redneck whites worked there. The base pay was a dollar sixty-five, but the average was three dollars. Of the black workers, I knew Sugar Daddy the best. His body carried two hundred and fifty pounds, armfuls of scars, and a long knife that made me jump when he brought it out from his boot without warning. At one time he had been a singer, and had cut a record in 1967 called *Love's Chance*, which broke into the R and B charts. But nothing came of it. No big contract, no club dates, no tours. He made very little from the sales, only enough for an operation to pull a steering wheel from his gut when, drunk and mad at a lady friend, he slammed his Mustang into a row of parked cars.

"Touch it," he smiled at me one afternoon as he raised his shirt, his black belly kinked with hair. Scared, I traced the scar that ran from his chest to the left of his belly button, and I was repelled but hid my disgust.

Among the Mexicans I had few friends because I was different, a *pocho*[1] who spoke bad Spanish. At lunch they sat in tires and laughed over burritos, looking up at me to laugh even harder. I also sat in tires while nursing a Coke and felt dirty and sticky because I was still living on the street and had not had a real bath in over a week. Nevertheless, when the border patrol came to round up the nationals, I ran with them as they scrambled for the fence or hid among the tires behind the warehouse. The foreman, who thought I was an undocumented worker, yelled at me to run, to get away. I did just that. At the time it seemed fun because there was no risk, only a goodhearted feeling of hide-and-seek, and besides it meant an hour away from work on company time. When the police left we came back and some of the nationals made up stories of how they were almost caught—how they out-raced the police. Some of the stories were so convoluted and unconvincing that everyone laughed *mentiras*,[2] especially when one described how he overpowered a policeman, took his gun away, and

[1] A derogatory term for Mexicans living in the United States who have forgotten their cultural heritage.
[2] Lies.

sold the patrol car. We laughed and he laughed, happy to be there to make up a story.

If work was difficult, so were the nights. I still had not gathered enough money to rent a room, so I spent the nights sleeping in parked cars or in the balcony of a church. After a week I found a newspaper ad for room for rent, phoned, and was given directions. Finished with work, I walked the five miles down Mission Road looking back into the traffic with my thumb out. No rides. After eight hours of handling tires, I was frightening, I suppose, to drivers since they seldom looked at me; if they did, it was a quick glance. For the next six weeks I would try to hitchhike, but the only person to stop was a Mexican woman who gave me two dollars to take the bus. I told her it was too much and that no bus ran from Mission Road to where I lived, but she insisted that I keep the money and trotted back to her idling car. It must have hurt her to see me day after day walking in the heat and looking very much the dirty Mexican to the many minds that didn't know what it meant to work at hard labor. That woman knew. Her eyes met mine as she opened the car door, and there was a tenderness that was surprisingly true—one for which you wait for years but when it comes it doesn't help. Nothing changes. You continue on in rags, with the sun still above you.

I rented a room from a middle-aged couple whose lives were a mess. She was a school teacher and he was a fireman. A perfect set up, I thought. But during my stay there they would argue with one another for hours in their bedroom.

When I rang at the front door both Mr. and Mrs. Van Deusen answered and didn't bother to disguise their shock at how awful I looked. But they let me in all the same. Mrs. Van Deusen showed me around the house, from the kitchen and bathroom to the living room with its grand piano. On her fingers she counted out the house rules as she walked me to my room. It was a girl's room with lace curtains, scenic wallpaper of a Victorian couple enjoying a stroll, canopied bed, and stuffed animals in a corner. Leaving, she turned and asked if she could do laundry for me and, feeling shy and hurt, I told her no; perhaps the next day. She left and I undressed to take a bath, exhausted as I sat on the edge of the bed probing my aches and my bruised places. With a towel around my waist I hurried down the hallway to the bathroom where Mrs. Van Deusen had set out an additional towel with a tube of shampoo. I ran the water in the tub and sat on the toilet, lid down, watching the steam curl toward the ceiling. When I lowered myself into the tub I felt my body sting. I soaped a wash cloth and scrubbed my arms until they lightened, even glowed pink, but still I looked unwashed around my neck and face no matter how hard I rubbed. Back in the room I sat in bed reading a magazine, happy and thinking of no better luxury than a girl's sheets, especially after nearly two weeks of sleeping on cardboard at the church.

I was too tired to sleep, so I sat at the window watching the neighbors move about in pajamas, and, curious about the room, looked through the bureau drawers to search out personal things—snapshots, a messy diary, and a high school yearbook. I looked up the Van Deusen's daughter, Barbara, and studied her face as if I recognized her from my own school—a face that said "promise," "college," "nice clothes in the closet." She was a skater and a member of the German Club; her greatest ambition was to sing at the Hollywood Bowl.

After awhile I got into bed and as I drifted toward sleep I thought about her. In my mind I played a love scene again and again and altered it slightly each time. She comes home from college and at first is indifferent to my presence in her home, but finally I overwhelm her with deep pity when I come home hurt from work, with blood on my shirt. Then there was another version: Home from college she is immediately taken with me, in spite of my work-darkened face, and invites me into the family car for a milkshake across town. Later, back at the house, we sit in the living room talking about school until we're so close I'm holding her hand. The truth of the matter was that Barbara did come home for a week, but was bitter toward her parents for taking in boarders (two others besides me). During that time she spoke to me only twice: Once, while searching the refrigerator, she asked if we had any mustard; the other time she asked if I had seen her car keys.

But it was a place to stay. Work had become more and more difficult. I not only worked with Iggy, but also with the assistant foreman who was in charge of unloading trucks. After they backed in I hopped on top to pass the tires down by bouncing them on the tailgate to give them an extra spring so they would be less difficult to handle on the other end. Each truck was weighed down with more than two hundred tires, each averaging twenty pounds, so that by the time the truck was emptied and swept clean I glistened with sweat and my T-shirt stuck to my body. I blew snot threaded with tire dust onto the asphalt, indifferent to the customers who watched from the waiting room.

The days were dull. I did what there was to do from morning until the bell sounded at five; I tugged, pulled, and cussed at tires until I was listless and my mind drifted and caught on small things, from cold sodas to shoes to stupid talk about what we would do with a million dollars. I remember unloading a truck with Hamp, a black man.

"What's better than a sharp lady?" he asked me as I stood sweaty on a pile of junked tires. "Water. With ice," I said.

He laughed with his mouth open wide. With his fingers he pinched the sweat from his chin and flicked at me. "You be too young, boy. A woman can make you a god."

As a kid I had chopped cotton and picked grapes, so I knew work. I knew the fatigue and the boredom and the feeling that there was a good possibility you might have to do such work for years, if not for a lifetime. In fact, as a kid I imagined a dark fate: To marry Mexican poor, work Mexican hours, and in the end die a Mexican death, broke and in despair.

But this job at Valley Tire Company confirmed that there was something worse than field work, and I was doing it. We were all doing it, from foreman to the newcomers like me, and what I felt heaving tires for eight hours a day was felt by everyone—black, Mexican, redneck. We all despised those hours but didn't know what else to do. The workers were unskilled, some undocumented and fearful of deportation, and all struck with an uncertainty at what to do with their lives. Although everyone bitched about work, no one left. Some had worked there for as long as twelve years; some had sons working there. Few quit; no one was ever fired. It amazed me that no one gave up when the border patrol jumped from their vans, baton in hand, because I couldn't imagine any work that could be worse—or any life. What was out there, in the world, that made men run for the fence in fear?

How we arrived at such a place is a mystery to me. Why anyone would stay for years is even a deeper concern. You showed up, but from where? What broken life? What ugly past? The foreman showed you the Coke machine, the washroom, and the yard where you'd work. When you picked up a tire, you were amazed at the black it could give off.

INTERPRETATIONS

1. "There are two kinds of work: one uses the mind and the other uses muscles." How effectively does Soto support this thesis in his essay? Cite evidence.

2. Soto catalogs his first day at work in great detail. How do his sensory and visual descriptions not only enhance his essay but also serve his purpose?

3. What role does Iggy play in Soto's summer work experience? How is Iggy different from his co-workers? Does Soto ever resolve his doubts about Iggy's "dignity"? Explain.

4. Why does Soto include the Van Duesens? Is it digressive or does it add another dimension to his narrative? Explain.

5. In paragraphs 29 and 30, Soto contrasts being a field worker with his summer in the tire factory. Although field work pays less, why is it better in his view than the tire factory?

6. Most writers use their conclusions to summarize their essays. Why does Soto conclude his essay with a series of questions? To what effect?

Getting Close to the Machine

ELLEN ULLMAN

Ellen Ullman (b. 1948) graduated from Cornell University and was a soft-
ware engineer for twenty years when she began writing about her profession.
Her writing has appeared in Harper's, Salon, Wired, The Washington
Post, *and* The New York Times. *Ullman is the author of the memoir* Close
to the Machine: Technophilia and Its Discontent (1997) *and* The Bug,
a novel published in 2003. To what extent is your workplace dependent on
your relationship to machines? Explain.

PEOPLE IMAGINE that computer programming is logical, a process like
fixing a clock. Nothing could be further from the truth. Programming is
more like an illness, a fever, an obsession. It's like riding a train and
never being able to get off.

The problem with programming is not that the computer is
illogical—the computer is terribly logical, relentlessly literal. It demands
that the programmer explain the world on its terms; that is, as an algorithm that must be written down in order, in a specific syntax, in a
strange language that is only partially readable by regular human
beings. To program is to translate between the chaos of human life and
the rational, line-by-line world of computer language.

When you program, reality presents itself as thousands of details,
millions of bits of knowledge. This knowledge comes at you from one
perspective and then another, then comes a random thought, then you
remember something else important, then you reconsider that idea
with a what-if attached. For example, try to think of everything you
know about something as simple as an invoice. Now try to tell an idiot
how to prepare one. That is programming.

I used to have dreams in which I was overhearing conversations I
had to program. Once I dreamed I had to program two people making
love. In my dream they sweated and tumbled while I sat looking for the
algorithm. The couple went from gentle caresses to ever-deepening
passion, and I tried desperately to find a way to express the act of love
in the C computer language.

When you are programming, you must not let your mind wander. As
the human-world knowledge tumbles about in your head, you must
keep typing, typing. You must not be interrupted. Any break in your

concentration causes you to lose a line here or there. Some bit comes, then—oh no, it's leaving, please come back. But it may not come back. You may lose it. You will create a bug and there's nothing you can do about it.

People imagine that programmers don't like to talk because they prefer machines to people. This is not completely true. Programmers don't talk because they must not be interrupted.

This need to be uninterrupted leads to a life that is strangely asynchronous to the one lived by other human beings. It's better to send e-mail to a programmer than to call. It's better to leave a note on the chair than to expect the programmer to come to a meeting. This is because the programmer must work in mind time while the phone rings and the meetings happen in real time. It's not just ego that prevents programmers from working in groups—it's the synchronicity problem. Synchronizing with other people (or their representations in telephones, buzzers, and doorbells) can only mean interrupting the thought train. Interruptions mean bugs. You must not get off the train.

I once had a job in which I didn't talk to anyone for two years. Here was the arrangement: I was the first engineer to be hired by a start-up software company. In exchange for large quantities of stock that might be worth something someday, I was supposed to give up my life.

I sat in a large room with two other engineers and three workstations. The fans in the machines whirred, the keys on the keyboards clicked. Occasionally one of us would grunt or mutter. Otherwise we did not speak. Now and then I would have an outburst in which I pounded the keyboard with my fists, setting off a barrage of beeps. My colleagues might have looked up, but they never said anything.

Real time was no longer compelling to me. Days, weeks, months, and years came and went without much change in my surroundings. Surely I was aging. My hair must have grown, I must have cut it, it must have slowly become grayer. Gravity must have been working on my late-thirties body, but I didn't pay attention.

What was compelling was the software. I was making something out of nothing, I thought, and I admit that the software had more life for me during those years than a brief love affair, my friends, my cat, my house, or my neighbor who was stabbed and nearly killed by her husband. One day I sat in a room by myself, surrounded by computer monitors. I remember looking at the screens and saying, "Speak to me."

I was creating something called a device-independent interface library. ("Creating"—that is the word we used, each of us a genius in the attic.) I completed the library in two years and left the company. Five years later, the company's stock went public, and the original arrangement was made good: the engineers who stayed—the ones who had given seven years of their lives to the machine—became very, very wealthy.

If you want money and prestige, you need to write code that only machines or other programmers understand. Such code is called "low." In regular life, "low" usually signifies something bad. In programming, "low" is good. Low means that you are close to the machine.

If the code creates programs that do useful work for regular human beings, it is called "high." Higher-level programs are called "applications." Applications are things that people use. Although it would seem that usefulness is a good thing, direct people-use is bad from a programmer's point of view. If regular people, called "users," can understand the task accomplished by your program, you will be paid less and held in lower esteem.

A real programmer wants to stay close to the machine. The machine means midnight dinners of Diet Coke. It means unwashed clothes and bare feet on the desk. It means anxious rides through mind time that have nothing to do with the clock. To work on things used only by machines or other programmers—that's the key. Programmers and machines don't care how you live. They don't care when you live. You can stay, come, go, sleep—or not. At the end of the project looms a deadline, the terrible place where you must get off the train. But in between, for years at a stretch, you are free: free from the obligations of time.

I once designed a graphical user interface with a man who wouldn't speak to me. My boss hired him without letting anyone else sit in on the interview. My boss lived to regret it.

I was asked to brief my new colleague with the help of the third member of our team. We went into a conference room, where my co-worker and I filled two white boards with lines, boxes, circles, and arrows while the new hire watched. After about a half hour, I noticed that he had become very agitated.

"Are we going too fast?" I asked him.

"Too much for the first day?" asked my colleague.

"No," said our new man, "I just can't do it like this."

"Do what?" I asked. "Like what?"

His hands were deep in his pockets. He gestured with his elbows. "Like this," he said.

"You mean design?" I asked.

"You mean in a meeting?" asked my colleague.

No answer from the new guy. A shrug. Another elbow motion.

Something terrible was beginning to occur to me. "You mean talking?" I asked.

"Yeah, talking," he said, "I can't do it by talking."

By this time in my career, I had met many strange software engineers. But here was the first one who wouldn't talk at all. We had a lot of design work to do. No talking was certainly going to make things difficult.

"So how *can* you do it?" I asked.

"Mail," he said. "Send me e-mail."

Given no choice, we designed a graphical user interface by e-mail. Corporations across North America and Europe are still using a system designed by three people in the same office who communicated via computer, one of whom barely spoke at all.

Pretty graphical interfaces are commonly called "user-friendly." But they are not really your friends. Underlying every user-friendly interface is terrific contempt for the humans who will use it.

The basic idea of a graphical interface is that it will not allow anything alarming to happen. You can pound on the mouse button, your cat can run across it, your baby can punch it, but the system should not crash.

To build a crash-proof system, the designer must be able to imagine—and disallow—the dumbest action possible. He or she has to think of every single stupid thing a human being could do. Gradually, over months and years, the designer's mind creates a construct of the user as an imbecile. This image is necessary. No crash-proof system can be built unless it is made for an idiot.

The designer's contempt for your intelligence is mostly hidden deep in the code. But now and then the disdain surfaces. Here's a small example: You're trying to do something simple such as copying files onto a diskette on your Mac. The program proceeds for a while, then encounters an error. Your disk is defective, says a message, and below the message is a single button. You absolutely must click this button. If you don't click it, the program will hang there indefinitely. Your disk is defective, your files may be bollixed up, but the designer leaves you only one possible reply. You must say, "OK."

The prettier the user interface, and the fewer replies the system allows you to make, the dumber you once appeared in the mind of the designer. Soon, everywhere we look, we will see pretty, idiot-proof interfaces designed to make us say, "OK." Telephones, televisions, sales kiosks will all be wired for "interactive," on-demand services. What power—demand! See a movie, order seats to a basketball game, make hotel reservations, send a card to mother—all of these services will be waiting for us on our televisions or computers whenever we want them, midnight, dawn, or day. Sleep or order a pizza: it no longer matters exactly what we do when. We don't need to involve anyone else in the satisfaction of our needs. We don't even have to talk. We get our services when we want them, free from the obligations of regularly scheduled time. We can all live, like programmers, close to the machine. "Interactivity" is misnamed. It should be called "asynchrony": the engineering culture come to everyday life.

The very word "interactivity" implies something good and wonderful. Surely a response, a reply, an answer is a positive thing. Surely it signifies an advance over something else, something bad, something that doesn't respond. There is only one problem: what we will be interacting with is a machine. We will be "talking" to programs that are beginning to look surprisingly alike; each has little animated pictures we are supposed to choose from, like push buttons on a toddler's toy. The toy is meant to please us. Somehow it is supposed to replace the rewards of fumbling for meaning with a mature human being, in the confusion of a natural language, together, in a room, within touching distance.

As the computer's pretty, helpful face (and contemptuous underlying code) penetrates deeper into daily life, the cult of the engineer comes with it. The engineer's assumptions and presumptions are in the code. That's the purpose of the program, after all: to sum up the intelligence and intentions of all the engineers who worked on the system over time—tens and hundreds of people who have learned an odd and highly specific way of doing things. The system reproduces and re-enacts life as engineers know it: alone, out of time, disdainful of anyone far from the machine.

INTERPRETATIONS

1. "To program is to translate between the chaos of human life and the rational line-by-line world of computer language." What talents does a potential computer programmer need in addition to absolute concentration? Does Ullman make the job appealing? Why or why not?

2. Ullman distinguishes between "mind time" and "real time." How would you define both kinds of time? What activities do you associate with "mind time?" Is there a connection between creativity and "mind time"? Explain.

3. "I once had a job in which I didn't talk to anyone for two years." Review paragraphs 8 through 15 carefully and list the psychological costs of Ullman's isolation.

4. Why does she include paragraphs 16 through 31? What new element does she introduce? How might you respond in her situation?

5. "We can all live, like programmers, close to the machine." What predictions does Ullman make regarding human communication? Is she exaggerating? Explain.

CORRESPONDENCES

1. Review Soto's and Ullman's introductions. What makes them effective? Are they equally provocative? Explain.

2. According to Shrank's perspective, the workplace performs the function of community. To what extent do Soto and Ullman refute this concept?

APPLICATIONS

1. If you involve yourself with hard labor, the kind that Soto has described in his essay, what kind of literacy is acquired? For a few minutes, do an activity that requires the use of your muscles. For example, you might run a few sprints, lift weights, work vigorously in the garden, or split firewood. As you engage in this activity, pay attention to the physical sensations you experience. Write a few paragraphs about what you felt and came to understand about your body and physical activity.

2. Conduct an experiment with your group by logging for a week your use of communications technology including e-mail, faxes, ATMs, and the Web. What possibilities for human interactions did you eliminate? At what personal cost?

3. In the context of describing his summer job, Soto also focuses on the destructive effects of poverty. Write an analysis of the connections he makes between poverty and despair. How does poverty also contribute to emotional and intellectual paralysis?

4. Compare with your group your various experiences with summer jobs. Then focus on one that was particularly pleasant or unpleasant. What did you learn about yourself from this experience? Was it an effective rite of passage? Explain.

5. Step 1: Create a design using two geometric shapes (see examples below).

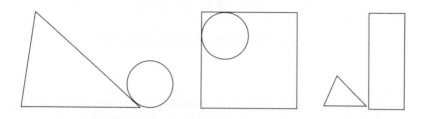

Step 2: Write a set of instructions that will help someone draw the *exact* image you have made.

Step 3: Exchange *only* your set of instructions with someone who has also created a geometric shape and a set of instructions. (Make sure that the images created by both you and your partner are concealed during this exchange!)

Step 4: As your partner draws from the set of instructions you produced, try to do the same. When you have both completed your drawings, sit together and show each other your work. Who produced the actual figure that was described? If the drawing does not match the model, why doesn't it? With your partner still sitting next to you, draw the object from his or her instructions. If the occasion arises, let your partner help you interpret the directions. Now, reconsider the reasons behind what went right and what didn't!

Step 5: In a whole class discussion of this exercise, consider the implications of vocabulary (diction), organization, and audience. What conclusions do you come to? Welcome to programming!

Warning: This Is a Rights-Free Workplace

BARBARA EHRENREICH

Barbara Ehrenreich (b. 1941) is a social activist and feminist who has written about healthcare, family, sex, and class for magazines that include The Nation, *the* Atlantic Monthly, *the* New Republic, The Washington Post Magazine, *and the* Progressive. *Ehrenreich is a contributing editor of* Harper's *and the author of* The Hearts of Men: American Dreams and the Flight from Commitment *(1983),* The Snarling Citizen *(1995),* Fear of Falling: The Inner Life of the Middle Class *(1989),* The Worst Years of Our Lives: Irreverent Notes for a Decade of Greed, *and* Blood Rites: Origins and History of the Passion of War *(1997). Ehrenreich's most recent book is* Nickel and Dimed: On (Not) Getting by in America, *which was published in 2001. Ehrenreich has a Ph.D. from the Rockefeller University and a B.A. from Reed College. She has been a regular teaching fellow at the UC Berkeley Graduate School of Journalism. As you read Ehrenreich's essay, compare her thoughts about freedom in the workplace with your own work experiences.*

IF THE LAWS OF ECONOMICS WERE ENFORCED as strictly as the laws of physics, America would be a workers' paradise. The supply of most kinds of labor is low, relative to the demand, so each worker should be treated as a cherished asset, right? But there have been only grudging gains in wages over the last few years, and in the realm of dignity and autonomy, a palpable decline.

In the latest phase of America's one-sided class war, employers have taken to monitoring employees' workplace behavior right down to a single computer keystroke or bathroom break, even probing into their personal concerns and leisure activities. Sure, there's a job out there for anyone who can get to an interview sober and standing upright. The price, though, may be one's basic civil rights and—what boils down to the same thing—self-respect.

Not that the Bill of Rights ever extended to the American workplace. In 1996, I was surprised to read about a grocery store worker in Dallas who was fired for wearing a Green Bay Packers T-shirt to work on the day before a Cowboys-Packers game. All right, this was insensitive of him, but it certainly couldn't have influenced his ability to keep the shelves stocked with Doritos. A few phone calls, though, revealed that his firing was entirely legal. Employees have the right to express their religious preferences at work, by wearing a cross or a Star of David, for example. But most other forms of "self-expression" are not protected, and strangely enough, Green Bay Packer fandom has not yet been recognized as a legitimate religion.

Freedom of assembly is another right that never found its way into the workplace. On a recent journalistic foray into a series of low-wage jobs, I was surprised to discover that management often regarded the most innocent conversation between employees as potentially seditious. A poster in the break room at one restaurant where I worked as a waitress prohibited "gossip," and a manager would hastily disperse any gathering of two or more employees. At the same time, management everywhere enjoys the right to assemble employees for lengthy anti-union harangues.

Then there is the more elemental and biological right—and surely it should be one—to respond to nature's calls. Federal regulations forbid employers to "impose unreasonable restrictions on employee use of the facilities." But according to Marc Linder and Ingrid Nygaard, co-authors of "Void Where Prohibited: Rest Breaks and the Right to Urinate on Company Time," this regulation is only halfheartedly enforced. Professionals and, of course, waitresses can usually dart away and relieve themselves as they please. Not so for many cashiers and assembly-line workers, some of whom, Linder says, have taken to wearing adult diapers to work.

In the area of privacy rights, workers have actually lost ground in recent years. Here, too, the base line is not impressive—no comprehensive right to personal privacy on the job has ever been established. I learned this on my first day as a waitress, when my fellow workers warned me that my purse could be searched by management at any time. I wasn't carrying stolen salt shakers or anything else of a compromising nature, but there's something about the prospect of a purse search that makes a woman feel a few buttons short of fully dressed. After work, I called around and found that this, too, is generally legal, at least if the boss has reasonable cause and has given prior notification of the company's search policies.

Purse searches, though, are relatively innocuous compared with the sophisticated chemical and electronic forms of snooping adopted by many companies in the '90s. The American Management Association reports that in 1999 a record two-thirds of major American companies monitored their employees electronically: videotaping them; reviewing their e-mail and voice-mail messages; and, most recently, according to Lewis Maltby, president of the Princeton-based National Workrights Institute, monitoring any Web sites they may visit on their lunch breaks. Nor can you count on keeping anything hidden in your genes; a growing number of employers now use genetic testing to screen out job applicants who carry genes for expensive ailments like Huntington's disease.

But the most ubiquitous invasion of privacy is drug testing, usually of urine, more rarely of hair or blood. With 81 percent of large companies now requiring some form of drug testing—up from 21 percent in 1987— job applicants take it for granted that they'll have to provide a urine sample as well as a résumé. This is not restricted to "for cause" testing— of people who, say, nod or space out on the job. Nor is it restricted to employees in "safety-sensitive occupations," like airline pilots and school-bus drivers. Workers who stack boxes of Cheerios in my local supermarkets get tested, as do the editorial employees of this magazine, although there is no evidence that a weekend joint has any more effect on Monday-morning performance than a Saturday-night beer.

Civil libertarians see drug testing as a violation of our Fourth Amendment protection from "unreasonable search," while most job-holders and applicants find it simply embarrassing. In some testing protocols, the employee has to strip to her underwear and urinate into a cup in the presence of an aide or technician, who will also want to know what prescription drugs she takes, since these can influence the test results.

According to a recent report from the American Civil Liberties Union, drug testing has not been proven to achieve its advertised effects, like reducing absenteeism and improving productivity. But it does reveal who's on antidepressants or suffering with an ailment that's expensive to treat, and it is undeniably effective at weeding out those potential "troublemakers" who are too independent-minded to strip and empty their bladders on command.

Maybe the prevailing trade-off between jobs and freedom would make sense, in the narrowest cost-benefit terms, if it contributed to a more vibrant economy. But this is hardly the case. In fact, a 1998 study of sixty-three computer-equipment and data-processing firms found that companies that performed both pre-employment and random drug testing actually "reduced rather than enhanced productivity"— by an eye-popping 29 percent, presumably because of its dampening effect on morale.

Why, then, do so many employers insist on treating their workers as a kind of fifth column within the firm? Certainly the government has played a role with its misguided antidrug crusade, as has the sheer availability of new technologies of snooping. But workplace repression signals a deeper shift away from the postwar social contract in which a job meant a straightforward exchange of work for wages.

Economists trace the change to the 1970s, when, faced with falling profits and rising foreign competition, America's capitalists launched an offensive to squeeze more out of their workers. Supervision tightened, management expanded and union-busting became a growth industry. And once in motion, the dynamic of distrust is hard to stop. Workers who are routinely treated like criminals and slackers may well bear close watching.

The mystery is why American workers, the political descendants of proud revolutionaries, have so meekly surrendered their rights. Sure, individual workers find ways to cheat on their drug tests, outwit the electronic surveillance and sneak in a bit of "gossip" here and there. But these petty acts of defiance seldom add up to concerted resistance, in part because of the weakness of American unions. The A.F.L.-C.I.O. is currently conducting a nationwide drive to ensure the right to organize, and the downtrodden workers of the world can only wish the union well. But what about all the other rights missing in so many American workplaces? It's not easy to organize your fellow workers if you can't communicate freely with them on the job and don't dare carry union literature in your pocketbook.

In a tight labor market, workers have another option, of course. They can walk. The alarming levels of turnover in low-wage jobs attest to the popularity of this tactic, and if unemployment remains low, employers may eventually decide to cut their workers some slack. Already, companies in particularly labor-starved industries like ski resorts and software are dropping drug testing rather than lose or repel employees. But in the short run, the mobility of workers, combined with the weakness of unions, means that there is little or no sustained on-site challenge to overbearing authority.

What we need is nothing less than a new civil rights movement—this time, for American workers. Who will provide the leadership remains to be seen, but clearly the stakes go way beyond "labor issues," as these are conventionally defined. We can hardly call ourselves the world's pre-eminent democracy if large numbers of citizens spend half of their waking hours in what amounts, in plain terms, to a dictatorship.

INTERPRETATIONS

1. What evidence does Ehrenreich cite to support her thesis that in many contemporary workplaces accepting a job may involve surrendering one's "civil rights"?

2. Ehrenreich devotes four paragraphs to the issue of drug testing in the workplace. With which of her positions do you agree or disagree?

3. What factors have contributed to "repression in the work force" according to Ehrenreich? Which do you find most convincing?

4. To what extent are American workers too passive? Do you agree with the author that they have "meekly surrendered their rights"? Why or why not?

CORRESPONDENCES

1. Review Terkel's perspective on work and discuss its relevance to Ehrenreich's essay. What examples of "violence of the spirit" does she cite?

2. The culture of the workplaces described by Soto and Ehrenreich minimize individual rights. What examples of repression in each essay do you find most affecting?

APPLICATIONS

1. Several sociological surveys indicate that job satisfaction is difficult to attain. Discuss with your group the implications of choosing a major in college based on job market trends or a major based on talents and interests.

2. Assume the role of manager and brainstorm with your group on creating strategies to make the workplace less regimented. Summarize your suggestions.

3. Describe someone with whom you work who obviously likes or dislikes his or her job. How much does that person communicate this in performance and attitude? How do such attitudes affect the workplace? Be specific.

4. Using Ehrenreich's essay as a guide, draw up your own "Workers' Bill of Rights." Then, with members of your small peer group, compare your list with the ones created by your classmates. Through negotiation and compromise, arrive at a consensus list. When your group shares its list with the lists generated by the other groups in your class, be attentive to those ideas that recur as well as those that do not.

Forty-Five a Month

R. K. NARAYAN

R. K. Narayan (1906–2001) was one of India's most prolific writers. During his lifetime Narayan wrote 34 novels, which include: Swami and Friends *(1935),* The English Teacher *(1953),* The Printer of Malgudi *(1957),* The Guide *(1958),* The Man-Eater of Malgudi *(1961),* The Vendor of Sweets *(1967),* The Painter of Signs *(1976), and* A Tiger for Malgudi *(1983). Narayan's short-story collections include:* Malgudi Days *(1982) and* The Grandmother's Tale and Selected Stories *(1994). As you read Narayan's story, think about how you would have reacted in Rao's situation.*

In 1947, India declared its independence from the British, who had controlled most of that country for about 300 years. Colonial India had at the same time been partitioned into Pakistan and India, creating in the same year about 12 million Hindu and Muslim refugees, of whom about 200,000 were killed. Mohandas K. Gandhi (known as the Mahatma), the leader of Indian independence who had advocated nonviolent civil disobedience and abolition of the Untouchable caste, was assassinated the year after independence. The Congress Party dominated Indian politics for forty years (from Independence until late 1989) under Prime Ministers Jawaharlal Nehru, his daughter Indira Gandhi (no relation to Mohandas), and her son Rajiv Gandhi. The Nehru-Gandhi dynasty ended when Rajiv Gandhi lost the November 1989 election and was assassinated while campaigning two years later. His successors have faced an electorate that is more assertive and more impatient, a new divergence between state and society, increasing clashes between Hindus, Sikhs, and Muslims, and ongoing tensions between India and its neighbors, particularly Pakistan.

Indian history, one of the oldest in the world, can be traced to at least 5,000 B.C. The founder of Buddhism lived in fifth-century India. In the third century B.C. Buddhism became the established religion; the native Hinduism revived, however, and eventually prevailed, and now claims well over three-quarters of the Indian population of 800 million.

SHANTA COULD NOT STAY IN HER CLASS any longer. She had done clay-modeling, music, drill, a bit of alphabets and numbers and was now cutting coloured paper. She would have to cut till the bell rang and the teacher said, "Now you may all go home," or "Put away the scissors and take up your alphabets—" Shanta was impatient to know the time. She asked her friend sitting next to her, "Is it five now?"

"Maybe," she replied.

"Or is it six?"

"I don't think so," her friend replied, "because night comes at six."

"Do you think it is five?"

"Yes."

"Oh, I must go. My father will be back at home now. He has asked me to be ready at five. He is taking me to the cinema this evening. I must go home." She threw down her scissors and ran up to the teacher. "Madam, I must go home."

"Why, Shanta Bai?"

"Because it is five o'clock now."

"Who told you it was five?"

"Kamala."

"It is not five now. It is—do you see the clock there? Tell me what the time is. I taught you to read the clock the other day." Shanta stood gazing at the clock in the hall, counted the figures laboriously and declared, "It is nine o'clock."

The teacher called the other girls and said, "Who will tell me the time from that clock?" Several of them concurred with Shanta and said it was nine o'clock, till the teacher said, "You are seeing only the long hand. See the short one, where is it?"

"Two and a half."

"So what is the time?"

"Two and a half."

"It is two forty-five, understand? Now you may all go to your seats—" Shanta returned to the teacher in about ten minutes and asked, "Is it five, madam, because I have to be ready at five. Otherwise my father will be very angry with me. He asked me to return home early."

"At what time?"

"Now." The teacher gave her permission to leave, and Shanta picked up her books and dashed out of the class with a cry of joy. She ran home, threw her books on the floor and shouted, "Mother, Mother," and Mother came running from the next house, where she had gone to chat with her friends.

Mother asked, "Why are you back so early?"

"Has Father come home?" Shanta asked. She would not take her coffee or *tiffin*[1] but insisted on being dressed first. She opened the trunk and insisted on wearing the thinnest frock and knickers, while her mother wanted to dress her in a long skirt and thick coat for the evening. Shanta picked out a gorgeous ribbon from a cardboard soap

---

[1]Midday snack.

box in which she kept pencils, ribbons and chalk bits. There was a heated argument between mother and daughter over the dress, and finally Mother had to give in. Shanta put on her favourite pink frock, braided her hair and flaunted a green ribbon on her pigtail. She powdered her face and pressed a vermilion mark on her forehead. She said, "Now Father will say what a nice girl I am because I'm ready. Aren't you also coming, Mother?"

"Not today."

Shanta stood at the little gate looking down the street.

Mother said, "Father will come only after five; don't stand in the sun. It is only four o'clock."

The sun was disappearing behind the house on the opposite row, and Shanta knew that presently it would be dark. She ran in to her mother and asked, "Why hasn't Father come home yet, Mother?"

"How can I know? He is perhaps held up in the office."

Shanta made a wry face. "I don't like these people in the office. They are bad people—"

She went back to the gate and stood looking out. Her mother shouted from inside, "Come in, Shanta. It is getting dark, don't stand there." But Shanta would not go in. She stood at the gate and a wild idea came into her head. Why should she not go to the office and call out Father and then go to the cinema? She wondered where his office might be. She had no notion. She had seen her father take the turn at the end of the street every day. If one went there, perhaps one went automatically to Father's office. She threw a glance about to see if Mother was anywhere and moved down the street.

It was twilight. Everyone going about looked gigantic, walls of houses appeared very high and cycles and carriages looked as though they would bear down on her. She walked on the very edge of the road. Soon the lamps were twinkling, and the passersby looked like shadows. She had taken two turns and did not know where she was. She sat down on the edge of the road biting her nails. She wondered how she was to reach home. A servant employed in the next house was passing along, and she picked herself up and stood before him.

"Oh, what are you doing here all alone?" he asked. She replied, "I don't know. I came here. Will you take me to our house?" She followed him and was soon back in her house.

Venkat Rao, Shanta's father, was about to start for his office that morning when a *jutka*[2] passed along the street distributing cinema

---

[2] A two-wheeled horse-drawn carriage.

handbills. Shanta dashed to the street and picked up a handbill. She held it up and asked, "Father, will you take me to the cinema today?" He felt unhappy at the question. Here was the child growing up without having any of the amenities and the simple pleasures of life. He had hardly taken her twice to the cinema. He had no time for the child. While children of her age in other houses had all the dolls, dresses and outings that they wanted, this child was growing up all alone and like a barbarian more or less. He felt furious with his office. For forty rupees[3] a month they seemed to have purchased him outright.

He reproached himself for neglecting his wife and child—even the wife could have her own circle of friends and so on: she was after all a grown-up, but what about the child? What a drab, colourless existence was hers! Every day they kept him at the office till seven or eight in the evening, and when he came home the child was asleep. Even on Sundays they wanted him at the office. Why did they think he had no personal life, a life of his own? They gave him hardly any time to take the child to the park or the pictures. He was going to show them that they weren't to toy with him. Yes, he was prepared even to quarrel with his manager if necessary.

He said with resolve, "I will take you to the cinema this evening. Be ready at five."

"Really! Mother!" Shanta shouted. Mother came out of the kitchen. "Father is taking me to a cinema in the evening."

Shanta's mother smiled cynically. "Don't make false promises to the child—" Venkat Rao glared at her. "Don't talk nonsense. You think you are the only person who keeps promises—"

He told Shanta, "Be ready at five, and I will come and take you positively. If you are not ready, I will be very angry with you."

He walked to his office full of resolve. He would do his normal work and get out at five. If they started any old tricks of theirs, he was going to tell the boss, "Here is my resignation. My child's happiness is more important to me than these horrible papers of yours."

All day the usual stream of papers flowed onto his table and off it. He scrutinized, signed and drafted. He was corrected, admonished and insulted. He had a break of only five minutes in the afternoon for his coffee.

When the office clock struck five and the other clerks were leaving, he went up to the manager and said, "May I go, sir?" The manager looked up from his paper. "You!" It was unthinkable that the cash and account section should be closing at five. "How can you go?"

---

[3]The rupee is an Indian unit of money.

"I have some urgent private business, sir," he said, smothering the lines he had been rehearsing since the morning: "Herewith my resignation." He visualized Shanta standing at the door, dressed and palpitating with eagerness.

"There shouldn't be anything more urgent than the office work; go back to your seat. You know how many hours I work?" asked the manager. The manager came to the office three hours before opening time and stayed nearly three hours after closing, even on Sundays. The clerks commented among themselves, "His wife must be whipping him whenever he is seen at home; that is why the old owl seems so fond of his office."

"Did you trace the source of that ten-eight difference?" asked the manager.

"I shall have to examine two hundred vouchers. I thought we might do it tomorrow."

"No, no, this won't do. You must rectify it immediately."

Venkat Rao mumbled, "Yes, sir," and slunk back to his seat. The clock showed 5:30. Now it meant two hours of excruciating search among vouchers. All the rest of the office had gone. Only he and another clerk in his section were working, and of course, the manager was there. Venkat Rao was furious. His mind was made up. He wasn't a slave who had sold himself for forty rupees outright. He could make that money easily; and if he couldn't, it would be more honourable to die of starvation.

He took a sheet of paper and wrote: "Herewith my resignation. If you people think you have bought me body and soul for forty rupees, you are mistaken. I think it would be far better for me and my family to die of starvation than slave for this petty forty rupees on which you have kept me for years and years. I suppose you have not the slightest notion of giving me an increment. You give yourselves heavy slices frequently, and I don't see why you shouldn't think of us occasionally. In any case it doesn't interest me now, since this is my resignation. If I and my family perish of starvation, may our ghosts come and haunt you all your life—" He folded the letter, put it in an envelope, sealed the flap and addressed it to the manager. He left his seat and stood before the manager. The manager mechanically received the letter and put it on his pad.

"Venkat Rao," said the manager, "I'm sure you will be glad to hear this news. Our officer discussed the question of increments today, and I've recommended you for an increment of five rupees. Orders are not yet passed, so keep this to yourself for the present." Venkat Rao put out his hand, snatched the envelope from the pad and hastily slipped it in his pocket.

"What is that letter?"

"I have applied for a little casual leave, sir, but I think . . ."

"You can't get any leave for at least a fortnight to come."

"Yes, sir, I realize that. That is why I am withdrawing my application, sir."

"Very well. Have you traced that mistake?"

"I'm scrutinizing the vouchers, sir. I will find it out within an hour . . ."

It was nine o'clock when he went home. Shanta was already asleep. Her mother said. "She wouldn't even change her frock, thinking that any moment you might be coming and taking her out. She hardly ate any food; and wouldn't lie down for fear of crumpling her dress. . . ."

Venkat Rao's heart bled when he saw his child sleeping in her pink frock, hair combed and face powdered, dressed and ready to be taken out. "Why should I not take her to the night show?" He shook her gently and called, "Shanta, Shanta." Shanta kicked her legs and cried, irritated at being disturbed. Mother whispered, "Don't wake her," and patted her back to sleep.

Venkat Rao watched the child for a moment. "I don't know if it is going to be possible for me to take her out at all—you see, they are giving me an increment—" he wailed.

INTERPRETATIONS

1. Why do you think Narayan focuses on the daughter at the outset of the story?

2. "For forty rupees a month they seemed to have purchased him outright." Is this an accurate portrayal of Rao's situation? How does his personality contribute to his dissatisfaction at work?

3. Analyze the mother's role in the story. Does she share her husband's antipathy toward his job? How do you know?

CORRESPONDENCES

1. Ehrenreich and Narayan focus on rights in the workplace from different vantage points and cultural perspectives. What conversation can you imagine them sharing?

2. Review Terkel's perspective on work and discuss its relevance to the texts by Narayan and Ehrenreich.

APPLICATIONS

1. Imagine yourself in Shanta's position and write a journal entry on your emotional responses to your father's broken promise.

2. Narayan's stories often reflect the conflict between tradition and individuality. How are both reflected in "Forty-Five a Month"? Analyze the elements of the conflict.

3. Brainstorm with your group on images of power. Do you associate power with the workplace? In what context? Is it possible to have power within the constraints of the employee–employer relationship? Summarize the group's discussion.

4. In the story "Forty-Five a Month," the plot seems to follow directly from the beginning to the end. Despite the hopes and expectations of both Shanta and a reader, Venkat Rao will not attend the cinema that evening. What, however, do you think would have happened if Rao had said his piece and left his resignation with his manager? How would this twist in plot affect not only what happens in the story but characterization, setting, and theme? After considering the possibilities, write your version of a section of the story that takes into account the twist in plot offered above. Try as best you can to match Nayaran's style and literary technique (e.g., attention to detail, use of dialogue, involvement of the narrator).

Free and Equal

LALITA GANDBHIR

Lalita Gandbhir (b. 1938) works as a physician in the Boston area, where she has lived since coming to the United States in 1963. She has published stories in the Toronto South Asian Review, *the* Massachusetts Review, Spotlight, *and other journals, as well as two collections of short stories in India. Before reading her short story, freewrite about your association with its title.*

RAMESH CAREFULLY STUDIED his reflection in the mirror hung in the hallway. His hair, shirt, tie, suit, nothing escaped his scrutiny. His tie seemed a little crooked, so he undid it and fixed it with slow deliberate movements. Then he reexamined the tie. A conservative shade of maroon, not too wide, not too narrow, just right for the occasion, for the image he wanted to project.

All of a sudden he was aware of two eyes staring at him. He turned to Jay, his little son. Jay sat on the steps leading to the second floor, his eyes focused on his father.

"Why are you staring at me?" Ramesh inquired.

"Going to work now?" Jay intimated the reason for the surprised stare.

Ramesh understood the reason behind Jay's confusion. He used to go to work dressed like this in the mornings. Jay had not seen him dressed in a suit in the evening.

For a moment Ramesh was proud of his son. "What a keen observer Jay is!" Ramesh thought to himself. "For six months I have not worked, yet he noticed a change in my old routine."

However, the implications behind the question bothered Ramesh.

"I am going to a job fair," he answered irritably and again attempted to focus on his tie.

"Can I come?" Jay promptly hurled a question in Ramesh's direction. To him a fair was a fun event. He had been to fairs with his mother before and did not wish to miss this one.

"Jay, this is not the kind of fair you are thinking of. This is a job fair."

"Do they sell jobs at job fairs?"

"Yes." Jay's question struck a sensitive spot. "No, they don't sell jobs. They are buyers. They shop for skills. It's me who is selling my skills. Unfortunately, it's a buyer's market."

The question stimulated Ramesh's chain of thought. "Is my skill for sale?" Ramesh wondered. "If that is true, then why did I dress so carefully? Why did I rehearse answers to imaginary questions from interviewers?"

"No, this job hunting is no longer a simple straightforward business transaction like it used to be when engineers were in demand. I am desperate. I am selling my soul. The job market is no longer a two-way street. I have no negotiating power. I just have to accept what I can get."

Ramesh pulled on his socks mechanically and longingly thought of the good old days like a sick old man thinking of his healthful youth.

Just ten years ago he had hopped from job to job at will. Money, interesting work, more responsibility, benefits, a whim for any reason that appealed to him, and he had switched jobs. Responding to advertisements was his hobby. Head hunters called him offering better and better situations. He went to job fairs casually dressed and never gave a second thought to his attire.

He had job offers, not one or two, but six or seven. The industry needed him then. It was so nice to be coveted!

Ramesh wiped his polished, spotless shoes with a soft cloth.

How carefree he used to be! He dressed like this every morning in five minutes and, yes, Jay remembers.

He never polished his shoes then. His hand moving the cloth on his shoes stood still for a minute. Yes, Rani, his wife, did it for him. Nowadays she seemed to do less and less for him. Why? He asked himself.

Rani had found a part-time job on her own when companies in the area had started to lay off engineers. She had not bothered to discuss the matter with him, just informed him of her decision. In a year she accepted a full-time slot. "How did she manage to receive promotions so soon?" Ramesh wondered.

Rani still ran the home and cared for their young children. Ramesh had seen her busy at all kinds of tasks from early morning until late at night.

Over the last three months she did less and less for Ramesh. She no longer did his laundry or ironing. She had stopped polishing his shoes and did not wait up for him when he returned late from job fairs.

"She is often tired," Ramesh tried to understand, but he felt that she had let him down, wronged him just when his spirit was sinking and he needed her most.

"She should have made an effort for the sake of appearance. It was her duty toward a jobless, incomeless husband."

He pushed all thoughts out of his mind.

He tied his polished shoes, dragged his heavy winter coat out of the closet, and picked up his keys.

"Tell your Ma that I have left," he ordered Jay, and closed the door without saying good-bye to Rani.

In the car, thoughts flooded his mind again.

Perhaps he made a mistake in coming to study abroad for his Master's in engineering. No! That was not the error. He should not have stayed on after he received his Master's. He should have returned home as he originally planned.

He intended to return, but unfortunately he attended a job fair after graduation just for fun and ended up accepting a job offer. A high salary in dollars converted into a small fortune in rupees, proved impossible to resist. He always converted dollars into rupees then, before buying or selling. He offered himself an excuse of short-term American experience and stayed on. The company that hired him sponsored him for a green card.

He still wanted to return home, but he postponed it, went for a visit instead and picked Rani from several prospective brides, married her and returned to the United States.

The trip left bitter memories, especially for Rani. He could not talk his mother out of accepting a dowry.

"Mother, Rani will earn the entire sum of a dowry in a month in the United States. A dowry is a hardship for her middle-class family. Let us not insist on it. Just accept what her family offers."

But Mother, with Father's tacit support, insisted. "You are my only son. I have waited for this occasion all my life. I want a proper wedding, the kind of wedding our friends and relatives will remember forever."

Ramesh gave in to her wishes and had a wedding with pomp and special traditional honors for his family. His mother was only partially gratified because she felt that their family did not get what was due them with her foreign returned son! The dowry, however, succeeded in upsetting Rani, who looked miserable throughout the ceremony.

"We will refund all the money once you come to the United States," Ramesh promised her. "It's a minor sum when dollars are converted to rupees."

Instead of talking in his conciliatory tone, Rani demanded, too harshly for a bride, "If it's a minor sum, why did you let your family insist on a dowry? You know my parents' savings are wiped out."

Over a few years they refunded the money, but Rani's wounds never healed and during fights she referred to the dowry spitefully.

Her caustic remarks did not bother Ramesh before, but now with her income supporting the family, they were beginning to hurt. "Write your mother that your wife works and makes up for part of the dowry her father failed to provide!" she had remarked once.

"Don't women ever forgive?" he had wondered.

"I am extra sensitive." He brushed off the pain that Rani's words caused.

The job fair was at a big hotel. He followed the directions and turned into a full parking lot. As he pulled into the tight space close to the exit, he glanced at the hotel lobby. Through the glass exterior wall, underneath a brightly lit chandelier, he could see a huge crowd milling in the lobby.

Panic struck him. He was late. So many people had made it there ahead of him. All applicants with his experience and background might be turned away.

Another car approached and pulled into the last parking space in the lot. The engine noise died and a man roughly his height and build stepped out, just as Ramesh shut his car door. Out on the walkway Ramesh heard a greeting.

"Hello, how are you?"

Ramesh looked up.

In the fluorescent lights his eyes met friendly blue eyes. He noticed a slightly wrinkled forehead and receding hairline, like his own.

"Hello," Ramesh responded.

The stranger smiled. "Sometimes I wonder why I come to these fairs. In the last six months I must have been to at least ten."

"Really? So have I!" He must have been laid off at the same time, Ramesh thought.

"We must have attended the same ones. I don't remember seeing you," the newcomer said.

"Too many engineers looking for a job—you know," Ramesh offered as explanation.

The pair had approached the revolving lobby doors. Ramesh had a strong urge to turn back and return home.

"Come on, we must try." The newcomer apparently had sensed the urge. "My name is Bruce. Would you like to meet me at the door in an hour? We will have a drink before we go home. It will—kind of lift my spirits."

"All right," Ramesh agreed without thinking and added, "I am Ramesh."

Bruce waited for Ramesh to step into the revolving door.

Ramesh mechanically pushed into the lobby. His heart sagged even further. "With persons like Bruce looking for a job, who will hire a foreigner like me?" he wondered. He looked around. Bruce had vanished into the crowd.

Ramesh looked at a row of booths set up by the side wall. He approached one looking for engineers with his qualifications. A few

Americans had already lined up to talk to the woman screening the applicants.

She looked at him and repeated the same questions she had asked applicants before him. "Your name, sir?"

He had to spell it. She made a mistake in noting it down. He had to correct her.

"Please fill out this application." He sensed a slight irritation in her voice.

"Thank you," he said. His accent seemed to have intensified. He took the application and retreated to a long table.

He visited six or seven booths of companies who might need—directly, indirectly, or remotely—someone of his experience and education; challenge, benefit package, location, salary, nothing mattered to him anymore. He had to find a job.

An hour and a half later, as he approached the revolving door, he noticed Bruce waiting for him.

During the discussion over drinks, he discovered that Bruce had the same qualifications as himself. However, Bruce had spent several years wandering around the world, so he had only four years of experience. Ramesh had guessed right. Bruce had been laid off the same time as himself.

"It's been very hard," Bruce said. "What little savings we had are wiped out and my wife is fed up with me. She thinks I don't try hard. This role reversal is not good for a man's ego."

"Yes," Ramesh agreed.

"I may have to move but my wife doesn't want to. Her family is here."

"I understand."

"I figure you don't have that problem."

"No. You must have guessed I'm from India."

After a couple of drinks they walked out into an empty lobby and empty parking lot.

Two days later Bruce called. "Want to go to a job fair? It's in Woodland, two hundred miles from here. I hate to drive out alone." Ramesh agreed.

"Who will hire me when Americans are available?" he complained to Rani afterward.

"You must not think like that. You are as good as any of them," Rani snapped. "Remember what Alexander said."

Ramesh remembered. Alexander was a crazy history student with whom he had shared an apartment. Rani always referred to Alexander's message.

Ramesh had responded to an advertisement on his university's bulletin board and Alexander had answered the phone.

"You have to be crazy to share an apartment with me. My last roommate left because he could not live with me."

"What did you do? I mean, why did he leave?" Ramesh asked.

"I like to talk. You see, I wake up people and tell them about my ideas at night. They call me crazy Alexander . . ."

"I will get back to you." Ramesh put the receiver down and talked to the student who had moved out.

"You see, Alexander's a nut. He sleeps during the day and studies at night. He's a history buff. He studies revolutions. He wakes up people just to talk to them, about theories, others and his own! He will offer to discount the rent if you put up with him."

Short of funds, Ramesh moved in with Alexander.

Much of Alexander's oratory bounced off Ramesh's half-asleep brain, but off and on a few sentences made an impression and stuck in his memory.

"You must first view yourself as free and equal," Alexander had said.

"Equal to whom?"

"To those around you who consider you less than equal . . ."

"Me? Less than equal?"

"No! Not you, stupid. The oppressed person. Oppression could be social, religious, foreign, traditional."

"Who oppressed me?"

"No! No! Not you! An imaginary oppressed person who must first see himself as the equal of his oppressors. The idea of equality will ultimately sow seeds of freedom and revolution in his mind. That idea is the first step. You see . . . stop snoring . . . That's the first step toward liberation."

Soon Ramesh walked like a zombie.

In another month, he too moved out.

After his marriage he told Rani some of his conversations with Alexander.

"Makes sense," she said, looking very earnest.

"Really! You mean you understand?" Rani's reaction amazed Ramesh.

"Yes, I do. I am an oppressed person, socially and traditionally. That's why my parents had to come up with a dowry."

A month went by and Ramesh was called for an interview.

Bruce telephoned the same night. He and some other engineers he knew had also been called. Had Ramesh received a call, too?

Ramesh swallowed hard. "No, I didn't." He felt guilty and ashamed. He had lied to Bruce, who was so open, friendly, and supportive, despite his own difficulties.

Ramesh's ego had already suffered a major trauma. He was convinced that he would not get a job if Americans were available and he did not wish to admit to Bruce later on, "I had an interview, but they didn't hire me." It was easier to lie now.

The interview over, Ramesh decided to put the job out of his mind. His confidence at a low ebb, he dared not hope.

Three weeks went by and he received a phone call from the company that interviewed him. He had the job.

"They must have hired several engineers," Ramesh thought, elated.

Bruce called again. "I didn't get the job. The other guys I know have also received negative replies."

The news stunned Ramesh. He could not believe that he had the job and the others did not. As he pondered this, he realized he owed an embarrassing explanation to Bruce. How was he going to tell him that he had the job?

As Bruce jabbered about something, Ramesh collected his courage.

"I have an offer from them," he stated in a flat tone and strained his ear for a response.

After a few unbearable seconds of silence, Bruce exclaimed, "Congratulations! At least one of us made it. Now we can all hope. I know you have better qualifications."

Ramesh knew that the voice was sincere, without a touch of the envy he had anticipated.

They agreed to meet Saturday for a drink, a small celebration, Bruce suggested.

"Rani, I got the job. The others didn't." Ramesh hung up the receiver and bounded up to Rani.

"I told you you are as good as any of them," Rani responded nonchalantly and continued to fold laundry.

"Maybe . . . possibly . . . they needed a minority candidate," Ramesh muttered.

Rani stopped folding. "Ramesh," she said as her eyes scanned Ramesh's face, "You may have the job and the knowledge and the qualifications, but you are not free and equal."

"What do you mean?" Ramesh asked.

INTERPRETATIONS

1. Alexander, for all his eccentricities, is portrayed as the voice of wisdom. How does his "message" of free and equal relate to the problems of job seeking? To the problems of competition between foreign and native-born job seekers? To the problem of dowries?

2. How realistic is Bruce's lack of resentment that Ramesh got a job? How well does the story make us believe in Ramesh's "better qualifications"?

3. From your own experience, what is the usual relationship between two candidates competing in a limited job market? Do they confide in each other or share tips? Does the first one to get a job feel guilty?

CORRESPONDENCES

1. Soto and Gandbhir discuss how one's job affects self-respect. Which examples did you find most convincing?

2. What was Gandbhir's purpose in writing this story? Is she trying to show human nature in action, or to entertain, or to persuade? How does her purpose compare with Narayan's?

APPLICATIONS

1. "You may have the job and the knowledge and the qualifications, but you are not free and equal." Discuss Rani's assessment of her husband. Is it possible for Ramesh to be "free and equal" in the United States? Why or why not?

2. Discuss with your group your images of success. To what extent do they involve economic prosperity? Your self-image? Is it possible for everyone to be successful? Do individual strivings for success affect communal values? How?

3. Discuss with your group issues of discrimination in the workplace involving race, gender, disabilities, and/or seniority. What suggestions would you make to cope with these situations?

A View of Affirmative Action in the Workplace

MICHAEL GNOLFO

Michael Gnolfo was born in Brooklyn, New York, in 1951. He grew up in Queens, and lives in Nassau County on Long Island with his wife and son. He works for a major utility company as a customer-service supervisor. He returned to college after a sixteen-year absence and is now a graduate of Queensborough Community College. Before reading Gnolfo's essay, write a journal entry on your views on affirmative action.

AFFIRMATIVE ACTION IS BY DEFINITION any plan or program that promotes the employment of women and members of minority groups. This has come about to right all the wrongs suffered by these groups in the past. It is intended to be a positive force for civil rights.

Directly or indirectly, because of Affirmative Action women and minorities have increasingly found more opportunity where none existed for them. Traditional role separation is disappearing. Society is realizing an untapped wealth of talent, and business is reaping a whirl-wind of benefits from this new diversity.

Jobs that were traditionally male-dominated have had major inroads by women. Bus drivers, construction workers, telephone technicians and pilots now count women among their numbers as do the management staffs of many corporations. The reverse is also true. Men have increasingly entered such fields as nursing, secretarial sciences and flight attendants, which have been traditionally female occupations. It seems that no barriers exist to an individual with the skills to perform a job.

While all of this is good and the proper course to pursue, there are problems. We can all agree that the protection and promotion of one group in society is wrong. So, when does a program designed to promote fairness become discriminatory? When capable people are neglected at the expense of less capable or similarly capable politically correct/connected candidates. A glaring example of this is the New York City Police exam and requirements. A comparison of physical requirements from today versus thirty years ago reveals a less demanding test of strength and physique. The requirements were relaxed to allow lesser physical candidates to pass. Minority candidates with lower written test marks are also taken over other candidates if a certain percentage of those minorities are not represented on the force. We are legislating mediocrity at best. What is more desirable, a competent organization or a gender/racially correct structure?

Private business is doing just the same. It is especially true in any large company that is contractually obligated to the government or is regulated by it. Those not included in Affirmative Action become less likely to be successful despite qualification. They are fast becoming a new oppressed minority. Companies are zealous in their adherence to Affirmative Action not out of altruism but of fear of loss of contract or stiffer regulation. Remember that while there has been much progress by minorities in business there is a dearth of minority CEOs in the major corporations, and that says so much about the reality of Affirmative Action.

The time is right for another step in the evolution of American society. We all realize the positive contributions of the groups protected by Affirmative Action. They have been valuable additions to our society. But abuses have now surfaced. Let's not make the same mistakes we made before. We need a Positive Fairness principle to replace Affirmative Action. Qualification and achievement should be the deciding factors in society and business. Quotas are abhorrent. Discrimination is bad, be it directed toward a race, gender, religion or anyone for any reason. Affirmative Action is becoming a racist, sexist instrument that is quickly turning into a tool of those who would replace one form of dominance with another. Contrary to the belief of feminists, the best man for the job is not a WOMAN but the most qualified individual.

INTERPRETATIONS

1. Gnolfo says that the purpose of Affirmative Action has been "to right all the wrongs suffered by these groups in the past." If this was once a worthwhile goal, has the goal been met? Are there perhaps other reasons for Affirmative Action (such as diversification) that make it still worthwhile?

2. What is the relationship between economic hard times and Affirmative Action in the workplace?

3. What is the legal status of Affirmative Action? Gnolfo says that companies don't practice Affirmative Action out of "altruism." What difference would it make if it were voluntary? Would it still accomplish its goal without the "abuses" Gnolfo attributes to it?

4. Comment on the relationship between Gnolfo's first three paragraphs and the rest of the essay. How effective is this two-part organization?

CORRESPONDENCES

1. Gnolfo examines the effects of Affirmative Action in the workplace. What conversation can you imagine him having with Ramesh in "Free and Equal"?

2. "Affirmative Action is becoming a racist, sexist instrument that is quickly turning into a tool of those who would replace one form of dominance with another." To what extent do you agree or disagree? Compare Gnolfo's assessment of Affirmative Action with that expressed in Steinem's perspective on work.

APPLICATIONS

1. Affirmative Action is a controversial issue. If you are a member of a minority group who could benefit from Affirmative Action, write an essay citing reasons why your choice to do so is ethical. If you are in a position to be hurt by Affirmative Action, write an essay citing reasons why Affirmative Action programs offer unfair opportunities to minorities. Be as specific as you can.

2. Discuss Gnolfo's thesis that, "Contrary to the belief of feminists, the best man for the job is not a WOMAN but the most qualified individual."

3. Write an essay analyzing the causes and effects of women's entry into the workplace in the nineties. You might focus on *one* of the following issues: the responsibility of the employer or the state to provide adequate child care, or the impact of working mothers playing multiple roles.

4. In his third paragraph Gnolfo states, "Jobs that were traditionally male dominated have had major inroads by women." Do you agree with this statement? Check these sites to support your opinions.

    http://www.gendercenter.org/genderwork.htm

    http://www.census.gov/population/
    pop-profile/2000/chap20.pdf

    ftp://ftp.bls.gov/pub/special.requests/lf/aat10.txt

The Knowing Eye

Linda Stanley

READING IMAGES

1. What kinds of work are the people in the photographs doing? In general, are cultural values placed upon some kinds of work more than others? Explain your answers to these questions.

2. To an extent, the language we speak is also the language of the gestures we make with our bodies. Focus upon the hands and arms of the people in the photographs. What do these gestures seem to be saying?

Zachary Rutkin

MAKING CONNECTIONS

1. The photograph of the man and woman shows them working; however, this image recalls the theme of Chapter 3 ("Gender Issues"). Do you agree or disagree with this observation? Explain your answer in detail.

2. In "Living Up the Street Black Hair," Gary Soto writes about his observations and feelings when working in a tire shop. How do you think the workers in the fish market would relate to Soto's essay?

WORDS AND IMAGES

1. How are these images similar to and different from each other? Write an essay (you might use comparison and contrast form) that presents your findings and that also comes to a conclusion about the photographs.

2. There is a saying that a picture is worth a thousand words. Pick one photograph and write an essay that expresses your thoughts about it. Be sure to create a focused essay, using a clear thesis statement and body paragraphs to support it.

Additional Writing Topics

1. Economic success has long been associated with the American dream. View two videos on this topic made approximately 50 years apart—*Death of a Salesman* and/or the more recent *Field of Dreams*, *Wall Street*, or *Boiler Room*. Write a review of both films comparing and contrasting their perspectives on success and failure.

2. Reflect on your reasons for pursuing your education. To what extent are they related to your professional goals? Are your goals market driven or based on personal preference? Write a journal entry on these issues.

3. How do you define ambition? Are your personal ambitions contingent on your professional aspirations? How have familial expectations affected your choice of profession?

4. Review Sayers's perspective on work (page 230) and test its validity by interviewing people you know in various occupations on their attitudes toward working and the workplace. What conclusions did you reach? Write an analysis based on their responses.

5. Recent sociological surveys indicate that overworked parents in the U.S. are unable to provide a sense of family and community for their children. Discuss this with your group. How is it pertinent to the concept of latchkey children? How would you classify that lifestyle and its effects on family life? What solutions can you think of?

6. Working with your group, construct your own Bill of Rights for a changing workplace. You might consider such issues as:

   > Drug testing
   > Health benefits
   > Retirement plans
   > Child care
   > Flexible hours
   > Promotional opportunities
   > Tuition reimbursement for upgrading skills

   Write a brief rationale for the inclusion of each item in your "Bill."

7. Sociologists argue that despite stress, boredom, and burnout in the workplace, many Americans are unable to enjoy leisure time in simple pursuits. Do you agree? Why is it difficult for people to

relax off the job? Have leisure activities become more sophisticated, expensive, and complex? To what extent have they become
a burden?

8. Is there a career that has captured your imagination that you would
    like to pursue? Do you dream of being a musician, talk show host,
    archeologist, or lawyer? Write an essay explaining what draws you
    to this career. How do you intend to make it a reality?

CHAPTER

6

Traditions

THE IDEA OF TRADITION or heritage is inherent in most definitions of culture. A culture incorporates the shared knowledge, expectations, and beliefs of a group of people. The human imagination has always been captivated by the idea of the past and its connections to the present. Stories from the oral traditions of ancient cultures as well as our own evoke the powers and mysteries of the past by recreating a time in which myths, fables, legends, and archetypes dictated the values of human actions within the community. The ritual of orality—of storytelling— was an integral part of communal life, as tribe members from the oldest to the youngest listened to, recalled, or retold stories about creation, good and evil, war and peace, life and death.

In the United States we tend to value the new over the old; to seek solutions to problems that often involve breaking with the past. Older cultures like that of the Native Americans seek to preserve old ways handed down through generations. Paula Gunn Allen, a leading Native American writer and anthologist, writes in *Who Is Your Mother? Red Roots of White Feminism* (p. 14), "Rejection of tradition constitutes one of the major features of American life." Americans, continues Allen, can and should learn from Native Americans to value tradition: "The Native-American view, which highly values maintenance of traditional customs, values, and perspectives . . . has the advantage of providing a solid sense of identity and lowered levels of psychological and interpersonal conflict."

Robert Bellah qualifies this line of argument. He feels that the tendency of Americans to reject tradition does not necessarily eliminate its influence: "In our forward-facing society, we are more apt to talk about the future than the past . . . yet even in the debate about our future, our cultural tradition, in its several strands, is still very much present . . ."

(*Habits of the Heart: Individualism and Commitment in American Life,* 1985, p. 27). Thus it is no surprise that our attitude toward tradition is ambivalent. (We want it, but we want to be free of it; we love part of the tradition but also hate part of it.) Tradition is both past and future, both history and destiny: "So long as it is vital, the cultural tradition of a people—its symbols, ideas, and ways of feeling—is always *an argument about the meaning of the destiny its members share. Cultures are dramatic conversations* about things that matter to their participants, and American culture is no exception" (italics ours). Americans need to learn to participate in such conversations about our own traditions and those of other, older cultures.

It is no accident that several texts in this chapter come out of a very old culture: Bantu, Mayan, Native American, Northern European, Chinese, and Indian. Our purpose is to explore the significance of these traditions—both our own and those of others. These opening selections demonstrate the universal importance of traditions but also celebrate their diversity. They show that the "dramatic conversations about things that matter" are continuous and may lead to a number of conclusions. They suggest an astonishing variety of tradition in its "several strands": rituals, ceremonies, customs, "symbols, ideals, and ways of feeling." Little wonder, then, that *intra*-cultural (and, less wonder, *inter*-cultural) conversation is sometimes argument. You can see such arguments variously in progress in Yael Yarimi's reflections on the importance of cultural mourning and in Salman Rushdie's meditations on Bombay, his "lost city."

When "dramatic conversation" stops—when tradition is unquestioningly accepted or revered—it can stifle, maim, or kill. So, at least, suggests John King Fairbank as he looks at footbinding, a thousand-year-old custom that ended only in this century. In "The Lottery," a cautionary tale set in a New England village in the 1940s, Shirley Jackson also suggests that blind adherence to custom can be deadly. A similar point is made by Mark Fineman in his factual account of a tradition obsessed in his 1970s essay "Stone-Throwing in India: An Annual Bash."

Participation in conversations about your own traditions and those of other cultures can be challenging, even disturbing, since it may involve new ways of listening and seeing. It invites you to suspend judgment and avoid making unfavorable comparisons by looking at the value of a people and their culture through a different lens. Although it is impossible to be totally free of ethnocentrism, we hope that the overheard conversations in this chapter will deepen your appreciation of cultural pluralities.

Perspectives

History has a way of intruding upon the present.

—*Louise Erdrich*

Every man, every woman, carries in head and mind the image of the ideal place, the right place, the one true home, known or unknown, actual or visionary.

—*Edward Abbey*

Contemporary man has rationalized the myths, but he has not been able to destroy them.

—*Octavio Paz*

I was born a thousand years ago, born in the culture of bows and arrows . . . born in an age when people loved the things of nature, and spoke to it as though it had a soul.

—*Chief Dan George*

The past is a foreign country: they do things differently there.

—*L. P. Hartley*

I have found that life persists in the midst of destruction, and therefore, there must be a bigger law than that of destruction.

—*Mohandas K. (Mahatma) Gandhi*

The position of women in a society provides an exact measure of the development of that society.

—*Gustav Geiger*

Memory is the diary that we all carry about with us.

—*Oscar Wilde*

Tradition is a guide and not a jailor.

—*W. Somerset Maugham*

True places are not found on maps.

—*Herman Melville*

To everything there is a season, and a time to every purpose under the heaven: a time to be born, and a time to die; a time to plant, and a time to pluck up that which is planted; a time to kill, and a time to heal; a time to break down, and a time to build up; a time to weep, and a time to laugh; a time to mourn, and a time to dance; a time to cast away stones, and a time to gather stones together; a time to embrace, and a time to refrain from embracing; a time to get, and a time to lose; a time to keep, and a time to cast away; a time to rend, and a time to sew; a time to keep silence, and a time to speak; a time to love, and a time to hate; a time of war, and a time of peace. What profit hath he that worketh in that wherein he laboreth?

—Ecclesiastes 3:1–10

History is the present. That's why every generation writes it anew. But what most people think of as history is its end product, myth.

—E. L. Doctorow

We do not remember days, we remember moments.

—Cesare Pavese

We have to do with the past only as we can make it useful to the present and the future.

—Frederick Douglass

We want to remain curious, startled, provoked, mystified, and uplifted. We want to glare, gaze, gawk, behold, and stare. We want to be given opportunities to change, and ultimately we want to be told that we can become kings and queens, or lords of our own destinies. We remember wonder tales and fairy tales to keep our sense of wonderment alive and to nurture our hope that we can seize possibilities and opportunities to transform ourselves and our worlds.

—Jack Zipes

Memory is something we reconstruct, something we create. Memory is a story we make up from snatches of the past.

—Lynne Sharon Schwartz

Myths are public dreams, dreams are private myths.

—Joseph Campbell

Each act of creation shall leave you humble, for it is never as great as your dream and always inferior to that most marvelous dream of God which is nature.

—Gabriela Mistral

Gratitude is the heart's memory.

—French Proverb

To be ourselves we must have ourselves—possess, if need be repossess, our life-stories. We must "recollect" ourselves, recollect the inner drama, the narrative, of ourselves. A man needs such a narrative, a continuous inner narrative, to maintain his identity, his self.

—Oliver Sachs

Where I come from, the words that are most highly valued are those which are spoken from the heart, unpremeditated and unrehearsed. Among the Pueblo people, a written speech or statement is highly suspect because the true feelings of the speaker remain hidden as he reads words that are detached from the occasion and the audience.

—Leslie Marmon Silko

APPLICATIONS

1. Wilde and Schwartz comment on the relationship between memory and identity as well as its importance in the rituals of storytelling. Discuss their perspectives with your group. To what extent is it true that we all have stories to tell?

2. Analyze the points of view expressed in three perspectives on aspects of traditions. On what functions of traditions do they focus? What do they suggest about the roles of traditions? Do you agree that our attitude toward tradition is ambivalent? Write an essay using these questions as a framework.

3. To what extent do stories help us to know who we are? Is there a story that made an impression on you as a child? Summarize this story for your group and analyze the reasons for its effect.

Here are two different stories about how the world was created. The first is a legend from the Bantu, a diverse black people inhabiting a large part of southern Africa south of the Congo and speaking many languages (including Zulu and Swahili) and dialects. The second is the opening of the Popol Vuh, the sacred saga of the Quiché, a branch of the great Mayan civilization. The Quiché Maya live in what is now western Guatemala.

In the Beginning: Bantu Creation Story

AFRICAN LEGEND

IN THE BEGINNING, in the dark, there was nothing but water. And Bumba was alone.

One day Bumba was in terrible pain. He retched and strained and vomited up the sun. After that light spread over everything. The heat of the sun dried up the water until the black edges of the world began to show. Black sandbanks and reefs could be seen. But there were no living things.

Bumba vomited up the moon and then the stars, and after that the night had its light also.

Still Bumba was in pain. He strained again and nine living creatures came forth: the leopard named Koy Bumba, and Pongo Bumba the crested eagle, the crocodile, Ganda Bumba, and one little fish named Yo; next, old Kono Bumba, the tortoise, and Tsetse, the lightning, swift, deadly, beautiful like the leopard; then the white heron, Nyanyi Bumba, also one beetle, and the goat named Budi.

Last of all came forth men. There were many men, but only one was white like Bumba. His name was Loko Yima.

The creatures themselves then created all the creatures. The heron created all the birds of the air except the kite. He did not make the kite. The crocodile made serpents and the iguana. The goat produced every beast with horns. Yo, the small fish, brought forth all the fish of all the seas and waters. The beetle created insects.

Then the serpents in their turn made grasshoppers, and the iguana made the creatures without horns.

Then the three sons of Bumba said they would finish the world. The first, Nyonye Ngana, made the white ants; but he was not equal to the task, and died of it. The ants, however, thankful for life and being, went searching for black earth in the depths of the world and covered the barren sands to bury and honour their creator.

Chonganda, the second son, brought forth a marvellous living plant from which all the trees and grasses and flowers and plants in the world have sprung. The third son, Chedi Bumba, wanted something different, but for all his trying made only the bird called the kite.

Of all the creatures, Tsetse, lightning, was the only troublemaker. She stirred up so much trouble that Bumba chased her into the sky. Then mankind was without fire until Bumba showed the people how to draw fire out of trees. "There is fire in every tree," he told them, and showed them how to make the firedrill and liberate it. Sometimes today Tsetse still leaps down and strikes the earth and causes damage.

When at last the work of creation was finished, Bumba walked through the peaceful villages and said to the people, "Behold these wonders. They belong to you." Thus from Bumba, the Creator, the First Ancestor, came forth all the wonders that we see and hold and use, and all the brotherhood of beasts and man.

Quiché-Mayan Creation Story

QUICHÉ-MAYAN LEGEND

BEFORE THE WORLD WAS CREATED, Calm and Silence were the great kings that ruled. Nothing existed, there was nothing. Things had not yet been drawn together, the face of the earth was unseen. There was only motionless sea, and a great emptiness of sky. There were no men anywhere, or animals, no birds or fish, no crabs. Trees, stones, caves, grass, forests, none of these existed yet. There was nothing that could roar or run, nothing that could tremble or cry in the air. Flatness and emptiness, only the sea, alone and breathless. It was night; silence stood in the dark.

In this darkness the Creators waited, the Maker, Tepeu, Gucumatz, the Forefathers. They were there in this emptiness, hidden under green and blue feathers, alone and surrounded with light. They are the same as wisdom. They are the ones who can conceive and bring forth a child from nothingness. And the time had come. The Creators were bent deep around talk in the darkness. They argued, worried, sighed over what was to be. They planned the growth of the thickets, how things would crawl and jump, the birth of man. They planned the whole creation, arguing each point until their words and thoughts crystallized and became the same thing. Heart of Heaven was there, and in the darkness the creation was planned.

Then let the emptiness fill! they said. Let the water weave its way downward so the earth can show its face! Let the light break on the ridges, let the sky fill up with the yellow light of dawn! Let our glory be a man walking on a path through the trees! "Earth!" the Creators called. They called only once, and it was there, from a mist, from a cloud of dust, the mountains appeared instantly. At this single word the groves of cypresses and pines sent out shoots, rivulets ran freely between the round hills. The Creators were struck by the beauty and exclaimed, "It will be a creation that will mount the darkness!"

INTERPRETATIONS

1. In the Bantu story "The creatures themselves then created all the creatures": Fish produced fish, birds produced birds (except for the predatory kite), and so on. How "scientific" is this explanation?

2. Why is there almost no explanation of Bumba's identity (other than his being white and "the Creator, the First Ancestor") or of his sickness? Are such details better omitted? Can you supply the missing explanation?

3. In the Bantu story what purpose does the retching incident serve? What tone does it set?

4. What is the purpose of the Bantu story?

5. How important in the Quiché creation story is language?

6. In the Quiché story what are the Creators' main attributes? How are they demonstrated in the story?

7. What seems to be the Creators' main motive in creating "a man" in the Quiché story?

8. Interpret the last sentence of the Quiché story. What explanation does it provide for the Creation?

CORRESPONDENCES

1. Review the perspective from Ecclesiastes (page 279). Compare the concepts in Ecclesiastes with those in the Bantu and Quiché stories. Which account do you prefer? How do they differ in implication?

2. Compare the tones and meanings of the two creation stories.

APPLICATIONS

1. Working in your group, discuss the roles and function of creation texts. Why is it important to become aware of different cultural explanations of the origins of the natural world? Analyze the significance of the motifs of light and darkness in both creation stories. What do they suggest about the nature of good and evil?

2. Review Zipes's perspective and write an essay in which you seek to persuade your audience on the importance of preserving a sense of wonder about yourself and the world. Be specific.

3. Write an essay discussing the importance of storytelling in your family. Have any of the stories become family traditions? What elements account for their popularity? How have the stories affected your sense of identity and that of your family?

Footbinding

JOHN KING FAIRBANK

John King Fairbank (1907–1991) was born in South Dakota and received degrees from Harvard and Oxford universities. He was the director emeritus of Harvard's East Asian Research Center and enjoyed a distinguished career in the field of Asian studies. His numerous books on China include Modern China: A Bibliographical Guide to Chinese Works, 1898–1937 *(1950);* The United States and China *(1971);* Chinabound: A Fifty-Year Memoir *(1983); and* China Watch *(1987). Before reading Fairbank's essay, consult a dictionary for a definition of footbinding.*

China, one of the world's oldest civilizations (dating at least to 5000 B.C.) with a fifth of the world's population (about a billion inhabitants), has had a tumultuous history, especially in the last two centuries. For thousands of years, beginning with the Shang Dynasty (about 1500–1000 B.C.), a succession of dynasties ruled China and expanded Chinese political and cultural domination of East Asia. In 1644 a foreign invader, the Manchus, established the Ch'ing Dynasty without destroying the underlying culture. The nineteenth century was a time of increasing stagnation and rebellion. European powers took advantage of internal strife to take control of large parts of the country. The country became a republic in 1912, but lost much of its territory to the Japanese, both before and during World War II. The People's Republic of China was declared in 1949 under the leadership of Mao Zedong, by which time footbinding—but not its effects—had vanished. In the excerpt that follows, Fairbank describes the rise of the custom of footbinding in the tenth century, details its mechanics and its influence on domestic life, and advances reasons for its longevity.

OF ALL THE MANY UNEXPLORED FACETS of China's ancient history, the subjection of women has been the least studied. Women were fitted into the social and cosmic order (which were a continuum) by invoking the principles of Yang and Yin. All things bright, warm, active, male, and dominant were Yang while all things dark, cold, passive, female, and yielding were Yin. This dualism, seen in the alternation of night and day or the contrast of the sun and moon, was a ready-made matrix in which women could be confined. The subjection of women was thus a sophisticated and perfected institution like the other Chinese achievements, not a mere accident of male biceps or female childbearing as might be more obviously the case in a primitive tribe. The inequality between the sexes was buttressed with philosophical underpinnings and long-continued social practices. Symbolic of woman's secondary status was her bridal night: she expected to be deflowered by a stranger, a husband selected by her family whom she had never seen before. Even though the facts may often have been less stark, the theory was hard-boiled.

Out of all this complex of theory and custom by which the Chinese world was given an enduring and stable order, the most neglected aspect is the institution of footbinding. This custom arose at court in the tenth century during the late T'ang and spread gradually among the upper class during the succeeding Sung period. By the Ming and Ch'ing eras after 1368 it had penetrated the mass of the Han Chinese population. It became so widespread that Western observers in the nineteenth century found it almost universal, not only among the upper class but throughout the farming population.

Footbinding spread as a mark of gentility and upper-class status. Small feet became a prestige item to such an extent that a girl without them could not achieve a good marriage arrangement and was subjected to the disrespect and taunts of the community. In short, bound feet became *de rigueur*, the only right-thinking thing to do for a daughter, an obligation on the part of a mother who cared about her daughter's eventual marriage and success in life. The bound foot was a must. Only tribal peoples and exceptional groups like the Manchu conquerors or the Hakka Chinese migrant groups in South China or finally the mean people, that lowest and rather small group who were below the social norms of civility, could avoid binding their daughters' feet.

The small foot was called a "golden lotus" or "golden lily" *(chin-lien)* and was much celebrated in poems and essays by male enthusiasts. Here is the early Sung poet Su Tung-p'o (1036–1101):

Anointed with fragrance, she takes lotus steps;
Though often sad, she steps with swift lightness.
She dances like the wind, leaving no physical trace.
Another stealthily but happily tries on the palace style,
But feels such distress when she tries to walk!
Look at them in the palms of your hands, so wondrously
small that they defy description.

The Sung philosophers stressed women's inferiority as a basic element of the social order. The great Chu Hsi (1130–1200) codified the cosmology of China as magistrally as his near contemporary Thomas

Aquinas (d. 1274) codified that of Western Christendom. When he was a magistrate in Fukien province, Chu Hsi promoted footbinding to preserve female chastity and as "a means of spreading Chinese culture and teaching the separation of men and women."

By the Ming period the overwhelming majority of Han Chinese women all over the country had artificially small feet. The Manchu emperors many times inveighed against it in hortatory edicts, but to no avail. Male romanticizing on the subject continued unabated as in this poem of the fourteenth century:

> Lotus blossoms in shoes most tight,
> As if she could stand on autumnal waters!
> Her shoe tips do not peek beyond the skirt,
> Fearful lest the tiny embroideries be seen.[1]

There can be no doubt that footbinding was powered by a sexual fetish. Chinese love manuals are very specific about the use of bound feet as erogenous areas. All the different ways of taking hold of the foot, rubbing it with the hands, and using the mouth, tongue, and lips are explicitly catalogued. Many cases are recorded with the verisimilitude of high-class pornography. Meanwhile, the aesthetic attractiveness of the small shoes with their bright embroidered colors was praised in literature, while the tottering gait of a bound-foot woman was considered very fetching as a symbol of feminine frailty, which indeed it was. In fact, of course, bound feet were a guarantee of chastity because they kept women within the household and unable to venture far abroad. Lily feet, once formed, could not be unlocked like a chastity belt. By leaving only men able-bodied, they ensured male domination in a very concrete way.

Thus the prevalence of footbinding down to the 1920s, while the movement against it began only in the 1890s, vividly index the speed and scope of China's modern social revolution. This may be less comprehensible to white American males than to white women, or especially to black Americans, for Chinese women within the present century have had an emancipation from veritable slavery.

While footbinding is mentioned in so many foreign books about China, it is usually passed by as a curious detail. I don't think it was. It was a major erotic invention, still another achievement in Chinese social engineering. Girls painfully deformed themselves throughout their adolescence in order to attract desirable husbands who, on their part,

---

[1]Howard Levy, *Chinese Footbinding: The History of a Curious Erotic Custom* (New York: Walton Rawls, 1966), p. 47.

subscribed to a folklore of self-fulfilling beliefs: for example, that footbinding made a vagina more narrow and muscular and that lotus feet
were major foci of erotic sensitivity, true erogenous zones, a net addition of 50 percent to the female equipment. Normal feet, we are now
told by purveyors of sexual comfort, are an underdeveloped area sen-
sually, but one must admit they are a bit hard to handle—whereas small
lotus feet could be grasped, rubbed, licked, sucked, nibbled, and bitten.
The garrulous Jesuit Father Ripa, who spent a decade at the court of
K'ang-hsi in the early 1700s, reported that "Their taste is perverted to
such an extraordinary degree that I knew a physician who lived with a
woman with whom he had no other intercourse but that of viewing and
fondling her feet."[2] Having compacted all their nerve endings in a
smaller area, golden lilies were far more sensitive than, for example, the
back of the neck that used to bewitch Japanese samurai. After all, they
had been created especially for male appreciation. When every proper
girl did it, what bride would say that her sacrifice, suffering, and inconvenience were not worth it? A bride without small feet in the old China
was like a new house in today's America without utilities—who would
want it? Consequently in the 1930s and '40s one still saw women on
farms stumping about on their heels as they worked, victims of this old
custom.

A girl's foot was made small, preferably only three inches long, by
pressing the four smaller toes under the sole or ball of the foot (plantar)
in order to make it narrower. At the same time it was made shorter by
forcing the big toe and heel closer together so that the arch rose in a
bowed shape. As a result the arch was broken and the foot could bear
no weight except on the heel. If this process was begun at age five, the
experience was less severe than if a little girl, perhaps in a peasant
household, had been left with normal feet until age eight or ten so that
she could be of more use in the household.

> When I was seven [said one woman to Ida Pruitt], my mother . . .
> washed and placed alum on my feet and cut the toenails. She
> then bent my toes toward the plantar with a binding cloth ten
> feet long and two inches wide, doing the right foot first and then
> the left. She . . . ordered me to walk but when I did the pain
> proved unbearable. That night . . . my feet felt on fire and I
> couldn't sleep; mother struck me for crying. On the following
> days, I tried to hide but was forced to walk on my feet . . . after
> several months all toes but the big one were pressed against the

[2]Fortunato Prandi, ed. and trans., *Memoirs of Father Ripa* (London: John Murray, 1855),
p. 58.

inner surface . . . mother would remove the bindings and wipe the blood and pus which dripped from my feet. She told me that only with removal of the flesh could my feet become slender . . . every two weeks I changed to new shoes. Each new pair was one-to-two-tenths of an inch smaller than the previous one . . . In summer my feet smelled offensively because of pus and blood; in winter my feet felt cold because of lack of circulation . . . four of the toes were curled in like so many dead caterpillars . . . it took two years to achieve the three-inch model . . . my shanks were thin, my feet became humped, ugly and odoriferous.[3]

After the first two years the pain lessened. But constricting the feet to a three-inch size was only the beginning of trouble. By this time they were very private parts indeed and required daily care, washing and manicuring at the same time that they had to be kept constantly bound and shod night and day. Unmanicured nails could cut into the instep, bindings could destroy circulation, blood poisoning or gangrene could result. Massage and applications of hot and cold water were used to palliate the discomfort, but walking any distance remained difficult. It also produced corns on the bent-under toes, which had to be pared with a knife. Once deformed to taste, bound feet were of little use to stand on. Since weight was carried entirely on the heels, it had to be constantly shifted back and forth. Since the bound foot lacked the resilience of a normal foot, it was a tiring and unsteady support.

Footbinding, in short, had begun as an ostentatious luxury, which made a girl less useful in family work and more dependent on help from others. Yet, once the custom had spread among the populace, lotus feet were considered essential in order to get a good husband. Marriages, of course, were arranged between families and often by professional matchmakers, in whose trade the length of the lily foot was rated more important than beauty of face or person. When the anti-footbinding movement began at the end of the nineteenth century, many mothers and daughters, too, stubbornly clung to it to avoid the public shame of having large feet. The smallness of the foot, in short, was a source of social pride both to the family and to the victim. First and last one may guess that at least a billion Chinese girls during the thousand-year currency of this social custom suffered the agony of footbinding and reaped its rewards of pride and ecstasy, such as they were.

---

[3]Ida Pruitt, *A Daughter of Han: The Autobiography of a Chinese Working Woman* (New Haven: Yale University Press, 1945), p. 22.

There are three remarkable things about footbinding. First, that it should have been invented at all—it was such a feat of physio-psycho-sociological engineering. Second, that once invented it should have spread so pervasively and lasted so long among a generally humane and practical-minded farming population. We are just at the beginning of understanding this phenomenon. The fact that an upper-class erotic luxury permeated the peasantry of Old China, for whom it could only lower productivity, suggests that the old society was extraordinarily homogeneous.

Finally, it was certainly ingenious how men trapped women into mutilating themselves for an ostensibly sexual purpose that had the effect of perpetuating male domination. Brides left their own homes and entered their husband's family in the lowest status, servants of their mothers-in-law. Husbands were chosen for them sight unseen, and might find romance in extra-marital adventures or, if they could afford it, bring in secondary wives. But a woman once betrothed, if her husband-to-be died even as a child, was expected to remain a chaste widow thereafter. Mao remarked that "women hold up half the sky," but in the old China they were not supposed to lift their heads. The talent that one sees in Chinese women today had little chance to grow and express itself. This made a weak foundation for a modern society.

INTERPRETATIONS

1. What is Fairbank's purpose in describing "the principles of Yang and Yin"? How does this relate to the topic of footbinding? Does the intellectual theory (Yang-Yin) really explain any important aspects of Chinese behavior? Or is it a rationalization? A pretext? An emblem?

2. According to Fairbank, "there are three remarkable things about footbinding." What are they and why are they significant?

3. What examples can you give of elaborate psychological or other theories in contemporary America that have the aura of science or intellect but really explain very little? Do these theories affect our society for good or for ill, or do they simply remain in the realm of theory? If you find they have practical effects on people's behavior, what effects?

CORRESPONDENCES

1. Review the Douglass perspective on traditions (page 280). How does it apply to the selection by Fairbank? To what extent was footbinding "useful" in the culture of its day?

2. Review the Geiger perspective (page 279). How does it apply to "Footbinding"? To which other selections in this chapter is it also relevant? In what way?

APPLICATIONS

1. Fairbank estimates that "at least a billion Chinese girls during the thousand-year currency of this social custom suffered the agony of footbinding . . ." What does Fairbank's essay suggest about re-evaluating the custom?

2. What is the general relationship between tradition and individual desires? For example, are the traditional ethnic or tribal costumes you are familiar with calculated to promote individual beauty (or sex appeal) or the beliefs and values of the tribe or collective? Write an essay responding to these questions with specific examples.

3. A fetish is an inanimate object or charm thought to possess magical powers such as good luck or protection from evil. In psychiatry, fetishism is associated with an abnormal sexual attraction to an inanimate object such as a shoe. What associations do you and your group have with fetishes or fetishism? Summarize your discussion.

4. In "Footbinding," Fairbank writes about the physical subjugation of women. Do you think that such practices continue to exist? Check the following Web sites for information that you might use to formulate an argument.

   http://www.towson.edu/%7Eloiselle/foot.html

   http://outlawtv.com/333/016.htm

   http://www.nefilim.de/addfiles/myth/nephilim/articles/cranial_deformation.htm

The Algonquin Cinderella

NATIVE AMERICAN MYTH

The small Algonquin tribe of Canada was one of the first with whom the French formed alliances. Because of their mingling with whites, little remains of Algonquin culture. Their name, however, came to be used to designate other nearby tribes, and their language family (known as Algonquian) is one of the most widespread of all North American Indian languages, extending from New Brunswick to the Rocky Mountains. Among Indian languages in the Algonquian stock are the Arapaho, the Cheyenne, the Blackfoot, the Potawatami, the Ottawa, the Passamaquoddy, the Penobscot, the Delaware, and the Cree. Record your memory of the first fairy tale that impressed you as a child.

THERE WAS ONCE A LARGE VILLAGE of the MicMac Indians of the Eastern Algonquins, built beside a lake. At the far end of the settlement stood a lodge, and in it lived a being who was always invisible. He had a sister who looked after him, and everyone knew that any girl who could see him might marry him. For that reason there were very few girls who did not try, but it was very long before anyone succeeded.

This is the way the test of sight was carried out: at evening-time, when the Invisible One was due to be returning home, his sister would walk with any girl who might come down to the lakeshore. She, of course, could see her brother, since he was always visible to her. As soon as she saw him, she would say to the girls:

"Do you see my brother?"

"Yes," they would generally reply—though some of them did say "No."

To those who said that they could indeed see him, the sister would say:

"Of what is his shoulder strap made?" Some people say that she would enquire:

"What is his moose-runner's haul?" or "With what does he draw his sled?"

And they would answer:

"A strip of rawhide" or "a green flexible branch," or something of that kind.

Then she, knowing that they had not told the truth, would say:

"Very well, let us return to the wigwam!"

When they had gone in, she would tell them not to sit in a certain place, because it belonged to the Invisible One. Then, after they had helped to cook the supper, they would wait with great curiosity, to see him eat. They could be sure that he was a real person, for when he took off his moccasins they became visible, and his sister hung them up. But beyond this they saw nothing of him, not even when they stayed in the place all the night, as many of them did.

Now there lived in the village an old man who was a widower, and his three daughters. The youngest girl was very small, weak and often ill: and yet her sisters, especially the elder, treated her cruelly. The second daughter was kinder, and sometimes took her side: but the wicked sister would burn her hands and feet with hot cinders, and she was covered with scars from this treatment. She was so marked that people called her *Oochigeaskw*, the Rough-Faced-Girl.

When her father came home and asked her why she had such burns, the bad sister would at once say that it was her own fault, for she had disobeyed orders and gone near the fire and fallen into it.

These two elder sisters decided one day to try their luck at seeing the Invisible One. So they dressed themselves in their finest clothes, and tried to look their prettiest. They found the Invisible One's sister and took the usual walk by the water.

When he came, and when they were asked if they could see him, they answered: "Of course." And when asked about the shoulder strap or sled cord, they answered: "A piece of rawhide."

But of course they were lying like the others, and they got nothing for their pains.

The next afternoon, when the father returned home, he brought with him many of the pretty little shells from which wampum was made, and they set to work to string them.

That day, poor Little Oochigeaskw, who had always gone barefoot, got a pair of her father's moccasins, old ones, and put them into water to soften them so that she could wear them. Then she begged her sisters for a few wampum shells. The elder called her a "little pest," but the younger one gave her some. Now, with no other clothes than her usual rags, the poor little thing went into the woods and got herself some sheets of birch bark, from which she made a dress, and put marks on it for decoration, in the style of long ago. She made a petticoat and a loose gown, a cap, leggings and a handkerchief. She put on her father's large old moccasins, which were far too big for her, and went forth to try her luck. She would try, she thought, to discover whether she could see the Invisible One.

She did not begin very well. As she set off, her sisters shouted and hooted, hissed and yelled, and tried to make her stay. And the loafers around the village, seeing the strange little creature, called out "Shame!"

The poor little girl in her strange clothes, with her face all scarred, was an awful sight, but she was kindly received by the sister of the Invisible One. And this was, of course, because this noble lady understood far more about things than simply the mere outside which all the rest of the world knows. As the brown of the evening sky turned to black, the lady took her down to the lake.

"Do you see him?" the Invisible One's sister asked.

"I do, indeed—and he is wonderful!" said Oochigeaskw.

The sister asked:

"And what is his sled-string?"

The little girl said:

"It is the Rainbow."

"And, my sister, what is his bow-string?"

"It is the Spirit's Road—the Milky Way."

"So you *have* seen him," said his sister. She took the girl home with her and bathed her. As she did so, all the scars disappeared from her body. Her hair grew again, as it was combed, long, like a blackbird's wing. Her eyes were like stars; in all the world there was no other such beauty. Then, from her treasures, the lady gave her a wedding garment, and adorned her.

Then she told Oochigeaskw to take the *wife's* seat in the wigwam; the one next to where the Invisible One sat, beside the entrance. And when he came in, terrible and beautiful, he smiled and said:

"So we are found out!"

"Yes," said his sister. And so Oochigeaskw became his wife.

INTERPRETATIONS

1. Why does Oochigeaskw succeed where her sisters failed?

2. What explanation does the story offer or imply for Oochigeaskw's ability to see the Invisible One? How is this ability related to Oochigeaskw's persecuted position in the family?

3. How do the clothes Oochigeaskw makes or assembles for herself indicate a reverence for tradition? What effect do you think this reverence might have on her success in winning the Invisible One?

4. What part do moccasins play in the story?

CORRESPONDENCES

1. Compare the Native American version of the Cinderella story with the standard version you read as a child. What motifs do they have in common? How do they differ?

2. Review Chief Dan George's perspective on nature and discuss its relevance to "The Algonquin Cinderella."

APPLICATIONS

1. Write a contemporary version of a favorite childhood fairy tale and analyze the significance of your changes. To what extent do they reflect your values?

2. Is there anything positive to be learned from the Cinderella story? What does it teach about sibling rivalry? How might identifying with Cinderella be helpful to some children?

3. From ancient times to the present, poets and lyricists have used nature as their subject. Share with your group a favorite poem or lyric about nature. What aspects of nature emerged in the various texts? To what extent were the writers' attitudes toward nature influenced by their cultural backgrounds?

Cinderella's Stepsisters

TONI MORRISON

Toni Morrison (b. Chloe Anthony Wofford, 1931) received a B.A. in English from Howard University and an M.A. from Cornell University. Morrison made her debut as a novelist in 1970 with the acclaimed The Bluest Eye. *Morrison's other novels include:* Sula *(1973),* Song of Solomon *(1977),* Tar Baby *(1981),* Beloved *(1987),* Jazz *(1992), and* Paradise *(1998).* Love, *Morrison's most recent work, was published fall 2003. Morrison has received the National Book Critics Circle Award, the American Academy and Institute of Arts and Letters Award, the Pulitzer Prize, and the Robert F. Kennedy Award. Since 1988, Morrison has held a Professorship at Princeton University. Before reading Morrison's essay record your first memory of hearing the words "once upon a time."*

LET ME BEGIN BY TAKING YOU BACK A LITTLE. Back before the days at college. To nursery school, probably, to a once-upon-a-time time when you first heard or read, or, I suspect, even saw "Cinderella." Because it is Cinderella that I want to talk about; because it is Cinderella who causes me a feeling of urgency. What is unsettling about that fairy tale is that it is essentially the story of a household—a world, if you please—of women gathered together and held together in order to abuse another woman. There is, of course, a rather vague absent father and a nick-of-time prince with a foot fetish. But neither has much personality. And there are the surrogate "mothers," of course (god- and, step-), who contribute both to Cinderella's grief and to her release and happiness. But it is her stepsisters who interest me. How crippling it must have been for those young girls to grow up with a mother, to watch and imitate that mother, enslaving another girl.

I am curious about their fortunes after the story ends. For contrary to recent adaptations, the stepsisters were not ugly, clumsy, stupid girls with outsize feet. The Grimm collection describes them as "beautiful and fair in appearance." When we are introduced to them they are beautiful, elegant women of status, and clearly women of power. Having watched and participated in the violent dominion of another woman, will they be any less cruel when it comes their turn to enslave other children, or even when they are required to take care of their own mother?

It is not a wholly medieval problem. It is quite a contemporary one: feminine power when directed at other women has historically been wielded in what has been described as a "masculine" manner. Soon you will be in a position to do the very same thing. Whatever your background—rich or poor—whatever the history of education in your family—five generations or one—you have taken advantage of what has been available to you at Barnard and you will therefore leave both the economic and social status of the stepsisters *and* you will have their power.

I want not to *ask* you but to *tell* you not to participate in the oppression of your sisters. Mothers who abuse their children are women, and another woman, not an agency, has to be willing to stay their hands. Mothers who set fire to school buses are women, and another woman, not an agency, has to tell them to stay their hands. Women who stop the promotion of other women in careers are women, and another woman must come to the victim's aid. Social and welfare workers who humiliate their clients may be women, and other women colleagues have to deflect their anger.

I am alarmed by the violence that women do to each other: professional violence, competitive violence, emotional violence. I am alarmed by the willingness of women to enslave other women. I am alarmed by a growing absence of decency on the killing floor of professional women's worlds. You are the women who will take your place in the world where *you* can decide who shall flourish and who shall wither; you will make distinctions between the deserving poor and the undeserving poor; where you can yourself determine which life is expendable and which is indispensable. Since you will have the power to do it, you may also be persuaded that you have the right to do it. As educated women the distinction between the two is first-order business.

I am suggesting that we pay as much attention to our nurturing sensibilities as to our ambition. You are moving in the direction of freedom and the function of freedom is to free somebody else. You are moving toward self-fulfillment, and the consequences of that fulfillment should be to discover that there is something just as important as you are and that just-as-important thing may be Cinderella—or your stepsister.

In your rainbow journey toward the realization of personal goals, don't make choices based only on your security and your safety. Nothing is safe. That is not to say that anything ever was, or that anything worth achieving ever should be. Things of value seldom are. It is not safe to have a child. It is not safe to challenge the status quo. It is not safe to choose work that has not been done before. Or to do old work in a new way. There will always be someone there to stop you. But in pursuing your highest ambitions, don't let your personal safety diminish the safety of your stepsister. In wielding the power that is deservedly yours, don't permit it to enslave your stepsisters. Let your might and your power emanate from that place in you that is nurturing and caring.

Women's rights is not only an abstraction, a cause; it is also a personal affair. It is not only about "us"; it is also about me and you. Just the two of us.

INTERPRETATIONS

1. How much of the Cinderella fairy tale do you remember from childhood? Why is Morrison particularly interested in the stepsisters? What contemporary relevance does she find in their story?

2. "I am alarmed by the violence that women do to each other: professional violence, competitive violence, emotional violence." What examples does Morrison cite to support her statement? To what extent do you agree with her?

3. What distinction does Morrison make between "masculine" and "feminine" power? Do men and women think differently about competition, ambition, and success? Explain.

CORRESPONDENCES

1. Review Gandhi's perspective (page 279) and discuss its application to Morrison's text.

2. Morrison's purpose is to persuade. How would you characterize her tone? How do her purpose and tone compare with that of "The Algonquin Cinderella"?

APPLICATIONS

1. Discuss with your group Morrison's comments in paragraph 7 about safety and security. How plausible is it that "power emanates from that place in you that is nurturing and caring"?

2. Write an essay analyzing the implications of Morrison's conclusion. Be specific.

3. Write an essay about a character in a fairy tale that you identified with, or rejected as a child. What factors determined your

responses? In retrospect, was the experience negative or positive? Cite reasons.

4. What do you think Cinderella herself would reply to Toni Morrison? Write a letter from Cinderella to Morrison that addresses issues that are raised in "Cinderella's Stepsisters."

The Way to Rainy Mountain

N. SCOTT MOMADAY

N. Scott Momaday (b. 1934) spent a year teaching on an Apache reservation after graduating from the University of New Mexico. He won a poetry fellowship to the creative writing program at Stanford University and earned a doctorate in 1963. After Momaday's first novel House Made of Dawn *(1969) was awarded the Pulitzer Prize for Fiction, he began teaching at the University of California at Berkeley. Momaday's additional books include:* Angle of Geese and Other Poems *(1974),* The Names *(1976),* The Ancient Child *(1989),* In the Presence of the Sun *(1991),* Circle of Wonder: A Native American Christmas Story *(1993), and* The Native Americans: Indian Country *(1993). Momaday has taught at the University of Arizona since 1982.*

In the following excerpt from The Way to Rainy Mountain, *Momaday traces the migration of his tribe from their origins in Montana to Oklahoma. He chronicles alliances of the Kiowas with other tribes (the Comanches and the Crows) and their subjugation by the United States Army. Notice how Momaday uses the memories of his grandmother's death to evoke the importance of preserving tribal traditions.*

After 1840 the Kiowas, occupying the Arkansas River region of western Oklahoma, allied with the Comanches and others against eastern tribes that had moved west. This provoked the United States Army to move against both groups. By 1874, the Kiowa were devastated; their horses had been killed, and their leaders had been deported to Florida. They surrendered at Fort Sill. By 1879, most of the tribe had been moved to a reservation in southwest Oklahoma, between Fort Sill and the Washita River—the very landscape Momaday describes so dramatically here.

A SINGLE KNOLL rises out of the plain in Oklahoma, north and west of the Wichita Range. For my people, the Kiowas, it is an old landmark, and they gave it the name Rainy Mountain. The hardest weather in the world is there. Winter brings blizzards, hot tornadic winds arise in the spring, and in summer the prairie is an anvil's edge. The grass turns brittle and brown, and it cracks beneath your feet. There are green belts along the rivers and creeks, linear groves of hickory and pecan, willow and witch hazel. At a distance in July or August the steaming foliage seems almost to writhe in fire. Great green-and-yellow grasshoppers are everywhere in the tall grass, popping up like corn to sting the flesh, and tortoises crawl about on the red earth, going nowhere in the plenty of time. Loneliness is an aspect of the land. All things in the plain are isolate; there is no confusion of objects in the eye, but *one* hill or *one* tree or *one* man. To look upon that landscape in the early morning, with the sun at your back, is to lose the sense of proportion. Your imagination comes to life, and this, you think, is where Creation was begun.

I returned to Rainy Mountain in July. My grandmother had died in the spring, and I wanted to be at her grave. She had lived to be very old and at last infirm. Her only living daughter was with her when she died, and I was told that in death her face was that of a child.

I like to think of her as a child. When she was born, the Kiowas were living that last great moment of their history. For more than a hundred years they had controlled the open range from the Smoky Hill River to the Red, from the headwaters of the Canadian to the fork of the Arkansas and Cimarron. In alliance with the Comanches, they had ruled the whole of the southern Plains. War was their sacred business, and they were among the finest horsemen the world has ever known. But warfare for the Kiowas was preeminently a matter of disposition rather than of survival, and they never understood the grim, unrelenting advance of the U.S. Cavalry. When at last, divided and ill-provisioned, they were driven onto the Staked Plains in the cold rains of autumn, they fell into panic. In Palo Duro Canyon they abandoned their crucial stores to pillage and had nothing then but their lives. In order to save themselves, they surrendered to the soldiers at Fort Sill and were imprisoned in the old stone corral that now stands as a military museum. My grandmother was spared the humiliation of those high gray walls by eight or ten years, but she must have known from birth the affliction of defeat, the dark brooding of old warriors.

Her name was Aho, and she belonged to the last culture to evolve in North America. Her forebears came down from the high country in western Montana nearly three centuries ago. They were a mountain people, a mysterious tribe of hunters whose language has never been positively classified in any major group. In the late seventeenth century they began a long migration to the south and east. It was a long journey toward the dawn, and it led to a golden age. Along the way the Kiowas were befriended by the Crows, who gave them the culture and religion of the Plains. They acquired horses, and their ancient nomadic spirit was suddenly free of the ground. They acquired Tai-me, the sacred Sun Dance doll, from that moment the object and symbol of their worship, and so shared in the divinity of the sun. Not least, they acquired the sense of destiny, therefore courage and pride. When they entered upon the southern Plains, they had been transformed. No longer were they slaves to the simple necessity of survival; they were a lordly and dangerous society of fighters and thieves, hunters and priests of the sun. According to their origin myth, they entered the world through a hollow log. From one point of view, their migration was the fruit of an old prophecy, for indeed they emerged from a sunless world.

Although my grandmother lived out her long life in the shadow of Rainy Mountain, the immense landscape of the continental interior lay like memory in her blood. She could tell of the Crows, whom she had never seen, and of the Black Hills, where she had never been. I wanted to see in reality what she had seen more perfectly in the mind's eye, and traveled fifteen hundred miles to begin my pilgrimage.

Yellowstone, it seemed to me, was the top of the world, a region of deep lakes and dark timber, canyons and waterfalls. But, beautiful as it is, one might have the sense of confinement there. The skyline in all directions is close at hand, the high wall of the woods and deep cleavages of shade. There is a perfect freedom in the mountains, but it belongs to the eagle and the elk, the badger and the bear. The Kiowas reckoned their stature by the distance they could see, and they were bent and blind in the wilderness.

Descending eastward, the highland meadows are a stairway to the plain. In July the inland slope of the Rockies is luxuriant with flax and buckwheat, stonecrop and larkspur. The earth unfolds and the limit of the land recedes. Clusters of trees and animals grazing far in the distance cause the vision to reach away and wonder to build upon the mind. The sun follows a longer course in the day, and the sky is immense beyond all comparison. The great billowing clouds that sail upon it are shadows that move upon the grain like water, dividing light. Farther down, in the land of the Crows and Blackfeet, the plain is yellow. Sweet clover takes hold of the hills and bends upon itself to cover and seal the soil. There the Kiowas paused on their way; they had come to the place where they must change their lives. The sun is at home on the plains. Precisely there does it have the certain character of a god. When the Kiowas came to the land of the Crows, they could see the dark lees of the hills at dawn across the Bighorn River, the profusion of light on the grain shelves, the oldest deity ranging after the solstices. Not yet would they veer southward to the caldron of the land that lay below; they must wean their blood from the northern winter and hold the mountains a while longer in their view. They bore Tai-me in procession to the east.

A dark mist lay over the Black Hills, and the land was like iron. At the top of a ridge I caught sight of Devil's Tower upthrust against the gray sky as if in the birth of time the core of the earth had broken through its crust and the motion of the world was begun. There are things in nature that engender an awful quiet in the heart of man;

Devil's Tower is one of them. Two centuries ago, because they could not do otherwise, the Kiowas made a legend at the base of the rock. My grandmother said:

> Eight children were there at play, seven sisters and their brother. Suddenly the boy was struck dumb; he trembled and began to run upon his hands and feet. His fingers became claws, and his body was covered with fur. Directly there was a bear where the boy had been. The sisters were terrified; they ran, and the bear after them. They came to the stump of a great tree, and the tree spoke to them. It bade them climb upon it, and as they did so, it began to rise into the air. The bear came to kill them, but they were just beyond its reach. It reared against the tree and scored the bark all around with its claws. The seven sisters were borne into the sky, and they became the stars of the Big Dipper.

From that moment, and so long as the legend lives, the Kiowas have kinsmen in the night sky. Whatever they were in the mountains, they could be no more. However tenuous their well-being, however much they had suffered and would suffer again, they had found a way out of the wilderness.

My grandmother had a reverence for the sun, a holy regard that now is all but gone out of mankind. There was a wariness in her, and an ancient awe. She was a Christian in her later years, but she had come a long way about, and she never forgot her birthright. As a child she had been to the Sun Dances; she had taken part in those annual rites, and by them she had learned the restoration of her people in the presence of Tai-me. She was about seven when the last Kiowa Sun Dance was held in 1887 on the Washita River above Rainy Mountain Creek. The buffalo were gone. In order to consummate the ancient sacrifice—to impale the head of a buffalo bull upon the medicine tree—a delegation of old men journeyed into Texas, there to beg and barter for an animal from the Goodnight herd. She was ten when the Kiowas came together for the last time as a living Sun Dance culture. They could find no buffalo; they had to hang an old hide from the sacred tree. Before the dance could begin, a company of soldiers rode out from Fort Sill under orders to disperse the tribe. Forbidden without cause the essential act of their faith, having seen the wild herds slaughtered and left to rot upon the ground, the Kiowas backed away forever from the medicine tree. That was July 20, 1890, at the great bend of the Washita. My grandmother was there. Without bitterness, and for as long as she lived, she bore a vision of deicide.

Now that I can have her only in memory, I see my grandmother in the several postures that were peculiar to her: standing at the wood stove on a winter morning and turning meat in a great iron skillet; sitting at the south window, bent above her beadwork, and afterwards, when her vision had failed, looking down for a long time into the fold of her hands; going out upon a cane, very slowly as she did when the weight of age came upon her; praying. I remember her most often at prayer. She made long, rambling prayers out of suffering and hope, having seen many things. I was never sure that I had the right to hear, so exclusive were they of all mere custom and company. The last time I saw her she prayed standing by the side of her bed at night, naked to the waist, the light of a kerosene lamp moving upon her dark skin. Her long, black hair, always drawn and braided in the day, lay upon her shoulders and against her breasts like a shawl. I do not speak Kiowa, and I never understood her prayers, but there was something inherently sad in the sound, some merest hesitation upon the syllables of sorrow. She began in a high and descending pitch, exhausting her breath to silence; then again and again—and always the same intensity of effort, of something that is, and is not, like urgency in the human voice. Transported so in the dancing light among the shadows of her room, she seemed beyond the reach of time. But that was illusion; I think I knew then that I should not see her again.

INTERPRETATIONS

1. According to tribal myth, the Kiowa "entered the world through a hollow log." From what sort of world did they consider themselves to have emerged? How might this tradition have shaped the Kiowas' attitude toward life and death?

2. Momaday says his grandmother regarded the last Kiowa Sun Dance (1887) as "a vision of deicide," or god-killing. Do you agree? Was it the death of a god or of a people?

3. What portrait of Momaday's grandmother emerges from the essay? How would you describe his relationship to her?

4. What is the significance of Momaday's equating family with tribe?

5. How does Momaday use description of the setting (the mountains and plains, the great spaces of the West) to control the mood or tone of his essay?

CORRESPONDENCES

1. Review Sachs's perspective on the importance of life-stories (page 281) and discuss its application to Momaday's essay. To what extent does Momaday's return to his grandmother's house help him to "recollect" himself?

2. Review Paz's perspective on myth (page 281). How does it apply to the history of Momaday's ancestors? What changes occur in the myth of the Kiowa tribe as a result of their migration from the mountains to the plains?

APPLICATIONS

1. Discuss with your group what you were taught about Native Americans. What did you learn about their traditions, culture, and values? Do you think you were made sufficiently aware of their history? Write a concise summary of your discussion.

2. Write an essay about a person you associate with a specific place. Try to convey through sensory and other details why the place and the person seem inseparable to you.

3. Brainstorm about your associations with nature. Try to recall an experience with nature that was negative or positive and recreate the event with as many details as you can.

4. If there were a soundtrack to the essay "The Way to Rainy Mountain," what would it be? Write an essay describing the music that you perceive. (Or, create and record a song that you hear.)

Seven Days of Mourning

YAEL YARIMI

Yael Yarimi was born in Qiryat Eqron, Israel, a daughter of Jews of Yemenite descent. Like the majority of the sabras (first generation who were born in the new land), Yael had a communication problem with the old generation, who tried to practice the culture they had brought with them. The gaps that were created among the generations were very common in the country in which they lacked identity. Naturally, Yael pursued the Western lifestyle, the dominant one in Israel, and deserted the one of her ancestors, since the latter seemed to her obsolete. Yael rediscovered the richness of her roots only after she arrived in the United States in the late 1980s, when she reexamined her heritage.

In this essay, she expresses both appreciation and regret for the ignorance she had toward her heritage. She dedicates this essay to her parents Shalom and Yona ("peace" and "dove"), who endured many great ordeals when they came to the Holy Land. Going through a similar experience in America, Yael can now profoundly realize the high price her parents paid for their passage from the familiar to the strange. This is her way of thanking them for raising her with pride and confidence in spite of all the difficulties.

Tuesday

Dear Diary,

It is eleven p.m. I hear unclear words coming from the next room. It is as if Mom and Dad entered an unfamiliar state and are speaking in a strange language . . . Among these odd words I can only understand one sentence Mom just said: "We must call everybody and inform them about the funeral time". . . Now I hear my father crying. Oh my God! This is the first time in my life I have ever heard him crying just like us—the children.

I WAS TWELVE and too young to digest the significance of my grandfather's death. However, I was bothered with the notion that I would never see him again. I couldn't sleep. Constantly hiding my diary under the pillow, I remember trying to strangle my weeping under the blanket. Threatening pictures emerged and floated in my mind.

I cannot forget the scene: our front yard that was also our play-ground, turned overnight into a huge black tent made of strong, plastic canvas sheet and a great number of supporting rods. Strange people were unloading dozens of long tables and benches into the tent.

By the afternoon, all my relatives, neighbors and some other people had already arrived. Naturally, the men formed into a big rectangular pattern and began praying in loud voices, while the women were trans-ferring large cooking pots from our house to the back of the tent. There, they installed a giant cooking stove which could be big enough for an army division. These volunteer ladies looked as if they were in a hurry. They worked so skillfully, that one might have thought that their lives depended on it.

We—the children—were running around between the legs and were scolded with blaming fingers. We were asked to be quiet. "This is not a time for joy" rebuked one of the ladies while holding my little brother by his ear. He was then sent away promising to keep quiet. Everything had happened very fast.

My father's eyes were an unforgettable sight. As the son of the deceased, my father was sitting on the ground, in one of the tent cor-ners. Suddenly, he seemed so old, so infirm. My father, who was natu-rally a strong man, a towering figure, changed before my eyes into a helpless man with a saddened feeling of inner rage.

Not far from the men, in another corner, the mourning women were sitting on the ground as well. In the center of them, a woman I had never seen before was mourning in a heartbreaking wailing voice and caused all the other women to cry with her. I still remember her holding a square handkerchief with one hand on her forehead in a way that cov-ered her entire face. Accompanying her sad songs, she then moved her upper body from side to side in a steady rhythm. Her mourning songs were interrupted by her outcries after every two stanzas that described my grandfather. I could see my grandmother's pleading facial expres-sion as if she was trying to stop these words from being said.

I then was wondering how the mourning woman could cry and sob in such an honest way as if she knew my grandfather. I also could not understand why she had to add more agony to the already sad situation.

Dear Diary,
    I hate Aunt Rina, I hate her so much. She had no right to push me and ask me to help the working ladies . . . I feel so sad today . . . I couldn't enter the cemetery this afternoon; Mom says that women with periods are not clean; therefore I couldn't be present when my grandfather was buried. It is so corny . . .

Grandpa, I know you hear me. I know you are watching me from heaven . . . This is a mad house. Mom says its going to be like that every day for the next seven days . . . My friend Sara, remember her?, the one you used to call "The Russian"?, she says they never cooked for funerals . . . She says our funeral is like camping. You would have been proud of me if you heard what a lecture I gave her about us, about our dream that came true; to be in the land of the Jews, about all the things you used to tell me.

I am still astonished each time I recall the dedication of the Yemenite Jewish Community during the Shiva—the seven days of mourning in Jewish tradition in which all the community has to console and help the family to get over the loss.

All men rose at dawn and were praying three times a day. After each prayer, meals were served, in a religious ceremony, first to the men, then to the mourning women and last to the congregation. Deep, stiff, plastic dishes were filled with soup and meat in the Yemenite style. Scattered pita breads were laid along the tables by the side of small round dishes that contained a spicy dip called *hilba*—made of herbs. Hilba is used to flavor the soup. People then were eating with their hands, and there were no conversations during the eating time.

Dear Diary,

It has been a couple days that people are sleeping in my house. Everywhere I turn I encounter people, it's as if my house has turned into a hostel . . . Today it is an important day that's why I marked it in red ink. Today I have received my very first kiss.

Eddie, my cousin and I climbed the lemon tree in our back yard and kissed . . . I love him so much . . . Dad must not know; he will kill me, like the time he beat me when I played with Eric.

I closed the diary, which had aged with the years. I held it to my bosom and allowed myself to cry. I can still feel the pain and the insult of the blows I received from my father. It was eighteen years ago, but I still remember him saying outrageously "Kiss is a half intercourse," then came a second round of blows.

Knocking on the door, my husband woke me up from the journey to my past. "Everybody is leaving," he shouted. "Hurry up." I wore a black dress with a black scarf as is customary at mourning in my family.

By the time we arrived at the cemetery, my grandmother had already been buried. Women were spread out on the grave, yelling and pulling their hair. Grandmother was eighty-nine years old when she died. I was so sorry that distance did not enable me to see her before.

Living in the Diaspora, I find myself torn apart between the home I am trying to establish with my American husband, and the great, rich and embracing tradition I have left in my land of birth. I miss the togetherness, the caring and the warmth among my people so much that I sometimes contemplate leaving everything I have accomplished here and just returning to my roots, to the familiar, and run away from the ambiguous coldness I feel in America.

Entering the tent, my husband and I were sitting on the benches, in front of the same old tables, listening to the same heartbreaking weeping but this time from a different lady.

New generation of kids in our family were laughing and running around happy for the opportunity that brought them all together. Some of the traditional rituals will probably vanish among the new generation of Yemenite Jews in Israel, but in appearance only. I believe the essential tradition will remain forever.

INTERPRETATIONS

1. How do you feel about the custom of a leader causing "all the other women to cry with her" even though the leader didn't know Yarimi's grandfather? What purpose does it serve?

2. Why do you think food has such an important place in these ceremonies? How common in other traditions is this attention to food?

3. Does moving away from one's home or native land strengthen or weaken the importance of tradition? What examples can you provide from your own experience?

4. What is added to this narrative by seeing most of it from the point of view of a twelve-year-old?

CORRESPONDENCES

1. Review Schwartz's perspective on memory (page 280) and discuss its application to "Seven Days of Mourning." What do the journal entries reveal about the narrator's memories? What is Yarimi's purpose in linking her grandfather's death to the present?

2. The Algonquin Cinderella and Yarimi both focus on the importance of ritual and the preservation of traditions. To what extent do you agree that preserving both adds dimension to individual and communal living? What examples can you cite?

APPLICATIONS

1. Discuss with your group Yarimi's ambivalence about living in the Diaspora. Should she run away from the "ambiguous coldness of America"? What consensus did you reach?

2. Are all of Yarimi's memories pleasant? What portrait of her father emerges in her journal? What do the entries reveal about the writer?

3. How important are mourning rituals in your culture? Are prescribed gender roles involved? Is the food served part of the rituals? Will you teach your children these customs? Why or why not?

4. On page 308, Yael Yarimi describes the scene at her house following her grandfather's funeral. What sights do you see? Make a drawing that takes into account your interpretation of Yarimi's work. Pay attention to color as well as content and composition.

from Imaginary Homelands

SALMAN RUSHDIE

Ahmed Salman Rushdie (b. 1947) was born in Bombay, India and sent to Rugby School in England when he was fourteen. After graduating in 1968 from King's College, Cambridge, he worked in television in Pakistan. In 1975, Rushdie made his debut with the novel Grimus. *Rushdie's next novel,* Midnight's Children *(1981) won the Booker Prize. In 1988 he won the Whitebread Award with his fourth novel,* The Satanic Verses, *which was banned in several countries. This book forced him to go into hiding after Ayatollah Khomeini called for Rushdie and his publishers to be killed. Although Rushdie lived outside publicity after the decree, he published three novels:* The Moor's Last Sigh *(1995),* The Ground Beneath Her Feet *(1999), and* Fury *(2001). Although others have offered rewards for Rushdie's death, in 1998 the Iranian government announced that the state would not put the fatwa against him into effect. According to interviews, Rushdie has decided to end his hiding. Before reading Rushdie's essay, speculate in your journal on the meaning of his title.*

AN OLD PHOTOGRAPH in a cheap frame hangs on a wall of the room where I work. It's a picture dating from 1946 of a house into which, at the time of its taking, I had not yet been born. The house is rather peculiar—a three-storied gabled affair with tiled roofs and round towers in two corners, each wearing a pointy tiled hat. "The past is a foreign country," goes the famous opening sentence of L. P. Hartley's novel *The Go-Between*, "they do things differently there." But the photograph tells me to invert this idea; it reminds me that it's my present that is foreign, and that the past is home, albeit a lost home in a lost city in the mists of lost time.

A few years ago I revisited Bombay, which is my lost city, after an absence of something like half my life. Shortly after arriving, acting on an impulse, I opened the telephone directory and looked for my father's name. And, amazingly, there it was; his name, our old address, the unchanged telephone number, as if we had never gone away to the unmentionable country across the border. It was an eerie discovery. I felt as if I were being claimed, or informed that the facts of my faraway life were illusions, and that this continuity was the reality. Then I went to visit the house in the photograph and stood outside it, neither daring nor wishing to announce myself to its new owners. (I didn't want to see how they'd ruined the interior.) I was overwhelmed. The photograph had naturally been taken in black and white; and my memory, feeding on such images as this, had begun to see my childhood in the same way, monochromatically. The colors of my history had seeped out of my mind's eye; now my other two eyes were assaulted by colors, by the vividness of the red tiles, the yellow-edged green of cactus-leaves, the brilliance of bougainvillaea creeper. It is probably not too romantic to say that that was when my novel *Midnight's Children* was really born; when I realized how much I wanted to restore the past to myself, not in the faded grays of old family-album snapshots, but whole, in Cinema-Scope and glorious Technicolor.

Bombay is a city built by foreigners upon reclaimed land; I, who had been away so long that I almost qualified for the title, was gripped by the conviction that I, too, had a city and a history to reclaim.

It may be that writers in my position, exiles or emigrants or expatriates, are haunted by some sense of loss, some urge to reclaim, to look back, even at the risk of being mutated into pillars of salt. But if we do look back, we must also do so in the knowledge—which gives rise to profound uncertainties—that our physical alienation from India almost inevitably means that we will not be capable of reclaiming precisely the thing that was lost; that we will, in short, create fictions, not actual cities or villages, but invisible ones, imaginary homelands, Indias of the mind.

Writing my book in North London, looking out through my window onto a city scene totally unlike the ones I was imagining onto paper, I was constantly plagued by this problem, until I felt obliged to face it in the text, to make clear that (in spite of my original and I suppose somewhat Proustian ambition to unlock the gates of lost time so that the past reappeared as it actually had been, unaffected by the distortions of memory) what I was actually doing was a novel of memory and about memory, so that my India was just that: "my" India, a version and no more than one version of all the hundreds of millions of possible versions. I tried to make it as imaginatively true as I could, but imaginative truth is simultaneously honorable and suspect, and I knew that my India may only have been one to which I (who am no longer what I was, and who by quitting Bombay never became what perhaps I was meant to be) was, let us say, willing to admit I belonged.

This is why I made my narrator, Saleem, suspect in his narration; his mistakes are the mistakes of a fallible memory compounded by quirks of character and of circumstances and his vision is fragmentary. It may be that when the Indian writer who writes from outside India tries to reflect that world, he is obliged to deal in broken mirrors, some of whose fragments have been irretrievably lost.

But there is a paradox here. The broken mirror may actually be as valuable as the one which is supposedly unflawed. Let me again try and explain this from my own experience. Before beginning *Midnight's Children,* I spent many months trying simply to recall as much of the Bombay of the 1950s and 1960s as I could; and not only Bombay—Kashmir, too, and Delhi and Aligarh, which, in my book, I've moved to Agra to heighten a certain joke about the Taj Mahal. I was genuinely amazed by how much came back to me. I found myself remembering what clothes people had worn on certain days, and school scenes, and whole passages of Bombay dialogue verbatim, or so it seemed; I even remembered advertisements, film posters, the neon Jeep sign on Marine Drive, toothpaste ads for Binaca and for Kolynos, and a footbridge over the local railway line which bore, on one side, the legend "Esso puts a tiger in your tank" and, on the other, the curiously contradictory admonition: "Drive like Hell and you will get there." Old songs came back to me from nowhere. . . .

I knew that I had tapped a rich seam; but the point I want to make is that of course I'm not gifted with total recall, and it was precisely the partial nature of these memories, their fragmentation, that made them so evocative for me. The shards of memory acquired greater status, greater resonance, because they were *remains;* fragmentation made trivial things seem like symbols, and the mundane acquired numinous qualities. There is an obvious parallel here with archaeology. The broken pots of antiquity, from which the past can sometimes, but always provisionally, be reconstructed, are exciting to discover, even if they are pieces of the most quotidian objects.

It may be argued that the past is a country from which we have all emigrated, that its loss is part of our common humanity. Which seems to me self-evidently true; but I suggest that the writer who is out-of-country and even out-of-language may experience this loss in an intensified form. It is made more concrete for him by the physical fact of discontinuity, of his present being in a different place from his past, of his being "elsewhere." This may enable him to speak properly and concretely on a subject of universal significance and appeal.

But let me go further. The broken glass is not merely a mirror of nostalgia. It is also, I believe, a useful tool with which to work in the present.

John Fowles begins *Daniel Martin* with the words: "Whole sight: or all the rest is desolation." But human beings do not perceive things whole; we are not gods but wounded creatures, cracked lenses, capable only of fractured perceptions. Partial beings, in all the senses of that phrase. Meaning is a shaky edifice we build out of scraps, dogmas, childhood injuries, newspaper articles, chance remarks, old films, small victories, people hated, people loved; perhaps it is because our sense of what is the case is constricted from such inadequate materials that we defend it so fiercely, even to the death. The Fowles position seems to me a way of succumbing to the guru-illusion. Writers are no longer sages, dispensing the wisdom of the centuries. And those of us who have been forced by cultural displacement to accept the provisional nature of all truths, all certainties, have perhaps had modernism forced upon us. We can't lay claim to Olympus, and are thus released to describe our worlds in the way in which all of us, whether writers or not, perceive it from day to day. . . .

The Indian writer, looking back at India, does so through guilt-tinted spectacles. (I am of course, once more, talking about myself.) I am speaking now of those of us who emigrated . . . and I suspect that there are times when the move seems wrong to us all, when we seem, to ourselves, post-lapsarian men and women. We are Hindus who have crossed the black water; we are Muslims who eat pork. And as a result— as my use of the Christian notion of the Fall indicates—we are now partly of the West. Our identity is at once plural and partial. Sometimes we feel that we straddle two cultures; at other times, that we fall between two stools. But however ambiguous and shifting this ground may be, it is not an infertile territory for a writer to occupy. If literature is in part the business of finding new angles at which to enter reality, then once again our distance, our long geographical perspective, may provide us with such angles.

INTERPRETATIONS

1. Review the first paragraph of Rushdie's essay and explain what the mirror represents to him.

2. Paragraph 7 begins "But there is a paradox here. The broken mirror may actually be as valuable as the one which is supposedly unflawed." What is the meaning of the paradox to which Rushdie refers?

3. What points does Rushdie make concerning memory in paragraph 8? To what extent do you agree or disagree? Explain.

4. Rushdie's identity as a person and a writer has been shaped by his experiences in England and India. What does he cherish most about his Indian experiences? His Western identity?

CORRESPONDENCES

1. Review Schwartz's perspective on memory (page 280) and discuss its applications to Rushdie's essay. Focus on paragraphs 8–12. What connections does Rushdie make between memory and the writer?

2. A sense of place is central to the selections by Fineman and Rushdie. What techniques do they use to establish the relationship between places and traditions?

APPLICATIONS

1. Although Rushdie describes Bombay as "his lost city," he still retains a deep emotional attachment to it. Write a journal entry explaining why this is the case.

2. Discuss with your group Melville's perspective on places (page 279). Is there a "place" that you cherish that fits his description? How has this "place" affected your sense of identity? Write a summary of your responses.

3. Rushdie writes that all immigrants have an identity that is both "plural" and "partial." What does he mean? If you share his experience as an immigrant, write a journal entry on your own identity that supports or refutes Rushdie's thesis.

4. In the second paragraph of this essay, Rushdie writes: "The photograph had naturally been taken in black and white; and my memory, feeding on such images as this, had begun to see my childhood in the same way, monochromatically." Examine the photograph on page 330. What colors do you imagine to exist? Which one is dominant? What subtle shades are visible? How does the absence of color make you feel?

The Lottery

SHIRLEY JACKSON

Shirley Jackson (1919–1965) was born and raised in California. In 1933, she moved with her family to Rochester, New York, where she briefly attended the University of Rochester. Notable publications include the novel Hangsaman *(1951) and the play* We Have Always Lived in the Castle *(1962). In "The Lottery" (1948), a frequently anthologized piece, Jackson scrutinizes scapegoating. Record in your journal your associations with "scapegoating."*

THE MORNING OF JUNE 27TH was clear and sunny, with the fresh warmth of a full-summer day; the flowers were blossoming profusely and the grass was richly green. The people of the village began to gather in the square, between the post office and the bank, around ten o'clock; in some towns there were so many people that the lottery took two days and had to be started on June 26th, but in this village, where there were only about three hundred people, the whole lottery took less than two hours, so it could begin at ten o'clock in the morning and still be through in time to allow the villagers to get home for noon dinner.

The children assembled first, of course. School was recently over for the summer, and the feeling of liberty sat uneasily on most of them; they tended to gather together quietly for a while before they broke into boisterous play, and their talk was still of the classroom and the teacher, of books and reprimands. Bobby Martin had already stuffed his pockets full of stones, and the other boys soon followed his example, selecting the smoothest and roundest stones; Bobby and Harry Jones and Dickie Delacroix—the villagers pronounced this name "Dellacroy"—eventually made a great pile of stones in one corner of the square and guarded it against the raids of the other boys. The girls stood aside, talking among themselves, looking over their shoulders at the boys, and the very small children rolled in the dust or clung to the hands of their older brothers or sisters.

Soon the men began to gather, surveying their own children, speaking of planting and rain, tractors and taxes. They stood together, away from the pile of stones in the corner, and their jokes were quiet and they smiled rather than laughed. The women, wearing faded house dresses and sweaters, came shortly after their menfolk. They greeted one another and exchanged bits of gossip as they went to join their husbands. Soon the women, standing by their husbands, began to call to their children, and the children came reluctantly, having to be called four or five times. Bobby Martin ducked under his mother's grasping hand and ran, laughing, back to the pile of stones. His father spoke up sharply, and Bobby came quickly and took his place between his father and his oldest brother.

The lottery was conducted—as were the square dances, the teenage club, the Halloween program—by Mr. Summers, who had time and energy to devote to civic activities. He was a round-faced, jovial man and he ran the coal business, and people were sorry for him, because he had no children and his wife was a scold. When he arrived in the square, carrying the black wooden box, there was a murmur of conversation among the villagers, and he waved and called, "Little late today, folks." The postmaster, Mr. Graves, followed him, carrying a three-legged stool, and the stool was put in the center of the square and Mr. Summers set the black box down on it. The villagers kept their distance, leaving a space between themselves and the stool, and when Mr. Summers said, "Some of you fellows want to give me a hand?" there was a hesitation before two men, Mr. Martin and his oldest son, Baxter, came forward to hold the box steady on the stool while Mr. Summers stirred up the papers inside it.

The original paraphernalia for the lottery had been lost long ago, and the black box now resting on the stool had been put into use even before Old Man Warner, the oldest man in town, was born. Mr. Summers spoke frequently to the villagers about making a new box, but no one liked to upset even as much tradition as was represented by the black box. There was a story that the present box had been made with some pieces of the box that had preceded it, the one that had been constructed when the first people settled down to make a village here. Every year, after the lottery, Mr. Summers began talking again about a new box, but every year the subject was allowed to fade off without anything's being done. The black box grew shabbier each year; by now it was no longer completely black but splintered badly along one side to show the original wood color, and in some places faded or stained.

Mr. Martin and his oldest son, Baxter, held the black box securely on the stool until Mr. Summers had stirred the papers thoroughly with his hand. Because so much of the ritual had been forgotten or discarded, Mr. Summers had been successful in having slips of paper substituted for the chips of wood that had been used for generations. Chips of wood, Mr. Summers had argued, had been all very well when the village was tiny, but now that the population was more than three hundred and likely to keep on growing, it was necessary to use something that would fit more easily into the black box. The night before the lottery, Mr. Summers and Mr. Graves made up the slips of paper and put them in the box, and it was then taken to the safe of Mr. Summers's coal company and locked up until Mr. Summers was ready to take it to the square next morning. The rest of the year, the box was put away, sometimes one place, sometimes another; it had spent one year in Mr. Graves's barn and another year underfoot in the post office, and sometimes it was set on a shelf in the Martin grocery and left there.

There was a great deal of fussing to be done before Mr. Summers declared the lottery open. There were the lists to make up—of heads of families, heads of households in each family, members of each household in each family. There was the proper swearing-in of Mr. Summers by the postmaster, as the official of the lottery; at one time, some people remembered, there had been a recital of some sort, performed by the official of the lottery, a perfunctory, tuneless chant that had been rattled off duly each year; some people believed that the official of the lottery used to stand just so when he said or sang it, others believed that he was supposed to walk among the people, but years and years ago this part of the ritual had been allowed to lapse. There had been, also, a ritual salute, which the official of the lottery had had to use in addressing each person who came up to draw from the box, but this also had changed with time, until now it was felt necessary only for the official to speak to each person approaching. Mr. Summers was very good at all this; in his clean white shirt and blue jeans, with one hand resting carelessly on the black box, he seemed very proper and important as he talked interminably to Mr. Graves and the Martins.

Just as Mr. Summers finally left off talking and turned to the assembled villagers, Mrs. Hutchinson came hurriedly along the path to the square, her sweater thrown over her shoulders, and slid into place in the back of the crowd. "Clean forgot what day it was," she said to Mrs. Delacroix, who stood next to her, and they both laughed softly. "Thought my old man was out back stacking wood," Mrs. Hutchinson went on, "and then I looked out the window and the kids was gone, and then I remembered it was the twenty-seventh and came a-running." She dried her hands on her apron, and Mrs. Delacroix said, "You're in time, though. They're still talking away up there."

Mrs. Hutchinson craned her neck to see through the crowd and found her husband and children standing near the front. She tapped Mrs. Delacroix on the arm as a farewell and began to make her way through the crowd. The people separated good-humoredly to let her through; two or three people said, in voices just loud enough to be heard across the crowd, "Here comes your Missus, Hutchinson," and "Bill, she made it after all." Mrs. Hutchinson reached her husband, and

Mr. Summers, who had been waiting, said cheerfully, "Thought we were going to have to get on without you, Tessie." Mrs. Hutchinson said, grinning, "Wouldn't have me leave m'dishes in the sink, now, would you, Joe?" and soft laughter ran through the crowd as the people stirred back into position after Mrs. Hutchinson's arrival.

"Well, now," Mr. Summers said soberly, "guess we better get started, get this over with, so's we can go back to work. Anybody ain't here?"

"Dunbar," several people said. "Dunbar, Dunbar."

Mr. Summers consulted his list. "Clyde Dunbar," he said. "That's right. He's broke his leg, hasn't he? Who's drawing for him?"

"Me, I guess," a woman said, and Mr. Summers turned to look at her. "Wife draws for her husband," Mr. Summers said. "Don't you have a grown boy to do it for you, Janey?" Although Mr. Summers and everyone else in the village knew the answer perfectly well, it was the business of the official of the lottery to ask such questions formally. Mr. Summers waited with an expression of polite interest while Mrs. Dunbar answered.

"Horace's not but sixteen yet," Mrs. Dunbar said regretfully. "Guess I gotta fill in for the old man this year."

"Right," Mr. Summers said. He made a note on the list he was holding. Then he asked, "Watson boy drawing this year?"

A tall boy in the crowd raised his hand. "Here," he said. "I'm drawing for m'mother and me." He blinked his eyes nervously and ducked his head as several voices in the crowd said things like "Good fellow, Jack," and "Glad to see your mother's got a man to do it."

"Well," Mr. Summers said, "guess that's everyone. Old Man Warner make it?"

"Here," a voice said, and Mr. Summers nodded.

A sudden hush fell on the crowd as Mr. Summers cleared his throat and looked at the list. "All ready?" he called. "Now, I'll read the names—heads of families first—and the men come up and take a paper out of the box. Keep the paper folded in your hand without looking at it until everyone has had a turn. Everything clear?"

The people had done it so many times that they only half listened to the directions; most of them were quiet, wetting their lips, not looking around. Then Mr. Summers raised one hand high and said, "Adams." A man disengaged himself from the crowd and came forward. "Hi, Steve," Mr. Summers said, and Mr. Adams said, "Hi, Joe." They grinned at one another humorlessly and nervously. Then Mr. Adams reached into the black box and took out a folded paper. He held it firmly by one corner as he turned and went hastily back to his place in the crowd, where he stood a little apart from his family, not looking down at his hand.

"Allen," Mr. Summers said, "Anderson . . . Bentham."

"Seems like there's no time at all between lotteries any more," Mrs. Delacroix said to Mrs. Graves in the back row. "Seems like we got through with the last one only last week."

"Time sure goes fast," Mrs. Graves said.

"Clark . . . Delacroix."

"There goes my old man," Mrs. Delacroix said. She held her breath while her husband went forward.

"Dunbar," Mr. Summers said, and Mrs. Dunbar went steadily to the box while one of the women said, "Go on, Janey," and another said, "There she goes."

"We're next," Mrs. Graves said. She watched while Mr. Graves came around from the side of the box, greeted Mr. Summers gravely, and selected a slip of paper from the box. By now, all through the crowd there were men holding the small folded papers in their large hands, turning them over and over nervously. Mrs. Dunbar and her two sons stood together, Mrs. Dunbar holding the slip of paper.

"Harburt . . . Hutchinson."

"Get up there, Bill," Mrs. Hutchinson said, and the people near her laughed.

"Jones."

"They do say," Mr. Adams said to Old Man Warner, who stood next to him, "that over in the north village they're talking of giving up the lottery."

Old Man Warner snorted. "Pack of crazy fools," he said. "Listening to the young folks, nothing's good enough for *them*. Next thing you know, they'll be wanting to go back to living in caves, nobody work any more, live *that* way for a while. Used to be a saying about 'Lottery in June, corn be heavy soon.' First thing you know, we'd all be eating stewed chickweed and acorns. There's *always* been a lottery," he added petulantly. "Bad enough to see young Joe Summers up there joking with everybody."

"Some places have already quit lotteries," Mrs. Adams said.

"Nothing but trouble in *that*," Old Man Warner said stoutly. "Pack of young fools."

"Martin." And Bobby Martin watched his father go forward. "Overdyke . . . Percy."

"I wish they'd hurry," Mrs. Dunbar said to her oldest son. "I wish they'd hurry."

"They're almost through," her son said.

"You get ready to run tell Dad," Mrs. Dunbar said.

Mr. Summers called his own name and then stepped forward precisely and selected a slip from the box. Then he called, "Warner."

"Seventy-seventh year I been in the lottery," Old Man Warner said as he went through the crowd. "Seventy-seventh time."

"Watson." The tall boy came awkwardly through the crowd. Someone said, "Don't be nervous, Jack," and Mr. Summers said, "Take your time, son."

"Zanini."

After that, there was a long pause, a breathless pause, until Mr. Summers, holding his slip of paper in the air, said, "All right, fellows." For a minute, no one moved, and then all the slips of paper were opened. Suddenly, all the women began to speak at once, saying,"Who is it?" "Who's got it?" "Is it the Dunbars?" "Is it the Watsons?" Then the voices began to say, "It's Hutchinson. It's Bill." "Bill Hutchinson's got it."

"Go tell your father," Mrs. Dunbar said to her older son.

People began to look around to see the Hutchinsons. Bill Hutchinson was standing quiet, staring down at the paper in his hand. Suddenly, Tessie Hutchinson shouted to Mr. Summers, "You didn't give him time enough to take any paper he wanted. I saw you. It wasn't fair!"

"Be a good sport, Tessie," Mrs. Delacroix called, and Mrs. Graves said, "All of us took the same chance."

"Shut up, Tessie," Bill Hutchinson said.

"Well, everyone," Mr. Summers said, "that was done pretty fast, and now we've got to be hurrying a little more to get done in time." He consulted his next list. "Bill," he said, "you draw for the Hutchinson family. You got any other households in the Hutchinsons?"

"There's Don and Eva," Mrs. Hutchinson yelled. "Make *them* take their chance!"

"Daughters drew with their husbands' families, Tessie," Mr. Summers said gently. "You know that as well as anyone else."

"It wasn't *fair*," Tessie said.

"I guess not, Joe," Bill Hutchinson said regretfully. "My daughter draws with her husband's family, that's only fair, And I've got no other family except the kids."

"Then, as far as drawing for families is concerned, it's you," Mr. Summers said in explanation, "and as far as drawing for households is concerned, that's you, too. Right?"

"Right," Bill Hutchinson said.

"How many kids, Bill?" Mr. Summers asked formally.

"Three," Bill Hutchinson said. "There's Bill, Jr., and Nancy, and little Dave. And Tessie and me."

"All right, then," Mr. Summers said. "Harry, you got their tickets back?"

Mr. Graves nodded and held up the slips of paper. "Put them in the box, then," Mr. Summers directed. "Take Bill's and put it in."

"I think we ought to start over," Mrs. Hutchinson said, as quietly as she could. "I tell you it wasn't *fair*. You didn't give him time enough to choose. *Every*body saw that."

Mr. Graves had selected the five slips and put them in the box, and he dropped all the papers but those onto the ground, where the breeze caught them and lifted them off.

"Listen, everybody," Mrs. Hutchinson was saying to the people around her.

"Ready, Bill?" Mr. Summers asked, and Bill Hutchinson, with one quick glance around at his wife and children, nodded.

"Remember," Mr. Summers said, "take the slips and keep them folded until each person has taken one. Harry, you help little Dave." Mr. Graves took the hand of the little boy, who came willingly with him up to the box. "Take a paper out of the box, Davy," Mr. Summers said. Davy put his hand into the box and laughed. "Take just *one* paper," Mr. Summers said. "Harry, you hold it for him." Mr. Graves took the child's hand and removed the folded paper from the tight fist and held it while little Dave stood next to him and looked up at him wonderingly.

"Nancy next," Mr. Summers said. Nancy was twelve, and her school friends breathed heavily as she went forward, switching her skirt, and took a slip daintily from the box. "Bill, Jr.," Mr. Summers said, and Billy, his face red and his feet overlarge, nearly knocked the box over as he got a paper out. "Tessie," Mr. Summers said. She hesitated for a minute, looking around defiantly, and then set her lips and went up to the box. She snatched a paper out and held it behind her.

"Bill," Mr. Summers said, and Bill Hutchinson reached into the box and felt around, bringing his hand out at last with the slip of paper in it.

The crowd was quiet. A girl whispered, "I hope it's not Nancy," and the sound of the whisper reached the edges of the crowd.

"It's not the way it used to be," Old Man Warner said clearly. "People ain't the way they used to be."

"All right," Mr. Summers said. "Open the papers. Harry, you open little Dave's."

Mr. Graves opened the slip of paper and there was a general sigh through the crowd as he held it up and everyone could see that it was blank. Nancy and Bill, Jr., opened theirs at the same time, and both beamed and laughed, turning around to the crowd and holding their slips of paper above their heads.

"Tessie," Mr. Summers said. There was a pause, and then Mr. Summers looked at Bill Hutchinson, and Bill unfolded his paper and showed it. It was blank.

"It's Tessie," Mr. Summers said, and his voice was hushed. "Show us her paper, Bill."

Bill Hutchinson went over to his wife and forced the slip of paper out of her hand. It had a black spot on it, the black spot Mr. Summers had made the night before with the heavy pencil in the coal-company office. Bill Hutchinson held it up and there was a stir in the crowd.

"All right, folks," Mr. Summers said. "Let's finish quickly."

Although the villagers had forgotten the ritual and lost the original black box, they still remembered to use stones. The pile of stones the boys had made earlier was ready; there were stones on the ground with the blowing scraps of paper that had come out of the box. Mrs. Delacroix selected a stone so large she had to pick it up with both hands and turned to Mrs. Dunbar. "Come on," she said. "Hurry up."

Mrs. Dunbar had small stones in both hands, and she said, gasping for breath, "I can't run at all. You'll have to go ahead and I'll catch up with you."

The children had stones already, and someone gave little Davy Hutchinson a few pebbles.

Tessie Hutchinson was in the center of a cleared space by now, and she held her hands out desperately as the villagers moved in on her. "It isn't fair," she said. A stone hit her on the side of the head.

Old Man Warner was saying, "Come on, come on, everyone." Steve Adams was in the front of the crowd of villagers, with Mrs. Graves beside him.

"It isn't fair, it isn't right," Mrs. Hutchinson screamed and then they were upon her.

INTERPRETATIONS

1. What do the villagers mean by "fairness"? What is implied by the fact that the only villager to complain about the lottery's consequences is Tessie Hutchinson?

2. Why does Jackson use a flat, reportorial style to describe an event that would normally be headline news? Consider the role of irony in this story.

3. How important is it that the story is set in roughly contemporary New England? How, for example, would its influence differ if the story were set in Aztec Mexico, a culture that routinely practiced human sacrifice?

4. The tradition here depicted brings summary execution or reprieve. What traditions do we participate in that have life-or-death consequences, in either the short or the long run?

Stone-Throwing in India: An Annual Bash

MARK FINEMAN

Mark Fineman (b. 1952) has had a varied career in journalism since receiving his degree from Syracuse University. He has worked for The Chicago Sun-Times; *the Allentown, Pennsylvania,* Call-Chronicle; *and* The Philadelphia Inquirer. *At present he is based in Miami as Caribbean bureau chief for* The Los Angeles Times. *To what extent do you find Fineman's title engaging? Is there anything unusual about it?*

PANDHURNA, INDIA—To most of the 45,000 seemingly normal residents of this sleepy little town on the banks of the River Jam, Anil Sambare is nothing more than a spoilsport.

To some, he is something worse. A troublemaker, some say. An idealistic radical, according to others. Some even think him a traitor to his hometown.

And all because the twenty-seven-year-old high school teacher has dedicated his life to stopping his entire town from going completely berserk once a year in a frenzied festival of destruction—a daylong event in which thousands of people try to stone each other to death in the name of fun, tradition and, now, stardom.

The annual event is called the Gotmaar Festival—literally, "stone-hitting"—and it is an ancient Pandhurna tradition, unique and brutal even by Indian standards.

No one here remembers exactly how ancient it is, although older people say that it dates back at least three centuries. And no one knows exactly why they do it every year, year after year, despite scores of deaths and thousands of injuries, although the myth behind it is a compelling one.

All the Pandhurnans really know for sure is that once a year, on the day of the new moon in the Hindu month of Sharawan, when the drums start beating along the River Jam, the time for the madness has begun again.

Within minutes, thousands of male Pandhurnans, ranging in age from six to sixty, many of them deeply scarred or limping from festivals of years past, divide into two groups, gather their huge piles of stones on opposite sides of the river and, for the next six-and-a-half hours, try to kill, maim and mangle as many fellow townsfolk as they can.

When sunset comes, and the drumbeat stops, the two sides drop their rocks, come together, shake hands, nurse each other's wounds and return to the peaceful monotony of rural Indian life.

This year, the Gotmaar carnage, which took place two weeks ago, left four dead and 612 injured. But there were a few new twists this year that speak volumes about India's struggle to enter the modern age.

First, there was Anil Sambare and his signature drive to end the carnage, which drew the ire of almost everyone. Second, this is an election year in India, which meant that Sambare's signature campaign was doomed to failure. And finally, there was the introduction of a new evil, videotape equipment, which is likely to ensure that Pandhurna's sado-masochistic ritual will continue for many years to come.

The story of the Pandhurnans and their bizarre, ancient rite of stoning is a living illustration of the paradoxes of a modern-day India, as well as a freeze-frame glimpse at the ironies and distortions resulting from Indian Prime Minister Rajiv Gandhi's five-year-old pledge to modernize rural India.

Pandhurna, in central Madhya Pradesh state, is hardly what one would call a backwater. In many ways it is a model of Rajiv Gandhi's rural modernization plan.

There are 10,000 television sets in Pandhurna, 340 telephones and even 100 videocassette players. More than ninety percent of the homes have electricity. Everyone has access to clean drinking water. Unemployment is under five percent, and there are even beauty parlors doing booming business.

"There is just this one little thing that sets us apart," said Bhargao Pandurang Bhagwatkar, who has taught in the local high school for the last forty-one years. "We all know it is barbaric. It is a kind of madness. And it has no reason at all. But it has been with us since Day 1, and, on that day every year, we just cannot help ourselves."

Day 1, as myth has it, was sometime in the 1600s, according to local historians, police and other local officials, who say they and their predecessors have been trying to stop it every year for the last half-century.

On Day 1, it seems, Pandhurna's brutal battle began as a love story.

"The way the old ones tell it," town official M. M. Singh explained, "a boy from the Pandhurna side of the river eloped with a girl from the village on the other side, which was then known as Sawargaon but since has merged into Pandhurna.

"As the amorous young couple was trying to flee across the river, the Sawargaon people began throwing stones at them. The Pandhurnans heard about this and quickly ran to the river bank, where they began stoning the Sawargaons.

"The couple, of course, died in the cross-fire. And it's on the spot where they died that the people now put the tree every year."

"The tree?" the stranger asked.

"Oh, the tree. The tree is the main object of the game."

The Pandhurnans who actually play "the game," which is what everyone here except Sambare calls the annual stoning battle, explained that the tree is cut the day before the festival from a special grove of flame trees beside a temple to the Hindu god of destruction, which is where legend states that the mythical young couple first met.

The tree is then "planted" in the middle of the River Jam, and the object of "the game" is to chop down the tree with an ax, without, of course, getting stoned to death in the process.

Enter the videotape.

Unlike previous years, in which an average of two or three Pandhurnans were stoned to death during the festival, the four deaths this year were from drowning.

"These boys had climbed the tree, and were posing for the camera," Sambare explained. "They were so preoccupied with the video camera, they didn't see the stones coming. They got hit in the head, fell into the river and drowned."

Sambare knows what he's talking about. He lives on Stone-hitting Road, in a riverfront house with a view of the battle zone. And he jumped into the river and saved four other "players" from the same fate this year, getting hit in the back with stones in the process.

But that's not why Sambare is so committed to ending the carnage of Gotmaar. It's not even because his uncle was stoned to death twenty-seven years ago, or because he cannot stop his own younger brother from joining in—"imagine, my own brother bought five different outfits and changed clothes five times during the stone-hitting this year because he wanted to look good for the camera."

"No, I am fighting this because it is a perversion, because it is barbaric and because it puts all of India in a very poor light," said Sambare, who has a masters degree in mathematics.

"This is not a game. This is madness. And now, with this videotape, there is all of a sudden a renewed interest in joining in. Everyone wants to show off their bravado."

Enter Rajiv Gandhi's high-tech revolution.

The videotape was the government's idea. And the local police actually paid 5,000 rupees (about $300) in government funds to a local video contractor to film the festival this year.

"The idea was to minimize the killing," said Krishna Kohle, the enterprising Pandhurnan who got the video contract. "It was, how do you call it, a compromise."

For decades, local officials said, the authorities have attempted to end the festival. Two years ago, the police even opened fire on the festival, killing two Pandhurnans, in an attempt to end it after a passing constable was accidentally stoned to death.

"I myself have seen too many deaths and very much want this madness to end," said Dr. Ratan Singhvi, a local physician who is Pandhurna's equivalent of mayor and the local head of Gandhi's ruling Congress-I party.

"I have seen people with eyes bulging out, ears sheared off, noses broken, teeth shattered, skulls and legs fractured to bits. But we've never been able to stop it. My God, the people like it.

"Of course, an additional problem is these people are all dead drunk when they're playing the game, and the game gives them a good excuse to get drunk. They look forward to it all year long."

Enter politics.

"The people of Pandhurna, you see, are very sentimental about this festival," Singhvi said. "And such things are very important to our local voters. Had we stopped the Gotmaar this year, for example, the Congress Party definitely would be sent away in the next elections. So what we did instead was try to cut down on the deaths—we banned the slingshot."

Called *gofans*, the handmade slingshots came into vogue two years ago and clearly escalated the conflict. They turned the stones into speeding bullets, tripling the death toll and ultimately forcing the police to step in. The *gofan* was outlawed. And, in an effort to enforce that ban, police hired the video man to film violators for prosecution.

"I guess it backfired," said Kohle, who conceded he is now making a tidy profit renting out copies of the Gotmaar video to townspeople who want to relive their moments of bravery and endurance.

INTERPRETATIONS

1. Explain the myth that serves as the catalyst for the town's annual stone-hitting event.

2. "This is not a game. This is madness. And now with this videotape, there is all of a sudden a renewed interest in joining in." To what extent do you agree with Sambare? How has the video camera affected the stone-hitting activities?

3. What are Sambare's reasons for protesting against his town's tradition? Do you think he will succeed? To what extent is he foolish to try?

CORRESPONDENCES

1. Review the Maugham perspective on traditions (page 279) and explain its meaning. How does it apply to the texts by Jackson and Fineman?

2. Imagine a conversation between Anil Sambare and *one* of the characters depicted in Shirley Jackson's short story "The Lottery" (e.g., Old Man Warner, Mrs. Hutchinson, Mr. Summers). What would these two people say to each other? Write down the conversation that you think they would have. Try to extend this discourse for twenty lines.

APPLICATIONS

1. A symbol is something that stands for something else. In Jackson's story, a reader may look at the lottery, the black box, or Old Man Warner as signifying something more than a literal meaning.

2. Select a work that you have already written. How might you use a symbol to represent an idea that you are discussing? What modifications must you make in your piece to accommodate your use of this symbol? Once you consider these questions, revise your essay to include your symbolic treatment of your topic.

3. When Jackson's story was first published in *The New Yorker* in 1948, she received hundreds of letters from people "who wanted to know where these lotteries were held, and whether they could go there and watch." Discuss with your group what the responses to "The Lottery" reveal about human nature. What is your response?

4. By showing how familiar the process of each event is to the townspeople involved, what are the authors implying about traditions, mass psychology, and social pressure? To what extent does your group's response to this question compare with that of other groups in your class?

5. Review the titles of the texts by Jackson and Fineman. What are your associations with a lottery or an annual bash? What images do the words evoke? How do these underscore the ironies in both titles?

The Knowing Eye

Freesockphotos.com

READING IMAGES

1. What is happening in these photographs? What is familiar to you? What is unfamiliar? To what extent are you able to relate to what is depicted in each photograph?

2. What is the relationship between the setting of each photograph and the people in it? How has the photographer chosen to use backgrounds and foregrounds?

Lu Feng

MAKING CONNECTIONS

1. Which photograph do you think best applies to the Shirley Jackson story "The Lottery"? Explain your answer fully.

2. What kinds of traditions are depicted by these photographs? How are these types represented in the essays of this chapter?

WORDS AND IMAGES

1. What is a sacred tradition that you or your family participate in? What is a secular tradition that you uphold? Write an essay about these traditions, how they are similar to and different from each other.

2. What music do you think would be listened to by the woman
    dancer in the photograph? What details in the image help you to
    make this determination? Try to locate an example of this music
    and listen to it. Next, write a description of this music that includes
    how it makes you feel and what it helps you to think about.

Additional Writing Topics

1. Many writers in this chapter recall aspects of their family's traditions—weddings, funerals, and religious customs. Focus on a ritual that you would like to record, and do so from a cross-generational or a cross-cultural perspective. Interview members of your family and extended family on their memories and associations. Write an account of these recollections that illustrates and explains their importance.

2. In the Cinderella tales and Fairbank's "Footbinding," various traditions (or magic powers) are used to confine women, to control them in some way(s). In every case, women escape the controls or turn them, at least in part, to their advantage. Discuss for these works the advantages and consolations that women in these cultures find even in their arduous and rigidly ordered lives. What qualities of human nature do they reveal, and are the qualities common to both men and women, or not?

3. All cultures observe holidays of national or international importance. What functions do these observances serve? Write an essay about the holidays your family celebrates and the rituals you observe. How "traditional" are these observances—and your role in them?

4. Write a journal entry on what you know about your own roots. What else would you like to discover about them? Which members of your immediate and extended family might you consult? What sources—letters, journals, family photographs—might be useful? After compiling information from these various sources, write a narrative essay on what you discovered about your origins.

5. Several writers in this chapter recall and describe a place at a moment when a major truth comes into focus for them. Recall some major awakening in your past life—love, death, religion, hatred—and then describe briefly but exactly the place where the awakening occurred so that your mood is also evident.

6. Review Bellah's statement in the chapter introduction: "In our forward-facing society, we are more apt to talk about the future than the past . . . yet even in the debate about our future, our cultural tradition, in its several strands, is still very much present." To what extent do the selections in this chapter support or refute Bellah? What is your own point of view?

7. According to Cesare Pavese, "We do not remember days, we remember moments." Freewrite about a moment of special significance for you. Then expand on the memory and its importance in a fully developed essay. Why do you remember it so vividly? What do you remember? How might you best explain its effects on you?

8. Past experiences—their own or others—are important to Momaday, Yarimi, and Rushdie. Does the fact that each essay is about a particular culture and its traditions have any relevance to the writer's purpose? Have you had a similar experience that could be valuable to record? Before writing your essay, decide whether your purpose is to inform or persuade.

9. Review Erdrich's perspective on the relation between the past and the present. How do the texts in this chapter support or refute her theory that "history has a way of intruding upon the present?" What is your point of view?

CHAPTER

7

Cultural Encounters

Peaceful encounters among cultures take many forms: treaties, trade, tourism, art exhibits, drama, movies, dance, student exchanges, exchange of scientific information, world fairs, conferring of awards and honors like the Nobel Prizes, sports events, musical events, conferences, emergency and other aid, cooperation in law enforcement, the United Nations. In general these encounters please, intrigue, or interest us. Variety enhances—in food, dress, language, religion, art, celebrations, government. However, as the Senegalese folktale that begins this chapter implies, there is another side to human nature, and it is bleak. People may be so fond of their vested arrangements, so afraid that change will be for the worse, that they prefer falsehood to truth. Exposure to other cultures, the sifting of truth, the juxtaposition of another's knowledge and our ignorance, for example, are sometimes more than we can stand: "Better the devil we know than the devil we don't" expresses an enduring attitude that quickly surfaces when cultures compete rather than complement. Such clashes exact a price and take various forms.

Are our encounters with people affected by our culture? Indeed they are. "The American Dream," for example, is more than a slogan adorning a T-shirt; it is a shorthand expression of a widespread belief among Americans that freedom, social justice, and improvement in material standards are desirable and possible for all. But lack of awareness of cultural differences or the assumptions of one cultural group that another is inferior often results in encounters that are patriotic power struggles. Although the United States continues to be a nation of immigrants (a recent survey reported that 70 percent of New York City's population is comprised of immigrants) in search of that dream, many groups have felt excluded from the right to equality promised in the Declaration of Independence of 1776. They are challenging the monocultural concept that was first expressed in Hector St. Jean de Crevecoeur's 1781 statement that "individuals of all nations are melted down in a new race of men" and which has shaped the collective consciousness of North America for almost two centuries.

In fact, in a 1991 interview, the Asian-American writer Bharati Mukherjee proposed that the metaphor of a "fusion chamber" in which elements interact but do not melt, has perhaps become a more appropriate metaphor to describe the new multiracial democracy of the twenty-first century. The African-American novelist Toni Morrison concurs: "We have to acknowledge that the thing we call 'literature' is pluralistic now, just as society ought to be. The melting pot never worked." Isabelle de Courtivron, professor of language and literature at Massachusetts Institute of Technology goes further in a recent article. "I think that one can surely belong to a gender, a country, a language, a culture, a religion, a race,—or to several of each—without having to make consistently unilateral identifications with any of them."

Several of the personal encounters in this chapter involve confronting cultural and ethnic stereotypes. Michael T. Kaufman reflects on losing contact with a former schoolfriend because of his own "prejudice and stupidity" and on a school system that tracked students even in elementary school. Brent Staples is forced to deal with other people's stereotypes in his essay "Black Men and Public Spaces"; in "Passion and the Dream," Linda Stanley records how a jury in Queens, New York, had to reexamine their concepts of the American dream.

Encounters also often involve personal and cultural reevaluations. Garrett Hongo, for example, in "Fraternity," struggles with the "punishment" and "exclusion" of racism inflicted by members of his own and another ethnic group, as well as the personal rejection of his Portuguese girl friend. Taneisha Grant, in "To Speak Patois," contrasts her personal and communal experiences of living in Jamaica until early adolescence with the personal and cultural adjustments she had to make as a college student in New York City. Jay Ford, in "20/20 Hindsight" works to integrate his experiences of being raised in a middle-class African-American family with the effects of a semester in Kenya, where he gains a different perspective on the value of simple human relationships.

As you read about the cultural encounters in this chapter, consider how factors such as race, ethnicity, and social class have contributed to or detracted from your own position of privilege in American society. You might consider also professor Henry Louis Gates's challenge to graduating students at Hamilton College's 1999 commencement address as you forge your own identity in the multicultural world of the twenty-first century.

Perspectives

The United States, by its very nature, by its very development, is the essence of diversity. It is diverse in its geography, population, institutions, technology; its social, cultural, and intellectual modes. It is a society that at its best does not consider quality to be monolithic in form or finite in quantity, or to be inherent in class. Quality in our society proceeds in large measure out of the stimulus of diverse modes of thinking and acting; out of the creativity made possible by the different ways in which we approach things; out of diversion from paths or modes hallowed by tradition.

—Arturo Madrid

Culture is that which binds men together.

—Ruth Benedict

The greatest distance between people is not space but culture.

—Jamake Highwater

People and their cultures perish in isolation, but they are born or reborn in contact with other men and women, with men and women of another culture, another creed, another race. If we do not recognize our humanity in others, we will not recognize it in ourselves.

—Carlos Fuentes

As long as you keep a person down, some part of you has to be down there to hold him down, so it means you cannot soar as you otherwise might.

—Marian Anderson

Man is an animal suspended in the webs of significance which he himself has created. I take culture to be those webs.

—Clifford Geertz

I speak to the black experience, but I am always talking about the human condition—about what we can endure, dream, fail at, and still survive.

—Maya Angelou

No man is an island, intire of it selfe; every man is a peece of the Continent, apart of the maine; if a Clod bee washed away by the Sea, Europe is the lesse, as well as if a Promontorie were, as well as if a Mannor of thy friends or of thine owne were; any man's death diminishes me, because I am involved in Mankinde; And therefore never send to know for whom the bell tolls; It tolls for thee.

—John Donne

Americans are wedded by proximity to a common culture.

—Richard Rodriguez

Culture regulates our lives at every turn. From the moment we are born until we die there is, whether we are conscious of it or not, constant pressure upon us to follow certain types of behavior that other men have created for us.

—Clyde Kluckhohn

It is a terrible, an inexorable, law that one cannot deny the humanity of another without diminishing one's own; in the face of one's victim one sees oneself.

—James Baldwin

Where justice is denied, where poverty is enforced, where ignorance prevails and where any one class is made to feel that society is in an organized conspiracy to oppress, rob and degrade them, neither persons nor property will be safe.

—Frederick Douglass

There are are two ways of spreading light: to be the candle or the mirror that receives it.

—Edith Wharton

There is wisdom in turning as often as possible from the familiar to the unfamiliar; it keeps the mind nimble, it kills prejudice, and it fosters humor.

—George Santayana

We travel, initially, to lose ourselves; and we travel, next, to find ourselves.

—Pico Iyer

It's that same old, same old story. We all have an immigrant ancestor, one who believed in America, and who, daring or duped, took sail.

—Fae Myeene Ng

The alien resident mourns even as she chooses to abandon. Her memory, like her guilt and early love, is involuntary but her choice of the United States is willful.

—Shirley Geok-lin Lim

As social equality spreads there are more and more people who, though neither rich nor powerful enough to have much hold over others, have gained or kept enough wealth and enough understanding to look after their own needs. Such folk owe no man anything and hardly expect anything from anybody. They form the habit of thinking of themselves in isolation and imagine that their whole destiny is in their own hands.

Thus, not only does democracy make men forget their ancestors, but it also clouds their view of their descendants and isolates them from their contemporaries. Each man is forever thrown back on himself alone, and there is danger that he may be shut in the solitude of his own heart.

—Alexis de Tocqueville

The only way to make sure people you agree with can speak is to support the rights of people you don't agree with.

—Eleanor Holmes Norton

APPLICATIONS

1. Discuss Madrid's perspective on the United States (page 337). To what extent do you agree with his point of view? Consider how aspects of other cultures including food, fashion, music, or movies influence your daily lives. Is it possible to appreciate multiculturalism without losing cultural identity?

2. Select two perspectives with which you disagree and, in your journal, record and analyze the reasons for your point of view.

3. The perspectives of Ng and Lim focus on aspects of the immigrant experience. Review them with your group and summarize your discussion in your journal.

The Falsehood of Truth

SENEGALESE MYTH

Senegal is a republic in western Africa, which gained independence from France in 1960. Explain the paradox in the title of the Sengalese myth.

FENE-FALSEHOOD AND DEUG-TRUTH started out on a journey one day.

Fene-Falsehood said, "Everyone says that the Lord loves truth better than falsehood, so I think that you had better do all the talking for us."

Deug-Truth agreed, and when they came to a village, Deug-Truth greeted the first woman they met and asked if they could have a drink. She gave them a filthy bowl full of lukewarm water and then sat down in the doorway of her hut and began to eat a big meal of rice. While the two travelers were still there, the woman's husband came home and asked for his supper.

"It's not ready," replied the woman insolently.

The husband then turned to the two strangers who were watching and asked, "What would you say about a woman like that?"

"I would say that she is the worst wife I have seen in a long time. It's bad enough for her not to be hospitable to strangers, but it is really disgraceful when she doesn't feed her own husband," replied Deug-Truth. Fene-Falsehood didn't say a word.

The woman became furious and began to yell and scream louder than either of the two travelers had ever heard anyone scream before. "Are you going to stand by and let these strangers insult me!" she screamed to her husband. "If so, I will go home to my father and you will have to raise a bride-price for a new wife."

Then the husband, too, became angry and chased the two strangers out of town.

So Deug and Fene continued their travels and next came to a village where they found several children dividing up a bull that had just been slaughtered. They thought that this was rather strange, for it was the custom that meat was always divided by the head-man. While they were still watching, they saw the chief come up and take a very poor share of meat which the children handed him. The chief saw the two strangers and asked, "Who do you think is the leader in this village?"

Fene said nothing but Deug immediately answered, "It seems to me that these children must be the leaders of this village, for they are dividing the meat."

The chief immediately became angry and chased them out of that village.

As they continued to walk along, Fene said to Deug, "It is said that the Lord loves you the best, but I am beginning to wonder if man is not rather different from God. It seems to me that men do not like you very well. I think I will try my luck at the next village."

At the next village, they found that all the people were weeping because the favorite wife of the king had just died. Fene thought for a minute and then said, "Go tell the king that a man is here who can raise people from the dead."

Soon Fene was brought before the king and said, "I will raise your wife from the dead if you will give me half of your fortune."

The king immediately agreed and Fene had a hut built above the family grave. The king and all of the people waited outside and listened to the strange noises. First they heard huffing and panting and strange chants, but then they began to hear Fene talking loudly as if he were arguing. Finally he burst out of the door and slammed it shut—holding it tightly.

"Oh, dear," he said, "you did not tell me that your whole family was buried in there. When I woke your wife up, your father and your grandfather both came out too. I thought I had better check before I let them all out."

The king and his advisers began to look frightened, for the king's father had been a very cruel king and the new king and his friends had given his death a little assistance.

"I think you had better leave them all," said the king. "We would have a lot of trouble here with three kings."

"Well, it's not that easy," said Fene slyly. "Your father has offered me half of his property to let him out. I am certainly not going to send him back for nothing."

"I will still give you half of my property," said the desperate king. "Just get rid of them all."

So Fene received half of the king's fortune and concluded that while truth might have the favor of God, falsehood was the best way to get ahead with men.

INTERPRETATIONS

1. Are the incidents along the journey effective illustrations of the moral? To what institutions does falsehood apply? How do you respond to the choices made by the husband and the king?

2. The Senegalese myth is an allegory about abstractions like falsehood and truth. What associations do you have with myths or fables? What expectations do characters based on abstractions set up?

3. What does this fable teach about human attitudes toward absolutes like truth and falsehood? Are they relevant only to Senegalese culture? Explain.

The Wise Rogue

JEWISH FOLKTALE AS TOLD BY MOSES GASTER

The editor of A Harvest of World Folk Tales *describes the origins of "The Wise Rogue" as follows:*

> *The keynotes of Jewish folk story are wisdom, humor, and piety, and its favorite form is the parable. It is plainly the product of a society that was in its early days priestly and in its later days persecuted. Rare are the mighty, muscular heroes (Samson was one, of course, but David against Goliath and Judith against Holofernes seem much more characteristic); nor are there any authentic fire breathing dragons or broom-riding witches. The heroes of the Jews are wise kings, learned rabbis, or rogues who live by their wits; their dragons are the Devil and the Temptations; their witches are those who have historically oppressed them. Even their humor is of a wordly wise or satiric sort; and their sillies, the Wise Men of Helm, are not so much numskulls as absent-minded philosophers, men whose heads are filled with more than is commonly useful.*

A MAN WHO WAS ONCE CAUGHT stealing was ordered by the king to be hanged. On the way to the gallows he said to the governor that he knew a wonderful secret, and it would be a pity to allow it to die with him, and he would like to disclose it to the king. He would put a seed of a pomegranate in the ground, and through the secret taught to him by his father he would make it grow and bear fruit overnight. The thief was brought before the king, and on the morrow the king, accompanied by the high officers of state, came to the place where the thief was waiting for them. There the thief dug a hole and said, "This seed must be put in the ground only by a man who has never stolen or taken anything which did not belong to him. I being a thief cannot do it." So he turned to the vizier who, frightened, said that in his younger days he had retained something which did not belong to him. The treasurer said that in dealing with large sums he might have entered too much or too little, and even the king owned that he had kept a necklace of his father's. The thief then said, "You are all mighty and powerful and want nothing, and yet you cannot plant the seed, whilst I who have stolen a little because I was starving am to be hanged." The king, pleased with the ruse of the thief, pardoned him.

INTERPRETATIONS

1. "The king, pleased with the ruse of the thief, pardoned him." Usually people do not enjoy being tricked; what was different about this case? How would you have felt if the trick had been played on you?

2. What does this story imply about the relationship between justice and mercy?

3. What is the tone of this story? How does it affect the meaning?

CORRESPONDENCES

1. In folk literature, the trickster is the antithesis of the cultural hero, and his role is to destabilize the status quo by introducing the unexpected. How does the trickster function in both the Senegalese and the Jewish fables?

2. Review the Geertz perspective. What does it mean? How does it relate to "The Wise Rogue"? What does the story imply?

APPLICATIONS

1. The folktale, in contrast to literature, which is transmitted through written texts, is communicated orally primarily through memory and tradition. Create a folktale with your group members. Before beginning, decide on the moral you wish to communicate and think of humorous ways to include it.

2. Do you think of yourself as an idealist or a realist? An optimist or pessimist? Introvert or extrovert? Honest or dishonest? Are these categories adequate or too absolute to be accurate? Write a short essay on your attitude toward labeling.

3. What do the Senegalese and the Jewish stories suggest about success? Are rogues likely to achieve success? What examples can you think of? Discuss these questions in your group and record your conclusions.

20/20 Hindsight

JAY FORD

Jay Ford (b. 1969) was raised and educated in New York City. He graduated from Wesleyan University, majoring in African-American history and is a graduate of Boston College's Law School. In his junior year, he spent a semester in Kenya as part of an international exchange program. His essay "20/20 Hindsight" is an account of what he learned there—about himself and Kenyan culture.

Kenya, located on the eastern coast of Africa with a population of twenty-three million, is slightly smaller in area than Texas. Having won independence from Great Britain in 1963, Kenya has until recently had a relatively free political life, and has shown steady growth in industry and agriculture. The official language is Swahili. The Kikuyu account for twenty-one percent of the population and are the largest of Kenya's many ethnic groups. Thirty-eight percent of Kenyans are Protestant, twenty-six percent Roman Catholic, and six percent Muslim. Tourists and other visitors account for $355 million of Kenya's annual budget of $2 billion.

BORN INTO A MIDDLE-CLASS African-American family on the upper west side of Manhattan, I have spent most of my life chasing the (white) American dream. Absorbing the rhetoric brewed by the media, school curricula, and, more important, my teachers, I was graduated from high school with the goal of travelling to Europe, achieving a college degree, becoming a corporate lawyer and, eventually, marrying a spouse who would be most likely white or a light-skinned black. We would have two homes and probably three children. This was my rough sketch of my future, one with which I was satisfied. I would be a success and this was very important because I clearly represent what W. E. B. DuBois coined as the "talented tenth." Therefore, I had a responsibility to my people to succeed, to vanquish the disabilities associated with my color and earn my place in white America, my America.

In starting off on my journey to success, I met my first obstacle as I neared the end of my sophomore year in college. The student body had taken over the administration building in hopes of persuading the University to divest monies invested in corporations in South Africa. A meeting between the students and the administration had been

346 CHAPTER 7 • CULTURAL ENCOUNTERS

arranged during which the administration had thoroughly explained its position on divestment. Now it was the students' turn to respond. As student after student approached the microphone, explaining what he/she believed to be the most important reasons for disinvesting, an unsettling feeling began to overwhelm me. Although all of the explanations were more than legitimate reasons to disinvest, none of them had touched my personal reasons for protesting the University's position on divestment.

When it was my turn, I did not actually know what I wanted to say, but I was determined to say something. "My name is Julius J. Ford. I am an Afro-American. Inherent in my title is the word African, meaning 'of Africa.' My ancestry is from Africa. Africans are therefore my people, my history. So as long as you continue to oppress my people through violence or investment or silence, you oppress me. And as long as you oppress me, I will fight you! I will fight you!" As I returned to my seat, my friend leaned over, patted me on the back and said, "That was great, I never really knew you felt that way." I turned to him and said, "Neither did I."

It was this event that made me question myself. How could I be satisfied with my sketch of success when it had no background or depth? Why had I not felt this strongly about Africa or Africans before? Why was I more attracted to women who possessed European features (straight hair, light skin, thin nose) than those who possessed African features? Why did I feel that Europe was so great and Africa so primitive? Why did I choose to call myself an African-American when I knew virtually nothing about Africa? These questions would trouble my soul for the remainder of the year. In fact, they would push me to apply to a student exchange program in East Africa, Kenya.

Called "An Experiment in International Living," the program would offer me travel throughout the country, during which time I would live in both rural and urban areas, in both huts and hotels, for approximately four months from February through mid-May, 1989. I would be equipped with two academic directors with numerous university and government contacts and ensured a variety of learning opportunities, as I would stay with native families and be allowed to venture off on my own.

Even though this program seemingly presented an optimum opportunity to find answers to all my pending questions, I was still apprehensive about my decision to go. But, perhaps if there was one specific incident that canceled any wavering on my part, it was that Friday afternoon at drama class. On Fridays, I taught drama to about twenty 9–14-year-old kids from predominantly black families with low incomes at a community center about twenty minutes from my college.

On this particular day I had decided to ask the class what they thought about my taking a trip to Africa. They shot off these responses: "Why would you want to go to Africa to get even blacker than you are now?", "Why don't you take a trip somewhere nice like Paris, London, Rome?", "But they say in Africa every one is backwards, they can't teach you anything," "People are so black and ugly there." And, although some of the comments from the children were said specifically to make the other children laugh, many of them were exemplifications of how our educational system and other forms of external social propaganda affect a black child's mind.

When I first arrived in Kenya, we stayed in its capital city, Nairobi. Surprisingly enough, my first impression of Nairobi was that it was just like any American city: skyscrapers, movie theatres, discos, and crime. In fact, I was a bit disappointed, feeling that I had travelled fifteen hours in a Pan Am jet just to come back to New York City. But upon more detailed observation, I realized that this city was quite different from any other I had visited before. This city was black and, when I say black, I'm not talking your coffee-colored Atlanta, Oakland, Harlem black people. I mean black! I mean when you were small and used to play games and chose to embarrass the darkest kid on the block by calling him "midnight," "shadow," and "teeth black."

But the lesson to be learned in Nairobi was that all shades of black were equally attractive and the small children did not penalize attractiveness according to shade of skin, or length of hair, or size of nose. Furthermore, being in a black city, knowing I was in a mostly black country that sits on a predominantly black continent, enhanced my confidence and hence my actions. For the first time in my life I felt as though I could do anything, fit in anywhere, be welcomed by everyone because of my color. This was the feeling I had often assumed blacks felt during the Twenties, the period of the Harlem Renaissance. It was wonderful! I would go for days without being aware of my color. It did not seem to matter.

It was only a few weeks into the program, however, when I began to notice racial insecurities developing within my peer group (of twenty-four I was the only black). As many as half a dozen of the other students declared that they had begun to view black children as more beautiful than white, that black women and black features were more pleasing to the eye than white ones. Others simply segregated themselves from the black society as much as possible, refusing to stay with families without another white person present. Perhaps, then, inherent in the role of minority come feelings of inferiority, a certain lack of confidence, insecurity.

Because there is much tribalism in Kenya, the first title I had to drop was African-American. When people around me refer to themselves as

Masai or Kikuyu as opposed to Kenyan or East African, then how could I refer to myself as an African? Furthermore, the language I spoke, my values, morals and education were not African. So this put me in an awkward position. No one could question my ancestry as African because of my color, so I enjoyed most benefits of majority status. Yet, to many Kenyans, I was much more similar to a white American than an African so there was a wide gap between us.

It was here I realized that to be an accepted descendant of Africa I had a lot of work to do. I needed to learn a new language and a new culture. I needed to assimilate, and I figured that that shouldn't be too hard as I had twenty years of experience in that in the United States. But, the difference between my American and Kenyan assimilations is that in Kenya it seemed to be welcomed if not encouraged by the majority. The more knowledge I attained of Kenya and the more I left my English at home and spoke Swahili or another tribal language, the more cultural doors opened to me. For example, as I became increasingly familiar with Gidiam tribal customs and my use of Kiswahili improved, I was able to travel along the coast for days never worrying about food or lodging. I was often given the opportunity to sit and discuss with elders, and take part in tribal ceremonies and had responsibilities bestowed on me by elder men, *Mzees*, or my temporary *Mama*. In fact, toward the end of my trip, when travelling alone, it was often difficult for me to convince people that I was African-American. They would tell me, *"Una toka Africa qwa sababo una weza kusema Kiswahili na una famhamu Africa life"* (You are from Africa because you are able to speak Kiswahili and you understand African life). The more I learned, the more comfortable I was with the title African-American.

I also took more pride in myself. Here it was important to learn that the black empowerment was not from sheer numbers, it was from the fact that the blacks in Africa possess a communal sense of self, a shared past that is never to be forgotten, that has passed through generations, and is used as a reference for modern-day experiences. An exemplification of this concept is the way in which Kenyans and Africans in general treat their elderly. In Kenya you are told that you never grow to equal your parents' authority or knowledge. Your elders will forever be your elders and respected as such. In Kenya, elderly people are cherished not forgotten.

As we visited small villages in the areas of Kisumu, Nakru, and on the coast, villages which by American standards were far below the poverty line, we were welcomed with feasts of foods, drinks, people and music. To them we were guests paying them the honor of visitation. Even on a more individual level, most Kenyan families were extraordinarily hospitable. To be welcomed into a stranger's home and be offered food, wine, and a bed for an unlimited number of days is shocking to Americans and even more so to a New Yorker.

This humanistic view was very difficult to adapt to because it affected every level of Kenyan society. For example, Kenyans have a very limited concept of personal space (but in a country with a population growth rate of 4.3 percent that is quite understandable). So it was often difficult for me to discover that my four newly acquired brothers were also my newly acquired bedmates, to change money at the bank while the people behind me were looking over my shoulder examining my passport and money exchange papers, and, to learn not to tell your family that you would like to be left alone because crazy people stay by themselves.

Also, Americans are lost outside of a linear society. We are taught from kindergarten to stay in line. Order for us is symbolically represented by the line, and we therefore choose to see all other forms of non-linear collective activity as chaotic. Kenyans, however, do not have this same view of order. They choose to mass together, aggressively seeking out their desires and bringing new meaning to the words "organized chaos." Mobs catch buses, herds are seen at ticket counters, and, unfortunately, until your adjustment period is complete, you stand apart from the chaos, "jaw dropped," staring at the stampede of people. As a result, you do not obtain a ticket or get on the bus.

This conception of order plus the Kenyan view of personal space make for exciting moments in the public sphere. For example, there is a type of Kenyan public transportation called *matatus*. Matatus are small privately owned minivans that serve as buses for local citizens. To ride a matatu is like taking the most crowded New York City subway car during rush hour, placing that car on Broadway, and allowing a taxicab driver to control the wheel. Matatus do not actually stop at designated bus stops; in fact, they do not actually stop at all. Instead, they simply slow down and those who need to get off push and shove their way to the front of the van and jump out. And as for those who wish to board, they simply chase the matatu down and shove and push their way onto the van. As with circus clown cars, there is always room for one more.

Another linear concept I was introduced to was time. In rural areas there would sometimes be days when we would have no activities planned. It was at these moments when I would curse my directors for poor planning. But I was soon to learn that doing nothing was not necessarily wasted time. This time to think, relax, conversationalize was most important for a peaceful state of mind. I finally understood that it is not imperative even in America to eat breakfast, read the paper in the street while you are running to the subway, or to work two jobs just to pay off your life insurance bill. Here there was not "so much to do and so little time"; here there was a great deal to do but also the belief that that which is supposed to get done will get done in time.

For example, during the last month of my stay in Kenya I visited a small farm in Kisumu Kaubu, Uganda, with a woman and her three sons. I was only to stay for a day and one night. I had come to visit just prior to the time the rains were expected, so I had assumed that the family was going to spend very little time relaxing with me because it was imperative that the soil and seeds for the year be prepared for the rains which could come at any moment.

However, once I arrived, we did very little field work. We talked instead—about the history of her people, about America, and about American perceptions of Kenya. Of course this was hard work since their English was very limited and my Swahili is fair at best. And as the day crept on to the night, I asked her how she could afford to give her attentions to me when the threat of the rains could come at any day now. "*Pole Pole, bwana*," she replied (We have not neglected our work to the fields. We have only delayed our work so to welcome our new son, who by joining us will ease our workload). I then asked her, "But, Mama, it is already 11:00 and I leave tomorrow at 9:00." She replied, "Don't worry, bwana, we start to work the cattle (plow) at 2:00 A.M. Good night."

It seemed as though Kenyan culture chose to be humanistic rather than materialistic. The value placed on human life and interaction is much greater than in the States. To shake hands, to share a meal or even your home with a foreigner is an honor, not a burden. And, for you as a guest to turn down that hand, meal, or bed is an insult. How wonderfully strange to travel to a foreign land where people who can hardly understand what language you speak are ready to take you home and make you part of the family. They wouldn't last too long in New York, I thought.

In most places in Kenya, it was common knowledge for one to know his/her environment. People could name the types of trees along the roads, tell you animals indigenous to the area, and explain which types of soil were best for growing specific crops. They could tell you the staple foods of different parts of Kenya *or* even the United States. In fact, their world geography was superior to that of most American college students. Access to information, whether at home or in schools, was a privilege to be appreciated by those involved and then passed down to younger generations orally. I wonder why I did not feel this way. My country offers more educational opportunities than any other in the world and yet seldom are these opportunities fully exploited. American students go to school, but they do not go to learn. They go to get A's and move up economically. They go to play the game, the educational game of success that I like to refer to as DT (Diploma Training), a process that verifies one's intelligence by certificate as opposed to action or common sense.

Furthermore, along with this overwhelming appreciation for knowledge, Kenyans show reverence for everyday simplicities which we in America take for granted: the appreciation for candlelight, running water, a toilet with a seat cover, a long hot shower every day. Learning to live is to stay in Kenya and survive with twenty-three other people living mostly off rain water, sleeping in huts, and eating many fruits and vegetables with only the occasional beef meal. I felt as though Kenya taught me a new dimension of life, a rebirth of sorts. It put objectives, time, goals, values into a new perspective. It did not tell me, "Please be aware of how much water you use because a drought warning is in effect." It gave me a gallon of water and told me to drink and bathe for an undetermined period. It did not tell me of the beauties of nature, rather it revealed them to me by greeting me in the morning with the sights of Mt. Kenya, Kilimanjaro, and Lake Victoria. I saw no need for National Geographic or wildlife television, for when it wanted to introduce me to animals, a monkey, leopard, or family of raccoons would become my fellow pedestrians. There was no urge to tell me of the paradox of zoos when it could show me national parks with hundreds of acres of land.

In Kenya I felt more free than I have ever felt before. The only thing holding me captive was the earth which would grow the food, the sky which would quench the earth of its thirst, and the sun which would warm and help all things to grow. But these masters were sure to give back all that you have put in. When you worked hard, your rewards were great and if you chose to relax so would your crop and cattle. And with a give-and-take relationship like this, one learns that it is okay to take time, time for others, for oneself, time to enjoy and appreciate all that life and earth offer. Some choose to call this type of relationship religion, a covenant with the Lord and her divinity (sky, earth, and animals) and I will not deny that there was a strong sense of God or Allah or Sa or Buddha.

A forest burning to the ground germinates the soil, allowing new life to grow. The omnipotence of nature—floods, lightning, hurricanes, earthquakes, the beauty of a cheetah or giraffe running, an open field, the sky, the mountains, the sea—is overwhelming and foreign to me living so long in a concrete jungle. When all of this engulfed me and I took the time to embrace it, I became convinced that there exists a master craftsperson of this creation, that there exists a God.

Kenya has more than (just) given me a new perception of the world; Kenya has widened my world view. I now realize that there are other significant cultures in the world besides a western one. I no longer think of the world in First, Second, and Third World terms. There are aspects of Kenyan values which should be regarded as more First World than American: humanistic sentiments, importance of family, pride of ancestry, appreciation and respect for other peoples' differences.

Also, whereas I ventured off to Kenya to learn about a new culture and its new people, I found that most of the more important discoveries and evaluations were about myself. Upon leaving Kenya I feel that I have grown more confident about my African-Americanness, my perceptions of the world around me, and my expectation of 21/21 vision and beyond. I do not believe I could have gone anywhere else on earth and been as personally challenged.

INTERPRETATIONS

1. Was the author wrong to assume that the dreams of "white America" should or could also be the goals of a black American? Why? To what extent are the aspirations ("rhetoric") he mentions in the first paragraph misguided? Why? How does the speech made before students and administration relate to these aspirations and the identity crisis raised by the label "African-American"?

2. What does the title mean? What is the author scrutinizing with 20/20 hindsight? How successfully does he combine the story of an identity crisis with cultural commentary? Support your conclusion.

3. What did the author's young drama-class students teach him about attitudes of American blacks toward Africa? How does this attitude contrast with what he found among children in Nairobi? How reliable are children's conversation and vocabulary as indicators of widespread but unconscious attitudes?

4. "Perhaps . . . inherent in the role of minority come feelings of inferiority . . ." Can you offer evidence from your own life that supports or refutes this idea? Does the author's evidence (the white group's behavior in Kenya) convince you? How does this idea relate to Ford's later assertion that "black empowerment [in Africa] was not from sheer numbers" but from long and rich cultural traditions?

CORRESPONDENCES

1. Review Benedict's perspective on cultural interactions (page 337) and discuss its relevance to Ford's essay. What is the most important

insight that Ford gains about himself as a result of his experiences in Kenya?

2. Ford's semester in Kenya also changed his perspective: "I no longer think of the world in First, Second, and Third World terms." What evidence does he cite? To what extent does his experience reinforce or contradict Kluckhohn's perspective on cultural interactions (page 338)?

APPLICATIONS

1. "American students go to school, but they do not go to learn. They go to get A's and move up economically." Ford wrote his essay in 1989. To what extent does it apply to your aspirations educationally and economically? Write an essay disagreeing or agreeing with Ford citing evidence for your point of view.

2. "In Kenya, elderly people are cherished not forgotten." How might such an attitude affect social and cultural aspirations? How does it compare to prevailing attitudes toward older people in the United States?

3. In his conclusion, Ford notes that his most important discoveries in Kenya were evaluations about himself. If you have spent time in another culture, write an essay about what you learned about yourself through this encounter.

4. After reading Ford's essay, what are your feelings about living in America? Make a chart that divides positives and negatives. Fill out your chart and tally your results. Write an essay about what you have learned from your reading and chartmaking.

Becoming American, by Degrees

JIM FUSILLI

Jim Fusilli (b. 1953) has written for a variety of publications, most notably
The Wall Street Journal. *He says he particularly enjoys writing personal
essays. "When I get to write about things that allow me to examine my childhood, it gives me a new opportunity to see how it affected me. It either rein-
forces my perspective or gives me a new one. That's pretty healthful, I think."*

I'VE RECENTLY COME TO REALIZE that, for a native, an understanding of
what it means to be an American isn't so much a matter of heritage as a
matter of consciousness. It's a matter of awareness that comes in degrees, sometimes slowly, if at all.

For me, this consciousness, this awareness, began when I started to
travel often outside the U.S., a fairly recent activity for me. I imagine for
a young child who is well traveled from birth, toted along with the lug-
gage, it may occur on a subconscious level, like the awareness of race,
class and organized religion (though faced with bigotry these deeply
rooted identities surface to the conscious level with the power of a thun-
derbolt). For me, whose idea of an adventure in travel as a child was a
25-cent bus ride to an adjoining town, there was no such opportunity.

We lived in an immigrant community, within sight of the Statue of
Liberty and Ellis Island; a steady flow of imposing yet magnificent ships
brought European immigrants to the piers at the other end of our mile-
square town. If memory serves, in kindergarten I had classmates whose
parents had recently come from Italy, Germany, the Netherlands and
Yugoslavia.

But if this was a form of training for life in a multinational environment, I was unaware of it. It seemed to me these families were remark-
ably similar, sharing the same basic characteristics: They worked hard
and aspired to assimilate. A few remnants of their native culture remained—music and food, in particular—but they came to America to
be American.

At the same time, though, the seeds of my American identity were
sown: I was something others aspired to become. But this wasn't an
active thought by any means—I was not yet old enough to have active
thoughts about much of anything—but, I see now, it's in there. Fortunately, it appears to manifest itself as a kind of quiet self-confidence

rather than ugly American arrogance. I've now come to see that I'm lucky that way.

As a boy, I struggled with national identity. My Irish-American mother had married a second-generation Italian, and they drew, if not the wrath, a level of scorn from her family, though not so much as to cause her to actively side with her husband. In fact, we lived among my mother's family, and they never ceased to remind me that I was an outsider. Something stubborn within me made me emphasize what was the other in me; and I still look at life as not what I ought to be, not what I am being coaxed to be, but what I am and what I can be, and that too gives me self-confidence, though as a boy I very often felt isolated and had to learn to thrive by myself. (This, I think, is the shared, fundamental characteristic of all writers: the ability to live comfortably, at times preferably, in a world of our own creation. But, another time for that.)

The idea of an American character came to me as it did to most people my age: through the mass media. Of course, in school we learned of Thomas Paine and John Adams and Abraham Lincoln and Woodrow Wilson. But, so upstanding were they, and completely without human foibles, they might as well have been literary devices to advance a fictional story of a country of gods. But, via mass media—glimmering images at the Fabian Theater, our only movie house; the flopping picture on our black-and-white TV; New York City's myriad newspapers, all available at nearby candy stores—I learned of the American character: Jimmy Stewart as good, honest, self-sacrificing George Bailey in "It's a Wonderful Life"; the steel-jawed determination of Robert Ryan in "The Longest Day"; James Cagney as George M. Cohan, "a real live nephew of my Uncle Sam, born on the Fourth of July"; clean-cut John Glenn orbiting the earth in *Friendship 7*; Leonard Bernstein, patiently teaching us the joys of Copeland; and Superman, "who, disguised as Clark Kent, mild-mannered reporter for a great metropolitan newspaper, fights a never-ending battle for truth, justice and the American Way."

Frankly, at that age, with the exception of Superman, it was impossible to tell who was real and who was fictional, for they shared one absolute: They did, or were doing, the right thing for us, the Americans. Even John Wayne, who massacred a few hundred Indians in the promotion of our standard, had God on his side.

I must confess that as a boy I had no real heroes, besides the almost-mandatory sports idols. Men in the neighborhood had served and had been wounded in the second World War, but, seeing them every day, they hardly seemed heroic. Sadly, through drink and intolerance, some seemed smaller, not larger, than life. My father adored Frank Sinatra, a native of our town, but he made my skin crawl with his ring-a-ding-ding, booze-

and-broads routine. To my grandfather's peers, men who had come from Italy to establish a new life in America, Joe DiMaggio was an idol: Joe D, a man of enormous dignity, a baseball legend *and* husband to Marilyn Monroe. (Madonna mio! *That's* assimilation.) I thought Joe Namath was pretty neat, and since he had dark hair and a kind of appealing, post-Sinatra swagger, I imagined he might have some Italian blood in him. Maybe he was a half-breed, like me.

The idea of what is the American character, what are the inherent characteristics of an American, began to be challenged during the Vietnam War–era by hippies, assertive feminists, pop psychologists, contrarians of all kinds, and I had the best view of this debate: a tad too young to have to serve in the war, a bit too young to have to deal with assertive women, often alone, willingly assaulted by media, and interested enough to observe. Perhaps confused by all of it—there really was nobody to root for then, save slaughtered saints like Martin Luther King and the unpenetrables like Bob Dylan and Miles Davis; and so many loathsome worms like the crook Nixon and his (execrable) subordinates—I withdrew, thus avoiding the subject of what it really means to be an American.

Avoidance, to be frank, was easy. My experiences in college were extremely limited: I attended a college to which virtually everyone commuted from nearby communities, and in my class were at least a dozen people with whom I'd gone to high school. I had a full-time night job, so I stayed pretty close to home. I'd joined the college newspaper and began interviewing people from different backgrounds, which was somewhat enlightening: only somewhat, because most of my subjects were Anglo-Saxon musicians, a narrowly focused group, I can assure you. So insulated was I that I remember as I spoke with the Grateful Dead's Jerry Garcia that he was the first person I'd ever met from California.

My exposure to the other began in earnest about five years after graduation when I fell into the company of world-class journalists at a major daily newspaper, people who had dodged the Khmer Rouge, been detained by the KGB, conversed with Castro, Deng, Khomeini, walked the streets of Baghdad, Palestine, Johannesburg. They had been eyewitnesses to every historic event of the past 20 years and knew how to relate their experiences with vivid color and nuance, even over coffee or a quick lunch. And among these reporters were men and women born in India, Taiwan, Egypt and Japan as well as all parts of the English-speaking world. They had an entirely different perspective on things, and it was enlightening to try to see as they did. When a question was raised, it was impossible to anticipate what the answer could be, and when the topic was an event occurring in America—be it political, economic, social, the arts—I soon realized they weren't merely addressing the subject, they were talking about America and its nature.

And this was a revelation to me. Despite attempts to avoid it, I'd heard echoes of the public debate on the American character, and knew it had degenerated into diatribes shouted from the polar fringes, with all forms of recrimination and bilge replacing thoughtful analysis. Remember, this was the era of family values promoted by men and women who couldn't keep their own families together, and the whining of the well-off who demanded more personal liberties without a shred of discussion about community and responsibility. Had I not been privy to the considered comments of those editors and reporters, I would've come to believe self-indulgence, insincerity and intolerance were our defining features now. But, no, they knew this was all so much babble, and that real issues could be solved, or at least prudently addressed, by a people who were better than their leaders, either elected or self-appointed. They knew quality when they saw it.

After leaving the company of those journalists, I began working for an organization with headquarters in Paris, France, and offices in more than 100 countries. I suddenly found myself a part of a global team with members from each country in Western Europe as well as Hungary and several countries in South America, all of whom spoke, in addition to their native language, French and, thankfully, English. With these people, I had no identity other than American. They didn't much care that I was from New Jersey (which they knew was close to New York City) or that I considered myself an Italian-American. "My grandfather is from Foggia," I told my colleague from Milan. She replied, "Ah, you speak Italian?" "No," I admitted. At that moment, I lost my hyphen.

It was early in my tenure that I first heard the expression "You Americans." While traveling across the south of France, a British colleague who was based in Brazil tapped me on the shoulder and said, "Say, James, where do you stand on the issue of the coloreds?"

"What?" I was hoping I misunderstood.

"Well, I know you Americans are of two minds on this issue—"

"I'm not," I snapped.

(An imperial bore on many issues, he was fired shortly thereafter.)

But most allusions to "you Americans" were complimentary; in fact, some were over the top. I was riding in a New York City subway with a colleague from Paris, and the crowded car was filled with a tension typical of certain lines at certain times of the day. After we surfaced, he asked me if I was afraid on the train. No, I replied, and that was true: I took that line every day for several years. "Yes," he said, "you Americans are never afraid." Too many John Wayne movies, I thought.

As I became integrated into the team, my opinion was sought, perhaps more often than that of others with more experience than I. "Let's get the American viewpoint" was how it was often presented. And I gave the American viewpoint, as if there was such a thing, and I tried to be as humble and unobtrusive as possible: I was new, still, and I understood that these people were accommodating me by conducting meetings in English. I did know enough French to overhear one colleague say, "He's not a typical American" as I quietly acquiesced to some now-forgotten scheme. I wasn't sure what she meant, but I took the comment as a mild insult and determined to be a bit more assertive. Maybe a bit more daring and steel-jawed determination, and a little less self-sacrifice.

Once the team became comfortable with me, and I with them, we found common ground on subjects that transcended nationality and language. I knew at least a little about Stendhal and Baudelaire, Manet and Seurat, Truffault and Godard, and they knew rock 'n' roll and American movies. I was sitting in a cafe by the water in Stockholm with a colleague who spoke no English. The ships in the harbor reminded me of my hometown and I suddenly felt compelled to tell her about my childhood. In carefully crafted French, I asked her if she ever saw a movie called "On the Waterfront" with Marlon Brando, Eva Marie Saint, Lee J. Cobb and Rod Steiger. She brightened and nodded. "Ma ville," I said proudly.

These relationships have become precious. People from many countries know my family and me, and I know some of their children. My Italian colleague has researched my grandfather's hometown and presented me with her findings. The daughters of my German colleague wear Oshkosh jeans I purchased at a New Jersey mall. My wife, daughter and I saw "Turnadot" performed at the Acropolis, and when I ranted about the experience at a team meeting the next morning, these people looked at me with benign bemusement: They liked it that the American was pleased. The goodwill continues: Diet Coke is kept in the refrigerator at headquarters in Paris. My colleagues wear baseball caps.

Meanwhile, back at home, I've become irrationally proud of American things: geysers in Yellowstone National Park. Pathfinder on the surface of Mars. Windows 95. A New England clam bake. Walt Whitman. David Mamet. Thelonious Monk . . .

INTERPRETATIONS

1. How did Fusilli's cultural encounters as a child in his neighborhood shape his awareness of what it means to be an American?

2. "As a boy, I struggled with national identity." What role did his family play in this process?

3. Fusilli examined at some length the extent to which figures from mass media helped form his generation's ideas about American culture. With how many of the people he mentions are you familiar?

4. How did traveling and being part of an international group of professionals add to his perspective as an American?

CORRESPONDENCES

1. Review and interpret Fuentes's perspective on cultural encounters (page 337). To what extent does it apply to Fusilli's essay?
2. Compare and contrast the role of travel in the cultural encounters of Grant and Fusilli.

APPLICATIONS

1. Fusilli lists movie stars and sports figures who influenced his generation. Update that list for your generation with the assistance of your group. How have these celebrities shaped your ideas of what being an American means?
2. Have you, like Fusilli, had an experience that "transcended language and culture"? What insights did you gain from it? Write an essay recounting your experience and its impact on your life.
3. In a journal entry, explore your own sense of ethnic identity. If you are biracial, how do you choose to categorize yourself? Have you ever felt compelled to "choose" an ethnic identity?

Fraternity

GARRETT HONGO

*Garrett Hongo (b. 1951) was born in Hawaii and received an M.F.A. at the
University of California at Irvine. Hongo's publications include:* Budding
Bandits Down Highway 99, *with Lawson Inada and Alan Lau (1978);* The
River of Heaven *(1988), which was the Lamont Poetry Selection of The
Academy of American Poets and a finalist for the Pulitzer Prize, and* Yellow
Light *(1982). His most recent book,* Volcano: A Memoir of Hawaii, *was
published in 1995. Hongo has received fellowships from the Guggenheim
Foundation, the National Endowment for the Arts, and the Rockefeller Foun-
dation. He is currently Professor of Creative Writing at the University of
Oregon at Eugene. Before reading Hongo's essay, record in your journal your
definition of fraternity.*

IT WAS HIGH SCHOOL IN GARDENA. I was in classes mostly with Japanese
American kids—*kotonks*. Mainland Japanese, their ethnic pet name originated, during the war, with derisive Hawaiian GIs who thought of the
sound of a coconut being hit with a hammer. Sansei *kotonks* were sons
and daughters of the Nisei *kotonks* who had been sent off to the concentration camps during World War II. School was tepid, boring. We
wanted cars, we wanted clothes, we wanted everything whites and
blacks wanted to know about sex but were afraid to tell us. We "bee-
essed" with the black kids in the school parking lot full of coastal fog
before classes. We beat the white kids in math, in science, in typing. We
ran track and elected cheerleaders. We *ruled*, we said. We were dumb,
teeming with attitude and prejudice.

Bored, I took a creative writing class with an "academically mixed"
bunch of students. There were Chicanos, whites, a black woman, and a
troika of Japanese women who sat together on the other side of the room
from me. They said nothing—*ever*—and wrote naturalistically correct
haiku. Suddenly among boisterous non-Japanese, I enjoyed the gabbing,
the bright foam of free talk that the teacher encouraged. An aging man
in baggy pants that he wore with suspenders, he announced he was
retiring at the end of the year and that he wanted no trouble, that he was
going to read "Eee-bee White" during our hour of class every day, that
we were welcome to read whatever we wanted so long as we gave him a
list ahead of time, and that we could talk as much as we wanted so long

as we left him alone. We could read, we could write, we could jive each other all class long. It was freedom. And I took advantage.

I sat next to a Chicano my age named Pacheco and behind a white girl a class younger than me named Regina. Behind us was a curly-headed white guy who played saxophone in the marching band. He'd been in academic classes with me, the only Caucasian among Japanese, a Korean, and a few Chinese. He was a joker, and I liked him, but usually stayed away—we didn't fraternize much across the races, though our school was supposed to be an experiment in integration.

Gardena H. S. wasn't so much a mix or blend as a mosaic. Along with a few whites and blacks, Japanese were in the tough, college-prep, "advanced placement" scholastic track. Most whites and blacks were in the regular curriculum of shop, business skills, and a minimum of academic courses. The "dumb Japs" were in there with them. And the Chicanos filled up what were called the *remedial* classes, all taught imperiously only in English, with no provision for language acquisition. We were a student body of about three thousand, and we walked edgily around each other, swaggering when we could, sliding the steel taps on our big black shoes along the concrete outdoor walkways when we wanted to attract a little attention, making a jest of our strut, a music in the rhythm of our walking. Blacks were bused in from Compton; the whites, Japanese, and Chicanos came from around the town. Girls seemed to me an ethnic group of their own too, giggling and forming social clubs, sponsoring dances, teaching some of us the steps.

Crazes of dress moved through our populations—for Chicanos: woolen Pendletons over thin undershirts and a crucifix; big low-top oxfords; khaki work trousers, starched and pressed; for the *bloods*: rayon and satin shirts in metallic "fly-ass" colors; pegged gabardine slacks; cheap moccasin-toed shoes from downtown shops in L.A.; and for us *Buddhas*: high-collar Kensingtons of pastel cloths, A-tapered "Racer" slacks, and the same moccasin shoes as the bloods, who were our brothers. It was crazy. And *inviolable*. Dress and social behavior were a code one did not break for fear of ostracism and reprisal. Bad dressers were ridiculed. Offending speakers were beaten, tripped walking into the john, and set upon by gangs. They *wailed* on you if you fucked up. A girl was nothing except pride, an ornament of some guy's crude power and expertise in negotiating the intricacies of this inner-city semiotic of cultural display and hidden violence. I did not know girls.

I talked to Regina, saying "white girl" one time. She told me not to call her that, that she was *Portuguese* if anything, that I better *know* that white people were *always* something too. From vague memories of Hawaii, I reached for the few words in *Portuguese* that I knew, I asked her about the sweet bread her mother baked, about heavy donuts fried in oil and rolled in sugar. I said *bon dea* for "good day" to her. I read the books she talked about—Steinbeck, Kesey, Salinger, and Baldwin. Her mother brought paperbacks home from the salon she worked in, putting up other women's hair—*rich* women's. We made up our reading list from books her mother knew. I wanted desperately to impress her, so I began to write poetry too, imitating some melancholy rock and country-and-western lyrics. She invited me to her house after school. It was on the way, so I walked her home. It became a practice.

Her father was a big, diabetic man from Texas. With his shirt off, he showed me how he shot himself with insulin, poking the needle under the hairy red skin on his stomach, working it over the bulge of fat around his belly. He laughed a lot and shared his beer. There were other guys over too—white guys from the football team, a Filipino, and one other Japanese guy who played left tackle. They were tough, raucous, and talked easily, excitedly. I stood alone in the front yard one day, holding a soft drink in my hand, the barbecue party going on around me. Regina and her mother were baking bread inside. No one knew exactly what was going on, and I was still trying to pretend all was casual.

I took photographs of her. We had a picnic on the coast by the lighthouse near Marineland, on the bluffs over the Pacific. It was foggy, mist upon us and the tall, droopy grasses in the field we walked through, but we made do. She wrapped herself in the blanket she'd brought for us to sit on. We were in the tall grasses of the headlands far from the coast road. She posed. I changed lenses, dropping film canisters, other things. She waved to me, unbuttoning the blouse she was wearing, her body full of a fragrance. The warm, yeasty scent of her skin smelled like bread under bronze silk.

We couldn't be seen together—not at the private, car-club-sponsored Japanese dances out in the Crenshaw District, not at the whites-dominated dances after school in the high school gym. Whites did not see Buddhas, and Buddhas did not see bloods. We were to stay with our own—*that* was the code—though we mixed some in the lunch line, in a few classes, on the football field, and in gym. We segregated ourselves.

Regina and I went to the Chicano dances in El Monte. Pacheco introduced us to them. Regina, tanned Portuguese, passed for Chicana, so long as she kept her mouth shut and her lashes long. Pacheco showed her what skirts to wear, his quick hands fluttering through the crinolines and taffetas in her closet at home. He advised me to grow a mustache and let my black hair go long in the back, to slick it down with pomade and to fluff it up in front, then seal it all in hair spray. I bought brown Pendletons and blue navy-surplus bell-bottoms. I bought hard, steel-toed shoes, We learned trots and tangos. We learned *cuecas* and polkas. We *passed, ese*, and had a good time for a couple of months.

One day, Regina got hurt. She was stopped by one of the football players at the beach. She was stepping onto a bus when he came up behind her and grabbed her arm. She tried to twist away, and the arm snapped. She crumpled. Everyone ran. She rode in a friend's car to the hospital that day and had the arm set. She didn't call me.

I heard about it after school the next day, crossing the street against the light. It was summer, and I was taking classes while Regina spent her days at the beach. I'd see her weekdays, stopping at her house on the way home. I was going to her when, just outside the gates of our school, a guy I knew taunted me with the news. He was Japanese, and it was strange to hear him say anything about Regina. I hadn't realized anyone from my crowd knew about us.

I wanted to run the rest of the way to her house. I crossed over a rise of bare earth, then down to a bedded railway—a strip line so that scrap steel and aluminum could be shipped from the switching stations and railyards downtown to steel and aeronautical factories near our school. Brown hummocks rose above eye level and masked the track of crossties, steel rails, and the long bed of gravel. I was set upon there by a troop of Japanese boys. A crowd of them encircled me, taunting, then a single gangly fellow I recognized from gym class executed most of the blows. They beat me, grinding my face in the gravel, shouting epithets like *inu* ("dog"), *cow-fucker*, and *paddy-lover*.

I've seen hand-sized reef fish, in a ritual of spawning, leave their singular lairs, gathering in smallish, excitable schools—a critical mass—and, electrified by their circling assembly, suddenly burst the cluster apart with sequences of soloing, males alternating, pouncing above the finning group, clouding the crystalline waters above the circle with a roll of milt.

All spring and summer, I'd been immune, unaware of the enmity of the crowd. I hadn't realized that, in society, humiliation is a force more powerful than love. Love does not exist in society, but only between two, or among a family. A kid from Hawaii, I'd undergone no real initiation in shame or social victimization yet and maintained an arrogant season out of bounds, imagining I was exempt. It was humiliating to have been sent to Camp. The Japanese American community understood their public disgrace and lived modestly, with deep prohibitions. I was acting outside of this history. I could cross boundaries, I thought. But I was not yet initiated into the knowledge that we Japanese were *not* like anyone else, that we lived in a community of violent shame. I paid for my naïveté with a bashing I still feel today, with cuts that healed with scars I can still run my fingers along. I can still taste the blood, remember the split skin under the mustache on my upper lip, and feel the depth of an anger that must have been *historical, tribal*, arising from fears of dissolution and diaspora.

Separated societies police their own separations. I was hated one day, and with an intensity I could not have foreseen. I was lifted by my clothes, the hands of my schoolmates at the nape of my shirt collar and the back of the waistband of my trousers, and I was hurled against the scrawny trunk of a little jacaranda tree and beaten there, fists cracking against my arms as I tried to cover my face, thumping along my sides and back, booted feet flailing at my legs. I squirmed, crawled, cried out. And I wept. Out of fear and humiliation and a psychic wounding I understand only now. I was *hated*. I was high and needed lowering. My acts were canceled. Regina was canceled. Both by our own peoples, enacting parallel vengeances of their own, taking our bodies from us.

Our trystings were over, and, later that summer, Regina simply moved away. Her father was retiring, she said, and had found a nice trailer park up by Morro Bay. She wouldn't see me before she left. I had to surprise her at a Laundromat one Saturday. She gave me a paperback book. She laughed, made light of everything, but there was a complete *fear* of me that I felt from her, deeply, one I had not felt before—at least, it had never registered. *Race*. It is an exclusion, a punishment, imposed by the group. I've felt it often since. It is a fear of *fraternity*. A fraternity that is forbidden. I wept, but let her go.

INTERPRETATIONS

1. In paragraph one, Hongo describes his ethnic group. What portrait does he create?

2. "Gardena H.S. wasn't so much a mix or blend as a mosaic." What evidence supports his thesis?

3. "Dress and social behavior were a code one did not break for fear of ostracism and reprisal." What evidence resonates with your experiences in high school?

4. List the highlights of Hongo's relationship with Regina. Why does he devote so much space to this experience?

5. Hongo's brutal beating by his Japanese classmates was traumatic. Characterize your response to this incident.

CORRESPONDENCES

1. Review Fuentes's perspective on cultural interactions (page 337). To what extent do you agree with it? What conversation on this subject can you imagine Hongo and Fuentes sharing?

2. Review Santayana's perspective and show how Hongo's experience refutes it.

APPLICATIONS

1. Brainstorm about "fraternity." What images and associations does it evoke? What new meanings does Hongo's memoir create?

2. Discuss with your group Hongo's concept that "in society humiliation is a force more powerful than words." How does his concept of community compare to yours? Have you ever been punished for "crossing boundaries"?

3. Hongo describes race as "an exclusion," "a punishment," and a "fear of fraternity." Write an essay on your definition of race, supporting it as does Hongo with examples from your own experience.

4. In "Fraternity," Hongo tells a powerful story of his attempt to cross cultural boundaries. What story do you think Regina would tell? Create two journal entries written by Regina. Let the first one address her thoughts and feelings about culture before meeting Hongo. Direct the second entry to her thoughts and feelings after meeting him.

To Speak Patois

TANEISHA GRANT

Taneisha Grant received her B.S. degree from the City College of the City University of New York in 1999. She matriculated at the Albert Einstein College of Medicine of Yeshiva University in fall of 2000 and is currently pursuing her M.D. degree.

Her essay "A Writing History: From Reluctant and Redundant to Raving and Rampant" was published in the December 1995 issue of "The Compositor," a newsletter from the CCNY English Composition Program. She also won the Lucia Santorsa/Beatrice Coviello Award for the same essay. Before reading Grant's essay, consult a dictionary on the definition of patois.

AT FOURTEEN YEARS OLD, I thought I knew everything there was to know about everything worth knowing—life, people, and relationships. My mind felt full, especially full of academic knowledge, and I felt that if given ample time for gathering a little experience in the field of teaching, I would be able to teach math and science. I had only completed the introductory levels of these classes but my ambition was not to be deterred by such trivialities. In my opinion, I was already armed with the foundation—more advanced math and science classes were mere applications of the basic concepts. I was also sure that if my "skills" as a relationship expert were to be tested, I would prove myself exceedingly gifted. I counselled all my peers because I knew how Kivette should cope with not having her boyfriend, Rory, call in all of a week, and why Tashika was "keeping malice" with Odetle over something Tashika supposedly hadn't done. I longed for the everyday rigors of life that my mother and her friends were always speaking about on my verandah. I was being anchored by high school—I needed a challenge.

I was born on the tropical West Indian Island of Jamaica, which is just south of Florida. I lived in a beautiful white house on a two-and-a-half acre plot of land. My neighbors and I were surrounded by the greenery that was mango, orange, cherry, avocado, guava, apple, and June plum trees. The neighborhood children would relish in sucking on the hard June plum covered with salt on their ways home until they got to the spiky seed. This sweetish-sourish fruit was particularly satisfying if eaten when "turned" (the point of just ripening). Those school evenings were filled with the lively chatter of noisy students, tired from the day's work but with just enough energy left over to play a game of scruchie. This was a game in which two people stood about ten feet apart passing a ball between each other while all other participants ran back and forth to face the person with the ball. The object of the game was to skirt the ball as creatively as possible and not to get hit. Our "ball" was made from a juice box stuffed with paper and it really stung upon contact. Needless to say, none of us wanted to get hit and got quite a workout trying to avoid that juice box ball!

The rainy nights of May were a lot of fun because my sister and I were allowed to stay up past our bedtimes and await my cousins' return from crab hunting. The occasional sunshine warmed the water collected in the crab holes. These times were very unwelcomed by the crabs because they would have to leave their holes and would have nowhere to hide if attacked. It was on nights like these, under cover of the darkness, that my cousins went crab hunting by lamp light. Their catch was often plenty and the entire neighborhood would have a big feast of peppered crabs and boiled green bananas. On one of these nights, punctuated by the slightly hissing sounds of crickets, I happened to overhear my mother speaking on the verandah. She was telling Miss Vivene of our upcoming and permanent departure to the United States.

Growing up in Jamaica was everything one could wish for. From its white sandy beaches and crystal-clear waters to its unique reggae music, year-round sunshine, fruit trees, games of sidewalk scruchie, and delicious midnight crab feasts—this island was some sort of NICE! But quite unknown to me, sugar cane and spiced bun were not all that this island was made of. It also held a high cost of living and limited higher education. My parents thought it best for us to relocate (our home) and seize the more abundant educational opportunities offered by the United States.

I was very upset and afraid of leaving Jamaica's familiar sights, sounds, activities of daily living, my friends, my home, my country. My surroundings had always lent a partial definition to who I am. I was Taneisha who attended Titchfield High School, Taneisha who did scripture readings in church on Sundays, rode her bike to Mr. Browning's shop, and Taneisha who could find her way home blindfolded by counting the bumps in the road. I was now Taneisha leaving the familiar and all those other Taneishas behind, and that was heart-wrenching.

I had longed for a challenge and I certainly got one by moving to New York! Living here has been culturally shocking. Though the educational opportunities have been tremendously rewarding, the transition was difficult. Having to adjust to the drastic temperature change, the restrictions that go with being cautious in a more violent society, and the different educational system have quite fulfilled the challenge I sought. The sights and sounds are different, and the feeling of protection that is almost innate in a Jamaican society is lacking here.

There are many places in New York with high Jamaican populations, and there the culture and environment are closely simulated, but it's just not quite the same. I feel a deep-rooted guilt for leaving Jamaica. Though my family's situation was extenuating, I do feel as if I've abandoned my country. I speak Patois—the Jamaican dialect—as much as I can because one really can't help becoming a little culturally "dilute" when abroad. "Settled" is probably a better word, and it's an effort to keep yourself "shaken up" so as not to betray your country's memory by becoming too well-adapted/too well-mixed. I speak Patois because it serves as a verbal transport back to my homeland. I speak Patois to rekindle, "shake up" the memory of other identities and realize that I am still those Taneishas, the one who lives in New York State and also the Taneisha who will be going home.

I am now nineteen years old and I don't know a whole lot about life, relationships, or people. But I do know that I knew nothing of the rigors for which I longed or of change and the growth that it brings.

Turning points are moments
of conscious or unconscious
decisions to release stability
for a time.

Change is scary because
it means releasing the
comforts of the familiar
in order to embrace the
possibilities that newness
can bring.

Adjustments—coping mechanisms
to deal with changes—
can sometimes subdue the
memories of what was once
precious familiarity.

Dialects and other cultural
signatures help in maintaining
a firmer grasp on the old familiars.

I speak Patois.
Growth is the emotional and/or
physical manifestation of change
—of new.

INTERPRETATIONS

1. What characteristics does the author reveal about herself in the introductory paragraph?
2. How does she portray Jamaica visually, culturally, and psychologically?
3. Characterize her impression of life in New York City. Do you think she regrets having left her homeland? Cite evidence for your point of view.
4. What is the effect of ending the memoir with a poem? What does the poem mean?

CORRESPONDENCES

1. Compare and contrast the concept of assimilation presented in the essays by Hongo and Grant.
2. Review Kluckhohn's perspective on culture (page 338) and discuss its application to Grant's essay.

APPLICATIONS

1. Review Geok-lin Lim's perspective and discuss its relevance to Grant's essay. What evidence is there of sorrow and guilt for leaving Jamaica?
2. Write a journal entry on the significance of Grant's title.
3. Analyze Grant's poem with your group. How do you respond? Are the issues raised in the poem different from those in the essay? How?

Passion and the Dream

LINDA STANLEY

Linda Stanley is a professor of English at Queensborough Community College in New York City, where she teaches many recent immigrants. She has a Ph.D. in comparative literature from New York University, and for many years has been interested in, and has published on, the changing responses of people in other countries to the American experience as F. Scott Fitzgerald portrays it in The Great Gatsby. *Brainstorm on your associations with Stanley's title. To what extent is it appropriate?*

RESIDENTS OF QUEENS, NEW YORK, we are on jury duty, and, as juries do, we find a lot in common. We learn early that most of us are Catholic, with a couple of Protestants and one Orthodox Jew for some variety. Almost all are college graduates (two teachers, two engineers, a copy editor, a nurse, a personnel officer, a sales manager), and each sex and age group are equally represented. Irish, English, Danish, French, German, Croatian, Cuban, Polish, Romanian, Italian, Austrian, African-American—we are representative of early, for the most part European, immigrations to Queens. With only one exception, we are at least second-generation Americans, and some of us go much further back.

Each day we spend most of our time together outside the courtroom, either surrounding the table in the cramped closet of a jury room or, for at least an hour and a half each day, eating lunch together. We tell stories. Stories about childhood games, of what we were doing during the Vietnam War, of parenthood and grandparenthood, of travels, of sports and other leisure activities, of jobs, of events in the news. The stories form a fragile bond between us and keep us going for the two weeks, one day and one night of being almost constantly together.

Controversial topics, like the current trial of the four policemen accused of the Rodney King beating, are treated as newstories and not as topics for discussion. Those who are Republicans are matched by an equal number of Democrats, the young men drink alcohol while the middle aged feel the need to work out, and the single women are matched by the married and so we are careful. We know all Americans do not agree, and we do not want disharmony. By their sheer existence, our stories relieve us of our discomfort at being thrust in this situation. We also find pleasure in their content, and we laugh constantly.

We find varying degrees of pleasure in discussing the case. Some object to our doing so because the judge has admonished us not to. To ignore the courtroom is impossible because, next to the stories, we have the case in common. But our discussions are tangential to the issue of guilt as we admire the appearance of the young, female assistant district attorney, express wariness about the sternness of the judge, evaluate the cut of the defendant's suits, and relive the hilarity of the account of one of the witnesses. We do not feel we are prematurely closing our own minds or those of others through these discussions.

We discover early that the ethnic makeup of this defendant, plaintiff and witnesses represents much of the current immigration to Queens. The defendant and his brother, who witnesses for him, are Egyptian; his wife is from Ecuador; another witness is from India. Only one witness, from Greece, represents an earlier nationality on the scene, but he too is a first-generation American.

We on the jury are gradually gripped by the intensity of both the defendant and his wife. At first, we feel sorry for the wife, who sobs her way through her testimony. Too, we feel annoyed when the judge points out that the defendant does not have to testify because, as he tells us, in the American system the defendant is considered innocent and need not defend himself. Rather, he explains, it is up to the prosecution to prove he is guilty. Well, we think, that seems arrogant on the part of someone with so many charges of reckless endangerment against him. Our sympathies are with his wife, the tearful wife.

But when the defendant testifies, our sympathies slowly shift. An intense and nervous man, he blinks constantly. He also weeps. When the assistant district attorney finally gets up to cross-examine him, we wonder, with surprise, how she can ever hope to destroy such agonized testimony.

The passions are what move us. We cannot be told the reasons why the alleged crime has taken place, we can be told only the facts. The truth is denied us, but we can imagine their stories. They have come from so far with so many hopes to this city, the possessors of the same brave American Dream that all immigrants to America have dreamed. We know that he went first to Italy to learn to cook Italian food, perhaps knowing that Egyptian food is not in demand in America, and has prospered, now owning a medallion cab and a house. She has left behind a mother and a sister in Ecuador whom she returns to with her three children when all is not well between her and her Egyptian. Even when she comes back to New York, she leaves the children behind where they learn Spanish, a language their father cannot speak. The command of English of this pair is not conducive to easy communication and, we think, this has perhaps complicated their difficulties.

But their passion for their children is communicated in a universal language. His tears are for the children he had not been allowed to see for nine months, hers are for the terror of his taking them one pleasant Sunday morning in May on the street outside her new home in Queens.

We know that we will have to agree that what he has done is illegal. We have also discussed with disapproval how many Latin American women leave their children behind when coming to work in New York. We are suspicious of their actions, but we are not suspicious of their passions. Despite, or perhaps because of what we hear and know of many Americans' seeming callousness towards the fate of their own children, we are gripped by what these people so freely communicate to us about their love of their "babies."

Because of the many charges against the defendant, a unanimous decision does not come easily. We are taken to a hotel to be sequestered overnight. We eat dinner together and share rooms. For the first time, we share stories of significant events and people in our lives, of parents who have died and of the distress of their deaths. Breakfast finds us valued friends.

Back in the jury room, we unanimously decide we do not want to find him guilty of all charges. Yes, he hit his wife with a meat tenderizer when she protested his taking the children and, yes, he sped through the neighborhood with the three children held only by the arms of another person in the two-seater van, but we see his face even as we deliberate, and we cannot find him guilty of reckless endangerment in the first degree. He loves those children and is not callously indifferent to their fates. We settle on reckless endangerment in the second degree as well as to the assault charge and proceed to the courtroom.

There, the verdict is read by our foreman, a religious person who feels great sympathy for the defendant. The defendant, of course, is not aware of the foreman's agony as he begins to agonize himself. He shields his face with his hand and cries. His brother, who is present, cries also. When his lawyer asks for a poll of our votes, we have difficulty concentrating as each charge is read, and we must collect our thoughts occasionally before answering. Many of us feel tears welling up in our own eyes.

In the jury room once again, we feel the intensity of the experience keenly. We are very aware that we have supported each other through a difficult time. We make plans to meet again. We ask our court officer if all juries feel such intense camaraderie, and he can think of only one.

Fifteen minutes later, we prepare to leave the courthouse for the last time. As we pass through the lobby outside the courtroom, the defendant's brother stands weeping still.

Their passion has touched us profoundly. In losing their bright new world, they have shared with us the passions of an old world that they have been unable to leave behind. We have thought of inviting the defendant and his family to our reunion. We want them to understand what has transpired during the trial, that the dream is behind us all in its raw, most innocent form but that regeneration is possible. In a way that they can probably neither understand nor appreciate, they have made it possible for us.

INTERPRETATIONS

1. Why do you think Stanley implies that members of a jury always "find a lot in common"? From your own experience, do people thrown together always discover that they share common interests? To what extent does the essay suggest that, more than most groups, serving on jury duty might heighten common bonds?

2. What do we learn about the jurors from the essay? Why do they discuss stories rather than controversial issues? To what extent do you agree that the characteristics they have in common might have been overwhelmed by their political, marital, and sexual differences?

3. "The passions are what move us." How does the author build up to this statement? To what extent might the courtroom procedure of allowing only facts pertinent to the case encourage juries to interpret for themselves the "truth" of the case and to react to emotions expressed?

4. To what extent, based on the evidence Stanley presents, do you agree with the jury's decision to settle for "reckless endangerment in the second degree"? How convincing a rationale has she built for this lesser verdict?

5. Explain the meaning of the last paragraph of the essay. What "dream" does the author refer to? Why does this dream need regeneration and how does the author think the defendant and his wife have provided it?

CORRESPONDENCES

1. To what extent does Stanley's essay support Rodriguez's perspective that "Americans are wedded by proximity to a common culture"?

2. Is Stanley's purpose to inform or persuade? Is the tone of her essay similar to that of Hongo? Explain.

APPLICATIONS

1. Discuss the effect on our national life of the language barrier between many Americans. Is there, as the author suggests, a "universal language" that permits Americans to communicate with even the most recent immigrants?

2. To what extent do you think second- and third-generation Americans are generally as sympathetic to new immigrants as this jury is? How might you have responded as a member of the jury?

3. Alienation from the mainstream is a recurrent theme in several texts in this chapter. If you are a person of color who has felt like an outsider, write an analysis of that experience. If you are Caucasian and have felt excluded in a group, analyze the causes and effects in a brief essay.

4. Who is America? Check the following Web sites to learn the composition of inhabitants of the United States. Then, compare your findings to the jury described by Stanley in her essay.

   http://factfinder.census.gov

   http://www.socccd.cc.ca.us/ref/almanac/demographics/uspop.htm

   http://quickfacts.census.gov/qfd/index.html

Black Men and Public Spaces

BRENT STAPLES

Brent Staples (b. 1951) is from Chester, Pennsylvania. He has a Ph.D. in psychology from the University of Chicago and is currently on the editorial board of The New York Times, *where he writes on culture and politics. His autobiography,* Parallel Time: Growing Up in Black and White, *was published in 1994. We asked him why he selected* Ms. *for the publication of his essay "Black Men and Public Spaces" and he responded:*

> Ms. *is a women's magazine. Women are more vulnerable to street violence, and judgments about who is safe and who is dangerous is an urgent priority for them.*

MY FIRST VICTIM WAS A WOMAN—white, well dressed, probably in her early twenties. I came upon her late one evening on a deserted street in Hyde Park, a relatively affluent neighborhood in an otherwise mean, impoverished section of Chicago. As I swung onto the avenue behind her, there seemed to be a discreet, uninflammatory distance between us. Not so. She cast back a worried glance. To her, the youngish black man—a broad six feet two inches with a beard and billowing hair, both hands shoved into the pockets of a bulky military jacket—seemed menacingly close. After a few more quick glimpses, she picked up her pace and was soon running in earnest. Within seconds she disappeared into a cross street.

That was more than a decade ago. I was 22 years old, a graduate student newly arrived at the University of Chicago. It was in the echo of that terrified woman's footfalls that I first began to know the unwieldy inheritance I'd come into—the ability to alter public space in ugly ways. It was clear that she thought herself the quarry of a mugger, a rapist or worse. Suffering a bout of insomnia, however, I was stalking sleep, not defenseless wayfarers. As a softy who is scarcely able to take a knife to a raw chicken—let alone hold it to a person's throat—I was surprised, embarrassed, and dismayed all at once. Her flight made me feel like an accomplice in tyranny. It also made it clear that I was indistinguishable from the muggers who occasionally seeped into the area from the surrounding ghetto. That first encounter, and those that followed, signified that a vast, unnerving gulf lay between nighttime pedestrians—particularly

375

women—and me. And I soon gathered that being perceived as danger-ous is a hazard in itself. I only needed to turn a corner into a dicey situa-tion, or crowd some frightened, armed person in a foyer somewhere, or make an errant move after being pulled over by a policeman. Where fear and weapons meet—and they often do in urban America—there is always the possibility of death.

In that first year, my first away from my hometown, I was to become thoroughly familiar with the language of fear. At dark, shad-owy intersections in Chicago, I could cross in front of a car stopped at a traffic light and elicit the *thunk, thunk, thunk, thunk* of the driver—black, white, male, or female—hammering down the door locks. On less trav-eled streets after dark, I grew accustomed to but never comfortable with people who crossed to the other side of the street rather than pass me. Then there were the standard unpleasantries with police, doormen, bouncers, cab drivers, and others whose business it is to screen out troublesome individuals *before* there is any nastiness.

I moved to New York nearly two years ago and I have remained an avid night walker. In central Manhattan, the near-constant crowd cover minimizes tense one-on-one street encounters. Elsewhere—visiting friends in SoHo, where sidewalks are narrow and tightly spaced build-ings shut out the sky—things can get very taut indeed.

Black men have a firm place in New York mugging literature. Nor-man Podhoretz in his famed (or infamous) 1963 essay, "My Negro Prob-lem—And Ours," recalls growing up in terror of black males; they "were tougher than we were, more ruthless," he writes—and as an adult on the Upper West Side of Manhattan, he continues, he cannot constrain his nervousness when he meets black men on certain streets. Similarly, a decade later, the essayist and novelist Edward Hoagland extols a New York where once "Negro bitterness bore down mainly on other Negroes." Where some see mere panhandlers, Hoagland sees "a mugger who is clearly screwing up his nerve to do more than just *ask* for money." But Hoagland has "the New Yorker's quick-hunch posture for broken-field maneuvering," and the bad guy swerves away.

I often witness that "hunch posture," from women after dark on the warrenlike streets of Brooklyn where I live. They seem to set their faces on neutral and, with their purse straps strung across their chests ban-dolier style, they forge ahead as though bracing themselves against being tackled. I understand, of course, that the danger they perceive is not a hallucination. Women are particularly vulnerable to street violence, and young black males are drastically overrepresented among the perpetra-tors of that violence. Yet these truths are no solace against the kind of alienation that comes of being ever the suspect, against being set apart, a fearsome entity with whom pedestrians avoid making eye contact.

It is not altogether clear to me how I reached the ripe old age of 22 without being conscious of the lethality nighttime pedestrians attributed to me. Perhaps it was because in Chester, Pennsylvania, the small, angry industrial town where I came of age in the 1960s, I was scarcely noticeable against a backdrop of gang warfare, street knifings, and murders. I grew up one of the good boys, had perhaps a half-dozen first fights. In retrospect, my shyness of combat has clear sources.

Many things go into the making of a young thug. One of those things is the consummation of the male romance with the power to intimidate. An infant discovers that random flailings send the baby bottle flying out of the crib and crashing to the floor. Delighted, the joyful babe repeats those motions again and again, seeking to duplicate the feat. Just so, I recall the points at which some of my boyhood friends were finally seduced by the perception of themselves as tough guys. When a mark cowered and surrendered his money without resistance, myth and reality merged—and paid off. It is, after all, only manly to embrace the power to frighten and intimidate. We, as men, are not supposed to give an inch of our lane on the highway; we are to seize the fighter's edge in work and in play and even in love; we are to be valiant in the face of hostile forces.

Unfortunately, poor and powerless young men seem to take all this nonsense literally. As a boy, I saw countless tough guys locked away; I have since buried several, too. They were babies, really—a teenage cousin, a brother of twenty-two, a childhood friend in his mid-twenties—all gone down in episodes of bravado played out in the streets. I came to doubt the virtues of intimidation early on. I chose, perhaps even unconsciously, to remain a shadow—timid, but a survivor.

The fearsomeness mistakenly attributed to me in public places often has a perilous flavor. The most frightening of these confusions occurred in the late 1970s and early 1980s when I worked as a journalist in Chicago. One day, rushing into the office of a magazine I was writing for with a deadline story in hand, I was mistaken for a burglar. The office manager called security and, with an ad hoc posse, pursued me through the labyrinthine halls, nearly to my editor's door. I had no way of proving who I was. I could only move briskly toward the company of someone who knew me.

Another time I was on assignment for a local paper and killing time before an interview. I entered a jewelry store on the city's affluent near north side. The proprietor excused herself and returned with an enormous red Doberman pinscher straining at the end of a leash. She stood, the dog extended toward me, silent to my questions, her eyes bulging nearly out of her head. I took a cursory look around, nodded, and bade her good night. Relatively speaking, however, I never fared as badly as another black male journalist. He went to nearby Waukegan, Illinois, a couple of summers ago to work on a story about a murderer who was born there. Mistaking the reporter for the killer, police hauled him from his car at gunpoint and but for his press credentials would probably have tried to book him. Such episodes are not uncommon. Black men trade tales like this all the time.

In "My Negro Problem—And Ours," Podhoretz writes that the hatred he feels for blacks makes itself known to him through a variety of avenues—one being his discomfort with that "special brand of paranoid touchiness" to which he says blacks are prone. No doubt he is speaking here of black men. In time, I learned to smother the rage I felt at so often being taken for a criminal. Not to do so would surely have led to madness—via that special "paranoid touchiness" that so annoyed Podhoretz at the time he wrote the essay.

I am uneasy with the word "paranoid" in this context because the term refers to a delusionary state, something wholly imagined. But what do we say of a man who is driven to distraction by very real irritations, by a culture that consistently views him as sinister, for example? Since it isn't possible to unpack the entire issue here, we must let "paranoid" stand for the time being, even though it falls far short of describing the state of mind in question.

I take precautions to make myself less threatening. I move about with care, particularly in the late evening. I give a wide berth to nervous people on subway platforms during the wee hours, particularly when I have exchanged business clothes for jeans. If I happen to be entering a building behind some people who appear skittish, I may walk by, letting them clear the lobby before I return, so as not to seem to be following them. I have been calm and extremely congenial on those rare occasions when I've been pulled over by the police.

And on late-evening constitutionals along streets less traveled by, I employ what has proved to be an excellent tension-reducing measure: I whistle melodies from Beethoven and Vivaldi and the more popular classical composers. Even steely New Yorkers hunching toward nighttime destinations seem to relax, and occasionally they even join in the tune. Virtually everybody seems to sense that a mugger wouldn't be warbling bright, sunny selections from Vivaldi's *Four Seasons*. It is my equivalent of the cowbell that hikers wear when they know they are in bear country.

INTERPRETATIONS

1. What evidence does Staples provide to make a convincing case that "being perceived as dangerous is a hazard in itself"?

2. ". . . [S]ome of my boyhood friends were finally seduced by the perception of themselves as tough guys." Do you think being perceived as tough has a natural appeal to boys and/or men of any race? What's the difference between virility (or manliness) and toughness?

3. To what extent does Staples think there is any justification for New York women's precautions against young black males?

4. Has our society had any success so far in reducing "touchiness" of blacks and the fears of whites? What more can be done? Does an essay like this one contribute to the solution or to the problem? Explain.

Of My Friend Hector and My Achilles' Heel

MICHAEL T. KAUFMAN

Michael T. Kaufman (b. 1938) attended the City College of New York and Columbia University. He spent 42 years at The New York Times *as a reporter, foreign correspondent, editor, and bureau chief. He also edited the magazine* Transitions *that covered the post-communist sphere in the Czech Republic. Kaufman's most recent book,* Soros: The Life and Times of a Messianic Billionaire, *was published in 2003. Record in your journal your responses to Kaufman's introduction.*

THIS STORY IS ABOUT PREJUDICE and stupidity. My own.

It begins in 1945 when I was a seven-year-old living on the fifth floor of a tenement walkup on 107th Street between Columbus and Manhattan Avenues in New York City. The block was almost entirely Irish and Italian, and I believe my family was the only Jewish one around.

One day a Spanish-speaking family moved into one of the four apartments on our landing. They were the first Puerto Ricans I had met. They had a son who was about my age named Hector, and the two of us became friends. We played with toy soldiers and I particularly remember how, using rubber bands and wood from orange crates, we made toy pistols that shot off little squares we cut from old linoleum.

We visited each other's home and I know that at the time I liked Hector and I think he liked me. I may even have eaten my first avocado at his house.

About a year after we met, my family moved to another part of Manhattan's West Side and I did not see Hector again until I entered Booker T. Washington Junior High School as an eleven-year-old.

The class I was in was called 7SP-1; the SP was for special. Earlier, I recall, I had been in the IGC class, for "intellectually gifted children." The SP class was to complete the seventh, eighth and ninth grades in two years and almost all of us would then go to schools like Bronx Science, Stuyvesant or Music and Art, where admission was based on competitive exams. I knew I was in the SP class and the IGC class. I guess I also knew that other people were not.

Hector was not. He was in some other class, maybe even 7-2, the class that was held to be the next-brightest, or maybe 7-8. I remember I was happy to see him whenever we would meet, and sometimes we played punchball during lunch period. Mostly, of course, I stayed with my own classmates, with other Intellectually Gifted Children.

Sometimes children from other classes, those presumably not so intellectually gifted, would tease and taunt us. At such times I was particularly proud to have Hector as a friend. I assumed that he was tougher than I and my classmates and I guess I thought that if necessary he would come to my defense.

For high school, I went uptown to Bronx Science. Hector, I think, went downtown to Commerce. Sometimes I would see him in Riverside Park, where I played basketball and he worked out on the parallel bars. We would acknowledge each other, but by this time the conversations we held were perfunctory—sports, families, weather.

After I finished college, I would see him around the neighborhood pushing a baby carriage. He was the first of my contemporaries to marry and to have a child.

A few years later, in the 60s, married and with children of my own, I was once more living on the West Side, working until late at night as a reporter. Some nights as I took the train home I would see Hector in the car. A few times we exchanged nods, but more often I would pretend that I didn't see him, and maybe he also pretended he didn't see me. Usually he would be wearing a knitted watch cap, and from that I deduced that he was probably working on the docks as a longshoreman.

I remember quite distinctly how I would sit on the train and think about how strange and unfair fate had been with regard to the two of us who had once been playmates. Just because I had become an intellectually gifted adult or whatever and he had become a longshoreman or whatever, was that any reason for us to have been left with nothing to say to each other? I thought it was wrong and unfair, but I also thought that conversation would be a chore or a burden. That is pretty much what I thought about Hector, if I thought about him at all, until one Sunday in the mid-70s, when I read in the drama section of this newspaper that my childhood friend, Hector Elizondo, was replacing Peter Falk in the leading role in "The Prisoner of Second Avenue."

Since then, every time I have seen this versatile and acclaimed actor in movies or on television I have blushed for my assumptions. I have replayed the subway rides in my head and tried to fathom why my thoughts had led me where they did.

In retrospect it seems far more logical that the man I saw on the train, the man who had been my friend as a boy, was coming home from an Off Broadway theater or perhaps from a job as a waiter while taking acting classes. So why did I think he was a longshoreman? Was it just the cap? Could it be that his being Puerto Rican had something to do with it? Maybe that reinforced the stereotype I concocted, but it wasn't the root of it.

No, the foundation was laid when I was eleven, when I was in 7SP-1 and he was not, when I was in the IGC class and he was not.

I have not seen him since I recognized how I had idiotically kept tracking him for years and decades after the school system had tracked both of us. I wonder now if my experience was that unusual, whether social categories conveyed and absorbed before puberty do not generally tend to linger beyond middle age. And I wonder, too, that if they affected the behavior of someone like myself who had been placed on the upper track, how much more damaging it must have been for someone consigned to the lower.

I have at times thought of calling him, but kept from doing it because how exactly does one apologize for thoughts that were never expressed? And there was still the problem of what to say. "What have you been up to for the last forty years?" Or "Wow, was I wrong about you!" Or maybe just, "Want to come over and help me make a linoleum gun?"

INTERPRETATIONS

1. Comment on the significance of Kaufman's title. (If necessary, refer to a book on Greek mythology for the meaning of the names "Hector" and "Achilles.")
2. Evaluate the effectiveness of Kaufman's opening sentences. Does his essay support his self-judgment?
3. Analyze the causes and effects of the changes that occur in Kaufman and Hector's relationship over the years.

CORRESPONDENCES

1. Analyze the significance of stereotyping in the essays by Kaufman and Staples. To what extent do you agree that people often make judgments based on stereotypes rather than their own social encounters?
2. Analyze the role of ethnicity and social class in the essays by Kaufman and Staples. What insight did you gain from their experiences?

APPLICATIONS

1. "This story is about prejudice and stupidity." Write a journal entry applying Kaufman's statement to your own experience.

2. Speculate about Kaufman's purpose in writing this essay. Is he trying to clarify this experience for himself? Is there evidence that he would like to influence his readers? Explain.

3. Brainstorm with your group on "racism" and "stereotyping." How do they differ in meaning and connotation? Was the woman in Staples's essay a racist because she was responding to a stereotype? On what basis did Kaufman decide that Hector was a longshoreman? Does that make him a racist? Summarize the highlights of your discussion.

The Man I Killed

TIM O'BRIEN

Tim O'Brien (b. 1946) was drafted into the Vietnam War shortly after receiving a B.A. from Macalester College. After returning from two years in the service, O'Brien began postgraduate studies at Harvard. The New York Times *named his war memoir,* If I Die in a Combat Zone, Box Me Up and Ship Me Home, *Outstanding Book of 1973. Going After Cacciato (1978) was also based on O'Brien's war experiences. O'Brien's other novels include:* Northern Lights *(1975),* The Nuclear Age *(1985),* The Things They Carried *(1990),* In the Lake of the Woods *(1994), and* Tomcat in Love *(1998). O'Brien's most recent novel,* July, July, *was published in 2002. Before reading O'Brien's text, record your initial responses to his title.*

HIS JAW WAS IN HIS THROAT, his upper lip and teeth were gone, his one eye was shut, his other eye was a star-shaped hole, his eyebrows were thin and arched like a woman's, his nose was undamaged, there was a slight tear at the lobe of one ear, his clean black hair was swept upward into a cowlick at the rear of the skull, his forehead was lightly freckled, his fingernails were clean, the skin at his left cheek was peeled back in three ragged strips, his right cheek was smooth and hairless, there was a butterfly on his chin, his neck was open to the spinal cord and the blood there was thick and shiny and it was this wound that had killed him. He lay face-up in the center of the trail, a slim, dead, almost dainty young man. He had bony legs, a narrow waist, long shapely fingers. His chest was sunken and poorly muscled—a scholar, maybe. His wrists were the wrists of a child. He wore a black shirt, black pajama pants, a gray ammunition belt, a gold ring on the third finger of his right hand. His rubber sandals had been blown off. One lay beside him, the other a few meters up the trail. He had been born, maybe, in 1946 in the village of My Khe near the central coastline of Quang Ngai Province, where his parents farmed, and where his family had lived for several centuries, and where, during the time of the French, his father and two uncles and many neighbors had joined in the struggle for independence. He was not a Communist. He was a citizen and a soldier. In the village of My Khe, as in all of Quang Ngai, patriotic resistance had the force of tradition, which was partly the force of legend, and from his earliest boyhood the man I killed would have listened to stories about the heroic Trung sisters and Tran Hung Dao's famous rout of the Mongols and Le Loi's final victory against the Chinese at Tot Dong.[1] He would have been taught that to defend the land was a man's highest duty and highest privilege. He had accepted this. It was never open to question. Secretly, though, it also frightened him. He was not a fighter. His health was poor, his body small and frail. He liked books. He wanted someday to be a teacher of mathematics. At night, lying on his mat, he could not picture himself doing the brave things his father had done, or his uncles, or the heroes of the stories. He hoped in his heart that he would never be tested. He hoped the Americans would go away. Soon, he hoped. He kept hoping and hoping, always, even when he was asleep.

"Oh, man, you fuckin' trashed the fucker," Azar said. "You scrambled his sorry self, look at that, you *did*, you laid him out like Shredded fuckin' Wheat."

"Go away," Kiowa said.

"I'm just saying the truth. Like oatmeal."

"Go," Kiowa said.

"Okay, then, I take it back," Azar said. He started to move away, then stopped and said, "Rice Krispies, you know? On the dead test, this particular individual gets A-Plus."

Smiling at this, he shrugged and walked up the trail toward the village behind the trees.

Kiowa kneeled down.

"Just forget that crud," he said. He opened up his canteen and held it out for a while and then sighed and pulled it away. "No sweat, man. What else could you do?"

Later, Kiowa said, "I'm serious. Nothing *anybody* could do. Come on, stop staring."

The trail junction was shaded by a row of trees and tall brush. The slim young man lay with his legs in the shade. His jaw was in his throat. His one eye was shut and the other was a star-shaped hole.

Kiowa glanced at the body.

"All right, let me ask a question," he said. "You want to trade places with him? Turn it all upside down—you *want* that? I mean, be honest."

The star-shaped hole was red and yellow. The yellow part seemed to be getting wider, spreading out at the center of the star. The upper lip and gum and teeth were gone. The man's head was cocked at a wrong angle, as if loose at the neck, and the neck was wet with blood.

"Think it over," Kiowa said.

[1]The Trung sisters led a Vietnamese rebellion against Chinese rule in A.D. 40; Tran Hung Dao repelled a Mongol attack in 1287; Le Loi defeated the Chinese in 1426.

Then later he said, "Tim, it's a *war*. The guy wasn't Heidi—he had a weapon, right? It's a tough thing, for sure, but you got to cut out that staring."

Then he said, "Maybe you better lie down a minute."

Then after a long empty time he said, "Take it slow. Just go wherever the spirit takes you."

The butterfly was making its way along the young man's forehead, which was spotted with small dark freckles. The nose was undamaged. The skin on the right cheek was smooth and fine-grained and hairless. Frail-looking, delicately boned, the young man would not have wanted to be a soldier and in his heart would have feared performing badly in battle. Even as a boy growing up in the village of My Khe, he had often worried about this. He imagined covering his head and lying in a deep hole and closing his eyes and not moving until the war was over. He had no stomach for violence. He loved mathematics. His eyebrows were thin and arched like a woman's, and at school the boys sometimes teased him about how pretty he was, the arched eyebrows and long shapely fingers, and on the playground they mimicked a woman's walk and made fun of his smooth skin and his love for mathematics. The young man could not make himself fight them. He often wanted to, but he was afraid, and this increased his shame. If he could not fight little boys, he thought, how could he ever become a soldier and fight the Americans with their airplanes and helicopters and bombs? It did not seem possible. In the presence of his father and uncles, he pretended to look forward to doing his patriotic duty, which was also a privilege, but at night he prayed with his mother that the war might end soon. Beyond anything else, he was afraid of disgracing himself, and therefore his family and village. But all he could do, he thought, was wait and pray and try not to grow up too fast.

"Listen to me," Kiowa said. "You feel terrible, I know that."

Then he said, "Okay, maybe I *don't* know."

Along the trail there were small blue flowers shaped like bells. The young man's head was wrenched sideways, not quite facing the flowers, and even in the shade a single blade of sunlight sparkled against the buckle of his ammunition belt. The left cheek was peeled back in three ragged strips. The wounds at his neck had not yet clotted, which made him seem animate even in death, the blood still spreading out across his shirt.

Kiowa shook his head.

There was some silence before he said, "Stop *staring*."

The young man's fingernails were clean. There was a slight tear at the lobe of one ear, a sprinkling of blood on the forearm. He wore a gold ring on the third finger of his right hand. His chest was sunken and poorly muscled—a scholar, maybe. His life was now a constellation of possibilities. So, yes, maybe a scholar. And for years, despite his family's poverty, the man I killed would have been determined to continue his education in mathematics. The means for this were arranged, perhaps, through the village liberation cadres, and in 1964 the young man began attending classes at the university in Saigon, where he avoided politics and paid attention to the problems of calculus. He devoted himself to his studies. He spent his nights alone, wrote romantic poems in his journal, took pleasure in the grace and beauty of differential equations. The war, he knew, would finally take him, but for the time being he would not let himself think about it. He had stopped praying; instead, now, he waited. And as he waited, in his final year at the university, he fell in love with a classmate, a girl of seventeen, who one day told him that his wrists were like the wrists of a child, so small and delicate, and who admired his narrow waist and the cowlick that rose up like a bird's tail at the back of his head. She liked his quiet manner; she laughed at his freckles and bony legs. One evening, perhaps, they exchanged gold rings.

Now one eye was a star.

"You okay?" Kiowa said.

The body lay almost entirely in shade. There were gnats at the mouth, little flecks of pollen drifting above the nose. The butterfly was gone. The bleeding had stopped except for the neck wounds.

Kiowa picked up the rubber sandals, clapping off the dirt, then bent down to search the body. He found a pouch of rice, a comb, a fingernail clipper, a few soiled piasters, a snapshot of a young woman standing in front of a parked motorcycle. Kiowa placed these items in his rucksack along with the gray ammunition belt and rubber sandals.

Then he squatted down.

"I'll tell you the straight truth," he said. "The guy was dead the second he stepped on the trail. Understand me? We all had him zeroed. A good kill—weapon, ammunition, everything." Tiny beads of sweat glistened at Kiowa's forehead. His eyes moved from the sky to the dead man's body to the knuckles of his own hands. "So listen, you best pull your shit together. Can't just sit here all day."

Later he said, "Understand?"

Then he said, "Five minutes, Tim. Five more minutes and we're moving out."

The one eye did a funny twinkling trick, red to yellow. His head was wrenched sideways, as if loose at the neck, and the dead young man seemed to be staring at some distant object beyond the bell-shaped flowers along the trail. The blood at the neck had gone to a deep purplish black. Clean fingernails, clean hair—he had been a soldier for only a single day. After his years at the university, the man I killed returned with his new wife to the village of My Khe, where he enlisted as a common rifleman with the 48th Vietcong Battalion. He knew he would die quickly. He knew he would see a flash of light. He knew he would fall dead and wake up in the stories of his village and people.

Kiowa covered the body with a poncho.

"Hey, you're looking better," he said. "No doubt about it. All you needed was time—some mental R&R."

Then he said, "Man, I'm sorry."

Then later he said, "Why not talk about it?"

Then he said, "Come on, man, talk."

He was a slim, dead, almost dainty young man of about twenty. He lay with one leg bent beneath him, his jaw in his throat, his face neither expressive nor inexpressive. One eye was shut. The other was a star-shaped hole.

"Talk," Kiowa said.

INTERPRETATIONS

1. How does the opening paragraph of O'Brien's story set up the pages that follow?

2. Who are Azar and Kiowa? What do they want O'Brien to do? Why?

3. Why does O'Brien, the writer, include the paragraphs of narration in his story? What do these paragraphs tell you about Tim, the soldier?

4. What facts does the narrator of the story absolutely *know* about the man he killed? What does he *surmise*?

CORRESPONDENCES

1. In what ways do you think the essays by O'Brien, Hongo, and Staples are linked thematically? How are the narrators and the stories they tell related?

2. What does it mean to be an "American"? How do you think Tim O'Brien, Jim Fusilli, and Linda Stanley would answer this question?

APPLICATIONS

1. What do you learn about war from O'Brien's story? What preconceptions about war has this story changed? Within your small discussion group, talk with your classmates about the ideas you had about war before reading this story and those you formed after

reading it. Write a journal entry about what you have learned as a result of this exploration.

2. "War is hell." Do you think that this maxim is true or false? Write an essay that explores fully your response to this statement.

3. O'Brien's story seems to end unresolved. What do you think he is feeling when the story concludes? Why doesn't he say anything to Kiowa? If you found the ending to be unsatisfying, rewrite the last several paragraphs after reflecting on the previous questions. Alternatively, pick up the action after a period of three months and continue the story in a way that presents your thoughts about the previous questions.

Literacy Narratives

Gloria Naylor and Kenneth Woo focus on the paradoxes of language. Naylor reveals the potential of language to wound, even destroy, while Woo discovers finally that words can create and liberate the self. As you reflect on their experiences, think about your encounters with language in the community and in other cultures. How do their cultural and educational experiences compare with yours? When did you first realize that words have the potential to imprison and liberate the self?

What's in a Name?

GLORIA NAYLOR

Gloria Naylor (b. 1950) was born in New York City to parents who were share-croppers from Mississippi. In 1968 she became a Jehovah's Witness, which she practiced for seven years. From 1975–1981 Naylor worked as a switchboard operator, pursued writing, and received a B.A. from Brooklyn College in English. Naylor did graduate work in Afro-American studies at Yale. Her first novel, The Women of Brewster Place *(1982), won a National Book Award. Naylor's other novels include:* Linden Hills *(1985),* Mama Day *(1988),* Bailey's Cafe *(1990), and* The Men of Brewster Place *(1998). Naylor is currently working on another novel. As you read Naylor's narrative, record the connotations you think of to the names she refers to in her essay.*

LANGUAGE IS THE SUBJECT. It is the written form with which I've managed to keep the wolf away from the door and, in diaries, to keep my sanity. In spite of this, I consider the written word inferior to the spoken, and much of the frustration experienced by novelists is the awareness that whatever we manage to capture in even the most transcendent passages falls far short of the richness of life. Dialogue achieves its powers in the dynamics of a fleeting moment of sight, sound, smell and touch.

I'm not going to enter the debate here about whether it is language that shapes reality or vice versa. That battle is doomed to be waged whenever we seek intermittent reprieve from the chicken and egg dispute. I will simply take the position that the spoken word, like the written word, amounts to a nonsensical arrangement of sounds or letters without a consensus that assigns "meaning." And building from the meanings of what we hear, we order reality. Words themselves are innocuous; it is the consensus that gives them true power.

I remember the first time I heard the word nigger. In my third-grade class, our math tests were being passed down the rows, and as I handed the papers to a little boy in back of me, I remarked that once again he had received a much lower mark than I did. He snatched his test from me and spit out that word. Had he called me a nymphomaniac or a necrophiliac, I couldn't have been more puzzled. I didn't know what a nigger was, but I knew that whatever it meant, it was something he shouldn't have called me. This was verified when I raised my hand, and in a loud voice repeated what he had said and watched the teacher scold him for using a "bad" word. I was later to go home and ask the inevitable question that every black parent must face—"Mommy, what does 'nigger' mean?"

And what exactly did it mean? Thinking back, I realize that this could not have been the first time the word was used in my presence. I was part of a large extended family that had migrated from the rural South after World War II and formed a close-knit network that gravitated around my maternal grandparents. Their ground-floor apartment in one of the buildings they owned in Harlem was a weekend mecca for my immediate family, along with countless aunts, uncles and cousins who brought along assorted friends. It was a bustling and open house with assorted neighbors and tenants popping in and out to exchange bits of gossip, pick up an old quarrel or referee the ongoing checkers game in which my grandmother cheated shamelessly. They were all there to let down their hair and put up their feet after a week of labor in the factories, laundries and shipyards of New York.

Amid the clamor, which could reach deafening proportions—two or three conversations going on simultaneously, punctuated by the sound of a baby's crying somewhere in the back rooms or out on the street—there was still a rigid set of rules about what was said and how. Older children were sent out of the living room when it was time to get into the juicy details about "you-know-who" up on the third floor who had gone and gotten herself "p-r-e-g-n-a-n-t!" But my parents, knowing that I could spell well beyond my years, always demanded that I follow the others out to play. Beyond sexual misconduct and death, everything else was considered harmless for our young ears. And so among the anecdotes of the triumphs and disappointments in the various workings of their lives, the word nigger was used in my presence, but it was set within contexts and inflections that caused it to register in my mind as something else.

In the singular, the word was always applied to a man who had distinguished himself in some situation that brought their approval for his
strength, intelligence or drive:

"Did *Johnny* really do that?"

"I'm telling you, that nigger pulled in $6,000 of overtime last year.
Said he got enough for a down payment on a house."

When used with a possessive adjective by a woman—"my nigger"—it became a term of endearment for husband or boyfriend. But it
could be more than just a term applied to a man. In their mouths it
became the pure essence of manhood—a disembodied force that chan-
neled their past history of struggle and present survival against the
odds into a victorious statement of being: "Yeah, that old foreman found
out quick enough—you don't mess with a nigger."

In the plural, it became a description of some group within the
community that had overstepped the bounds of decency as my family
defined it: Parents who neglected their children, a drunken couple who
fought in public, people who simply refused to look for work, those
with excessively dirty mouths or unkempt households were all "trifling
niggers." This particular circle could forgive hard times, unemployment, the occasional bout of depression—they had gone through all of
that themselves—but the unforgivable sin was a lack of self-respect.

A woman could never be a "nigger" in the singular, with its connotation of confirming worth. The noun girl was its closest equivalent in
that sense, but only when used in direct address and regardless of the
gender doing the addressing. "Girl" was a token of respect for a woman.
The one-syllable word was drawn out to sound like three in recognition
of the extra ounce of wit, nerve or daring that the woman had shown in
the situation under discussion.

"G-i-r-l, stop. You mean you said that to his face?"

But if the word was used in a third-person reference or shortened
so that it almost snapped out of the mouth, it always involved some element of communal disapproval. And age became an important factor in
these exchanges. It was only between individuals of the same generation, or from an older person to a younger (but never the other way
around), that "girl" would be considered a compliment.

I don't agree with the argument that use of the word nigger at this
social stratum of the black community was an internalization of racism.
The dynamics were the exact opposite: the people in my grandmother's
living room took a word that whites used to signify worthlessness or
degradation and rendered it impotent. Gathering there together, they
transformed "nigger" to signify the varied and complex human beings
they knew themselves to be. If the word was to disappear totally from
the mouths of even the most liberal of white society, no one in that room

was naïve enough to believe it would disappear from white minds. Meeting the word head-on, they proved it had absolutely nothing to do with the way they were determined to live their lives.

So there must have been dozens of times that the word "nigger" was spoken in front of me before I reached the third grade. But I didn't "hear" it until it was said by a small pair of lips that had already learned it could be a way to humiliate me. That was the word I went home and asked my mother about. And since she knew that I had to grow up in America, she took me in her lap and explained.

INTERPRETATIONS

1. Naylor writes that "words themselves are innocuous; it is the consensus that gives them true power." Do you agree with this position? Can you think of an example that supports it?

2. What are the effects of juxtaposing the rich multiple meanings of "nigger" in African-American culture with the derogatory label of the third grader? How does this juxtaposition support meanings being dependent upon context?

APPLICATIONS

1. Describe a time when you heard a familiar word in a new way.

2. In her opening paragraph, Naylor distinguishes between the *written* and the *spoken* word. To what extent do these different terms represent differences in *literacy*? Explain your answer.

3. What kind of literacy is the child in Naylor's narrative exposed to and forced to engage in? When was there a time in your life that you were thrown into the adult world and a new type of literacy? What kind of literacy were you confronted with? How did you begin to negotiate this new literacy?

4. What kind of literacy is being described and exemplified in paragraphs 4 through 13? As she becomes more aware of this type of literacy, what distinctions does Naylor come to understand?

Konglish

KENNETH WOO

I NEVER REALLY LIKED TO WRITE. Whenever I thought of English, or English class, there was only one word that popped into my head: essays. I always felt this feeling of nausea, "got to finish the essay by a certain date and what in the world am I supposed to write." I constantly saw myself as a science and math "buff" (majoring in computer science) and viewed English as an obstacle. I would think to myself, "why must I keep learning how to write, isn't the knowledge I already know enough to get by?" But there are a few instances in my life in which writing greatly affected my life, changing the way I perceived the art form of a brush (the pen) painting emotions on a blank white canvas (paper).

Moving from Flushing, New York to Douglaston was going to be a huge alteration in my life. Though I was only in second grade, I dreaded the thought of moving. What I feared the most was attending a new school: beady little eyes from strangers gazing at me because I was the new kid on the block. It was like those nightmares where I find myself standing naked in front of a laughing audience. The school I attended (P.S. 94) was one of the most academic achieving schools in the city, being number one or two in every imaginable category.

I remembered I had a poem to write about something that was close to your heart. I thought to myself, "I'm in the second grade, how am I supposed to write a poem?" I really thought a second grader writing a poem was outrageous. But I had no choice, and the poem was due the next day. So I sat in my miniature desk and tried to cook up something worthy since this was my first assignment at school. All of a sudden I thought about my grandfather. I had no idea what he looked like (since he died before I was born), what his favorite dish was; my grandfather was basically a stranger to me. So my pen started to dance and I called the poem, "I Wonder." I handed the poem to my teacher and waited for the poem to be marked. When the class received their poems back, I didn't receive back the piece I wrote. "Did I do something wrong? Great, what a great first impression." I never had the guts to ask her what happened to my poem, so I did what my father always said to do when in doubt: keep your lips shut. So I kept my lips shut. By the end of the class, I heard, "Ken, can you stay after school? I want to talk to you about your poem." What did I write in that poem? Was it wrong to write about my grandfather? I remembered my hands were sweating like bullets and my legs couldn't help but shake.

I approached the teacher cautiously, as if she were the enemy over the war line. I waited for my educator to shoot and assassinate my poem. "Yes, Mrs. Nazarro?" She leaned over my shivering body and said, "This is one of the best poems I ever read in my entire life. I read this piece in front of my Queens College lecture, and half the audience fell into tears. Ken, you have a gift—a gift of writing."

What my teacher said hit me like a ton of bricks. I couldn't understand what she was saying. I didn't want to write the poem, I didn't even feel like I put effort into it. But I kept all my emotions in and replied, "Thank you, Mrs. Nazarro." This was the first time I ever accomplished a writing experience, and I didn't like the feeling. I felt a sort of embarrassment, feeling "cheesed out." For some reason or another, I took this writing skill I had and shoved it deep into my soul, never seeing it again. I didn't see this ability to write until fifteen years later.

Time went by, from essays here and boring compositions there, and I finally graduated high school. When I attended SUNY Albany, I registered my classes so that I wouldn't have to take an English course for a while. After a semester, my mother decided it was time for me to go to the motherland, Korea. I didn't think much of the trip, "what's the big deal?" I thought going to summer school would have been a lot more productive in using my time but I had no say. So I jumped on a 747 and twelve hours later, ended up in this strange land they called the Land of the Morning Calm.

When my feet first touched Kimpo Airport, I was stunned and in awe. I never had seen a place where everyone was Korean. It took my eyes a while to get adjusted to, and I stared at the passengers that walked by. After my gazing, I took the next train to Korea University. At this university, I had registered for two courses, Business Management and Structure of Korea, and Introduction to Korean. I was really excited about the business course, but oh no, not Korean. Thinking about having to take a Korean course reminded me of the English courses I was forced to take.

For the first couple of weeks, we only attacked the basic stuff. From vowels to consonants, I felt like I was back in kindergarten. Han-gul (the Korean alphabet) is pretty much a simple concept to follow. It's basically our alphabet but circles and slashes are the A's, B's, and C's. The challenging part of the language, like English, is the numerous vocabulary words that had to be learned. Quickly, the Han-gul dictionary became a friend. When I was in Korea, it was hard. Everyone around me talked Korean while I struggled trying to say, "Hello, my name is Kenneth Woo, and how are you doing today?"

For lunch, I would walk to the local McDonald's. I preferred to eat there more than the local native cuisine because Ronald McDonald reminded me of home. I clearly remembered the first time I stepped in, as if it happened yesterday. I attempted to read the red and yellow alien language that gawked into my eyes. "What does that say?" I stood there for an eternity trying to figure out what it said when it finally whacked me. I was staring at Big Mac, only it was in the Korean alphabet. I suddenly noticed how much trouble I was in.

There was only one thing left to do—to conquer what I didn't know. I attacked the books and studied the Korean language as if my life depended on it (at the time, my survival in the country did rely on it). From the alphabet and days of the week, to learning their way of grammatical structure, it was a challenge I did not believe I could accomplish. However after some time, I was getting the hang of the language. I knew the consonants and vowels forwards and backwards, and was able to read the whole McDonald's menu.

Attending classes wasn't a problem. Most of the students never attended because they would get so drunk and wasted the night before, still drunk when they woke up. Wednesday was a problem for me. During the other days of the week I had classes and on the weekends I stayed at a relative's house, but Wednesday was a killer. I usually stayed in my room, smoking a cigarette as each minute passed by. Then one day in my dorm room, I approached a flier that read, "Free Brush-Painting classes on Wednesday . . . Rm 101 1:00 P.M." I decided to be brave and attend the mysterious class. When I walked in, there was one thing I noticed: I was the only male. This didn't bother me at all since a couple of my classmates looked attractive but I questioned myself what I was doing there. I ended up staying and I saw a dorky, black-dressed (like the WWF wrestler Undertaker), slothful man with a clean brush. He introduced himself as Mr. Lim, Master of the Brush. I chuckled at the title and waited for my lesson. Like the Korean language class, we went over the basic brush stroking techniques and went over some of the Chinese characters. What amazed me the most was how hard it was to hold an authentic Asian character brush. The tip was wide yet pointy, short yet heavy. The proper grip of the brush is the ambitious part. It's like when a person first approaches a billiard table and has no idea how to hold the cue stick.

Following a few practices, the Master of the Brush instructed that we had to paint our name in Chinese characters with a couple of words describing ourselves. I thought about the task and had a notion to make a poem out of the assignment. So I worked on the poem and brushed it out on the thin rice paper and handed it in to Mr. Lim. He read what I wrote and stared into my eyes. He replied, "Wow, this is a great poem, simple but deep. You have a talent. Your brushstrokes are another thing, but your poetry. God . . ." I snatched my piece and responded that I had to go eat lunch. I was enraged, I had no idea why. What he said made my blood pump. I knew it was the part about me having a talent. I didn't care about my techniques as a brushpainter, I could have cared less. But how can a typical Korean-American have a gift of writing poems, it made no sense to me. Once again I was determined to keep my talent buried within myself, forever.

I walked outside and it was so humid that the sun had a hard time peeking through the smog. Sweat was pouring out my pores like Niagara Falls and I wanted to go to a cool, air-conditioned place. I went to my spot (McD's) and ordered a No. 3 combo, super-sized. I sat by the window and ate gradually. As people walked by, I would stare at them thinking about where they were going, what part of Korea they were from, if they had a romance going. Then something caught my eye. Across the street there was an elderly woman with a mid-sized shopping cart packed with things, from clothing to a rice-cooker. This was the only homeless person I had seen in my native land since my feet touched here. I was in shock, not because she was homeless, but the way people on the street treated her. They passed by, as if she were a parking meter. She would shake a noiseless cup and hear no coins rattling. I stepped outside and lit my cigarette, trying to ignore the situation. I pondered to myself, "It was none of my business."

I flicked my cigarette and at the moment two guys approached the helpless grandmother and yelled in Korean, "What a disgrace to our country. Get the fuck off my land." They laughed and walked away. From across the street I saw two little droplets of water stream down her powerless face. My gut told me to do something, so I walked over and told her that it was all right. I reached into my pockets and gave her 50,000 won (equivalent to thirty American dollars) and told her it was a token from my heart. Then like my pores from the heat, her eyes started streaming with water like a broken faucet and she kept thanking me. She then uttered out of nowhere, "Don't close your soul, leave it open and share it among other people. It's a gift." I didn't think much of what she said assuming that she was drunk. I informed her that crying and gratitude were not needed and walked away. As my feet marched down the street, I heard the words of thank you all the way to my dorm.

This situation brought the Socrates out of me. Philosophical questions started to burn my cranium. How can a country like Korea ignore the unfortunate? I decided to talk to my aunt about what had happened and she told me the naked truth. She said that even though Korea excelled from the rubbles of the Korean War, the country still has a lot to do. The country has no social security, no welfare, and doesn't care for the people who need aid the most. I thought to myself, "how can a

Third World country that turned into a First World forget about the helpless?" Then I told her what the homeless woman said to me about my soul. My aunt paused, then slowly she said, "People like that know what they are talking about. Americans might think they are crazy, but here, they are the wisest. Consider what she said and open your soul." I felt like I was in an episode of the "Twilight Zone." What in the world is everyone talking about? Is the kimchee or the rice getting to their heads? I left the question unanswered and just looked forward to touching down on Uncle Sam's land.

The plane ride was exhausting and my parents were all over me. They showered their kisses on my weak pale face, and I returned the love. I arrived home and the whole family was exhausted. The lights turned out, but I had a problem called jet lag. So I unpacked and walked around my house. I stumbled upon an old Reebok box and opened the ancient treasure chest. The cloud of dust cleared and I found ratty old papers. It was a box filled with my old school work. It had my "A" paper on World War II, the 100's I received on those ridiculous spelling tests, and then "BAM." Under all the debris, I found my spirit, "I Wonder." I thought I was dreaming and pinched my arms a couple of times. It was reality, and I took the poem to a light source and read it out loud. Wow, this brought back memories. It then hit me like a freight train. This was my breath of life, my soul. What Mrs. Nazarro, Mr. Lim, the homeless grandmother, and my aunt were talking about was in this poem. My special gift is writing broken sentences into funny stanzas to express my emotions. This was my soul and my talent. I remembered what the poor grandmother said and smiled.

I woke up my mom and handed her the poem. She read the poem and her face shined. She hugged me and I left the room so she could continue her beauty sleep. I walked outside my abode and lit a cancer stick. I looked at the weak full moon and the beautiful dawn sky. I then closed my eyes, unlocked the door to my soul, and threw the key into the sun. I don't need the key. From now on, there were going to be visitors in and out reading my talent.

INTERPRETATIONS

1. Woo's narrative reflects on his journey to creativity from second grade to his second year in college. Why was he so reluctant to pursue his poetic self? What impresses you most about his journey?

2. Woo now thinks of words as being powerful enough to unlock the door to his soul. How does he explain this transformation? How do you respond to his metaphor?

APPLICATIONS

1. Imagine having the opportunity to talk with Woo. What would you ask him? What literacy experience would you share with him?

2. What kinds of literacy does the author encounter? Present specific examples from the essay to support your views.

3. Why is the homeless person presented in paragraphs 13–14 important to Woo? What kind of literacy does she represent to the author?

4. How does Woo use the concept of literacy as a theme in this essay? How do your experiences with literacy help you to understand your own life? Explain your answers fully.

The Knowing Eye

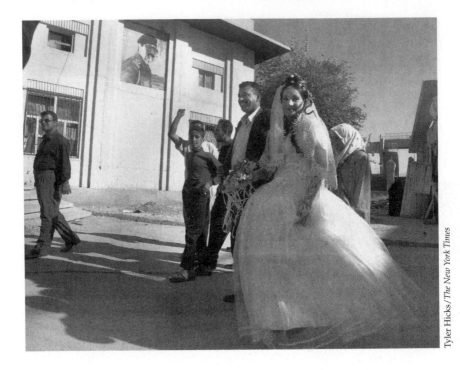

Tyler Hicks/*The New York Times*

READING IMAGES

1. At first glance, it might be difficult to discern the cultural encounter taking place in each photograph. What specific details show the encounter? What historical knowledge is useful to help you to see the cultural encounter as it applies to each photograph?

2. What emotions do you notice on the faces of the people in the photographs? To what extent does body posture reveal feelings?

MAKING CONNECTIONS

1. How do these photographs relate to ones that you have seen previously? In particular, review the images presented in "Family and Community," "Work," and "Traditions" (chapters 2, 5, and 6).

2. Which essays in this chapter seem to match these photographs best? What similarities do you notice between text and image?

Albert Simpson/National Archives and Records Administration

WORDS AND IMAGES

1. Which of these images do you like more? Why? Present your findings in an essay using argumentation/persuasion or comparison/ contrast. Be sure to include specific references to each photograph.

2. In reference to the photograph of the soldiers and civilians, what do you think these groups might be saying to each other? Write a dialogue of ten lines that communicates what you might have heard if you were in that scene.

Additional Writing Topics

1. As college campuses become more ethnically diverse, how might administrators, faculty, staff, and students work together to create a climate of inclusiveness that enhances educational, social, personal, and cultural encounters? Interview a cross-section of the college community on this issue. What suggestions did they make? What responsibilities are they willing to assume? Write a summary of your findings for your campus or local newspaper.

2. In the context of the American Dream, analyze how Hongo, Grant, and Stanley explore the themes of immigration, exile, and displacement. Take into account generational as well as cultural differences.

3. Review the Norton perspective (page 339). Is it easier to support theoretically than practically? To what extent do the interactions presented in the selections in this textbook reflect the kinds of tolerance of individual differences Norton advocates?

4. Write about a group you participated in recently. Analyze how the group members interact with one another. By what means do they communicate with one another? How do they handle disagreement or friction? Write an essay on what you learned about group relations.

5. Lack of awareness of cultural differences or the assumption by one cultural group that another is inferior results in interactions that are painful power struggles. Apply this thesis to any three selections in this chapter.

6. Although "the melting pot" is the traditional metaphor associated with the immigrant experience in the United States, many sociologists now believe that "the fusion chamber" is a more accurate description of current cultural interacting. Contrast the implications of both terms and, using any three essays in this chapter, justify your choice of metaphor.

7. Who are you? Create a pie chart that accurately represents your cultural heritage. When you have finished, write an essay that describes and explains your thoughts about each section of your pie.

8. To what extent do you agree that in spite of our enormous ethnic diversity and the hyphenated identity of the children of most immigrant parents, we are on the whole shaped by a common culture.

9. Review Iyer's perspective on travel and analyze its relevance to any three cultural interactions in this chapter.

8

Choices

C ULTURE, ACCORDING TO ANTHROPOLOGIST BRONISLAW MALINOWSKI, is the "artificial, secondary environment that human beings superimpose on nature." We human beings, then, are "in" both nature and culture, and both influence our choices. A diversity of cultures, which the following texts illustrate, makes for great choices and sometimes great difficulty of choices.

Choices are part of daily life. Some are anticlimactic, even repetitive, such as training ourselves to set the alarm clock and getting up when it rings. It becomes "second nature" and we are on time for work or school without having to think about it. When life runs its traditional course, unconscious habit often replaces conscious choice, but when crises arise, social, personal, or political habit is useless, and all kinds of choices must be made, even painful ones. Such choices may involve a conflict of values or test our personal or social commitments. They also shape the kind of people we become.

Is culture a limitation on freedom of choice, or does it allow more free play of individual wisdom and imagination? Do we increase our own choices to the degree we free ourselves from culture? The first selection in the chapter poses such a possibility. The young man in the Swahili tale chooses a wife and finds that the choice involves such cultural requirements as a bride price. The wife's culture denies her the choice of husband, but her wisdom, which is even greater than her beauty, reveals to her subsequent choices that allow her to triumph.

Although our ability to choose may not be limitless, several texts in this chapter present several choices open to us. Pete Hamill, for example, advocates choosing in favor of struggle to learn about ourselves rather than blind obedience to the concept of winning. In a crisis, habit can seldom ease the pain of choice.

The narrator of "Honor Bound" is forced into dramatic conversations with himself when confronted with unexpected choices; and in his memoir, "Homeplace," Scott Russell Sanders defends his choice to stay in one community despite most peoples' lack of commitment to a particular place.

It would be hard to imagine more difficult choices than those which confront the family in Hana Wehle's memoir "Janushinka." Set in the Auschwitz concentration camp, a young mother is faced with the choice of saving herself or going to her death with her child.

A change of environment may also alter the significance of moral, economic, and social choices. In "To the Border," Richard Rodriguez sympathetically and poetically recreated the emotional and wrenching choices of a boy who is one of the lonely "Mexicans without Mexico," while in "The Fender Bender," an illegal alien is the beneficiary of a moral choice by an Anglo driver.

Traditionally, college commencement speakers challenge students at what is viewed as a defining moment in their lives, and in her speech to the 1999 graduates of Mount Holyoke College, contemporary novelist and columnist Anna Quindlen urges the graduates to resist conformity and focus on making their own choices about their lives.

> This is the hard work of your life in the world: to make it all up as you go along, to acknowledge the introvert, the clown, the artist, the reserved, the distraught, the goofball, the thinker. You will have to bend all your will not to march to the music that all of those great "theys" out there pipe on their flutes. They want you to go to professional school, to wear khakis, to pierce your navel, to bare your soul. These are the fashionable ways. The music is tinny, if you listen close enough. Look inside. That way lies dancing to the melodies spun out by your own heart. This is a symphony. All the rest are jingles.

Perspectives

Growth demands a temporary surrender of security.

—Gail Sheehy

Life shrinks or expands in proportion to one's courage.

—Anaïs Nin

Which you want. A whipping and no turnips or turnips and no whipping?

—Toni Morrison

No trumpets sound when the important decisions for our lives are made. Destiny is made known silently.

—Agnes de Mille

. . . You don't get to choose how you're going to die or when. You can only decide how you're going to live now.

—Joan Baez

People are trapped in history and history is trapped in them.

—James Baldwin

If man's condition is unjust, he has only one alternative, which is to be just himself.

—Albert Camus

One doesn't throw the stick after the snake has gone.

—Liberian Proverb

Once to every man and nation comes the moment to decide
In the strife of truth with falsehood, for the good or evil side.

—James Russell Lowell

A new place brings out a new thing in man.

—D. H. Lawrence

Two roads diverged in a wood, and I—I took the one less traveled by, and that has made all the difference.

—Robert Frost

Every time a man has contributed to the victory of the dignity of the spirit, every time a man has said no to an attempt to subjugate his fellows, I have felt solidarity with his act.

—Frantz Fanon

No day comes back again; an inch of time is worth a foot of jade.

—Zen Proverb

There is, I think, an essential difference of character in mankind, between those who wish to do, and those who wish to have certain things.

—William Hazlitt

All life is an experiment. The more experiments you make the better.

—Ralph Waldo Emerson

If I had to choose between betraying my country and betraying my friend, I hope I should have the guts to betray my country.

—E. M. Forster

APPLICATIONS

1. What is implied in thinking about life as an experiment? Is it more appealing than a blueprint? How do they differ? To what extent are you free to conduct experiments in living?

2. Discuss with your group the perspective of the Zen proverb (above). What does it imply about time and choice? To what extent do you agree that time is more important than wealth?

3. Decisions are often the result of judgments. Consult a dictionary and thesaurus on the word and its connotations. Is there a choice that you made based on sound judgment? Write about it in your journal.

The Wise Daughter

SWAHILI FOLKTALE

Swahili is spoken widely in East Africa and is an official language of Kenya and Tanzania. What are your associations with the word "wise"?

THERE WAS ONCE A YOUNG MAN whose parents died and left him a hundred cattle. He was lonely after the death of his parents, so he decided to get married. He went to his neighbors and asked them to help him find a wife.

Soon one of the neighbors came to tell him that he had found the most beautiful girl in the country for him to marry. "The girl is very good and wise and beautiful, and her father is very wealthy," he said. "Her father owns six thousand cattle."

The young man became very excited when he heard about this girl. But then he asked, "How much is the bride price?"

"The father wants a hundred cattle," was the reply.

"A hundred cattle! That is all I have. How will we be able to live?" replied the young man.

"Well, make up your mind. I have to take an answer to the father soon," said the neighbor.

The young man thought, "I cannot live without this girl." So he said, "Go and tell the father that I want to marry his daughter."

So the two were married. But after they returned home, they quickly ran out of food, and the young man had to herd cattle for a neighbor to get anything to eat. What he got was not very much for a young lady who was used to eating well and living in style.

One day as the young wife was sitting outside the house, a strange man came by and was struck by her beauty. He decided to try to seduce her and sent a message to her. The young wife told him that she could not make up her mind and he would have to come back later.

Several months later, the girl's father came to visit. She was very upset because she did not have anything to feed him. But on that same day, the seducer came back. So the young wife told the seducer that she would give in to his requests if he would bring her some meat to cook for her father.

Soon the seducer returned with the meat and the girl went inside to cook it. Her husband returned, and he and her father sat down to eat and have a good time. The seducer was standing outside listening. Soon he became angry and went inside to see what was happening. The young husband, who was hospitable, invited him in.

The young wife then brought in the meat and said, "Eat, you three fools."

"Why do you call us fools?" the three men said all together.

"Well, Father," the girl replied. "You are a fool because you sold something precious for something worthless. You had only one daughter and traded her for a hundred cattle when you already had six thousand."

"You are right," said her father. "I was a fool."

"As for you, husband," she went on. "You inherited only a hundred cattle and you went and spent them all on me, leaving us nothing to eat. You could have married another woman for ten or twenty cows. That is why you were a fool."

"And why am I a fool?" asked the seducer.

"You are the biggest fool of all. You thought you could get for one piece of meat what had been bought for a hundred cattle."

At that, the seducer ran away as fast as he could. Then the father said, "You are a wise daughter. When I get home, I will send your husband three hundred cattle so that you shall live in comfort."

INTERPRETATIONS

1. Is this tale about how *not* to make choices? Explain your answer.

2. Evaluate the daughter's role in the story. Was she wise or just practical? What is the difference?

Flowers

AMANDA STELLMAN

*Amanda Stellman (b. 1991) is in seventh grade at Albert Leonard Middle
School in New Rochelle, New York. She wrote "Flowers" for a project in
mythology. Before reading her myth, record in your journal your first memory of "flowers."*

IN A VALLEY BETWEEN Mt. Embrasy and Mt. Ampado there lived a beautiful goddess named Fracas. Fracas lived with her family—her mom, her
dad, and her two brothers. They lived in a peaceful village where
neighbors shared food and clothing. They knew nothing of war or
crime or other injustices. They knew kindness and sharing.

One day clouds began to form over Mt. Embrasy. They were thick
and dark and threatening. Goddess Fracas and her family had never
seen clouds like that before. They were frightened. Their neighbors
were scared also. Goddess Fracas told her family that whenever she
was outside and the dark clouds were over Mt. Embrasy, she felt like
she couldn't keep her feet on the ground. "She felt there was a dark
force pulling her up the mountain."

Soon there came a time when dark, threatening clouds also hung
over Mt. Ampado to the left of the valley. She felt pulled in both directions now until her arms ached and she could no longer go outside without someone to hold her down. There was no more sunshine in the valley
and the crops they used for food began to die. The people of the village
looked up to the heavens and asked what was happening. They begged
for help. Suddenly, a bird flew down and sang to them. The bird sang
about the war between Memoo and Cuno. Each of them vowed never to
give up until he had won over the love of his life, the goddess Fracas.

Indeed the skies got darker and the dark forces pulling Fracas up
the mountain got stronger. The townspeople decided they needed to
take action. They consulted with the goddess of love, Rose Blossom.
She told them that goddess Fracas would never be safe while Memoo
and Cuno were fighting over her. Their hatred for each other had won
out over their love for her. The villagers prepared to carry out the secret
plan that they had made up with Rose Blossom.

The next day the family said goodbye to their sweet goddess, Fracas,
for they knew they would never see her again in the same way. They dug

a hole in the ground and Fracas climbed into it. The townspeople covered the hole with rich soil and watered it with love. Very soon after, flowers and crops began to grow all over the land, and the sun began to shine brightly again. The townspeople gathered outside with smiles on their faces. They took deep breaths and said hello to their dear goddess Fracas all over the land. Memoo and Cuno had no power over her any longer. Hatred had no power over her. Only the good find love.

INTERPRETATIONS

1. Why does Fracas feel "that there was a dark force pulling her up the mountain"?
2. What is Rose Blossom's role in the myth?
3. Is the author's purpose to inform or persuade? Explain.

CORRESPONDENCES

1. Compare and contrast the choices in "The Wise Daughter" and "Flowers."
2. Review the Nin perspective on choices and discuss its relevance to both texts. Which choice in your view is most courageous? Explain.

APPLICATIONS

1. Myths are often didactic. Compose with your group a short myth that involves a moral issue.
2. Write a journal entry about a choice that you regret having made. What did you learn from the experience?
3. Discuss with your group the relation between economics and choice in "The Wise Daughter." Does economics limit choices in the tale? How? To what extent do you base your choices on economics? Summarize your group's discussion.

Janushinka

HANA WEHLE

Hana Wehle (1917–1997) was born in Czechoslovakia. She was a survivor of the Theresienstadt, Auschwitz, and Stutthof concentration camps. After the defeat of the Nazis in 1945, she returned to Czechoslovakia, where she remarried. In 1951, she and her husband, also a survivor of Auschwitz, emigrated to the United States. She published several essays about her concentration camp experiences.

This is how she described her purpose in writing "Janushinka."

For Franz Kafka, "writing is a form of prayer." For me, writing is a form of conveying a message. I remember the time in Auschwitz, when every prisoner in our part of the camp was destined to die in the gas chambers. How much did I then want to live, so that I could bring the message to the world about the absurdity of our existence during that period of madness. I survived and I want to help young people understand this event through a form which is easier to grasp than a strictly historical account. I like to share my experiences with a college-age audience on the threshold of adult life, since they are the makers of the future. I wish to give them certain awareness of things they would not encounter otherwise. Last, but not least, I want them to understand that what I write contains an important message for them.

As you read "Janushinka," determine what message it contains for you.

WITH JANUSHINKA'S BIRTH the passionate bond was sealed. She was swept into the happy orbit of her parents, Henry and Pepinka, and became the focal point of their life. Whenever they looked at her, they transformed their souls into that look. They tasted with pleasure bordering on reverence every move, touch and exploration of the child, as well as, later, the cascade of words scrambled in nonsense combinations. Today, forty years later, I am still able to draw from my memory the sweet melody of Janushinka's laughs and cries coming from the nursery.

Henry was my father's cousin, a successful, hard working businessman, in his thirties. Pepinka, a few years younger, was a beautiful woman with velvety brown eyes radiating with love and happiness.

I stayed with them for a short time, after arriving in Prague from the German-occupied Sudetenland in the northern region of Bohemia.

Before long, I too gravitated toward the sweet little child. I remember how one or the other of us would tip-toe in and out of the nursery to make sure that the sleeping Janushinka was not too cold or too hot. When the weather became chilly and rainy, we would brace ourselves with a surgical cotton mask so that germs would not invade her delicate system. Unquestionably, Henry and Pepinka's happiness was also heavily tinted by shadows of fear and anxiety for the safety of their precious jewel.

At a time when love and affection still warmed every corner of their home, the German army already occupied Prague. My recollection of being frightened as the clatter of marching soldiers could be heard through the windows is still clear. The dissonance between the dim winter morning when the Germans marched into our city and the sanctity of that loving home was an unbearable experience.

Very soon the tide of the events turned against the Jews. The curtains of their homes were drawn, the lights went out. They were deported to an unknown destination . . . Also the lights in the nursery were turned out, the curtains drawn. The chuckle of Janushinka was silenced.

After I was deported to Auschwitz, I never thought that I would see Henry and his family again. However, it did happen in the "Familienlager," one of the many sections of Auschwitz-Birkenau. I was on my way to the "latrine" (toilet), a large wooden barrack, used by prisoners under the watchful eyes of the SS guards. Inside the large area on one side were women, on the other side were men, exposed to one another in utter humiliation. The entrance was always crowded with prisoners waiting for their turn. For some of them it was too late: they collapsed into their own excrement, unable to lift themselves from the muddy ground. We had to bypass these human forms as we moved on in silence.

The air was damp and the rags of clouds hung over us. As we were slowly inching away, I heard somebody softly calling my name. Carefully, so as not to dispel the feeble voice behind me, I turned my head in the direction of a tiny cloud steaming from the frozen mouth of a man. I looked at the still face and suddenly felt as if a sword were splitting the web of my brain. There stood Henry! His sunken eyes were fixed upon me and the narrow line of his mouth twisted into a strange, almost embarrassed smile. The unshaven face hung between his shoulders, and the once translucent, blue eyes signaled an unspeakable anguish. His rasping voice cut through the silence around us: "Janushinka is very sick. Pneumonia. Pepinka is desperately trying to save her life." In these words there was something that killed all hope.

The memory of the gulf between Henry in the nursery and the man standing in front of me that day will never allow me to forget the perversity of fate. I remember the dreamer's dreams and how they were shattered under the wheels of the trains rushing through the German and Polish countrysides, carrying in their dark bellies thousands of little Janushinkas, Henrys, and Pepinkas . . .

I slipped back through time and recaptured the fragrance of the little child in the nursery and the sight of Pepinka pulling the soft pink blanket over the sleeping Janushinka. Henry is lovingly watching the young woman in the bright opening of the door, as she steps out of the nursery. She then sets a bowl of steaming soup on the table covered with a starched, hand-embroidered table cloth; the silver spoons touching the fine porcelain send pleasant tinkles through the cozy dining room.

The urgency in Henry's eyes jolted me back into the present. I looked past Henry and glanced at the watch towers above the barbed wire surrounding the camp. What consolation could I offer to this man? I felt so cold and hungry. A picture of Pepinka and Janushinka struggling in some dark corner of a barracks pushed its way upon me. Janushinka's body is so thin that it appears translucent. Pepinka bends over the little girl and with an almost childlike expression hopes for a miracle. Her hand caresses the sweet forehead, covered with beads of sweat and her gentle lips brush the feverish face as she intently follows the quickening breath of her child, fighting for life . . . I leaned toward Henry and whispered: "Meet me here tomorrow at this time, I will bring you some soup." The crowd behind pushed us into the latrine barrack. As we parted, it seemed to me that Henry's face somewhat brightened.

Once in a while the workers at the camp post office got an additional portion of soup. I was one of them and, therefore, was able to share that precious "premium" with my mother, who had been deported with me to Auschwitz. Suddenly I panicked. What if I did not get the special soup tomorrow? Henry would be waiting . . . and what about my mother? How could I deprive her? Would she be able to understand?

The night seemed long because I could not sleep. Will I get the additional soup, and if I do, how shall I divide it? We all are so hungry! The barrels of soup paraded endlessly in front of my tired mind. Will any of them stop in front of me? Will there be some soup for Henry? The last barrel is finally set in front of me. What a relief! Eagerly I bend over the slippery edge of the barrel and realize with horror—the vessel is empty!

Finally daylight crept into our barrack. The dead were carried behind the barrack, the half dead and the healthy filed out for the roll-call. That day the counting and recounting of prisoners was endless.

It was almost midday before we could return. I could not rest. My eyes were glued to the road stretching between the rows of the wooden barracks. At last two women surfaced in the fog. Between them, they carried the long awaited barrel of soup. I followed eagerly the wooden clogs marching in unison with the swinging barrel suspended from two heavy poles. They headed toward us, the poles in the grip of their bony hands. Around their necks, attached to the poles, was a strong strap, which pulled their heads forward. As they came closer I could see their distorted faces reflecting the enormous strain of their bodies as they struggled to distribute the weight of the barrel between their arms and necks.

Finally they arrived at our barrack. Amid the pushing of the hungry prisoners a line was formed. There stood the vessel with a grayish, slimy liquid dripping down its sides. We all followed eagerly every drop. One full ladle was dropped into each bowl. My turn came . . . in an almost hypnotic trance I traced the movement of the ladle. It emptied once and dipped in—and emptied into my bowl again!

Victoriously I carried the full bowl to my place, where my mother was waiting for her share of the soup. I reluctantly explained to her why we would from now on divide the soup into three parts. She understood the urgency and shared in the sacrifice. I hurried with the rest of the soup to the latrine barrack. As I pushed my way through the waiting crowd to meet Henry, icy rain dropped into the soup. The hand on my shoulder was Henry's. His face seemed thinner than the day before. As I was transferring the soup into his dish, Henry's eyes were transfixed on that thick, gray stream barely filling the bottom of his bowl. He just nodded and disappeared into the crowd.

I met Henry several times, sometimes with the soup, sometimes without it. Meanwhile, Janushinka, he told me, was still in the grip of death. The question as to whether I could actually prevent her imminent death never left me. What if the recovery never took place?

The subhuman conditions in the camp were sapping the strength of Henry's frail body. His walking had become visibly slower, his back stooped increasingly and he was more listless. One day, however, I noticed some change. He tried to straighten his haggard body and across his face the cruel play of fear and hope was gone. The words rolled from his mouth like pieces of gold: "Janushinka's fever has subsided—she ate the soup!" Henry's and my eyes connected in a new alliance with life. In his face lingered a flicker of hope. For myself, I freed my conscience from the burden of guilt about having deprived my mother of the additional soup.

As Janushinka's health slowly improved so Henry's strength quickly evaporated. One day Henry did not show up. As usual, I waited

in front of the latrine barrack, the gelatinous soup cold in my bowl . . .
That day I returned to my mother's place, overtaken by fatigue. We
shared Janushinka's soup in silence.

The only place where men and women were able occasionally to
share a fleeting moment was the latrine barrack. For a long time
I looked into the faces around me in vain. I never saw Henry again.
At the far end of our camp was the so called children's block where
some of the mothers and their young children were housed; they
helped take care of the youngsters' needs. There Pepinka and
Janushinka lived also. Any contact between the occupants of the children's block and the rest of the camp prisoners was forbidden.
Apparently, Henry had found some clandestine way to get the soup
to Janushinka during her sickness. After his disappearance I lost
track of their whereabouts.

Not until the beginning of July 1944, when the prisoners of the
"Familien-lager" were about to be gassed, did I learn about Pepinka's
and Janushinka's fate. Daily selections, grouping and regrouping
of the old and young, the sick and healthy, took place. The younger
and more healthy men and women were transported to other camps
for work; the old and sick were exterminated in the gas chambers
and to the mothers of young children a choice was given: "Leave
your child behind and save yourself by joining the group of working
women, or—go to your death together with your children." Three
hundred young mothers made their choice: Pepinka was one of
them. She held the tiny hand of Janushinka as if she would lead the
child to school, like other mothers, in another world. In her lonely
hour of anguish once again Pepinka hoped for a miracle. This time,
however, there was none . . . Janushinka had to die, before she even
learned to live. By a twist of fate Janushinka's recovery had led to
Pepinka's death. Such was the notorious "law" in the world of
Auschwitz!

INTERPRETATIONS

1. What is Wehle's relationship to Janushinka and her family? What
   do the details of their lifestyle before the war suggest about their
   social class?

2. Reread paragraphs 3 through 5. Which details foreshadow the fate
   of many Jewish people during the Nazi regime?

3. What is the connotation of "rags" in the phrase "the mass of
   clouds" (paragraph 7)? Of "crept" in "Daylight crept into our barrack" (paragraph 12)?

4.   How does Wehle's mother's presence make her decision to help Janushinka more difficult? Would you have chosen differently? Explain.

5.   Do you think more people would have survived the war if they had not had parents, spouses, or children in the camp? Explain.

6.   How does Janushinka's recovery lead to Pepinka's death? Do you agree that "fate" was involved here? If so, how would you define "fate"? Is character also involved? Love? How would you characterize Pepinka?

Honor Bound

JOSEPH STEFFAN

*Joseph Steffan (b. 1964) was a senior in 1987 when he was discharged from
the United States Naval Academy after admitting that he was gay. After his
discharge, Steffan filed a lawsuit against the academy, became an advocate for
gay and lesbian military members, and wrote about his military career in*
Honor Bound *(1992). Steffan received a law degree from the University of
Connecticut in 1994. Before reading Steffan's essay, speculate as to the meaning of his title.*

I WALKED INTO THE COMMANDANT'S outer office and reported to his executive assistant, a junior officer assigned to serve as his aide. He said the
commandant would be right with me, and asked me to take a seat. The
strange quietness of the hallway seemed to permeate everything, and
although the EA's greeting had been cordial, there was an obvious tension in the air. He undoubtedly knew the purpose of this meeting as
well, and I began to wonder how long it would take before it leaked to
the rest of the brigade.

I tried to keep calm, but it was difficult to ignore the obvious importance of this meeting. What would happen in the next few moments
would likely determine, to a very large extent, the rest of my life. My
feelings were a strange mixture of fear, anger, and pride, and I was
determined that, no matter what, I was going to maintain my sense of
dignity.

Finally, the EA signaled that the commandant was ready and led me
into his office. The commandant of midshipmen, Captain Howard
Habermeyer, was waiting just inside the door as we entered. He greeted
me, shaking my hand, and motioned for me to sit as he returned to his
desk. The office was relatively opulent by military standards, with dark
wood paneling and blue carpeting. Behind the commandant's large
wooden desk stood the United States flag and the blue-and-gold flag of
the Brigade of Midshipmen. The walls were covered with pictures and
plaques, memorabilia from his service as an officer in the submarine
service.

Captain Habermeyer was tall, bespectacled, and quite thin, almost
to the point of frailty. He and the superintendent had taken over during the previous summer, replacing Captain Chadwick and Admiral

Larson, both of whom I had come to know quite well during my previous years. I regretted that they were not here now, and that my fate rested in the hands of two officers who barely knew me. I sometimes wonder if they had been there instead whether it would have changed the outcome at all. Perhaps it would at least have been more difficult for them.

I had first met Captain Habermeyer at a small leadership retreat held for the top incoming stripers of my class. The retreat was relatively informal and was held at an Annapolis hotel. At the time, he impressed me as an intelligent and articulate officer, and we had shared a conversation about his admiration of Japanese culture. It was an interest that had grown through several tours of duty he had in Japan.

I had heard since then that Captain Habermeyer was a stickler for regulations. He played everything exactly by the book. My suspicion was confirmed when the EA remained standing in the doorway as the commandant began to question me about my request. He had apparently been ordered to remain as a witness to the conversation. Despite an outward sense of cordiality, I was beginning to feel like a criminal under interrogation.

As with the previous officers, I refused to discuss the purpose of my request with the commandant, but he continued to question me. He finally stated that no one in the military has an inherent right to meet with anyone above his own commanding officer, which for midshipmen is technically the commandant. If I refused to disclose the purpose of the meeting, he would deny my request. When he again questioned me, I finally answered, "The meeting concerns a situation of which you are already aware."

"You're referring to the NIS investigation presently under way?" he asked.

"Yes, sir."

He responded, "Are you willing to state at this time that you are a homosexual?"

The moment of truth had arrived. In a way, I was surprised that he was even asking the question. Captain Holderby had already basically told him the answer. Was he offering me an out, a chance to deny it, to say that it was all a big misunderstanding? Was he offering me a chance to lie?

I looked him straight in the eye and answered, "Yes sir, I am."

It was a moment I will never forget, one of agony and intense pride. In that one statement, I had given up my dreams, the goals I had spent the last four years of my life laboring to attain. But in exchange, I retained something far more valuable—my honor and my self-esteem.

In many ways, the commandant's words were more than a simple question—they were a challenge to everything I believed in, and to the identity I had struggled to accept. In giving me the opportunity to deny my sexuality, the commandant was challenging that identity. He could just as well have asked, "Are you ashamed enough to deny your true identity in order to graduate?" More than anything I have ever wanted in my entire life, I wanted to be an outstanding midshipman and to graduate from the Naval Academy. And I firmly believe that if I had been willing to lie about my sexuality, to deny my true identity, I would have been allowed to graduate.

I had come to the academy to achieve my potential as an individual. These four years had been filled with trials and lessons from which I learned a great deal about life and about myself. But none of these lessons was more difficult, important, or meaningful than coming to understand and accept my sexuality—in essence, to accept my true identity. By coming out to myself, I gained the strength that can come only from self-acceptance, and it was with that added strength that I had been able to persevere through the many trials and difficulties of life at Annapolis.

The commandant's question was also a challenge to my honor as a midshipman. The Honor Concept at Annapolis is based on the tenet that personal honor is an absolute—you either have honor or you do not. No one can take it from you; it can only be surrendered willingly. And once it is surrendered, once it is compromised, it can never again be fully regained.

I knew that my graduation would mean absolutely nothing if I had to lie to achieve it, especially if that lie was designed to hide the very fact of my own identity. I would have given up my honor, destroying everything it means to be a midshipman. And I would have given up my identity and pride —everything it means to be a person.

The only way to retain my honor and identity, both as a midshipman and a person, was to tell the truth. I was honor bound not simply by the Honor Concept, but by its foundation: the respect for fundamental human dignity. The academy had the power to take away everything tangible that I had attained, but only I had the power to destroy my honor. Even if the academy discharged me for being gay, I could live with the knowledge that I had passed the ultimate test. I was willing to give up everything tangible to retain something intangible but far more meaningful: my honor and my identity. Even the military could not take them away from me now.

Captain Habermeyer said that he could not grant my request to speak with the superintendent because he would eventually sit in judgment over me. A performance board would be scheduled the next day, the first step toward discharge from Annapolis. Although I explained that I still desired to graduate, the commandant assured me that he did not believe the superintendent would allow it.

Before leaving, I looked at the commandant and said, "I'm sorry it had to end this way." He answered, "So am I." I truly believed him, which didn't make the imminent destruction of my life much easier to deal with. It would have been so much easier to have someone to hate, a person to blame for everything that was happening. But there was no one to blame. I couldn't blame myself because I had done what I believed right. There was only a military policy, a rule like countless others that define life in the military, rules that we learn to instinctively enforce and obey.

My perception of what was happening seemed almost detached at times, and I wondered how long it would be before I woke up to realize this was all a horrible dream. In retrospect, I don't doubt that I was suffering from shock, so completely overcome by emotion that I couldn't feel anything at all. I wanted to scream or cry or something, but there was too much to deal with, and I wondered if I would be able to stop once I started.

Not only was the nature of my life changing rapidly, but I was also anticipating how each of my relationships with other people would change. Would my parents and friends reject me as I had feared for so long, or was I not giving them enough credit? In any case, I knew it would be only a short time until the news of my disclosure would leak to the brigade, and I had to be prepared before then. I had heard a story about two male mids who were caught in bed together a year or two before I was inducted. That evening, they were both dragged from their rooms, wrapped in blankets and beaten by other mids in what was called a "blanket party." In a way, I doubted whether anyone would dare do that to me, but I wasn't too excited about the possibility.

There was no doubt in my mind that the story would leak, probably within twenty-four hours. After that, it would spread like wildfire. Annapolis is such a rumor mill that I could expect to hear about five hundred colorful variations of the story within a few hours. I decided that the best way to combat this inevitability was through a controlled release of information, and that release had to start with my closest friends at the academy.

I spent the rest of the afternoon telling six of my friends what was going on. Each of them was shocked and surprised, but they were universally supportive, even more so than I had hoped. I told them I wanted them to hear it from me first, but that they should keep it under wraps for now. I also took the time to go to each of the teachers I had in classes that semester to inform them personally. I felt a need to do this first out of respect for them, and second, to make sure that they knew I was not ashamed to face them. If I was going to leave the academy, I wanted it to be with the same level of pride I had felt as a battalion commander. I didn't want anyone to think I was running away, departing under a cloak of deserved shame. I wanted to show them I was the same person as before—exactly the same.

INTERPRETATIONS

1. Explain the significance of the title of Steffan's essay. Do you respect his courage to tell the truth about his sexuality in spite of the consequences he would confront? Why or why not?

2. What prompted Steffan to later tell his closest friends about his decision? To what extent were you surprised by their reactions? How might you have responded in their situation?

3. Why does Steffan describe the setting and the captain in such detail? How do these descriptions affect meaning?

CORRESPONDENCES

1. Review Camus's perspective on choices (page 405) and discuss its relevance to Steffan's decision. Do you agree that his situation was unjust? Why or why not?

2. Wehle and Steffan take risks because of their commitments to individual integrity. Under what circumstances can you imagine taking a similar risk to protect your honor?

APPLICATIONS

1. Rent the video "Sophie's Choice" and write an extended journal entry on your responses to the choices made by young mothers in the film. To what extent did the film confirm or change your response to Pepinka's choice in Wehle's essay?

2. The realities written about by Hana Wehle are unthinkable. In the final sentence of her essay she writes: "Such was the notorious 'law' in the world of Auschwitz!" What was the "world of Auschwitz"?

   http://remember.org/then-and-now/index.html

   http://www.holocaust-trc.org/wmp17.htm

3. In the last paragraph of this essay, Joseph Steffan informs his friends and teachers of his situation. What do you think he might have said to them? Create a conversation about twenty lines in duration that you think might have taken place between Steffan and a friend or a teacher.

Winning Isn't Everything

PETE HAMILL

Pete Hamill (b. 1935) was born in Brooklyn, New York. Using the educational benefits of the G. I. Bill of Rights, he attended Mexico City College. In 1960, Hamill began his long journalism career as a reporter for The New York Post. *Since then he has been a columnist for* The New York Post, The Daily News, *and* New York Newsday. *Hamill's pieces have also been published in* Esquire, New York, *and* The New York Times Magazine. *Hamill has also written eight novels and two collections of short stories. His 1997 novel,* Snow in August, *was a* New York Times *bestseller as was his memoir,* A Drinking Life. *He has also published collections of his journalism, a book about New York City, and an extended essay on the music of Frank Sinatra. Currently, Hamill is on the staff of* The New Yorker. *As you read Hamill's essay, compare your ideas of winning and losing with those of the author.*

ONE OF THE MORE WIDELY ACCEPTED maxims of modern American life was uttered on a frozen winter afternoon during the early sixties. The late Vince Lombardi, who coached the Green Bay Packers when they were the greatest team in football, said it. "Winning isn't everything," he declared. "It's the only thing."

Vince Lombardi's notion was immediately appropriated by an extraordinary variety of American males: presidents and lesser politicians, generals, broadcasters, political columnists, Little League coaches, heads of corporations, and probably millions of others. In fact, it sometimes seems that Lombardi's words have had greater impact than any sentence uttered by an American since Stephen Decatur's "our country, right or wrong."

That's surprising on many levels, beginning with the obvious: It's a deceptively simple premise. Winning *isn't* "the only thing." Such an idea muddles the idea of competition, not simply in sports, but in all aspects of our lives. We've learned the hard way in this century that the world is a complex place; it's certainly not the National Football League. Winning isn't the only thing in love, art, marriage, commerce, or politics; it's not even the only thing in sports.

In sports, as in so many other areas of our national life, we've always cherished gallant losers. I remember one afternoon in the fall of

1956 when Sal Maglie was pitching for the Brooklyn Dodgers against the hated Yankees. Maglie was an old man that year, as age is measured in sports. But this was the World Series, and he hauled his thirty-nine-year-old body to the mound, inning after inning, gave everything he had, held the Yankees to a few scattered hits and two runs—and lost. That day Don Larsen pitched his perfect game: no runs, no hits, no errors. Yet, to me, the afternoon belonged to Maglie—tough, gallant, and a loser.

There was an evening in Manila when Joe Frazier went up against Muhammad Ali for the third and final time. That night, Frazier brought his workman's skills into combat against the magic of the artist, called on his vast reservoir of courage and will, and came up empty at the end of fourteen rounds. Frazier was the loser, but that evening, nobody really lost. Because of that fight, Joe Frazier can always boast with honor that he made Muhammad Ali a great fighter. He was the test, the implacable force who made Ali summon all of his own considerable reserves of skill, heart, and endurance for a final effort. The contest consumed them both. Neither was ever again a good fighter. But during their violent confrontation, winning or losing was, in the end, a marginal concern; that all-consuming effort was everything.

There are hundreds of similar examples of losers who showed us how to be more human, and their performances make the wide accept-ance of Lombardi's notions even more mystifying. Lombardi's thesis, in fact, represented something of a shift in the nation's popular thought. Americans had been the people who remembered the Alamo or Pearl Harbor; we blew taps over the graves of those who lost at the Battle of the Bulge or Anzio or the Yalu Basin. Those soldiers had all been defeated, but we honored them for their display of a critical human quality: courage.

Ernest Hemingway once defined courage as grace under pressure, and that's always struck me as an eminently useful definition. The best professional athletes not only possess that kind of courage but, more important, are willing to display it to strangers. Baseball's Reggie Jackson or Richard ("Goose") Gossage, for instance, function most completely as athletes and as men when appearing before gigantic crowds under pres-sure: bases loaded, late innings, a big game. They come to their tasks with gladness and absolute focus, neither whimpering, complaining nor shirking when doing their job; they just try their best to get that job done. And, of course, sometimes they fail. Gossage gives up a single and his team loses. Jackson strikes out. No matter. The important thing is that such men keep their appointments with confidence and grace. Courage has become so deep a part of their character that they don't even think about it. (They certainly *want* to win. Sometimes they absolutely lust for victory. But they know that winning isn't everything. All a man can do is his best.)

Competition isn't really a problem for Americans. All sports, in one way or another, are competitive. But an individual's primary competition is with himself and all his attendant weaknesses. That's obviously true of boxing, where fear must be donated and made to work to the fighter's benefit. Yet it's also true for team sports, as well as such solitary endeavors as golf, where a player must learn control before anything else. The problem isn't competition, which is a part of life; it's in the notion of the necessity of triumph. A man can lose but still win. And the point of competition in sports is an old and not very fashionable one: It builds character.

That's especially true of prizefighters, the athletes I've known best. Outside the ring, almost all fighters are the gentlest of men. They carry themselves with the dignity of those who have little to prove, either to others or themselves. They're never bullies, rarely use their dangerous skills against ordinary citizens and avoid pointless confrontations. When a fighter hears that a colleague has been involved in a bar brawl or a swingout with a cop, he dismisses that fighter as a cowardly bum. Most of the boxers I know are honest, generous, funny. Yet they also know that as good as they are, there might be someone down the line who has their number. Again, they would prefer to be winners. But they're aware that losing, if a courageous effort is made, is never a disgrace. The highest compliment one fighter can pay another is to say that he has "heart."

There are lessons to be learned from such athletes that can be applied to how we live our lives. In the long run, we'll all come up losers because there's no greater loss than death. And since primitive man first began to think, we humans have devised strategies to deal with dying. Religion is the most obvious one, usually demanding that we adhere to a moral code on earth in exchange for a serene existence after death. Ideologies offer secular versions of the same instinct, insisting that we sacrifice now, directing our lives toward the ideal of a better future, with each man becoming an architect of his own utopia. Patriotism and nationalism carry some of the same fearful baggage.

An athlete's goals are less cosmic, his field of struggle less grandiose and therefore more applicable to ordinary citizens. Great athletes teach us that life is a series of struggles, not one giant effort. Just when we appear to have triumphed, we must stop like Sisyphus and again begin rolling the boulder up that mountain. The true athlete teaches us that winning isn't everything, but struggle is—the struggle to simply get up in the morning or to see hope through the minefields of despair.

Viewed that way, a marriage, or any relationship with another human being, is an ongoing struggle. The mastering of a skill or craft doesn't end with the granting of a diploma; it goes on for life. The relationship between parents and children doesn't end when the children turn eighteen. The running of a corporation isn't a one-shot affair, measured by a single year's statements of profits and losses; it's a continuing process, accomplished by human beings who learn from mistakes, plunge fearlessly into the struggle, take risks and prepare for the future.

It's probably no accident that American capitalism, with its often permanently infantile male executives, experienced a decline that coincided with the period when Vince Lombardi's values received their widest acceptance. The results are visible everywhere. Sit on a plane with American businessmen and they'll be chattering about the Pittsburgh Steelers. Join a group of Japanese businessmen and they'll be discussing twenty-first-century technology. One group is trapped in a philosophy that demands winning as its goal; the other cares more about patient, long-term growth—and for the moment at least, the latter is winning.

Another great maxim of the years of America's triumphs also came from the sports pages via the writer Grantland Rice. "It matters not who won or lost," declared the esteemed chronicler of the prewar years, "but how they played the game." By the time Vince Lombardi came along, such sentiments were being sneered at. We had then become a superpower, capable of blowing up the world. The man of grace, courage, endurance, and compassion was replaced in the public imagination by the swaggering macho blowhard; Humphrey Bogart gave way to John Wayne. With such attitudes dominating the landscape, we were certain to get into trouble, and we did. Vietnam and Watergate underscored the idea of winning at all costs. Yet today we seem incapable of admitting that an obsession with winning often leads to the most squalid of defeats.

Solid marriages are often built upon the experience of disastrous ones. Politicians who lose elections become tempered for the contests that follow, sometimes going on to solid, useful careers. Painters, playwrights, novelists, and other artists often learn as much from their failures as they do from those rare moments when vision, craft, and ambition come together to produce masterpieces. It's also that way in sports.

I remember a night when my friend José Torres, then a middleweight, was boxing Florentino Fernandez in Puerto Rico. I couldn't go to the fight, so I spent the night tuning in and out of the all-news radio stations, anxious about the result because Florentino was a great puncher. About three in the morning, Torres called.

"Oh, Pete," he said, close to tears. "I'm so sorry."

"What happened?"

"I got knocked out," Torres replied, his voice brimming with emotion, since he'd never lost as a professional. We started discussing what had happened. Emotions cooled; the talk became technical. Torres explained that he had learned some things about himself, about boxing. He now understood some of his flaws, and thought he could correct them. We talked for an hour. Then I asked what he was going to do next.

"Go to the gym," he said. "I'm going to be champion of the world."

Two years later, Torres *was* the world's light-heavyweight champion. He didn't quit after his first defeat. That night in San Juan he didn't say winning was the only thing, that it was time to pack it in. He had learned something from defeat, and knew that one violent night, somewhere down the line, he would show the world what he had learned. And that was precisely what he did. But he was aware of something else too: Sooner or later, someone might come along who was better than he was, for at least one evening. After all, even champions are human. Even champions eventually lose. That happened to José Torres as well. But then it didn't really matter. José Torres, like the rest of us, had learned that winning wasn't everything. Living was all, and in life, defeat and victory are inseparable brothers.

INTERPRETATIONS

1. What is your reaction to Hamill's point that winning has been overemphasized in our society?

2. Why does Hamill think that in sports courage is more important than winning? Do you agree with his reasons? Why or why not?

3. "An individual's primary competition is with himself and all his attendant weaknesses." What point is Hamill making? To what extent do you agree with him?

4. Does Hamill downplay the importance of winning or does he expand our concepts of it by examining other ways of looking at the issue?

CORRESPONDENCES

1. At several points in his essay, Hamill states that life is not about the importance of winning but the necessity of struggling. To what extent is this true of Steffan's experience in "Honor Bound"?

2. Review Baez's perspective (page 405) and discuss its relevance to Hamill's essay. To what extent do you agree with Baez?

APPLICATIONS

1. Record your group's responses to the title of Hamill's essay. On what issues did you disagree?

2. For what audience was Hamill writing? Do you think his essay would appeal only to people interested in sports? Why or why not?

3. Hamill writes: "Living was all, and in life, defeat and victory are inseparable brothers." To what extent do you agree or disagree? How is it possible to transform defeat into victory? If you have had such an experience, analyze its effects in a brief essay.

4. What does it feel like to win a sporting event or contest? What body posture accompanies this mental state? Conversely, what does it feel like to lose? What body posture accompanies *this* mental state? Try to shift back and forth between these mental states and body postures. What do you notice as you make these transitions? Quickly write down your perception of these experiences.

To the Border

RICHARD RODRIGUEZ

Richard Rodriguez (b. 1944) was born to Mexican immigrant parents and attended Stanford University and the University of California at Berkeley, where he earned a doctorate in English Renaissance literature. His memoir Hunger of Memory *(1982) deals with the distance he felt from his Mexican culture by learning English. Rodriguez is also the author of* Days of Obligation: An Argument with My Mexican Father *(1992) and most recently* Brown: The Last Discovery of America *(2002). He is also a contributing editor for* Harper's *and a commentator on public television's* MacNeil/Lehrer News Hour. *Review Rodriguez's headnote, and write a journal entry speculating on the location of the border in his title.*

YOU STAND AROUND. You smoke. You spit. You are wearing your two shirts, two pants, two underpants. Jesús says if they chase you, throw that bag down. Your plastic bag is your mama, all you have left: the yellow cheese she wrapped has formed a translucent rind; the laminated scapular of the Sacred Heart nestles flame in its cleft. Put it in your pocket. Inside. Put it in your underneath pants' pocket. The last hour of Mexico is twilight, the shuffling of feet. Jesús says they are able to see in the dark. They have X rays and helicopters and searchlights. Jesús says wait, just wait, till he says. Though most of the men have started to move. You feel the hand of Jesús clamp your shoulder, fingers cold as ice. *Venga, corre.*[1] You run. All the rest happens without words. Your feet are tearing dry grass, your heart is lashed like a mare. You trip, you fall. You are now in the United States of America. You are a boy from a Mexican village. You have come into the country on your knees with your head down. You are a man.

Papa, what was it like?
I am his second son, his favorite child, his confidant. After we have polished the De Soto, we sit in the car and talk. I am sixteen years old. I fiddle with the knobs of the radio. He is fifty.

---

[1] Go, run.

He will never say. He was an orphan there. He had no mother, he remembered none. He lived in a village by the ocean. He wanted books and he had none.

You are lucky, boy.

In the Fifties, Mexican men were contracted to work in America as *braceros*, farm workers. I saw them downtown in Sacramento. I saw men my age drunk in Plaza Park on Sundays, on their backs on the grass. I was a boy at sixteen, but I was an American. At sixteen, I wrote a gossip column, "The Watchful Eye," for my school paper.

Or they would come into town on Monday nights for the wrestling matches or on Tuesdays for boxing. They worked over in Yolo County. They were men without women. They were Mexicans without Mexico.

On Saturdays, they came into town to the Western Union office where they sent money—money turned into humming wire and then turned back into money—all the way down into Mexico. They were husbands, fathers, sons. They kept themselves poor for Mexico.

Much that I would come to think, the best I would think about male Mexico, came as much from those chaste, lonely men as from my own father who made false teeth and who—after thirty years in America—owned a yellow stucco house on the east side of town.

The male is responsible. The male is serious. A man remembers.

Fidel, the janitor at church, lived over the garage at the rectory. Fidel spoke Spanish and was Mexican. He had a wife down there, people said; some said he had grown children. But too many years had passed and he didn't go back. Fidel had to do for himself. Fidel had a clean piece of linoleum on the floor, he had an iron bed, he had a table and a chair. He had a coffeepot and a frying pan and a knife and a fork and a spoon, I guess. And everything else Fidel sent back to Mexico. Sometimes, on summer nights, I would see his head through the bars of the little window over the garage at the rectory.

The migration of Mexico is not only international, south to north. The epic migration of Mexico, and throughout Latin America, is from the village to the city. And throughout Latin America, the city has ripened, swollen with the century. Lima, Caracas, Mexico City. So the journey to Los Angeles is much more than a journey from Spanish to English. It is the journey from *tú*—the familiar, the erotic, the intimate pronoun—to the repellent *usted* of strangers' eyes.

It is 1986 and I am a journalist. I am asking questions of a Mexican woman in her East L.A. house. She is watchful and pretty, in her thirties, she wears an apron. Her two boys—Roy and Danny—are playing next door. Her husband is a tailor. He is sewing in a bright bedroom at the back of the house. His feet work the humming treadle of an old Singer machine as he croons Mexican love songs by an open window.

I will send for you or I will come home rich.

Mexico is poor. But my mama says there are no love songs like the love songs of Mexico. She hums a song she can't remember. The ice cream there is creamier than here. Someday we will see. The people are kinder—poor, but kinder to each other.

My mother's favorite record is *"Mariachis de Mexico y Pepe Villa con Orquesta."*

Men sing in Mexico. Men are strong and silent. But in song the Mexican male is granted license he is otherwise denied. The male can admit longing, pain, desire.

HAIII—EEEE—a cry like a comet rises over the song. A cry like mock weeping tickles the refrain of Mexican love songs. The cry is meant to encourage the balladeer—it is the raw edge of his sentiment. HAIII-EEEE. It is the man's sound. A ticklish arching of semen, a node wrung up a guitar string, until it bursts in a descending cascade of mockery. HAI. HAI. HAI. The cry of a jackal under the moon, the whistle of the phallus, the maniacal song of the skull.

Mexico is on the phone—long-distance.

A crow alights upon a humming wire, bobs up and down, needles the lice within his vest, surveys with clicking eyes the field, the cloud of mites, then dips into the air and flies away.

Juanito killed! My mother shrieks, drops the phone in the dark. She cries for my father. For light.

The earth quakes. The peso flies like chaff in the wind. The police chief purchases his mistress a mansion on the hill.

The door bell rings. I split the blinds to see three nuns standing on our front porch.

Mama. Mama.

Monsignor Lyons has sent three Mexican nuns over to meet my parents. The nuns have come to Sacramento to beg for Mexico at the eleven o'clock Mass. We are the one family in the parish that speaks Spanish. As they file into our living room, the nuns smell pure, not sweet, pure like candles or like laundry.

The nun with a black mustache sighs at the end of each story the other two tell. Orphan. Leper. Crutch. Dry land. One eye. Casket.

¡Que lástima![2]
Tell me, Papa.
What?
About Mexico.

I lived with the family of my uncle. I was the orphan in the village. I used to ring the church bells in the morning, many steps up in the dark. When I'd get up to the tower I could see the ocean.
The village, Papa, the houses too . . .
The ocean. He studies the polished hood of our beautiful blue De Soto.

Relatives invited relatives. Entire Mexican villages got re-created in three stories of a single house. In the fall, after the harvest in the Valley, families of Mexican adults and their American children would load up their cars and head back to Mexico in caravans, for weeks, for months. The schoolteacher said to my mother what a shame it was the Mexicans did that—took their children out of school.
Like Wandering Jews. They carried their home with them, back and forth; they had no true home but the tabernacle of memory.
Each year the American kitchen takes on a new appliance.
The children are fed and grow tall. They go off to school with children from Vietnam, from Kansas, from Hong Kong. They get into fights. They come home and they say dirty words.
The city will win. The city will give the children all the village could not—VCRs, hairstyles, drumbeat. The city sings mean songs, dirty songs. But the city will sing the children a great Protestant hymn.
You can be anything you want to be.
Your coming of age. It is early. From your bed you watch your mama moving back and forth under the light. The bells of the church ring in the dark. Mama crosses herself. From your bed you watch her back as she wraps the things you will take.
You are sixteen. Your father has sent for you. That's what it means. He has sent an address in Nevada. He is there with your uncle. You remember your uncle remembering snow with his beer.
You dress in the shadows. You move toward the table, the circle of light. You sit down. You force yourself to eat. Mama stands over you to make the sign of the cross on your forehead with her thumb. You are a man. You smile. She puts the bag of food in your hands. She says she has told *La Virgen.*

[2]What a pity!

Then you are gone. It is gray. You hear a little breeze. It is the rustle of your old black Dueña, the dog, taking her shortcuts through the weeds, crazy Dueña, her pads on the dust. She is following you.

You pass the houses of the village, each window is a proper name. You pass the store. The bar. The lighted window of the clinic where the pale medical student from Monterrey lives alone and reads his book full of sores late into the night.

You want to be a man. You have the directions in your pocket: an address in Tijuana and a map with a yellow line that leads from the highway to an X on a street in Reno. You are afraid, but you have never seen snow.

You are just beyond the cemetery. The breeze has died. You turn and throw a rock back at La Dueña, where you know she is—where you will always know where she is. She will not go past the cemetery. She will turn in circles like a *loca*[3] and bite herself.

The dust takes on gravel, the path becomes a rutted road which leads to the highway. You walk north. The sky has turned white overhead. Insects click in the fields. In time, there will be a bus.

I will send for you or I will come home rich.

INTERPRETATIONS

1. Who is the "you" in the first (and subsequent) sentence? What choice has been made?

2. What attitude did the sixteen-year-old Rodriguez have toward the Mexican farmworkers he saw downtown in Sacramento? How far removed from their situation was his? How does this account for his attitude?

3. What attitude toward the United States is revealed by the last line of the essay?

4. The last vignette of this essay describes the beginning of a voyage from the known to the unknown: ". . . each window is a proper name." What are some of the "knowns" the Mexican boy is leaving? Why do you think Rodriguez chose to include each of them? What is their combined impact?

5. Rodriguez avoids a bald statement of his main point or thesis, apparently preferring to create a mood and force his reader to intuit meaning. What is the mood and the point?

---

[3]Crazy woman.

CORRESPONDENCES

1. "So the journey to Los Angeles is much more than a journey from Spanish to English. It is the journey from *tú*—the familiar, the erotic, the intimate pronoun—to the repellant *usted* of strangers' eyes." What is Rodriguez implying about the personal costs involved in "choosing" to cross the border? Apply the Nin perspective (page 405) to Rodriguez's essay.

2. "The male is responsible. The male is serious. A man remembers." What point is Rodriguez making in these statements? What conversation can you imagine him having with Steffan? On what issues might they agree?

APPLICATIONS

1. Rodriguez writes that the Mexican migrant workers are "[l]ike Wandering Jews. They carried their home with them, back and forth; they had no true home but the tabernacle of memory." What is the meaning here of "tabernacle"? In what sense does memory serve as a refuge? At what price does one "choose" to become a migrant worker? Discuss the questions with your group.

2. To what extent do the expectations of other people—parents, friends, peers, relatives—influence choices? Is there a decision that you made based on outside pressure? If so, describe your dilemma and the factors that motivated your choice. In retrospect, was it the "right" choice?

3. Has your family chosen to leave their native culture to emigrate to the United States? If so, how has this choice affected their cultural and linguistic identities? To what extent have they assimilated? What changes have occurred in your family's lifestyle?

4. What soundtrack might accompany the essay "To the Border"? Write an essay that describes the music that you hear. (Or, if possible, record a song or two that you have composed.)

Living in Two Worlds

MARCUS MABRY

Marcus Mabry (b. 1967) received a Master of Arts degree from Stanford University and joined Newsweek *in 1989 as an associate editor. In 1996, Mabry and a colleague won the Overseas Press Club's Morton Frank Award for Best Business Reporting for their cover story, "End of the Good Life?" Mabry has also won the New York Association of Black Journalists award for Personal Commentary (1992), and a Lincoln University Unity Award in Media in 1991. Mabry is author of the 1995 memoir* White Bucks and Black-Eyed Peas: Coming of Age Black in White America. *He was named Chief of Correspondents for* Newsweek *in 2002. The following essay was originally published in the 1988 issue of* Newsweek on Campus. *Before reading Mabry's essay, record in your journal your responses to his title.*

A ROUND, GREEN CARDBOARD SIGN hangs from a string proclaiming, "We built a proud new feeling" the slogan of a local supermarket. It is a souvenir from one of my brother's last jobs. In addition to being a bagger, he's worked at a fast-food restaurant, a gas station, a garage and a textile factory. Now, in the icy clutches of the Northeastern winter, he is unemployed. He will soon be a father. He is nineteen years old.

In mid-December I was at Stanford, among the palm trees and weighty chores of academe. And all I wanted to do was get out. I joined the rest of the undergrads in a chorus of excitement, singing the praises of Christmas break. No classes, no midterms, no finals . . . and no freshmen! (I'm a resident assistant.) Awesome! I was looking forward to escaping. I never gave a thought to what I was escaping to.

Once I got home to New Jersey, reality returned. My dreaded freshmen had been replaced by unemployed relatives; badgering professors had been replaced by hard-working single mothers, and cold classrooms by dilapidated bedrooms and kitchens. The room in which the "proud new feeling" sign hung contained the belongings of myself, my mom and my brother. But for these two weeks it was mine. They slept downstairs on couches.

Most students who travel between the universes of poverty and affluence during breaks experience similar conditions, as well as the guilt, the helplessness and, sometimes, the embarrassment associated with them. Our friends are willing to listen, but most of them are unable to imagine the pain of the impoverished lives that we see every six months. Each time I return home I feel further away from the realities of poverty in America and more ashamed that they are allowed to persist. What frightens me most is not that the American socioeconomic system permits poverty to continue, but that by participating in that system I share some of the blame.

Last year I lived in an on-campus apartment, with a (relatively) modern bathroom, kitchen and two bedrooms. Using summer earnings, I added some expensive prints, a potted palm and some other plants, making the place look like the more-than-humble abode of a New York City Yuppie. I gave dinner parties, even a *soirée française.*

For my roommate, a doctor's son, this kind of life was nothing extraordinary. But my mom was struggling to provide a life for herself and my brother. In addition to working 24-hour-a-day cases as a practical nurse, she was trying to ensure that my brother would graduate from high school and have a decent life. She knew that she had to compete for his attention with drugs and other potentially dangerous things that can look attractive to a young man when he sees no better future.

Living in my grandmother's house this Christmas break restored all the forgotten, and the never acknowledged, guilt. I had gone to boarding school on a full scholarship since the ninth grade, so being away from poverty was not new. But my own growing affluence has increased my distance. My friends say that I should not feel guilty: what could I do substantially for my family at this age, they ask. Even though I know that education is the right thing to do, I can't help but feel, sometimes, that I have it too good. There is no reason that I deserve security and warmth, while my brother has to cope with potential unemployment and prejudice. I, too, encounter prejudice, but it is softened by my status as a student in an affluent and intellectual community.

More than my sense of guilt, my sense of helplessness increases each time I return home. As my success leads me further away for longer periods of time poverty becomes harder to conceptualize and feels that much more oppressive when I visit with it. The first night of break, I lay in our bedroom, on a couch that let out into a bed that took up the whole room, except for a space heater. It was a little hard to sleep because the springs from the couch stuck through at inconvenient spots. But it would have been impossible to sleep anyway because of the groans coming from my grandmother's room next door. Only in her early 60s, she suffers from many chronic diseases and couldn't help but moan, then pray aloud, then moan, then pray aloud.

This wrenching of my heart was interrupted by the 3 A.M. entry of a relative who had been allowed to stay at the house despite rowdy behavior and threats toward the family in the past. As he came into the house, he slammed the door, and his heavy steps shook the second floor as he stomped into my grandmother's room to take his place, at the foot of her bed. There he slept, without blankets on a bare mattress. This was the first night. Later in the vacation, a Christmas turkey and a Christmas ham were stolen from my aunt's refrigerator on Christmas Eve. We think the thief was a relative. My mom and I decided not to exchange gifts that year because it just didn't seem festive.

A few days after New Year's I returned to California. The Northeast was soon hit by a blizzard. They were there, and I was here. That was the way it had to be, for now. I haven't forgotten; the ache of knowing their suffering is always there. It has to be kept deep down, or I can't find the logic in studying and partying while people, my people, are being killed by poverty. Ironically, success drives me away from those I most want to help by getting an education.

Somewhere in the midst of all that misery, my family has built, within me, "a proud feeling." As I travel between the two worlds it becomes harder to remember just how proud I should be—not just because of where I have come from and where I am going, but because of where they are. The fact that they live in the world in which they live is something to be very proud of, indeed. It inspires within me a sense of tenacity and accomplishment that I hope every college graduate will someday possess.

INTERPRETATIONS

1. Compare and contrast Mabry's two worlds. In which does he feel most himself?

2. Review the last paragraph of the essay. To what extent has his background contributed to his survival?

3. Identify the tone of his essay. Is it appropriate for the subject? Explain.

CORRESPONDENCES

1. Compare and contrast the ramifications of the personal choices made in "To the Border" and "Living in Two Worlds."

2. Review Baldwin's perspective on choices (page 405). How does it apply to "Living in Two Worlds"? To what extent is Mabry "trapped in history"? Cite evidence for your point of view.

APPLICATIONS

1. Discuss with your group the inequities of social class as described in Mabry's essay. What is ironic about his success?

2. Is Mabry a divided self? Characterize his "two worlds." How have his choices contributed to his emotional conflicts? To what extent is he an outsider in both worlds? Can you imagine making a similar choice?

3. Assume you and your family had to forcibly leave your home. What three items would you carry with you? Write a short essay on your emotional attachment to each.

4. What do you think one of Marcus Mabry's relatives would say to him after reading "Living in Two Worlds"? Using the voice of that individual, write a letter to Mabry that expresses your thoughts and feelings.

The Fender-Bender

RAMÓN "TIANGUIS" PÉREZ

Ramón "Tianguis" Pérez is an undocumented alien. Of necessity he does not disclose information about his life or his whereabouts. "The Fender-Bender" is an excerpt from his book Diary of an Undocumented Immigrant *(1991) and gives a glimpse of his life in this country.*

ONE NIGHT AFTER WORK, I drive Rolando's old car to visit some friends, and then head towards home. At a light, I come to a stop too late, leaving the front end of the car poking into the crosswalk. I shift into reverse, but as I am backing up, I strike the van behind me. Its driver immediately gets out to inspect the damage to his vehicle. He's a tall Anglo-Saxon, dressed in a deep blue work uniform. After looking at his car, he walks up to the window of the car I'm driving.

"Your driver's license," he says, a little enraged.

"I didn't bring it," I tell him.

He scratches his head. He is breathing heavily with fury.

"Okay," he says. "You park up ahead while I call a patrolman."

The idea of calling the police doesn't sound good to me, but the accident is my fault. So I drive around the corner and park at the curb. I turn off the motor and hit the steering wheel with one fist. I don't have a driver's license. I've never applied for one. Nor do I have with me the identification card that I bought in San Antonio. Without immigration papers, without a driving permit, and having hit another car, I feel as if I'm just one step away from Mexico.

I get out of the car. The white man comes over and stands right in front of me. He's almost two feet taller.

"If you're going to drive, why don't you carry your license?" he asks in an accusatory tone.

"I didn't bring it," I say, for lack of any other defense.

I look at the damage to his car. It's minor, only a scratch on the paint and a pimple-sized dent.

"I'm sorry," I say. "Tell me how much it will cost to fix, and I'll pay for it; that's no problem." I'm talking to him in English, and he seems to understand.

"This car isn't mine," he says. "It belongs to the company I work for. I'm sorry, but I've got to report this to the police, so that I don't have to pay for the damage."

"That's no problem," I tell him again. "I can pay for it."

After we've exchanged these words, he seems less irritated. But he says he'd prefer for the police to come, so that they can report that the dent wasn't his fault.

While we wait, he walks from one side to the other, looking down the avenue this way and that, hoping that the police will appear.

Then he goes over to the van to look at the dent.

"It's not much," he says. "If it was my car, there wouldn't be any problems, and you could go on."

After a few minutes, the long-awaited police car arrives. Only one officer is inside. He's a Chicano, short and of medium complexion, with short, curly hair. On getting out of the car, he walks straight towards the Anglo.

The two exchange a few words.

"Is that him?" he asks, pointing at me.

The Anglo nods his head.

Speaking in English, the policeman orders me to stand in front of the car and to put my hands on the hood. He searches me and finds only the car keys and my billfold with a few dollars in it. He asks for my driver's license.

"I don't have it," I answer in Spanish.

He wrinkles his face into a frown, and casting a glance at the Anglo, shakes his head in disapproval of me.

"That's the way these Mexicans are," he says.

He turns back towards me, asking for identification. I tell him I don't have that, either.

"You're an illegal, eh?" he says.

I won't answer.

"An illegal," he says to himself.

"Where do you live?" he continues. He's still speaking in English.

I tell him my address.

"Do you have anything with you to prove that you live at that address?" he asks.

I think for a minute, then realize that in the glove compartment is a letter that my parents sent to me several weeks earlier.

I show him the envelope and he immediately begins to write something in a little book that he carries in his back pocket. He walks to the back of my car and copies the license plate number. Then he goes over to his car and talks into his radio. After he talks, someone answers. Then he asks me for the name of the car's owner.

He goes over to where the Anglo is standing. I can't quite hear what they're saying. But when the two of them go over to look at the dent in the van, I hear the cop tell the Anglo that if he wants, he can file charges against me. The Anglo shakes his head and explains what he had earlier explained to me, about only needing for the police to certify that he wasn't responsible for the accident. The Anglo says that he doesn't want to accuse me of anything because the damage is light.

"If you want, I can take him to jail," the cop insists.

The Anglo turns him down again.

"If you'd rather, we can report him to Immigration," the cop continues.

Just as at the first, I am now almost sure that I'll be making a forced trip to Tijuana. I find myself searching my memory for my uncle's telephone number, and to my relief, I remember it. I am waiting for the Anglo to say yes, confirming my expectations of the trip. But instead, he says no, and though I remain silent, I feel appreciation for him. I ask myself why the Chicano is determined to harm me. I didn't really expect him to favor me, just because we're of the same ancestry, but on the other hand, once I had admitted my guilt, I expected him to treat me at least fairly. But even against the white man's wishes, he's trying to make matters worse for me. I've known several Chicanos with whom, joking around, I've reminded them that their roots are in Mexico. But very few of them see it that way. Several have told me how when they were children, their parents would take them to vacation in different states of Mexico, but their own feeling, they've said, is, "I am an American citizen!" Finally, the Anglo, with the justifying paper in his hands, says goodbye to the cop, thanks him for his services, gets into his van and drives away.

The cop stands in the street in a pensive mood. I imagine that he's trying to think of a way to punish me.

"Put the key in the ignition," he orders me.

I do as he says.

Then he orders me to roll up the windows and lock the doors.

"Now, go on, walking," he says.

I go off taking slow steps. The cop gets in his patrol car and stays there, waiting. I turn the corner after two blocks and look out for my car, but the cop is still parked beside it. I begin looking for a coat hanger, and after a good while, find one by a curb of the street. I keep walking, keeping about two blocks away from the car. While I walk, I bend the coat hanger into the form I'll need. As if I'd called for it, a speeding car goes past. When it comes to the avenue where my car is parked, it makes a turn. It is going so fast that its wheels screech as it rounds the corner. The cop turns on the blinking lights of his patrol car and leaving black marks on the pavement beneath it, shoots out to chase the speeder. I go up to my car and with my palms force a window open a crack. Then I insert the clothes hanger in the crack and raise the lock lever. It's a simple task, one that I'd already performed. This wasn't the first time that I'd been locked out of a car, though always before, it was because I'd forgotten to remove my keys.

INTERPRETATIONS

1. Compare and contrast the attitudes of the Anglo driver and the Chicano cop at the scene of the fender-bender.

2. Why do you think the Anglo chooses not to report the illegal alien to Immigration? Does it surprise you that the cop is intent on punishing the Mexican? Why or why not?

3. Characterize the tone of the narrative. Is it objective? Subjective? Ironic?

CORRESPONDENCES

1. Review Fanon's perspective on choices (page 406) and discuss its relevance to "The Fender-Bender."

2. Rodriguez and Pérez portray aspects of the illegal immigrants' experience in the United States. Characterize your response to both selections.

APPLICATIONS

1. Discuss with your group stereotyping in "The Fender-Bender."

2. Review the last paragraph of the essay. What does it reveal about the attitude of the "illegal" toward his situation? Write an essay discussing the thematic implications of the author's use of irony in "The Fender-Bender."

3. The rights and status of illegal aliens became the subject of national debate in the last decade resulting in severe penalties and legal restrictions. What is your point of view? Do you think, for example, that "illegals" pose a threat to the job market given the fact that most of them are involved in menial tasks and paid below minimum wage? Summarize your discussion.

Homeplace

SCOTT RUSSELL SANDERS

Scott Russell Sanders (b. 1945) is a distinguished Professor of English at Indiana University, where he currently directs the Wells Scholars Program. Sanders is a frequent contributor to journals such as Audubon, Harper's, Orion, North American Review, *and* Utne Reader *among others. His novels include* Bad Man Ballad *(1986),* The Invisible Company *(1989),* The Engineer of Beasts *(1988), and* Terrarium *(1985). Sanders's non-fiction includes:* Essays: Scott Russell Sanders *(1998),* Writing From Center *(1995),* Wilderness Plots *(1983),* The Paradise of Bombs *(1987),* Fetching the Dead *(1984),* In Limestone Country *(1991),* Secrets of the Universe *(1993),* Staying Put *(1993), and* Hear the Wind Blow *(1985). Sanders's work has also been selected for* The Best American Essays, *the PEN Syndicated Fiction Award, and the Gamma Award. Write a journal entry on your associations with "Homeplace."*

As a boy in Ohio, I knew a farm family, the Millers, who suffered from three tornadoes. The father, mother, and two sons were pulling into their driveway after church when the first tornado hoisted up their mobile home, spun it around, and carried it off. With the insurance money, they built a small frame house on the same spot.

Several years later, a second tornado peeled off the roof, splintered the garage, and rustled two cows. The Millers rebuilt again, raising a new garage on the old foundation and adding another story to the house. That upper floor was reduced to kindling by a third tornado, which also pulled out half the apple trees and slurped water from the stock pond. Soon after that I left Ohio, snatched away by college as forcefully as by any cyclone. Last thing I heard, the family was preparing to rebuild yet again.

Why did the Millers refuse to move? I knew them well enough to say they were neither stupid nor crazy. Plain stubbornness was a factor. These were people who, once settled, might have remained at the foot of a volcano or on the bank of a flood-prone river or beside an earthquake fault. They had relatives nearby, helpful neighbors, jobs and stores and schools within a short drive, and those were all good reasons to stay. But the main reason, I believe, was that the Millers had invested so much of their lives in the land, planting orchards and gardens, spreading manure on the fields, digging ponds, building sheds, seeding pastures. Out back of the house were groves of walnuts, hickories, and oaks, all started by hand from acorns and nuts. April through October, perennial flowers in the yard pumped out a fountain of blossoms. This farm was not just so many acres of dirt, easily exchanged for an equal amount elsewhere; it was a particular place, intimately known, worked on, dreamed over, cherished.

Psychologists tell us that we answer trouble with one of two impulses, either fight or flight. I believe that the Millers exhibited a third instinct, that of staying put. They knew better than to fight a tornado, and they chose not to flee. Their commitment to the place may have been foolhardy, but it was also grand. I suspect that most human achievements worth admiring are the result of such devotion.

The Millers dramatize a choice we are faced with constantly; whether to go or stay, whether to move to a situation that is safer, richer, easier, more attractive, or to stick where we are and make what we can of it. If the shine goes off our marriage, our house, our car, do we trade it for a new one? If the fertility leaches out of our soil, the creativity out of our job, the money out of our pocket, do we start over somewhere else? There are voices enough, both inner and outer, urging us to deal with difficulties by pulling up stakes and heading for new territory. I know them well, for they have been calling to me all my days. I wish to raise here a contrary voice, to say a few words on behalf of staying put, learning the ground, going deeper.

Claims for the virtues of moving on are familiar and seductive to Americans, this nation founded by immigrants and shaped by restless seekers. From the beginning, our heroes have been sailors, explorers, cowboys, prospectors, speculators, backwoods ramblers, rainbow chasers, vagabonds of every stripe. Our Promised Land has always been over the next ridge or at the end of the trail, never under our feet. In our national mythology, the worst fate is to be trapped on a farm, in a village, in the sticks, in some dead-end job or unglamorous marriage or played-out game.

Stand still, we are warned, and you die. Americans have dug the most canals, laid the most rails, built the most roads and airports of any nation. In a newspaper I read that, even though our sprawling system of interstate highways is crumbling, politicians think we should triple its size. Only a populace drunk on driving, a populace infatuated with the myth of the open road, could hear such a proposal without hooting.

Novelist Salman Rushdie chose to leave his native India for England, where he has written a series of brilliant books from the perspective of a cultural immigrant. In his book of essays *Imaginary*

Homelands he celebrates the migrant sensibility: "The effect of mass migrations has been the creation of radically new types of human being: people who root themselves in ideas rather than places, in memories as much as in material things." He goes on to say that "to be a migrant is, perhaps, to be the only species of human being free of the shackles of nationalism (to say nothing of its ugly sister, patriotism)." Lord knows we could do with less nationalism (to say nothing of its ugly siblings, racism, religious sectarianism, and class snobbery). But who would pretend that a history of migration has immunized the United States against bigotry? And even if, by uprooting ourselves, we shed our chauvinism, is that all we lose?

In this hemisphere, many of the worst abuses—of land, forests, animals, and communities—have been carried out by "people who root themselves in ideas rather than places." Migrants often pack up their visions and values with the rest of their baggage and carry them along. The Spaniards devastated Central and South America by imposing on this New World the religion, economics, and politics of the Old. Colonists brought slavery with them to North America, along with smallpox and Norway rats. The Dust Bowl of the 1930s was caused not by drought but by the transfer onto the Great Plains of farming methods that were suitable to wetter regions. The habit of our industry and commerce has been to force identical schemes onto differing locales, as though the mind were a cookie cutter and the land were dough.

I quarrel with Rushdie because he articulates as eloquently as anyone the orthodoxy that I wish to counter: the belief that movement is inherently good, staying put is bad; that uprooting brings tolerance, while rootedness breeds intolerance; that to be modern, enlightened, fully of our time is to be displaced. Wholesale displacement may be inevitable in today's world; but we should not suppose that it occurs without disastrous consequences for the earth and for ourselves. People who root themselves in places are likelier to know and care for those places than are people who root themselves in ideas. When we cease to be migrants and become inhabitants, we might begin to pay enough heed and respect to where we are. By settling in, we have a chance of making a durable home for ourselves, our fellow creatures, and our descendants.

The poet Gary Snyder writes frequently about our need to "inhabit" a place. One of the key problems in American society now, he points out, is people's lack of commitment to any given place;

> Neighborhoods are allowed to deteriorate, landscapes are allowed to be strip-mined, because there is nobody who will live there and take responsibility; they'll just move on. The

reconstruction of a people and of a life in the United States depends in part on people, neighborhood by neighborhood, county by county, deciding to stick it out and make it work where they are, rather than flee.

But if you stick in one place, won't you become a stick-in-the-mud? If you stay put, won't you be narrow, backward, dull? You might. I have met ignorant people who never moved; and I have also met ignorant people who never stood still. Committing yourself to a place does not guarantee that you will become wise, but neither does it guarantee that you will become parochial.

To become intimate with your home region, to know the territory as well as you can, to understand your life as woven into the local life does not prevent you from recognizing and honoring the diversity of other places, cultures, ways. On the contrary, how can you value other places if you do not have one of your own? If you are not yourself *placed*, then you wander the world like a sightseer, a collector of sensations, with no gauge for measuring what you see. Local knowledge is the grounding for global knowledge. Those who care about nothing beyond the confines of their parish are in truth parochial, and are at least mildly dangerous to their parish; on the other hand, those who *have* no parish, those who navigate ceaselessly among postal zones and area codes, those for whom the world is only a smear of highways and bank accounts and stores, are a danger not just to their parish but to the planet.

Since birth, my children have regularly seen images of the earth as viewed from space, images that I first encountered when I was in my twenties. Those photographs show vividly what in our sanest moments we have always known—that the earth is a closed circle, lovely and rare. On the wall beside me as I write there is a poster of the big blue marble encased in its white swirl of clouds. That is one pole of my awareness; but the other pole is what I see through my window. I try to keep both in sight at once.

For all my convictions, I still have to wrestle with the fear—in myself, in my children, and even in some of my neighbors—that our place is too remote from the action. This fear drives many people to pack their bags and move to some resort or burg they have seen on television, leaving behind what they learn to think of as the boondocks. I deal with my own unease by asking just what action I am remote *from*—a stock market? a debating chamber? a drive-in mortuary? The action that matters, the work of nature and community, goes on everywhere.

Since Copernicus, we have known better than to see the earth as the center of the universe. Since Einstein, we have learned that there is no center; or alternatively, that any point is as good as any other for observing the world. I find a kindred lesson in the words of the Zen master Thich Nhat Hanh: "This spot where you sit is your own spot. It is on this very spot and in this very moment that you can become enlightened. You don't have to sit beneath a special tree in a distant land." If you stay put, your place may become a holy center, not because it gives you special access to the divine, but because in your stillness you hear what might be heard anywhere.

I think of my home ground as a series of nested rings, with house and family and marriage at the center, surrounded by the wider and wider hoops of neighborhood and community, the bioregion within walking distance of my door, the wooded and rocky hills of southern Indiana, the watershed of the Ohio Valley, and so on outward—and inward—to the ultimate source.

The longing to become an inhabitant rather than a drifter sets me against the current of my culture, which nudges everyone into motion. Newton taught us that a body at rest tends to stay at rest, unless it is acted on by an outside force. We are acted on ceaselessly by outside forces—advertising, movies, magazines, speeches—and also by the inner force of biology. I am not immune to their pressure. Before settling in my present home, I lived in seven states and two countries, tugged from place to place in childhood by my father's work and in early adulthood by my own. This itinerant life is so common among the people I know that I have been slow to conceive of an alternative. Only by knocking against the golden calf of mobility, which looms so large and shines so brightly, have I come to realize that it is hollow. Like all idols, it distracts us from what is truly divine.

I am encouraged by the words of a Crow elder, quoted by Gary Snyder in *The Practice of the Wild*: "You know, I think if people stay somewhere long enough—even white people—the spirits will begin to speak to them. It's the power of the spirits coming up from the land. The spirits and the old powers aren't lost, they just need people to be around long enough and the spirits will begin to influence them."

As I write this, I hear the snarl of earth movers and chain saws a mile away destroying a farm to make way for another shopping strip. I would rather hear a tornado, whose damage can be undone. The elderly woman who owned the farm had it listed in the National Register, then willed it to her daughters on condition they preserve it. After her death, the daughters, who live out of state, had the will broken, so the land could be turned over to the chain saws and earth movers. The machines work around the clock. Their noise wakes me at midnight, at three in the morning, at dawn. The roaring abrades my dreams. The sound is a reminder that we are living in the midst of a holocaust. I do not use the word lightly. The earth is being pillaged, and every one of

us, willingly or grudgingly, is taking part. We ask how sensible, educated, supposedly moral people could have tolerated slavery or the
slaughter of Jews. Similar questions will be asked about us by our
descendants, to whom we bequeath an impoverished planet. They will
demand to know how we could have been party to such waste and ruin.

What does it mean to be alive in an era when the earth is being
devoured, and in a country that has set the pattern for that devouring?
What are we called to do? I think we are called to the work of healing,
both inner and outer: healing of the mind through a change in consciousness, healing of the earth through a change in our lives. We can
begin that work by learning how to inhabit a place.

"The man who is often thinking that it is better to be somewhere
else than where he is excommunicates himself," we are cautioned by
Thoreau, that notorious stay-at-home. The metaphor is religious: To
withhold yourself from where you are is to be cut off from communion
with the source. It has taken me half a lifetime of searching to realize
that the likeliest path to the ultimate ground leads through my local
ground. I mean the land itself, with its creeks and rivers, its weather,
seasons, stone outcroppings, and all the plants and animals that share
it. I cannot have a spiritual center without having a geographical one;
I cannot live a grounded life without being grounded in a *place*.

In belonging to a landscape, one feels a rightness, an at-homeness,
a knitting of self and world. This condition of clarity and focus, this
being fully present, is akin to what the Buddhists call mindfulness,
what Christian contemplatives refer to as recollection, what Quakers
call centering down. I am suspicious of any philosophy that would
separate this-worldly from other-worldly commitment. There is only
one world, and we participate in it here and now, in our flesh and our
place.

INTERPRETATIONS

1. How effective is it that Sanders begins his essay with the story of
   the Millers? Do you share his admiration for their choosing to
   rebuild their house after each tornado? Why or why not?

2. Review paragraph 6. How do you interpret "national mythology"?
   To what extent do you agree that Americans are seduced by the
   virtues of moving on?

3. Sanders believes that people who remain in one place are more
   likely to be involved in community service. To what extent do you
   agree? Do you share his commitment to civil responsibility? Cite
   reasons for your answer.

CORRESPONDENCES

1. Imagine a conversation between Rodriguez and Sanders on the subject of home. What points are they likely to disagree on? What experiences would you bring to the discussion?

2. Review Lawrence's perspective on place (page 405). What is your response? How does it apply to Sanders's essay?

APPLICATIONS

1. Are you someone who likes to be on the move or who prefers to stay in one place? As you contemplate the future, are you likely to change your opinion? Depending on your stand on this issue, what factors would you consider in deciding to stay or move? Write a brief essay on the subject.

2. Freewrite on your concept of home. Focus on the images and associations that the word evokes. Then write an essay defining what home means to you.

3. Discuss with your group Sanders's thesis that "Committing yourself to a place does not guarantee that you will become wise, but neither does it guarantee that you will become parochial." Frame your discussion by defining "wise" and "parochial" and make a summary of your findings.

4. Being in motion or staying still—these are the choices explored by Sanders in his essay. Walk around a room briskly for five minutes. Then sit still for five minutes. Write down your thoughts pertaining to what you perceive about each of these five-minute sessions. How do your responses relate to what Sanders has written about in his piece?

One of These Days

GABRIEL GARCÍA MÁRQUEZ

Gabriel García Márquez (b. 1928) was born in Aracataca, Colombia and raised by grandparents who told him many fables and fairy tales. García Márquez dropped out of law school to pursue a career in journalism, and was a regular contributor to El Espectador *and other newspapers before dedicating himself to writing fiction full time. His first book* Leaf Storm and Other Stories, *was published in 1955.* One Hundred Years of Solitude, *García Márquez's most successful and popular novel, was written in 1967. García Márquez's other major literary works include:* Chronicle of a Death Foretold *(1981),* Love in the Time of Cholera *(1988),* The General in His Labyrinth *(1990),* Of Love and Other Demons *(1994), and* News of a Kidnapping *(1996). García Márquez's memoir,* Living to Tell the Tale, *was published in the United States in fall 2003. Before reading Márquez's story, record in your journal your thoughts on the concept of revenge.*

García Márquez's Colombia, which is about the size of California and Texas, is located in northwestern South America and bordered by Panama, Venezuela, Brazil, Peru, and Ecuador. Like many South American countries, Colombia has a long history of violence and political upheaval. A brutal civil war began in 1899 and lasted until 1902. 1946–1958 is known as the La Violencia period, since hundreds of thousands of lives were lost due to insurrection and banditry. The emergence of the infamous guerilla Marxist groups like the National Liberation Army (ELN) and the Revolutionary Armed Forces of Colombia (FARC) in the 1960s and 1970s, drove the country further into violence and instability. During the 1970s and 1980s Colombia was known around the world for its international drug cartels. Colombia's long history of political and social instability accounts for the millions of natives who have fled in recent years. Alvaro Uribe, who won the presidential election of 2002, has been working with the United States to implement an aggressive campaign against Colombia's drug trade.

MONDAY DAWNED WARM and rainless. Aurelio Escovar, a dentist without a degree, and a very early riser, opened his office at six. He took some false teeth, still mounted in their plaster mold, out of the glass case and put on the table a fistful of instruments which he arranged in size order, as if they were on display. He wore a collarless striped shirt, closed at the neck with a golden stud, and pants held up by suspenders. He was erect and skinny, with a look that rarely corresponded to the situation, the way deaf people have of looking.

When he had things arranged on the table, he pulled the drill toward the dental chair and sat down to polish the false teeth. He seemed not to be thinking about what he was doing, but worked steadily, pumping the drill with his feet, even when he didn't need it.

After eight he stopped for a while to look at the sky through the window, and he saw two pensive buzzards who were drying themselves in the sun on the ridgepole of the house next door. He went on working with the idea that before lunch it would rain again. The shrill voice of his eleven-year-old son interrupted his concentration.

"Papá."

"What?"

"The Mayor wants to know if you'll pull his tooth."

"Tell him I'm not here."

He was polishing a gold tooth. He held it at arm's length and examined it with his eyes half closed. His son shouted again from the little waiting room.

"He says you are, too, because he can hear you."

The dentist kept examining the tooth. Only when he had put it on the table with the finished work did he say:

"So much the better."

He operated the drill again. He took several pieces of a bridge out of a cardboard box where he kept the things he still had to do and began to polish the gold.

"Papá."

"What?"

He still hadn't changed his expression.

"He says if you don't take out his tooth, he'll shoot you."

Without hurrying, with an extremely tranquil movement, he stopped pedaling the drill, pushed it away from the chair, and pulled the lower drawer of the table all the way out. There was a revolver. "O.K.," he said. "Tell him to come and shoot me."

He rolled the chair over opposite the door, his hand resting on the edge of the drawer. The Mayor appeared at the door. He had shaved the left side of his face, but the other side, swollen and in pain, had a five-day-old beard. The dentist saw many nights of desperation in his dull eyes. He closed the drawer with his fingertips and said softly:

"Sit down."

"Good morning," said the Mayor.

"Morning," said the dentist.

While the instruments were boiling, the Mayor leaned his skull on the headrest of the chair and felt better. His breath was icy. It was a poor office: an old wooden chair, the pedal drill, a glass case with ceramic bottles. Opposite the chair was a window with a shoulder-high cloth curtain. When he felt the dentist approach, the Mayor braced his heels and opened his mouth.

Aurelio Escovar turned his head toward the light. After inspecting the infected tooth, he closed the Mayor's jaw with a cautious pressure of his fingers.

"It has to be without anesthesia," he said.

"Why?"

"Because you have an abscess."

The Mayor looked him in the eye. "All right," he said, and tried to smile. The dentist did not return the smile. He brought the basin of sterilized instruments to the worktable and took them out of the water with a pair of cold tweezers, still without hurrying. Then he pushed the spittoon with the tip of his shoe, and went to wash his hands in the washbasin. He did all this without looking at the Mayor. But the Mayor didn't take his eyes off him.

It was a lower wisdom tooth. The dentist spread his feet and grasped the tooth with the hot forceps. The Mayor seized the arms of the chair, braced his feet with all his strength, and felt an icy void in his kidneys, but didn't make a sound. The dentist moved only his wrist. Without rancor, rather with a bitter tenderness, he said:

"Now you'll pay for our twenty dead men."

The Mayor felt the crunch of bones in his jaw, and his eyes filled with tears. But he didn't breathe until he felt the tooth come out. Then he saw it through his tears. It seemed so foreign to his pain that he failed to understand his torture of the five previous nights.

Bent over the spittoon, sweating, panting, he unbuttoned his tunic and reached for the handkerchief in his pants pocket. The dentist gave him a clean cloth.

"Dry your tears," he said.

The Mayor did. He was trembling. While the dentist washed his hands, he saw the crumbling ceiling and a dusty spider web with spider's eggs and dead insects. The dentist returned, drying his hands. "Go to bed," he said, "and gargle with salt water." The Mayor stood up, said goodbye with a casual military salute, and walked toward the door, stretching his legs, without buttoning up his tunic.

"Send the bill," he said.

"To you or the town?"

The Mayor didn't look at him. He closed the door and said through the screen:

"It's the same damn thing."

Translated by J. S. Bernstein

INTERPRETATIONS

1. What kind of man do you think Aurelio Escovar is? What specific details can you find to support your view?

2. Aurelio Escovar chooses to remove the Mayor's tooth without using anesthetic. Why does he do this? Do you believe him? Why or why not?

3. Note the dialogue between Aurelio Escovar and his son (see paragraphs 4 through 16). What do you learn about the dentist from these paragraphs? How does this information prepare you for what comes next in the story?

4. Why does the dentist open the drawer in paragraph 17? What do you think he intends to do with the object he finds inside? Explain your reasoning fully.

5. In paragraph 29, the dentist says, "Now you'll pay for our twenty dead men." Why did he choose to utter this statement exactly at this time? What does this statement add to your understanding of the relationship between the dentist and the mayor? How might it help explain the dentist's behavior earlier in the story?

CORRESPONDENCES

1. Both Joseph Steffan and Aurelio Escovar are men concerned with honor. How is honor defined and lived up to in "Honor Bound"? What is the point of honor in "One of These Days"? To what extent are Steffan and Escobar similar to and/or different from each other in the choices they make and the actions they perform in the name of honor?

2. How do Rodriguez and García Márquez use setting (time, place, atmosphere) in their respective works? How does setting help the authors get their points across? How does their use of setting affect a reader's responses to the works?

APPLICATIONS

1. What do you think is the primary theme of the story "One of These Days"? Write an essay that explains this idea and that supports it with carefully presented examples from the text.

2. How do you feel when you go to the dentist? How do your experiences compare with those depicted in paragraphs 22–33? What writing techniques does Márquez use to capture this moment? Write a narrative essay that tells the story of a meaningful dental visit. Try to emulate Márquez in making your experience come alive to a reader!

3. Oftentimes, writers *tell* about an experience or situation by explaining and analyzing carefully. It is also possible to achieve the same purpose by *showing* what has occurred or is occurring. Generally, *showing*, rather than *telling*, will help you to gain and retain a reader's interest, thereby making this descriptive technique quite effective. For example, what specific details do you notice in "One of These Days"? Why do you think that Márquez has chosen to include them?

    Review an essay that you have written. Where might you include specific details to *show* a reader what you mean? What exact details will accomplish the goal of showing rather than telling?

4. How does Márquez use *setting* to bring readers into the world he has created in the story "One of These Days"? Which specific details stick out to give you a sense of *time, place,* and *atmosphere*?

    Now, write a story that has as its first sentence: "_____ rode into the _____ on horseback." Supply the name of a person in the first blank and a type of place (e.g., mansion, apartment building, shack, log cabin, hunting lodge) in the second. Continue to write! As you work, pay particular attention to setting. Notice how elements of your first sentence help you to establish setting. Try to apply some of the techniques you observe Márquez using to bring *your* readers into *your* world!

Flight by Night

YAMIT NASSIRI

Yamit Nassiri (b. 1976) was born in Israel and moved to New York City with her American husband in 2000. She graduated from Queensborough College in January 2004 and is currently enrolled in the Linguistic Degree program at Queens College (CUNY). Record in your journal your memory of your "first flight" and your responses to this experience.

THE WEDDING RING on my left ring finger carries an essential part of my life behind it. Not only does it symbolize a change in my personal status, but the significant choices I have made. Every time the sheen of the white-gold metal reflects towards my eye, or when my thumb naturally plays with it, I recall my wedding night underneath the huppah (canopy). I remember the decisive moment when I said "I do" to my husband who was standing to my left, looking into my eyes with such excitement and adoration. He understood perfectly that my part of the vow "I do," meant that I agreed to leave my family and my country in order to become his wife.

It was a hot June night and everyone's face was covered with sweat. I noticed the tears on my mother's cheeks, but never dared to ask her why, so that she would not get the chance to say the unnecessary words: "I miss you already," or "I need you." How could I possibly deal with that then? It would have hurt too much. But . . . maybe it was only my imagination. Mothers always cry on their children's wedding day. Certainly my mother cried out of happiness and gratitude to God for sending her daughter a sweet, loving and caring man. She prayed all her life for that to happen, and indeed, her wish was granted.

As a little girl, I remember my mom saying that "no matter what happens to you, it is determined in advance by your fate," she explained, "but in a way, you can control your destiny by making your own decisions and making the choice to act upon them." Her philosophy regarding fate and destiny was not so clear to me, until I met Maurice and decided to marry him. To do so, I had to desert my family, my homeland, and move to the United States. Although I liked the idea of acquiring more freedom, it did not make my decision easier.

After my parents' divorce, I became an important figure at home, fulfilling the roles of mother and father. While my mother was working hard, I was taking care of the household, working outside to help pay the bills, and basically raising my sister (who is nine years younger than me). It hurt me that I could not afford college or even a driver's license, while my friends easily could. I was not able to discover myself or explore my abilities or talents. As a result, I grew resentful and felt deprived of opportunities for personal growth.

By accepting Maurice's proposal, I was letting go of my duties and responsibilities to my family. Part of me felt guilty. Yet the guilt did not make me give up my love. Had I done so, I would have hated myself. The uncertainty was my main concern, since I did not know what to expect. I was leaving the familiar behind and heading towards a new beginning.

My first year in New York City was difficult to deal with. I was terrified by the new environment, the unfamiliar faces, language, and customs. Unlike Israel, everything around me looked extremely big: buildings, roads, shopping malls, and streets. New York was a gigantic mountain compared to Israel, which was like a grain of sand. I was completely lost. Immigration laws made me wait to get my social security card, work permit, driver's license, and eventually my green card. I hated the jobs that paid the minimum salary and felt exploited, which filled me with bitterness. More than anything, I felt lonely. There was no one to confide in since all my friends lived in Israel.

My unhappiness affected my relationship with Maurice, and we argued more often. I cried a lot. Even small arguments made me cry. I accused him of tearing me away from my family and friends. He kept saying that it was only a matter of time and that I needed to be more patient. The idea of going back to Israel had crossed my mind a few times. Yet I wasn't ready to give in and let myself down. It would have been too easy.

Significant changes occurred in the following year and thereafter that shaped my identity and future goals. College contributed a lot. At first, I was worried about having difficulties with the language, and I was confused about choosing a major. But with strong will and determination I managed to set goals for myself and receive excellent results. The fact that English wasn't my first language required me to work harder than the other students (in class) in order to keep up. In my first semester I took ESL classes to improve my reading and writing skills. It was fulfilling to see myself advancing, and it was then that I got the idea of becoming an ESL teacher, with encouragement from my professor. I started taking advanced English classes and combined them with dance classes, since I have always loved to dance ballet, jazz, latin, and hip-hop. It was (and still is) a sort of relaxation and escape.

It was interesting also to meet so many people from different cultures and countries, since I felt less like a stranger. My social life improved significantly as well when I made good friends in school, which also contributed to my education. Now that I had my own circle of friends, I craved the independence, the space that I had in Israel. So I told Maurice that once a week I needed to spend some time with my girlfriends, because that would give me time to breathe. At first, he wasn't thrilled about the idea of "girls' night out," but gradually he understood its importance. He realized that it was my way of surviving in this new country, and furthermore, it improved our relationship.

Consciously or unconsciously, I became part of my new environment. Today, after four years, the process of Americanization continues. I speak the language, watch American movies, eat American food, wear American clothes, and "hang out" with American friends. Everyday I absorb more information about the country and the people, about the history, customs, and values. Yet accepting American values has not made me forget my own customs and traditions. I feel that my heart is closer to my country today, and as a result, I care more about observing Jewish holidays. I constantly think about my mom in Israel, and wherever I go I carry with me the small Bible she gave me ten years ago, which gives me strength.

Being with Maurice, I have a lot more opportunities. I am able to grow and find new dimensions in myself, which I wasn't able to do when living with my mom. Besides his love and affection, Maurice makes me feel confident and secure, which I cherish. My achievements in college make me believe in myself more, and I am less afraid of challenges. Sometimes I try to imagine what is possible and then hope to surpass the boundaries. Doing the things I want to do gives me peace of mind, so that I am better to myself and to the people around me. Despite all the initial obstacles, I am now able to look at my ring with such delight.

INTERPRETATIONS

1. What symbol does Nassiri use to unify her essay? How does it also enhance theme?

2. Characterize Nassiri's mother. How has her philosophy of fate and destiny affected the writer?

3. Nassiri has to negotiate between her responsibilities to her mother and her husband. What strategies does she use to accomplish this while creating space for herself?

4. To what extent has the process of assimilation affected her attitude toward the customs and traditions of her homeland? Explain.
5. Characterize Maurice. How does he contribute to her "new self"?

CORRESPONDENCES

1. Review Emerson's perspective and discuss its relevance to Nassiri's essay. What evidence is there of experimentation?
2. Review Lawrence's perspective and discuss its application to Nassiri's essay. What new things did she discover about herself in her new country?

APPLICATIONS

1. To what extent is pain an element of choice? What role does emotion play in making choices? Write an essay on a choice that you made involving pain—your own or others.
2. Imagine yourself in Nassiri's situation. Would you have made a different choice? Explain. Compare your responses to those of your group and summarize your responses.
3. Write an essay analyzing the reasons for a choice you would make between the security of the familiar (job, vocation, person) and taking a risk involving the unknown. What factors would influence your choice?

The Knowing Eye

Tamar Michal Friedner

READING IMAGES

1. What are some of the choices that may be interpreted from each of these photographs?

2. Which photograph are you able to relate to more? Be sure to explain how the *tone* of each photograph influences your response.

Ken Hammond/USDA

MAKING CONNECTIONS

1. Compare the photograph of the person in the doorway with the image of the partial faces in Chapter 3 (page 153). How do these representations seem similar or different?

2. How would you characterize the choices written about in this chapter's essays? Which of these photographs best illustrates the nature of choice that you have read about?

WORDS AND IMAGES

1. In our lives we are always making decisions. Write an essay about a decision that you had to make. As you think about your topic, let your responses to the photographs guide you. For example, will you write about a decision that you made recently or one that you made as a child? Will your topic concern a decision made privately or one that was made in the company of others?

2. What is the person standing in the doorway thinking? Make a drawing of what you perceive to be this individual's thoughts. Write a journal entry that describes how you came to your conclusion and the process you went through to create your drawing.

Additional Writing Topics

1. Review the Frost perspective (page 405). What does it imply about the nature of choice? Under what circumstances might you make a similar choice? In an essay, analyze your reasons for a choice you would make to take "the road less traveled."

2. View the videotape *El Norte* and/or review the selections by Rodriguez and Pérez, and write an analysis of the cost of being a migrant worker or illegal alien in the United States.

3. Although in many ways the Holocaust was "unthinkable," Wehle is asking her readers to think about it. What are some of the conclusions thinking might force on one who reads about the Holocaust?

4. Each chapter in this textbook begins with a myth, a folktale, or a story that teaches a lesson. Collaborate with members of your group on composing a moralistic tale that, like "The Wise Daughter," teaches a moral lesson on choices.

5. To what extent are the selections by Rodriguez, Mabry, and Pérez concerned with the "American Dream"? How do their dreams compare with yours?

6. Is culture, like nature, a limitation on freedom of choice, or does it allow more free play of individual wisdom and imagination? Do we increase our own choices to the degree that we free ourselves from culture? Limit your discussion to any three selections in this chapter.

7. Hamill warns against being too competitive. What are your views on competition? Are they similar to or different from those of your parents? From Hamill's? In what areas of life do you consider yourself least or most competitive?

8. Wehle and Steffan discuss the importance of individual integrity. Write an essay discussing your views on integrity and its impact on choices you have made.

9. Imagine yourself confronting a choice that involves taking a risk. Write an essay analyzing the reasons for the choices you would make between the security of the familiar (job, vocation, person), and taking a risk involving the unknown. What factors would influence your choice?

CHAPTER

9

Popular Culture

IN PREVIOUS CHAPTERS we explored the degree to which our identities, relationships, education, and careers are influenced by the many people in our private and public worlds. In this chapter we will focus on another instrument for shaping our thoughts and behavior: popular culture. Traditionally, as we have seen, cultures are social. They inculcate human achievements, particularly those that serve the good of the people. The world of culture is a world in which values are realized and conserved. What then is popular culture? "Popular" may be defined as "in relation to the general public, the majority," and the culture it encompasses includes media images of contemporary life and culture. Popular culture is dynamic, transitory, and an initiator of change. Through sophisticated technology it introduces us to worlds far from our local communities, enlarging our perspectives of cultural realities at home and abroad. Popular culture also creates a commonality that cuts across traditional barriers of geography, language, education, economics, ethnicity, and class.

The essays in this chapter reflect aspects of popular culture you encounter daily in magazines, television, films, and music. As you analyze each medium individually and in your groups, you will be asked to think critically about issues in contemporary culture and to develop an awareness of the extent to which the medium not only influences our ideas but often directs our daily actions, including what to wear and what music to listen to, films to see, and television programs to watch.

Robyn Meredith, for example, examines the implications of the decision by the owners of Minnesota's Mall of America to place a curfew on teenagers on weekend nights, while Kathleen Carlin analyzes the degree to which clothes are indicators of personal identity and social

461

class. In "The Signs of Shopping," Anne Norton analyzes the impact of consumerism in the United States, and how obsession with dressing in the latest style, for instance, is often constructed, reinforced, even dictated by displays in shopping malls, the rhetoric of catalogs, and the manipulation by announcers on the "Home Shopping Network."

The influences of film and television are all pervasive. No consideration of the forces that have helped shape the history of the century could ignore the impact of the media. From the birth of film, movies have among other things documented events, informed our ideas of romantic love, physical beauty, heroism, and personal and national identity. Culturally, they have exposed us not only to subcultures and countercultures within the United States but throughout the world.

Hollywood is the focus of two essays in this unit: Benjamin DeMott's "Class Struggle in Hollywood" and Sylvester Monroe's "Hollywood: The Dark Side." DeMott discusses several recent American movies about class differences that in his view often gloss over the complexities of upward mobility, inequities of power among economic classes, and differences in social behavior. Monroe addresses the failure of most Hollywood script writers and producers to present African-Americans as real people instead of "stereotypical characters" who "verbally bludgeon one another with insulting 'one-liners'."

Perhaps the aspect of popular culture that has most influenced the values of the present generation is music. Emma Wunsch, for example, in "Closer to Fine: My Parents' Music and Mine," contrasts the degree to which the music of her parent's generation influenced her childhood with that of the impact that the lyrics of the Indigo Girls had in her adolescence. Jay Ford in his essay "What Is Hip Hop?" writes from a different perspective. His purpose is to reach audiences who in his view need to be informed about the personal, social, political, ethical, and cultural implications of this music written and performed primarily by young African-Americans. The appeal of their music, he believes, extends far beyond the inner city, addressing such controversial issues as racism, sexuality, and violence.

In sum, the icons and images of popular culture pervade all aspects of contemporary culture, nationally and globally. Critical analyses of the texts in this chapter should provide catalysts for your evaluation of the issues they address as well as their impact on your life.

Perspectives

Most of our movies have been pro the underdog, concerned with injustice, relatively anti-authority. There's usually a system—or a bureaucracy—to triumph over.

More often than not, American movies have been affirmative and hopeful about destiny. They're usually about individuals who control their own lives and their fate. In Europe, the system was so class-bound and steeped in tradition that there was no democratization of that process.

There's no prior education required to assimilate American movies or American culture. American culture is general, as opposed to the specificity of Japanese or Indian culture. America has the most easily digestible culture.

—Sydney Pollack

It is a misunderstanding of the American retail store to think we go there necessarily to buy. Some of us shop. There's a difference. Shopping has many purposes, the least interesting of which is to acquire new articles. We shop to practice decisionmaking. We shop to be useful and productive members of our class and society. We shop to remind ourselves how much is available to us. We shop to remind ourselves how much is to be striven for. We shop to assert our superiority to the material objects that spread themselves before us.

—Phyllis Rose

Two out of every three adults in the United States say they fidget, fuss, take furtive glances in windows and mirrors, and study other people's reaction to the way they look. It is not overstating it to report that a solid majority of the American people are close to being obsessed with their physical appearance.

—Louis Harris

The hip hop industry in general, is stronger than it's ever been, in terms of units sold, in terms of the number of releases . . . Rap has proved itself to be the rock-and-roll of the '90s.

—Brian Turner

Resigning one's self to living off the table scraps of the American Century is what twentystuff culture is all about. It's about recycling anger into irony, pain into poses.

—Walter Kirn

All objects, all phases of culture are alive. They have voices. They speak of their history and interrelatedness. And they are talking at once.

—*Camille Paglia*

I am my body.

—*Marge Piercy*

In America, the photographer is not simply the person who records the past but the one who invents it.

—*Susan Sontag*

It is easier to understand a nation by listening to its music than by learning its language.

—*Anonymous*

What's swinging in words? If a guy makes you tap your foot and if you feel it down your back, you don't have to ask anybody if that's good music or not. You can always feel it.

—*Miles Davis*

Along with the idea of romantic love, she was introduced to another— physical beauty. Probably the most destructive ideas in the history of human thought. Both originated in envy, thrived in insecurity, and ended in disillusion. In equating physical beauty with virtue, she stripped her mind, bound it, and collected self-contempt by the heap. She forgot lust and simple caring for. She regarded love as possessive mating, and romance as the goal of the spirit. It would be for her a well-spring from which she would draw the most destructive emotions, deceiving the lover and seeking to imprison the beloved, curtailing freedom in every way.

—*Toni Morrison*

The truest expression of a people is in its dances and its music. Bodies never lie.

—*Agnes de Mille*

It should not be surprising that all sorts of Americans—not only the bed- and house-ridden—find solace in the mythically stable communities of soap operas. Some soap communities, after all, have lasted over thirty years. All potential viewers are members of a society that has been in constant transformation through geographic mobility and the loss of extended families. Loneliness, we are repeatedly told, has become pandemic in America, and the longing for community is a palpable need. Whether through region, clubs, associations, or support groups—or through daily immersion in a favorite soap—many Americans search for some kind of communal life to counter varying degrees of social isolation and alienation.

—*Ruth Rosen*

If Poe were alive, he would not have to invent horror; horror would invent him.

—*Richard Wright*

The mall is a common experience for the majority of all youth: they have probably been going there all their lives.

—*William Severini Kowinski*

The image is freedom, words are prison.

—*Jean Luc Godard*

The success of modern advertising, its penetration into every corner of American life, reflects a culture that has itself chosen illusion over reality.

—*Jack Solomon*

Movies are still the most seductive and powerful of artistic mediums, manipulating us with ease by a powerful combination of sound and image.

—*Jessica Hagendorn*

Piercing is a return to flesh as fashion—and a revitalized rite of passage.

—*D. James Romero*

When I was young, the movies definitely had an effect on me. I found role models in them. I was a kid who liked to be adventurous, who wanted to fly like Superman or be a pilot or a Jedi knight in Star Wars. My dreams of being a hero made life exciting to me.

—*Dave Zimecki*

Movies are not a good source of role models or heroes. It appears that the majority of today's films focus on violence and crime. Since we live in a nation where crime is the cause of many social problems that exist, I do not think that portraying criminals and violent characters as heroes is good for children. By doing this, the film industry tells the audience that violent people are admirable and that their values should be embraced. I feel there should be more positive role models in movies and on television so that young people can actually have someone to look up to who represents positive values.

—*Celeste Armenti*

Consumer culture is a one-dimensional world, a wafer-thin world, a world low on significance and high on glitz, a world without yesterday.
—*James B. Twitchell*

APPLICATIONS

1. Review the perspectives on movies and discuss each with your group. On what issues did you agree and disagree?

2. The perspectives of Harris and Morrison focus on the preoccupation with physical beauty in contemporary American culture. To what extent do you and your group members disagree with their points of view? Compose three perspectives of your own on the topic.

3. Is piercing as important as clothing in constructing identity? Does it also make a statement about individuality or is it a reflection of conformity to current fashion trends? Discuss these issues in a short essay.

The Signs of Shopping

ANNE NORTON

Anne Norton (b. 1954) received a B.A., M.A., and Ph.D. from the University of Chicago and has been a Professor of Political Science at the University of Pennsylvania since 1993. Norton's articles have been published in numerous journals and reviews including Political Theory, The University of Chicago Law Review, *and* Social Text. *Norton's most recent books are,* 95 Theses on Politics, Culture, and Method *(2003) and* Blood Rites of the Post-Structuralists: Word, Flesh and Revolution *(2002). Norton is also the author of* Republic of Signs: Liberal Theory and American Popular Culture *(1993),* Reflections on Political Identity *(1988), and* Alternative Americas: A Reading of Antebellum Political Culture *(1986). Brainstorm on your associations with "shopping."*

Shopping at the Mall

THE MALL HAS BEEN THE SUBJECT of innumerable debates. Created out of the modernist impulse for planning and the centralization of public activity, the mall has become the distinguishing sign of suburban decentralization, springing up in unplanned profusion. Intended to restore something of the lost unity of city life to the suburbs, the mall has come to export styles and strategies to stores at the urban center. Deplored by modernists, it is regarded with affection only by their postmodern foes. Ruled more by their content than by their creators' avowed intent, the once sleek futurist shells have taken on a certain aura of postmodern playfulness and popular glitz.

The mall is a favorite subject for the laments of cultural conservatives and others critical of the culture of consumption. It is indisputably the cultural locus of commodity fetishism. It has been noticed, however, by others of a less condemnatory disposition that the mall has something of the mercado, or the agora, about it. It is both a place of meeting for the young and one of the rare places where young and old go together. People of different races and classes, different occupations, different levels of education meet there. As M. Pressdee and John Fiske note, however, though the mall appears to be a public place, it is not. Neither freedom of speech nor freedom of assembly is permitted there. Those who own and manage malls restrict what comes within their confines. Controversial displays, by stores or customers or the plethora of organizations and agencies that present themselves in the open spaces of the mall, are not permitted. These seemingly public spaces conceal a pervasive private authority.

The mall exercises its thorough and discreet authority not only in the regulation of behavior but in the constitution of our visible, inaudible, public discourse. It is the source of those commodities through which we speak of our identities, our opinions, our desires. It is a focus for the discussion of style among peripheral consumers. Adolescents, particularly female adolescents, are inclined to spend a good deal of time at the mall. They spend, indeed, more time than money. They acquire not simple commodities (they may come home with many, few, or none) but a well-developed sense of the significance of those commodities. In prowling the mall they embed themselves in a lexicon of American culture. They find themselves walking through a dictionary. Stores hang a variety of identities on their racks and mannequins. Their window displays provide elaborate scenarios conveying not only what the garment is but what the garment means.

A display in the window of Polo provides an embarrassment of semiotic riches. Everyone, from the architecture critic at the *New York Times* to kids in the hall of a Montana high school, knows what *Ralph Lauren* means. The polo mallet and the saddle, horses and dogs, the broad lawns of Newport, Kennebunkport, old photographs in silver frames, the evocation of age, of ancestry and Anglophilia, of indolence and the Ivy League, evoke the upper class. Indian blankets and buffalo plaids, cowboy hats and Western saddles, evoke a past distinct from England but nevertheless determinedly Anglo. The supposedly arcane and suspect arts of deconstruction are deployed easily, effortlessly, by the readers of these cultural texts.

Walking from one window to another, observing one another, shoppers, especially the astute and observant adolescents, acquire a facility with the language of commodities. They learn not only words but a grammar. Shop windows employ elements of sarcasm and irony, strategies of inversion and allusion. They provide models of elegant, economical, florid, and prosaic expression. They teach composition.

The practice of shopping is, however, more than instructive. It has long been the occasion for women to escape the confines of their homes and enjoy the companionship of other women. The construction of woman's role as one of provision for the needs of the family legitimated her exit. It provided an occasion for women to spend long stretches of time in the company of their friends, without the presence of their husbands. They could exchange information and reflections, ask advice, and receive support. As their daughters grew, they would be brought increasingly within this circle, included in shopping trips and lunches with their mothers. These would form, reproduce, and restructure communities of taste.

The construction of identity and the enjoyment of friendship outside the presence of men was thus effected through a practice that constructed women as consumers and subjected them to the conventions of the marketplace. Insofar as they were dependent on their husbands for money, they were dependent on their husbands for the means to the construction of their identities. They could not represent themselves through commodities without the funds men provided, nor could they, without money, participate in the community of women that was realized in "going shopping." Their identities were made contingent not only on the possession of property but on the recognition of dependence.

Insofar as shopping obliges dependent women to recognize their dependence, it also opens up the possibility of subversion.[1] The housewife who shops for pleasure takes time away from her husband, her family, and her house and claims it for herself. Constantly taught that social order and her private happiness depend on intercourse between men and women, she chooses the company of women instead. She engages with women in an activity marked as feminine, and she enjoys it. When she spends money, she exercises an authority over property that law and custom may deny her. If she has no resources independent of her husband, this may be the only authority over property she is able to exercise. When she buys things her husband does not approve—or does not know of—she further subverts an order that leaves control over property in her husband's hands.[2]

Her choice of feminine company and a feminine pursuit may involve additional subversions. As Fiske and Pressdee recognize, shopping without buying and shopping for bargains have a subversive quality. This is revealed, in a form that gives it additional significance, when a saleswoman leans forward and tells a shopper, "Don't buy that today, it will be on sale on Thursday." Here solidarity of gender (and often of class) overcome, however partially and briefly, the imperatives of the economic order.

Shoppers who look, as most shoppers do, for bargains, and salespeople who warn shoppers of impending sales, see choices between

---

[1]Nuanced and amusing accounts of shopping as subversion are provided in John Fiske's analyses of popular culture, particularly *Reading the Popular* (Boston: Unwin Hyman [now Routledge], 1989), pp. 13–42.

[2]See R. Bowlby, *Just Looking: Consumer Culture in Dreiser, Gissing, and Zola* (London: Methuen, 1985), p. 22, for another discussion and for an example of the recommendation of this strategy by Elizabeth Cady Stanton in the 1850s.

commodities as something other than the evidence and the exercise of freedom. They see covert direction and exploitation; they see the withholding of information and the manipulation of knowledge. They recognize that they are on enemy terrain and that their shopping can be, in Michel de Certeau's term, a "guerrilla raid." This recognition in practice of the presence of coercion in choice challenges the liberal conflation of choice and consent.

Shopping at Home

Shopping is an activity that has overcome its geographic limits. One need no longer go to the store to shop. Direct mail catalogues, with their twenty-four-hour phone numbers for ordering, permit people to shop where and when they please. An activity that once obliged one to go out into the public sphere, with its diverse array of semiotic messages, can now be done at home. An activity that once obliged one to be in company, if not in conversation, with one's compatriots can now be conducted in solitude.

The activity of catalogue shopping, and the pursuit of individuality, are not, however, wholly solitary. The catalogues invest their commodities with vivid historical and social references. The J. Peterman catalogue, for example, constructs the reader as a man of rugged outdoor interests, taste, and money.[3] He wears "The Owner's Hat" or "Hemingway's Cap," a leather flight jacket or the classic "Horseman's Duster," and various other garments identified with the military, athletes, and European imperialism. The copy for "The Owner's Hat" naturalizes class distinctions and, covertly, racism:

> Some of us work on the plantation.
> Some of us own the plantation.
> Facts are facts.
> This hat is for those who own the plantation.[4]

Gender roles are strictly delineated. The copy for a skirt captioned "Women's Legs" provides a striking instance of the construction of the gaze as male, of women as the object of the gaze:

[3]I have read several of these. I cite *The J. Peterman Company Owner's Manual No. 5*, from the J. Peterman Company, 2444 Palumbo Drive, Lexington, Kentucky 40509.

[4]Ibid., p. 5. The hat is also identified with the Canal Zone, "successfully bidding at Beaulieu," intimidation, and LBOs. Quite a hat. It might be argued against my reading that the J. Peterman Company also offers the "Coal Miner's Bag" and a mailbag. However, since the descriptive points of reference on color and texture and experience for these bags are such things as the leather seats of jaguars, and driving home in a Bentley, I feel fairly confident in my reading.

just when you think you see something, a shape you think you recognize, it's gone and then it begins to return and then it's gone and of course you can't take your eyes off it.

Yes, the long slow motion of women's legs. Whatever happened to those things at carnivals that blew air up into girls' skirts and you could spend hours watching.[5]

"You," of course, are male. There is also the lace blouse captioned "Mystery": "lace says yes at the same time it says no."[6] Finally, there are notes of imperialist nostalgia: the Sheapherd's Hotel (Cairo) bathrobe and white pants for "the bush" and "the humid hell-holes of Bombay and Calcutta."[7]

It may no longer be unforgivable to say that the British left a few good things behind in India and in Kenya, Singapore, Borneo, etc., not the least of which was their Englishness.[8]

As Paul Smith observes, in his reading of their catalogues, the *Banana Republic* has also made capital out of imperial nostalgia.[9]

The communities catalogues create are reinforced by shared mailing lists. The constructed identities are reified and elaborated in an array of semiotically related catalogues. One who orders a spade or a packet of seeds will be constructed as a gardener and receive a deluge of catalogues from plant and garden companies. The companies themselves may expand their commodities to appeal to different manifestations of the identities they respond to and construct. Smith and Hawken, a company that sells gardening supplies with an emphasis on aesthetics and environmental concern, puts out a catalogue in which a group of people diverse in age and in their ethnicity wear the marketed clothes while gardening, painting, or throwing pots. Williams-Sonoma presents its catalogue not as a catalogue of things for cooking but as "A Catalog for Cooks." The catalogue speaks not to need but to the construction of identity.

---

[5]Ibid., p. 3. See also pp. 15 and 17 for instances of women as the object of the male gaze. The identification of the gaze with male sexuality is unambiguous here as well.

[6]Ibid., p.17.

[7]Ibid., pp. 7, 16, 20, 21, 37, and 50.

[8]Ibid., p. 20.

[9]Paul Smith, "Visiting the Banana Republic," in *Universal Abandon?* ed. Andrew Ross for Social Text (Minneapolis: University of Minnesota Press, 1988), pp. 128–148.

The Nature Company dedicates its spring 1990 catalogue "to trees," endorses Earth Day, and continues to link itself to *The Nature Conservancy* through posters and a program in which you buy a tree for a forest restoration project. Here, a not-for-profit agency is itself commodified, adding to the value of the commodities offered in the catalogue.[10] In this catalogue, consumption is not merely a means for the construction and representation of the self, it is also a means for political action. Several commodities are offered as "A Few Things You Can Do" to save the earth: a string shopping bag, a solar battery recharger, a home newspaper recycler. Socially conscious shopping is a liberal practice in every sense. It construes shopping as a form of election, in which one votes for good commodities or refuses one's vote to candidates whose practices are ethically suspect. In this respect, it reveals its adherence to the same ideological presuppositions that structure television's Home Shopping Network and other cable television sales shows.

Both politically informed purchasing and television sales conflate the free market and the electoral process. Dollars are identified with votes, purchases with endorsements. Both offer those who engage in them the possibility to "talk back" to manufacturers. In television sales shows, this ability to talk back is both more thoroughly elaborated and more thoroughly exploited. Like the "elections" on MTV that invite viewers to vote for their favorite video by calling a number on their telephones, they permit those who watch to respond, to speak, and to be heard by the television. Their votes, of course, cost money. On MTV, as in the stores, you can buy as much speech as you can afford. On the Home Shopping Network, the purchase of speech becomes complicated by multiple layers and inversions.

Each commodity is introduced. It is invested by the announcer with a number of desirable qualities. The value of these descriptions of the commodities is enhanced by the construction of the announcer as a mediator not only between the commodity and the consumer but between the salespeople and the consumer. The announcer is not, the format suggests, a salesperson (though of course the announcer is). He or she is an announcer, describing goods that others have offered for sale. Television claims to distinguish itself by making objects visible to the eyes, but it is largely through the ears that these commodities are constructed. The consumer, in purchasing the commodity, purchases the commodity, what the commodity signifies, and, as we say, "buys the salesperson's line." The consumer may also acquire the ability to

---

[10]*The Nature Company Catalog*, The Nature Company, P.O. Box 2310, Berkeley, California 94702, Spring 1990. See pp. 1–2 and order form insert between pp. 18 and 19. Note also the entailed donation to Designs for Conservation on p. 18.

speak on television. Each purchase is recorded and figures as a vote in a rough plebiscite, confirming the desirability of the object. Although the purchase figures are announced as if they were confirming votes, it is, of course, impossible to register one's rejection of the commodity. Certain consumers get a little more (or rather less) for their money. They are invited to explain the virtue of the commodity—and their purchase—to the announcer and the audience. The process of production, of both the consumers and that which they consume, continues in this apology for consumption.

The semiotic identification of consumption as an American activity, indeed, a patriotic one, is made with crude enthusiasm on the Home Shopping Network and other video sales shows. Red, white, and blue figure prominently in set designs and borders framing the television screen. The Home Shopping Network presents its authorities in an office conspicuously adorned with a picture of the Statue of Liberty.[11] Yet the messages that the Home Shopping Network sends its customers—that you can buy as much speech as you can afford, that you are recognized by others in accordance with your capacity to consume—do much to subvert the connection between capitalism and democracy on which this semiotic identification depends.

INTERPRETATIONS

1. At the end of paragraph 2 Norton writes of shopping malls that "These seemingly public spaces conceal a pervasive private authority." What does she mean? What evidence does she cite?

2. Do you agree with Norton that shopping in the mall teaches familiarity with "the language of communities"? What examples would you add?

3. How, according to Norton, has shopping affected women's identities, including their relationships? Do you agree with her gender analysis? Why or why not?

4. How is the language of mail-order catalogs intended to influence consumers? Is their awareness of audience sophisticated? Explain.

5. What evidence does Norton cite to support her thesis that the Home Shopping Network presents "consumption" as a "patriotic" activity?

[11]This moment from the Home Shopping Network was generously brought to my attention, on videotape, by Peter Bregman, a student in my American Studies class of fall 1988, at Princeton University.

CORRESPONDENCES

1. Review Rose's perspective on shopping (page 463). To what extent does her perspective reinforce or contradict Norton's? With whom do you agree? Explain your answer.

2. Review Solomon's perspective on advertising. How does it reinforce Norton's view of consumerism in the United States? What new dimension does it introduce?

APPLICATIONS

1. Test Norton's thesis on the targeting of window displays to a particular audience by visiting a shopping mall and focusing on one or two displays. Pay attention to special details and write an analysis of how effectively they appeal to their intended audience.

2. To what extent have current advertisers included models from all ethnic groups? Flip through two or three catalogs and/or magazines. Which groups are represented? For what products? Are the advertisements free of stereotypes? Write a brief report on your findings.

3. Do you agree with the concept that "you are what you buy"? Select three purchases you made recently and write a brief essay on how each reflects aspects of your identity.

4. Review these online catalogues. How do they support or refute what Norton has written in her essay?

   http://www.jpeterman.com

   http://www.bananarepublic.com

   www.smith-hawken.com

   www.williams-sonoma.com

You Become What You Wear

KATHLEEN CARLIN

Kathleen Carlin was born in Elyria, Ohio. She left a career as a surgical nurse to return to Rocky Mountain College in Montana for a B.A. in English and a B.S. in sociology and anthropology. She serves at the Family Support Network of Montana where she specializes in cases of child abuse and neglect and also works with crime victims at the Yellowstone County Sheriff's Office. Write a journal entry on your responses to Carlin's title.

A STANDARD CRITICISM of sociological research projects is that they go to great lengths to prove what most people with common sense already know. Without exactly taking sides for or against that criticism, I want to describe a sociological exercise that might seem to validate it— except that, for me and a classmate (and maybe for some who read this account), the experience made a truism come alive.

What we did: During spring break from a local college, my friend and I went downtown to shop. First, however, we made ourselves virtually unrecognizable to our friends and even to our families. We wore clothing slightly inappropriate for the weather, clean but wrinkled, clearly out of sync with the styles worn by most visitors to the area. We carried plastic bags of nameless possessions. Both of us were slightly unkempt. My friend wore a faded flannel shirt and T-shirt, a wrinkled skirt over sweat pants. I wore a wool hat that concealed my hair, an unfashionable coat and scarf, and glasses with clip-on sun shades.

The aim was to look like street people and to observe what difference that made in the way other people responded to us—whether the appearance of poverty would place a stigma on us. We were also prepared to act out some mildly unusual behaviors that might speak of some emotional disabilities, without appearing seriously disturbed or dangerous. As it turned out, there was no need for histrionics; people turned us off or turned us out on the basis of appearance alone.

Our first stop (after parking our cars near the railroad tracks) was in the bargain store of a local charity, where we politely asked access to a bathroom and were refused. Next we entered the lobby of a large hotel, where we asked for a coffee shop and a bathroom. The bellhop said, "You must go to the twentieth floor." We weren't up to trying our gig at an exclusive restaurant, so we wandered around the first floor and left. From there we went to a pawnshop, where we more or less blended with the patrons, and then on to the upper-scale stores and coffee shops during the lunch hour.

It was stigma time. Some of the children we encountered stared, pointed, and laughed; adults gave us long, incredulous looks. Clerks in stores followed us around to watch our every move. In a lunchroom a second assistant hurried to the side of the cashier, where they took my $2 check without asking for an ID; it seemed worth that price to have us out the door. At one doorway a clerk physically blocked the entrance apparently to discourage our entry.

We had money to cover small purchases, and, apart from wearing down-scale clothing, we did nothing in any of these settings to draw attention to ourselves; we merely shopped quietly in our accustomed manner. At one establishment we did blow our cover when we ordered croissants with a latté and an espresso; that may have been too far out of character for "bag ladies." Elsewhere we encountered derision, mockery, distrust, and rude stares.

So what did we learn? Mostly what we expected, what everybody knows; people judge by appearances. Just looking poor brings with it a stigma, accompanied by the withdrawal of much of the social civility most of us take for granted. Lacking the culturally acceptable symbols of belonging in this milieu, we became, to a degree, objects, with less inherent dignity as persons.

There was, however, one surprise—more accurately, a shock. It became clear most strongly at the shop I mentioned earlier, the one where a clerk conspicuously positioned herself in the entryway on seeing us. I had just noticed the place and had turned to my companion, saying, "I've never seen this store. Let's go in." She looked at me with dismay. "You're not really going in there, are you?"

I knew what she meant and shared her feeling. The place felt out of bounds for us. In a very few hours, we found ourselves accepting and internalizing the superficial and biased judgments of ourselves that prevailed among the people we met; we stigmatized ourselves. It's a good lesson to learn, maybe especially for sociologists.

INTERPRETATIONS

1. Analyze the significance of Carlin's title.

2. Review paragraph 5. What examples best support that it was "stigma time"?

3. Reread paragraphs 8 and 9. What shock does Carlin describe? How does paragraph 9 relate to the essay's title?

CORRESPONDENCES

1. Review Harris's perspective and discuss its relevance to Carlin's essay.

2. Compare and contrast the tone of the texts by Carlin and Norton. How does their tone affect purpose? Audience?

APPLICATIONS

1. Carlin's experience demonstrates how clothing affects society's perceptions as well as the extent to which the wearer accepts that judgment. Should people be denied respect because they lack the interest or the financial resources to make a fashion statement? To what extent do you agree that clothing and identity are inseparable?

2. To what extent do you and your group members buy brand name clothing? What current brand names are mandatory? Less popular? What images do brand names project?

3. Imagine you have the resources to open a clothing store targeted for your generation. What site would you choose? How would you decorate it? What images would you like to project? What kind of clothing would you stock? How would you advertise your opening? Write an essay explaining the criteria for your choices.

4. When you think of "street" and "establishment" people, who do you see in your mind's eye? Create a drawing that represents your vision of these individuals.

Big Mall's Curfew Raises Questions of Rights and Bias

ROBYN MEREDITH

Robyn Meredith writes about Asian business for Forbes *and* Forbes Global *magazine. She was the Detroit correspondent for* The New York Times *and a business reporter for* USA Today. *This article was originally published in the September 4, 1996* New York Times. *Brainstorm on your associations with malls. Is there a particular age group to which they appeal?*

BLOOMINGTON, MINN., AUG. 29—Marcus D. Wilson, eighteen, has been coming to the Mall of America here once or twice a week since it opened four years ago. He buys tapes, plays video games and sees his friends, especially his girlfriend.

But starting September 20, his habits will be disrupted by the mall's new chaperon policy. People under 16—including his 15-year-old girlfriend, Stephanie E. Jones—will be barred from the mall on Friday and Saturday nights unless they bring a parent or other grownup over 21. Teenage shoppers who were interviewed recently said they would not be caught dead with their parents at the Mall of America, the biggest mall in the country and the coolest spot in town.

The Mall of America is one of the nation's first shopping centers to impose curfews on unchaperoned teenagers. Malls from New Jersey to California are watching the effort as they, too, struggle to control rowdy teenagers.

The new policy here touches on many serious social issues: safety, race relations, parental responsibility and civil liberties. Malls have always been magnets for teenagers, but rising levels of juvenile violence have put pressure on shopping centers to limit who walks in the door.

Although the rule means that his girlfriend will be excluded on Fridays and Saturdays after 6 P.M., Mr. Wilson favors the rules because he thinks they will make the mall safer. But Miss Jones, who works at a shoe store, said "If I can work in the mall, I know how to handle myself." But she added, "I understand what they're trying to get at."

Every weekend night, at least 2,000 teenagers gather at the Mall of America. On wintry Minnesota Saturday nights, 3,000 teenagers swarm the shopping mall, disturbing other shoppers with chases, practical jokes and fistfights, said Teresa A. McFarland, a mall spokeswoman.

Still, Mr. Wilson called the policy "a little racist" because weekend nights are the only time large groups of black teenagers, like him, show up at the suburban mall, which is near the Minneapolis airport. Mall workers already tend to hand him a copy of the mall's rules for behavior as he walks in the door, not bothering to give copies to the white teenagers nearby, he said. Ms. McFarland bristled at the suggestion, saying the mall's policy was to hand all young people a copy of the rules.

That sentiment is one reason some local community groups are concerned about the mall's policy and how it will be enforced. Yusef Mgeni, president of the Minneapolis chapter of the Urban Coalition, a public policy research and advocacy group, said, "This policy has been drawn up in reaction to and in large part because of the large number of young people of color who congregate in the mall in the evening."

"The policy itself is neutral," said Mr. Mgeni (pronounced em-JANE cy). "How they implement it will determine whether it is unfair."

Virgil H. Heatwole, a mall manager, denied that the policy was directed at children of color. "It is fair; it is across the board," he said. "We are not targeting any individual, any group, any ethnic group."

Under the policy, security officers posted at each of the mall's twenty-three entrances will ask unchaperoned youths to prove that they are at least 16 before letting them inside. Other workers will sweep the halls, ejecting those who are under 16.

Mr. Heatwole said he hoped the policy would result in children bringing their parents to the mall. "I think society itself, we need to look at where parents are today," he said.

The mall's policy is opposed by the American Civil Liberties Union. "It infringes on the rights of young people," said Chris Hansen, a senior staff counsel at the A.C.L.U. in Manhattan. "It ought to be the parents, not the mall or the government who decide whether unchaperoned children can come to mall," he said.

"We don't object at all to the mall setting up rules of behavior," Mr. Hansen said. "But we do object to punishing the good kids for the behavior of kids that aren't behaving."

Federal courts have ruled in past cases that shopping malls are not considered public spaces and that First Amendment rights may be restricted inside them, Mr. Hansen said. But state courts are nearly evenly divided on the issue. New York holds that malls are private property, while California courts have ruled that shopping centers "now occupy the civic role that downtown used to," Mr. Hansen said.

Minnesota does not apply First Amendment principles to shopping malls, said Kathleen M. Milner, legal counsel for the Minnesota Civil

Liberties Union, part of the A.C.L.U. For that reason, her group does not plan to sue over the chaperon rules.

While many shopping centers draw customers from only their immediate communities, the Mall of America draws people of differing generations and cultures. Families from across the country, here on two-day shopping binges, mix with local teenagers, who include rebellious suburbanites with spiked hairdos as well as poorer children from nearby Minneapolis and St. Paul. It is an uneasy combination.

Of course, security concerns at the mall pale compared with those in cities like New York. "This is not like walking into the Port Authority at 3 o'clock in the morning," said Billy Ellis, a Manhattan native who manages the mall's Rainforest Cafe, where there has never been a drunk at the bar. Many people here leave their cars unlocked in the mall's parking lot, he said.

While the mall has more than 400 stores and is so big that its indoor amusement park sports a roller coaster and log ride, teenagers congregate on the weekends along the railings to the mall's four floors, where they can peer at one another. Parents are nowhere to be seen, and mall workers have found children as young as 12 caring for 2-year-old siblings as they wander the mall.

Young people and adults agree that the teenagers can be obnoxious. They race down the halls in groups, scattering shoppers in their paths. They use foul language when shouting to their friends two floors above. Some even drop food or spit over the railings, aiming at shoppers below.

Recently, the fun and games have taken an alarming turn. Security officers broke up a fight between two 15-year-old boys who were quarreling about a pair of red tennis shoes. One boy had lifted the other's feet off the ground as if he intended to throw him over the railing, which "could have killed him," Mr. Heatwole said.

Perhaps the worst incident came one Saturday in June. Nancy A. Bordeaux and her family came to the Mall of America from Portland, Oregon. They were eating hot dogs when a gang of Asian-American teenagers chased a group of black teenagers through a food court. One boy pointed a gun at her 16-year-old son, Felix, who is black, apparently mistaking him briefly for one of those being chased, Mrs. Bordeaux said.

Although no one was seriously hurt, "it was really pretty frightening," said Mrs. Bordeaux, who praised the mall's chaperon policy.

While the problems seem magnified here because of the mall's sheer size, they are common on a smaller scale at shopping centers around the country, mall managers and others in the industry said.

"It is a subject that was probably hardly ever discussed fifteen years ago, and now it is at the top of the agenda for a lot of management companies, and that reflects societal changes," said Mark J. Schoifet, a spokesman for the industry trade group, the International Council of Shopping Centers, based in New York.

"Malls are put in the position of being baby sitters," Mr. Schoifet said. "These are mall managers, not social workers."

The Mall of America said it had partly patterned its policy after a shopping center in Asheville, North Carolina, that three years ago began requiring teenagers to have chaperons on Saturday nights. Sunrise Mall in Corpus Christi, Texas, requires children under 14 to be accompanied by an adult at all times. But the mall's general manager, Brian K. Giffin, said the rule was enforced only when unaccompanied children caused trouble.

Few malls restricted teenagers' access, Mr. Schoifet said, because their spending power tops $90 billion a year. "Nobody in our business wants to alienate this group in any way," he said. "It is a quandary."

Malls around the country will watch to see if the Mall of America's approach works, and some might follow its example, he added.

Some stores at the Mall of America have had their business hurt by the teenage crowd. One is the Security Store, which sells personal security items on the first floor, near a stage where families, most of them white, gather by day to hear storytellers or children's songs.

But on Friday and Saturday nights, that part of the mall seems transformed, said the store's manager, Paul T. Barnes. One evening, as he stood outside his store, someone poured a chocolate shake on his head from the floor above.

On weekend nights, Mr. Barnes said, the crowds are younger. Thousands of teenagers swarm near his store, "seventy percent of them under the age of 20 and minority and wearing gang-related apparel," Mr. Barnes said. Many of his older customers are scared away. "A lot of people are not used to seeing large numbers of kids and large numbers of minority kids," he said.

Some young black shoppers said the new chaperon policy would only add to their sense that they were under added scrutiny at the Mall of America. Martino M. Landrum, 15, said. "Every time we go to a store, we've got the owner following us, and they let the white people alone." Mr. Landrum said he knew that black gang members came to the mall, but he said white skinheads did as well. He opposes the mall's policy and said it was aimed at blacks.

Most teenagers interviewed in the mall last week said they thought the policy was unfair because it would punish all young people, not just the ones who cause trouble.

Jackie M. Soucek, 14, one of three girls outside the mall waiting for a bus to her suburban home one night, said, "They just took away the best shopping days." She and her friends had already visited the mall twice that week, and they vowed never to be seen there with their parents.

INTERPRETATIONS

1. Meredith begins by interviewing people who frequent the mall. What is their attitude toward the decision of the mall owners to ban unescorted teenagers on weekend nights? What is your reaction?

2. Are you convinced that the curfew decision was not ethnically based? Why or why not?

3. Where do you stand on the issue of malls as private or public properties? What arguments on this issue do you find convincing?

4. What points regarding mall security does Meredith raise? Are the concerns legitimate in your view?

CORRESPONDENCES

1. Review Kowinski's perspective (page 465) and discuss its relevance to Meredith's essay.

2. Is Meredith's purpose to inform or is she also seeking to persuade her audience? How does the tone of her essay compare with that of Norton?

APPLICATIONS

1. Speculate with your group as to why the mall is the hangout of choice for many teenagers. You might conduct interviews with several adolescents of both genders and use their responses as a basis for your discussion.

2. Visit your local mall and interview personnel including shop owners, shoppers, and security guards on their impressions of how teenagers affect life at the mall. Using their responses, write an essay analyzing the effects of their presence on the mall's social and economic environment.

3. Visit your local mall and jot down your visual and sensory impressions. What are its dominant colors? Is the space designed to stimulate social interactions? How do people use the space? What does

their body language indicate about their responses to being there? Write an analysis of your findings.

4. In her essay, Meredith reports varied perspectives presented by several individuals. From the essay, select *one* person in favor of the curfew and *one* who is not. In the voice of *each* person you have chosen, write a letter to the president of the city council that either supports or does not support the mall restrictions.

Hollywood: The Dark Side

SYLVESTER MONROE

*Sylvester Monroe (b. 1951) might be best known for his 1987 Newsweek
cover story "Brothers." For this article, which he co-wrote with Peter Gold-
man, Monroe used childhood friends as a springboard to look at black men in
society. A paperback version of* Brothers *was published in 1989. Currently
Monroe is a correspondent for* Time *Magazine, which he joined in 1989. He
continues to report on social issues, including trends in ethnic and minority
communities. As you read Monroe's essay, list at least three examples of "the
dark side" of Hollywood.*

JOAN MOSLEY IS A LOVING BUT TOUGH single mother raising three children,
among them a five-year-old foster child, in South Central Los Angeles.
When she discovers that her teenage son is planning to buy a beeper,
every Black mother in America can appreciate her concern. "The day you
get a beeper is the day after you become a doctor," she admonishes. And
when she overhears him exclaim "That bitch is fine!" she comes down so
hard on him that every woman in America is on her side. "Am I a bitch?
Is your sister a bitch?" she asks rhetorically, driving her point home.

Joan Mosley, the protagonist of the half-hour show from 20th Century Fox Television called *South Central*, is the mirror image of millions
of African-American mothers who can be found in almost any city in
America. Where she cannot be found is on major network television.
Executives at CBS had "reservations" and passed on it; ABC and NBC
weren't interested either. So what has been described as a "refreshing
and realistic" portrayal of a significant slice of African-American life
remains at 20th Century Fox Television in the mini network's winter
lineup.

Why was it so difficult to get the show on the air? Rose Catherine
Pinkney, the former director of programming for 20th Century Fox
Television, now with Uptown Entertainment, helped develop *South
Central* and was assigned to cover its progress; she says the answer is
that *South Central* is a different type of Black comedy. "It's a realistic but
positive depiction of life in the nineties," explains Pinkney. "If you're
expecting 'ha, ha, ha' every two minutes, you're not going to enjoy this
show. But if you want honest laughs from an honest family when it's
right, then you'll like it."

South Central is like too many intelligent Black projects that often never make it to prime-time TV or that vanish forever after a few airings. Their chief flaw is that they don't fit neatly into the Black-sitcom formula—that electronic never-never land where stereotypical characters verbally bludgeon one another with insulting one-liners.

"As long as we're funny, as long as the public is allowed to laugh at us, then everyone seems to be comfortable dealing with us," says Leisa M. Henry, director of marketing and public relations for new-writer recruitment at Warner Brothers Television. "It's okay to be ethnic. It's okay to wear dreadlocks if you are making people laugh. But as soon as we cross the line and become serious, when we have to be contended with as adults facing serious real-life issues, then we're no longer marketable."

Clowns, Cutups, and Buffoons

After all these years, Hollywood still doesn't get it. On the big screen, films like *Boyz N the Hood, Juice* and *Menace II Society* have been applauded by both critics and Black moviegoers for their more honest portrayals. The frustration is their sameness. Studio executives seem to think that hard-core inner-city life is the only slice of Black life there is.

Flick on the small screen, and you're likely to be bombarded with stereotypes of a different stripe: Black men and women depicted mainly as clowns, cutups and loud-mouthed buffoons. "We are more or less told who we are, rather than asked," testified veteran actress and Hollywood activist Maria Gibbs at a hearing held last June by the U.S. Commission on Civil Rights. "We sing, we dance, we tell jokes—that's all we are allowed to do. We entertain."

Among Tinseltown's most vocal critics is one of its biggest stars, Bill Cosby. Temporarily shedding his own comic Jell-O–pudding persona, the most successful African-American in television history took the occasion of his induction into the Academy of Television Arts and Sciences Hall of Fame to urge the industry to cut it out. "Stop this horrible massacre of images that are being put on the screen now," he chided his network peers. "I'm begging you, because it isn't us."

Saundra Sharp, an outspoken African-American actress, writer and independent filmmaker, blames the poor quality of Black TV fare on the nature of the business. "Every once in a while something positive sneaks through like *Frank's Place*," she says. "But I don't hold much hope for Hollywood. The mentality is too low and the greed, too high."

But Sharp complains that too many Blacks in the industry have succumbed to the very same dollar-driven shallow way of thinking. Sharp, a former member of the Writers Guild of America, West, Inc., cofounded the activist Black Anti-Defamation Coalition to protest the negative images of Blacks on-screen in the early eighties. She says that if the coalition were still active, they would probably be going after their own people.

"Back then we were going to White producers complaining about how we were being represented as pimps and whores," she says. "But as more and more Blacks got into positions as producers and writers, they began to create the same images."

It's About Power and Control

In all fairness, Black executives are still too few and too low on the organizational chart to wield much clout. "There is not one Black person who can 'green light' a television project, who can say, 'Yes, let's make that film or put that show on the air,'" observes veteran actor and producer Tim Reid, who starred in *WKRP in Cincinnati* and *Simon & Simon* before coexecutive-producing the highly acclaimed but short-lived *Frank's Place*. "It's very difficult for a Black person to be taken seriously at the level we are talking about. It's about power and control, and those who have it do not want to relinquish it."

Simply casting more Black actors and actresses in the countless major and minor character roles that routinely go to Whites would go far in getting beyond the same old tired clichés. But with only about eight or ten established Black casting directors for TV and film—that's out of hundreds—Black names, other than those of a star like Denzel Washington, are unlikely to be mentioned. "You can't rely on political correctness," explains Reuben Cannon, veteran Black casting director and producer. "When there's not a person of color in the room when casting is taking place, you can end up with a film that is set in America, yet doesn't have a Black face in it."

Television's biases are so blatant that media scholars and the few outspoken activists within the industry are becoming increasingly vocal in calling for change. George Gerbner, a professor at the University of Pennsylvania's Annenberg School for Communication, directed a ten-year study of the industry commissioned by the Screen Actors Guild and the American Federation of Television and Radio Artists. The study, released last year, found that White males under forty work more and earn more than any other group in television. Women, non-Whites and the elderly—in other words, most of America—are greatly underrepresented. That helps explain the enormous diversity of White male characters—from villains to superheroes and just about everything imaginable in between—while everyone else is mainly a type.

"Television seems to be frozen in a time warp of obsolete and damaging representations that deprive millions of people of the chance to see themselves growing up with the same opportunities, values and potential as everyone else," Gerbner said.

Another study, commissioned by the Writers Guild of America, West, Inc., found that both the television and the film industries have been shamefully lax in employing women and non-White writers. In 1991 White males still accounted for more than 70 percent of employed television writers and more than 80 percent of the working writers on feature films. In contrast, non-Whites comprise a mere 4 percent of the guild's 7,648 members. That's 3.9 percent of television writers and 2.6 percent of film writers. The result, says the report, is a "numbness and sameness in the storytelling."

The Lowest Common Denominator

Hollywood's long-standing race problems can be explained in large part by an old-fashioned blend of racism and ignorance plus a healthy dose of the industry's legendary arrogance. When it comes to writing for Black characters, for example, most Blacks in the industry would agree that while some White writers can write for Blacks, Black writers are critical to doing it consistently. Most White executives see it differently. "This industry still feels that Whites can write for Black characters simply because they have the power to do it," says Warner Brothers' Leisa M. Henry.

Particularly infuriating to many Blacks in the business is watching White writer-producers become specialists in producing Black shows, while Black writers and producers are routinely locked out of the process. The White husband-wife team of Andy and Susan Borowitz, for example, are the creators of a long list of Black shows, including *The Fresh Prince of Bel-Air*. But industry insiders say it wasn't until Black writer Winifred Hervey became the show's executive producer in June 1991 that it stopped being what one critic described as "a Black caricature of a White caricature" and began noticeably improving.

The industry's flaws are magnified by television's tendency to reduce everyone and everything to its lowest common denominator. "One of the things television does is take reality and pour it into convenient packages of an hour or half hour," says Bridget Potter, senior vice-president of original programming for HBO, "and the process of stereotyping happens."

Television executives concede that their industry is the last place to look for displays of multiculturalism. "What the studios have been doing for years is playing to middle-class White Americans," says David Gerber, who was the longtime chairman of the MGM/UA Television Group until the studio phased out its TV operations. "As a result you won't see Black family shows outside the sitcom genre, and you won't see Jewish family shows. I'm not sure you have any typical family on television other than a White middle-class one, because the view is that they won't work in a mass audience." He shrugs, "After all, there are only about 30 million African-Americans. But there are 200 million White Americans."

That leaves many African-Americans in the industry in a bind. "If you're working on a show with White executive producers, they have their perceptions of what Black people are like," says P. Karen Raper; Raper and her writing partner, Eunetta Boone, are the only Blacks on a nine-writer staff for the NBC sitcom *Getting By*. "They just don't get it, and in their life they don't have to get it," adds Boone. "It's our job to help them get it." But the burden of speaking up for an entire race can take its toll on even the best Black writers, particularly those working on Black shows. Boone and Raper, who were story editors on *Roc* and *The Fresh Prince of Bel-Air* before writing for *Getting By*, say that at times it's easier *not* to write on Black shows.

"It's easier to sit by and let a White character look stupid," says Raper. "But I am at the point where I am tired of having to defend my race against people who know nothing about our culture. So you are in a position of constantly having to give history lessons to people who act as if you've only existed since 1954. They know nothing about you, and they don't care to know anything about you."

Few people better understand the industry's resistance to quality Black programming than Frank Dawson and his partners in 2002 Communications. For nearly two years the company has had a promising Black dramatic series called *Fox Hills* languishing in "development hell." It's about a thirty-something African-American couple, both lawyers, in an upper-middle-class Los Angeles neighborhood. The series follows their return from Chicago to Los Angeles, where the husband works for a Fortune 500 company and the wife runs a community law practice in South Central L.A.

Although there hasn't been a dramatic series about an African-American family on network TV since the early 1980's, *South Central* remains tough to sell. "At the studio, they're saying the writing is strong, but they're still not sure whether mainstream audiences want to see these characters on a weekly basis," says Dawson, who spent almost ten years at CBS and Universal Studios before hitting the glass ceiling. "What we're battling are long-standing perceptions not rooted in any truth at all."

It doesn't have to be this bad. African-American viewers, today Hollywood's largest and most loyal audience, could make a difference. According to a 1989–90 Nielsen survey, we watch an average of 72 hours of television each week. That's 24 hours, or 49 percent more than

non-Blacks watch. We're also frequent moviegoers—by various estimates accounting for between 10 and 25 percent of theater audiences.
That puts us in a good position to demand—through petitions, letter
writing and telephone campaigns—Black love stories, family dramas
and westerns and to see ourselves portrayed as something other than
fly girls and clowns from the 'hood. The tragedy is that we rarely exercise our collective power to improve the quality of what we watch.

"Black television audiences are not selective, and they are not
vocal," complains Debra Lynn Langford, vice-president of television at
Quincy Jones/David Salzman Entertainment. "When we like a show,
we don't write in, we don't call in." Nor do Blacks have a group like the
influential Viewers for Quality Television, which saved the popular
Cagney & Lacey from cancellation nearly half a dozen times when network executives tried to ax the show because of low ratings.

Angry viewers did launch a letter-writing campaign against CBS's
decision to drop *Frank's Place*. Unfortunately, it came after the show had
already been canceled. Black protest did make a difference in deep-
sixing an offensive CBS half-hour pilot for a proposed series based on
the film *Driving Miss Daisy*. Similarly, if Black viewers want to see *South
Central*'s Joan Mosley handling the challenges of raising three kids
alone in South Central L.A. or any number of other distinctly American
issues from an authentic African-American perspective, it will be up to
us to start writing letters and making calls to Fox and the other net-
works and their advertisers.

"It's about teaching people *how* to watch television," says Rose
Catherine Pinkney. For many of us, that could turn out to be worth
much more than the price of the ticket.

INTERPRETATIONS

1. *"South Central* is like too many intelligent Black projects that often
    never make it to prime-time TV or that vanish forever after a few
    airings." What evidence does Monroe offer to support his claim?

2. To what extent do you agree with Monroe that most sitcoms
    "reduce everyone and everything to its lowest common denomi-
    nator"? What examples can you cite?

3. Monroe's original audience was *Essence*, an African-American
    magazine. Does his essay appeal only to that readership? Explain
    your answer.

4. Monroe's purpose is to persuade. Does he appeal to his audience's
    emotions, logic, or ethics? Cite examples to justify your answer.

Class Struggle in Hollywood

BENJAMIN DEMOTT

Benjamin DeMott (b. 1924) is a Mellon Professor of Humanities at Amherst College. DeMott writes widely on race, class, and media. His most recent books include The Trouble With Friendship: Why American Can't Think Straight About Race *(1995),* Created Equal: Reading and Writing About Class in America *(1996), and* Killer Women Blues: Why Americans Can't think Straight About Gender and Power *(2000). Before reading DeMott's essay, record in your journal your definition of "class struggle."*

INCREASINGLY IN RECENT YEARS movies have been dealing with power issues and class relationships—interactions between masters and servants, executives and underlings, yuppies and waitresses, millionaires and hookers, rich aristocrats and social-nobody lawyers. Think of "Reversal of Fortune" and "The Bonfire of the Vanities." Think of "White Palace" and "Pretty Woman." Think of Michael Corleone's struggle for social acceptance in "The Godfather Part III." Think of "Working Girl," or "Driving Miss Daisy" or "Dirty Dancing." Script after script links up clout and cloutlessness, often to stunning box-office effect.

Not every movie version of the power theme speaks specifically about class relationships, and some versions are only loosely linked to social reality. The two worlds of "Edward Scissorhands," for example— hilltop mansion and tract house; solitary helpless artist versus artist-baiting mob—are derived less from everyday experience than from fairy tales, allegory and satire.

Usually, though, conventional realism is the chosen mode, and class skirmishes are sketched. The camera in "White Palace" studies St. Louis's fancier suburbs and its rundown Dog Town; class conflict erupts at the movie's crisis point. Nora, the waitress-heroine (Susan Sarandon), listens smolderingly to her yuppie lover's upper-middle friends and relations uttering their hypocritical socio-political pieties, and explodes. Storming her way out, she cries: "*I'm* working class!"

At first glance the angry explicitness of her outcry and the movie's declaration of difference look promising. They could signify that Hollywood is reaching toward maturity, trying to teach itself and the nation how to think straight about social hierarchy—the realities of class and class power. The need for such instruction is patent. This country has an ignoble tradition of evading social facts—pretending that individual episodes of upward mobility obviate grappling with the hardening socio-economic differences in our midst. Movies that deal responsibly with class relationships could, in theory, moderate the national evasiveness.

But, regrettably, contemporary "class movies" don't deal responsibly with class. The tone of their treatment of rich and poor is new; it is harsher and meaner than that of Frank Capra's "little guy" sagas or George Cukor's social comedies or John Ford's populism that were pleasing to our parents and grandparents in the 30s, 40s and 50s.

The harsher tone, however, doesn't bespeak fundamental change. At their best, Hollywood's new-style "class movies" nod at realities of social difference—and then go on to obfuscate them. At their worst these films are driven by near-total dedication to a scam—the maddeningly dangerous deceit that there are no classes in America.

One favorite story line stresses discovery: people who think firm class lines exist come to discover, by the end of the tale, that they're mistaken; everybody's really the same.

In the 1988 blockbuster "Working Girl," Tess McGill (Melanie Griffith), initially a bottom-dog secretary-gofer, is positive she can make it to the top. But her peers in the word-processing pool regard her aspirations as foolish. They tell her, flat out, that the real world has lines and distinctions and that her daydreams of glory and business power are foolish. "I sing and dance in my underwear," says one pal, "but I'm not Madonna." The implicit message: Get real, Tess. Accept the reality of levels.

But Tess, of course, accepts no such thing. She reads *W*, takes classes to improve her accent, seizes her boss's office when the latter breaks her leg skiing—and winds up not only doing deals but ordering the boss (Sigourney Weaver) to get her bony bottom out of sight. What does it take to get to the top? Desire, period. Tess's desire flies her straight up to a managerial perch, allowing her to become, almost effortlessly, all she can be: no problem, few barriers, class dismissed. In the final frame the doubters in the secretarial pool acknowledge their error; they rise to applaud the heroine who proved them wrong.

A second familiar story line involves upendings: characters theoretically on the social bottom shake the cages of characters who try to use their position to humiliate those below. The top dogs are so stupid they don't realize that socioeconomic power only lasts for a second and that they can be overcome by any intrepid underling.

Consider "Pretty Woman," the 1990 film that became one of the highest-grossing movies ever and is now near the top of video bestseller and rental charts. The would-be humiliators in this movie are snobbish salespeople on chic Rodeo Drive. Vivian (Julia Roberts), a hooker, runs afoul of them when she is sent on a shopping spree by the corporate raider (Richard Gere) who has hired her for a week. The raider wants elegance and the hooker aims to oblige—but on her first pass at the Drive she's suited up in hooker garb, and the salespeople are offended. "I don't think we have anything for, you. *Please leave.*" Quickly the snobs are undone. The corporate raider flashes plastic, and tells a shop manager that they'll be spending big and need appropriate cosseting. In minutes—through instruction in fork-tine-counting, for instance—the raider effects the few alterations of manners required to transform Vivian the street hooker into grandeur.

Regally togged, her arms filled with sleek clothes boxes, Vivian returns to the salespeople who were mean to her and sticks it to them in economic not moral terms. If they had been nice to her, they would have made a killing. ("You work on commission, don't you?")

Power is temporary and snobs are dopes—so goes the message. Ostracize a hooker in midmorning and she'll ruin you before tea. *Class dismissed.*

Comparable dismissals occur in movies drawing huge audiences of high school students. They usually have plot lines showing bottom dogs gliding smoothly and painlessly to the top. In "Dirty Dancing" (1987), Patrick Swayze, playing a talented working-class dancer (he has a card in the "housepainters and plasterers union"), competes for esteem with a Yale medical school student—and wins in a breeze.

In John Hughes's "Some Kind of Wonderful" (1987) and "Pretty in Pink" (1986), working-class heroes or heroines become romantically interested in classmates who rank above them, in terms of money and status, in the school society. As the attachments develop, the poor students commence to display gifts and talents that prove them equal to or intrinsically superior to the arrogant, insecure characters in whom they've become interested.

Once the nonclass, merit-based order or hierarchy has been established, and superficial, class-based gradations have been eliminated, the poor boy or girl chooses whether to continue the relationship with the pseudo-superior as an equal or to end it. Either way, the experience bolsters the belief that, in school and out, social strata are evanescent and meaningless.

But what is truly striking is the array of ploys and devices by which movie makers bring off escapes from significant confrontation with class realities. The Vietnam War film "Platoon" (1986), for example, lets on at the beginning that it will show us an upper-middle white soldier learning about differences between himself and the sons of the working class who compose the majority of his comrades in arms.

But in place of the experience of learning, we're offered liberal platitudes and star turns. The hero writes his grandmother that his fellow soldiers are the salt of the earth (little corroboration supplied); the soldiers themselves—particularly the blacks among them—are brought on for a succession of amusing monologues, following which they disappear, shipped out dead or alive; at no point is the gritty stuff of class difference even momentarily engaged.

In the much-acclaimed "Driving Miss Daisy" (1989), the early intimation is that the focus will be on relations between white employers and black servants. But almost immediately the outlines of that social difference are blurred. The white employer is Jewish and her synagogue is bombed; poor black and rich white become one, joint victims of discriminatory violence. ("You're my best friend, Hoke.") Class dismissed once more.

The story is nearly the same even in those unusual movies that focus solely on minority communities. Social difference is glanced at, defined in a few snippets of dialogue—and then trashed, often by means of a joke. In "House Party," Reginald Hudin's 1990 film about teenage life, the joke is about sex. Through establishing shots and talk, two girlfriends are placed at a social distance from each other. One lives in "the projects," the other in an expensively middle-class suburban home.

The film offers a single moment of reflection on the social difference in question; a young man points out that there is plenty of space for making out in the rich girl's house, none where the projects girl lives. Yet once more, class dismissed.

It's hardly surprising that the notion of America as a classless society emerges at its most schematic in movies aimed at relatively youthful, unsophisticated audiences. But the same impulse to paper over social differences surfaces in many more ambitious films purporting to raise subjects considered controversial by Hollywood standards (social injustice, war, the treatment of minorities).

And not infrequently that impulse drives film makers—such as Francis Ford Coppola in "The Godfather Part III" and Barry Levinson in "Avalon"—to overplay ethnic influence and underplay class influence on character.

The reason all this matters is simple. Treating class differences as totally inconsequential strengthens the national delusion: that class power and position are insignificant. It encourages the middle-class—those with the clearest shot at upward mobility—to assume, wrongly, that all citizens enjoy the same freedom of movement that they enjoy. And it makes it easier for political leaders to speak as though class power had nothing to do with the inequities of life in America. ("Class is for

European democracies or something else," says George Bush. "It isn't for the United States of America. We are not going to be divided by class.")

Movies that deal responsibly with class relationships might help to embolden leaders to begin talking candidly, about real as opposed to phony issues of "fairness." But movies obviously can't do this as long as their makers are in terror of allowing class permanently out of the closet.

It's true that occasional moments occur when movie audiences can grasp the substantive dimensions of social difference. A person reached toward from above or below is seen to possess inner, mysterious resources (or limits) about which someone differently placed on the social scale can have no inkling, and can't conceivably lay claim.

There is one such moment in "Working Girl." Following orders, Tess, as secretarial underling, books her boss, Katharine Parker (Ms. Weaver), into a chalet for a ski weekend. She is helping Katharine fasten her new ski boots in the office when she is asked where in the chalet the room is located. Tess doesn't know; Katharine dials the resort and at once a flood of flawless German fills the room.

The camera angle shows us Tess's awe; we gaze up with her (from the glossy white boots that she, as footman, is buckling) to this animated, magical, Ivy-educated mistress of the world, self-transformed into Europe, performing in another language. Katharine is demonstrating quite casually that bottom dogs have no exact knowledge of what lies between them and their ideal, that top dogs possess secret skills nobody learns overnight, as in charm class, or by changing hairstyles—skills traceable to uncounted indulgent hours of tutoring, study and travel.

The bottom dog's eyes widen as frightening truth dawns. If a talent so mesmerizing—this poured-forth foreign self—can be invisible until now, must there not be others equally well-concealed? Maybe this dream to be her *is* foolish. What unimaginable barriers stand between me and my desire?

In the movie culture the answer to such questions is, of course: no real barriers, none. "Be all you can be" means, at the bottom as at the top, "Be whatever you wish," fear no obstacle, see no obstacle, there are no obstacles. "Working Girl" is, finally, a story about how ambitious working girls just can't lose—one more movie that obliterates class.

"White Palace," for all its initial explicitness about the reality of social differences, is, finally, a story asserting that such differences simply don't matter; pure passion erases them every time.

The other week Senator Daniel Patrick Moynihan told a *Wall Street Journal* reporter that the fundamental issue in this country is "class, not race." It's essential, he said, "to at least start thinking about it, start talking about it. Let's be honest. We're not doing that."

One reason we're not is that movies remain firmly resolved against letting us.

INTERPRETATIONS

1. "At their best, Hollywood's new-style 'class movies' nod at realities of social difference—and then go on to obfuscate them. At their worst these films are driven by near-total dedication to a scam—the maddeningly dangerous deceit that there are no classes in America." What evidence does DeMott offer to support this thesis? To what extent do you agree with his point of view?

2. According to DeMott, movies like *House Party* and *Driving Miss Daisy* that focus on different ethnic groups also present the myth of classlessness in the United States. What evidence does he offer for his point of view? Is it convincing? Why or why not?

CORRESPONDENCES

1. Read Pollack's perspective on American movies (page 463). How does it contradict or reinforce DeMott's thesis that most American films on class differences "strengthens the national delusion: that class, power, and position are insignificant"? With whose point of view do you agree?

2. Characterize Monroe's tone. Is it neutral, serious, bitter, or argumentative? What does his tone suggest about his attitude toward his subject? How does it compare to that of DeMott in "Class Struggle in Hollywood"?

APPLICATIONS

1. For a period of one hour flip channels on your television. Record the nationality, race, gender, and economic position of the people on the screen that you encounter during this time. How well do your observations match the composition of individuals present in the United States? Check your figures against U.S. census data.

   http://www.census.gov/

   http://www.socccd.cc.ca.us/ref/almanac/demographics/uspop.htm

   http://faculty.vassar.edu/lenevare/2003a/soci254/1990race.html

2. View one of the movies cited by DeMott and write your analysis of its treatment of class or ethnic differences.

3. To what extent are soap operas and sitcoms reflections of mainstream attitudes toward ethnicity? Are the images they project free of stereotypes? Cite examples.

Why We Crave Horror Movies

STEPHEN KING

Stephen King (b. 1947) is one of the best-selling novelists of our time and is famous worldwide for his horror fiction. He graduated from the University of Maine and began writing short stories in order to supplement his teaching salary. Carrie, *King's first novel, was a phenomenal success in both print and on the screen. Among King's many novels are:* The Shining *(1977),* Pet Sematary *(1983), and* Misery *(1989). King's most recent books are* Dream Catcher *(2001) and* From a Buck 8 *(2002). As you read King's essay, underline the statements with which you are in agreement or disagreement.*

I THINK THAT WE'RE ALL MENTALLY ILL; those of us outside the asylums only hide it a little better—and maybe not all that much better, after all. We've all known people who talk to themselves, people who sometimes squinch their faces into horrible grimaces when they believe no one is watching, people who have some hysterical fear—of snakes, the dark, the tight place, the long drop . . . and, of course, those final worms and grubs that are waiting so patiently underground.

When we pay our four or five bucks and seat ourselves at tenth-row center in a theater showing a horror movie, we are daring the nightmare.

Why? Some of the reasons are simple and obvious. To show that we can, that we are not afraid, that we can ride this roller coaster. Which is not to say that a really good horror movie may not surprise a scream out of us at some point, the way we may scream when the roller coaster twists through a complete 360 or plows through a lake at the bottom of the drop. And horror movies, like roller coasters, have always been the special province of the young; by the time one turns 40 or 50, one's appetite for double twists or 360-degree loops may be considerably depleted.

We also go to re-establish our feelings of essential normality; the horror movie is innately conservative, even reactionary. Freda Jackson as the horrible melting woman in *Die, Monster, Die!* confirms for us that no matter how far we may be removed from the beauty of a Robert Redford or a Diana Ross, we are still light-years from true ugliness.

And we go to have fun.

Ah, but this is where the ground starts to slope away, isn't it? Because this is a very peculiar sort of fun indeed. The fun comes from

498 CHAPTER 9 • POPULAR CULTURE

seeing others menaced—sometimes killed. One critic has suggested that if pro football has become the voyeur's version of combat, then the horror film has become the modern version of the public lynching.

It is true that the mythic, "fairytale" horror film intends to take away the shades of gray . . . It urges us to put away our more civilized and adult penchant for analysis and to become children again, seeing things in pure blacks and whites. It may be that horror movies provide psychic relief on this level because this invitation to lapse into simplicity, irrationality and even outright madness is extended so rarely. We are told we may allow our emotions a free rein . . . or no rein at all.

If we are all insane, then sanity becomes a matter of degree. If your insanity leads you to carve up women like Jack the Ripper or the Cleveland Torso Murderer, we clap you away in the funny farm (but neither of those two amateur-night surgeons was ever caught, heh-heh-heh); if, on the other hand your insanity leads you only to talk to yourself when you're under stress or to pick your nose on the morning bus, then you are left alone to go about your business . . . though it is doubtful that you will ever be invited to the best parties.

The potential lyncher is in almost all of us (excluding saints, past and present; but then, most saints have been crazy in their own ways), and every now and then, he has to be let loose to scream and roll around in the grass. Our emotions and our fears form their own body, and we recognize that it demands its own exercise to maintain proper muscle tone. Certain of these emotional muscles are accepted—even exalted—in civilized society; they are, of course, the emotions that tend to maintain the status quo of civilization itself. Love, friendship, loyalty, kindness—these are all the emotions that we applaud, emotions that have been immortalized in the couplets of Hallmark cards and in the verses (I don't dare call it poetry) of Leonard Nimoy.

When we exhibit these emotions, society showers us with positive reinforcement; we learn this even before we get out of diapers. When, as children, we hug our rotten little puke of a sister and give her a kiss, all the aunts and uncles smile and twit and cry, "Isn't he the sweetest little thing?" Such coveted treats as chocolate-covered graham crackers often follow. But if we deliberately slam the rotten little puke of a sister's fingers in the door, sanctions follow—angry remonstrance from parents, aunts and uncles; instead of a chocolate-covered graham cracker, a spanking.

But anticivilization emotions don't go away, and they demand periodic exercise. We have such "sick" jokes as, "What's the difference between a truckload of bowling balls and a truckload of dead babies?" (You can't unload a truckload of bowling balls with a pitchfork . . . a joke, by the way, that I heard originally from a ten-year-old.) Such a joke may surprise a laugh or a grin out of us even as we recoil, a possibility that confirms the thesis: If we share a brotherhood of man, then we also share an insanity of man. None of which is intended as a defense of either the sick joke or insanity but merely as an explanation of why the best horror films, like the best fairy tales, manage to be reactionary, anarchistic, and revolutionary all at the same time.

The mythic horror movie, like the sick joke, has a dirty job to do. It deliberately appeals to all that is worst in us. It is morbidity unchained, our most base instincts let free, our nastiest fantasies realized . . . and it all happens, fittingly enough, in the dark. For those reasons, good liberals often shy away from horror films. For myself, I like to see the most aggressive of them—*Dawn of the Dead*, for instance—as lifting a trap door in the civilized forebrain and throwing a basket of raw meat to the hungry alligators swimming around in that subterranean river beneath.

Why bother? Because it keeps them from getting out, man. It keeps them down there and me up here. It was Lennon and McCartney who said that all you need is love, and I would agree with that.

As long as you keep the gators fed.

INTERPRETATIONS

1. An effective introduction should capture the reader's interest. Review King's first paragraph. What is his thesis? What evidence does he offer to support? Do you agree or disagree with his point of view? Did he gain your attention? Why or why not?

2. What are King's three main reasons for the popularity of horror movies? Which did you find most convincing?

3. What is King's purpose in writing this essay? Is he mainly seeking to inform or does he want also to persuade his reader? Explain.

CORRESPONDENCES

1. Review Wright's perspective on horror (page 465) and discuss its application to King's essay.

2. Review Armenti's perspective on movies (page 465). What conversation can you imagine him having with Stephen King? To what extent does Armenti's point of view on movies reflect yours?

APPLICATIONS

1. Many of King's novels, including *The Shining* (1980), *Pet Sematary* (1989), or *Sleepwalkers* (1992), have been adapted for the screen.

View one of them and write two paragraphs responding to King's comment in an interview that "Horror isn't a hack market now, and never was. The genre is one of the most delicate known to man, and it must be handled with great care and more than a little love."

2. Write an essay defending or attacking King's thesis that horror movies are a safe release for expressing behavior that might otherwise be considered abnormal, even criminal. Include videos and/ or computer games also perceived as "dangerous" to reinforce your point of view.

3. Conduct an experiment with your group by monitoring for a day the violent images you encounter on television, video games, Web sites or magazines. Compare your list with other group members. What consensus, if any, did you reach?

4. What's *really* scary? Check this Web site!

www.phobialist.com/

What Is Hip Hop?

JAY FORD

Jay Ford (b. 1969) is a writer, singer, composer, activist, and lawyer. He currently resides in New York City, where he is developing a legal magazine for the general public called Pro Bono. *It is his sincerest hope that the music he shares and the reflection of life he provides will bring change, both personal and societal. Do you agree with Ford, that "Hip Hop" can bring about positive societal change?*

WHEN I WAS A YOUNG MAN, my grandmother told me that I should not do what the white boys did. She said, "You are different from the white boys. Their ways will not benefit you." She advised me "to discover and appreciate my 'difference,' and follow the way of my own people." My grandmother was teaching me the importance of culture. For her, a person's culture is the life-generating energy behind his or her human experience. It reflects both external and internal forces and often brings clarity to the past, perspective to the present, and direction for the future.

Much of the culture of American-Africans is expressed through music. Their traditions and customs have been passed down through the beat of the master drum, their sacred source of communication. In Africa, the drum was used in ceremonies to celebrate the crowning of the king. The beating of its sacred skin could talk to the dead and summon the gods to do the people's bidding. American-Africans used the drum to communicate to neighboring villages hundreds of miles away or to announce the birth of new life into the world. The drum provided the life energy needed to conquer foes in war and to celebrate peace when conflict ended.

When Africans were taken from their homeland by Europeans and Arabs, the drum came with them. In captivity, the drum continued to enable them to stay connected with Africa and to each other. In the face of degrading treatment, it reminded them of their magnificent history and ancestral legacy. It allowed them to teach their children their own significance in life and provided a cultural foundation for them in a strange and hostile land. It was the sacredness of the drum that enabled lessons to be taught under the noses of their enemies.

Unfortunately, their captors soon understood the power of the drum and forbade their using it. In fact, many plantations made it a serious crime to be caught drumming or in possession of drum-making material. People were whipped, beaten, and sold to faraway plantations. Lies and misinformation were spread about the drum and people who chose to drum. What the captors did not realize, however, is that the power of the master drum was not the drum itself but the drum beat, and that beat was inside of the American-Africans. In other words, the captors could take the people away from the drum but they could not take the drum out of the people.

So even without the physical presence of the drum, American-Africans continued to play music and pass culture from generation to generation. They used farm tools, water jugs, spoons, washtubs, wash boards, and tapped their feet, all in the name of their drum. They sang work songs, plantation songs, freedom songs, and civil rights songs, all in the name of the drum. By being denied the physical use of the drum they were forced to expand the sounds and rhythms that carried their culture. Something from nothing became the motto, and with hard work they fused old customs with new traditions, all in an attempt to define a new American-African culture.

From this new culture came a tradition of music that has forced the world to reflect. The music of their children today is Hip Hop, and like Jazz before it, it has revolutionized the way the world dresses, speaks, wears its hair, dances, views drugs, and treats its youth. It has charmed the fashion industry. It has rejuvenated a jejune record industry. It has been debated in Congressional hearings and has been argued in the Supreme Court. It has conquered the children of Africa, Europe, Asia, Russia, and everywhere else it has been heard. And it has physically, economically, and spiritually empowered and embraced a generation of young people that many ignore or are afraid to love.

My generation was the first to grow up during this musical era. In fact, many of us remember when Hip Hop first began, with the crews battling each other for DJ equipment and bragging rights. The new jazz, street wise, on the edge, limitless, unpredictable, and above all real, was a true expression of life from the souls of those who lived it. Songs were sung because they must be sung for both therapeutic purposes and cultural survival, and at that time the songs were uncorrupted by record labels, money, and image exploitation.

I was introduced to Hip Hop music through the radio. In those days most radio stations would not play rap music at all. To hear some Hip Hop I was forced to stay up late and listen to Mr. Magic's Rap Attack on WBLS or some local college stations who played Rap way after midnight. Or I could go to the clubs that played Hip Hop music, like the Roof Top on 155 Street in Harlem. My parents did not let me out to the Roof Top, so I had to be content with late night radio.

First came the sound, then the break dancing, then the beat and the language, and I was hooked. Everything to me was Hip Hop. It expressed my emotions, often saying what I felt but dared not say. Its flamboyance and pride in being Black gave me great self-esteem. And its master drum motivated me to move in ways that I often could not understand or control.

I do not contend to be an expert on Hip Hop, and there are many who understand its history better than I. However, it is important to understand that you are a part of the Hip Hop era, whether you know it or not. From block parties to political debates, styles of dress, the deaths of Tupac Shakur and Christopher Wallace (a.k.a. Biggie Smalls), the Million Man March, the Million Woman March, Hip Hop has and will continue to influence your world. It is the voice of my peers and my children, sometimes rude, often crude, but always an honest reflection of American life.

Further, true to the spirit of the African tradition, Hip Hop has provided and continues to provide an avenue of oral expression and hope for a segment of society that is overwhelmingly bombarded with death, prison, poverty, negativity, drugs, and hopelessness. American-Africans make up twelve percent of the American population and represent nearly sixty percent of its prison population. American-African men have been disenfranchised by felony convictions. The death rate of American-Africans is equal to or worse than the death rate of many so-called Third World countries. AIDS has now become the leading cause of death for American-Africans between the ages of 25 and 44.

In fact, American-Africans are disproportionately represented in all negative quality-of-life indicators in America, including but not limited to life expectancy, poverty, unemployment, and literacy. Hip Hop has helped to peacefully and creatively focus frustrations with society. It has provided them with a self-created job market, and it has even prevented many from acting violently toward others. For example, Trech, from the group "Naughty by Nature" warned, "If I was not doing this Hip Hop thing, I would probably be in your house right now, stealing your shit!"

This is not to say that everything about Hip Hop is good. Many Hip Hop lyrics echo the self-hatred and anger that are the residue of slavery: Black codes, Jim Crow laws, police brutality, and Eurocentric force feedings. European colonialism and white supremacist ideologies have done a great deal to set back the strongest of Africa's children. Much of American-African suffering is due to mental blocks that have many believing that someone apart from themselves, or God, ultimately controls their destinies. They have become a people who do not believe in what they cannot physically see. Many artists will complain that the music industry is controlled by lawyers, CEOs, video producers, radio stations, and distribution companies that are from a different culture from their own. Yet they forget that their ancestors faced twice the obstacles that they face today, with half the resources at their disposal, and they still kept hope alive.

This is not to discredit or undermine their anger about the way things are. The mechanisms of power and money are seemingly in the hands of a few while the majority fight for the scraps at the bottom. This unresolved anger about mastering one's own fate is a large part of Hip Hop. The critics of Hip Hop's reckless, oftentimes anti-white, or anti-American spirit, do not understand that this behavior reflects grieving for the lack of control over lives. Further, the assassinations and/or removal of an entire generation of African elders during the sixties and the seventies has left a void in their cultural lineage and unresolved anger in regard to their own country. From Fred Hampton and Bobby Hutton to Assata Shackur, Mumia Abu Jamal, Jeronimo Pratt, and Patrice Lamumba, and Steven Biko, the absence of these elders has resulted in miscommunication, confusion concerning right and wrong, and feelings of hopelessness and desperation among the young.

Many have become so filled with anger and resentment that they have forgotten that Africans are the moral fabric of America. The human rights struggle in America is their legacy. That is their strength. That is their master drum beat. Some today have a greater desire to be capitalistic. They have subconsciously or consciously become the very people that they wish to strike out against. By surrendering to the philosophies of "money over people" and "procedure over substance" they have now become the "pig," and they spit in the faces of their fathers and mothers, who gave their lives to deconstruct the thinking that some American-Africans now possess.

This inner struggle and generational conflict are also reflected in their music. Hip Hop is all of this: the good, the bad, the ugly, and the confused. It is a standing record of the American-African's inner struggle to be both African and American. It exposes the earnest quest to be God-like as well as the repulsive arrogance to have no fear of and faith in God. It reeks of the frustration of knowing exactly where you are in time, and yet having no idea of where you belong within the continuum of your own legacy.

Finally, Hip Hop is a historical journal of people who are often left out of white American historical texts. Listen as it bravely focuses on the concerns and struggles of everyday people as well as the heroes, sheroes, and villains of our time. Reflect, as it speaks of religion, money, and power and gauges our societal priorities without excuses and/or judgment. And what is most important, honor it as it stays true to its culture, following the beat of the master drum with an oral tradition focused on spiritual resurrection.

INTERPRETATIONS

1. "Their traditions and customs have been passed down through the beat of the master drum." What evidence does Ford provide to support this thesis?

2. Review paragraph 6. To what extent do you agree with Ford that Hip Hop has permeated popular culture? What other examples would you cite?

3. What portrait of contemporary African-American culture emerges in Ford's essay?

4. According to Ford, "Many Hip Hop lyrics echo the self-hatred and anger that are the residue of slavery." What evidence did you find most convincing? Do you agree with Ford's point of view? Why or why not?

5. What do you make of Ford's use of "American-African" for "African-American" throughout his essay? How does this wording affect your reading of this selection?

CORRESPONDENCES

1. Compare and contrast the influence of music on the identities of Wunsch and Ford.

2. Monroe and Ford discuss aspects of African-American culture from a different generational perspective. On what issues do they agree and disagree?

APPLICATIONS

1. Discuss with your group the portrayal of white culture in Ford's essay. To what extent do you agree or disagree with his analysis? Is it possible to control your destiny? Why or why not?

2. Working with your group, construct your definition of Hip Hop. How does your interpretation of the lyrics of Hip Hop compare to Ford's? How do you account for differences?

3. Compare and contrast a current male and female rap video. How are gender roles presented in the lyrics? Do they challenge or

perpetuate traditional stereotypes? Explain. What elements of Hip Hop are there?

4. As you read "What Is Hip Hop," by Ford, what music do you hear? If there are changes to these musical forms, where do they occur? What in the text suggests these changes to you?

Closer to Fine:
My Parents' Music and Mine

EMMA WUNSCH

Emma Wunsch (b. 1975) holds a B.A. from Binghamton University and expects to receive an M.F.A. from Brooklyn College in 2004. Wunsch has published in the Aura Arts Literary Review, PoetryMemoirStory, New England Writers Network, *and* Hanging Loose. *Her short story "Sugar Cereal" was published in 2003 in the* Vermont Literary Review. *Write a journal entry on your responses to Wunsch's title.*

UNLIKE MANY CHILDREN of my generation—the so-called X Generation—I was not raised on nursery rhymes, "Rock-a-Bye-Baby," or "Mary Had a Little Lamb."

I was raised on harder stuff.

My bedtime songs consisted of Jimi Hendrix's "The Wind Calls Mary," Pink Floyd's "Us and Them," "Aqualung," by Jethro Tull. By the time I was ten, I had been to more Grateful Dead concerts than Girl Scout meetings. My parents were hippies, big hippies, and they raised me on what had influenced them and their personal rebellions: music. Their music.

My parents were married in 1972 and I was born in 1975; a time when my parents were becoming disillusioned with contemporary music and moved to Westchester County, New York, where I was supposed to be Tom's Petty's "American Girl." Nice house, nice parents, nice car, and therefore nice kid. But there was something wrong: there was no "Great Wide Open" in the songs that my parents played for me. There was something missing. It took me thirteen years to realize, because of hearing the song of two lesbians with acoustic guitars from Georgia, that my parents' music collection (over 500 LPs) lacked women.

It wasn't that there were no women represented in the music my parents listened to; they were just scarce. The number of male groups that make up both my and my parents music is dominated by the male gender. Obviously this isn't the "fault" of my parents. Rock-'n'-roll has historically marginalized female artists. Of course there were the few women who broke through the chords of domination. I listened to

Janis Joplin, but when I did, I thought of her crazy past: how she died of alcohol and drugs. She wasn't a role model: she was "crazy." But for some reason, male rock stars who had similar lives of drugs and alcohol seemed "cool." (My father had a framed picture of Hendrix in his study.) Plus, Joplin's songs like "Down on Me" and "Get It While You Can" didn't seem to advocate much agency of female power. And Joni Mitchell, Judy Collins, and countless other women it seems, looking back, were never given as much air play on my parents' stereo as were Neil Young, Bob Dylan, Eric Clapton.

In "New Woman, New History" Rosemary Hennesey writes "Like literature, history is one of the preeminent transmitters of hegemonic culture and tradition. The stories it tells serves to legitimate standards of value and define the boundaries of intelligibility and subjectivity" (100). Hennesey's idea can easily be applied to the music my parents raised me on. They said their music was good; therefore I believed it was "classic." But this notion of "classic" rock led me to problematic constructions. I wanted to play the drums because Jon Bonham, the drummer of Led Zepplin, was "cool." Never mind the fact that like Joplin, Bonham too had died of substance abuse. The male classic rock bands that my parents played for me had indeed as Hennesey wrote, served "to legitimize [my] standards of value . . ." Of course, happily singing along to "Under My Thumb" by the Rolling Stones, at eight years old, I had no idea of the problems my parents' music was perpetuating.

When I was thirteen, we moved to another town in Westchester. I was in seventh grade and felt, like many, that I didn't belong anywhere. I had braces, few friends, and all the wrong clothes. According to biology, I was supposed to be embarking on womanhood. In December of 1989, I had my bat mitzvah and was supposed to be, according to Jewish tradition, a woman. Instead I felt alone, confused, and young. In June of that year, my parents sent me to sleep-away camp, in the hope that spending time away from them would make me more confident.

I grew up a lot that summer (when I came home after eight weeks in the Berkshire Hills of Western Massachusetts, I had sprouted almost three inches). But it wasn't camp that made me grow up. It was a two-woman band from Georgia called The Indigo Girls, with their acoustic guitars and poetic lyrics, who not only made me rethink a lot of the constructions of male classic rock stars, but also helped develop a lot of who I am today.

"I'm trying to tell you something about my life/Maybe give me insight between black and white," sings Emily Saliers in "Closer to Fine" on the band's first album "Indigo Girls," released in 1989. The first time I heard those words, I was sitting in my bunk stringing a bead necklace, and I insisted that I couldn't go eat lunch with my bunkmates until I heard every song on this new album. Twice. On the one hand, it was the personal element I felt from hearing Salier sing "my life" that made me skip lunch that hot summer day. I felt for the first time that I was the one being sung to. Unlike Bob Dylan singing about how angry he was, or other groups singing about how much they were in love, I actually felt like the Indigo Girls were singing to me. I wasn't angry like Bob Dylan was and I was too young to know what it felt like to be in love. But like the Indigo Girls, I too wanted "insight between black and white."

I had so many questions and the Indigo Girls were the first band that seemed to have questions too. I was supposed to be a woman, growing up. I was going to high school the following year. Was I going to start dating? Wear makeup? Carry a purse like my mother? I felt like I had all these questions, but no one had the time to tell me the answers. The Indigo Girls sang "there's more than one answer to these questions pointing me in a crooked line." I'm not going to lie and say that as soon as I heard the Indigo Girls sing the above line everything in my life was clear. Of course I was confused throughout my teenage years. I'm still confused in my early twenties. But there was something about the Indigo Girls . . . Something about hearing them for the first time in my bunk in the Berkshires, away from my parents for the first time, that made me feel a little "closer to fine."

Analyzing the lyrics of the Indigo Girls, I realize that part of the reason I related (and still do) to them much more than to the lyrics of the male rock-'n'-roll stars of my parents' generation is that their songs can be seen as postmodern. By postmodern I am defining the often problematic term as Linda Hutcheon does in "Representing the Postmodern" as "fundamentally contradictory, resolutely historical and inescapably political." Looking back at the lyrics of "Closer to Fine," I can now see the fundamental contradictions that I related to so well. The girls sing that life is "black and white," a typical modernist view, but then go on to say that "there's more than one answer." This is pure postmodern ideology; there are myriad answers and possibilities to everything in life. In "Closer to Fine" the women admit trying many different things in order to find answers. "I went to the doctor, I went to the mountains/I looked to the children, I drank from the fountain/I went to see the doctor of philosophy/I stopped at a bar at 3 A.M." The contradictions of this song go even further to empower the group. Even if they did find the answers, the road they are on is crooked, unlike the straight road of modernism. The Indigo Girls' philosophy is clear in "Closer to Fine."

Life is not black and white: it is crooked and will take you in a multitude of directions and even if you get "answers" from various sources, they are not the only ones. Because "the less [you] seek [your] source for something definitive, the closer [you] are to fine." And if that's hard to take, the girls reassure us that "it's only life after all."

The songs on many of the band's albums are historical as well. The Indigo Girls are always, in their postmodern mentality, looking back to the past that constructed their songs. Michele Foucault writes in "Space, Power and Knowledge" that nothing "just happens"; everything is connected to some kind of historical framework. In a Foucauldian way, the band often applies the theorist's idea of "discursive formations" to their contemporary music. In "Least Complicated" the group asks "What makes me think I could start clean slated?" Like Foucault, the Girls know that no slate is ever "clean." History is always involved. Other Indigo Girls' songs are historical as well and range from paying homage to Virginia Woolf ("Virgina Woolf"), calling to Jonas and Ezikiel ("Jonas and Ezikiel") to thanking Galileo Galilei ("Galileo").

The band shows their own self-reflexive positionality and history in "History of Us": "So we must love while these moments are still called today . . . stretching our youth as we must, until we are ashes to dust/Until time makes a history of us." In a refreshing, nondidatic way, the Indigo Girls are always aware of time, age, and history. They never take on positions of privilege: "this is my situation, it's not pictures or privilege, it's just self preservation." The band shows not only their awareness of history when they sing "I'm just a mirror of a mirror of myself, the things that I do," but also of their own limitations. And by hearing these women sing about their own shortcomings, at thirteen I was a little more confident in my own.

To me the Indigo Girls will always be "resolutely historical" simply because they entered my life at a significant time in my own personal history. In 1989, I was embarking on the journey of my teenage years . . . years in which my life would change more rapidly than it had ever before. In the ten years of my teens, I would enter and graduate high school, begin college, get my first boyfriend, develop physically and mentally, make new friends, get my first job, break up with my first boyfriend, read hundreds of new books and authors, get my second job, get drunk, and so on. In "Kid Fears" the band asks, "Hey little girl—how much have you grown? Are you on fire from the years? What would you give for your kid fears?" At times I would give a lot for my "kid fears," but I like to think that because of the Indigo Girls, I wouldn't give too much.

INTERPRETATIONS

1. Wunsch's earliest musical preferences were shaped by the music to which her parents introduced her. How does she evaluate their music's influence on her preadolescent identity?

2. "Rock-'n'-roll has historically marginalized female activists." What evidence does Wunsch cite to support her thesis? To what effect?

3. The year 1989–1990 is a crucial one for Wunsch. What experiences contributed to her growing up? How did the music of the Indigo Girls affect her self-concept and philosophy? Be specific.

CORRESPONDENCES

1. The anonymous perspective on page 464 links music and national identity. To what extent might it apply also to Wunsch's essay on music and personal identity?

2. Wunsch is a member of the X Generation. Review Kirn's perspective on "Twentystuff Culture" (page 464) and apply it to Wunsch's essay. What conclusions did you reach?

APPLICATIONS

1. Is there a rock group that has shaped your identity as the Indigo Girls did Wunsch's? Write an essay citing as she does specific lyrics to support your thesis.

2. According to music critic Susan Douglas, "popular music is probably the most girl-friendly medium going. The movies remain dominated by hard-body, big-gun action films; the news media either ignore or trivialize issues of central importance to young women; and most TV programming aimed at teenage girls features skinny, poreless women who screw up at work and obsess about dating." Discuss Douglas's assessment with your group. To what extent do you agree or disagree? On what evidence do you base your opinion?

3. Musically, what does "cool" sound like? What does "crazy" sound like? What characterizes these musical distinctions that Wunsch speaks of in her essay? What other distinctions might you characterize?

On Reading a Video Text

ROBERT SCHOLES

Robert Scholes is a Professor of Modern Culture and Media and Professor Emeritus of English and Comparative Literature at Brown University. He holds degrees from Yale and Cornell Universities. He is the author of more than a dozen books including: The Cornell Joyce Collection: A Catalogue *(1961),* Elements of Poetry *(1969),* Semiotics and Interpretations *(1985),* The Rise and Fall of English *(1998), and* The Crafty Reader *(2001). Scholes has published in many periodicals including,* Tri Quarterly, Sewanee Review, College English, *and* Critical Inquiry. *His many awards include a Guggenheim fellowship, a David H. Russell Research Award, and an honorary doctorate from the Universite Lumiere at Lyon, France. Scholes has been elected President of the Modern Language Association for 2004. Record in your journal your process for "reading a video text."*

THE MOMENTS OF SURRENDER proposed to us by video texts come in many forms, but all involve a complex dynamic of power and pleasure. We are, for instance, offered a kind of power through the enhancement of our vision. Close-ups position us where we could never stand. Slow motion allows us an extraordinary penetration into the mechanics of movement, and, combined with music, lends a balletic grace to ordinary forms of locomotion. Filters and other devices cause us to see the world through jaundiced or rose-colored optics, coloring events with emotion more effectively than verbal pathetic fallacy and less obtrusively. These derangements of normal visual processing can be seen as either constraints or extensions of visual power—that is, as power over the viewer or as extensions of the viewer's own optical power, or both. Either way they offer us what is perhaps the greatest single virtue of art: change from the normal, a defense against the ever-present threat of boredom. Video texts, like all except the most utilitarian forms of textuality, are constructed upon a base of boredom, from which they promise us relief.

Visual fascination—and I have mentioned only a few of its obvious forms—is just one of the matrices of power and pleasure that are organized by video texts. Others include narrativity and what I should like to call, at least tentatively, cultural reinforcement. By narrativity, of course, I mean the pleasures and powers associated with the reception of stories presented in video texts. By cultural reinforcement, I mean the process through which video texts confirm viewers in their ideological positions and reassure them as to their membership in a collective cultural body. This function, which operates in the ethical-political realm, is an extremely important element of video textuality and, indeed, an extremely important dimension of all the mass media. This is a function performed throughout much of human history by literature and the other arts, but now, as the arts have become more estranged from their own culture and even opposed to it, the mass media have come to perform this role. What the epic poem did for ancient cultures, the romance for feudalism, and the novel for bourgeois society, the media—and especially television—now do for the commodified, bureaucratized world that is our present environment.

It is time, now, to look at these processes as they operate in some specific texts. Let us begin with a well-known Budweiser commercial, which tells—most frequently in a format of twenty-eight seconds, though a longer version also exists—the life story of a black man pursuing a career as a baseball umpire. In this brief period of time, we are given enough information to construct an entire life story—provided we have the cultural knowledge upon which this construction depends. The story we construct is that of a young man from the provinces, who gets his "big break," his chance to make it in the big city, to rise to the top of his profession. We see him working hard in the small-time, small-town atmosphere of the minor leagues, where the pace of events is slower and more relaxed than it is "at the top." He gets his chance for success—the voice-over narrator says, "In the minors you got to make all the calls, and then one day you *get* the call"—after which we see him face his first real test. He must call an important and "close" play correctly and then withstand the pressure of dispute, neither giving ground by changing his mind (which would be fatal) nor reacting too vigorously to the challenge of his call by an offended manager. His passing of this test and being accepted is presented through a later scene in a bar, in which the manager who had staged the protest "toasts" the umpire with a bottle of Budweiser beer, with a chorus in the background singing, "You keep America working. This Bud's for you." From this scene we conclude that the ump has now "made it" and will live happily ever after. From a few scenes, then, aided by the voice-over narration and a music track, we construct an entire life. How do we do this? We draw upon a storehouse of cultural information that extends from fairy tales and other basic narrative structures to knowledge about the game and business of baseball.

In processing a narrative text we actually construct the story, bringing a vast repertory of cultural knowledge to bear upon the text that we are contemplating. Our pleasure in the narrative is to some extent a constructive pleasure, based upon the sense of accomplishment we achieve by successfully completing this task. By "getting" the story, we prove our competence and demonstrate our membership in a cultural community. And what is the story that we "get"? It is the myth of America itself, of the racial melting pot, of upward mobility, of justice done without fear or favor. The corporate structure of baseball, with minor leagues offering a path for the talented to the celebrity and financial rewards of the majors, embodies values that we all possess, we Americans, as one of the deepest parts of our cultural heritage or ideology. It is, of course, on the playing field that talent triumphs most easily over racial or social barriers. Every year in baseball new faces arrive. Young men, having proved themselves in the minors, get their chance to perform at the highest level. Yale graduates and high-school dropouts who speak little or no English are judged equally by how well they hit, run, throw, and react to game situations. If baseball is still the national pastime, it is because in it our cherished myths materialize—or appear to materialize.

The commercial we are considering is especially interesting because it shows us a black man competing not with his body but with his mind, his judgment and his emotions, in a cruelly testing public arena. Americans who attend to sports are aware that black athletes are just beginning to find acceptance at certain "leadership" positions, such as quarterback in professional football, and that there is still an active scandal over the slender representation of blacks at baseball's managerial and corporate levels. The case of the black umpire reminds viewers of these problems, even as it suggests that here, too, talent will finally prevail. The system works, America works. We can take pride in this. The narrative reduces its story to the absolutely bare essentials, making a career turn, or seem to turn, on a single decision. The ump must make a close call, which will be fiercely contested by a manager who is deliberately testing him. This is a story of initiation, in that respect, an ordeal that the ump must meet successfully. The text ensures that we know this is a test, by showing us the manager plotting in his dugout, and it gives us a manager with one of those baseball faces (Irish? German?) that have the history of the game written on them. This is not just partisan versus impartial judge, it is old man against youth, and white against black. We root for the umpire because we want the system to work—not just baseball but the whole thing: America. For the story to work, of course, the ump must make the right call, and we must know it to be right. Here, the close-up and slow motion come into play—just as they would in a real instant replay—to let us see both how close the call is and that the umpire has indeed made the right call. The runner is out. The manager's charge from the dugout is classic baseball protest, and the ump's self-control and slow walk away from the angry manager are gestures in a ritual we all know. That's right, we think, that's the way it's done. We know these moves the way the contemporaries of Aeschylus and Sophocles knew the myths upon which the Greek tragedies were based. Baseball is already a ritual, and a ritual we partake of mostly through the medium of television. The commercial has only to organize these images in a certain way to create a powerful narrative.

At the bar after the game, we are off stage, outside that ritual of baseball, but we are still in the world of myth. The manager salutes the ump with his tilted bottle of beer; the old man acknowledges that youth has passed its test. The sword on the shoulder of knighthood, the laying on of hands, the tilted Bud—all these are ritual gestures in the same narrative structure of initiation. To the extent that we have wanted this to happen we are gratified by this closing scene of the narrative text, and many things, as I have suggested, conspire to make us want this ending. We are dealing with an archetypal narrative that has been adjusted for maximum effect within a particular political and social context, and all this has been deployed with a technical skill in casting, directing, acting, photographing, and editing that is of a high order. It is very hard to resist the pleasure of this text, and we cannot accept the pleasure without, for the bewildering minute at least, also accepting the ideology that is so richly and closely entangled with the story that we construct from the video text. To accept the pleasure of this text is to believe that America works; and this is a comforting belief, itself a pleasure of an even higher order—for as long as we can maintain it. Does the text also sell Budweiser? This is something only market research (if you believe it) can tell. But it surely sells the American way first and then seeks to sell its brand of beer by establishing a metonymic connection between the product and the nation: a national beer for the national pastime.

An audience that can understand this commercial, successfully constructing the ump's story from the scenes represented in the text and the comments of the narrative voice, is an audience that understands narrative structure and has a significant amount of cultural knowledge as well, including both data (how baseball leagues are organized, for instance, and how the game is played) and myth (what constitutes success, for example, and what initiation is). At a time when critics such as William Bennett and E. D. Hirsch are bewailing our ignorance of culture, it is important to realize that many Americans are not without culture; they simply have a different culture from that of Bennett and Hirsch. What they really lack, for the most part, is any way of analyzing and criticizing the power of a text like the Budweiser commercial—not its power to sell beer, which is easily resisted, especially once you have tasted better beer—but its power to sell America. For the sort of analysis that I am suggesting, it is necessary to recover (as Eliot says) from the surrender to this text, and it is also necessary to have the tools of ideological criticism. Recovery, in fact, may depend upon critical analysis, which is why the analysis of video texts needs to be taught in all our schools.

Before moving on to the consideration of a more complex textual economy, we would do well to pause and consider the necessity of ideological criticism. One dimension of the conservative agenda for this country has been conspicuously anticritical. The proposals of William Bennett and E. D. Hirsch, for instance, different as they are in certain respects, are both recipes for the indoctrination of young people in certain cultural myths. The great books of past ages, in the eyes of Bennett, Hirsch, and Allan Bloom, are to be mythologized, turned into frozen monuments of Greatness in which our "cultural heritage" is embodied. This is precisely what Bloom does to Plato, for instance, turning the dialectical search for truth into a fixed recipe for "greatness of soul." The irony of this is that Plato can only die in this process. Plato's work can better be kept alive in our time by such irreverent critiques as that of Jacques Derrida, who takes Plato seriously as an opponent, which is to say, takes him dialectically. In this age of massive manipulation and disinformation, criticism is the only way we have of taking something seriously. The greatest patriots in our time will be those who explore our ideology critically, with particular attention to the gaps between mythology and practice. Above all, we must start with our most beloved icons, not the ones we profess allegiance to, but those that really have the power to move and shake us.

INTERPRETATIONS

1. Why does Scholes devote so much space to an analysis of the Budweiser commercial? What points does he raise about it in paragraph 3? What did you learn about analyzing a TV commercial?

2. To what extent do you agree that "If baseball is still the national pastime, it is because in it our cherished myths materialize—or appear to materialize"? What examples does Scholes cite? What examples would you add?

3. According to Scholes, "Baseball is already a ritual." What does he mean? What are your associations with rituals? Are they important to you and your family? Why would advertisers focus on

rituals when promoting products? Can you think of another commercial with the components of ritual?

4. The subtext of many print and visual commercials links patriotism and consumerism. What are your associations with both words? Is consumerism intrinsically patriotic? What is the purpose of advertisers connecting these concepts?

CORRESPONDENCES

1. Review Solomon's perspective and discuss its relevance to Scholes's text. What critical skills are necessary to prevent "our being susceptible to visual deception" according to Scholes? What would you add?

2. Review Paglia's perspective and discuss its relevance to Scholes's text. To what extent is it possible to "hear" the interrelated voices of culture if they "are talking at once"?

APPLICATIONS

1. "A picture is worth a thousand words." Discuss with your group your associations and experiences with this expression. Is there a pattern that emerges? Are they private or communal experiences? Do they validate the concept? Write a summary of your findings.

2. According to Neal Postman, a media critic and communications professor, "we are now a culture whose information, ideas, and epistemology are given form by television, not the printed word." Write an essay that refutes or supports Postman's thesis using specific examples to support your point of view.

3. Create with your group a specific set of criteria for reading and analyzing a video text. Your audience is high school and college students targeted by Madison Avenue. What guidelines would you offer for distinguishing between image and reality?

Arnie's Test Day

BARRY PETERS

Barry Peters lives in Ohio. He received his M.A. from Wright State University in 1995 and teaches English at Centerville High School.

ARNIE WATSON, facing five tests on a spring Friday of his junior year at Riverdale High School, sat in his bedroom at five a.m. and wrote all over his clothes. Beneath the bill of his Chicago Bulls cap, Arnie wrote in Spanish twenty of the vocabulary words from a list that he was provided with by Señora Martin on Monday and told to memorize by Friday. Certainly Arnie would have memorized those words, just as he had done with vocabulary lists all year, had he not been on the phone for two hours Thursday night trying to convince Marilou Spencer not to break up with him. Dismayed when Marilou slammed the phone in his ears, Arnie couldn't concentrate on his Español the rest of the night. Exasperated, he rose early on Friday and meticulously wrote those twenty words and shorthand definitions in fine black ink on the underside of the cap's red bill.

Frankly, Arnie didn't have the chance to study history, either, that week. Gus Finley and Arnie were going to meet at the Riverdale Library on Tuesday and study the amendments to the Constitution, but Arnie got stuck in the house after a fight with his parents. How are you going to get into a real college, they yelled, a Michigan or a Duke or a Stanford, if you fall out of the top five percent of your class, if you bring home any more eighty percents in your honors classes? It won't be possible, they said. Just you wait and see, Arnie retorted, storming upstairs to his bedroom.

Knowing that he couldn't leave the house after such a scene, Arnie didn't meet Gus at the library, which is why on that Friday morning before school, Arnie wrote abbreviated versions of the amendments on the inside collar of his Reebok polo shirt, actually needing to write on the inside of the shirt itself, repealing Prohibition just above his heart.

Luck ran against Arnie that week in English, too. Mr. Phelan, the Riverdale basketball coach, told his players they had better be at spring conditioning OR ELSE. Naturally, Arnie wanted to stay on Phelan's good side for his senior season, so Arnie ran and lifted weights with the rest of the team after school that week, precluding him from reading all but the first chapter of *The Great Gatsby*. On Friday morning, then, Arnie wrote "Jay Gatsby" and "Nick Caraway" and "Tom Buchanan" and "Daisy Buchanan" on the tanned inside of his belt along with a very brief synopsis of their literal and metaphorical roles in the novel; on the pale blue inside waistband of his jeans, Arnie elaborated on Fitzgerald's symbolism, even drawing a pair of spectacles overlooking a map of East Egg and West Egg, Gatsby's mansion, a heap of ashes and a skyscraper representing New York City, praying that the information he had gleaned from *Cliff's Notes* would be useful on Mrs. Schenck's in-class essay.

Possibly the most difficult test for Arnie would be physics. Quantum theory was hard enough for Arnie to understand during lectures and labs: finding time to memorize formulas for Friday's test was another problem.

Right when he opened his notebook on Wednesday night, Arnie's grandmother called to say that Grampa had been admitted to Riverdale Hospital with chest pains. So Arnie and his parents spent three hours at the hospital, where Arnie read *People* magazine instead of *Introduction to Physics* while waiting for the doctors to report Grampa's condition. They said Grampa would have surgery on Friday—Arnie's test day— only a few hours after Arnie wrote quantum physics formulas on the outside of his polyester white socks.

Unusual as it was, Arnie faced a fifth test that Friday in trigonometry. Vindicating himself for being required to attend Riverdale Lutheran Church choir practice last night—after basketball conditioners and before his devastating phone call to Marilou Spencer, after lying to his parents that no, he did not have any tests on Friday, after answering countless questions from other choir members about his grandfather's impending heart operation—Arnie wrote trigonometry notes on the bottom white soles of his Air Jordan basketball shoes. Why me, Arnie thought, and next to the silhouette logo of Michael Jordan flying above the world, Arnie charted trigonometic patterns. X-axis: the function of pressure is on the rise. Y-axis: the probability exists that Arnie will be forced to use his crib notes. Z-axis: the arc of trouble in Arnie's life increases at an extremely sharp angle, the black line speeding unheeded toward infinity.

INTERPRETATIONS

1. What specific *facts* does Barry Peters provide about Arnie Watson? What might you guess at about Arnie from information that has been stated indirectly?

2.   Why has Arnie decided to cheat on his tests? What priorities has he established for himself?

3.   What do you observe about the writing style that Peters has used for this story? How do you think the style is related to the content of "Arnie's Test Day"?

CORRESPONDENCES

1.   The essays "You Become What You Wear," by Carlin, and "Holly-wood: The Dark Side," by Monroe, concern perception. How is illusion and reality a theme of each of these essays? To what extent is the character Arnie Watson truth or fiction? From your own experiences, how effective—in terms of illusion and reality—is Peters's depiction of the world that Arnie inhabits?

2.   In "Arnie's Test Day," Peters takes a snapshot of the story's protagonist. What realities confront Arnie Watson? What does the story's last line predict for his future? Given Arnie's current situation—and his fate—how does he fit into the partial portrait of today's youth provided by Meredith in "Big Mall's Curfew Raises Questions of Rights and Bias"?

APPLICATIONS

1.   "Español," "the amendments to the Constitution," "*The Great Gatsby*," "Quantum theory," "trigonometry." These are the subjects Arnie is to be tested on. Remembering back to your high school days, did you find these topics to be valuable? Should they have been replaced by other—more relevant—subjects? Write an essay explaining your position.

2.   "To cheat or not to cheat . . . ?" Why do you agree or disagree with Arnie's solution to his dilemma? What arguments are you able to develop in support of your decision?

3.   Create a list of specific details that you find in "Arnie's Test Day." Look over your list carefully. Which details do you like the most? Which are most striking?

When writers use exact details, they hope to generate interest in their work and to draw a reader into the world inhabited by their characters. How does Peters's use of details affect *your* response to the story?

Choose something that you have written for this class that you would like to revise. When making your changes, focus upon how you might include specific details to engage your readers as you make your point. Remember to pay attention to your five senses— they will often reveal details that are clear and effective. As you work on your text, do you think there is a point at which a piece cannot support additional details? If so, why is this the case?

The Knowing Eye

Elissa R. Schlau

READING IMAGES

1. What is your response to the photograph with the bicycles? Would you classify the objects in the photograph as popular culture or as art? If there is a difference between these terms, what is it and how might it influence your interpretation of the objects in the photograph and the photograph itself?

2. What kind of music is being played by the person in the photograph? What details in the image help you to form your opinion?

MAKING CONNECTIONS

1. These photographs recall specific aspects of popular culture. What additional kinds are identified in the essays presented in this chapter?

2. Review the photographs that have appeared in earlier chapters. Which ones show evidence of popular culture? What specific details can you locate to support your claims?

Arnold Asrelsky

WORDS AND IMAGES

1. What music do you think would be listened to by the person in the photograph? Create a tune in this style and write a brief explanation of the music you have composed and how you came to create it.

2. What is "popular culture"? Write an essay that defines this term. What will you include by virtue of your definition? What will you exclude? After you have completed your essay, add photographs that you have found or taken that will enhance and exemplify your definition.

Additional Writing Topics

1. Write an essay attacking or defending the statements that "advertisements are designed to exploit the discontentments fostered by the American Dream, the constant desire for social success and the material rewards that accompany it." You may use commercials on television or advertisements from magazines as supporting evidence for your point of view.

2. To construct a contemporary profile of gender images in our culture, select several issues of magazines targeted for men and women and compare and contrast the advertisements in each. What techniques do they use to reflect and influence their readership? What is the profile of their intended audiences?

3. Compare the social situations depicted in *Boyz N the Hood* and *Do the Right Thing*. How do the different settings and intercultural circumstances affect character behavior and the issues of race relations in each case?

4. You are enrolled in a film class and your assignment is to create a short film that depicts race relations in your age group or discrepancies between social classes. Discuss with your group your ideas and point of view for such a film.

5. Write a persuasive essay comparing and contrasting your responses to seeing a movie in the theater as opposed to viewing it at home on the VCR. Provide as many specific examples as you can to convince your targeted audience.

6. Choose an influential rock or movie star popular with your generation. Review your tapes of him or her, and write an essay analyzing the causes and effects of his or her influence on your age group. Support your analysis with creative, specific examples.

7. Review Toni Morrison's perspective on physical beauty and romantic love (page 464). To what extent do you agree that both are destructive? Is physical attractiveness a reflection of a person's character? Write an analysis of the emphasis that media places on physical beauty. Focus on examples from movies, or television, *or* print media.

8. Bring to class a recent issue of *Time, Newsweek*, or *People Magazine*. Study the advertisements with your group. Who is their target

audience? To which social class are the advertisements aimed? Do they reinforce or refute Carlin's essay?

9. Write an analysis of the role of music in movies. Cite three specific films in which the music detracts from or contributes to theme, setting, and characterization.

Rhetorical and Cultural Glossary

Abstract   Without physical, tangible existence in itself; a concept as opposed to an object. A "child" is a concrete object that our senses can perceive, but "childishness" is an abstract quality. *See* Concrete.

Addition   A revising technique that enables you to add information to your draft. Words, phrases, or paragraphs may be inserted to clarify or enhance what you have written.

Analogy   A comparison that points out a resemblance between two essentially different things. Sleep and death are analogous, although certainly not identical. Often an analogy is drawn to explain simply and briefly something that is complex or abstract by pointing out one way in which it resembles something that is simpler or more concrete. To explain how the mind processes and stores information in its memory, an analogy might be drawn to the way in which a bank processes and stores deposits.

Antonym   A word of opposite meaning from another word, "Good" is an antonym of "bad." *See* Synonym.

Argumentation   In persuasive essays, a unit of discourse meant to prove a point or to convince; the process of proving or persuading.

Audience   A work's intended readership, the author's perception of which directly affects style and tone. As a rule, the more limited or detailed the subject matter, the more specific the audience. An author may write more technically if the intended audience is composed of specialists in the field and may write less technically if the writing is for the general public.

Brainstorming   A prewriting technique in which you rapidly write down ideas in list form. Each idea is usually represented by only one or two words.

Cause and Effect   A type of exposition used primarily to answer the questions "Why did this occur?" and "What will happen next?" The structure of a cause-and-effect essay is a series of events or conditions, the last of which (the effect) cannot occur without the preceding ones (causes). When you write a cause-and-effect essay, it is helpful to keep chronology clearly in mind: remember, causes always create effects and effects are derived from causes.

Class   A group of related objects or people. Those who share the same economic status in a society are said to be of the same social class, such as working class, middle class, upper class.

Cliché   An expression so overused that it has lost its ability to convey a sharp image or fresh idea. Clichés, such as "busy as a bee," diminish clarity and precision. Familiarity reduces them to little more than vague generalizations.

Coherence   The sense of connection and interrelationship present among the parts of a work. In a coherent piece of writing each sentence leads reasonably to the next sentence, and each paragraph follows reasonably from the preceding paragraph. A lack of coherence is evident when gaps are left between parts. The reader of a poorly written essay might begin to ask, "Why does the writer say this here?" or "How did the writer get to this idea from the preceding idea?" *See* Transition and Unity.

Colloquialism   A conversational or folksy word or phrase deemed inappropriate in formal writing. Using colloquialisms ("booze" for "whiskey" or "loosen up" for "relax") imparts a less dignified, less studied quality to one's writing. *See* Slang.

Combining   A rearrangement strategy that helps you to concentrate information in a draft by taking ideas expressed in two or more locations and placing them together. Such a change can improve essay organization and the logical presentation of main ideas.

Comparison and Contrast   A type of exposition that states or suggests similarities and differences between two or more things. Two types of organization for comparison and contrast essays are point by point and subject by subject.

Conclusion   A summing up or restatement of the writer's thesis. A strong conclusion imparts a sense of completion and finality to a piece of writing. The conclusion may be no more than a sentence in a short essay; it may be many paragraphs in a long report. A short conclusion may restate the writer's thesis in a memorable way, place the specific topic being discussed within or against a broader framework, or suggest answers to questions raised in the essay. A summary of the writer's main points may be effective as the conclusion to a long paper, but in a short essay it will seem unnecessarily repetitious.

Concrete   Specific and tangible as opposed to general and abstract. "Wealth" is an abstract concept of which "gold" is a concrete form. The use of concrete details, examples, and illustrations is a key to clear and effective writing. *See* Abstract.

Connotation   The implication(s) and overtones, qualities, feelings, and ideas a word suggests. Connotation goes beyond literal meaning or dictionary definition. "Sunshine" denotes the light rays of the sun, but connotes warmth, cheer, happiness, and even prosperity. *See* Denotation.

Culture   The total pattern of human (learned) behavior embodied in thought, speech, action, and artifacts. It is dependent on the human capacity for learning and transmitting knowledge to succeeding generations through the use of tools, language, and systems of abstract thought.

Deduction   A logical or argumentative appeal in persuasive essays; deductive reasoning elicits a specific conclusion from a generalization. Deduction as a logical approach proceeds from the general to the particular. For example, if we assume that cigarette smoking causes cancer, we may deduce that a person who smokes is liable to contract the disease. *See* Induction.

Definition   A type of exposition that explains the meaning of a word or concept by bringing its characteristics into sharp focus. An **extended definition** explores the feelings and ideas you attach to a word. Extended definitions are suited to words with complex meanings, words that are subject to interpretation, or words that evoke strong reactions. Such definitions are an appropriate basis for organizing exposition. A **dictionary definition** places a word in a class with similar items but also differentiates it from members of the same class.

Deletion   The revising strategy that enables you to remove unnecessary information from your draft. Words, phrases, or paragraphs may have to be dropped if you find they clutter or digress.

Denotation   The literal meaning of a word as defined in a dictionary. *See* Connotation.

Description   A method of paragraph development that conveys sensory experience through one or more of the five senses: sight, hearing, touch, taste, and smell. Description is generally either objective or subjective and can be organized in three broad categories: spatial, chronological, or dramatic. *See* Mode.

Diction   The writer's choice of words. Writers are said to employ proper diction when the words they choose to express their ideas are accurate and appropriate; that is, when what they write says exactly what they mean. Poor diction stems from choosing words whose denotation does not accurately convey the author's intended meaning or from choosing words regarded as inappropriate because they are nonstandard ("ain't"), colloquial, or obsolete.

Editing   The final stage of revising, not to be substituted for careful revision. Changes in punctuation, spelling and word choice are all editing changes.

Epiphany   A moment of insight for a character, often resulting in a turning point.

Exposition   A mode or form of discourse that conveys information, gives directions, or explains an idea that is difficult to understand.

Fetishism   The worship of inanimate objects believed to have magical or transcendent powers. Some people obtain sexual arousal and satisfaction from an object, for example, gloves or shoes.

Figure of Speech   An imaginative phrase and comparison that is not meant to be taken literally. "He ran as fast as the wind" is a figure of speech known as a simile. *See* Analogy, Hyperbole, Metaphor, Personification, Simile, and Understatement.

Freewriting   A prewriting activity that requires you to write down thoughts about a subject as they occur to you. Essentially, you are taking dictation from your brain.

Function   The utility of an object, as opposed to its cultural meaning.

Generalization   A broad statement, idea, or principle that holds a common truth. Despite many possible exceptions, it is generally true that a soldier's job is to go to war. Writing that relies too much on generalization is likely to be vague and overly abstract. *See* Specificity.

High Culture   Classical music, serious novels, poetry, dance, high art, and other cultural products that are usually appreciated by a small number of educated people.

Hyperbole   Obvious exaggeration, an extravagant statement, intentionally designed to give the reader a memorable image. A fisherman who brags that the one that got away was "big as a whale" almost certainly is speaking hyperbolically. *See* Understatement.

Image   In writing, an image is a picture drawn with words, a reproduction of persons, objects, or sensations that are perceived through sight, sound, touch, taste, or smell. Often an image is evoked to visually represent an idea. *See* Symbol.

Impressionistic   Depicting a scene, emotion, or character so that it evokes subjective or sensory impressions. An impression is an effect produced upon the mind or emotions. The more writing emphasizes the effects on the writer of scenes, persons, and ideas, the more impressionistic, and hence the less objective, it will be. *See* Objectivity and Subjectivity.

Induction   The process by which one draws a generalized conclusion from specifics. If it is a fact that a high percentage of people who die from lung cancer each year also smoke cigarettes, one might safely induce that cigarette smoking is a contributing factor in the disease. *See* Deduction.

Introduction   An introduction sets forth the writer's thesis or major themes and establishes tone (attitude toward one's subject), and—particularly in a long paper—suggests an organizational plan. The introduction, or opening, of an essay should capture the reader's attention and interest. Like the conclusion, it may be no more than a sentence or it may be many paragraphs.

Irony   The undermining or contradicting of someone's expectations. Irony may be either verbal or dramatic. **Verbal irony** arises from a discrepancy, sometimes intentional and sometimes not, between what is said and what is meant, as when a dog jumps forward to bite you, and you say, "What a friendly dog!" **Dramatic irony** arises from a discrepancy between what someone expects to happen and what does happen: for example, if the dog that seemed so unfriendly to you saves your life. *See* Sarcasm and Satire.

Jargon   The specialized language of a trade, profession, or other socioeconomic group. Truck drivers employ a jargon on their citizen's band radios that sounds like gibberish to most people. Writing that employs contextless jargon is inappropriate.

Journal   A daily written record of ideas, memories, experiences, or dreams. A journal can be used for prewriting and as a source for formal writing.

Journalism   The profession of writing for newspapers, magazines, wire services, and radio and television. Journalistic writing emphasizes objectivity and factual reportage; the work of editorial writers, columnists, and feature writers often is a more subjective form of reportage.

Literal   The ordinary or primary meaning of a word or expression. Dwelling on literal meaning can promote erroneous thinking. The sentence "Childhood is a time of sunshine" should be read figuratively, not literally. (The sun does not always shine during childhood: rather, childhood is a happy time.)

Metaphor   A figure of speech in which, through an implied comparison, one object is identified with another and some qualities of the first object are ascribed to the second. *See* Simile.

Mode   A conventional form or usage. Writing includes four customary modes of discourse: description, narration, exposition, and persuasion (argumentation).

Multiculturalism   Assimilation of several cultures while allowing each culture to retain its separate identity.

Myth   A traditional or legendary story with roots in folk beliefs.

Narration   A narrative essay is a story with a point; narration is the technique used to tell the story. When writing a narrative essay, pay close attention to point of view, pacing, chronology, and transitions.

Objectivity   Freedom from personal bias. A report about a scientific experiment is objective insofar as facts in it are explained without reference to the writer's feelings about the experiment. But not even the most factual piece of writing is completely uncolored by the writer's attitudes and impressions. Objectivity is best thought of as a matter of degree, increasing in direct proportion with the writer's distance from the work. *See* Subjectivity.

Paradox   A statement that sounds self-contradictory, even absurd, and yet expresses a truth. It is paradoxical, though nonetheless true, to say that one person can simultaneously feel both love and hatred for another person.

Parallel Structure   The association of ideas phrased in parallel ways, thus giving a piece of writing balance and proportion. "He loves wine, women, and singing" lacks parallelism. "He loves wine, women, and song" is parallel; the verbal noun "singing" interrupts the series of nouns.

Personification   A figure of speech in which abstract concepts or inanimate objects are represented as having human qualities or characteristics. To write that "death rides a pale horse," for example, is to personify death.

Persuasion   The art of moving someone else to act in a desired way or to believe in a chosen idea. Logic and reason are important tools of persuasion. Equally effective may be an appeal either to the emotions or to the ethical sensibilities.

Point of View   The vantage point from which an author writes. In expository prose, an author may adopt a first-person or a third-person point of view. *See* Style and Tone.

Politics   The practice of promoting one's interests in a competitive social environment. It does not only have to do with running for government office; there are office politics, academic politics, classroom politics, and sexual politics.

Popular Culture   Sometimes called mass culture. It is accessible to everyone and is dominated by sports, television, films, and popular music.

Purpose   A writer's reason for writing. A writer's purpose is clarified by his or her answer to the question "*Why* am I writing?"

Rearrangement   The revising process that enables you to reorganize your draft by changing the placement of information. Three subsidiary rearrangement techniques are moving, combining, and redistributing.

Redistributing   A rearrangement strategy that helps you to reorganize your essay by taking a block of information and breaking it up into smaller units. Such a revision might help you to explain ideas more carefully or divide main ideas into more understandable units.

Revising   The writing process that enables you to change what you have written. Revising implies rethinking, rereading, and rewriting and does not necessarily come after a whole essay is created. Revising helps you bring what you have written into line with what you want to write.

Sarcasm   An expression of ridicule, contempt, or derision. Sarcastic remarks are nasty or bitter in tone and often characterized by irony that is meant to hurt. You might express your displeasure with those who have given you a hard time by sarcastically thanking them for their help. *See* Irony.

Satire   A genre of writing that makes various use of irony, sarcasm, ridicule, and broad humor in order to expose, denounce, or reform. Satires dwell on the follies and evils of human beings and institutions. The satirist's tone may range from amusement and gentle mockery to harsh contempt and moral indignation.

Simile   A figure of speech including *like* or *as* and stating a direct, explicit comparison between two things: he ate *like* a pig; her heart felt light *as* a feather. *See* Metaphor.

Slang   Colloquialisms and jargon are deemed inappropriate in formal writing. Whether a word or phrase is considered colloquial or slang is often a matter of personal taste. Also, slang often gains acceptance in time. A word such as *uptight*, once considered slang by cultivated people, is now an acceptable colloquialism. *See* Colloquialism and Jargon.

Specificity   Precision, particularity, concreteness. Specificity, like generalization, is a matter of degree; the word *horse* is more specific than *animal* but more general than *stallion*. *See* Generalization.

Style   The "fingerprint," the identifying mark, of a writer—both as an individual and as a representative of his or her age and culture. An author's style is the product of the diction employed, sentence structure and organization, and the overall form and tone in which thoughts are expressed. Style is variously described, depending on the analyzer's purpose. It may be simple or complex, forthright or subtle, colloquial or formal, modern or classical, romantic or realistic, "logical" or poetic. It may be anything, in short, that reflects the writer's personality, background, and talent. *See* Point of View and Tone.

Subjectivity   The personal element in writing. The more subjective a piece of writing, the more it is likely to be focused on the writer's opinions and feelings. *See* Objectivity.

Substitution   A revising strategy that allows you to replace unsatisfactory words, phrases, or paragraphs with ones that are more desirable. Substitution uses both addition and deletion in the same place in the draft.

Syllogism   A high formal three-part form of deductive logic. The syllogist argues that if a generalization (major premise) is true and a specific case of the generalization (minor premise) is also true, then any conclusion reached is necessarily true. If the major premise is "smoking causes cancer" and the minor premise is "John Doe smokes," then the conclusion is "John Doe will contract lung cancer." Syllogisms often sound logical, but are not true because one or both premises are faulty. *See* Deduction.

Symbol   Something that stands for something else. An eagle is a conventional symbol of the United States. Any word, image, or description, any name, character, or action that has a range of meanings and associations beyond its literal denotation may be symbolic, depending on who is interpreting it and the context in which it appears. The word eagle, therefore, may bring to mind different images or ideas; it may connote freedom or power or solitude.

Synonym   One of two or more words having approximately the same meaning. "Happiness" and "joy" are synonyms. *See* Antonym.

Tautology   Inherent or pointless repetition. To write that a person was treated with "cruel inhumanity" is tautological: inhumanity is always cruel.

Thesis   The main idea or theme of an essay. In expository prose, the writer usually states the thesis clearly in the introduction. The thesis statement should establish point of view, the primary point(s) intended for discussion, and the writer's attitude toward it.

Tone   Tone of voice; an author's attitude toward his or her subject, and, at times, audience. Tone is caught in the "sound" of a piece of writing. The tone of an essay may be angry, resigned, humorous, serious, sentimental, mocking, ironic, sarcastic, satirical, reasoning, emotional, philosophic—anything, in short, that echoes the voice of the author. One tone may predominate or many tones ("overtones") may be heard in any work. *See* Style.

Topic Sentence   The sentence in a paragraph that states clearly the main theme or point of the paragraph.

Transition   A bridge between one point or topic or idea and another. The logical movement from sentence to sentence and paragraph should be easy to follow if a piece of writing is coherent. This logic is often emphasized by means of transitional expressions such as *therefore, hence, similarly, however, but, furthermore, also,* and *for example. See* Coherence.

Understatement   An obvious downplaying or underrating of something. It is the opposite of hyperbole, although use of either may create a memorable image or an ironic effect. To say that "after they ate the apple, Adam and Eve found life a bit tougher," is to understate their condition. *See* Hyperbole.

Unity   The basic focus or theme that permeates a piece of writing, thus lending the piece a sense of wholeness and completeness. The words and sentences and paragraphs, the images and ideas, the explanations and examples, the characters and actions, the descriptions and arguments—all should be relevant to the overriding purpose or point of a work. *See* Coherence.

Geographic Index

Selections are listed in the Index by both subject matter and the author's national or ethnic background. Authors from the United States are listed by ethnic groups only when the selection involves the writer's ethnic background.

Africa

Asia

Central America and the Caribbean

South America

Europe

Middle East

United States: Ethnic Groups

United States

Credits

Luke 10:29-37, "The Good Samaritan." From the *New English Bible*, © Oxford University Press and Cambridge University Press, 1961, 1970.

Tom Montgomery-Fate, "In Search of Balance." Reprinted by permission of Tom Montgomery-Fate.

Dana Wehle, "We Kissed the Tomato and Then the Sky." Reprinted by permission of Dana Wehle.

Steve Tesich, "Focusing on Friends." Reprinted by permission of International Creative Management, Inc. Copyright © 1983 by The New York Times Co.

Maxine Hong Kingston, from "White Tigers." From *The Woman Warrior* by Maxine Hong Kingston. Copyright © 1975, 1976 by Maxine Hong Kingston. Reprinted by permission of Alfred A. Knopf, a Division of Random House, Inc.

Amy Tan, "Mother Tongue." © Amy Tan. First published in *Threepenny Review*, 1990.

Mahwash Shoaib, "Treasures." Reprinted by permission of Mahwash Shoaib.

Shirley Geok-lin Lim, from *Among the White Moon Faces: An Asian-American Memoir of Homelands*. Reprinted, by permission of the author and The Feminist Press at The City University of New York, from Shirley Geok-lin Lim, *Among the White Moon Faces: An Asian-American Memoir of Homelands* (New York: The Feminist Press at The City University of New York, 1996). Copyright © 1996 by Shirley Geok-lin Lim.

Lewis (Johnson) Sawaquat, "For My Indian Daughter." From "My Turn," published in *Newsweek* magazine, September 5, 1983. Reprinted by permission of Lewis Sawaquat.

Danit Wehle, "Noah." Reprinted by permission of Danit Wehle.

Emma Wunsch, "Learning to Fly." First appeared in *Hanging Loose* magazine. Reprinted by permission of Emma Wunsch.

Sherman Alexie, "The Joy of Reading and Writing: Superman and Me." Reprinted by permission of Sherman Alexie.

Susan G. Madera, "One Voice." Reprinted by permission of Susan G. Madera.

Paul Theroux, "The Male Myth." Copyright © 1983 by Paul Theroux. First published in *The New York Times*. Reprinted with the permission of The Wylie Agency.

Rose Del Castillo Guilbault, "Americanization Is Tough on 'Macho.'" Reprinted by permission of Rose Del Castillo Guilbault.

Jerry Rockwood, "Life Intrudes." © 1988 by Jerry Rockwood. Reprinted by permission.